A RICHER HERITAGE

A Richer

THE

RICHARD

HAMPTON

JENRETTE

SERIES IN

ARCHITECTURE

AND THE

DECORATIVE

ARTS

Heritage

HISTORIC PRESERVATION IN THE TWENTY-FIRST CENTURY

EDITED BY ROBERT E. STIPE

The University of North Carolina Press

Chapel Hill and London

Designed by April Leidig-Higgins
Set in Ehrhardt by Copperline Book Services, Inc.
Manufactured in the United States of America

The paper in this book meets the guidelines for permanence and
durability of the Committee on Production Guidelines for Book
Longevity of the Council on Library Resources.

In Chapter 4, much of the material in the section entitled
"Planning for Preservation," under "Regulating Preservation: The
Heart of the Matter," has been adapted from Robert E. Stipe, "On
Preservation Plans and Planning," *Alliance Review*
(January–February 2001): 1–4, (March–April 2001): 4–5, 15.

The publisher wishes to thank the Historic Preservation
Foundation of North Carolina, Inc., for its many efforts in support
of this book's development and publication.

Library of Congress Cataloging-in-Publication Data
A richer heritage: historic preservation in the twenty-first century /
edited by Robert E. Stipe.
p. cm.—(The Richard Hampton Jenrette series in architecture &
the decorative arts)
Includes bibliographical references and index.
ISBN 0-8078-2779-7 (cloth: alk. paper)
ISBN 0-8078-5451-4 (pbk.: alk. paper)
1. Historic preservation—United States.   2. United States—
Cultural policy.   3. Historic sites—Conservation and restoration
—United States.   I. Stipe, Robert E.   II. Series.
E159 .R535   2003
363.6'9'0973—dc21   2003004109

cloth   07 06 05 04 03   5 4 3 2 1
paper   07 06 05 04 03   5 4 3 2 1

Contents

Part Three. The Human Face of Preservation

Part Four. Historic Preservation in the Twenty-first Century

Preface

This book has its origins in a number of informal conversations between the editor and various college and university educators and other professionals over a period of several years. All of them agreed on the need for a new textbook on historic preservation in America. As these conversations took place, it became increasingly clear that such a text should not only describe the who-does-what-and-how of preservation at the beginning of the new century, but should also provide a larger, long-term perspective that would trace important changes that have taken place in American preservation in recent decades. This volume is the result. I hope that it will be not only a useful text for those who intend to enter the field of historic preservation as professionals, but also a source of ideas for administrators, volunteers, and preservation policymakers at all levels of government and in the private sector.

In a very real sense, the progenitor of this work is an earlier volume entitled *With Heritage So Rich*, the book most often credited with the passage by Congress of the National Historic Preservation Act of 1966, which catapulted the movement forward and gave us the unified national system that has been in effect ever since.

This book does not pretend to have the political clout or prestige of that earlier volume. It is not sponsored by the U.S. Conference of Mayors and the National Trust for Historic Preservation, nor will it be distributed to every member of Congress. It does not advocate a comprehensive, top-to-bottom remake of the American preservation system then considered urgent, although the passage of time mandates some changes. The historic preservation scene, the people and institutions that make it work, and, indeed, its underlying values have changed significantly since that earlier time. A reappraisal is in order.

The machinery of historic preservation has now come mostly into the hands of a younger generation that brings to the movement new and different—and sometimes controversial—visions of what is important. These new preservationists add many more strands to the preservation rope, but it is not yet woven into a single, strong, politically viable cable. Whether and how that might be made to happen are among the important topics discussed.

A special concern of this book is to look beyond the events and policies embedded in the 1966 legislation and to provide an account of the major developments in the preservation movement since the early 1980s, when it began to expand and to enter its present, more mature phase. The data presented are those available to us as of the date of going to press in the summer of 2002. A secondary purpose is to attempt to speculate in an ordered way about where the movement might want to head next, how it might get there, and some of the obstacles it might face along the way.

The book is ordered according to several themes. The introduction describes the principal ideas and events that have characterized American preservation from the days of Ann Pamela Cunningham and Mount Vernon to the present, told largely as a sequence of benchmark ideas and events in the continuing story of where the movement has come from and how it arrived at its present state.

Part I of the book largely serves the singular purpose of explaining the workings—legal, administrative, and fiscal—of the layered federal, state, and local government partnership put in place by Congress in 1966. The system created by that legislation is best described by two words: "partnered" and "layered." Not to denigrate the preservation programs of state and local governments before 1966, but the new act established a system in which the three layers of American government became partners in a unified effort, each layer fulfilling the special role assigned to it under our constitutional system of government —each presenting and presented with special opportunities and problems along the way (Chapter 1).

Although Part I tends to emphasize the federal role, the reader would do well to bear in mind throughout the book that the states are the sovereign governments within our system (Chapter 1) and that although the preservation story begins with what is considered by many as the top layer in Washington, D.C., the heavier burdens of responsibility increase as preservation tasks are undertaken by state and local governments. Chapters 2, 3, and 4 treat with each of these layers, and Chapter 5 describes how these government programs and policies meld into a single preservation ethic.

Part II of the book is devoted to several special topics that have come to the fore since approximately 1980. The preservation of American landscapes, large and small, designed and vernacular, has begun to assume importance almost equal to that of our traditional preoccupation with the preservation of buildings as such (Chapter 6). Historic landscape preservation has, in turn, begun to rub against the larger environmental protection movement, presenting both opportunities and conflicts described in a companion essay (Chapter 7).

Ultimately, however, the successful preservation of buildings *or* landscapes depends on the availability and creative use of money. The essay (Chapter 9) on the role of the private sector describes where private money for preservation comes from, directly and indirectly, how it works its will on preservation projects, and the role of investor expectations in the process. Since the early 1980s there have been two major developments with fiscal implications for preservation. One has been the growing influence of tax policies on preservation efforts, and the other has been the increasing number and influence of nonprofit organizations on the implementation of preservation projects (Chapter 10). Two other developments have characterized the last two decades. The first has been the changing role of archaeology and archaeological thinking about preservation as it moves away from a preoccupation with excavations and artifacts and toward a concern for the discovery of patterns in the new field called cultural resource management (Chapter 8). The second is the shrinking nature of the world itself. As it becomes smaller, the global context of preservation has presented us with a variety of opportunities and challenges for the import and export of preservation ideas to and from other countries (Chapter 11).

Part III relates to an increasingly voiced criticism of American preservation efforts: that they have from the beginning been overly preoccupied with saving "stuff"—buildings and the artifactual content of our environment—and insufficiently concerned with the impact of preservation on people. Chapter 12 considers the increasing interest in the social and ethnic aspects of historic preservation, followed by Chapter 13 dealing with the emerging role of Native Americans in preservation. The challenge to our traditional focus on buildings and other artifacts is met by an essay on folklife and the preservation of what has come to be called, rightly or wrongly, the "intangible" American cultural heritage (Chapter 14). Here, again, are challenges and opportunities.

Part IV is an attempt, similar in some respects to the progenitor volume, *With Heritage So Rich*, to look broadly at the field of American preservation at the beginning of the twenty-first century and to suggest how some of its parts may be made to work more smoothly and effectively in the rapidly changing social, technological, and economic context of the country as a whole. Although each contributor has expressed his or her own view of that future, these last opinions are those of the editor, and only the editor.

The reader will notice wide variations in the way individual contributors have approached their subjects. Some chapters are laden with descriptive detail. Others are essentially philosophical. Some are scholarly and formal; others tend toward the more conversational. A few are highly prescriptive regarding the needs and directions of their special fields of interest; some offer only questions. Occasionally there are conflicting views about the value or efficacy of the same federal, state, or local preservation program. However, all of them are highly personal—tailored to the individual author's personal feelings about how we should go about achieving a richer heritage for the generations to come. All, without exception, are partisan on behalf of preservation. The contributors to the book bring to their chapters a special competence, born both of experience and a passion for preservation as an essential component of a well-ordered society.

These variations in style and approach are always frustrating to an editor, who, with an editor's typical conceit, will wish to weave them into one easily readable, stylistically uniform whole. Advancing years have made clear to me that it is best to give carefully selected contributors their lead—they, after all, are the experts—and to restrain the tendency to "improve things." The distinctive, personal views of individuals free to say what they think will always trump an easy read, and I hope that the unique experience and personality that each contributor has brought to this project has not been unduly tampered with. To each and all of them for their contributions, and for their patience and (mostly) good humor with a nagging editor over the several years it has taken to pull this book together, go my special thanks.

Our very special thanks are extended to the individuals and organizations that have so generously funded the preparation of the book manuscript: Dr. Henry M. Jordan, Chairman Emeritus of the National Trust for Historic Preservation; the Claniel Foundation of Philadelphia; Barbara Timken and the Montauk Foundation of Washington, D.C.; Joan Davidson and the J. M. Kaplan Fund of New York; the Marion S. Covington Foundation of Greensboro, North Carolina; and the College of Fellows of the American Institute of Architects. Generous contributions to its publication have also been made by Preservation North Carolina, the Marion S. Covington Foundation, Myrick Howard and Brinkley Sugg, and the editor and his wife, Josie Stipe. Thanks are also extended to the Board of Trustees of Preservation North Carolina, and to Myrick Howard, its executive director, for serving as the fiscal agent for the project. I am grateful to Terry B. Morton of Silver Spring, Maryland, who was instrumental in helping to raise funds for preparation of the manuscript, and to Antoinette J. Lee of Arlington, Virginia, who read and commented on a number of the chapters during the earlier stages of the project.

My deep gratitude is extended to Dr. Elizabeth Lyon, retired Georgia Historic Preservation Officer and former Chair of the National Center for Preservation Technology and Training, who, in her usual fashion, helped pull everything together when it all appeared to be falling apart. Historic preservation has never had a better friend.

Thanks are due also to Professor Martha Jo Leimenstoll, AIA, of the University of North Carolina at Greensboro; to Dan Becker, Executive Director of the Raleigh, North Carolina, Historic Districts Commission; to David Brook, Deputy State Historic Preservation Officer of North Carolina; and to Josie Stipe, my wife, for her hundreds of favors large and small. Elizabeth Watson and Brenda Barrett provided inspiration and help when it was badly needed, as did Anne Miller, editor of the *North Carolina Historical Review*. All of these individuals substantially assisted with a difficult and prolonged editorial process. For their help I am most appreciative.

Finally, the reader will note that there exist among the eighteen contributors to this volume inconsistencies, disagreements, and differences of opinion, sometimes strongly expressed, on matters of preservation policy. Some are liberal in their views; a few are conservative. A few are young and relatively new to the field, but they make no less a contribution for that. Most, like the editor, have been around for a while. All of us care deeply and believe profoundly in the preservation movement. However much the reader (or the editor) agrees or disagrees with the opinions expressed, I have attempted conscientiously to allow each author to state his or her views without undue interference in the hope that this may provoke a dialogue among readers that will eventually lead to improvement in our present way of doing things.

Robert E. Stipe
Chapel Hill, North Carolina

Why Preserve?

This book begins with a basic question that is not often asked: "Why preserve?" Why do so many of us care about what we call "historic preservation"? Is preservation at all important to society? Which parts of society? What is worth preserving, and what is not? Why we seek to preserve anything is central to these and other questions confronting the movement at the beginning of a new century. Those of us who tend the historic preservation vineyard are inclined to take it for granted. To us, it *is* important, and at a personal level each of us knows why. By extension, we think it should also be important to the rest of society. But in our more thoughtful moments, we recognize that there is no escaping the fact that for the public at large, historic preservation is not as high a priority as we might wish. That public is entitled to hear "why" we think it is important. That is the starting point for this book.

About thirty years ago, in the July 1972 issue of the National Trust's monthly newspaper, *Preservation News*, I outlined seven reasons why historic preservation was important. That small essay bears repeating here as a prologue to this book:

First, we seek to preserve our heritage because our historic resources are all that physically link us to our past. Some portion of that patrimony must be preserved if we are to recognize who we are, how we became so, and, most importantly, how we differ from others of our species. Archives, photographs and books are not sufficient to impart the warmth and life of a physical heritage. The shadow simply does not capture the essence of the object.

Second, we strive to save our historic and architectural heritage simply because we have lived with it and it has become part of us. The presence of our physical past creates expectations—expectations that are important parts of our daily lives. We should replace them only when they no longer have meaning, when other needs are more pressing, and we should do so only with great caution—knowing how our environment creates us, as well as how we create our environment.

Third, we save our physical heritage partly because we live in an age of ever more frightening communication and other technological abilities, as well as in an era of increasing cultural homogeneity. In such a situation we subconsciously reach out for every opportunity to maintain difference, individuality and personal identity.

Fourth, we preserve historic sites and structures because of their relation to past events, eras, movements, and people that we feel are important to honor and understand. The preservation of structures and places is an outgrowth of our respect for the past, which created our today. In making it accessible we are sometimes able to have the past live for us as it cannot when viewed as a printed page or a piece of celluloid. Nostalgia and patriotism are important human motivations for preservation, and important human emotions must be served. But the historic associations inherent in preserved structures and sites should encourage much more than mere nostalgia and patriotism. They are potential sources of imagination and creativity in our attempts to understand and appreciate the past—a past distant from us, but a time that can still offer much to guide us.

Fifth, we seek to preserve the architecture and landscapes of the past simply because of their intrinsic value as art. These structures and areas were designed by some of America's greatest artists. They are as important to our artistic heritage as our decorative arts, our painting and sculpture. . . . If we were to value historic structures as we honor our other works of art, much wanton destruction might be prevented.

Sixth, we seek to preserve our past because we believe in the right of our cities and the countryside to be beautiful. Here, regretfully, we must recognize the essential tawdriness of much contemporary design and construction. Much of it is junk. It assaults our senses. Thus, we seek to preserve the past, not only because it is unique, exceptional, architecturally significant, or historically important, but also because in many cases what replaces it is inhuman and grotesque. Potentially, of course, many old buildings could be demolished and replaced with contemporary structures of equal functional or aesthetic value. Yet, recent experience tells us that this is not likely, and until it is we shall preserve our past in order to preserve what is left of our pleasing and humane urban and rural landscape.

Seventh, *and most important of all*, we seek to preserve because we have discovered—all too belatedly—that preservation can serve important human and social purposes in our society. Ancestor worship and aesthetic motivations are no longer enough. Our traditional concern with great events, great people, and great architects will not serve the larger society in any full measure.

The problem now is to acknowledge that historic preservation is but one aspect of a much larger problem, basically an environmental one, of enhancing, or perhaps providing for the first time, a better quality of life for people. Especially is this so for the growing numbers of our population who must confront an increasingly dismal existence in a rapidly deteriorating urban environment. No one needs to be reminded that our cities are still falling apart. If preservation is not to fall into the black hole of total irrelevance, we must look beyond our traditional preoccupation with architecture and history, and beyond our elitist intellectual and aesthetic mind set. We must turn our preservation energies to a broader, more constructive and inclusive social purpose. We must move beyond the problem of saving architectural artifacts and begin to think about how we can conserve urban neighborhoods, rural landscapes, and natural resources for human purposes.

This is particularly urgent at a time when some special interest and ethnic groups, in an effort to discover their own heritage, have begun to isolate themselves even more, rejecting the notion of a common heritage for all Americans and placing a new emphasis on social and ethnic differences. Success in preservation in this day and age requires that we give as much of our attention to such problems as housing, schools, garbage collection, employment, and racial conflict as we have traditionally given to architecture and history. The importance of our nostalgic, patriotic and intellectual drives cannot be denied, but they are no longer a sufficient motivation for what we preservationists are about.

Basically, it is the saving of people and lives and cities—not just buildings —that is important to all of us. We have before us an unparalleled opportunity, if we are determined, to contribute significantly to upgrading the quality of human existence. If we can achieve this, to some extent at least, the architecture and the history will fall into place.[1]

Abbreviations

ACHP	Advisory Council on Historic Preservation
AHLP	Alliance for Historic Landscape Preservation
AIA	American Institute of Architects
APE	area of potential effect
APT	Association for Preservation Technology
ARPA	Archaeological Resources Protection Act
ASLA	American Society of Landscape Architects
BECA	Bureau of Educational and Cultural Affairs
CDBG	Community Development Block Grant
CFR	Code of Federal Regulations
CLG	Certified Local Government
CLR	cultural landscape report
CRM	cultural resource management
DOE	Determination of Eligibility
DOT	U.S. Department of Transportation
EA	environmental assessment
EIS	environmental impact statement
FAIA	Fellow, American Institute of Architects
FASLA	Fellow, American Society of Landscape Architects
FHWA	Federal Highway Administration
FPO	federal preservation officer
FY	fiscal year
GIS	geographic information system
GPS	global positioning satellite
GSA	U.S. General Services Administration
HABS	Historic American Buildings Survey
HAER	Historic American Engineering Record

HBCUS	historically black colleges and universities
HCRS	Heritage Conservation and Recreation Service
HPF	Historic Preservation Fund
HUD	U.S. Department of Housing and Urban Development
ICCROM	International Centre for the Study and Conservation of Cultural Property in Rome
ICOMOS	International Council on Monuments and Sites
IRS	Internal Revenue Service
ISTEA	Intermodal Surface Transportation Efficiency Act
ITC	Investment Tax Credit
MOA	memorandum of agreement
NAAAHP	National Association for African American Historic Preservation
NADB	National Archaeological Database
NAGPRA	Native American Graves Protection and Repatriation Act
NAOP	National Association of Olmsted Parks
NAPC	National Alliance of Preservation Commissions
National Register	National Register of Historic Places
NCPE	National Council for Preservation Education
NCPTT	National Center for Preservation Technology and Training
NCSHPO	National Conference of State Historic Preservation Officers
NCSL	National Conference of State Legislatures
NEPA	National Environmental Policy Act
NHA	National Heritage Area
NHL	National Historic Landmark
NHPA	National Historic Preservation Act
NPS	National Park Service
NRIS	National Register Information System
NTHP	National Trust for Historic Preservation
PA	Preservation Action

SAA	Society of American Archaeology
SAH	Society of Architectural Historians
SAT	Save America's Treasures
Secretary's Standards	Secretary of the Interior's Standards for Preservation (including Rehabilitation)
SHPO	state historic preservation officer
TCF	The Conservation Fund
TEA-21	Transportation Equity Act for the Twenty-first Century
THPO	tribal historic preservation officer
TNC	The Nature Conservancy
TPL	Trust for Public Land
TPO	tribal preservation office
UN	United Nations
UNESCO	United Nations Educational, Scientific, and Cultural Organization
USAID	U.S. Agency for International Development
US/ICOMOS	U.S. National Committee of the International Council on Monuments and Sites
WHSR	U.S. Conference of Mayors, Special Committee on Historic Preservation, comp., *With Heritage So Rich: A Report* (New York: Random House, 1966)
WMF	World Monuments Fund
World Heritage Convention	Convention Concerning the Protection of the World Cultural and Natural Heritage

A RICHER HERITAGE

America's Preservation Ethos
A Tribute to Enduring Ideals

Historic preservation has flowered and endured in the United States because the very concept incorporates some of this nation's most profoundly defining ideals. The concept of preservation is built on a finely wrought and sustained balance between respect for private rights on the one hand and a concern for the larger community on the other. It reflects long-held beliefs concerning appropriate roles for each level of government and government incentives for the private sector, which bears most of the burden of preserving the nation's heritage. Preservation in America is about nurturing the grass roots and assisting communities with the preservation of physical structures, objects, and settings that tell the story of our collective experience.

Preservation in America is an evolving phenomenon. Led by elite individuals and groups at its inception in the nineteenth century, it broadened its base with the advent of government programs in the twentieth century. The saving of early shrines to individuals and events of the Revolutionary War period represented a beginning that over time evolved into a national effort to preserve community history and identity. To understand the process by which preservation has come to its current state, it is necessary to look back on several major milestones in the preservation movement and on the influences that shaped them.

Early Roots of the Preservation Movement:
The Historic House Museum

The strongest initial impetus for preservation in America was the new country's conscious effort to memorialize the heroes of the Revolutionary War. One of the first buildings to be preserved as a shrine to the Revolution was Philadelphia's Old State House, later called Independence Hall. The deteriorated building was purchased in 1813 by the city, which intended to sell it and subdivide the surrounding land into building lots. Community activists opposed to the plan argued that as the 1776 venue of the Second Continental Congress, where Jefferson's Declaration of Independence was signed, and as the site in 1787 of the Constitutional Convention of the United States, the Old State House should be preserved as a public building. Their arguments prevailed. The city of Philadelphia withdrew its development plan and restored the building.

Although many early preservation efforts were launched in urban settings, the mid-nineteenth century's crowning achievement was the preservation of Mount Vernon in tidewater Virginia by the Mount Vernon Ladies Association. In 1858 this national organization secured a charter to hold and manage George Washington's ancestral home and much of its original plantation setting. Preservationists' earlier petitions to Congress and the Commonwealth of Virginia to buy the home and land had fallen on deaf ears, and developers were pushing to acquire the house and its two-hundred-acre site. But in 1853 Ann Pamela Cunningham rallied women from every state in the Union to solicit contributions to save Mount Vernon. With the organizational skills of a general and the preeminent icon of the Revolutionary period as her standard, Cunningham succeeded in raising the then-staggering sum of $200,000 to purchase Mount Vernon "and all its sacred associations."[1]

The successful drive by the Mount Vernon Ladies Association to preserve a house and its landscape by converting the residence to a house museum is typical of the private initiatives that remain the main strength of the historic preservation movement in America. The association called upon concerned citizens—in this case, relatively privileged citizens and for the most part women —and sallied forth to save the home and grounds. Cunningham's legacy is seen today in the thousands of historical and preservation societies that rally to preserve their communities' irreplaceable buildings and places.

The Mount Vernon effort inspired the formation of other groups, such as the National Society of Colonial Dames and the Daughters of the American Revolution. Established in the last decade of the nineteenth century, those organizations saved countless historic homes and public buildings, using the resources of their members' time, dedication, and organizational skills.[2]

Almost immediately after it was formed, the Mount Vernon Ladies Association became the source of inspiration and information for a spate of house museums celebrating other national heroes. Among the most notable efforts to emulate the Mount Vernon Ladies are the Kenmore Association, which preserved the home of George Washington's sister near Fredericksburg, Virginia; the Robert E. Lee Memorial Association, which protects Stratford Hall, associated with three signers of the Declaration of Independence as well as Lee's birthplace; and the Ladies Heritage Association, established in 1889 to operate and protect Andrew Jackson's home, which was purchased and preserved in 1856 by the state of Tennessee. Through associations like these, many historic homes have been sensitively adapted to house museums, both preserving our past and becoming increasingly popular as tourism sites.[3]

The Philadelphia Centennial Exposition of 1876, the first grand-scale exposition in the United States, introduced Americans to their country's decorative arts and architectural legacy. Popular fascination with eighteenth-century architecture eventually resulted in the recognition of a style called Colonial Revival, still prominent in residential design today. The exposition stimulated a new popularity of buildings representing early structural types and distinct architectural styles and introduced an enriched public vision of what was worthy of attention and, eventually, preservation.[4]

While preservationists in the East were expanding their concept of what was worth preserving in the built environment, the federal government took the first steps to protect the great scenic landscapes of the West and Southwest. In 1872 Congress established the world's first national park, Yellowstone, comprising over two million acres of public land in Montana, Wyoming, and Idaho. The purchase of this incomparably beautiful wilderness area heralded the U.S. government's acceptance of responsibility for conserving the nation's natural wonders.[5]

Increasing population density in the East generated interest in municipal parks and the preservation of landscapes. A design competition for what would become New York's Central Park catalyzed the development of several municipal parks and the preservation of urban open space, largely in the Northeast and Midwest, during the last half of the nineteenth century. In 1858 landscape architects Frederick Law Olmsted and Calvert Vaux won the New York park design competition with their "Greensward" plan, a plan supported by a report accurately predicting the rapid growth of New York City's population. The report justified the park's large acreage and emphasized the importance of buffering the populace from nearby noisome industries and incompatible uses.[6]

During this period several organizations emerged in response to the growing popular interest in historic landscapes and their preservation. In 1890 landscape architect Charles Eliot helped organize the Trustees of Reservations to protect Massachusetts's disappearing historic sites and scenic natural areas, thereby forging the first specific link between the two movements. In 1895 the Trustees of Scenic and Historic Places and Objects was formed in New York State, modeled after the Trustees of Reservations. Later named the American Scenic and Historic Preservation Society, the New York organization was in one sense an early forerunner of today's National Trust for Historic Preservation (NTHP). The activities of such groups advanced the state parks and reservations movement as well as historic preservation.[7]

In 1910 William Sumner Appleton, a Boston architectural historian and former real estate broker, helped found the Society for the Preservation of New England Antiquities (SPNEA). His stated goal for the six New England states was to save buildings "which are architecturally beautiful or unique, or have special historical value." Appleton purchased structures, restored them, and placed covenants on them requiring that their original uses be retained. His regional approach to saving buildings paralleled the preservation of regional landscapes by the Massachusetts Trustees of Reservations. Appleton deserves a special place in the preservation movement for his decision to preserve buildings for their beauty and uniqueness as well as for their historic associations.[8]

An additional spark to the incipient preservation movement was struck by the Columbian Exposition of 1893 in Chicago. There preservation became associated with civic improvement efforts that expressed themselves in handsome, centrally located public buildings and orderly city plans as antidotes to the congestion and seemingly disorderly growth of nineteenth-century cities. The Columbian Exposition, with its classically derived, magnificent buildings contained within a site designed by Olmsted and his colleague, Chicago architect Daniel H. Burnam, gave rise to a new vision of urban America that came to be known as the "City Beautiful."

Looking Back on the Twentieth Century

In the early twentieth century the City Beautiful movement brought together professionals from the fields of preservation, architecture, landscape architecture, and city planning—a new discipline—and spawned numerous community improvement associations. It also led to the construction of majestic civic centers in San Francisco and Cleveland and to the building of landscaped roadways linking public monuments, buildings, and parks. The first of these, still in place today, was the Benjamin Franklin Parkway in Philadelphia.[9]

The Antiquities Act of 1906 was designed to protect another kind of monument — fragile Native American archaeological sites on federal lands. The passage of this legislation was a congressional response to the growing need to preserve the artifacts of the continent's earliest inhabitants and provided government support for the protection of these endangered prehistoric monuments.[10]

In 1916, as City Beautiful precepts were helping to redefine the city in America, the National Park Service (NPS) was established in the U.S. Department of the Interior. Foreseeing the need to administer and protect the growing roster of federally owned lands, the department persuaded Congress to create a separate bureau "to conserve the scenery and the natural and historic objects and the wildlife therein and to provide for the enjoyment of same and in such a manner as will leave them unimpaired for the enjoyment of future generations."[11]

From modest beginnings—a $19,500 budget, a director, an assistant, and a clerk— the NPS has grown into a multibillion-dollar agency responsible for millions of acres of national parks, historical parks, monuments, military parks, memorial parks, battlefields, battlefield parks, battlefield sites, historic sites, memorials, cemeteries, seashores, parkways, recreational areas, the parks of the national capital city, and presidential homes. The expansion occurred gradually, as the U.S. government consolidated federal land management programs within the Park Service. The NPS emerged as the principal source of governmental preservation expertise in the early to mid-1930s, a benefit of its close cooperation with the civilian experts hired to accomplish the restoration of Colonial Williamsburg and of the momentum and visibility gained through the preservation-related federal work projects of the Great Depression.[12]

Colonial Williamsburg and the Outdoor Museum Village

In 1926 John D. Rockefeller Jr. authorized the Reverend W. A. R. Goodwin to commission Boston architect William G. Perry to begin drawings for the restoration of Williamsburg, Virginia's 1699 capital. The beauty and scale of the project appealed to Rockefeller, and he voiced his enthusiasm for the opportunity to restore an entire colonial town and keep it "free from inharmonious surroundings." The scope of the Williamsburg restoration required an interdisciplinary approach to preservation that enlisted some of the country's best historians, architects, landscape architects, archaeologists, engineers, and craftsmen.[13]

The team of experts assembled for the Williamsburg project also provided guidance and advice to preservation efforts of the NPS. Williamsburg's experts offered crucial assistance in the difficult task of researching and reconstructing George Washington's birthplace in Westmoreland County, Virginia. They also supplied useful consultation when, in 1928, the Park Service undertook construction of a twenty-three-mile historic parkway linking the Yorktown battlefield with Colonial Williamsburg and Jamestown, the site of the first English settlement in America.[14]

Goodwin's greatest contribution to Williamsburg was his determination that it be both authentic and an educational experience, goals that Rockefeller ardently shared. Today, the site encompasses the entire range of characteristics most sought by visitors: a recognized destination, a place with historical interest, an educational setting, and a variety of activities.[15] The opening of the partially completed restoration in 1934 created a vogue for Williamsburg architecture, furnishings, and garden design that dominated American tastes throughout the 1940s and 1950s. By 1960 Colonial Williamsburg had become the nation's number-one tourist attraction, and in the 1990s it drew more than one million visitors a year.[16]

Although Colonial Williamsburg is one of John D. Rockefeller Jr.'s best-known historical legacies to the nation, he and other family members also assisted with the purchase of lands that later were incorporated into the NPS holdings. These included the Great Smoky Mountains National Park and the Grand Tetons National Park. These premier natural parks testify to the Rockefellers' interest in the preservation of both natural and cultural areas for their value in teaching and promoting patriotism and good citizenship.[17]

Just as Mount Vernon had been the model for several mid-nineteenth-century historic house museums honoring statesmen and military heroes, Williamsburg inspired the creation of four museum villages in the 1930s and 1940s: Henry Ford's Greenfield Village in Dearborn, Michigan; Albert Wells's Old Sturbridge Village in Sturbridge, Massachusetts; Stephen Clark's The Farmer's Museum in Cooperstown, New York; and Mr. and Mrs. Charles Flynt's Deerfield Village in Deerfield, Massachusetts. Each was the product of individual philanthropy stimulated by a desire to preserve historic artifacts and educate the museum-going public, and each adhered to the stringent standards of architectural and historic authenticity that guided the Williamsburg restoration.[18] Though each museum village is impressive for the scope and variety of its collections and the zeal of its creator, it is Deerfield Village that provides an appropriate counterpoint to Williamsburg's exquisite historical set piece underpinned by comprehensive research. In Deerfield Village, the past is "lived in": daily life continues in the museum's assembled group of buildings, which now form one of New England's prettiest towns. It accomplished from the outset what living cities like Charleston, South Carolina, and Savannah, Georgia, achieved later: keeping the past alive while adjusting to the inevitable changes intrinsic to a viable community.[19]

Old and Historic Charleston

In 1931, seven years after the Williamsburg restoration was begun, the city of Charleston adopted the first historic district zoning ordinance in the nation and established a Board of Architectural Review to approve plans for exterior details on any construction in the Old and Historic Charleston District. This innovative ordinance was the result of an effective coalition of preservationists and government officials who hired James Allen of the Pittsburgh planning firm of Morris Knowles to draft a comprehensive zoning ordinance for Charleston. Charleston's experiment moved preservation firmly into the realm of land-use controls. For the first time, preservation was supported by an effective coalition of public and private leadership and funding.[20] The goal was to address historic areas as a whole.

In the process, the Charleston project introduced a concept that was later to be described as the *tout ensemble*—the idea that the character of an area is derived from its entirety, or the sum of its parts, rather than from the character of its individual buildings—an important advance in preservation thinking. Previously, preservationists tended to focus on individual places and buildings as something quite apart from the larger context.

Charleston provided a model for communities across the nation. It led some of the country's most important cities, including New Orleans, Louisiana, and Annapolis, Maryland, to establish historic districts regulated by ordinances and protected by boards of architectural review. Charleston's other enduring legacy to preservation was its development of America's first revolving fund. The privately organized Society for the Preservation of Old Dwellings, which had spearheaded the effort to preserve the city's historic architecture, helped owners finance restoration of their properties through use of a loan fund known as a "revolving fund." Though the society advanced the dollars for purchasing and renovating the historic structures, it received its money back when the properties were sold or rented on the open market.[21] Charleston continued to refine its concept of preservation and preservation planning with the preparation of a citywide survey of historic and architecturally significant buildings, published in 1942 as *This Is Charleston*, and a 1959 revision to the zoning ordinance that granted the board of architectural review powers over demolition.

Great Depression Programs

The Great Depression was an economic decline so severe that by 1932 one in every four U.S. workers was unemployed.[22] Yet during this period of social and political upheaval, historic preservation made some of its most significant gains. The Roosevelt administration's response to the depression—the New Deal— provided back-to-work projects administered by the NPS and the new Civilian Conservation Corps (CCC), as well as a variety of other federal agencies. In 1933 the government put jobless architects and photographers to work preparing measured drawings of major historic buildings. The Historic American Buildings Survey (HABS) thus became the country's first national audit of historic architecture.[23]

Two years later the Historic Sites Act of 1935 called upon the secretary of the interior to conduct surveys of historic places throughout the nation and to identify properties that might be included in the National Park System. Privately owned, nationally significant properties that were not likely candidates for parks were cited as National Historic Landmarks (NHLs). This modest list of holdings would, in time, form the basis for the National Register of Historic Places.

As the depression took its toll on artists, historians, writers, photographers, and others, the federal government created documentation programs to record important aspects of the nation's cultural heritage. These included extensive photographs, recordings, transcriptions, and other records of rural life that today still provide important insights into historic places and traditions in all of the states.[24]

Post–World War II Developments

At the end of World War II, the United States entered a period of relative stability. The American people were eager to put the deprivations of the depression and the war years behind them. Widespread access to automobiles and a decline in gasoline prices initiated the first wave of historic tourism; soon national parks, battlefield parks, and museum towns like Colonial Williamsburg were enjoying record numbers of visitors.

At the same time, returning veterans sought to fulfill a long-established American dream: ownership of a single family house on an individual lot, away from the congestion and other problems associated with central cities. Federal government housing subsidies strongly supported this migration to the suburbs and with the Housing Act of 1949 began to address central-city problems with new programs of slum clearance and urban redevelopment.

Meanwhile, natural, historic, and cultural areas were also under siege. Ronald F. Lee, chief historian for the NPS, described the postwar era's threats as "inflation, suburban developments, highway building, exploration for oil, construction of office buildings, the possible sale of surplus forts, and the destruction of archeological sites through water control projects."[25] Although the nature of these threats remained open to debate, Lee's comments reflected the views of many preservationists.

To combat these problems, a select group of preservationists turned their energies to the formation of a quasi-public advocacy group that could accomplish what the NPS could not do alone. In 1947 representatives of the nation's major cultural and preservation organizations chartered the National Council for Historic Sites and Buildings in Washington, D.C. The council immediately set about obtaining a congressional charter for the National Trust, a nongovernmental agency that could enlist voluntary support and act as a liaison between public and private agencies. The result was the NTHP, which became the standard-bearer for an expanded preservation movement. Chartered by Congress on October 17, 1949, the Trust was empowered to own important historic properties and to provide leadership and support for preservation, giving the movement national scope and visibility.[26]

By 1951 the National Trust had acquired its first historic property, Woodlawn Plantation in Mount Vernon, Virginia. As an owner and preserver of historic properties, the Trust was influential in expanding the definition of what might be preservable. Its 1956 criteria for evaluating historic sites and buildings emphasized the importance of a broad cultural, political, economic, or social history of the nation, state, or community, adding that mere antiquity was not a sufficient basis for selection. Although many of its early supporters came from the historic house museum and museum village constituency, there was growing acknowledgment that a wider view of preservation was necessary.

Through its energetic circuit-riding attempts to supply "practical preservation" assistance to local organizations and through its publication *Historic Pres-*

ervation, the NTHP helped to restructure the preservation movement. The Trust went on to encourage the enlargement of acceptable time periods to admit Victorian and twentieth-century contributions as historic architecture and to promote adaptive use as a major preservation tool.[27]

Important Benchmarks

By the mid-1960s the full impact of the postwar public construction programs was evident. The creation of the massive interstate and defense highway system, said to be the largest public work since the building of the pyramids, was largely an Eisenhower-era response to the Cold War. With federal government assistance, new interstate highways began to crisscross the nation, but they destroyed historic urban neighborhoods by cutting them up for major street and highway projects.

Perceptions of urban decay were met with programs that encouraged the redevelopment of whole sections of cities. Many of these programs caused older communities to be swept away and new development to rise in their place. However, successive changes to national housing legislation through the 1960s moved away from complete clearance and redevelopment to more sensitive, less destructive projects of urban renewal and conservation. Eventually, the U.S. Department of Housing and Urban Development (HUD) subsidized path-breaking demonstration historic preservation and housing rehabilitation studies in Providence, Rhode Island, New Orleans, and Savannah. Integrated approaches to area preservation involving the highly coordinated use of zoning regulations, nonprofit organizations, revolving funds, and urban renewal projects came to the fore, providing early models for many of today's local conservation programs.

A Clarion Call

Due partly to gains and losses experienced during urban renewal and partly to the advocacy of a number of state officials and the National Trust, a new sense of urgency arose about the need for the federal government to establish a comprehensive national historic preservation program. The case for preservation was eloquently stated in *With Heritage So Rich*, a report sponsored by the U.S. Conference of Mayors and mobilized by a special Committee on Historic Preservation formed during the 1965 White House Conference on Natural Beauty.

Congress's response to the report was the National Historic Preservation Act of 1966 (NHPA), the most far-reaching preservation legislation ever enacted in the United States. NHPA expanded the National Register of Historic Places and for the first time included historic properties of local and statewide significance. It also authorized matching funds to states for surveys, preservation planning, preparation of National Register nominations, and the acquisition and preservation of historic sites and buildings. Finally, the statute established a watchdog federal agency, the Advisory Council on Historic Preservation (ACHP).

The shift in emphasis from the 1935 Historic Sites Act was palpable. *With Heritage So Rich* was a clarion call to preserve not just nationally significant landmarks, but all historic places important to communities in order to provide "orientation to the American people."[28] In time, state governments enlarged their historic preservation programs to participate in the national program, thereby expanding local programs as well. Vastly broadened approaches to preservation at the state level led to the establishment of state financial incentives, state registers, and, in some cases, state-level advisory councils modeled on the ACHP. Building on the incentives and interest provided by the national program, some states began to subsidize preservation through direct grants or by tax relief in one form or another. More recently, some states have begun to emphasize preservation planning, thereby linking preservation with related growth management and other resource protection programs.[29] It is simply impossible to overstate the importance or incentive value of the 1966 act.

Early Years of the National Historic Preservation Act

Following passage of the 1966 measure, work began to implement its provisions. The NPS assembled a small staff to develop criteria for the expanded National Register and to develop a process for nominating properties for listing. Procedures were put in place to provide for the review of federal government projects and undertakings by the ACHP. An important requirement of the new federal law was that states formulate statewide plans for historic preservation.[30]

At the beginning, many properties that had already been documented were nominated and listed in the National Register. As time passed, new properties were identified, documented, and nominated. By the end of the first decade of the national program, many federal and state officials were confident that the National Register could be completed, and they could thereafter focus on preserving the properties listed. But it quickly became clear that, in light of the broadened scope of the register to account for new areas of historical and archaeological research, as well as changing attitudes about what was worth preserving, the listing process would be a never-ending one. In May 1971 President Richard M. Nixon issued Executive Order 11593 directing federal agencies to accept preservation responsibility for properties under their ownership or jurisdiction, whether listed or merely eligible for listing in the National Register.

Historic Preservation as a Mainstream Activity

By the time of the Bicentennial in 1976, the results of historic preservation could be observed from coast to coast. The Bicentennial was in fact many celebrations, and it generated publications, events, and other activities that sensitized many Americans to the concept of historic preservation for the first time. Because of the largely local nature of Bicentennial celebrations, a variety of topics associated with the nation's diverse character came to the fore, and ideas about what was worth preserving began to broaden in the public mind. For example, an NPS-sponsored survey of African American historic places inspired a concerted effort to inventory historic properties associated with other ethnic groups.

Partly as a result of federal tax legislation passed in 1976 and 1981, the adaptive use of historic buildings began to accelerate. The Tax Reform Act of 1976 provided "modest incentives for rehabilitating historic properties and eliminated certain tax benefits for demolition."[31] The later Economic Recovery Tax Act of 1981 offered benefits far superior to those of the 1976 act. So strong were these incentives that preservationists began to think in terms of the "business" of historic preservation.

In the 1970s and 1980s that business was fueled in large part by the growing numbers of individual homeowners and intrepid entrepreneurs who began renovating historic properties for their personal residences; adapting historic structures to income-producers like bed-and-breakfasts; and acquiring, renovating, and reselling historic properties for financial gain. Encouraged by the preservation tax credits and sensitized to quality-of-life issues emerging from the environmental movement, thousands of fledgling preservationists purchased their first old houses.

In 1973, the year the nation celebrated its first Historic Preservation Week, a newsletter called *The Old-House Journal* was published in an 1883 Brooklyn brownstone. One of the earliest of what is today a plethora of popular technical journals and magazines designed to address the how-tos of old house building technology, the *Journal* espoused the tenets of good preservation and renovation, distinguishing among rehabilitation, renovation, remodeling, and restoration. This publication, and many like it, gave the general public access to information that had been disseminated in seminars and pamphlets of the National Trust, the American Association for State and Local History, and the Association for Preservation Technology. Among the benefits of the preservation publications—which eventually spawned programs like public television's *This Old House*, made famous by Bob Vila—was the continuing discussion of what could be considered worthy of preservation. Late Victorian styles were the first to be analyzed and made acceptable. Then vernacular styles were acknowledged and praised, and for a brief period in 1985 *The Old-House Journal* considered publishing a separate magazine for post-Victorian and early-twentieth-century-style homes.[32]

About this time, attention began to focus strongly on the need to revitalize downtowns and to reposition central-city commercial areas to compete with postwar suburban shopping malls. In 1976 urban visionary and developer James Rouse used virtually all of the redevelopment tools then available to renovate Boston's Quincy Market and Faneuil Hall as the nation's first Festival Market Place. Featuring shops, restaurants, and a huge food emporium in the old market building, the project became known as the quintessential inner-city rehabilitation project. Rouse and many imitators went on to create festival markets in other cities.[33]

Preservation and commercial area revitalization proved to be an ideal match in still another way during the 1980s, as the National Trust's Main Street program became one of the most successful ventures built on these foundations. Following a highly fruitful pilot program in two midwestern cities—Galesburg, Illinois, and Hot Springs, South Dakota—the NTHP created a formal program to rebuild downtown commercial areas in cities of less than 100,000 residents. By the end of 1987 more than $1 billion had been reinvested by public and private sources in 650 so-called Main Street communities.[34] The program soon became known as "the best idea the Trust ever had" and remains extremely popular and effective today.

Other special preservation interests called out for support. The National Trust took a serious interest in maritime preservation, while other groups clamored for a greater focus on roadside development under the banner of "commercial archaeology." Attention also turned to the preservation of rural areas, to the need for a joining of interests between the built and natural environments, and to a greater emphasis on integrating preservation into local planning and growth management programs.[35] There was also a growing interest in moving beyond the preservation of buildings and structures into what came to be called our "intangible cultural heritage."[36]

In a real sense, preservation continued to become much more localized in the early 1980s. The lead-in to this development was the important *Penn. Central* decision of the U.S. Supreme Court in 1978 (described below), which greatly strengthened the hand of local governments in the use of preservation regulations. In 1980 amendments to the National Historic Preservation Act provided for the creation of Certified Local Governments (CLGs), which were not only to receive a portion of each state's federal preservation funds, but were also entitled to participate directly in some aspects of the national program.[37]

Localization had a downside, however. Not only did the 1980 NHPA amendments give individual owners a veto over the actual listing of their properties in the National Register, but also the emerging view of preservation as being primarily a state and local activity resulted in severe congressional budget cuts to the programs of the NTHP, the NPS, and the ACHP. This shift in attitude appeared even before the Reagan administration took office, and it was not confined to Congress. In Washington, for example, HUD's Urban Development Action Program Grants (UDAGS) were configured in a manner adverse to preservation interests,[38] and in the heartland the city of St. Louis, Missouri, fought hard against inclusion of its three-hundred-acre downtown business district in the National Register.[39]

In the four years of the Carter administration, responsibility for the national historic preservation program was removed from the NPS and merged with the programs of the Bureau of Outdoor Recreation (BOR) to form the Heritage Conservation and Recreation Service (HCRS). This combination of cultural, natural, and recreational programs seemed a constructive alliance of common interests, and the move may yet have implications for the future of the preservation movement. The principle of allied interests lives on in the many heritage areas that have been established by Congress and state governments. But implementation of the HCRS was unsuccessful, and the Reagan administration returned the national preservation and recreational programs to the NPS.[40]

Despite the positive direction of the National Main Street Program and the new ideas put forth during this period, the decade was characterized by a rising tide of conservatism and a growing preoccupation with individual property rights in both the national and state government. Historic preservation was viewed as a "liberal" activity and thus subject to reining-in by politicians. For instance, some members of Congress joined the Reagan administration to zero out the Historic Preservation Fund (HPF), which supported the state historic preservation offices and, indirectly, new CLG programs. The new conservatism was also evident as lobbyists for corporations attempted to limit the scope of NHPA by restricting federal involvement to nationally significant properties.[41]

In 1986 the federal preservation tax credits that had fueled the reclamation of innumerable historic buildings and neighborhoods across the nation suffered a major setback. Reacting to concern that wealthy investors were abusing the federal tax credits introduced in the Economic Recovery Tax Act only five years earlier, a bipartisan Congress passed the 1986 Tax Reform Act reducing the 25 percent credits to 20 percent for income-producing properties and to 10 percent for nonresidential buildings constructed before 1936.[42]

These restrictions and a general cooling of the real estate market nationwide seemed to present significant new challenges, even a severe blow, to the historic preservation field. But by the end of the century, it was clear that this had not happened. In 1999 the NPS director reported: "Since its inception in 1977, the historic rehabilitation tax credit has generated more than $20 billion in historic preservation activity. Last year, in 1998, the rehabilitation tax credit program approved more than 900 projects, creating more than 42,000 jobs, and leveraged nearly $1.8 billion in private investment."[43] As of October 2001, the figure stood at more than $23 billion in leveraged private investment.

Expanding the Vision

Much of the recent success of preservation at the local level has rested on the spectacular, if narrow, 5–4 decision of the Supreme Court in 1978 upholding New York City's landmark preservation law in *Penn. Central Transportation Co. et al. v. New York City Co. et al.*[44] The majority opinion by Justice William Brennan put to rest any lingering doubts about the constitutionality of regulating the designation of individual historic landmarks by local governments. In the new climate created by that decision, preservation enjoyed many local successes in the late 1980s and early 1990s. It fared well when the New York Supreme Court (the state's trial court) upheld landmark designation of twenty-two theaters in New York City. That decision, following the demolition of the Helen Hayes Theater for a hotel site, led to a renaissance in the theater district.[45] New York scored yet another preservation victory in 1990 when a U.S. Court of Appeals denied a request by St. Bartholomew's Church to build a forty-seven-story office tower on the site of its Park Avenue community house.[46]

Inspired, in part, by these victories, individuals, cities, and new coalitions made significant commitments to a variety of preservation-related projects and programs. Land conservation and the protection of historic and scenic landscapes made headlines when, in 1990, rock music star Don Henley joined forces with the Trust for Public Lands to option twenty-five acres of Walden Woods in Massachusetts. Made famous by author Henry David Thoreau, the idyllic setting was included by the National Trust on its Most Endangered Properties List.[47] Heritage tourism received major attention when the National Trust selected Indiana, Tennessee, Texas, and Wisconsin to participate in a pilot tourism development program to demonstrate that historic places can attract visitors and form the basis for considerable economic development.[48] New Orleans, the second city after Charleston to adopt a historic preservation ordinance, entered into its third public-private nonprofit partnership made possible by HUD programs to renovate the Flint-Goodridge Apartments as low-income housing for the elderly.[49]

An enhanced public understanding of cultural diversity began to appear in large and small preservation projects when the National Register broadened its concept of what was worth preserving and added vernacular, industrial, and natural resources to its nomination criteria. In New York, the Ellis Island main building reopened after a seven-year, $150 million restoration funded largely from private sources.[50]

The Power of Place, a small nonprofit Los Angeles organization, successfully mounted an exhibit in a parking garage on the site of the home of Billy Mason, an African American slave who in 1856 sued for her freedom.[51] The Black Heritage Trail, following the Alabama march route from Selma to Montgomery, opened as a National Historic Trail in one of the most significant moves by Congress to preserve artifacts of the African American community and the civil rights movement.[52] These and other innovative projects, often entailing significant financial, social, or political risks, spanned economic and cultural differences, were often regional or national in scope, and spoke effectively of a new era of state participation in the preservation process.

Anticipating the reauthorization of the federal Highway Trust Fund, the U.S. Department of Transportation (DOT) adopted the concept of a national system of scenic highways.[53] The idea of historic transportation corridors also received a boost when the Delaware and Lehigh Navigation Canal National

Heritage Corridor was designated as the third such corridor.[54] The concept of heritage areas found adherents in Congress and an increasing number of state legislatures and now constitutes a major preservation-conservation tool.

Emerging interest in preservation planning, begun in the 1980s, accelerated during the 1990s. State legislation and programs that parallel section 4(f) of DOT legislation and Section 106 of NHPA are in place in a number of states. Some of these measures, specifically oriented to preservation, have been incorporated into state-mandated planning activities. Vermont's comprehensive planning statute, known as the Growth Management Act of 1988, mandated approval of all state construction projects by a state regional planning commission to minimize potentially harmful effects on historic properties. Maryland and Rhode Island went even further, requiring all municipalities to prepare comprehensive plans that included historic preservation elements.[55] At the local level, cities such as Providence, Rhode Island,[56] Seattle, Washington, and Portland, Oregon, have adopted integrated and comprehensive approaches to planning, regulations, and fiscal procedures covering preservation activity.[57]

The historic house museums and outdoor museum villages that pioneered the historic preservation movement in the United States enjoyed a resurgence in the 1990s. Though some preservationists believed that such properties were no longer important to the preservation field, individual properties like Mount Vernon and Monticello and museum villages like Colonial Williamsburg became internationally renowned laboratories producing ground-breaking research in such fields as archaeology, textile conservation, slavery, and horticulture. Once again, these treasured properties proved popular with the public as well as with scholars. The preservation movement had begun to redefine itself.

A New Agenda

As the twentieth century entered its final decade, the agenda set forth in NHPA had largely been completed. In 1966 the major threat to historic places was seen to arise from federal government programs and federally funded development. Some twenty-five years later, and even today, privately funded development, rather than federally sponsored programs, is seen as the greater threat. The changing demographics and settlement patterns of the nation, the rise of a technology-oriented society, and a pervasive decline in public interest in our history and in the teaching of it now constitute some of the major challenges facing the preservation field.

The 1990s saw a search for a new mandate for the preservation movement, including its integration with a larger economic and social community, joining business, industry, and culturally diverse groups as well as traditional colleagues in government conservation and planning. The first prospective mandates appeared in the "Charleston Principles"—eight guidelines to community conservation formally adopted at the 1990 annual meeting of the National Trust.[58] Reading like a summary of all the preservation knowledge gained in the previous one hundred years, the Charleston Principles reflected a search for preservation theory that could guide and shape policies, plans, and development at the local level. They emphasized historic preservation as a major element of every community's economic success, called for the recognition of every community's multicultural nature, and urged the empowerment of a diverse constituency to "acknowledge, identify, and preserve America's cultural and physical resources."[59]

In 1991 the National Preservation Conference held in San Francisco was to be a celebration of the twenty-fifth anniversary of NHPA and a convocation on the challenges of the next quarter-century. Based on the theme "When Past Meets Future," the conference's purpose was to develop a new agenda. The sessions underscored five major themes for the future: the growing multicultural nature of the American people, the development of technologies that would revolutionize American society as a whole, the importance of integrating preservation concerns into land-use decision making, how to use preservation tools to address the increasing abandonment of the central cities, and how preservation could address the cultural illiteracy of a nation in which few young people knew the basic facts of their own national history.[60]

Tools to achieve some of the goals of the Charleston and San Francisco conferences were handed to preservationists in 1991 with the enactment by Congress of one of the most significant government funding packages ever made available for urban revitalization projects and open-space plans. Led by Senators Daniel Patrick Moynihan and Charles Chafee, and advised by the Surface Transportation Policy Project (STPP), the Intermodal Surface Transportation Efficiency Act (ISTEA) recognized that national transportation policy should be built upon more than new highways. It encouraged diverse modes of travel, including those that incorporated historic and recreational activities. ISTEA mandated that individual states set aside 10 percent of their allocated funds for options known as "enhancements," which covered a variety of people-friendly facilities as well as the purchase of scenic easements and development of historic highway programs.[61] ISTEA was reauthorized in 1998 as the Transportation Equity Act for the Twenty-first Century (TEA-21). The new legislation authorized and provided funding for downtown street improvements, the rehabilitation of historic neighborhoods, the restoration of rail depots, the creation of pedestrian paths, and the recovery of urban waterfronts.[62]

Whereas some agenda items from the Charleston and San Francisco conferences were addressed by transportation and tax incentives, others were reflected in the 1992 amendments to NHPA. These provided for the recognition of tribal historic preservation officers (THPOs), a move that gave Native American groups a seat at the table with federal agencies, state historic preservation offices, local government preservation programs, and the private sector. The amendments also directed the secretary of the interior to assist minority colleges and universities with the development of preservation training and degree programs.[63]

Future Directions for Historic Preservation

Historic preservation has evolved over nearly two hundred years to become an energetic, effective national movement. It began in the early nineteenth century with small localized efforts to preserve patriotic monuments and grew over the next hundred years into a national network of dedicated individuals, voluntary organizations, and local governments promoting the preservation of larger, mostly urban, historic environments.

The post–World War II era produced many of the social and infrastructural problems that eventually led to the passage of NHPA and the creation of federal, state, local, and private mechanisms to implement its mandate.[64] The 1980s and 1990s saw the emergence of the business of preservation and of efforts to incorporate the heritage of all the nation's people. Now, early-twenty-first-century preservationists are facing an interesting challenge: what post–World War II historic places to preserve. At issue are the Levittowns and other period subdivisions, glass box office buildings, shopping centers, suburban school buildings, and other elements of the midcentury sprawl.

Preservation is now an art, a business, an inexact science, and, for many, a passion. Its imperatives attracted a whole generation of baby boomers into preservation careers, or, at least, into restoring their own old houses. Many preservationists have been transformed from zealots into pragmatic bureaucrats. Today, the 1960s pioneers and their successors can rest assured that preservation values have penetrated many hearts and minds. Yet preservation has yet to become as pervasive a national priority as recycling, energy conservation, or the protection of endangered species.

In the early twenty-first century, preservation in America looks back upon the footprints of its history to Ann Pamela Cunningham and the Mount Vernon Ladies, the Reverend W. A. R. Goodwin, the Charleston Society, the advocates for the natural splendor of Yellowstone, the Main Streets of the heartland, and the routes of civil rights marches. That trail and those who walked it have vitalized the ideals that continue to inform the American national character and experience. They have laid a strong foundation for the preservation of the nation's cultural heritage as an essential part of the national identity.

I

Preservation Comes of Age

Some Preservation Fundamentals

The context of preservation has greatly changed over the last half century. Like the editors and contributors to *With Heritage So Rich* forty years ago,[1] we are faced with a host of new issues, as well as some old ones. Like its predecessor, this book is biased toward traditional values, but it also represents an attempt to deal with the preservation issues of our own day as a new century beckons. The prologue to this book poses a question, "why preserve?," that is still unasked and unanswered for a majority of the public. We thus must confront a major public educational task, one even greater and more complex than in 1966. How we approach that task and how well we succeed in completing it depends, first, on how well we understand the larger context of preservation as an emerging phenomenon in America.

Changing Values

Preservation's basic values have vastly changed since 1966. The early associative values centered almost exclusively on history and architecture as the most valued cultural resources. In recent years, however, we have moved beyond that narrow view. For example, National Register Criterion A ("the broad patterns of our history") has in most states become as important as style and design in architecture, and archaeology is a prominent value in the western states. A wide variety of specialized resources such as battlefields, designed and vernacular landscapes, mines, recent buildings, entire inner-city neighborhoods, and vernacular buildings are now widely accepted, as are a broad range of newly popular resources: highway commercial "strip business" developments, early filling stations, ships, lighthouses, outstanding contemporary buildings, and post–World War II subdivisions. Racial, tribal, and ethnic interests are firmly embedded in our preservation programs, and many would agree that such intangible cultural values as music, dialect, and storytelling should be added to the mix. American Indian tribes now have a special role in preservation programs, in recognition of their status as sovereign nation-states, and as the world grows smaller, the local traditions and preservation techniques of one nation seem to migrate ever more quickly to others. Monuments and sites of special international importance to all of humankind are threatened or lost as a result of war, neglect, or the march of progress, and the international dimension of preservation takes on a special significance. Cultural homogenization has become an issue.

The Preservation System

At first glance, the American historic preservation system seems terribly complex. However, in broad outline it is not, *provided* one has a solid understanding of three basic concepts. The first and perhaps most important is the general structure of the American federal system of government. The second is the universal nature of the preservation-conservation process itself. And the third is the nature of our free market economic system. To deal effectively with preservation problems, one must first be able to comprehend all three of these basic phenomena. The remaining sections of this chapter consider these fundamental concepts.

The Structure of Government

The first aspect of preservation in America that must be understood is our three-tiered, federal-state-local system of government. Most Americans— and most preservationists—neither appreciate nor fully grasp this system. Each of the three layers of government confronts us with both incentives and obstacles to historic preservation, and it is an unusual preservation situation that does not, in some manner, involve all three.

At the federal level, some of the obstacles we face are embedded in our Constitution, which is almost impossible to change or amend, as well as in congressional mandates and bureaucratic regulations and attitudes, which are also changed only with difficulty. The same is true at the state level, except that each of the fifty states has its own constitution, legislation, and traditions of

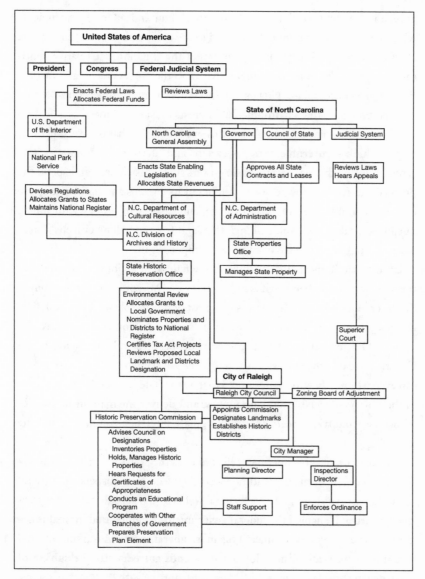

Organization of preservation responsibilities in North Carolina. This diagram dramatically illustrates the complexity of our layered, interconnected system of federal, state, and local governments involved in historic preservation, each with its own executive, legislative, and judicial system. Although it outlines how preservation functions in North Carolina, similar but equally complex relationships exist in all other states. Understanding these relationships is the starting point to effective participation in historic preservation activities. (Linda Harris Edmisten and Robert E. Stipe)

governing and preservation problem solving. Thousands of local governments with their own ways of doing things add to the complexity of the problem. At all of these levels there will be the politics of the situation, the relative political strength of the contestants themselves, and the bureaucracies and institutions representing them. This usually presents the most difficult hurdle that preservation and other environmental interests must overcome.

The starting point in sorting all of this out is to ask: What is government? It helps to think of governments as "sovereign" and "derivative." A *sovereign* government is one that has certain basic powers: to tax its citizens and spend the proceeds; to regulate the personal conduct of its citizens and the way they use their land; and to acquire, own, manage, and dispose of property for public purposes—taking or "condemning" that land from unwilling citizens if necessary for public use on payment of fair compensation.

Unfortunately, most citizens think of the federal or national government as the most important, because it is in Washington, D.C., or because it is "above" the others, and because it has access to almost unimaginable wealth. But in fact, it is not our basic government, nor even a "sovereign" government as just described. Our federal or national government was created by the states in the Constitution of 1787 and is thus a *derivative* government in the sense that it can exercise only those powers granted to it by the states in that document, such as the power to declare war, coin money, and deliver the mail; make treaties with other countries; create an army; regulate interstate commerce; and the like.

This narrow view is sometimes referred to as the "old" federalism. But Article 1, Section 8, of the Constitution also gives Congress unspecified, general power to pass legislation for the "general welfare," a power that over the years has, it is argued, enabled the federal government to embrace additional functions not specifically mentioned. This more liberal approach is often referred to as the "new" federalism. How far it extends is frequently the subject of lively debate.

What is important to remember, however, is that the states did not give away all their sovereign or inherent power to the federal government when they created it. They retained for themselves, in Amendments 9 and 10 to the Constitution, the basic power to regulate citizens in their personal conduct and the use of their property. This retained power is called the "police power," and it includes the power to regulate historic buildings.

This bit of history notwithstanding, there are indeed a lot of federal regulations pertaining to preservation and many other matters. But if there is no in-

Cartoon: "I Want You!" How should a committed preservationist react to a statement like the one implied in this editorial page cartoon? Most of us would probably accept some of the federal activities shown as quite proper and reject others. Overall, however, the cartoon intones the widely held, conservative bias of many who believe that the "old" federalism would probably exclude federal involvement in activities like historic preservation. (Gary Brookins, *Richmond [Va.] Times-Dispatch*)

herent federal regulatory authority, as just noted, what are these federal regulations? In short, federal regulations pertaining to historic preservation, the use of land, and hundreds of other activities are, in effect, a ritual form of bribery, mostly enacted under the "new" federalism of Article 1, Section 8, of the Constitution, which also gives Congress the authority to levy taxes and provide for the general welfare. Much of the federal government's so-called regulatory authority thus derives from the fact that Washington has tremendous wealth derived from personal and corporate income taxes, which it may "give back" to state and local governments with strings attached—strings adopted in general by Congress and later detailed by federal agencies. These are commonly called "federal regulations" and are found in the Code of Federal Regulations (CFR), which is cited in various places in this book.

Since all federal aid is subject to conditions set in Washington, federal regulations are a kind of string on loans, grants, and other forms of assistance from the national government. If they are violated, they result only in the potential loss of assistance to carry out federal programs in accordance with national policies—for instance, historic preservation, highways, housing, hospitals, schools, welfare, airports, libraries, parks, education, and just about everything else done or built by state and local governments. These days little happens that is not done in part with federal money or is not subject to a federal permit. Thus, disregarding federal policies or failing to abide by federal regulations means losing federal "aid"; this creates political problems at the state and local levels, like raising taxes to make up the loss or forgoing programs that citizens want.

Under our system, the truly sovereign or primary unit of government is, in fact, the state. After all, it was the states that got together and created a national government of thirteen states, now fifty in number, and they continue to hold all the basic powers not specifically given to the federal government in the Constitution of 1787 and its amendments. Of particular importance to preservation is that the states retained the "police power," or the power to regulate citizens' personal behavior (assault, murder, swearing in public, stealing, etc.) and the use of property (zoning, historic districts, landmark designation, building codes, etc.).

Cities, like the federal government, are created by the states and are also derivative governments. And though the states, as sovereign governments, have not delegated the police power "up" to Washington, they can and have delegated much of their regulatory authority "down" to cities and counties. (Counties, historically speaking, are local branches of state government spread over larger geographic areas to better provide state services locally—such as schools, law enforcement, care of the poor, roads, running the courts, holding elections, keeping real estate records, and other functions). The governmental powers delegated "down" to cities are somewhat different than those of counties in that they center on the needs of citizens living closely together: water and sewer services, police and fire protection, recreation programs, libraries, and so forth. These include land-use regulations like the creation of historic districts and the designation of landmarks, enforcement of subdivision and zoning ordinances, and other growth management measures. Today, in addition to their traditional responsibilities, many counties have been given the same powers as cities and have therefore also assumed responsibilities that involve historic preservation.

All of this explains how it is that local governments can simultaneously embrace nonregulatory National Register historic districts or buildings, designated by the U.S. Department of the Interior, and at the same time adopt and enforce local historic district and landmark ordinances passed by the city or county government under its state-delegated regulatory or police power over the same property. It also explains why National Register property owners are generally free to do whatever they want to their buildings so long as no federal money, permit, or other federal program is involved. But if those same property owners also hold property in a local historic district, or live in a designated landmark established by the local government pursuant to the sovereign police power of the state, they can be jailed or fined for violating a local historic district or landmark ordinance. As it works, a single historic property can be in one district and not the other, or the other and not the one—or both.

This may sound like a lot of theory, but in application it is very, very real. It is imperative that this underlying theory be understood, because the failure of most citizens, politicians, and administrators to comprehend these distinctions creates more problems for preservation than any other cause.

The Preservation Process

The second basic concept to understand is that from a procedural standpoint, preserving old buildings or neighborhoods is fundamentally no different from preserving a threatened or endangered animal or plant species, a coral reef, or the scenic character of a rural landscape. Conceptually, as well as at a practical level, the sequential steps are, first, setting standards or criteria that define what is worth preserving; second, undertaking a survey to locate and describe resources potentially to be saved; third, evaluating the resources discovered in the survey against the standards established in step one; fourth, giving those that qualify "official status" in some way; and fifth, following up with protective measures. These five steps are always involved and follow exactly that sequence in preserving anything—whether a mountain trail, the endangered Red Cockaded Woodpecker, or an old building. The objects or resources to be preserved or protected may be different, but the process itself never changes. Understanding the purpose and sequence of these steps, and why each step must be done correctly, is essential.

In our system, a basic standard of what is worth preserving is articulated in the various criteria established by the National Register of Historic Places in some instances, but state or local criteria may also come into play in others. Notwithstanding that new associative values—townscapes, vernacular and designed landscapes, marine resources, ethnic and racial history, and others—have crept into the system since 1966, architecture and history are still regarded by many as the bedrock associative values. In practice, most of our standards are derived from earlier, narrower views about what is worth preserving. Thus is maintained a tradition that extends back to the mid-1930s, when a New Deal, depression-era program, the Historic American Buildings Survey, was created to put unemployed architects back to work. Although the National Register standards are heavily weighted in favor of traditional thinking about architecture as art and history as a series of events, new words like "culture" and "historic places" appeared in the 1966 act and left the door open for the eventual admission of new concepts about what is important to preserve. Individual states and local governments may have their own standards of value, subject only to state and local preservation incentives and sanctions.

The second step, the survey, involves simply the creation of a database—no more. It is unnecessary at this point to dwell on the distinction between surveys and inventories, or whether they should be geographically or thematically organized. It is more important to emphasize that solid scholarship and professional competence are required to complete them, since faulty or sloppy work may result in serious adverse legal consequences at a later stage of the process when government benefits or penalties come into play. States, which oversee most of this work on behalf of themselves and the national government, are heavily dependent on historians, architectural historians, and archaeologists for the survey work. A few, like Florida and Georgia, have invited the participation of folklorists, cultural anthropologists, landscape architects, geographers, and other specialists.

Aside from their costly nature, a major problem is that surveys chase a moving target in both time and content. What was not old enough twenty years ago to be regarded as "historic" may have aged sufficiently in the interim to now be worth recording. Or it may now meet a standard that has changed in the interim or its context may be greatly modified. For all practical purposes, the surveys that count the most today are those that in one way or another can be related to the National Register. However, some states also maintain their own registers for some collateral or supplemental state purpose. Occasionally a survey will be undertaken locally without reference to either, but this is the exception rather than the rule.

The third step is to examine each surveyed property to determine whether it passes the test established by the criteria adopted in stage one. Those that do not are literally (as well as sometimes legally) "non-contributing"—a strange designation according to today's seemingly broadened preservation ethic. This aspect of the decision-making process is an imperfect one, as will be seen in later chapters. Is the resource "significant?" and to whom?—a local, state, or national constituency? Is it a Grade One resource that passed the threshold easily, or is it a Grade Five, only marginally worth being included? Are the criteria followed honestly, or do fiscal or political motives creep into the process?—as is often the case. Who or what group of individuals decides whether a resource is "in" or "out" is an important question, legally and politically. In the case of historic buildings, it may be a local governing board, a landmark commission, a state historical commission or historic preservation officer, or the Keeper of the National Register. The answer will eventually present legal consequences of one kind or another, regardless of whether we are evaluating plants, animals, air or water quality, people, buildings, neighborhoods, or landscapes.

The fourth step of this universal process is to bestow official status upon resources that pass the threshold test of acceptability, typically some form of registration. There are local "registers" (we call them landmark or historic district ordinances); state registers, with their own criteria in some cases; and a National Register. Designation or listing, however titled, is inevitably an "official" process, whether by a local, state, or national official, board, or commission—or all of them! It is from this step that legal and financial consequences flow. Again, it is part of a universal process of discrimination, which is implicit but rarely discussed in those terms. The designation process is that stage that ultimately determines what is important, why it is important, and who says so.

The final stage of this universal process is to determine the extent and nature of any protection or benefit to be accorded a designated resource that has been recognized by a process agreed to be socially, politically, and legally acceptable. The recognition may be as mild as the award of an official plaque, or it may provoke further nonbinding discussion among officials before it or its immediate environment may be altered or destroyed, as in some environmental review procedures. Or there may be sanctions that restrict the owner in the use of the property, perhaps the grant or denial of a required permit, or a delay or prohibition against alteration or demolition of the property. Additional consequences of this protective process may be in the form of government loans or grants directly from the public treasury; or an indirect subsidy, as in some form of income or property tax relief.

Whatever the consequences of designation, the process itself is always one of setting standards, locating and describing the resource, evaluating it according to the standards, giving it some kind of official status, and then following through with a variety of protective measures or preservation assistance. It is a universal process in all resource protection programs. Understanding how the various steps of this process are carried out and by whom is essential.

For simplicity's sake, it is helpful to categorize the major protective measures. One category protects cultural resources against the bad deeds of their owners or neighbors, such as demolishing or defacing buildings in ways that destroy their architectural or historic fabric, or damaging the surrounding environment—as it is often said, "protecting them against the hand of man." Protective measures run the gamut from mild environmental review and comment to regulatory programs that contemplate prison or fines or, in rare cases, to the actual acquisition of the property by government. Which approaches are used will depend on many factors, of which the political climate and the availability of public funds will be the most crucial. The success of increasingly widespread regulatory approaches is intimately related to how citizens feel about the basic power of government to tell them what they may or may not do with their property. All of these measures tend to put the cost of preservation on the individual property owner or citizen.

The second basic category of protective measures involves protecting the resource against the hand of time, to which empty buildings are always the most susceptible through simple deterioration.[2] This approach is basically one in which the government or some other entity, such as a nonprofit organization, provides financial assistance to stabilize, preserve, or restore the property. Such assistance can be direct and take the form of loans or grants from government funds given directly to the owner to help with preservation costs. Or it can be indirect and provided through reduced federal, state, or local taxes, thus freeing up the owners' resources for preservation work instead of sending them to the local, state, or federal treasury.

The important thing to remember is that everything we do in preservation is a combination of one or the other or both of these two basic approaches. This brings us to the central question of the impact of a market-oriented society on historic preservation processes.

Preservation as a Market Phenomenon

In addition to understanding the underlying nature of our federal system of government and the basic sequence of steps of the preservation process, one must also recognize that preservation always has been, presently is, and always will be primarily a matter of market economics. It follows that saving a resource of any kind will necessarily involve both the public and the private sectors of our capitalist, market economy. Historic preservation can rarely succeed unless both public and private sectors are operating together in a mutually supportive manner. That is because buildings, neighborhoods, landscapes, Main

Street—whatever one attempts to save or preserve—must always fulfill the basic investment expectations of the owner or owners of the property or the area. If they do not, they will inevitably be lost.

Many owners of old buildings and historic sites will accept that they have cultural value and importance, and often take pride in that and forgo financial benefits. But most owners' primary view of property is its ability to return current income or capital gains.[3] Thus, the preservation or loss of cultural property is almost always the result of economic feast or famine in the local real estate market. In a very bullish real estate market in which the value of the building exceeds the value of the site, there are heavy pressures on the owner to tear it down and replace it with something more profitable, whether a parking lot, a high-rise building, or a fast-food establishment. In a bearish market in which there is no active, profitable use for the property and thus little or no economic return to the owner, the building simply stays empty and decays—whether the neglect is deliberate or not. But in both situations, the building is lost or the site—which can include entire neighborhoods—is soon or eventually put to a more profitable use.

It follows that all of our approaches to preservation—again, with the exception of private homes, museums, public buildings, and the like—are an attempt to subsidize the cost of maintaining an economically unproductive piece of real estate, however important it may be in a cultural or environmental sense. By restricting the owner's options through state and local regulatory processes, by placing federal or state environmental reporting obstacles in the owner's path, by providing government or foundation grants, loans, or tax relief, or by some combination of all of these, we are aiming to bring the owner's return from the property up to his or her economic expectations.

Regulatory controls, whether historic district or landmark regulations, or some other restriction on the use of private property, shift some of the cost of preservation directly to the owner. When government (federal, state, or local) makes financial assistance available to the owner, it is transferring some of these costs to the larger society.

Government grants and loans are what I call "front-door" assistance. Whether and how much assistance to grant are debated and allocated in public as part of a political process through which citizens have an opportunity to participate, directly or through elected representatives, in a fair and open forum that decides how they are to be taxed and how their money is spent. Tax relief or incentives, on the other hand, can be thought of as "back-door" assistance, in the sense that they are off-budget and politically easier to obtain. That both forms of assistance work well is unquestioned. The American preservation movement has been heavily dependent on back-door public assistance since 1976.

The same basic rules of economics that apply to buildings apply as well to neighborhoods and large areas. Real estate markets, whether in Hoboken, New Jersey, or San Francisco, California, are driven to a substantial extent by fashion. Run-down, undesirable neighborhoods may suddenly become desirable for various reasons, including easy access to center-city jobs, an appreciation of the architecture, reasonably priced houses for young couples, and changing market conditions. In the same way, however, the problems of preserving rural buildings and landscapes typically arise from a depressed rural economy.

Often many of the best buildings are owned by institutions or individuals who are least able to maintain them, including financially pressed local governments, universities, churches, and other charitable, nonprofit enterprises that face special challenges. Endowments do not produce the same income as when interest rates were high, the cost of renovating while meeting handicapped, environmental, and other code standards rise ever higher, and someone always needs the parking space to be gained by demolishing the building. Universities are strapped for cash, central-city church congregations move to the suburbs, and the old sanctuary or Sunday school building sits on increasingly valuable urban land with commercial potential. With notable exceptions, most local governments in the United States place a relatively low priority on preservation. Most would strongly prefer to demolish the old city hall for a new office building. In all of these situations, the result is the same: the building is lost.[4]

These basic realities affecting preservation—the structure of government, the nature of the preservation process, and the underlying economic realities of preservation—constitute themes and issues that are not usually apparent and often lie just below the surface of all preservation efforts. Success or failure in any preservation endeavor is the result of success or failure in understanding where things went well or where they failed and—most important—why.

The Federal Preservation Program

The federal role in the national historic preservation program owes its form to the creators of the National Historic Preservation Act (NHPA) of 1966. Building on a well-established but narrow federal effort up to that time, the authors of *With Heritage So Rich* proposed a federal leadership role embodied in a series of innovative measures that formed the essential framework of today's program. Indeed, one might argue that little new has been added to that original vision and that progress since then has largely consisted of fleshing out the details of that vision and adapting it to the evolving circumstances of American society.[1] The 1965 report called for a federal preservation effort that encompassed:

- an expansive inventory of properties reflecting the full range of the national heritage,
- a mechanism to protect those properties from unnecessary harm caused by federal activities,
- a program of financial incentives, embracing both grants and tax incentives, to encourage the preservation of nonfederally owned historic properties, and
- an independent federal preservation body to coordinate the actions of federal agencies affecting historic preservation.

The resulting NHPA was signed into law by President Lyndon B. Johnson on October 15, 1966.[2] The federal program that has since evolved adheres closely to the founding principles and organizational framework embodied in NHPA.

The underlying theme of American preservation is that of an effective partnership among federal, tribal, state, and local governments and the private sector. The current blend of governmental activity evolved from the initial leadership role assumed by the federal government early in the twentieth century. However, this partnership has always recognized that most preservation happens outside the federal government and, for the most part, in the private sector. Today the partnership is firmly and largely grounded in the legislative provisions of NHPA.

The Federal Players

The federal role embraces the activities of both those agencies specifically charged with historic preservation as their principal mission and the larger number of agencies for which preservation is but one of many policies that must be considered when an agency mission is pursued—be it defense, transportation, education, or something else. The interplay between these two groups of agencies both defines the nature of the federal preservation program and produces its strengths and weaknesses.

The secretary of the interior and the Advisory Council on Historic Preservation have a primary mission of historic preservation. However, the many federal agencies that own or control historic properties or that affect historic resources outside federal ownership account for most of the impact that the federal government has on the nation's heritage. Each of these various agencies has program responsibilities specified by NHPA. They are usually distinct, but occasionally they overlap. More important, the actions of these agencies, regardless of the priority preservation commands, significantly affect how historic properties are actually treated in communities nationwide.

The National Park Service

Most federal preservation activities, though legally entrusted to the secretary of the interior, are delegated to the director of the NPS.[3] This has led to the creation of a substantial bureaucracy, which has evolved as new laws have been enacted and priorities shifted. Organizationally distinct from the park management component of the NPS, the historic preservation program comprises a range of activities. The organization chart of the program has varied greatly over the years, reflecting the differing management philosophies of NPS leadership and the political demands of any given period. But the "core" historic preservation activities have remained fairly constant.[4]

At the heart of the NPS historic preservation structure is the National Register of Historic Places and related survey and identification programs such as the National Historic Landmarks program. Closely related is the Historic

American Buildings Survey, with its spin-off Historic American Engineering Record (HAER). These and similar activities with a more targeted purpose, such as the National Maritime Initiative, form the core of the increasingly sophisticated federal program to identify, evaluate, recognize, and record the national patrimony.

Of paramount importance to implementing NHPA are those program elements that manage NPS grants to states, Indian tribes, and localities, and that coordinate the partnership. These set uniform national standards for state, tribal, and local programs; provide educational and technical assistance; and generally work with these other governmental bodies to take full advantage of NHPA's provisions. The NPS provides similar assistance to federal agencies in conducting their own internal preservation programs.

The NPS also administers federal tax incentives for historic preservation. It promulgates standards for acceptable work, certifies the eligibility of individual properties, and reviews the completed rehabilitation work on individual properties to ensure that the standards are met. Historically, the NPS has played a leading role in implementing federal laws and programs concerned with the protection of archaeological resources. Interior's role in archaeology dates back to the Antiquities Act of 1906 (which actually predated the establishment of the NPS by ten years) and continues as a key NPS preservation program component. It has expanded over the years, most recently by the 1992 amendments to NHPA and by the Native American Graves Protection and Repatriation Act (NAGPRA),[5] discussed below and in Chapter 13. A particularly noteworthy current initiative is the National Archaeological Database, a systematic approach to disseminating information on archaeological resources that has been accumulated by the federal government.

Also worthy of note are those NPS programs that are not limited to historic properties, but that promote related historic preservation program goals. Examples include the Land and Water Conservation Fund and the Wild and Scenic Rivers Program, which are primarily natural resource programs, and the National Heritage Areas (NHAS), American Heritage Rivers, and the Rivers, Trails, and Conservation programs, which bring cultural and natural interests together.[6] These programs often benefit historic preservation, although the long-sought goal of many preservationists to unite cultural and natural heritage programs remains elusive.

Finally, mention must be made of the National Center for Preservation Technology and Training (NCPTT). Created as a semi-independent entity by the 1992 NHPA amendments, the center was located by law in Nachitoches,

Louisiana, and charged with promoting preservation training and technology. Over the years, the center has addressed significant preservation and materials conservation problems through partnerships with educational institutions and preservation organizations but, in the face of declining resources, has struggled to meet its legislative mandate. It still pursues the advancement of preservation education with grants and cooperative activities and stimulates the development and application of cutting-edge technologies. But it has lost much of its initial autonomy and is becoming more of an NPS component program.

While these core program activities have grown steadily in scope and impact over the years, the organizational structure has changed to reflect larger NPS priorities. Currently, it emphasizes partnership with nonfederal parties. This not only mirrors a fundamental philosophy of NHPA, but also espouses a holistic approach to managing a variety of natural and environmental resources. The NPS program structure also demonstrates the special attention periodically focused on a particular category of resources.[7] Some argue that these special efforts, which often reflect priorities set by Congress or the administration, distort the core program. Others retort that this is the only way that traditionally underrepresented resources and slighted constituencies can muscle their way into the established program. Regardless of these viewpoints, the fact remains that NPS priorities, like those of other agencies, are shaped by forces embedded in the political process. Although the preservation of the nation's patrimony relies to a high degree on objective professional actions and activities, the reality is that the federal preservation programs will wither if they lack the support of the public or its elected representatives.

The Advisory Council on Historic Preservation

The National Park Service shares its federal preservation leadership role with the Advisory Council on Historic Preservation, created by NHPA in 1966 as an independent agency to advise the president and Congress on preservation matters generally, and to comment on federal actions affecting historic properties specifically.[8] The ACHP comprises twenty cabinet officers and presidential appointees representative of the preservation community and the public at large and is intended to bring a balanced view to preservation issues confronting the federal government. Federal representatives include the secretaries of the interior and agriculture and the heads of four other federal agencies designated by the president. Preservation interests are represented by the chairman of the National Trust for Historic Preservation, the president of the National Con-

ACHP meeting. The mixed composition of the ACHP membership brings a unique perspective to federal preservation issues. Combining senior federal officials, presidentially appointed citizens, representatives of state and local government, and preservation experts infuses the ACHP's policy recommendations and Section 106 opinions with a balanced view of the public interest. (ACHP)

ference of State Historic Preservation Officers, and four experts appointed by the president. A governor and a mayor appointed by the president represent the interests of state and local government. A Native American or Native Hawaiian is appointed by the president to provide the perspective of native peoples. The Architect of the Capitol and four members named by the president from the general public round out the membership. The ACHP chairman is one of the four members appointed from the general public.

The statutory duties of the ACHP include policy advice, interagency coordination, training and education, and protection of historic properties. The ACHP advises the administration and Congress on such preservation issues as tax policy, federal agency program improvement, and pending legislation. The ACHP occasionally reviews the activities of federal agencies and their state and local government partners, and makes recommendations to improve the effectiveness of the national preservation program.[9] It provides training for federal, tribal, state, and local officials on how to incorporate preservation values into project planning, and it oversees U.S. participation in the International Centre for the Study and Conservation of Cultural Property in Rome (ICCROM).

The ACHP's most visible role in the federal preservation program is its administration of the protective process established by Section 106 of NHPA. Given statutory authority to issue regulations to implement Section 106, the ACHP established an administrative process that influences the way the federal government treats historic properties (see "Protecting Historic Properties: The Section 106 Process," below).

The ACHP's unique structure determines how it does business; and it differs sharply from the normal executive branch agency, which answers to a single political appointee. The ACHP itself establishes the general policies and priorities; thereafter ACHP staff implement these policies, working closely with the chairman, who provides policy oversight. Unlike most federal agencies, the ACHP has a full-time professional staff reporting to a membership comprised of individuals who serve only intermittently. This has tended to insulate the ACHP from direct political control, which has both benefits and drawbacks. It allows the professional staff more freedom from politically motivated decisions, but it also removes the ACHP itself from policy-level deliberations within the administration.

The preservation activities of the NPS and the ACHP essentially complement one other. The National Park Service sets the professional standards and criteria for the program and manages day-to-day inventory, grants, tax incentives, and technical assistance programs. The ACHP independently conducts general oversight, makes recommendations, and takes other steps to resolve conflicts between historic preservation and other federal needs. Occasionally, their specific activities may overlap, but by and large there is good coordination between them.

Federal Program Agencies

Over time, NHPA has focused more on those federal agencies whose primary mission is something other than preservation. These agencies, through the issuance of federal permits, the management of federally owned historic properties, or the granting of federal assistance, directly affect the federal government's impact on the historic environment. That impact may be good or bad, depending on how well agencies fulfill their responsibilities under NHPA and how effectively the NPS and the ACHP do their jobs.

The moving force behind NHPA was public reaction to the destruction of historic resources caused by the public works projects of the 1950s and 1960s — in particular, urban redevelopment, urban renewal, and highway building.[10] Although tempered by NHPA's protective measures and by other environmental statutes, federal and federally assisted projects continue to threaten historic properties. These range from the obvious effects of federally aided highway construction to more subtle cases involving Corps of Engineers permits for private development. Regardless of their scale, federally supported development activities always carry the potential to alter the nation's historic fabric. The actual impact depends on how an agency responds to the policies and directives of federal historic preservation laws.

On the positive side, federal programs designed for other purposes often provide significant opportunities for preservation. Some are apparent, such as the use of Community Development Block Grants (CDBGs) to rehabilitate housing stock in historic neighborhoods or grants from federal transportation agencies to enhance historic properties associated with transportation projects. But most programs are far less obvious and more difficult to evaluate. For example, the General Services Administration (GSA) spends substantial amounts of money in maintaining its historic properties. The Federal Highway Administration (FHWA) and the Corps of Engineers spend sizable sums to mitigate the loss of archaeological resources during highway or dam construction, funding high-quality archaeological research. Examples are myriad. The point is that these funds do not come from sources earmarked as preservation dollars. In fact, the amounts far exceed appropriations for the Historic Preservation Fund in any given year. However, these effects, both positive and negative, demonstrate the tremendous impact of federal activities on historic properties.

The Federal Preservation Program:
The Key Components

The central elements called for in *With Heritage So Rich* still best define the major components of the federal preservation program. These include maintaining the national inventory of historic properties, protecting them through a planning process, providing financial assistance for the public and private sectors, and constructively managing federally owned resources. An examination of each of these areas not only reveals the nature and scope of the federal role in historic preservation, but also illustrates the roles of the various federal players and the partnership that characterizes preservation in the United States.

Defining What Is Historic:
The National Register Program

NHPA built on the existing Registry of National Historic Landmarks to create a more comprehensive catalog of the nation's heritage. The resulting National

Register of Historic Places was envisioned to be the basic inventory of significant historic properties. The National Register is maintained by the NPS and currently contains more than 73,000 listings of properties deemed significant in American history, architecture, archaeology, engineering, and culture. Listing on the National Register certifies that a property possesses significance, mandates its consideration in the planning of federal or federally assisted projects, and qualifies it for federal tax benefits and preservation grant assistance.

The National Register program tells us much not only about the national preservation partnership, but also about the challenges faced by preservation today. Criteria for entry in the National Register are derived from the language of NHPA itself. They embrace a wide range of properties: districts, sites, buildings, structures, and objects of national, state, and local importance. Significance may be based on association with events or persons, embodiment of distinctive architectural characteristics or high artistic values, collective importance as an entity whose components may individually lack significance, or the possession of information important in prehistory or history.[11]

There are qualifications, however. The NPS generally excludes cemeteries, birthplaces, graves, religious properties, structures that have been moved from their original locations, reconstructed historic buildings, commemorative properties, and properties achieving significance within the past fifty years. Still, under certain circumstances, even these properties may be listed. For example, a religious property primarily significant for its architecture or history or a property less than fifty years old may be listed if it is of exceptional importance.

The National Register today contains a broad, but by no means complete, catalog of historic properties. It consists of nominations from state governments and, to a lesser extent, federal, tribal, and local government sources. Of the more than 73,000 entries, more than 11,000 are historic or archaeological districts comprised of numerous individual buildings or sites. NPS estimates place the actual number of individual properties in the National Register at more than one million. Most of these are of local significance; only a few are of significance to the nation as a whole. Approximately 2,300 of the current entries are classified as NHLS.[12]

The National Register program has had a pervasive impact on preservation in the United States, as well as on the federal preservation program itself. Nomination to the register completes a complex process of locating, documenting, and evaluating potentially significant properties. Through professional surveys of each state's historic resources, often based on similar efforts at the local level, state historic preservation officers (SHPOS) have compiled extensive inventories

Artillery emplacement at Dutch Harbor, Aleutians. Whereas many federally owned historic resources, such as courthouses, parks, and public buildings, will be readily recognized by the public, a large proportion are less obvious. They include ranger stations and fish hatcheries, traditional cultural places, technical facilities, and a wide range of properties associated with the nation's military history. An example of the latter is this abandoned World War II artillery emplacement. (ACHP)

using the professional standards set by the NPS. The use of national criteria has promoted a high degree of consistency in historic survey efforts throughout the nation.

Many nominations have originated with federal agencies that own historic properties—a requirement originating in Executive Order 11593 of 1971, later embodied in 1980 amendments to NHPA.[13] This requirement not only forced federal agencies to recognize and evaluate their own historic holdings, but it also sensitized federal property managers to their special needs regarding maintenance and use. The impact has been significant. The GSA, for example, has 455 buildings on or eligible for the National Register, representing about one-quarter of its inventory of office space. The GSA has developed a highly sophisticated system for managing these buildings, recognizing both their inherent value and special management requirements.[14] Similarly, the Department of Defense, the Bureau of Land Management, and the Forest Service recognize that they have extensive holdings of historically significant properties, resulting in the adoption of a variety of constructive operational procedures regarding their stewardship.[15]

The National Register of Historic Places has dramatically shaped the national preservation program, well beyond its direct effects on the federal government. With National Register eligibility as the basic requirement for federal financial assistance or protection, the breadth of the eligibility criteria has greatly expanded the scope of the federal government's involvement in preservation over the past three decades. But the impact of the program is even more pervasive. The criteria established to judge eligibility have influenced the assessment of historic properties nationwide, at all levels of government and for a variety of purposes. Many state and local preservation laws either incorporate or closely follow the federal criteria. Likewise, the administrative structure that supports the National Register has fostered the federal, tribal, state, and local government cooperation that is central to the national historic preservation program.

Although the National Register program has undoubtedly surpassed the expectations of its creators in many ways, its growth has introduced another set of challenges. One is the recognition that the register has not fulfilled the original goal of becoming the all-inclusive list of what is significant in the nation's history. Chronically inadequate funding for surveys and nominations has seriously hampered the program. Although the number of listings is impressive, so is the number of properties that have not been identified, evaluated, and formally listed. This limits the utility of the register as a comprehensive planning tool and denies the protection, assistance, or simple recognition that significant properties deserve.

At the other end of the spectrum is a growing concern that too much is on the National Register and that the criteria for eligibility are too loosely applied. This objection is most frequently voiced by those agencies and organizations required to follow the protective procedures that attach to listing or eligibility for listing.

The significance of this debate cannot be understated. The historic preservation program has fared reasonably well since the 1960s because it has wide, if not deep, political support. Strong reaction to perceived abuses, especially when stated by politically powerful interests (such as the mining or energy industry), can erode this support and result in diminished federal financial support or weakening of the underlying law. This has happened in the past when powerful interests resisted the inclusion of their properties in the National Register.[16] Indeed, such reaction in 1980 brought about the owner objection provisions in the current NHPA. At the beginning of the new century, these concerns remain a serious point of debate and a looming threat to the growth of the National Register program.

Protecting Historic Properties:
The Section 106 Process

The authors of *With Heritage So Rich* identified the need for a mechanism to ensure that federal agencies adequately considered the potential impacts of their actions on historic properties. Since 1966, the "Section 106 process," named for Section 106 of NHPA, has evolved into the centerpiece of federal protection for historic properties.

The statutory basis is simple and straightforward. NHPA requires federal agencies that carry out, assist, or approve actions that may affect historic properties to take into account the effects of these actions on those resources and to afford the ACHP a reasonable opportunity to comment.[17] Through regulations, interpretation by the courts, occasional statutory amendment, and continued usage, this legislative directive has been integrated into the daily planning procedures of federal agencies.[18] The process now has a significant impact on the way the federal government treats historic resources.

The basic elements of the system have remained largely unchanged over the years. Essentially, it has five steps:

- Identification of historic properties that a federal action may affect
- Evaluation of the historic significance of potentially affected properties
- Assessment of the action's effects on historic properties
- Resolution of adverse effects on historic properties through consultation with the federal agency and other stakeholders
- Execution of an agreement embodying project modifications and mitigation, or, absent such agreement, obtaining advisory comments from the ACHP

Although these key features have remained relatively constant, an examination of how the Section 106 process works today reveals certain trends that will shape its growth in the future.

At the outset, it is important to note the scope of protection that Section 106 provides. First, the review process applies only when there is federal involvement in a project. This limitation on federal legal protection for historic properties is well grounded in American law and politics, which traditionally assign the authority to regulate private property to state and local governments. Federal preservation requirements do not control purely private actions that threaten historic resources.[19] Indeed, absent some form of federal involvement, the national government is left with only jawboning or outright purchase of a

ACHP hearing on Pasadena, California, Freeway. The Section 106 process embraces a wide range of federally supported activities that affect historic properties nationwide. By doing so, it provides citizens with a unique opportunity to participate in the federal decision-making process and influence its outcome. Here the mayor of South Pasadena stresses a point with the ACHP chairman at a public meeting on a controversial freeway project. (ACHP)

threatened historic property, voluntarily or through the exercise of eminent domain. The former technique yields only occasional results, and the latter is rarely exercised due to political and budgetary constraints.[20]

The second limitation is the inability of the federal preservation agencies to impose solutions. Under Section 106, the ultimate decision maker as to whether and how a federal action will affect a historic property is the head of the agency carrying out the action. Once the review process is completed, the agency head may determine that the public benefits outweigh the preservation costs and choose to move forward with a highly destructive project. Regardless of the significance of the property or the degree of harm to it, no veto is given to the ACHP or the secretary of the interior. The underlying premise is that conflicts between historic resources and the operations of government will be resolved through the administrative and political process. Although arguments that this should be changed surface regularly when amendments to NHPA are considered, the chances of eroding the power of federal program agencies are remote.

Despite these limitations, the Section 106 process has been surprisingly effective in promoting good preservation outcomes. It fosters assessment of impacts and alternatives and, when taken seriously, often produces agreed-upon solutions that allow federal projects to move forward with a realistic accommodation of historic preservation values.

The Section 106 Process in Operation

The ACHP has issued formal rules that guide federal agencies in meeting their legal responsibilities (36 Code of Federal Regulations, Part 800). Because the ACHP membership convenes only quarterly, the day-to-day administration of Section 106 rests primarily with the ACHP's professional staff. Given the large number of federal actions covered by the statute, the ACHP realized early on that it would have to rely on other participants to deal with the majority of cases. Thus, it turned to officials (the SHPOs) appointed by governors to coordinate their states' participation in the federal preservation program. Last amended in January 2001, the regulations continue a system that traces its primary elements to the late 1960s but that reflects many current trends in the national historic preservation program.

The Section 106 process begins when a federal agency proposes an undertaking that has the potential to affect historic properties. The scope of the term "undertaking" is broad. It includes direct federal construction and management activities (e.g., building federal office buildings, operating military bases, or approving timber sales), projects funded or assisted by federal agencies (constructing highways, building sewage treatment plants, or disposing of surplus federal property); and activities conducted by nonfederal parties requiring federal permits or licenses (building power plants, crossing rivers with bridges or transmission lines, or developing real estate affecting wetlands and navigable waterways). Undertakings also include activities with less direct or visible federal involvement, such as federal loan guarantees for privately financed construction and other types of indirect federal financial assistance to the private sector.[21] The critical element to trigger Section 106 is the presence of some form of federal decision making—the obligation to say yea or nay to support or approve the project.

When a federal undertaking is proposed, the Section 106 regulations prescribe a series of steps to be followed. First, the agency initiates a kind of historic preservation scoping process. This includes identifying areas likely to be affected, parties with interests in preservation issues, the need to involve the public, and how to coordinate Section 106 review with other planning and environmental review requirements. Of particular importance is the identification of those parties with a direct interest in the proposed action and its effects on historic properties. They may become "consulting parties," enabled to participate actively in Section 106 deliberations.

The principal consulting parties are the SHPO, and, if the action affects tribal lands, the tribal historic preservation officer (THPO).[22] These individuals represent the official preservation interests of the political jurisdiction in which the federal action occurs and thus have a prominent role in the Section 106 process. Other consulting parties may include Indian tribes that attach religious and cultural significance to potentially affected historic properties, applicants for federal assistance, local governments, property or business owners, preservation or community organizations, and other members of the public.

Next, the federal agency must identify potentially affected historic properties. Section 106 protection extends to all properties listed in the National Register and to those that meet the criteria for listing, even though they have not been formally nominated or entered in the register. Inclusion of the latter category of properties, added to NHPA in 1976, simply acknowledges that the effort to list all eligible U.S. properties in the register continues to be far from complete.

Identification of eligible properties has significant operational implications. Identifying properties already on the register requires only consulting a published list; locating eligible properties demands action by the federal agency and consultation with the appropriate SHPO to determine what actions are needed to identify eligible properties. Usually a survey is conducted, then the agency and SHPO review potentially eligible properties and determine which ones meet National Register criteria. Thereafter, for Section 106 purposes, no distinction is made between listed and eligible properties.[23]

The next step is to assess the federal action's effects on those properties. The agency continues its consultation with the SHPO and other parties, using criteria established by the ACHP to evaluate the nature of the effects. The criteria distinguish between those effects that are harmful and those that are not. Projects with harmless effects receive cursory review. Harmful effects, known as "adverse effects" in Section 106 jargon, trigger further consultation to seek ways of avoiding or minimizing them.

The Section 106 regulations define adverse effects broadly; they cover almost any alteration or environmental intrusion that diminishes the significant qualities of a historic property. Clearly included are direct impacts such as outright demolition or physical alterations. However, there is a wide range of more subtle impacts. These may be visual intrusions, such as an electrical transmission line running near a rural farm or incompatible new construction within a historic district; audible intrusions, such as noise from a nearby highway or an extended airport runway; and alterations that change the traditional relationship between a historic property and its setting, such as a tract housing development that severs the historic association between a rural village and the surrounding landscape. Adverse effects need not be immediate or direct. Section 106 has been invoked to consider long-term indirect impacts resulting from altered traffic patterns or growth-inducing activities that change the use or character of a significant property over time. In sum, the adverse effects criteria take an environmental approach to the notion of harm, recognizing that many kinds of impacts can degrade the significant features of historic properties.[24]

An adverse effect determination on a historic property requires the sponsoring federal agency to consult further with the SHPO and other parties to consider alternatives that may avoid or reduce the harmful impact. Consultation is intended to explore alternative locations and designs for the project and to seek mitigation measures. It usually results in project changes or conditions that the agency will adopt. The outcome is set forth in a binding memorandum of agreement (MOA), completing the Section 106 process.

An agreed-upon outcome under Section 106 is not usually a pure preservation solution. The objective of the process is to reach agreement on ways that the project can proceed with minimal harm to historic resources. Rarely is the "no-build" option given serious consideration, and the economic realities of the project are almost always dominant. Section 106 is successful when all of the participants enter the process with the shared objective of balancing preservation values with federal project needs.

Infrequently the parties are unable to reach agreement on how a project should proceed. In that event, the case is referred to the ACHP's membership, which renders its formal comments to the head of the sponsoring agency. Although the agency is obliged to consider the ACHP's opinion in reaching a decision on the project, it is not required to follow its advice. Thus, the ACHP may advise the secretary of transportation that a proposed highway project is ill-conceived, disastrously destructive of historic properties, and should not be built. The secretary is free to say "Thank you for your comments" and approve the project as originally proposed.[25]

Despite the seemingly easy path for an agency to go through the process, obtain ACHP comments, and then do what it wants to do, in reality the Section 106 process functions to promote agreement. Agreed-upon outcomes usually save time and avoid both the uncertainty that arises when the political leadership of a federal agency enters the decision-making process and the stigma that adheres to a case that has become a "problem." From the perspective of the federal project manager, inability to reach a negotiated solution smacks of failure and results in a loss of control over the outcome.

The Section 106 process is well integrated into federal project planning. The ACHP handles more than 2,500 cases annually, and nearly 100,000 cases are settled on the state level each year. The outcomes in specific cases vary widely, reflecting the importance of the historic properties, the complexities of the project, the availability of workable solutions, and, quite often, political considerations.

Other Federal Protections

Although Section 106 is NHPA's primary mechanism for protecting historic properties, other federal project planning requirements offer additional tools. These include Section 110(f) of NHPA, environmental laws such as the National Environmental Policy Act of 1969, and Section 4(f) of the Department of Transportation (DOT) Act of 1966.[26] They apply to federal agencies that are proposing to take actions that may impact historic properties, and, though generally developed outside the context of NHPA, they operate in a manner that is usually similar to the Section 106 process. Agencies are required to identify affected historic resources, evaluate the potential impact of the proposed action, and then consider ways to minimize or mitigate those impacts. However, each law has special requirements that must be met in order to bring its provisions to bear, and each has its own procedural peculiarities.

Section 110(f), added to NHPA in 1980, sets a higher standard of protection for nationally significant properties. Modeled on the provisions of Section 4(f) of the DOT act, it directs that federal agencies "to the maximum extent possible, undertake such planning and actions as may be necessary to minimize harm" to National Historic Landmarks. As with Section 106, Section 110(f) requires the federal agency to seek the comments of the ACHP before it approves an action affecting an NHL. Additional participation by the ACHP and the secretary of the interior in consultations embellishes the basic Section 106 process. This underscores the special importance of NHLs but offers no additional impediments to federal agency action that might seriously impair or destroy them. The basic statutory provision simply does not authorize stronger sanctions.

In operation, it is unclear how effective this legal requirement has been. Even before the enactment of Section 110(f) in 1980, the ACHP tended to put more weight on the protection of NHLs in the Section 106 process. This reflects the reality that, although all National Register–eligible properties must be considered in the Section 106 process, certain properties are given a closer look and held to a higher standard. Section 110(f) ensures that NHLs are singled out for special consideration. One criticism leveled at Section 110(f) has been that giving attention to nationally significant properties will cause federal agencies to regard properties of state or local importance as second class. So far there is little evidence to support this view.

Sections 106 and 110(f) of NHPA are directed at historic properties exclusively. However, two federal environmental statutes extend protection to both natural and cultural resources. Enacted in the 1960s, both the National Environmental Policy Act (NEPA) of 1969 and Section 4(f) of the DOT Act of 1966 have significantly strengthened federal protection of historic properties.

NEPA created a national policy of environmental protection that acknowledged that environmental quality is based on many factors, including the preservation of "important historic, cultural, and natural aspects of our national heritage."[27] Conceptually, NEPA's requirements are not much different from those of Section 106. Both are limited to actions of the federal government, both are essentially procedural statutes, neither provides a veto over a project that carries negative environmental effects, and both apply to all federal agencies and require consideration of a wide range of impacts. Procedurally, though, there are important differences.[28]

NEPA requires that federal agencies assess and consider the environmental consequences of their proposals. The agency prepares an environmental assessment (EA) to identify and evaluate the full range of anticipated environmental effects. Though most EAs result in a finding of no significant impact (FONSI), an environmental impact statement (EIS) is required for major federal actions with significant environmental effects. This is a full-blown assessment of affected resources, the nature of the impact, and alternatives that might alter those impacts.

In discharging its responsibilities under NEPA, a federal agency completes many of the same steps it would take to meet a corresponding requirement of Section 106. The agency must establish the significance of environmental values that its action may affect, and describe and assess the impact of the project on those values. It presents alternatives and mitigation proposals to respond to identified impacts. But once this information is assembled, NEPA and Section 106 place dramatically different obligations on the sponsoring agency.

Under NEPA, an agency must fully disclose the consequences of its action and permit the public an opportunity to express its concerns. Implementing regulations specify the content of the environmental documents, public notice requirements, and the opportunity for public review and comment. Once the requirements of public disclosure are met, the agency reviews the full environmental record and makes its final decision. By comparison, Section 106 obligates the agency not only to assess and disclose the effects of its action, but also to consult with state and federal preservation agencies and other stakeholders to seek ways to avoid or reduce the harm. The agency ultimately retains final authority for the decision, but in reality consultation normally results in negotiated solutions. Thus the protection afforded under Section 106 is significantly greater than that under NEPA.

One should not conclude that NEPA is redundant or offers little to historic preservation. Its broad scope has resulted in a greater awareness of its provisions by federal agencies and the public than the more narrow Section 106. This has made federal agencies more receptive to the integration of environmental review procedures, including Section 106, into their normal planning processes. NEPA also provides concerned citizens better opportunities to make themselves heard through legal action in the courts. The history of NEPA is marked by aggressive litigation and supportive court decisions that have made clear that federal agencies are not to take their environmental assessment duties lightly.

The environmental assessment procedure also serves to reinforce Section 106 as a practical matter. Federal agencies routinely use information gathered for NEPA to meet Section 106 needs and vice versa. In practice, the two procedures tend to be complementary rather than redundant. Indeed, recent trends in NEPA compliance have been to foster "one-stop shopping," gathering all federal environmental reviews, including Section 106, under the NEPA umbrella.

One of the most effective federal environmental laws, Section 4(f) of the DOT Act of 1966, has also been a useful tool for historic preservation, even though limited to the activities of a single federal department. Signed into law the same day as NHPA, Section 4(f) establishes a rigorous planning requirement for the development of federally assisted transportation projects. The procedures imposed by NEPA, Section 106, and Section 4(f) are roughly the same, but the latter provision adds a substantive standard that must be met when the final agency decision is reached.

Section 4(f) requires the secretary of transportation to determine that there is "no feasible or prudent alternative" to a transportation project that uses land from environmentally sensitive areas, including historic properties, and the courts have interpreted this standard to exceed simple procedural duties. The determination must show that alternatives are neither technically feasible nor prudent in terms of the entire range of concerns relevant to wisdom before the project can use a protected resource.

The Section 4(f) standard is high, but it applies only to DOT projects, such as highway and bridge construction (Federal Highway Administration), urban transit projects (Federal Transit Administration), airport development (Federal Aviation Administration), and river crossings and lighthouses (U.S. Coast Guard). Also, unlike the broad concepts of "effect" under Section 106 and "environmental impact" under NEPA, Section 4(f) requires that land from a historic property or other protected resource be "used," which has been interpreted to be narrower than the Section 106 definition of "adverse effect."

The impact of Section 4(f) on the projects that it does cover is significant. Several major highway projects that would have had serious negative impacts on historic properties were canceled by the DOT after 4(f) review, and others were halted by court action.[29] More important, Section 4(f) has forced federal transportation planners and their state counterparts who receive federal assistance for highways, mass transit, and airports to seriously consider the impact on historic resources. This results from the high legal standard for the "no feasible and prudent alternative" finding and the strict internal reviews that elevate the determination above the bureaucratic levels normally responsible for environmental decision making. Unsurprisingly, this regard for Section 4(f) has led transportation officials to a meticulous concern for their compliance with related laws such as Section 106 and NEPA.

The effect of Section 4(f) on historic preservation is not always positive. Stringent review requirements frequently tempt transportation planners to deny that an affected property is historic in order to avoid delay and complications. Although the close oversight given by SHPOs to transportation projects prevents this tactic from working often, the effort continues. A second problem has been the inflexible nature of Section 4(f), which requires transportation officials to undergo the same process regardless of the significance of the affected historic property. Thus, an archaeological site that everyone agrees should be excavated and paved over so a highway can be built is subjected to the same scrutiny as the demolition of a historic building of the highest national importance. This inability to relate the degree of protection to the nature and value of the resource complicates the project review process and often leads to costly avoidance of a use of historic properties, even when it is unnecessary to protect significant historic characteristics.

Federal Protections: A Last Look

The original concept of Section 106 has blossomed into the broad, decentralized preservation review process in place today. At the same time, additional protective mechanisms have emerged in response to specific concerns. Taken together, they represent a fairly comprehensive set of legal tools to deal with the impact of federal actions on the nation's historic environment and to protect those historic properties within the federal domain.

The protective provisions of federal law operate surprisingly well to minimize harm to historic properties caused by federal actions, considering that they neither compel a preservation solution nor enable a preservation agency to control the final decision of a project sponsor. The success of these provisions has been incremental, as procedures evolved and agency officials learned that they could not take their preservation responsibilities lightly. Energetic enforcement by the preservation community, most often at the administrative level by the ACHP and state historic preservation offices—but occasionally by citizens in the courts—has spurred this level of responsibility. Required compliance with NEPA, Section 4(f), and other agency-specific planning requirements has also reinforced NHPA preservation obligations.

Likewise, the emergence of more rigorous legal requirements for the management of federal lands, stemming from the growing power of the Native American community and increased concern over the destruction of archaeological resources, has strengthened the protective framework established by NHPA. Not all pieces fit together neatly, and few would suggest that the various authorities are coordinated in the most efficient manner, but the outcome is arguably more comprehensive and effective than the framers of NHPA anticipated in 1966.

Federal Preservation Assistance

The authors of *With Heritage So Rich* envisioned carrots to accompany the stick of Section 106. This was to take two complementary forms: a federal matching grants program to underwrite preservation projects and revision of the federal tax code to encourage private historic preservation. Both found their way into law, although at different times and with somewhat different consequences than were envisioned in 1966.

Grants-in-Aid. As enacted, NHPA endorsed the concept of direct federal financial support for the national historic preservation program.[30] There were two basic categories of assistance: grants for the acquisition and development of historic properties, and grants for survey and planning. The former were designed to support bricks-and-mortar work on historic properties and the latter to underwrite the cost of developing state historic preservation plans and nominations to the National Register. From the start, both were administered by the NPS. A third category was assistance to the National Trust for Historic Preservation for the conduct of its program activities. Each of these has made a significant contribution to the national historic preservation program over the past three and a half decades, but not as originally envisioned.

Understanding the actual impact of NHPA-authorized funding requires a brief review of the funding record of the historic preservation grant program, now known as the Historic Preservation Fund. Starting in 1967, the historic preservation grants program was never a massive source of federal funds for preservation. Until recently, with the exception of 1979 and 1980, the annual appropriation rarely exceeded $50 million. Appropriations for the first ten years of the program were more frequently in the vicinity of $5–6 million yearly. After 1981 they held steady at around $26 million for several years and then rose slowly. More recently, the level has reached around $40 million. In fiscal years (FYS) 1999–2003, an additional $30 million was added for a special, Millennium-related program called Save America's Treasures (SAT). This program provides matching grants for preservation and restoration of important historic properties.[31]

Through FY 2002, over $900 million had been appropriated for the grants program, but in terms of the total federal budget, the amount was minuscule. By comparison, the grants program of the National Endowment for the Arts received more than $4 billion during the same period. One need only mention the federal highway program, education, welfare, or national defense to place the HPF in its proper place as a federal priority. Nevertheless, these modest sums have been critical to the growth of the program, and to obtain even small increments in funding is regularly the highest annual legislative priority in the preservation community.

The most visible use of HPF grants has been the actual work on historic properties, but this has had the least impact on the long-term national program. NHPA authorized use of 50 percent matching grants for the acquisition and preservation of National Register properties. In the early years, approximately $121 million in grant funds went for a wide variety of projects, ranging from large public buildings such as courthouses to individual privately owned houses in historic districts. For the most part they were small grants, often no more than a few thousand dollars, which served as a catalyst to further investment or fund-raising. Projects originated with state and local governments, nonprofit organizations, and private individuals, and HPF funds were allocated by the SHPOs. In return for financial assistance, the NPS was assured that the property would be preserved and maintained over the long term. Although the amount of federal HPF money going directly for bricks and mortar was never great, its impact was significant since these modest sums were combined with other funding sources to make a restoration project successful.

This aspect of the grants program died when the expanded tax incentives of 1981 became law. The rationale was that tax incentives would substitute for the direct HPF subsidies. However, though tax incentives have since generated many times the amount of HPF grants, not all of the properties that qualify for HPF support are eligible for tax relief. Archaeological sites, owner-occupied houses, and properties owned by nonprofit organizations and museums are disqualified. Hence, many historic properties fall outside the scope of federal financial assistance actually available from the historic preservation program—a major step backward.

Recently, though perhaps reflecting the availability of federal budget surpluses, small amounts of bricks-and-mortar money have been quietly sneaking into the annual HPF appropriation. The SAT grants provide matching funds for the preservation of threatened historic properties. For several years, a new grant category for historically black colleges and universities (HBCUs) was a regular feature of the HPF appropriation but is no longer included. Likewise, the growing role of Indian tribes in the preservation program has been reflected in HPF funds provided for tribal activities.

The recent tendency to earmark HPF grants for certain programs of narrow focus is troubling to some. In particular, the growth of the HBCU grant allocation to approximately one-fifth of the annual appropriation has raised this concern.[32] The argument goes that these dollars should be funneled through the normal grants process, with decisions made at the state level, and that such earmarking displaces HPF moneys that would otherwise be more evenly spread across the program. The concern is in part a parochial one of who gets how much HPF money and in part the fear of a bad precedent for special interests to redirect HPF funds in a way that undercuts the intent and purposes of NHPA. Similar criticism has been leveled at the SAT program, which is allocated outside of the SHPO-administered system and has been increasingly subject to congressional earmarking. In reality, this phenomenon seems best described as pork barrel politics, whereby advocates for a particular cause use their power to send available funds to advance their goals. This is not to suggest that use of the money is not for a good purpose. It simply shows that the HPF is subject to the same forces that play on other government programs.

In contrast to the checkered history of the acquisition and development grants, the success of the HPF survey and planning grants probably exceeds most original expectations. These grants were originally intended to help states to conduct surveys for nomination of properties to the National Register and to prepare state historic preservation plans. The federal contribution was limited to a maximum of 50 percent until 1980, when it was raised to 70 percent. The 1980 amendments also expanded the range of eligible activities for which funds could be used:

- Administration, including routine office and program management
- Certification of local governments to participate in the national historic preservation program
- Activities related to the evaluation and nomination of properties to the National Register
- Development of statewide and regional preservation plans and planning processes
- Certifying properties and projects for federal tax incentives
- SHPO participation in the Section 106 process and related environmental review systems
- Field surveys and research to identify and document historic properties

Federal support for this broad range of state preservation activities has been a major factor in the growth of the current federal-state partnership. Though funding has been inadequate to achieve all the objectives set forth in the act, the catalyst of federal money tied to NPS professional standards has facilitated the development of competent administrative structures in each state. State legislatures have generally responded favorably, although sometimes grudgingly, appropriating the necessary matching share and often passing measures that enhance the state preservation program.

As described in Chapter 3, the primary government venue for implementing NHPA is the states. It is clear that the success of the program since 1966 is due largely to the state infrastructure, developed in response to the federal program incentives.

In 1992 Indian tribes were authorized to participate in the federal preservation program on much the same footing as state programs.[33] This has permitted tribes to receive HPF moneys to assist them in the development and operation of historic preservation programs. Tribal programs now share in the HPF. In 2001, $5.6 million was appropriated; as the number of approved tribal programs grows, it can be expected that their share of the HPF will increase.

HPF survey and planning grants have had a dramatic impact on the administrative structure for preservation at the state and local (and now tribal) levels. The NPS has established standards governing activities conducted by states with federal funds, ranging from the composition of preservation offices to the conduct of surveys. Through periodic program reviews, the NPS ensures that each program receiving HPF funds conforms to these requirements. This facilitates a certain level of professionalism in the conduct of preservation activities by the states and establishes a degree of uniformity throughout the country.

NHPA originally authorized 50 percent matching grants to the National Trust for the support of NTHP programs. The annual appropriation stabilized at about $5 million annually, representing approximately 25 percent of the Trust's yearly budget. Though federal support was critical to its operations over nearly three decades, congressional distaste for funding this private advocacy organization surfaced in the mid-1990s. As a result, the Trust's federal funding support was phased out and terminated in 1998. Interestingly, this has led to an arrangement that more closely tracks the original intent behind NHPA. Legislation passed in 2000 to reauthorize funding for the HPF included a provision that allows the Trust to seek HPF grants for specific preservation activities, but not for general administration. This amendment reintroduces the original concept of the Trust, serving as an alternative means of using federal dollars for preservation purposes.[34]

Although it has not lived up to original expectations as a funding source for bricks-and-mortar preservation, the HPF has admirably fulfilled the goals of the framers of NHPA. During the period when a large federal budget surplus was anticipated, a proposal that many once thought offered the hope of meeting NHPA's initial goals resurfaced. With varying degrees of bipartisan support in the last several sessions of Congress, the Conservation and Reinvestment Act continues to bubble up for consideration. This would provide an annual federal investment of $3 billion in broad-based conservation funding, including a yearly appropriation of $150 million for the HPF. What is unprecedented about the initiative is that the funds would be automatically appropriated each year, free of the annual tug-of-war over limited domestic discretionary spending. Although the future of this proposal is by no means certain, especially with the disappearance of the federal budget surplus, it is a refreshing counterpoint to the challenges of the past two decades when the struggle was to fend off budget cuts or threats to abolish the HPF outright.[35]

Embodying recommendations contained in *With Heritage So Rich*, NHPA authorizes other financial tools to promote historic preservation, although the bulk of these either have not been implemented by the federal government or have had little impact on preservation. For example, the 1980 amendments to the act directed the secretary of the interior to establish a loan guarantee program to finance private rehabilitation projects that would have provided federal loan insurance for private lender financing of preservation activities for National Register properties.[36] Due to budgetary constraints and a general lack of interest within the NPS as well as the preservation community, the program has never been implemented.

NHPA also authorizes a limited program of direct grants from the secretary of the interior for historic preservation, using 10 percent of the annual HPF appropriation.[37] The program includes preservation of threatened National Historic Landmarks, as well as World Heritage properties; demonstration projects; development of skilled labor in trades, crafts, analysis, and curatorial management; assistance to prevent small businesses from leaving historic districts; and preservation of the cultural heritage of Indian tribes and minority groups. Little has occurred under these authorizations, although some funds have been made available for threatened NHLs.

Tax Incentives for Historic Preservation. With Heritage So Rich included proposals for revising the Internal Revenue Code to promote private historic preservation. These included charitable deductions for contributions of preservation easements and expenditures by private parties to preserve or restore historic properties. Though Congress provided in NHPA for the direct federal financial assistance recommended by the report, a decade passed before revisions to the tax code were initiated.

In 1976, as part of the comprehensive Tax Reform Act, Congress amended the tax code to redress the imbalance between the tax treatment of new construction and rehabilitation of historic properties. As it then stood, provisions

Federal tax credits at work. A significant impact of the NPS external historic preservation program is the widespread use of the Secretary's Standards and guidelines for rehabilitation. Originally created to guide work for federal tax credits, the standards have been incorporated into many federal programs as well as state and local laws. They have become essentially the national norm of accepted preservation practice. (ACHP)

governing investment in real estate discriminated heavily against the preservation of historic properties and encouraged the replacement of older buildings with new structures. The 1976 amendments provided modest incentives for rehabilitating historic properties by allowing accelerated depreciation for rehabilitated historic structures and eliminated certain tax benefits for destruction of those properties.[38]

These changes spurred an increase in private preservation investment over the next few years, but it took the Economic Recovery Tax Act of 1981 to totally transform the economics of preservation. Until the benefits were circumscribed five years later in the Tax Reform Act of 1986, private investment in rehabilitation soared and surpassed all expectations, far exceeding the direct preservation grant funds distributed during the entire first twenty years of NHPA. Activity declined significantly after 1986, but the incentives remain as the most important part of federal financial support.[39]

The current tax incentive program offers a 20 percent credit for the "certified rehabilitation" of a "certified historic structure" and a 10 percent credit for the rehabilitation of nonhistoric structures built before 1936. The credit is based on the amount spent to rehabilitate the property and provides a dollar-for-dollar reduction of the amount of income tax due. To qualify, the project must meet specified criteria, and the taxpayer must follow a multistep process to establish the historic significance of the building and to obtain approval of the rehabilitation itself.[40]

Certified historic structures include buildings individually listed in the National Register and those located in, and certified as contributing to, historic districts. The historic district must be either listed in the National Register or designated pursuant to an enabling act approved by the secretary of the interior, who must also certify the district. In addition to being historic, a building has to be held for the production of income, thereby excluding most owner-occupied structures. *Certified rehabilitation* requires conformance with the Secretary of the Interior's Standards for Rehabilitation (Secretary's Standards). A further requirement is that the rehabilitation be "substantial," which means that rehabilitation expenses must exceed the adjusted basis of the building—the original cost of the building (less the land) with adjustments for improvements made or depreciation taken in previous years.

Owners of properties are required to submit certificates verifying the eligibility of the property for tax incentives and, later, demonstrating the appropriateness of the completed rehabilitation work. As with the National Register program and the Section 106 process, the primary responsibility for conducting the certification system falls on the SHPOs. They consult with property owners, assisting them in navigating the certification process, and make recommendations regarding both parts of the application. Final and formal approval lies by law with the secretary of the interior, through the NPS, but in practice, the SHPO's recommendations are usually accepted.

Due to the often significant financial consequences of being denied the tax incentives, applicants frequently invoke the appeals process and occasionally resort to litigation. More often than not, however, the NPS appeals officer, acting on behalf of the secretary of the interior, has sustained the initial ruling.

Since the introduction of the initial tax incentives in 1976, the NPS has reported that over $18 billion in private rehabilitation work can be attributed to them. More than 27,000 historic properties have been rehabilitated, many of which would have been lost to new construction without the tax benefits.[41] The relative importance of the tax incentives snaps into sharper focus when one considers that bricks-and-mortar preservation grant funding under the Historic Preservation Fund has totaled less than $250 million during the first thirty-five years of the program. Yet it must be recognized that the two incentive programs are complementary. The tax incentives cannot be used for properties owned by nonprofit organizations, Indian tribes, or state or local governments, which are the most frequent beneficiaries of HPF grants. Perhaps the lesson to be drawn is the woeful inadequacy of the funding for HPF grants since 1966.

The impact of tax credits—undreamed of by the most optimistic preservationists of the 1970s—is dramatic evidence of the role of the federal government in the national historic preservation program. Tax credit projects run the full gamut of the private development spectrum. The ACHP in 1983 noted that the average project was slightly less than $500,000 and that more than 40 percent of all projects were under $100,000.[42]

One of the outgrowths of the preservation tax incentives has been the development of policies and guidelines to implement the program. At the inception of the tax incentives program in 1977, the NPS adopted the Secretary's Standards, a broad, ten-point policy statement defining the boundaries of acceptable rehabilitation work. The Park Service further produced "Guidelines for Rehabilitating Historic Buildings," consisting of parallel practices, recommended and not recommended. Though developed to meet the immediate needs of certifying rehabilitation work for tax incentives, the Standards and "Guidelines" have become the Ten Commandments for preservation work throughout the country. They are regularly used by SHPOs and the ACHP in Section 106 cases to specify appropriate treatment for historic properties, integrated into contract specifications for federal preservation work, and used as the standard for a variety of state and local preservation laws that regulate how private property owners modify their historic properties. The Secretary's Standards are a prime example of how the federal government, without fully intending to do so and without either the desire or the ability to enforce them legally, exercises a leadership role in preservation nationwide.[43]

The *WHSR* recommendation that the value of an easement donated to preserve a historic property be allowed as a charitable contribution deduction from income was enacted in the Tax Reform Act of 1976. Preservationists have long recognized the value of easements for creating legally binding restrictions on a historic property, but questions concerning the deductibility of the easement's value had often inhibited their use.

The usefulness of this tax law change to protect historic properties across the nation was soon demonstrated. A 1983 ACHP report indicated that only 14 percent of recorded preservation easements were acquired before 1976. It also showed that developers were using the new easement provision to deduct the value of a facade easement on properties being rehabilitated for the preservation tax credit, thus providing an additional financial incentive for the developer while ensuring the long-term preservation of a property. Although there have been occasional questions about the valuation of donated easements, it appears that this simple change in the tax law has achieved the goals set by the framers of NHPA in 1965.[44]

Clearly, federal tax incentives have dramatically influenced historic preservation in the United States. It may be fittingly so, as the essence of the tax incentive program is the harnessing of the economic forces of the marketplace to the established social policy objective of preserving the national patrimony. Though this alliance may have its problems at times, its many successes demonstrate the resourcefulness of the preservation movement and its ability to tap necessary sources of support for a long-term, broad-based approach to the preservation of historic properties.

Assistance from Other Federal Programs. Not all of the financial assistance that the federal government provides for the preservation of historic properties comes from sources established for that specific purpose. Indeed, most federal monetary support for historic preservation originates in programs that appear on the surface to have little or nothing to do with it. No reliable estimate exists on the full extent of this support, but some examples will illustrate both its nature and magnitude.

At the outset it is useful to identify two basic categories of support. First are those grant funds that underwrite various developments at the state and local levels. These are most often community redevelopment, housing assistance, transportation, public works, and economic development programs. The second category consists of federal project funds used to mitigate unavoidable adverse effects on historic properties. Taken together, the two categories produce substantial and otherwise unavailable sources of federal funding to achieve preservation goals.

A prominent example of the grants category are the Community Development Block Grants administered by the U.S. Department of Housing and Urban Development.[45] The CDBG program originated in 1974 as a successor to many categorical grant programs. Initially, HUD programs were viewed as having a highly destructive potential as the result of the earlier experience with urban redevelopment and renewal in the 1950s and the 1960s. But as the focus of urban redevelopment shifted away from clearance to conservation and reuse, the use of these funds proved highly compatible with local preservation goals.

HUD's block grant funds are given to local governments for the general purpose of urban revitalization and are allocated to different local programs at the discretion of local government. As the preservation ethic spread at the local level and priorities shifted toward the adaptive use of existing structures, these funds were increasingly committed to rehabilitation. Since block grants are federal funds subject to review under Section 106, local governments are obliged to consider carefully the potential effects of their use on historic properties. Section 106 review, in turn, reinforces the efforts of local citizens to have these funds spent in a manner compatible with community preservation.

The result has been increasingly widespread use of block grant funds for conducting local historic property surveys and for carrying out renovation, code enforcement, and public improvement projects in a manner that enhances historic values. Hundreds of communities throughout the nation have Section 106 agreements in place to advance this objective. Through sensitive planning at the outset, usually involving the SHPO, these block grant funds often become preservation dollars.

In 1991 the massive Intermodal Surface Transportation Efficiency Act authorized the expenditure of $150 billion on transportation projects over six years. A revolutionary component of that law was the requirement that a portion of these funds be spent on "transportation enhancements" designed to improve quality of life.[46] Thus, $2.6 billion was authorized for enhancements over a six-year period. Of the specified enhancement categories, such as building bicycle trails and preserving scenic areas, a number dealt with historic preservation. These included acquisition of historic properties and preservation easements, development of historic highway preservation and interpretative programs, landscape and street furniture improvements in historic areas, preservation of historic buildings and structures for transportation-related purposes, and archaeological planning and research. To be eligible, a project must be "related" to surface transportation activities, although in practice the "relationship" has often been attenuated.

Decisions regarding the use of enhancement funds were left in the hands of state transportation departments, many of which were reluctant to spend transportation dollars on what were viewed as frills. When persuaded to use the money as intended, they were more inclined to support projects that looked like transportation, such as bike trails and pedestrian facilities. Nevertheless, an exceptional amount of money found its way into activities that could be fairly called historic preservation. These included bricks-and-mortar projects, such as restoration of a train station or urban street furniture rehabilitation, as well

Savannah, Georgia, Landmark Rehabilitation Project. Most federal assistance for historic preservation does not come from designated preservation grant programs but from the wide range of federal programs established to provide housing, transportation, and other public services. An outstanding example of the successful marriage between a HUD-funded housing program and local preservation objectives is this Savannah project, which has provided hundreds of units of affordable housing in rehabilitated historic buildings. (ACHP)

as important preservation planning products, such as compilation of a historic bridge survey and development of a statewide geographic information system (GIS)–based archaeological database. Creativity has not been lacking, either in innovative projects or in the rationales that link them to transportation activities.

Despite opposition from highway advocates, the 1998 successor to ISTEA, the Transportation Efficiency Act for the Twenty-first Century, not only continued the enhancement program but expanded it.[47] Again a six-year program, TEA-21 raised the amount of enhancement funds available to $3.6 billion and added two new categories that apply to historic preservation: visitors' centers for related scenic and historic sites and transportation museums. Increasing sophistication on the part of grant seekers and some state transportation departments and growing acceptance of the program by funding agencies have improved the climate. Through 2001, an estimated $800 million of ISTEA and TEA-21 funds have supported historic preservation projects. For the next few years, transportation funds will be the single largest source of federal dollars for historic preservation.

A major factor in the expanded use of federal funds to advance preservation while carrying out their primary mission is the increasing responsiveness of state and local government to preservation issues. This, in turn, is testament to the growing sophistication of preservationists and their ability to work effectively within the political process. The creation of a special fund in a major public works program, as exemplified by ISTEA and TEA-21, is perhaps the ultimate statement in this respect. By no means are all federal programs effectively integrating preservation purposes into their funding decisions, but the trend appears to be in that direction and an increasing number of success stories act as illustrations.

The second leading source of undesignated federal funds going into historic preservation are the many dollars that agencies expend to mitigate the adverse impacts of their projects. For example, under the Archaeological and Historic Preservation Act of 1974, agencies are authorized to use up to 1 percent of the total project budget to recover historical and archaeological data that would otherwise be lost.[48] This becomes a significant figure when one considers the magnitude of a single extensive federal construction project, such as a dam. Though no precise figures are available, according to one estimate as much as $200 million of federal project funds are expended annually just to conduct archaeological data recovery in advance of construction. This represents about six times the amount spent to support the administrative structure of the state preservation offices for one year.

Even more difficult to measure accurately are the additional expenditures by federal agencies to redesign projects to avoid or minimize harm to historic properties as required by the Section 106 process. Agencies generally consider these costs to be one more element of the project budget and often use contingency funds to cover the realignment of a highway segment or a change of building materials to meet a preservation concern. Although the ACHP urges agencies to relate the cost of mitigation to the significance of the values affected, not all of these decisions are made based on a careful analysis of cost and preservation benefit. A 1999 decentralization of the Section 106 process makes it more likely that a federal agency will simply yield to the demands of an SHPO, Indian tribe, or other party that a particular mitigation strategy be pursued without regard for either cost or benefit. It would be misleading, however, to suggest that federal agencies expend more on mitigation of impacts on historic resources than they do on other kinds of negative environmental effects.

A final source of federal preservation support comes from those agencies that fund preservation activities as part of their primary mission, although they are not usually regarded as preservation agencies as such. For example, the National Endowment for the Arts funds innovative preservation efforts as part of its broader program to advance architecture, community planning, and the design arts. The National Endowment for the Humanities supports research in history, archaeology, and other scholarly disciplines related to preservation. The National Science Foundation makes grants to conduct archaeological and anthropological research. Such funding is rarely large—usually measured in the thousands of dollars. But, collectively, these programs make a significant contribution to the federal government's support for historic preservation, filling a gap rarely met by any other source of public support.

Taken together, these varied federal funds greatly overshadow the modest sums appropriated for the primary federal historic preservation programs. Although difficult to quantify, they put the federal government clearly in the forefront of benefactors of the preservation movement. Under close scrutiny, much of the preservation work for publicly owned facilities and properties throughout the nation would reveal at least trace—and often sizable—amounts of federal dollars in their budgets.

Federal Management of Historic Properties

Significant legal mechanisms have been designed exclusively to ensure preservation of the extensive properties owned by the federal government. These responsibilities affect properties already set aside for preservation and properties having intrinsic historic significance. The resources range from the internationally recognized gems of the National Park System to real estate that barely passes the threshold of National Register eligibility. Property types span the full spectrum of historic properties, from expansive battlefields to individual buildings and bridges, and from prehistoric petroglyphs to artifacts of the space program. Likewise, the uses to which this vast array of properties is put range from enshrinement for posterity to supporting the daily changing needs of cutting-edge technological and scientific programs.

Tracing its origins to Congress's establishment of Yellowstone National Park in 1872, today's National Park System contains many of the crown jewels of the nation's patrimony. The evolution of the system includes the addition in the early 1900s of exceptional prehistoric sites in the Southwest, such as Mesa Verde, and in the 1930s the transfer of the Civil War battlefields from the War Department to the NPS. Most others were created by the express action of Congress, with specific legislation authorizing the creation of the park and defining its boundaries. Today, approximately 189 historical units of the 384 units of the

Manzanar National Historic Site, California. While most people associate the national parks with national shrines like Independence Hall and scenic wonders like the Grand Canyon, the NPS has become more embracing of the full range of the nation's cultural heritage. A recent example is this site of a World War II Japanese internment camp. (ACHP)

National Park System are classed as historic parks or sites. These properties illustrate the full spectrum of American history, from events and personages of the Revolutionary War to the varying social, intellectual, and economic currents that have shaped the nation.[49]

Historic properties located within the National Park System are usually there for the express purpose of preservation and interpretation. Consequently, preservation is the primary mission of the managing agency, the NPS. The complete control exercised by the NPS over a property has the potential to ensure the highest form of long-term preservation, but admittedly this does not always happen.

Threats to these properties are both external and internal. External threats present the most serious problem, and current federal law provides little help. As the spread of the nation's urban centers continues to engulf more and more of the surrounding rural landscape, many heretofore isolated national parks are threatened with urban encroachment. Many NPS officials view this incessant expansion of urbanization as a primary challenge to their mission for the foreseeable future. Particularly affected are Civil War battlefields in Maryland and

Virginia, as well as Revolutionary War sites in Pennsylvania and New England. Few would argue that locating housing developments and shopping malls on the boundaries of the Manassas Battlefield Park or cellular communications towers in the viewshed of the Antietam Battlefield do not seriously impact the integrity of these resources. Unfortunately, there are few alternatives to the costly acquisition of the adjoining lands to prevent these incursions.

Internal threats may be more subtle, but they are equally important. These are the actions that affect the actual fabric of the resource itself. Maintaining the integrity of a particular resource is not necessarily consistent with meeting the visitation expectations of an increasingly affluent and mobile American public. This threat is not unique to buildings in the National Park System; indeed, it is the superstar natural areas, Yellowstone and Yosemite, where this problem has been most publicized. Nevertheless, balancing the needs of preservation and use presents the NPS with its most formidable internal challenge.

Closely tied to this challenge is the chronic underfunding of park maintenance and restoration needs. Though one always hopes that the federal government will raise the level of investment in maintaining its National Park System, years of deferred maintenance have taken their toll, and it is currently estimated that $5 billion or more will be needed to erase the backlog of deferred maintenance. The Bush administration has made meeting this need a budget priority, but budget priorities can change quickly, as the events of September 2001 demonstrate.

A second category of internal threats is far less publicized, and probably few outside the preservation establishment are even aware of it. Virtually all historic parks are created to commemorate, preserve, and interpret a particular historical event, person, or theme. To best interpret the primary resource, it may be necessary to eliminate the vestiges of subsequent development unrelated to the primary theme or purpose for which the park was created. Thus the nineteenth-century additions to an eighteenth-century house may be stripped away to restore a property to its 1780 appearance. A corollary of this problem is found in the natural areas of the National Park System, where historic resources, such as early tourist facilities or mining structures, may be viewed as incompatible with the primary emphasis on preservation and interpretation of natural values.

Over time, the NPS has been compelled to confront another development that exacerbates these challenges. As the NPS completes its cultural resource inventories to determine the National Register eligibility of its holdings, it is finding that many properties meet the register criteria but are not compatible with the primary purpose for which the park was created. At best, acknowledgment of these additional historic properties places a further burden on limited maintenance and rehabilitation funds. At worst, it forces park managers to face up to difficult choices: Should an important ecological area be restored, or should an existing collection of early twentieth-century cabins that comprise a National Register historic district be retained?

These problems are perplexing and the answers unclear. Individual cases often divide professionals who share preservation goals. Most often the secondary resource is sacrificed, and this may sometimes be the most appropriate solution. But many times the loss of the lesser property is not so clearly warranted, and some allege that important elements of the nation's heritage are being destroyed by those who are specifically entrusted with their preservation.

It must be remembered that NPS properties, significant as they are, constitute but a small portion of the total universe of historic resources under federal jurisdiction. Due to the sheer size of the government's landholdings, federal responsibility for management of historic resources is extensive and has a great impact on the overall achievements of the national historic preservation program.[50]

Federal courthouses, post offices, and office buildings were intentionally created to be symbols of the power of the federal government and from the beginning of the Republic were designed by leading architects in high styles exemplifying the best of public architecture. Many of these structures are in relatively unaltered condition. Military and naval installations also contain buildings associated with significant historical events, ranging from the Revolutionary War to the development of the atomic bomb and the exploration of space. National forests and the public lands of the United States contain uncounted sites of prehistoric and historic archaeological significance, as well as structures associated with the mining and railroad industries and more recent social phenomena, such as the Civilian Conservation Corps. All but a few lighthouses built before World War I meet the National Register criteria, and most of those are owned by the federal government.

The list embraces thousands of properties. Their most important shared feature is that, while possessing historic significance, they are still used to provide public services. They are not set aside as museums or units of the National Park System. Rather, they are put to daily use in a variety of ways that are often inconsistent with the preservation of significant features. Indeed, many of the daily property management decisions of federal agencies fly beneath the radar of Section 106 and other historic preservation requirements. Property managers are often unaware that a property is historic or that a maintenance deci-

Former Battle Creek, Michigan, Post Office. The federal presence in cities and towns across the country has been marked by public buildings of high quality and intimate association with the local community. As the function of these buildings changes, adaptive use provides an opportunity to continue their role in the community. This structure was abandoned as a postal facility in 1968 and now houses city offices. (ACHP)

sion, like replacing a deteriorated window, has an impact on a property's historic integrity.

Executive Order 11593, issued by President Richard Nixon in 1971, attempted to correct this situation.[51] Recognizing that only a small proportion of federally owned historic properties were evaluated for the National Register, the order directed agencies to undertake surveys that might yield additional nominations and to exercise caution when considering actions affecting potentially eligible properties. This effectively extended the Section 106 process to properties eligible for the National Register but not yet listed.

In 1980 amendments to NHPA incorporated most of the executive order's federal property management requirements into Section 110 of the act. This section directs federal agencies to "assume responsibility for the preservation of historic properties" under their ownership or control. The 1992 NHPA amendments directed federal agencies to establish historic preservation programs, consistent with guidelines issued by the secretary of the interior. Each program is to ensure that:

• historic properties under the agency's control are identified, evaluated, and nominated to the National Register,

- the agency's historic properties are managed and maintained in a way that considers the preservation of their historic values in compliance,
- the agency has procedures for compliance with Section 106 consistent with governmentwide ACHP regulations, and
- the agency appoints a federal preservation officer (FPO) responsible for coordinating its historic preservation program.

In 1998 the secretary of the interior issued guidelines to implement these provisions.[52] It is fair to say that most agencies now have a "historic preservation program." But the quality of these programs varies widely, and few would fully meet the benchmarks set in the secretary's guidelines or approach the expectations of Section 110. The best programs, such as those of the NPS, the GSA, and the U.S. Army, embody the major components specified by the statute and guidelines and demonstrate a reasonable commitment of staff and resources. Most, though, are a patchwork of preexisting policies and procedures, limited staff and funding, and an unclear relation to the decision-making apparatus of the agency.

Almost all federal agencies have designated federal preservation officers, but their qualifications, placement in the agency, and effectiveness vary widely. Too often the FPO is a well-qualified and well-meaning preservation professional but operating at a grade level and in an organizational niche that makes it difficult, if not impossible, to effectively coordinate the agency's preservation-related activities. Many agencies have internal procedures implementing Section 106, although recent changes to Section 106 regulations require these to be updated. A few, most notably the regulations implementing the Corps of Engineers permit program for licensing construction that affects wetlands and navigable waterways, are considered by the preservation community to fall short of adequately fulfilling Section 106.[53]

Management and maintenance of historic properties consistent with mandates of Section 110 are hampered by funding constraints and a widespread lack of understanding as to what good preservation practice requires. To be sure, the level of federal agency sensitivity to historic preservation concerns greatly exceeds that of a decade ago, but the full promise and intent of Section 110 is far from being met. Money and staff available for historic preservation shrank as fiscal constraints were imposed on the federal budget in the 1990s. Preservation was and continues to be a low priority when budgets are tight. At the same time, the challenges that confront the NPS in managing its historic properties are faced by other property-managing federal agencies. Lack of resources, internal and external threats, and incompatibility of historic preservation needs and agency mission (perceived and occasionally real) dog federal agencies, despite the dedication of their cultural resource professionals.

Where a historic property can be used to meet an agency's program requirements, preservation has made progress. Reusing a historic property for federal office space, for example, uses program funds available for housing federal employees. With the application of Section 106 to ensure that such use improves rather than impairs the property in question, these moneys can become preservation dollars.

In an attempt to get agencies to better integrate historic preservation into the day-to-day pursuit of their statutory missions, Section 110(a) of NHPA directs agencies to use existing historic properties "to the maximum extent feasible" to carry out programs and to explore that use prior to acquiring, constructing, or leasing new buildings. To flesh out this somewhat nebulous statutory edict, President Bill Clinton issued Executive Order 13006 in 1998.[54] Designed to support an overall policy of locating federal office buildings in downtowns, it requires federal agencies to give preference to siting facilities in historic properties within historic districts. If that option does not exist, then federal agencies are to turn to historic properties outside of historic districts. This establishes a clear preference for using historic properties, although the qualifying words in the executive order—"when operationally appropriate and economically prudent"—provide a fair amount of room for agencies to avoid the mandate. In practice, the executive order has been reasonably successful in achieving its objectives.

Another tool for promoting the preservation of federally owned historic properties that has been successfully employed is found in Section 111 of NHPA.[55] This provision authorizes federal agencies to lease or exchange, or enter into contracts for the management of, historic properties under their jurisdiction to promote their preservation. This requires consultation with the ACHP to ensure that the preservation objectives are met. An important aspect of Section 111 is the authorization to use the proceeds of these leases to meet preservation costs. Without such an authorization, the proceeds would flow into the general treasury and be unavailable for preservation or maintenance. This provides an incentive to lease a property and to obtain lease funds that would otherwise have to be drawn from the agency's maintenance appropriation.

The Section 111 leasing authority has been used frequently in the case of federal surplus structures. An example is the leasing of obsolete lighthouses by the U.S. Coast Guard. The Coast Guard maintains its aid to navigation while allowing the lighthouse and its associated buildings and grounds to be used by the lessee. The controls retained by the leasing agency over the property ensure its proper care, and the proceeds are available to undertake repairs and upkeep as well as deferring the administrative cost of leasing the property. National Park properties have also benefited from this provision. To date, the NPS has leased more than sixty properties, resulting in the private sector rehabilitation of buildings exceeding $9 million. Although Section 111 has proven itself useful for preserving selected historic properties in the federal inventory, one limitation has emerged. Because the property must be surplus to federal needs, it prevents an agency such as the GSA from entering into a long-term lease to a private developer with a provision for a leaseback to the federal government. Were this possible, Section 111 leases could be used as an innovative method of financing the rehabilitation of historic federal buildings to provide needed federal office space.

Although federal stewardship laws and procedures appear to apply to all kinds of historic properties, the actual use of these tools has tended to focus on historic buildings and structures. The law has always recognized the special considerations associated with protecting archaeological resources. As a result, there exists a series of federal legal protections that are written specifically for the protection of archaeological resources on government lands. Here they are dealt with briefly; their application is covered in greater detail in Chapter 8.

The first law protecting archaeological sites on federal lands was the Antiquities Act of 1906, which authorized the president to designate national monuments. It established a permit system to control excavation activities and imposed criminal penalties on those who excavated archaeological official sites without permits.[56] The designation tool has been wielded by presidents from Theodore Roosevelt to Bill Clinton, most recently with the controversial establishment of two new national monuments in the West.[57]

The Archaeological Resources Protection Act (ARPA), resolving legal uncertainties in the 1906 act and expanding its coverage to lands held in trust for Indian tribes, was adopted in 1979. Under the 1979 act, archaeological resources now include "any remains of human life or activities which are at least 100 years of age, and which are of archaeological interest." This has been interpreted to encompass historic shipwrecks in addition to Native American antiquities. Anyone wishing to excavate or recover archaeological resources is required to apply to the federal land manager for a permit. The land manager must determine that the applicant is professionally qualified, that the proposed work is being undertaken to further archaeological knowledge in the public interest,

Archaeological site, Arizona. The unique nature of archaeological resources has long been recognized in the federal preservation program. Laws tailored to address archaeological issues range from the Antiquities Act of 1906 to the Native American Graves Protection and Repatriation Act of 1990. They control how archaeology is conducted on federal lands, such as this Bureau of Reclamation project in Arizona. (Bureau of Reclamation)

that the work is consistent with management plans for the lands involved, and that there is an appropriate repository for the recovered resources and records. Work must conform to the specific conditions of the permit. Archaeological resources removed from federal lands remain the property of the federal government, unless they come from Indian lands, in which case the tribe retains ownership. Penalties for violation, both civil and criminal, are severe.[58]

ARPA has been an effective tool against archaeological looting and pothunting on public lands. Aggressive criminal prosecutions and partnerships with citizens to monitor federal sites have given the law teeth. However, the principal problem in enforcing the act remains the vast expanse of the public domain, the scattering of archaeologically significant resources, and the woefully small number of people employed to enforce the law. ARPA's usefulness as a cultural resource management device has other limitations as well. It applies only to federal lands and regulates only nonfederal activities relating to archaeological resources. Unlike Section 106, it places no restrictions on what federal officials may decide to do on federal lands, and it does not extend to the protection of those historic properties that do not meet ARPA's definition of archaeological resources.

In part because of these limitations, Congress enacted the Native American Graves Protection and Repatriation Act in 1990.[59] A major requirement of NAGPRA is that federal agencies and museums must return human remains and Native American cultural items in their collections to Indian tribes. From the perspective of protecting historic sites, however, NAGPRA's greater impact lies in its protections for resources on federal lands and Indian reservations. Indeed, in NAGPRA lie the most restrictive provisions in federal historic preservation law.

Section 3(c) of NAGPRA prohibits the disturbance of Native American human remains and cultural items without obtaining an ARPA permit and coordinating the proposed action with any tribe that asserts a cultural affiliation with the resources. Thus, the disposition of any remains or cultural items must be accomplished in a manner satisfactory to the affiliated tribe. When human remains or cultural items are discovered during construction on federal or Native American lands, Section 3(d) requires the project manager to notify the responsible federal management official, cease construction near the discovery for thirty days, and make a reasonable effort to protect the affected resources.

The regulations implementing the act allow a federal agency to develop a "plan of action" in consultation with affected tribes and prescribes a course of action that the agency must follow if it encounters protected resources. Such matters as treatment, recording, reports, and custody are to be specified. If the activity occurs on federal lands, the federal agency is required to consult with interested tribes in developing the plan of action; if it occurs on tribal lands, then tribal consent is required for excavation.

As one of the most recent federal preservation laws, NAGPRA is one of the most stringent. It has brought an unprecedented level of protection to sites important to Native Americans and gives tribes a significant voice in the treatment of such sites. This is a noteworthy advance in federal land management policies, which have historically given little consideration to Native American views.

The federal stewardship role is thus extensive. As a result of a number of legislative enactments over the past decade, this responsibility is pursued with unprecedented vigor. The achievements in promoting the preservation of federally owned historic properties, especially since the passage of the 1992 amendments to NHPA, are noteworthy and increasingly frequent. Yet the realities of limited federal resources committed to protecting and maintaining historic properties in the government's care will continue to hamper the fulfillment of its stewardship role.

Conclusion

At the beginning of the new century, the federal role in the national historic preservation program largely fulfills the vision advanced by the framers of the National Historic Preservation Act thirty-five years earlier. Its structure is remarkably unchanged from the original blueprint. The basic concept of a partnership between government at all levels and the private sector continues to thrive. Both NHPA and its implementing administrative procedures have been remarkably adaptable to the dramatic changes that have occurred in the roles of the respective levels of government in the country's social and political life, giving vitality to the overall national historic preservation program. The federal role remains one of program leadership and support, the central role of state government has solidified, bridges to independently created local preservation programs have been built, and a growing number of tribal programs are being nurtured.

The current federal program contains the primary components that were the core recommendations of *With Heritage So Rich*. The National Register of Historic Places defines the scope of the national heritage in broad, expansive terms and stands as the benchmark for determining what historic resources will benefit from federal assistance and protection. The Section 106 process is firmly established as an effective mechanism to protect those properties from unnecessary harm caused by federal actions. A dual system of financial assistance, embracing direct grants and indirect tax incentives, encourages the preservation of nonfederal historic resources. An independent federal preservation body, the Advisory Council on Historic Preservation, coordinates the activities of federal agencies that affect historic properties.

With the exception of some important expansions—such as extending the scope of Section 106 to National Register–eligible properties and bringing Indian tribes and their unique interests into the program—the essential elements of the federal program are little changed since the mid-1960s. A hallmark of the program has been regular review and adjustment, both statutorily and administratively, to fill the gaps and bring the various aspects of the program into harmony with the broader political, social, and economic trends in

American society. Change has often originated with the partners, notably the states, and, more recently, Indian tribes. Regardless, the underlying vitality of the partnership has fostered a general spirit of cooperation that, despite occasional bumps and jerks, has moved the program forward.

Although the primary federal program elements are easily identifiable as products of *With Heritage So Rich*, there are important features that would surprise and perhaps shock the framers of NHPA. Only the most foresighted in 1966 would have anticipated that the National Register would encompass the vast number and wide range of properties now listed or eligible for listing. Whereas breaking down the pre-1966 constraint of national significance as the trigger for federal concern was readily accepted, the implications of that action were only partially understood at the time. Likewise, few people in 1966 would have foreseen the broad coverage of the Section 106 process today or the consultation-based process that it has become. On the other hand, the thirty-five-year history of parsimonious funding of NHPA-authorized preservation grants would shock the creators of the act, but this has been offset by the significant amounts of federal preservation money found in defense, transportation, and other programs.

By and large, support for the national preservation program, and the federal role in it, has risen above partisan politics. With a few notable exceptions where radical changes in the political landscape brought serious challenges to fundamental principles of preservation, the program has enjoyed fairly steady support regardless of who has occupied the White House or who has controlled Congress. This is not to say that all administrations or Congresses have smiled equally on the preservation program; obviously, they have not. But what its three-decade history does demonstrate is the almost constant acceptance of the federal preservation program's basic principles and, with varying degrees of passion and resources, a continuing commitment to keep it functioning.

At the same time, it is somewhat disturbing that, even in the best of times, the national program has not made quantum leaps forward. Funding support has remained sadly constant, federal project decisions regularly result in the loss of historic properties, and preservation rarely surfaces as a major concern of any elected official at the national level. In the preservation community, it is understood that political support is "a mile wide and an inch deep." But even in the relatively benign political environment of the Clinton administration and a period of unprecedented federal budget surpluses, dramatic changes in federal financial commitment or program expansion were not forthcoming.

So what does the future hold? Unquestionably, historic preservation is a mature, established component of the federal government, having weathered political onslaught, funding constraints, and periodic growing pains. It embraces the fundamental concepts of both federalism and the marketplace as the basis for carrying out statutory authorities, and these are the cornerstones of its success. Its history suggests a substantial capacity for adaptation to changing political and social currents. It is safe to say that the central element of governmental partnership will continue to drive the national program. The recent trend toward devolution of authority to state, tribal, and local governments is likely to continue. The major features have proven to be adaptable to administration outside of Washington, and federal policy leaders remain committed to moving in that direction, if only as a matter of fiscal and political necessity.

It is also likely that the current limits on the federal role in preservation will continue. Repeated reexamination of the Section 106 process, both legislatively and administratively, has reinforced the notion that the federal government will essentially regulate its own actions and its own lands, leaving more aggressive protections to state, tribal, and local governments. The current trend toward reassertion of state legal prerogatives suggests that the historic preservation program will continue to maintain the present limits in the federal protective process. Commitment to environmental values may result in enhanced protection for federally owned resources, but there is little evidence that Americans want, or that their government will give them, an expanded federal intervention in private decisions that affect historic properties.

Likewise, it appears that federal support for historic preservation activities is on a fairly flat trajectory. Even in an era of unprecedented financial well-being for the federal government and the nation at large, the Historic Preservation Fund remained static. With the recent evaporation of the federal budget surplus and the economic downturn, the prospect of dramatic increases in federal funding in the future is discouraging.

Still, the future of the program looks heartening. In recent years, more attention has been focused on how the federal government takes care of its own historic properties, and the emphasis on partnering with nonfederal parties—public and private—is growing stronger. It is reasonable to presume that these trends will continue and that the fundamental vitality of the program will be enhanced. The vision of the framers of the 1966 National Historic Preservation Act finds daily validation and continues to serve the nation well.

The States
The Backbone of Preservation

Since passage of the landmark National Historic Preservation Act of 1966, the states have become both the central point and the critical mechanism for the administration of the national-state-local historic preservation partnership. Absent the state programs, the national inventory of cultural resources, the distribution of historic preservation information, the administration of financial incentives, and the provision of technical assistance could not happen.

State preservation programs did, in fact, exist long before passage of the 1966 act, but prior to this, the state preservation agencies that administered them were widely scattered and primarily concerned with relics, ruins, and other historic properties. In the early twentieth century they focused on the interpretation of historic sites, museum properties, plaques, publications, and highway markers. Around midcentury, a number of states—Louisiana, Massachusetts, North Carolina, Rhode Island, Connecticut, Florida, and a few others—supported local preservation efforts by passing enabling acts for historic districts. Other state pioneering activities predating NHPA included surveys of both buildings and archaeological sites, and programs of financial assistance to local projects. The new federal law was still a decade in the future when some states began to establish preservation agencies specifically to respond to the destruction of historic properties by the massive public works of the post–World War II period.[1]

Turning Point, 1966–1980

With the passage of NHPA, the character and direction of state historic preservation programs changed quickly and expanded dramatically. National standards and guidelines for programs, supported with federal funding, created a new operational framework for the states and linked them together in a common effort. As noted in Chapter 2, to qualify for federal funding and assistance, the governors were required to appoint a state liaison officer (later changed to state historic preservation officer) and to prepare a statewide plan for historic preservation. These early plans summarized what was known about a state's historic and archaeological resources, indicated how future surveys would be conducted, and requested bricks-and-mortar funds for the preservation of specific properties. Federal funds did not become available until July 1968, but in such a small amount that many states were discouraged from participating in the new program. By 1976, however, all fifty states and five territories were competing for a total of almost $4.6 million in federal money.

Both the character and the level of state support for historic preservation were influenced by the location of the state historic preservation office within state government. Many state programs were set up in existing park and recreation agencies, in state archival agencies, and in state historical societies. Some states established new agencies to administer the program. Although by this time federal archaeological programs had already been merged with historic preservation efforts, their administration varied from state to state. Some continued in universities, state museums, and separate agencies, as before, while others either became separate divisions of the historical agency or were integrated with the new state preservation offices.[2]

The cornerstone of the new federal program was the National Register of Historic Places, which expanded its earlier focus on properties of national significance to include those of state and local significance. Early on, the National Park Service, with the states, developed a uniform survey approach to accommodate this wider variety of historic and archaeological properties and to create state inventories that would be necessary for effective preservation planning. However, limited funding meant that the work would be slow and would have to depend heavily on volunteers and consultants. Differing views developed about the usefulness of National Register listings. Some regarded listing as merely honorific. Others believed that the register would be a useful tool in public education and preservation planning.[3]

The states quickly become involved in the review-and-comment procedures of the Advisory Council on Historic Preservation mandated by Section 106. Though federal agencies were required as early as 1969 to consult the state historic preservation officer to determine effects on listed properties, much, if not most, of the actual work—providing information about the project area, recommending needed surveys, making determinations of National Register eligibility, and expressing opinions on the effects of federal projects on National Register sites and properties—fell to the states. The SHPO thus became an active participant at each stage of the review process; by 1976, 24 percent of the average SHPO budget was devoted to assisting federal agencies and their project applicants through the Section 106 process. By 1980 the states were conducting an average of more than two thousand reviews per state.

In addition to the workload created by surveys, National Register nominations, and the Section 106 review process, the provision of financial and technical preservation assistance to a rapidly growing citizen preservation constituency and local governments soon become a major component of state programs. On the one hand, participation in the new national program qualified states for federal funds, which could be used for a variety of purposes; but on the other, these had to be matched by 50 percent or more by the states or from other nonfederal sources. Unfortunately, matching funds lagged behind a rapidly growing demand. Essential state preservation services such as community education, surveys, and the provision of technical assistance had to compete with the more visible bricks-and-mortar projects.

From the outset, the new program required that professionally qualified historians, architectural historians, architects, and archaeologists be involved in new functions. The SHPOs soon realized that they were swimming in uncharted waters and came together to share experiences and compare methodologies, especially for the surveys in which they now found themselves involved. A 1969 meeting of SHPOs from the southeastern region led to the formation of a national organization, the National Conference of State Historic Preservation Officers (NCSHPO), whose principal purpose would be to foster communication among the states. Through the early 1970s, the NPS had provided the NCSHPO with a forum for discussion and dissemination of the developing preservation practice at yearly conferences for SHPOs and their staffs. But as issues of public policy and federal-state relations came to the fore toward the end of the decade, NCSHPO established a Washington office that more and more represented state interests in the national program and held a yearly conference as the medium through which many difficult issues faced by the states could be addressed.[4]

By the end of the 1970s state historic preservation offices had clearly become the central point in each state for the national historic preservation program. In 1980 the SHPOs, through the NCSHPO, initiated amendments to the federal law that not only confirmed the role of the states but also, equally important, recognized that it was time to share responsibility for the federal program with local governments by creating Certified Local Governments. At first, the CLG program was a response to political pressure from big-city mayors who wanted a veto over National Register designations. However, the SHPOs quickly turned it into one of the most positive elements of their programs. CLGs, essentially created as the result of state initiatives, have since become an increasingly important element of almost all state historic preservation programs.

Two Decades of Growth and Change, 1980 to the Present

The 1980 amendments to the National Historic Preservation Act were highly significant; they set the course for state programs for the next two decades. By legally codifying established program components previously set forth in administrative regulations and procedures, state-level programs and processes that had been developed by this time were given much more credibility. The new CLG program also enhanced the formal structure of preservation programs in each state by facilitating relationships with local governments. In 1992 the act was again amended, improving core programs as well as adding new sections for tribal programs and a National Center for Preservation Technology and Training. These amendments tried to address some of the administrative issues that had grown from reduced funding levels and helped to strengthen the position of the SHPOs heading into a new century.[5]

Program Structure and Support

For the most part, state historic preservation programs continued to reside in the agencies in which they were first established.[6] Building a qualified professional staff of historians, architectural historians, historical architects, and archaeologists in state governments unaccustomed to accommodating such personnel has not been easy. Adequate compensation in these fields has always been an important issue. Federal certification requirements that called for state staff in those disciplines to maintain program eligibility have been a key factor in obtaining state support for these new professionals. The rise of professionalism has also generated debate about professional standards, as well as continuing discussions among the NCSHPO, the NPS, and professional organizations on degree and experience requirements, and these have been aired more or less continuously for a long time.[7] A second set of issues has been whether state historic preservation programs have been sufficiently responsive to community ideas and values. These issues have not been resolved.

Federal funding to support SHPO program activities and subgrants to constituents and CLGs has consistently lagged behind state needs. From a 1979 high of $47.1 million, these funds have leveled off since 1981 and reached a low of $20 million in 1987. By slow and irregular increments they reached $46.5 million in 2001, only to drop back to $39 million for federal FY 2002.[8] In terms of inflation-adjusted dollars, federal support for the national preservation program is at present significantly worse off than in 1980.

Where states have been able to obtain state funding for grants and programs there has been growth, but congressional appropriations have never come close to the authorized level of $150 million annually for the national Historic Preservation Fund. As a result, there has been great frustration among the states over the growing discrepancy between what is expected of them and the financial resources available to them to do it. SHPOs and their staffs have been forced to balance an instinctive zeal to provide full service, on the one hand, with the reality of time, money, and sheer physical capacity on the other. The states have tried to address this problem through cooperative support networks that provide nonfederal matching funds for staff. Some states provide preservation services through established regional planning agencies, nonprofit organizations, or universities; a few work through city and county governments; and one or two rely on a network of volunteer professionals.[9]

Increasing constituent demands throughout a long period of stagnant funding have also led states to turn to the private sector. By the early 1980s many state offices had stopped preparing National Register nominations internally, thereby encouraging the growth of a private consultant workforce. States also coped with rising environmental review caseloads by forcing federal agencies to develop the appropriate professional expertise to handle their own Section 106 responsibilities. In 1995, for example, following an increasingly prevalent practice in the states, the Vermont SHPO informed all federal agencies working in his state that he and his staff would not perform any function that properly belonged to the agency under NHPA. The result was that the agencies hired either appropriate staff or consultants. Increasingly, states have also looked to wealthier state agencies for general financial assistance to support staff and operations.[10]

The CLG program, established in 1980, soon became a major component of many state preservation programs and has helped to take some of the load off state offices while expanding their outreach. CLGs have become an especially effective network for encouraging and working with local communities. For some states, like Colorado and Utah, they are the major coordination mechanism. From 1984, when the first nine cities were certified, to the present, this program has continued to grow, and by 2001 there were 1,262 CLGs. But this growth has been somewhat uneven, with some states having as few as two and others nearly one hundred programs. Both in size and content these programs vary from state to state, depending on state perspectives and ability to provide local technical assistance.[11]

Many state historic preservation offices place a high priority on assistance to local governments and to local preservation organizations. Accordingly, they have assisted in drafting the enabling legislation needed for local commissions to meet legal requirements, and they offer technical assistance, training, and encouragement in a variety of ways. SHPOs also administer the CLG certification process and the federal grants that CLGs have used for surveys, as well as design guidelines and public educational materials.

The special status of CLGs in relation to state and federal government programs has often been a catalyst for local government support of historic preservation, even in the face of minimal federal funding. The 1980 CLG legislation gave local governments the power to review and veto National Register nominations and to assume certain state responsibilities, such as environmental review. However, the majority of CLGs have not chosen expanded participation because the administration of local historic district and landmark regulations, carried out in large part by local volunteers in their spare time, has been enough to fully occupy them. To a remarkable degree, many CLGs have also taken steps to ensure that preservation planning is an integral part of local government planning. As a staff member of the Utah State Historic Preservation Office observed, "If the states are the backbone of preservation, then CLGs are all the other body parts—the eyes, ears, mouths, hands and feet."[12]

The new tribal preservation programs of the 1990s have changed the responsibilities of SHPOs for both historic and archaeological resources on American Indian tribal lands. As noted in Chapter 2, NHPA amendments authorized grants to tribes to develop preservation programs and empowered them to assume the functions of SHPOs on tribal lands. Recognizing the legitimate interest of Native Americans in the preservation of their own history and such issues as artifact removal and the reburial of human remains, the SHPOs strongly supported the initiation of tribal programs. Many SHPOs had already developed positive working relationships with the tribes in their states, but they worried that unless adequate professional expertise was available to the tribes, scientific information would be lost and cultural resources under tribal jurisdictions could not be protected.[13] Qualification standards for tribal programs and certification requirements that included consultation with SHPOs answered those concerns.

Program Components

Surveys. Recent decades have seen continued expansion by the states of core NHPA programs, the most fundamental of which is the survey of resources. When NHPA was passed in 1966, its authors thought that each state could complete its statewide survey within a few years.[14] But the low level of federal funding made that impossible. Moreover, it became increasingly evident that survey content would expand as time passed, as concepts of significance changed markedly, and as a broader understanding of the nation's history grew.[15] By 1980 states reported that 182,800 historic properties—predominantly National Register–eligible buildings—had been surveyed. The NPS required the states to promote survey activities during the eighties, and the percentage of SHPO staff time devoted to survey activities through 1987 was greater than any other program area. But the total number of properties inventoried each year generally declined after the mid-1980s as a result of insufficient funding and the growth of other program pressures, especially environmental review.[16]

As the size of the survey database grew, retrieval and distribution of the information housed in paper files in each office became a serious problem. Obtaining funding for computers and software to manage growing inventories proved to be a difficult task. As late as 1996 states reported as "notable accomplishments" the initiation of computer databases and GIS systems. Indeed, many states are still implementing GIS systems.[17] Through the years survey content has been expanded to include vernacular buildings, rural and cultural landscapes, and an ever-widening list of resources representing a broadened understanding of American history. Survey methods and reporting systems have also become more complex.

While states added historic and archaeological properties to their inventories in growing numbers, they continued to define their significance through the National Register of Historic Places. Since 1980 the states have shaped the national inventory of registered properties by nominating more than 90 percent of all National Register listings.[18] In 1980 states reported 3,600 nominations representing 47,300 historic properties and maintained this level to the late eighties, when the average declined to 1,765. The number of nominations produced by the states has continued to decrease, reaching 1,386 in FY 2001. In contrast, the states have increasingly recognized significant properties through the environmental review process of determining properties "eligible" for the National Register. Determinations of Eligibility (DOEs) increased from 1,700 to 10,000 annually in the 1980s and rose sharply during the 1990s, reaching 64,537 in FY 2001. DOEs have become an official part of the states' collective inventories.[19]

In addition to their National Register inventories, at least twenty-one states maintain state registers, typically for the purpose of qualifying properties for state grants, tax benefits, and other state financial incentives. Although these registers differ widely from state to state, almost all of them include individual National Register properties and contributing properties in National Register districts. A smaller number incorporate locally designated landmarks and districts. The motivations for these registers vary. Some were in existence long before the National Register. Some function as handy receptacles for politically important properties that the state does not wish to have placed on the National Register, whereas others serve as "consolation prizes" for significant properties that for one reason or another fail to meet National Register criteria.[20]

A Broader Context. As the national program developed, the National Register not only came to include the oldest sites and structures associated with national heroes, but also began to encompass a much broader view of history, a greater range of property types, and a higher proportion of locally significant properties and districts. Among those recognized by listing in the National Register are Gold Rush sites in Alaska; cattle ranches in Arizona; prehistoric pueblos in Colorado and New Mexico; California missions; shipwrecks and lighthouses in coastal and inland states; African American churches, schools, and homes in the Southeast; Civil War battlefields and industrial sites; early colonial sites in Virginia, Pennsylvania, and Massachusetts; and farm complexes and urban neighborhoods in virtually every state.

As the program has aged, the fifty-year requirement for listing has brought the resources of the mid-twentieth century into consideration. The eligibility of post–World War II resources is creating discomfort and conflict for some state preservation officers as they begin to evaluate Cold War properties and ranch house subdivisions. When serious studies of these resources, such as those being carried out for the Cold War, are available, defensible cases are possible.[21] As one deputy SHPO stated, the fifty-year threshold is less important than jus-

Farm complex, Delaware. Recognized as a farm owned by the same family for more than one hundred years, this property is typical of the many farms across the country that have been registered and honored by their states. Many SHPOs have established Centennial Farm programs to encourage the preservation of working farms. (Alice H. Guerrant, Delaware State Historic Preservation Office)

Mount Tonachaw, Micronesia. As participants in the national historic preservation program in "Free Association," the historic preservation officer of Micronesia is able to recognize a type of traditional cultural property that is found throughout the United States as well as in the South Pacific. The knobby top of Mount Tonachaw is the head of an octopus that spreads its tentacles over this area of the Pacific Ocean, connecting islands and uniting the people of Chuuk. (Photo by Lawrence E. Aten, courtesy of the NPS)

Rocket engine test complex, Stennis Space Center, Mississippi. Resources of recent significance such as this rocket engine test complex are now recognized as important historic features of the American landscape by their SHPOS through nomination to the National Register.
(Photo by Richard Cawthon, Mississippi Department of Archives and History)

tifying listings in terms of meaning and period of significance as, for example,
the Civil Rights sites of the 1960s. The real challenge is to encourage the development of historical and architectural perspectives and interpretive context.
Some have compared the current dilemma to the problems encountered in
evaluating depression-era resources fifteen years ago and note a steady growth
of scholarly attention to more recent periods.

The National Register is often viewed as an honor roll of the nation's premier historic and archaeological sites and monuments. But from the earliest
days the states have considered National Register designation more as a planning tool for protection and preservation—a "gateway," as one SHPO put it—
to a variety of federal preservation programs. Its role in triggering impact
reviews of federal and, in some cases, state projects has been especially important. Increasingly, however, in the decades since passage of the 1980 amendments, National Register status has functioned as a means of achieving community goals in older neighborhoods and historic downtowns. Listing qualifies
properties for financial incentives such as grants and tax credits, and these
have, in turn, served as a catalyst for private and local government investment.

Planning. State preservation plans and planning as a state preservation program component have changed greatly from the late 1960s, when the federal government first required the states to formulate such plans in order to qualify for federal funds. Whereas the earliest plans were primarily status reports regarding state activity, yearly plan submissions from the early 1980s until the present have listed a much broader mix of goals and programmatic material. All of the states now have plans that meet the secretary of interior's "Preservation Planning Standards," but they are based as much on the perceived needs and resources of the states as on specific federal requirements. However, the route to this more creative approach to statewide planning was achieved only after considerable agitation from the SHPOs.

In the mid-1980s NPS professional staff decided that a more orderly and comprehensive state planning process was needed, and Washington thereupon imposed on the states a "Resource Protection Planning Process (RP3)." This was an essentially top-down approach whereby the states were required to organize their history into study units and develop management plans for the different types of resources that fit into each unit. When the states found this process to be inappropriate and unsuited to the way in which they worked with their constituents, several years of highly contentious deliberations ensued. The RP3 controversy added greatly to existing tensions over how state product submissions were counted in annual reports to the NPS—widely known as "bean counting"—and used to determine yearly fund apportionments to the states. Most contentious was the difference in perspective between the NPS, a federal agency, and the states regarding what should be preserved and the role expected of a state office in imposing a federal scheme on communities.

Discussion lasted for several years before differences between the states and the NPS regarding what constituted an acceptable state plan were resolved. Model plans in Georgia and Maryland helped to gain recognition in the early nineties for the right of the states to embark on a more open and state-based planning process. By 1996 end-of-the-year reports from many SHPOs describing their efforts to prepare a statewide plan highlighted their public participation activities, which both the states and the NPS now agreed were critically important.[22] By 1997 all of the states had approved state plans based on goals developed with extensive local government and public participation. By 1999 summaries of these plans were available though the Internet and were being incorporated into comprehensive state government plans. Notably, some received awards from organizations of planners and government officials.

Review and Compliance. The process of identifying, evaluating, and determining effects under Section 106 is time consuming and requires the action of professionals representing a variety of disciplines within state offices. These issues have grown in complexity in a process that provides for disclosure and mediation of competing interests, memoranda of agreements, and mitigation of adverse effects.

Since 1980, as a result of the growing maturity of state programs, changes in regulations, and reductions in funding for the Advisory Council, states have played an increasingly dominant role in policing federal agencies and their applicants. The percentage of staff time devoted to compliance has grown to 26 percent of all federally funded activity, and by 1989 this percentage had surpassed even the effort devoted to surveys. Undertakings requiring SHPO review have ranged from highway construction and urban development to the disposition of properties defaulted to the Resolution Trust Corporation in the 1980s and those seized for illegal drug dealing in the 1990s. By 1980 the yearly number of state reviews of federally funded or licensed projects had reached 12,000 and by federal FY 2001 had skyrocketed to 105,803.[23]

Although the 1992 amendments strengthened the states' hand, the agitation produced among the regulated federal agencies when the Advisory Council began rewriting its regulations to implement the changes had a negative effect. Changes in congressional leadership and anti-environment and conservative property rights attitudes produced legislation that added to the confusion. The federal agencies, which by this time were heavily involved in compliance work, called for a streamlined process and expedited reviews. States, too, needed to make the environmental review process more efficient, and the reports from the mid-1990s contain many examples of SHPO and client agency coordination seeking to improve the system.

By 1996 the states were looking for more flexible and creative approaches to mitigation. SHPOs wanted alternatives to "document, and dig or destroy," which had become the standard treatment measures for architectural and archaeological resources. In 1996 and 1997, using information gained from SHPO meetings and surveys, NCSHPO suggested a new framework that allowed greater creativity at the state level.

For example, in addition to the then-standard HABS/HAER recording for buildings, data recovery for archaeological sites, and rehabilitation reviews for housing and community development activities, public benefit provisions in the form of publications, exhibits, school curricula, lectures, and tours were coming into use as mitigation measures. Other new mechanisms included the preparation of preservation plans and the development of historic context studies. In Pennsylvania the Corps of Engineers funded the entry of cultural data into the commonwealth's GIS as mitigation for the impact of a major flood control project. The construction of the McPhee Reservoir near Delores, Colorado, by the U.S. Bureau of Reclamation resulted in an extensive survey of ancient Pueblo sites and the establishment of a very successful museum, the Anasazi Heritage Center. In Minnesota, a narrow rural road—the Blue Earth County Highway—was converted to a paved roadway, resulting in the demolition of a National Register farmstead. Mitigation included the production and distribution of a publication on the value of historic farmsteads and the need to plan for their preservation.[24]

The federal Section 106 and 4(f) laws (see Chapter 2) served as models for the adoption of planning statutes for state undertakings that affected historic properties. By 1999 thirty-six states had state-level "106" laws providing for SHPO review of state undertakings, but, as a rule, state protection laws tended to be less stringent and comprehensive than federal laws. Though few states had passed the equivalent of Section 4(f) of the 1966 DOT Act, New Mexico imposed a state-level "Section 4(f)" standard of compliance in 1989 to protect properties listed in the National Register and the State Register of Cultural Properties. What is most unusual, however, is that New Mexico's law applies to both state *and* local government actions.[25] Laws to prevent disturbance of archaeological remains on state-owned land were in place by 1980 in virtually every state. Some states also passed laws to protect specific classes of resources such as covered bridges and county courthouses.[26]

Grants. Federal grants received by the states not only supported core programs of survey, National Register, review and compliance, CLGs, and federal tax incentive certifications, but also were subgranted to local governments and constituents. The amount of these financial incentives has fluctuated with changes in the political and economic climate of the 1980s and 1990s. When federal appropriations grew in the late 1970s to a high of $47 million in 1979 and 1980, it was possible for the SHPOs to assist bricks-and-mortar projects. This was no longer possible after 1981, which saw a 50 percent cut in congressional appropriations and administrative restrictions on development using federal funds. The situation changed briefly with passage of the federal Emergency Jobs Act of 1983, an exception that should have proved that rehabilitating historic buildings provides more jobs than new construction. By expeditiously distributing the funds under this act to significant buildings and compiling impressive economic figures, the states were able to demonstrate the effectiveness of using federal funds for preservation development.[27] Despite these successes, federal rehabilitation grants were prohibited until 1989, when, ironically, reduced funding levels kept most states from taking advantage of the lifting of the restriction. Looking back in 1996, the president of the NCSHPO observed that it was an odd turn of events when the states could use federal funds to identify historic properties but not to preserve them.[28]

In spite of these setbacks, the states continued to use the HPF to support their "survey and planning" activities. However, reduced or level funding for core programs meant that little money, with the exception of the required 10 percent pass-through to CLGs, was available. Since then, many states have had to curtail basic program services.[29] The CLG grants were generally small (between $5,000 and $10,000) but facilitated important work in local communities.[30]

Federal Rehabilitation Tax Incentives. Federal tax incentives (see Chapter 2), first enacted in 1976 and expanded in 1981, quickly became the major federal financial incentive available for the actual rehabilitation and preservation of historic buildings. An estimated $2–3 billion of private investment in historic properties nationwide each year has been the result. Although the largest programs are on the East Coast, all fifty state preservation offices, and those in the District of Columbia, Puerto Rico, and the Virgin Islands, have promoted and benefited from the program. They have also borne the brunt of a two-tiered, three-part review and certification process and worked laboriously with taxpayers to qualify their projects for certification. The process requires three stages of review: one to certify the significance of properties, a second for the proposed rehabilitation work, and a third for the completed project. In FY 2001 this meant that a total of 3,397 state-level reviews were conducted for 836 projects approved by the NPS. Despite the constantly increasing workload and the occasional friction caused by differing interpretations of the required standards between the NPS and the states, the states appreciate the benefits in historic properties preserved through this program and struggle to keep up with its public popularity and attendant workload.[31]

Public Education and Technical Assistance. Education and technical assistance were initially considered as an "Other" category of permitted activities by the NPS, as though they were unimportant. After all, much educational activity does not easily lend itself to "products" to be counted in performance reports, nor are there immediate observable benefits or consequences, such as those for

Lincoln Mill, Appleton, Wisconsin. A variety of building types, such as this previously abandoned mill in the Fox River Paper complex in Appleton, have been given new life through the
rehabilitation tax incentives administered by state historic preservation offices. As in many
states, the Wisconsin staff provided technical assistance to the developer who rehabilitated
this complex of historic buildings in the early 1990s for apartments. (Photo by Wisconsin Historical Society, Historic Preservation Division)

environmental review or tax act certifications, which involve mandates, dead-
lines, penalties, and profits for constituents. Nevertheless, the states have overcome the barriers that low funding has created by emphasizing education and
"customer service" through newsletters, fact sheets, publications, special pro-
motions of successful local projects, technical information, and a wide range of
other educational activities. These materials and programs were specially developed to meet particular state and local needs. State professional staffs offered property owner consultations and hands-on technical direction through
field visits to properties and communities. Ohio staff recently noted the twentieth year of their innovative "Building Doctor" workshops, which other states
have emulated. Minnesota created a technical assistance mechanism called "Re-
Use Studies" through which funds were provided for studies of the rehabilitation potential of endangered properties. Specific building types also received attention, as in Florida's *Historic Schools Reuse* booklet and the Texas
Courthouse Alliance, coordinated by the state historic preservation office.

Workshops and statewide conferences, which are more often than not joint

Restored Ohio state capitol. The Ohio State Historic Preservation Office provided technical assistance in the restoration of this National Historic Landmark. Some states have restored their historic capitols as combined working government offices and museum spaces. Others, such as Hawaii, have restored them as museums. Ohio preservation office staff served on the planning committee, reviewed restoration plans, consulted on archaeological investigations, and provided monument guidelines for the statehouse grounds. (Photo by Franklin B. Conaway)

ventures with statewide preservation and professional organizations, have served an especially important educational function by bringing people together to share successes and problems and to seek common solutions. Many states now hold annual statewide conferences on current preservation issues and practice. An innovative approach initiated by Indiana in 1994 was the "Grassroots Preservation Roundup Idea Exchange" intended to target local organizations and individuals who might not otherwise attend the statewide conference. Oklahoma and Louisiana have utilized the newsletter of a nonprofit organization to distribute information and articles about program activities. A majority of the states now provide newsletters, and many publish books and articles about the historic resources of their states and how to preserve them.[32] North Carolina, South Dakota, and Wisconsin have managed to produce major works on the architecture of their states; some states, like Maryland, have their own press.

States such as Maine and New Mexico have explored the use of other media, including public service announcements and television documentaries. Public outreach is a major activity in some of the territories, where the interpretation of local cultural history through publications, radio and television, and sign or highway marker programs is emphasized. With the assistance of SHPO staff and documentary resources, many statewide nonprofit organizations have taken the initiative to develop heritage educational programs with their school systems.[33] Most states also utilize the National Trust's annual designation of Preservation Week for a variety of promotional and educational events. Some, usually through nonprofit organizations, have also followed the National Trust's lead in using annual "Most Endangered Properties Lists" to encourage public attention and assistance to important properties. In a type of public educational event that began in the West and has now spread across the country, many states promote public interest and participation in archaeology through an annual Archaeology Week.

State Initiatives

In spite of declining federal funds since 1980, all of the states struggle to carry out the federally based core programs described above. But with federal commitment and leadership on the wane, state-based initiatives—some of them path breaking—have responded to the ever-expanding demand for preservation services.[34]

Before the 1966 act, direct federal grants to individual historic properties were unusual. By making the owners of qualified historic properties eligible for direct grants, the 1966 NHPA raised hopes and expectations; however, as a result of reduced federal funds, the states were forced to develop a variety of alternate incentives.[35] Florida, for example, built a stunningly successful program based on the natural tendency of elected legislators to want to "help" their constituents in the amount of $17 million annually in collaboration with a network of nonprofit preservation organizations. In a few other states funding levels have reached $1–2 million each year; Colorado now appropriates $14–16 million annually for preservation. In Arizona, Colorado, Florida, Maryland, Massachusetts, New York, North Carolina, Pennsylvania, and Virginia, the annual range of direct appropriations is $125,000 to $600,000 annually.[36]

The states have been especially creative in finding new funding sources. Some use bond issues and the proceeds from gambling and pari-mutuel betting. Colorado and several other western states have introduced special taxes on gambling—Colorado's deputy SHPO noted that these amount to more than twenty times the regular program funds![37] States have also provided a variety of indirect financial incentives through provisions in their tax codes—either income tax credits and/or property tax reductions and freezes. As of 2001, forty-five states offered some form of tax incentive, and twenty-six authorized local governments to provide property tax relief for historic properties.[38]

Limited federal and state resources also stimulated SHPOs to seek other types of federal funds to do the work of preservation. As noted in Chapter 2, they have for many years encouraged the use of federal CDBG funds in combination with the tax credits for building rehabilitation and historic neighborhood renewal.

The "enhancements" feature of the 1991 Intermodal Surface Transportation Act also produced a staggering $151 billion of available funding, but the number and quality of preservation projects undertaken by states heavily depended on the individual SHPO-DOT working relationship. Through creative interaction with state DOTs, SHPOs and state-level partners such as preservation and conservation organizations were able to channel enhancement funds into historic buildings and landscape improvements in historic districts and along historic roadways. SHPOs also encouraged state DOTs, which were more accustomed to contracting and engineering road building than to creating historic trails and restoring buildings, to use some of these funds for technical assistance through their state preservation offices.

Although transportation enhancement money is restricted to "transportation-related" projects, that definition has been creatively and expansively defined in practice. For instance, ISTEA funds paid for an intensive multistate survey of the original National Road. In North Carolina and New Hampshire, SHPOs used ISTEA money to create research and curation facilities for collections of archaeological artifacts, including those recovered from highway projects.[39] Ironically, the figure of $151 billion over the first five years of enhancement and scenic byway funding was equivalent to one thousand times the amount authorized from the HPF for the same period. The latest version of ISTEA, titled TEA-21, which passed into law in 1998, contains both enhancement and scenic byways funding.[40]

Other federal resource enrichment programs have also aided the work of the SHPOs. Through its "Legacy" program, the U.S. Department of Defense identifies and protects natural and cultural resources on its 25 million acres of land throughout the nation. State programs have specifically benefited from Legacy-funded initiatives such as the Naval Historical Center's effort to monitor, manage, and interpret historic shipwrecks. With the navy's help, the North Carolina and Maryland State Historic Preservation Offices were able to set up protected shipwreck diving preserves for the USS *Huron* near Nags Head and the German U-boat *U-1105* in the Potomac River off Piney Point, Maryland.[41] In California, Legacy funds made possible the creation of an electronic database and GIS system for the Mojave Desert and an overview of the history of the military in California from the Spanish period to the Cold War. As of 1994, Legacy's annual funding had reached $50 million—again, considerably more than the annual amount allocated to the states through the HPF.[42]

A major focus of state historic preservation offices since their creation has been local historic resources. The initiation of the CLG program in the early 1980s provided SHPOs with a visible, structured mechanism through which to assist citizens and local communities. Survey and National Register programs spurred local interest and helped communities realize the preservation value of their historic resources. Planning and technical assistance, grants and tax incentives have spurred community development projects and affordable housing. In addition, SHPOs found programs of other nonpreservation state agencies valuable to their work at the local level. Perhaps the most extensive and long lasting of these have been the National Trust's pilot Main Street programs. Often these were set up in state or local departments of economic development and community affairs, but many became programs of SHPO offices. Regardless of their location, Main Street programs utilized SHPO services in the revitalization of historic downtowns. Tourism departments, too, became cooperating partners as state governments began to recognize that a state's historic resources are a major source of tourist dollars. The majority of SHPOs have reported some type of coordination, information sharing, and promotion with their state tourism agency. Some SHPOs, like those in Florida and Maryland, are official members of their tourism councils; others have developed brochures and interpretive sign programs. Many work to promote the special historic and archaeological resources of their states, such as Gold Rush sites in Alaska and prehistoric resources in the Four Corners region of the Southwest.[43]

As state historic preservation programs matured, state initiatives grew and SHPOs became involved in some of the critical issues of the period: affordable housing, economic development in historic downtowns, neighborhood renewal, transportation planning, and growth management. Changes in the mid-1990s to the committee structure of the SHPOs' professional organization, the NCSHPO, reflected this breadth. In 1991 committees on the National Parks and Advisory Council were balanced by committees on state programs and critical issues that looked beyond Washington-oriented concerns. In 1994, when the NCSHPO surveyed member states to identify issues of greatest concern, they responded with affordable housing and rehabilitation standards, heritage education, property rights issues, transportation planning, and minority heritage, along with

Main Street program, Blytheville, Arkansas. Arkansas's Main Street program, like others nationwide, provides incentives for historic downtown revitalization. This business in Blytheville was rehabilitated using Model Business Grants as an example for others. (Photo by Main Street Arkansas/Arkansas Historic Preservation Program, Department of Arkansas Heritage)

program administration and funding.[44] The SHPOs' interaction with the larger political, social, and economic systems of the nation had not only become more evident, but now foretells a challenging future.

State Historic Preservation Officers: Values, Economics, Social Structure

The Political Context

The SHPOs administer programs that are firmly fixed in modern law and government, yet they struggle daily with recurring issues that arise from America's economic and political systems and contending philosophical values. The governmental framework within which the national preservation program operates is often overlooked. It is far down the ladder on the organization charts of the U.S. Department of the Interior. State programs are typically located in

Kiva on the Ute Reservation, southwestern Colorado. This kiva is typical of many archaeo-logical sites in the Four Corners region, where a coordinated tourism initiative of SHPOS and tourism agencies is under way to promote resource-sensitive heritage tourism. Colorado, Utah, Arizona, and New Mexico are partners in the Four Corners Heritage Council, whose mission is education, interpretation, and preservation. (Photo by Office of Archaeology and Historic Preservation, Colorado Historical Society)

the smaller units of larger departments of historic, cultural, or natural resources, or in semiautonomous state historical societies and commissions. The nature of state-level preservation programs is often misunderstood by other state agencies.

SHPOS are part of the executive function of state government. They are ap-pointed by and responsible to the governor. Yet they carry out the mandates of federal law made in Washington, D.C., enforcing and administering federal programs in state and local political environments that are frequently hostile. Not only are their programs often low in the bureaucratic organization and outside the realm of political influence among state agencies, they must often accommodate the fluctuating policies of changing administrations. To para-phrase former Speaker of the House Sam Rayburn, SHPO staff are often pres-sured to "go along" to "get along."[45]

Notwithstanding that state programs are said to be models of the "new fed-eralism," SHPOS are part of a decentralized national preservation network that simply could not function without them.[46] The irreducible truth is that the

Affordable housing in Greensboro, North Carolina. The positive role of state historic preservation offices in review and compliance is seen in this house purchased and rehabilitated with CDBG funds in the South Greensboro National Register Historic District. The rehabilitation occurred pursuant to a model Programmatic Agreement between the state SHPO, the city of Greensboro, and the federal Advisory Council on Historic Preservation. (Photo by Mike Cowhig, City of Greensboro)

National Park Service sets national standards and program priorities, and the SHPOs, as quasi-federal "agents," do the work. As might be expected with a program in which the federal government sets the rules and controls the funding, federal oversight has created tension between states and the NPS.

The NPS—by its mission, history, and all its instincts—places the greatest priority on its parks. Administratively relegated to a sideline category called "external" programs, the national preservation program was, from the SHPOs' point of view, operationally treated as the proverbial "red-headed step-child." Strains accompanied increased state responsibilities and program growth that have not been matched by commensurate increases in funding and staff. SHPOs grew to resent the ever-increasing federal paperwork and "micro-management" (bean counting) that accompanied the small federal grants awarded to the states.[47]

Through NCSHPO, NPS officials and staff on the one hand and SHPOs and their staff on the other had long been negotiating their differences about a fair grant apportionment formula among the states, administration of the program itself, and such substantive program issues as survey goals and guidelines. Other negotiated issues have included National Register criteria and documentation requirements, rehabilitation standards, and planning processes. Subsequent dialogue between the states and the NPS and the Advisory Council addressed other contentious issues such as tribal programs, Section 106 procedures, and rehabilitation standards encountered by the states in administering tax act reviews. Continued interaction has resolved many program issues.[48]

But several difficult administrative issues were not settled, and since 1985 many SHPOs have clamored for greater autonomy in setting program priorities and for an independent national agency outside the National Park Service solely dedicated to historic preservation.[49] These and other issues were first highlighted in discussions leading up to the NHPA amendments of 1992 and continued in a federal performance review process in 1993–94.

The outcome was essentially positive for preservation. During the negotiations of the early 1990s, NCSHPO backed away from its stance on the need for a separate agency—after all, an independent agency would be more visible and perhaps fiscally more vulnerable—and supported a consensus package of legislative amendments. Working with an ad hoc National Preservation Coordinating Council (comprised of representatives from the NCSHPO, Preservation Action [PA], the National Trust, and the Society of American Archaeology [SAA]), SHPOs gained a major legislative victory in 1992 that achieved four important objectives: it put the Section 106 process into statutory law, it prohibited anticipatory demolition by federal applicants for permits and grants, it required federal agencies to preserve historic properties on federal land, and it added new sections establishing tribal programs and a National Center for Preservation Technology and Training. Taken together, these were regarded as major preservation program improvements.

Through support for the new tribal programs, the SHPOs welcomed the Native American constituency into the national program. Although the SHPOs do not have a direct responsibility in the NCPTT program, they were consulted in planning for its creation and have benefited from its grants for research, training, and information management.[50]

The 1992 amendments did, in fact, accelerate an improved relationship between the federal government and state historic preservation programs, making them less subject to daily scrutiny and oversight by NPS.[51] The momentum toward program independence increased following a 1994 performance review of state programs by NPS that concluded that the states should be considered as "extensions of the service delivery hierarchy, rather than solely as recipients of service."[52] Although the SHPOs were disappointed that Department of the Interior streamlining prevented the creation of a proposed separate deputy directorate for external programs, the report sought to give states a somewhat freer hand in the federal-state partnership

A source of tension between NPS and the SHPOs that had grown into a major fault line by the late 1980s was a federal program review conducted every four years in each state. However, with the 1992 amendments, the 1994 performance review, and a subsequent downsizing of NPS staff, federal program reviews of the states became somewhat more collegial in spirit.

Despite all of these gains, the states continue to struggle with inadequate funding levels that have never come close to the $150 million authorization level for the Historic Preservation Fund. From 1981 and during each of its eight years in office, the Reagan administration earmarked NHPA funding to the states for total elimination on the grounds that grants to the states were for state, not federal, purposes, and that the federal-state partnership was a "start up" program with federal grants serving merely as a temporary incentive.[53] Contrary to the assertions of federal budget cutters that the states would assume all the costs of state administration of the national program, the states' real position was laconically summarized in the mid-1980s by the former SHPO of Idaho, Meryl Wells: "We have been pleased to give the federal government 50% grants all these years, but we can't afford to give the federal government 100% grants."[54]

Nonetheless—and fortunately—each year the states and the national preservation constituency have convinced Congress to put money back into the budget for the national historic preservation program. In terms of real purchasing power, however, the fund has gone from "merely inadequate" to "endangered." Further, state legislatures and budget offices can (and occasionally do) propose reductions in state funding, based on the incorrect assumption that the programs are solely federal in character.[55]

But most important, by the turn of the twenty-first century, the states were able to move beyond fighting for basic program survival and rights of partnership within the national program created by NHPA. They began looking for activities that would further enhance their national role, strengthen partnerships with all public and private preservation organizations, and make the case for increased financial resources and stronger preservation laws and incentives.[56]

The Challenge of Review and Compliance

The federal Review and Compliance program in which SHPOs work under ACHP procedures has been highly instrumental in saving thousands of historically and archaeologically significant properties from unnecessary destruction. It has also caused SHPOs many headaches and, occasionally, the loss of their jobs.

Perhaps nowhere is the position of the SHPO as a state government official responsible for federal procedures more significant and politically vulnerable at one and the same time. Many applicants for federal and state development grants and permits subscribe to long-held American philosophies and ideals of limited government, unfettered private property rights, and a free marketplace. Property owners, developers, and development-oriented officials are baffled by and resent any mandated stewardship enforced by public historians in what they perceive as a minor state office. On the other hand, citizens concerned about their neighborhoods and historic environment misunderstand the authority of the SHPOs and expect them to stop all unwanted development projects. Thus, the National Historic Preservation Act and its state-level equivalents have collided head-on with popular convictions that new is good, old is bad, and change always means progress.

A series of visible conflicts that illustrate the tide of thorny issues faced by SHPOs occurred in Virginia and engaged the attention of the nation due to the increasing interest in the Civil War as a defining moment in American history. Questions about property rights and development pressures that began in the early 1990s came to a head with resistance by property owners and developers to the historic designation and protection of Manassas, Bristoe Station, and Brandy Station—the latter being the site of the largest cavalry engagement of the war. Because National Register listings and determinations of eligibility for the register invoke Section 106, fierce opposition erupted against official findings of historical significance. In 1992, under intense political pressure, the secretary of the interior overturned a determination by the Virginia SHPO and the Keeper of the National Register that Brandy Station met the criteria for inclusion in the National Register. Partly as a consequence, an "owner consent" provision was added to the Virginia Landmarks Register law in April 1992. There was also an unsuccessful legislative effort to restrict professional preservation decisions by allowing local governments to veto determinations of eligibility, the linchpin of Section 106 effectiveness.[57]

Despite the actions of the secretary of the interior and the Virginia legislature, the state's historic preservation office stoutly maintained that Brandy Station was eligible. When a Formula One racetrack for automobiles was proposed for Brandy Station in 1993, the state office, with the help of the ACHP, successfully hammered out a memorandum of agreement with the project sponsors. Fortunately the Army Corps of Engineers, as the federal lead agency, agreed that the project was subject to Section 106. Facing the threat of lawsuits from project opponents such as the National Trust and the Brandy Station Foundation, the sponsors backed out even though the MOA was executed.[58]

In 1993 and 1994 the Disney Company's plans to build a 150-acre theme park at Haymarket, Virginia, threw the Old Dominion and the national preservation community into another preservation maelstrom. The Virginia General Assembly and the governor supported the Disney plan, which threatened the pristine cultural and natural setting of the entrance to the Shenandoah Valley. Arrayed against Disney and development-oriented Virginia politicians were the National Trust and twenty-four other preservation and conservation groups that condemned it as a "superscaled specimen of leapfrog development." Caught in the middle of the turmoil were the Virginia SHPO and staff, who entered into Section 106 consultations with pertinent federal and state agencies, and the developer applicants. Eventually, the considerable effort of the national historical and preservation community had its effect: recognizing that it had created a public relations fiasco, the Disney corporation abandoned the project.[59]

Although these events, viewed in a national context, were in some ways exceptional, they were not unusual in demonstrating a process that has been repeated across the nation. Federal regulations, usually seen negatively by citizens and public officials alike, nevertheless provide a mechanism for engaging a wider public in the issues of resource protection. Many SHPOs have experienced similar situations in which the regulatory reviews, in and of themselves, have not stopped projects without the active support and advocacy of the larger public.

In addition to the political trauma, the Virginia experience also illustrates another aspect of the compliance process that seems to be increasing: that is, the way in which it can bring competing interests together and produce a positive outcome. Virginia's governor subsequently supported a Virginia History Initiative, in which a volunteer group of business people, community planners, and public historians formulated goals and products to boost the state's historic resources. The objective was to put heritage stewardship on the policy agenda of as many Virginia communities as possible. To keep the momentum of the initial effort alive, the group formed a permanent Cultural Coordinating Council. In addition, the controversy led to a legislatively mandated study of the financial impact of historic designation. The ensuing report by the state preservation office was an articulate statement supporting historic designations and their beneficial economic impact that has since provided support to preservationists within and outside the state.[60]

There are many examples across the country in which the initial stresses created by the environmental review process have been resolved with positive results. MOAs often contain workable solutions for saving historic structures, while allowing a development-oriented agency or project to meet its goals. Among many success stories is that of Sauk Centre, Minnesota, where planned highway improvements through the "Main Street" that inspired native son Sinclair Lewis in his characterization of small-town America were mitigated under Section 106. As a result, a historic district was listed in the National Register, and improvements were added to the thoroughfare that actually helped to restore the area to its period of greatest historical significance. In the words of the SHPO staff, the local preservation picture was "refocused from a 'stop progress' image to one of community enhancement."[61]

Highway project reviews have generated much conflict over the years but are now beginning to produce positive results in many states. Some have had implications for all the states. Consultation between the New York State SHPO and the state Department of Transportation over projects for several notable postwar Long Island and Hudson Valley Parkways eventually led to more flexible construction standards that were approved by the Federal Highway Administration. These discussions, in turn, led to a National Register nomination, a HAER project, the restoration of landscape features, and a number of applications for Scenic Byway designations.[62]

The give-and-take of review and compliance has also encouraged private investment using state and federal tax incentives and has had a major impact on the private sector. The federal rehabilitation tax credit has provided SHPOs with a preservation option that greatly increases private sector willingness to consider preservation. In a blighted area of Chicago, for example, developers of a major HUD-funded project used the federal tax credits and the National Register nomination process recommended by the state preservation office.[63] This scenario was repeated throughout the nation hundreds, if not thousands, of times, to the benefit of many historic downtowns and neighborhoods. Sometimes through MOAs the review process saves buildings that many years later are rehabilitated. To illustrate, two very large Georgia mill complexes were saved during negotiations over a large transportation project but stood vacant for decades until federal and state tax credits provided the incentive for privately financed mixed-use projects that brought them back to life. In this case, as in many other depressed areas, Section 106 procedures kept buildings standing, giving states time to promote their reuse and offer financial incentives for private development.[64]

Natural and man-made disasters provide another type of situation in which SHPO responsibilities for review under Section 106 have been more widely and successfully applied. In crisis situations, officials are always under stress to act quickly. Calls for waivers or suspensions of preservation laws frequently occur. In 1993 midwestern governors requested waivers of Section 106 for flood relief efforts. Fortunately, ACHP rules that specifically addressed emergency undertakings, and a national programmatic agreement with the Federal Emergency Management Administration (FEMA) that could be tailored to specific situations, permitted expedited reviews that took preservation agencies out of the political line of fire.[65] The precedents established by the FEMA memorandum of agreement have since helped SHPOs in other states to deal with the impact of earthquakes, tornadoes, hurricanes, floods, oil spills, and a bombing.

Technical publications dealing with natural disasters, disaster relief plans that take historic preservation into account, and even the sharing of SHPO technical staff across state boundaries following emergencies have played a highly positive role in emergency recovery efforts, as has the administration of disaster relief funds by SHPOs. Examples include flood recovery booklets from Iowa and Georgia, a joint Missouri–Illinois–National Trust workshop on flood damaged masonry, hurricane response kits in Alabama, and disaster response plans in many states. What often began as an attempt to prevent unnecessary demolition became a much larger program of technical assistance to help communities all over the nation recover and preserve some continuity with their past.[66]

Notwithstanding the political and community tensions resulting from Section 106, the combination of incentives from NPS-managed programs and ACHP regulations has sometimes placed SHPOs between the standards of two preservation agencies. In 1996, when affordable housing became a contentious issue, the ACHP issued guidance to defuse the potential for conflict in an effort to relax strict rehabilitation standards as they applied to the interiors of simple buildings. The guidance provides flexibility but still leaves state historic preservation office staff coping with their personal conviction that preservation should be of benefit to low-income people, the stricter requirements of the NPS-administered Secretary of the Interior's Standards for Rehabilitation, and housing officials antagonistic to both historic preservation and the reuse of older structures.

In addition, the creative merger of federal preservation standards and affordable housing credits to benefit low-income families has been hampered by inconsistencies and conflicts among the Secretary's Standards, federal housing credits, and state-mandated local housing codes. In response, the Georgia SHPO organized a 1995 symposium of preservation and housing agency representatives, local officials, and housing architects to identify barriers and search for common ground. Recommendations adopted by the group were shared nationally, and some progress has been made.[67] A number of states, including Nebraska and Vermont, have since adopted more flexible, preservation-friendly codes that facilitate the cost-effective reuse of existing structures. In 1998, in North Carolina, the state historic preservation office, the city of Greensboro, and the ACHP reviewed and amended an earlier programmatic agreement that permitted the city's CDBG program to demolish historic buildings in a local National Register historic district. The highly successful affordable housing program that resulted is being used by the National Trust as a model for neighborhood revitalization through historic preservation.[68]

The Section 106 review and comment process has played a more important role than most realize. But it has generated an enormous workload for state preservation offices that shows no signs of abating. As the chair of the Advisory Council, herself an SHPO, observed in 1996, "The list of topics receiving Council attention from 1966–1996 serves as a virtual index to the national historic preservation agenda as well as the social and economic issues of the day." Examples included the 1970s energy crises, the 1980s tax issues, and a variety of preservation challenges in the 1990s, ranging from Native American consultation to low-income housing.[69]

Overall, the process works well if certain basic principles are understood. State historic preservation officers were reminded of these in 1995 by a relatively new SHPO who had recently survived a command visit to her governor's woodshed to explain her position on a contentious federal courthouse case. "The point . . . to remember," she said, "is that when we as SHPOs come under political pressure, our response should not be to retreat from our role as advocate for the resource. We must continue to give agencies the benefit of our best professional opinion, and we must insist that the federal agencies accept responsibility for the choices that must be made about costs and benefits." She added this important advice: "We should work constantly to develop a constituency for preservation within the general public . . . and insist that federal agencies fulfill their obligations and accept their responsibilities under the law."[70]

SHPOs in the American Scene

The larger trends in American society—among them increasing demographic diversity, rapidly changing technology, the economy, and sprawl—have affected all of the preservation programs of the SHPOs. Among the most far-reaching trends that will dramatically influence the future course of our national culture and ideas about historical significance is America's changing ethnic mix. One of the most notable and positive intellectual products of the modern preservation movement has been the broader understanding of the nation's history that has grown from SHPO programs of survey and study. Whereas surveys first tended to recognize the earliest history of an area and the most prominent state and national figures and buildings, the more recent work is more inclusive, both temporally and culturally. As David McCullough has said, the stage lights are coming up on a larger cast, illuminating the wide diversity of population groups and cultures that have contributed to present-day America.[71]

This more diverse culture is now widely reflected in state resource inventories, both in a wider selection of property types, from simple houses to cultural landscapes, and in a variety of special historic places such as those associated with the Civil War and women's history. It has also raised important questions of significance and evaluation criteria. Nevertheless, the historical professions have been slow to consider the research and analysis potential of this material. Serious syntheses could incorporate the broader picture of state and local history emerging from the work of state historic preservation offices into the nation's history and thus increase understanding of the richness of the American experience.[72]

The broader considerations of state and local history have brought new interests to the programs of the state offices. A 1990 NCSHPO survey found that many states were seeking to identify historic places associated with all facets of their history, and that many had established special committees to ensure that particular groups were represented. These efforts continue, but a gap identified in the 1990 survey, which continues today, lies within the preservation professions.[73] The new tribal programs established under the 1992 amendments

Selma to Montgomery March. This annual celebration, assisted by the work of Alabama's Black Heritage Council, the oldest of many state historic preservation office special African American preservation committees, attracts national attention. Among the speakers in 1997 was Congressman John Lewis, shown here in front of Brown's Chapel, a historic church building significant to the civil rights movement. (Photo by Ellen Mertins, Alabama Historical Commission)

are beginning to include Native American professionals, but other population groups are seriously underrepresented in state offices and programs. SHPOs have tried to address the issue of minority representation in their programs through staff hires and appointments to state National Register review boards.

The predominant discipline for minority participants in both staff and review boards continues to be history. The National Trust, NPS, NCSHPO, and National Council of Preservation Educators have periodically examined the issue of minority participation without determining fully either the reasons or the solutions. A sampling of responses from the states to a recent survey indicates a dearth of qualified applicants for positions and an apparent lack of interest and information, despite the increasingly broad attention to a variety of cultural resources representing the ethnic heritage of all Americans.[74]

In the mid-1990s, about the time when the National Center for Preservation Technology and Training was established (see Chapter 2), the states were becoming particularly aware of the impact of fast-changing technologies on their programs and resources as they struggled to obtain funding to utilize computer databases for growing resource inventories. The rapid development of the Internet and electronic mail systems added another dimension, which some states were able to master more rapidly than others. Surveys of the states by the NPS and the NCPTT in the late 1990s revealed that 44 percent of the states still had no computer databases for their inventories and 82 percent continued to rely on paper maps instead of GIS systems, which would facilitate the use of their inventory data in state and local planning.[75] In 1999 a working group that included the states, the NCPTT, and NPS Heritage Preservation Services began to coordinate technical developments and systems in an attempt to bring all the states into a workable system that could take advantage of state-of-the-art communications systems.[76] Communication links expanded further as the National Trust, in partnership with the NCPTT, began projects to bring statewide nonprofit organizations into the system. NCSHPO also used NCPTT funds to work with the National Conference of State Legislatures (NCSL) to establish an electronic database and website of state historic preservation laws.[77]

Technological change has also challenged state programs to find new methods for solving preservation problems and creating uses for many structures whose functions have become obsolete, such as barns, schools, bridges, filling stations, and tobacco warehouses. Nowhere is this as evident as in the NCSHPO e-mail listserv, where state staffs daily trade technical information on a range of problems such as the rehabilitation of schools and factories, the effects of increased traffic vibrations on historic buildings from widened highways, the effectiveness of various roofing materials, and the conservation of wood in water-logged wooden roads. Increasingly, the composition and characteristics of twentieth-century materials, including plastics and composition sidings, are becoming serious challenges as the buildings of the twentieth century reach the National Register's fifty-year qualifying mark. Some states have used NCPTT grant funds to look for solutions to technical problems like the energy efficiency of wooden windows (Vermont), the conservation of unique building materials such as tabby (Georgia), heating and air-conditioning in historic structures (New York), methods for economic analysis (New Jersey), and planning issues such as parking in historic downtowns (Kentucky), and to produce a video on lead paint abatement in historic buildings for distribution to all the SHPOs (Maryland).[78] Developing improved technical solutions to preservation problems and making them accessible within the states remains a daunting challenge.

Given the nature of SHPO programs and their impact on so many areas of community life, it is not surprising that they have collided head-on with a persistent philosophical viewpoint in some business and government circles that historic preservation is a nice but expensive frill. Public officials have often justified decisions leading to the demolition of historic buildings on the grounds that new construction will create more jobs and strengthen an area's tax base. It has been necessary to demonstrate that historic preservation is a productive, economic development tool—often more powerful than other more accepted approaches. The federal tax incentive process provided the statistics that allowed SHPOs to begin to respond to the economic climate of the 1980s with studies that demonstrated the potential economic benefit of historic preservation.

In addition to the national figures compiled each year by the NPS, New York (1983), Illinois (1984), Texas (1985), and Georgia (1986) published studies showing the amount of investment, the number of buildings and communities affected, and the increases in state and local taxes that certified rehabilitations had generated.[79] Beginning in the mid-1990s a new round of state studies, some initiated by private-sector preservation partners, continued and broadened the emphasis on preservation's economic benefits. Rhode Island in 1993 announced the results of a study of the economic impact on the state from more than twenty years of SHPO programs. Analyses of preservation's impact to the economies of Kentucky, Virginia, New Jersey, Oregon, North Carolina, Georgia, and Maryland, among others, followed.[80]

These newer studies have gone beyond certified tax rehabilitations to examine tourism, historic site maintenance and management, and Main Street programs and state incentives citing job and income growth, taxes generated, and wealth created. In New Jersey, research funding from the Task Force on New Jersey History, the Casino Reinvestment and Development Authority, and NCPTT supported the creation of a comprehensive model for determining preservation's effects by Rutgers University Center for Urban Policy Research.[81]

SHPOs have also become involved in the issue now known as "sprawl," as comprehensive planning has taken on greater significance in the many states that are trying to address the challenges and environmental impact of rapid growth. Accordingly, state historic preservation officers and their staffs have become more assertive in working within state governments to encourage anti-sprawl policies. In Maryland, the SHPO has been able to take advantage of a Smart Growth program that has become a national model for growth management, resource protection, and economic development. This generally activist antisprawl and managed growth activity has spread rapidly among the state historic preservation offices. Rhode Island and Michigan SHPOs have also undertaken notable initiatives in this area.[82]

Local comprehensive planning is another strategy through which SHPOs contribute to growth management. One feature of Maryland's Smart Growth is the requirement that local governments implement the program through their comprehensive master plans, which must be consistent with established state visions. In a process that has been used in several states, the Delaware State Historic Preservation Office in 1996 used its power of review and comment on local land-use plans through state law to encourage the insertion of historic preservation into the comprehensive plans of small towns. Driven by conservation and quality-of-life concerns, statewide land-use and Smart Growth planning laws have appeared with varying degrees of involvement by preservationists and varying degrees of protection or concern over historic properties in a number of states.[83]

SHPOs in the Larger Preservation Structure

As they have struggled to make their programs relevant to a changing society, SHPOs have depended heavily on the wider preservation community for support. Without the cooperation of the proliferating nonprofit organizations at every level, their effectiveness would have been limited. Local nonprofits were among the earliest proponents and users of state preservation programs, and the National Trust for Historic Preservation has helped the work of many states with innovative programs and supporting grants. One of the most important developments since the 1970s has been the growth of grass-roots, statewide, nonprofit preservation organizations, culminating most recently in the Statewides Partnership Initiative of the National Trust. The Trust has helped the organizations become professionally staffed and highlighted the benefits of cooperative working relationships with SHPOs. Statewides, together with local nonprofits and volunteer historical and archaeological organizations, offer the SHPOs financial and legal resources, advocacy services, survey fieldwork, National Register nomination research, and, for all practical purposes, additional staff services that would otherwise be unavailable.[84]

One of the essential outgrowths of these public-private partnerships has been strong preservation advocacy at every level of government. Preservation Action and the National Trust not only have protected federal funding and initiatives, but also are responsible for much state activity and legislation. As the struggles of the 1980s to maintain federal funding suggest, total elimination of funding for state programs remains a real possibility. The 1999 struggle even to reauthorize the national Historic Preservation Fund abundantly demonstrates the utter dependence of the preservation movement itself on these partnerships.[85] Despite thirty years of successful state and local preservation activities and the impressive economic benefits studies of the last few years, preservation as an economically viable community development and growth management strategy continues to be overlooked. Clearly, more effective public preservation education is needed. This is especially evident in the descriptions of the planning process in each state.

Making the connection between the technical assistance programs that citizens depend on in their communities to achieve their lofty goals and the means for that assistance in public preservation programs is a challenge. The SHPOs struggle to maintain their public education programs in the face of their legal responsibilities and the demands of constituents seeking particular actions such as tax project certifications. The recent economic benefits studies have given them a powerful tool, but if preservation is to become an integrated part of daily life and the decisions of planners and government officials, the SHPOs and their partners will have to make its accomplishments more widely visible and better understood. As one of these studies points out, historic preservation not only creates economic value, it also adds enrichment and educational value "to a community's overall quality of life."[86]

What of the Future?

SHPOs face the twenty-first century as the backbone of a national preservation system based on cost-effective partnerships with public and private, federal and local entities. The state historic preservation office has become the central distribution point in each state for a national program, as well as the state's focal point for historic preservation. To a greater or lesser degree, depending on circumstances and organizations in each state, the preservation office provides a vision for a better future. This is especially true in the recent state historic preservation plans that have consistently grown from a wider base of public participation.

State historic preservation programs have weathered a conservative backwash of political change that depressed funding and threatened their legal underpinnings. They have overcome the tensions created by overwhelming administrative and political pressures, maintained strong programs in spite of inadequate federal and state funding, and twice helped to strengthen the National Historic Preservation Act, which provides the program's framework. They have begun to turn around the negative implications of the regulatory processes they are required to carry out. State historic preservation offices have found strength in each other through the NCSHPO, and they have developed independent and innovative ways to accomplish their goals. Many have dealt with inadequate funding through partnerships with other agencies and organizations. Most important, they have learned to think strategically when faced with the conflicts of the review and compliance process, often finding creative solutions and utilizing the power of citizen involvement. They have emphasized the nonregulatory aspects of their programs such as grants and tax incentives, and technical assistance to historic property owners, business, and local governments, seeking willing partners for a variety of activities and programs that otherwise would not have been possible.

But they have also suffered much frustration because of the inadequacy of their operational resources and because historic preservation is not more widely recognized as a mechanism with which to meet contemporary problems. They, too, often find preservation needs brushed aside for what markets and decision makers deem to be more pressing tasks—highways, education, social security, and the war on terrorism. In a recent survey, SHPOs and their staffs indicated that for the most part their jobs were more satisfying than ten years earlier. Yet they found the lack of adequate funding demoralizing and in many cases the salaries too low. The requirements of Section 106 cast them into the role of regulators and absorbed too much of their operational resources. They were frustrated by their inability to provide the services that would directly and profoundly help their communities find what they perceived to be a better life.

Nevertheless, out of this adversity and frustration the SHPOs and their state and local partners have not just survived but in many cases have grown stronger. Thanks to NHPA, they have provided the American people with a remarkable level of historical understanding and appreciation. They have developed a collective historical memory and a panoply of preservation services and cost-effective technical assistance for thousands of private historical and preservation organizations and local governments that otherwise would have neither the financial resources nor the motivation to use preservation to improve the quality of community life. Their vision is a future in which every citizen appreciates the richness and diversity of community heritage, takes pride in maintaining and protecting that heritage, and embraces a role of stewardship for the significant historic features of the cultural landscape. Their success in fulfilling that vision can create a fuller sense in all citizens of what it means to be an American, of paramount importance in the smoldering wake of September 11, 2001.

Local Government Programs
Preservation Where It Counts

"Expansive, ebullient, optimistic and tolerant of change" is how one writer described the contemporary American preservation movement in 1987, a dramatic evolution from the "almost crisis-oriented" outlook expressed by the Special Committee on Historic Preservation in its report, *With Heritage So Rich*.[1] The spirit, perspective, and substance of the American preservation movement at all levels evolved at an even faster pace throughout the 1980s and 1990s and into the twenty-first century. How, why, and what brought about these changes and some issues for the future of preservation at the local level are addressed in this chapter.

Although local governments are the most important engines of preservation activity because of their close physical proximity to the citizens most directly affected, they do not act independently. Their regulatory authority is an exercise of delegated state power, and the fiscal incentives they can provide for preservation—grants, loans, tax breaks, revolving funds, easements, and the like—come from many sources, public, private, and nonprofit.

Local governments are thus both enabled and constrained—legally, politically, and practically—by many factors, and they do not act (or fail to act) entirely on their own. Federal and state resources, programs and policies, the state of the economy, and the availability of public-private-nonprofit partnerships thus dictate that in all the states, local governments will inevitably attack the same preservation problem in a different way. While the American preservation movement has moved beyond the saving of individual buildings, communities have the option of devising their own philosophy about what is important and how to preserve it. A few will go no further than preserving a historic house museum. Others will target entire neighborhoods. Others will merge traditional preservation interests with larger issues involving planning and growth management. This freedom for local governments to determine for themselves what they will seek to preserve, and how, is the real beauty of the American system.

As other chapters note, preservation at the local government level begins with some market fundamentals. In one way or another, we lose almost all cultural resources as a direct result of market imbalances, whether we are talking about individual buildings or whole neighborhoods.[2] Thus, when the value of a site greatly exceeds the value of its income-producing capability to the satisfaction of its owner, there is created inexorable pressure to tear down the building and put the site to a more productive use. In the opposite situation, when a building has little or no potential to satisfy the owner's economic expectations, it is lost through lack of maintenance and the inevitable rot that follows. All of our approaches to preservation—whether through planning, regulation, or economic subsidies of one kind or another—are aimed at the objective of producing just the right balance between too much and too little economic use. This is especially true at the local government level, always the source of real estate "value." The political aspects of most or all preservation controversies are inevitably related to the more fundamental economic considerations.[3]

Local Preservation Programs before 1980

Historically speaking, local governments have tended to back into historic preservation. Today, good practice would hold that a local preservation effort begins with surveys and plans of one kind or another, the development of priorities, and the integration of preservation efforts with larger, local land-use planning and growth management strategies. Only after these things are accomplished can it honestly be said that a local government has a real preservation program in effect.

But the first steps toward preservation in many cities have often been just the reverse: the hurried adoption of a controversial local historic district or landmark ordinance in response to a perceived preservation crisis, such as a landmark building threatened with Saturday night demolition. The first local historic districts were created in just this essentially retrograde way within the twenty-year period from 1931 to 1951, and, for the most part, they were often adopted independently of local planning programs. Nonetheless, these cities were the true pioneers of the American preservation movement at the local government level, and they deserve commendation here.

The real beginnings of preservation at the local level are to be found in the few local historic district ordinances passed between 1931 and the early 1950s, as recounted in the introduction to this book. The 1966 National Historic Preservation Act and other legislative initiatives of the Eighty-ninth Congress, taken together, virtually "locked local governments into a more active role in historic preservation" by tying local historic resources to federal funding and project status.[4] This was the real significance of the 1966 act.

NHPA established a number of significant new preservation mechanisms at the local level. The expanded National Register of Historic Places not only recognized properties of local and state significance, but made them routinely eligible for the first time to receive federal grants for planning, acquisition, and preservation. For the first time, locally valued properties came under the scrutiny of the systematic environmental review process created by Section 106.

Moreover, NHPA had a swift and far-reaching impact on the way local governments did business. Federal highway and urban renewal dollars could no longer be obtained without undergoing the Section 106 and Section 4(f) review and comment processes, and the federal courts held them to it.[5] Such court-enforced compliance had a pronounced effect on urban renewal projects. In addition to the NHPA connection between federal dollars and environmental review, a property's National Register status later became the trigger for federal tax incentives and often for state and local regulatory, funding, and planning programs as well.

The 1978 Supreme Court's decision in *Penn Central* (see Chapter 5) validated and legitimized local government preservation regulatory authority after years of uncertainty about the limits of the police power. It was a major victory and provided local preservation leaders confidence in the principal local government tools for preservation in use today.

Federal Influence on Local Preservation to 1980

The early, pre-1966 emphasis on a largely regulatory approach to preservation took a new direction in the 1950s and early 1960s. These were especially volatile years for preservation, largely because of the increasing role of the federal government in local government programs. Using the threat or power of eminent domain, the Urban Redevelopment Program embedded in the federal Housing Act of 1949 was directly responsible for the wholesale clearance of entire inner-city slum neighborhoods in many historic towns and cities across the country. Later federal housing acts shifted the emphasis away from clearance and redevelopment to more sensitive, area-specific, conservation and rehabilitation approaches, but damage to the inner-city historic fabric as the result of these programs was widespread. These early slash-and-burn projects were often carried out hand in hand with major street and highway projects that destroyed neighborhoods by slicing them apart with federal money and the aid of state "quick-take" road condemnation procedures. The extent and nature of destruction from these projects is by now well known and documented.

There were, of course, a few bright spots. One was a growing public sensitivity to the need for preservation. Another was an honest but very limited effort on the part of HUD itself to incorporate preservation values into urban renewal and housing programs, later characterized as "Model Cities" and "Demonstration Cities." Yet another was the Housing Act of 1954, which through Section 701 technical planning assistance grants gave rise to the concept of historic preservation plans as an important element in local planning programs. Wilmington, North Carolina, and Charleston, South Carolina, produced excellent studies of this kind, and HUD-financed demonstration projects in Providence, Rhode Island, and New Orleans, Louisiana, still stand as models. A few cities fought back with preservation efforts of their own. An innovative, precedent-setting local response to the threat of large-scale renewal and housing projects came from Philadelphia, which in 1956 gave its Historical Commission protective authority over historic buildings throughout the city.[6] A few of these measures had unintended consequences. Specially crafted, highly evocative design guidelines for the city of Savannah, Georgia, prepared as part of its overall preservation plan, were widely copied in other cities having no relationship whatever to the history, architecture, or spatial structure of Savannah.

What is not commonly realized is that the urban renewal program was sometimes used to fund a variety of preservation-related activities. These included surveys of historic resources, preservation and management plans, and demonstration projects. The demonstration plan volumes for the French Quarter of New Orleans and the College Hill area of Providence fall into this category.

Some cities proceeded on their own without federal help. The Pittsburgh, Pennsylvania, History and Landmarks Commission saved dozens of buildings in several declining neighborhoods by purchasing and rehabilitating buildings on a block-by-block basis, temporarily relocating the residents and returning them later through creative leasing arrangements with the local housing authority.

Several federal programs were created in the 1970s as partnership programs with local governments. The 1973 Urban Homesteading Program was designed to use preservation as a catalyst to revive inner-city neighborhoods. Tax-foreclosed properties could be purchased for as little as one dollar, with the stipulation that they be rehabilitated to code within a specified amount of time. Past taxes and penalties were forgiven by the local government in return for anticipated expanded tax bases. Homesteading programs were initiated for both residential and commercial properties. A second cooperative federal-local program, the Neighborhood Housing Service, was created to spur rehabilitation activities and new construction in older neighborhoods. Both programs coordinated preservation efforts with the goals of planning, community development, and capital projects.

Today, the preservation community can thank these pioneering efforts for the continuing presence of their remaining community historic resources. But in the larger scheme of things, the gains they generated were limited, and, as noted later, HUD is no longer a significant player in the preservation story—largely as the result of the replacement of these early categorical grant programs by block grants in 1974.[7]

Local Preservation Post-1980

Since 1980, changes in preservation programs have been more evolutionary than revolutionary. Since then, it can be said, there has been almost an explosion in the number of local preservation programs.

The 1980 amendments to the 1966 National Historic Preservation Act had a significant influence on local preservation operations and programming. The aim of these amendments was to decentralize federal historic preservation programs, placing former federal responsibility for programmatic decision making on local governments, including National Register nominations, environmental reviews, and funding decisions. A prime example of this decentralization was the creation of the Certified Local Government program. Local governments were to be allowed greater involvement in the National Register nomination process after certain standardized criteria demonstrating their capability to live up to program standards were satisfied. However, funding for the national Historic Preservation Fund was slashed at the same time the program was instituted, and the full potential of decentralization has never been reached. Nonetheless, the CLG program can certainly be credited for significantly boosting the effectiveness and credibility of local preservation programs.

In spite of this, tremendous gains have been scored at the local government level since 1980, as indicated by the almost explosive growth in the use of regulatory approaches to preservation. A good guess is that the number of preservation commissions has roughly doubled during each decade, from perhaps 500 in 1980, to 1,000 in 1990, to more than 2,000 at the end of the century. There have been gains not only in numbers, but in substance as well. The periods during which demolition is delayed or prohibited have tended to lengthen, controls over landscape elements and the regulation of color—which would have been seen as extreme twenty years ago—are now more common, and the extension of regulatory controls to rural areas is slowly gaining in popularity. An increasing number of cities are beginning to face the problem of demolition by neglect through regulatory programs, and local governments now have more general leeway, legally speaking, than in 1980 to enforce what were formerly characterized as "aesthetic" regulations. A related development has been the rapid growth and maturity of a national organization, the National Alliance of Preservation Commissions (NAPC), to provide research, training, and other support for local preservation commissions.[8]

Numbers are inexact, but there has been significant growth in the number of local nonprofit preservation organizations with responsibilities ranging from curatorial or management for individual properties to revolving or "endangered properties" funds. A single metropolitan area may contain many hundreds of such nonprofit organizations. (See Chapter 10.)

A collateral development since 1980 has been a significant increase in the number of local governments providing direct or indirect subsidies for preservation activities in the form of loan or grant funds or tax incentives of one kind or another. Some of the tax incentives have been modeled after federal and state incentive programs and include income tax credits or property tax exemptions or abatement. Some provide for the creation of special tax districts or tax increment financing, and an increasing number of cities give direct appropriations for preservation activities. As of 2001, nineteen states offer rehabilitation tax credits that more or less follow the 1981 federal model.

We must also acknowledge a huge increase in professional staffs with preservation responsibilities at the local level. This is partly the result of the increase in college and university preservation programs and an increase in the number of CLGs and the availability of federal funds to help create and staff local government positions. These positions tend to be administratively housed within local planning departments, which in turn brings preservation issues to the planning table. The growth in such positions is also attributable to local participation in state and federal environmental review programs.

In one sense, there is a multiplier effect to all of this. Not only has preservation become an important input to local comprehensive planning and to land-use and urban design planning efforts in some cities, it has also become an active and equal partner in neighborhood conservation and rehabilitation. In the large metropolitan areas, preservation has provided something of an economic development model, thus engaging and challenging the conservative "wise-use" movement. In all, though developments since 1980 are difficult to quantify precisely, they are nonetheless very real.

Partnerships

The successful preservation of historic resources at the local level is by no means the sole province of local government, but rather the result of a complex matrix of relationships. The preservation movement has created an impressive network comprised of federal, state, and local players in the public, private, and nonprofit sectors. Each of the elements in this network bears on the others in varying degrees, depending on the nature of the relationship, but none operates in isolation from the others.

Federal Programs and Local Government

In the last several decades, local preservation funding and activities have been strongly influenced, both positively and negatively, by the new federal laws and programs described in Chapter 2. These include highway construction and transportation-related historic resources (1982, 1991), tax reform (1976, 1981, 1986), and housing and neighborhood revitalization (1974, 1977). These are important because shifts in federal programs and funding have a major impact on local preservation programs. Generalities about their effect on such larger issues as sprawl and inner-city revitalization are difficult.

It is clear, however, that some federal programs, such as the funding of new expressways in urban areas, are not good for preservation. On the other hand, the Intermodal Surface Transportation Efficiency Act of 1991 contained clear benefits for preservation, as has its successor, the Transportation Equity Act for the Twenty-first Century.[9]

What is clear is that the earlier preservation emphasis on architecture as art and history for history's sake has constantly been expanded and invigorated with new values. New directions at the local level include preservation of the

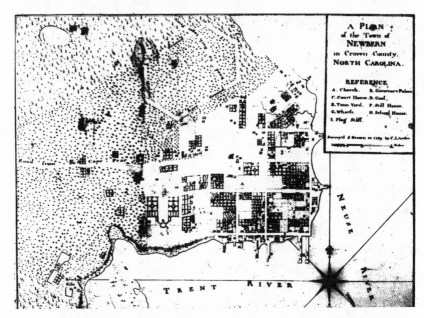

Sauthier map of New Bern, North Carolina, 1769. Suburban sprawl had early roots in North Carolina, as illustrated by the dispersion of single-family lots in New Bern, shown on this map by C. J. Sauthier. Individual homes on single-family lots are still the preferred housing type throughout the United States by families with children. How far to go in preserving post-1950s subdivisions is an unresolved issue. (North Carolina Historic Preservation Office)

John Mack Bridge across the Arkansas River. Built in 1930–31 of reinforced concrete, this eight-span, eight-hundred-foot bridge is the largest of its kind in the nation. ISTEA funds were critical to the $2.1 million restoration project. The success of the ad hoc citizen effort to save the bridge spawned the creation of the Wichita Preservation Alliance, the city's first nonprofit preservation organization. (Joseph J. Pullaro, Lichtenstein Consulting Engineers, Inc.)

Biff-Burger sign. This randomly chosen highway sign emphasizes that many of the landscape artifacts we deprecate today will one day become "historic," similar to the restored Shell Station in Winston-Salem, North Carolina, shown in Chapter 10. (Robert E. Stipe)

recent past, historic and cultural landscapes, commercial districts in addition to Main Street, ethnic and vernacular traditions, a larger "cultural" heritage, focused on people and the natural environment. This new, expanded program focus has brought with it a number of opportunities to broaden the local preservation constituency and to forge new partnerships.

Overall, local preservation processes and emphases have been most directly affected by the programs, requirements, and initiatives of the National Park Service. Since passage of the National Historic Preservation Act of 1966 and its amendments, the federal presence in preservation has helped shape its course at the local level. The various federal housing acts, NEPA, HUD block grants, the several federal tax acts, ISTEA, DOT legislation and programs all have had a direct and profound influence on local preservation efforts. In spite of limited funding, the CLG program has had an especially beneficial effect in helping local governments develop their own locally focused programs.

Altogether, these programs (most of them brought home locally through the states as "agents" of the federal government) have in one way or another stimulated local interest and much progress. At the same time, they have also had

Shotgun housing. Emblematic of minority and low-income shelters everywhere, shotgun houses pose special problems. One is how to bring them up to today's housing standards without compromising their integrity. Another is strong division of opinion among minority and ethnic communities. Some believe that these symbols of an unhappy past should be destroyed; others feel that they should be preserved as visible cautions against a recurrence of their early history. (Robert E. Stipe)

the effect of "federalizing" much preservation activity in terms of both philosophy and procedure. There is a growing tendency to define what is possible in local preservation programs in terms of what is available (grants, tax relief) from federal programs or what is proscribed (the Secretary's Standards). These can be a powerful stimulus, but they can also put blinders on local imagination. But the promise of permanent, direct funding embodied in the federal Historic Preservation Fund has never materialized, notwithstanding the tireless lobbying of Preservation Action for the Conservation and Reinvestment Act (HPF's current legislative incarnation), the National Trust, the National Conference of State Historic Preservation Officers, and others. In some respects, then, the *system* of preservation as it operates at the local level proceeds as an unfunded mandate, while individual projects may garner funding from one federal program or another.

Indirect federal subsidies for preservation at the local level embodied in our income tax legislation have provided significant incentives for local preservation. As Elizabeth Lyon and David Brook noted in Chapter 3:

Federal tax incentives . . . , first enacted in 1976 and expanded in 1981, quickly became the major federal financial incentive available for the actual rehabilitation and preservation of historic buildings. An estimated $2–3 billion of private investment in historic properties nationwide each year has been the result. Although the largest programs are on the East Coast, all fifty state preservation offices, and those in the District of Columbia, Puerto Rico, and the Virgin Islands, have promoted and benefited from the program.

Commercial properties in many historic downtowns have been given new life, as has rental housing in historic buildings and neighborhoods as well. In fact, in the last decade the most prevalent type of project receiving federal tax credits involved housing—between 40 and 57 percent, of which low-to-moderate-income units comprised between 19 and 48 percent. Yet recent projects include not only the conversion of limestone row houses in Newark, New Jersey, into low-income units but also a railroad roundhouse and shops in Aurora, Illinois, into a microbrewery and pub, and office towers in Manhattan's financial district into hotels and luxury apartments.[10]

The result of the tax incentives program has been a dramatic reshaping of the urban fabric across the country as old movie palaces, grand hotels, schools, railroad stations, and office buildings take on new lives. On a smaller scale, thousands of small commercial structures on the nation's main streets and residential rental properties that provide the character of individual communities have undergone successful renovation. The secondary impact on jobs, state and local tax bases, tourism, and the revitalization of decaying downtowns has also been significant. As intended by the framers of NHPA, the federal tax structure has been effectively revamped to favor, not discourage, the rehabilitation of historic properties.[11]

It is not often possible to predict the impact of national-level preservation incentive programs on local preservation efforts. For example, in addition to purely local sources of financial support, those local governments that enjoy CLG status under the national preservation program also have access to (unfortunately) small matching grants for planning, public education, and the restoration and rehabilitation of historic buildings. But federal funds for the CLG pass-through program are still very limited relative to need, and some local governments have even suggested that the resulting paperwork—that is, reporting and compliance requirements—make CLG designation only marginally worth the effort. Federal funding for Certified Local Governments has not kept pace with the increase in the number of CLGs, with the consequence that as more cities are designated as CLGs, the percentage of funds available for each local government is diminished, and to this extent the incentive for additional communities to achieve CLG status decreases. This aspect of federal-state support needs desperately to be substantially and permanently increased.

Federal legislation, programs, and appropriations (direct and indirect) over the years can therefore be seen to have worked in both positive and negative ways insofar as local preservation is concerned. It is impossible to predict with any degree of accuracy what the future holds in terms of the federal impact on local preservation efforts. Under the circumstances, however, it would seem prudent to assume that local governments will continue to have to bear more than a mere project matching-fund capability, as well as a greater substantive responsibility for both innovation and administration of local projects. Although there is no reason why this cannot be done in the context of existing federal and state programs, the very realization that they will in all probability be increasingly "on their own" should open the door to more imaginative ways of thinking about preservation and to a more precise tailoring of local programs to local needs and support.

Building Local Preservation Constituencies

The preservation movement in the United States has been a grassroots undertaking since its beginnings. At the 1991 National Preservation Conference in San Francisco, there was a resounding vote to keep preservation at the local level and not to abandon it totally to a one-size-fits-all national system dictated by the professional preservation community. The published findings and recommendations from that conference, *Past Meets Future*, reflect this concern by recognizing that grassroots preservationists represent the movement's front line.[12]

One source of frustration for preservation at the local level has been the inability of preservationists to build politically strong, viable, and visible constituencies generally respected by community leaders. In terms of accomplishment —buildings saved, sites protected—preservation has gained much ground during the last forty years. But compared with other local government programs such as education and protective services, it is still regarded as a special-interest, low-priority, fringe activity. Building an effective, nationally respected constituency for preservation as a community value at the local level must continue to be a major priority of the movement.

Traditionally, the extent of public involvement in preservation locally has ebbed and flowed. When a local site is threatened, citizen preservation interests become energized. Preservation fires burn hot, and public indignation is generated. If the threatened site is saved, the community congratulates itself and settles back, the battle won. But by this time its guard is often lowered, alliances become fragmented, and what was momentarily a united preservation front fades. When the next emergency arises, community empowerment must begin again from the ground up. Re-creating and reenergizing the local preservation constituency takes time and vigor that could better be directed toward the preservation effort itself. The grassroots preservation movement must give greater emphasis to engaging individuals on a continuing basis, not just in emergencies with an ad hoc, crisis response.

Constituency building is not typically seen as a priority preservation issue. The starting point is usually to build coalitions among existing groups that traditionally fail to communicate or that may even compete with one another. Historical societies concentrate on research and reminiscence. Preservation interests tend to zero in on one or more historic buildings or museum properties. Land trusts focus on a wide variety of endangered communities or resources. Bringing related interests together is a first step. Identifying leadership that can sell a broader vision to established special interests is another. Building continuing and productive relationships with community opinion makers, such as newspaper editorial boards and television and cable operators, is also essential. Overall, however, constituency building remains a significant challenge at the local level. We have become reasonably adept at regulating historic buildings and districts, and even at raising public funds from local governments for preservation. But the movement is still too often seen as a middle-class, ad hoc, special-interest endeavor, rather than as a potential source of solutions to broad community problems.

Volunteer Power

The 1991 National Preservation Conference also voted against abandoning preservation to the professionals. The felt need for such a resolution was itself evidence of a growing rift between the volunteer base of the preservation movement and the growing number of trained, paid individuals who provide professional and administrative expertise at all levels of government. Although this rift does not threaten the future of preservation in a serious way, it is enough of a problem to merit discussion here.

Growth in the number of professional preservationists is largely the result of the growth of federal and state preservation programs during the last quarter century and the availability of undergraduate and graduate training programs in preservation. Literally thousands of opportunities have been created in the fields of history, architectural history, archaeology, and related fields in response to the National Register and other programs, as well as fiscal incentives for preservation and environmental review programs. Colleges and universities have responded with generic certificate and degree programs in preservation, and, as a consequence, there has been a distinct tendency toward professionaliztion of the movement itself.

Thirty years ago, the response to a threatened, unexpected Saturday night demolition of an important local landmark would have been a march on city hall by volunteers with fire in their bellies. Now, the same situation may instead produce telephone calls to the local planning department preservation staff, the state historic preservation office, or the regional office of the National Trust with the expectation that professional staff will handle it.[13]

Preservation has always been driven by grassroots efforts. Lay preservationists predominate at every National Preservation Conference. Almost every local historical society and house museum is staffed by volunteers; many, in fact, have several layers of volunteers within their organizational structure. The trustees and boards of directors of all national, state, and local preservation nonprofits are invariably volunteers, as are the members of historic district and landmark commissions. The task forces and committees that fuel Main Street programs are largely community volunteers. Campaigns to stop the demolition of historic community resources are typically spearheaded by volunteers. The rehabilitation and restoration of historic buildings would not move forward without the governing board, planning and zoning commissions, and boards of appeal whose processes make preservation and development work.

Volunteers are central to the American way of governing. What they need are more and better educational and training programs. Indeed, the very success of the preservation movement in establishing an institutional presence in local governments across the country has created training requirements for local programs that are still largely unmet. The unfortunate reality is that the need for training far outstrips the resources of the National Trust, the National Park Service, and state historic preservation offices to provide it. The training programs that do exist tend to focus on improving the administration of federal and state programs of environmental review, tax act administration, and the like. The NAPC has begun important educational initiatives for district and landmark commissions in recent years, but too many commissions must operate without adequate training for lack of training opportunities and the funds to attend and participate in them.

Nonprofit organizations are the key to the development of a preservation constituency, and they too need additional tools to assist them in becoming more effective at creating and communicating a community's preservation voice. The availability of educational programs for nonprofit organizations that emphasize programming, fund-raising, and the essentials of corporate and fiscal management still falls short of what is required. Training in the areas of volunteer political leadership, tactics, fiscal management, and strategy is also desperately needed, as are broad-based educational programs for the public at large on the importance of preservation and what is worth preserving. Recently the professional preservation community has shown strong interest in vernacular architecture, post–World War II buildings, and rural landscapes. But the public at large has yet to be convinced that these are worth preserving in the first place—perhaps the result of an innate tendency of individuals not to see themselves or the events of their lifetimes as "historic."

Regulating Preservation: The Heart of the Matter

Though federal and state programs will always be important to preservation at the local level, the hard core of local preservation activity throughout the United States centers on the use by local governments of the states' sovereign authority to regulate citizens in their personal conduct and in the use of their property. That authority expresses itself in state authorizing or "enabling" legislation, which permits cities and counties to enact local ordinances covering new construction, additions to historic buildings, and moving and demolishing historic buildings. These we know as historic district ordinances, often as part of the zoning ordinance, or separate stand-alone ordinances designating historic districts and individual buildings as landmarks.

These ordinances were long considered to be a form of aesthetic regulation, not to be countenanced as a matter of state constitutional law because of their tenuous relationship between aesthetics on the one hand and public health, safety, and the general welfare on the other. However, early court decisions in Massachusetts took the position that such ordinances stabilized property values or produced economic benefits from increased tourism, and in so doing the regulations enhanced the tax base and could stand as furthering "the general welfare" of a community.[14] Tourism and an enhanced tax base were obvious enough justifications for the regulation of historic districts or places of special historic or architectural interest, such as the Back Bay in Boston, Massachusetts, and other architectural set pieces. But because individual, scattered landmark buildings standing by themselves could rarely be said to have an impact on surrounding property values or tourism, uncertainty about the regulation of landmark buildings continued until the Supreme Court decision in *Penn Central*, which resolved any lingering doubts.

In any case, state courts have recently tended to be more accepting of aesthetic regulation of all kinds, however motivated. For the last twenty or so years, the protection of historic buildings and areas through local regulation has greatly expanded. There are now estimated to be more than 2,300 active preservation commissions throughout the country, the number roughly doubling each decade since the 1930s.

Of course, establishment of the CLG program in 1980 has tended to promote this approach. In Georgia alone, the number of preservation commissions has grown by almost 500 percent since 1981.[15] Nationwide, 64 percent of these commissions operate in communities of less than 50,000, and, of these, a third function in communities under 10,000. But if we are to keep score by the numbers, so to speak, there are more than 22,000 city and county governments in the United States.[16] That approximately 85 or 90 percent of these have *not* opted to establish preservation commissions raises a question: Is the glass beginning to fill up, or is it still largely empty?

Although it is a narrow and essentially defensive approach to preservation, historic district and landmark ordinances are nonetheless the first line of defense at the local government level. This approach makes tremendous demands on the lay preservationist, especially with respect to following established legal procedures. State legislation for the most part requires a quasi-judicial approach to the review of applications for change or demolition in an evidentiary hearing. This is a highly ritualized activity involving lawyers, sworn testimony, binding findings of fact that may not usually be reopened on appeal, and elaborate, courtroomlike procedures spelled out in writing. Commissions must evaluate property owner requests against design guidelines and standards that inevitably require group interpretation and determination on technical, historical, and aesthetic grounds. In too many cases, however, guidelines are largely derived from National Register criteria or the Secretary's Standards, without sufficient emphasis placed on the special overall character of each local district so regulated. That is changing, thanks to the work of the NAPC, which is an in-

"Let's see... that's five votes in favor of saving the historic old hotel, and one vote for smashing it to bits and eating everyone inside."

To save or not to save a historic hotel. This cartoon lampoons the frequently heard reactionary voices of local district or landmark commission members. Appointed to the commission "to provide balance," they are an irritant to the preservation community. Others argue that they serve a useful purpose in keeping regulatory bodies from exceeding the limits of their authority. (Bradford Vesey, Marquette, Michigan)

creasingly beneficial influence in both the derivation of purely local guidelines in particular and the larger goals of local preservation generally.[17]

Historic district and landmark commission decisions have a direct and immediate impact on property values and the economic feasibility of what an individual property owner proposes to do. Typically, the commission's jurisdiction is limited to exterior appearance and, as a legal matter, focuses strongly on what can be seen from a nearby public street. Only rarely is there any commission control over preserving interiors or over landscape elements. These, like color, are often the subject of immediate political controversy. The emphasis is almost always on architectural features. The spatial structure of the neighborhood, its landscape, and general feeling, which we characterize as its *tout ensemble*, receive less if any attention. The property owner's extent of "economic hardship" as a consequence of compliance with the regulations is always a background issue, and the political implications of each case, both before the commission itself and on appeal, also factor into the commission's decisions.

There is a continuing challenge in finding individuals qualified to serve on these commissions, which operate independently of the local governing board. Known by various names, such as the "historic district commission" or "preservation commission," "board of architectural review," or some other title, their functions and processes are much the same everywhere. By and large, the owners of property within designated districts (or individually designated landmarks) may not change a designated property in any significant aspect without first having secured a "certificate of appropriateness" from the commission prior to the granting of any other needed permit or commencing construction. Unlike the determinations of advisory planning boards, the decisions of these commissions have a direct impact on the use of individual properties, and decisions regarding how they may be treated are thus generally held to a high standard of legal process. For many commissions, violations of their rules of procedure are fairly common, and the written record of individual cases—the only record that will go up to a court if an appeal is taken—will often be less than the law itself demands. Equal treatment of applicants required by federal and state constitutions is not always achieved, exposing the commissions to community criticism at the least, and lawsuits at the worst. The failure to follow these procedures not only violates the rights of individual property owners to equal treatment under the law, but also promotes an image of favoritism and arbitrary decision making on the part of local government, which all too easily can damage both the preservation movement and confidence in government generally.[18]

It follows that a high standard of personal qualifications should be required for membership on one of these commissions. Generalities are difficult because state legal requirements vary, but a typical board consists of five to ten members, a majority of whom are required to have professional qualifications or (no more than) an "interest" in preservation in order to serve. These are illusory requirements in many cases, since small towns rarely have enough professional architects, historians, architectural historians, archaeologists, and other credentialed specialists in residence. Under the best of circumstances, finding and keeping qualified members can be problematic. Professional individuals are reluctant to pass judgment on the work of their fellows, and conflicts of interest can arise when a client needs a permit. Ironically, conservative governing boards themselves are often reluctant to appoint known preservationists to the commission out of fear that they will take an activist position. There is also a tendency for governing boards to favor the appointment of members of the real estate and development communities in order to "balance" the interests of builders and preservationists. Thus, conflicts of interest, whether real or perceived, can be a serious problem for both small towns and larger cities. A few cities actually prohibit service by professional individuals on the grounds that conflicts of interest are inevitable. Others stack the deck in favor of real estate or building construction interests.

Given the very high standards of performance required by most state enabling acts, the challenge of educating district and landmark commission members on matters of substance and procedures is a serious and endemic problem. The proliferation of historic district and landmark commissions has not been accompanied by increased local, state, or federal budgets for the education of commission members. The educational programs that do exist are usually provided by the state through the CLG program, cosponsored workshops, private grants, or simply ad hoc publications or programs of statewide organizations. Unfortunately, some state historic preservation offices of necessity steer most of their available funds to survey and planning activities, to support of federal- or state-mandated environmental reviews, or to the processing of Tax Act applications, because they consider training and other forms of assistance to local commissions to be of secondary importance.

A recent NAPC survey found that 35 percent of Georgia commissions had not received any training in the last two years, that few commissions had funds to send their members for training even when programs were available, and that 79 percent of all Georgia commissions had no budget at all.[19] Once beyond the larger cities and metropolitan areas, which tend to be in better shape, this is probably representative of the situation for the country as a whole.

Given the heavy reliance of local governments on historic district and landmark ordinances as a principal tool for preservation, the issue of commissioner competence is serious and growing. Uninformed or poorly trained commissioners are more than likely incapable of rendering an informed judgment on preservation technique or design, and it is easy for them to overlook the larger neighborhood preservation issues. Many cannot read plans, sections, and elevations, and they may know little of the history of architectural styles. Some members are interested only in preserving the most important local buildings.

The NAPC has attempted to deal with the problem of training with some success. Given the proliferation of commissions in recent years, the National Trust, the National Park Service, state historic preservation officers, and statewide preservation organizations all have undertaken initiatives in this area. Whether they have been able to give the problem the priority it deserves remains uncertain. A related concern is that since many smaller cities and towns have to rely on outdated or incomplete surveys, many local commissions are not sufficiently aware of the resources they guard.

Planning for Preservation

Discourse about preservation planning is complicated by the fact that the word "planning" is used differently in different contexts. In the National Register context, planning usually refers to "project planning," which comes into play when a unit of government proposes to do or build something with federal involvement of one kind or another, at which point it is reviewed for potentially adverse impacts on a National Register or Register-eligible property. Project planning (really, "review") of this kind takes place under Section 106 of NHPA, Section 4(f) of the federal Department of Transportation Act of 1966, and many federal and state environmental policy acts. (See Chapters 2 and 5.)

Another approach to planning now coming back into favor is "comprehensive planning." This approach relies on the use of maps, or combinations of maps and text, to spell out in advance—typically within ten- and fifteen-year time frames—which areas of a city or county should be developed for what purposes, when, and how. These kinds of plans are based on population and economic projections, land capability analyses, land-use surveys, and the like. Land-use plan projections are accompanied by other comprehensive plan elements showing how new development will be serviced with public utilities and facilities (called "infrastructure") and how capital improvement budgets can be devised to pay for them. This approach to planning is, in a sense, a revival of the earlier, so-called master plan concept of the post–World War II era. It remains as *the* key element in all growth management strategies.

The ideal comprehensive plan package would include a variety of elements such as land use, transportation, public utilities and facilities, parks, open space, housing, historic preservation, and urban design.[20] Land-use projections

Jackson Ward, Richmond, Virginia. The preservation—from an architectural, housing, and economic standpoint—of minority neighborhoods like this one is essential to the success of central-city revitalization and maintenance. For decades, many cities shot revitalization efforts in the foot by zoning more land in the suburbs than the larger retail market could support as commercial interests followed middle- and upper-income customers to the outer suburbs. (Robert E. Stipe)

defining where and what kind of growth should or should not take place —increasingly identified as "growth boundaries"—as a matter of public policy are key.

In this larger context, most states still consider "planning" and "plans" just that: well-intentioned statements of policy always subject to change at the whim of a later elected governing board that had no hand in preparing or adopting it. Sadly, in most states there is a "huge disconnect," as Robert Stipe describes it, between the policies laid out in the official land-use plan and the zoning and other ordinances necessary to its implementation.[21] Maryland, Oregon, and a dozen or so other states are moving swiftly in the direction of this kind of planning, and it is to be hoped that it will "catch on" in a much more widespread way, whether as an aspect of Smart Growth or some other currently popular concept.[22] The National Trust for Historic Preservation has taken a forward-looking stance on this critical issue. Long-term, comprehensive land-use planning of this kind is slowly coming back into its own.

Historic preservation can and should be an essential element of every comprehensive plan. An increasing number of states, perhaps several dozen, specifically authorize the inclusion of a historic preservation element, although a smaller number actually mandate it. There are specific benefits to such a plan—some political, some financial, some legal. One is that the scheduling, financing, and acquisition of land for public improvements such as housing, open space, parks, and other public facilities within historic districts or old neighborhoods needing revitalization become possible. In this way historic districts begin to get the attention they deserve in the city's capital improvements budgeting and planning process, as well as in the annual operating budget. In short, a preservation element in the city's official comprehensive plan brings historic neighborhoods and cultural resources of all kinds into the real world of city hall in a forceful way that is hard to ignore. Second, historic neighborhoods tend to be cohesive geographic areas within which there exist, or can be organized, active political constituencies for conservation and preservation. Such a plan element provides the "public purpose" policy statement necessary to justify directing public resources toward them.

A preservation plan is especially useful in administering the local zoning ordinance. Amendments to the zoning map can be accomplished with a special protective eye to issues that have a direct bearing on the preservation of older areas and buildings—issues like infill development, density, building height, incompatible land uses, and parking. Most important, the plan will often provide an acceptable rationale for politically difficult decisions such as saying no to the mayor's brother-in-law, who may wish to tear down a listed building for a parking lot or put up a ten-story hotel in the wrong place. It also strengthens the always politically difficult argument in favor of regulating some property owners more strictly than others. Then, too, a written, officially adopted preservation plan provides continuity as key players, elected and bureaucratic, come and go in local government. This leaves less discretion to the whim of elected but always temporary officeholders, overly influential mayors and city managers, conservative city attorneys, and other boards and commissions that would otherwise operate with greater freedom.[23]

Finally, a preservation plan can provide important legal backup for landmark and historic district protection. This is because the Equal Protection and Due Process guarantees in the federal and state constitutions mandate that all property owners be treated alike. But zoning, by its nature, requires that some property owners be treated differently than others. Both legislatures and the courts have recognized that this situation is potentially open to abuse and, as

Nantucket, Massachusetts, waterfront. Maintaining the overall "feel" or *tout ensemble* of a historic area is often thought to be beyond the ability of most local preservation commissions. However, the watery character and atmosphere of Nantucket Island is clearly related to shoreline land-use controls and other environmental requirements that preservation commissions rarely deal with directly. A few preservationists now call for the control of the use of the water itself, and the New Mexico Heritage Preservation Alliance has listed the "night sky" as an endangered resource. (Robert E. Stipe)

safeguards, have required that zoning be "reasonable" in its application to individuals. The best possible way to convince a court that regulations are reasonable is to be able to show in the plan itself that preservation goals have been thoughtfully considered as part of the larger local comprehensive planning and zoning processes.

As a practical matter, all of these "plans" or types of "planning" have their uses in specific situations. Strategic planning, small area plans, the many forms of environmental review, planned unit development, and site plan review all have potentially useful applications in specific situations and are well embedded in the American public land management system. In the long term, however, bringing together all these different types of planning within the comprehensive plan approach holds by far the greatest potential for lasting results for preservation in particular and growth management generally.

If it is true that more is accomplished with honey than with vinegar, there is a clear case to be made that planning "honey" can do as much or more for preservation than all the regulations already on the books. That regulations are useful in protecting landmark buildings and neighborhoods is beyond question. But they have their procedural, substantive, and political limits, and in any case they do not come into play until the property owner needs a permit to do something. They are the back end of the planning process, and it is the front end that needs attention. Something more proactive than "Just say no" is desperately needed. There are still too few local jurisdictions in the United States that have adopted preservation plans as a standing, respected component of their official, local comprehensive plans. Potentially, CLG status could do much to encourage this kind of planning, which is the weakest link in the entire preservation process. Unfortunately, this is not yet a requirement for certification under the federal program.

Preserving the Urban Townscape: The *Tout Ensemble*

In 1987 *The American Mosaic* emphasized that the main purpose of historic district regulations is "the preservation of the entire district or neighborhood, *the tout ensemble* or the entire scene."[24] Yet, for all practical purposes, the Secretary's Standards—often adopted by local governments for use as design review standards—do not really address the preservation of the larger environment. Instead, they focus on the preservation of individual buildings and have little to offer about the context of the buildings or about larger environmental design issues. The same is true of National Register nominations, where, notwithstanding that it is a register of historic *places*, the day-to-day emphasis is on individual buildings, or, in the case of districts, collections of buildings, carefully noted as "contributing" or "noncontributing."

There is much more to a district than buildings. Spatial structure, landscape elements, and small details that provide character, legibility, and continuity of the feeling of a place are rarely spoken of. This is as much a problem with local regulatory historic districts as it is with National Register districts. In both cases, it is the result of a process dominated by historians and architectural historians, and by lay commissioners who are not trained to think in design terms. Commissions that insist on the historicity of every detail on buildings tend to assume that landscape values are a question of personal taste and therefore do not come under their jurisdiction. It follows that the designation, nomination, and review processes involving historic districts need to be opened up at all levels of government to a broader variety of skills and interests.

Planners and review commissions need to specially concern themselves with urban context. Historic landscapes and historic circulation patterns—both pedestrian and vehicular—are as important as the historic built environment. In planned cities like Savannah, Georgia, Hillsborough, North Carolina, and many planned suburban housing developments, the street layout or pattern is, in fact, the oldest surviving remnant of the concept on which it was founded. In such cities, extreme care must be taken not to taint these important historic qualities by closing lanes, modifying the size of streets, or reworking the shape of medians, parks, and squares to facilitate traffic flow. Failure to address such issues significantly devalues the larger historic context.

Neighborhood Conservation Districts

Another recent development in regulating historic resources is the increasing use of "neighborhood conservation areas" as something different from the traditional historic district. They are a relatively new phenomenon, perhaps best described as "Regulations-Lite" traditional historic districts, where tiered regulations tailored to local political sensitivities or the accomplishment of some special purpose such as affordable housing are sought. One writer speaks of them as "pre-natal historic districts," which have the potential to become full-fledged historic districts, but which have not yet acquired a sufficient patina of age.[25] Conservation districts are just now coming into their own, but with problems. According to Thompson Mayes:

> Establishing different standards for different historic districts or neighborhood conservation districts is viewed with suspicion by some preservationists, who consider the proliferation of varying standards as having the potential to weaken more stringent standards. The counter argument is that all historic resources are not the same and they should not be treated the same way. For example, some districts may be able to preserve the integrity and significance of properties without being restricted to the use of historically correct wood window sash as replacement for wood window sash. The trend toward more flexibility is partly a reaction to perceived overzealous regulation on the part of some historic district commissions, as well as an acknowledgment that not all neighborhoods are the same. In part, it is simply an acknowledgment of what the community will politically tolerate in terms of regulation.

Contemporary addition to San Francisco office building. Design guidelines in most historic district and landmark regulations deal gingerly, if at all, with the problem of contemporary additions to historic buildings. A few prohibit them altogether; some provide that they may not be denied, and many pass over the subject. Most readers will have a ready response one way or the other to the appropriateness of the additions shown to this building. (Robert E. Stipe)

The growing use of conservation districts is a challenge to the preservation community to examine its standards very carefully in determining what is appropriate for different historic resources. Not all communities wish to have all aspects of their buildings regulated. Some may seek simply to preserve the general character of their neighborhood and do not feel strongly about the retention of existing buildings, so long as replacement buildings are compatible in terms of size and scale.[26]

Preservation and Local Politics

Discussions about politics and preservation—whether arising separately or in conjunction with one another—inevitably generate widely divergent, passionate points of view. Truth is, failed preservation efforts and projects frequently mark the failure of political support at some stage of the planning, regulatory, or fiscal authority of local government. Without local political support, preservation efforts of every kind are impossible.

There is significantly more support for preservation in local government presently than there was twenty years ago, but it is still far short of what is needed. Worse, the failure of political support is not always obvious. Some anti-

Daffin Park, Savannah, Georgia. Public street rights-of-way provide important sight lines and links of continuity in historic districts. Urban spaces such as Daffin Park are especially important in maintaining local character. However, local preservation commissions rarely pay as much attention to the maintenance of character and control of change in public spaces as they do in privately owned property. (Rosetta Radtke)

preservation tactics lie somewhere between disingenuous and insidious—to put it politely. Failure to fund a project with the excuse, "We just don't have the money," is a case in point. Local governments *do* have the money for such projects. This is nothing more than saying, "We just don't want to spend it on preservation."

On the other hand, as noted in the discussion on constituency building, it might also be regarded as a failure by preservationists to justify the expenditure. Other examples range from failure to aggressively stop a Saturday night demolition when a local governing body or official had the clear authority to do so, to appointing conservative, antipreservation individuals to preservation and landmark commissions "in the interest of balance."

We must accept that, with only a few exceptions, preservation is still not as high a priority on local government agendas as we would like. At one level, failure of political will is related to the weak or failed educational agenda mentioned earlier. At another level, it is a failure of political "smarts." The preservation community rarely considers how essential it is to stake out elected officials *before* an election, rather than later. Later is too late. In most cases, active participation in political campaigns and campaign contributions are more important than a noble cause pleaded at the eleventh hour.

Why don't more local politicians and government officials support preservation? The answer varies with the community, of course. In some cases, it is mere lack of knowledge and understanding of preservation values and processes. In others, it is a built-in distrust of what is wrongly viewed as an elite interest or an instinctive predilection to approve any development that holds out the promise of providing jobs and adding to the local tax base. The bottom line is that those who do not support preservation are, for whatever reasons, not getting what they feel they need from it. Preservation is not seen as serving an important community purpose. As other chapters of this book make clear, strong preservation incentives and programs are in place at federal and state levels. But all preservation is local, and what happens on the ground happens locally. This is where the major educational and promotional efforts must take place.

Public Education and Public
Participation in Preservation

The key to the future of preservation is education. Richard Longstreth declares that "history is central to the real world of protecting valuable portions of the past."[27] From the beginning of the preservation movement in the United States, there has been an effort to educate the public about our past history and its importance in our present. Our early museum villages—Williamsburg, Virginia; Pendavis, Wisconsin; and Old Salem, North Carolina—are clear evidence of this. They are no less attractive to the public nor any less important to preservation education today.

Museum villages and restored buildings will always have an important contribution to make to tourism and local economic development, and vice versa. The critical issue is whether the kind of historical appreciation fostered by museum villages and historic landmarks will carry over to a wider enthusiasm for larger environmental issues and values. There is no hard evidence that it does or that it will. Clean air and water, open space, the safeguarding of farmland, the protection of endangered plant and animal species, and other programs not only beat out historic preservation as an environmental value; there is little evidence that the public at large values preservation except as an all-too-frequent ad hoc revulsion to the loss of treasured individual buildings and sites. When the choice of preservation versus "progress" does appear on a local public agenda, it often gives way to a wider enthusiasm for growth and new development.

Long-term benefits will be realized if more local preservation programs can place a greater priority on education. This is never easy in the face of day-to-day program demands and preservation emergencies, but in the increasing number of communities where preservation does enjoy a high degree of acceptance, somewhere in the equation one will find the influence of an educational program.

A growing number of federal, state, and local programs bring history to life in the classroom and in the field. In 1991 the NPS established its "Teaching with Historic Places" program. Targeting primarily middle and high school students, it uses National Register sites listed as resources for teaching different periods and facets of American history. The program is a team effort: curricula and lesson plans are developed by groups consisting of historians, preservationists, site interpreters, and other experts. At a particular site, students research primary sources, historical and contemporary photographs, maps and other documents, and the history of their own communities. This process serves as a bridge to the past and relates local history to the events that have shaped our larger history.[28] As Charles Lee, the longtime SHPO for South Carolina, liked to proclaim, "American history is nothing more than the sum of its state and local history."

The National Trust continues to develop programs that promise to improve the capacity of nonprofit organizations at the state and local levels. Its Statewide and Local Partnerships organizational development programs, Community Partners financial programs, Preservation Leadership Training, National Main Street Program, and six regional offices all work to meet needs for education and training.[29] The problem is membership turnover on commissions. The good members die, move, have babies, lose interest, and so forth, and training has to be undertaken a second time. As a practical matter, older "trained" members tend to dominate the proceedings, and newer members are intimidated, which often creates internal tensions among members who should be pulling together. If training is not a continuing effort, it may create as many problems as it solves.

At the college and university level, there have been exciting changes in the teaching of preservation. Traditionally, historic preservation has been taught in a bricks-and-mortar context, with concentration on the rehabilitation of landmark buildings, the architecture of neighborhoods, or the tangible, physical fabric of the city. In many programs, this is still the case. But in the last decade, the concept of preservation has expanded from the care of the built environment to the integrated investigation, protection, and interpretation of the larger culture that produced it. Historic and cultural landscapes, scenic roads and byways, minority history, and future planning and development must become central subjects in historic preservation. To engender any effective degree of public support, historic preservation must be studied in context, relating itself to the built and natural environments, to national events and local occurrences, to the less tangible aspects of our heritage—and integrating all with the physical and cultural makeup of a community. At the Fifty-fourth National Preservation Conference held in Los Angeles in 2000, National Trust president Richard Moe spoke of the mission of preservationists as "keepers of culture," recognizing the holistic role of preservation in our time and its ties to other conservation movements both in this country and in the rest of the world.[30]

Main Street Programs

In August 1976 Boston opened the refurbished Quincy Market in the center of the city. The product of a partnership between the city and the James Rouse Company, it was an unprecedented step in city revitalization and a last-ditch attempt to save the area from further decay. The day of the opening, Rouse and Boston mayor Kevin White did not know what to expect. What they found at the inaugural ceremonies were fifty thousand people ready to enjoy the revitalized market.[31] That occasion gave birth to the "festival markets" of the 1970s and 1980s and was a direct predecessor of the Main Street programs of today.

Boston, like many other cities, was suffering from business migration to the outskirts. Not to be blamed for this migration, businesses followed their customers to the suburbs. Mall parking was plentiful, and shopping malls were close to customers' homes. In the central city parking was limited, vacancies and crime abounded, and property values and tax revenues were declining. The natural reaction, which went back to the late 1950s, was to attempt a cosmetic central-city makeover that really did not work.

In the late 1970s community leaders from small midwestern towns approached the National Trust asking for help. A regional conference was organized to look for solutions, and a pilot revitalization program was developed for three communities: Galesburg, Illinois; Hot Springs, South Dakota; and Madison, Indiana. The Trust hired managers for each city who developed what has become the classic Main Street four-point approach: design (enhancing the physical appearance of the commercial district by rehabilitating historic buildings, encouraging supportive new construction, developing sensitive design management systems, and engaging in long-term planning); organization (building consensus and cooperation among the many groups and individuals who had a role in the revitalization process); promotion (marketing the traditional commercial district's assets to customers, potential investors, new businesses, local citizens, and visitors); and economic restructuring (strengthening the area's existing economic base while finding ways to expand it to meet new opportunities—and challenges from outlying development).[32]

Three years later, the results were visible in the three project cities. Downtown spending had increased by 25 percent, occupancy in once-vacant buildings had risen greatly, and the return on each dollar of administrative and improvement costs was eleven dollars. Today, the Main Street program has grown from the original 3 participants to more than 1,600 communities.

The most frequently heard criticism of the program is that it has had a tendency to merge preservation with stagecraft. The design emphasis in some Main Street projects centers on the quality of building rehabilitation and an artificial infill patina, rather than on the totality of the historic environment. The result is often a "Main Street look" emphasizing facades and achieved by pseudohistoric light standards and attractive but inappropriate sidewalk materials and street furniture. By failing to include historic landscape features as an integral project component, tension between historically appropriate buildings and their setting is created. As a consequence, beautification replaces or dilutes history, and historic context is lost. To avoid ersatz preservation, conscious design decisions should be made based on surveys and documentation. It may well be that elements of the historic landscape are found not to advance the vitality of the commercial district, but decisions should be based on an informed understanding of the district's historic features.

We hasten to emphasize that these concerns pale into insignificance when one considers the laissez-faire alternative. That the program has been hugely successful in revitalizing downtowns and commercial areas throughout the country is undeniable. The Main Street program from 1980 to 2000 reports these economic results:

- Total amount of public and private reinvestment in Main Street communities: $15.2 billion
- Number of net new businesses generated: 52,000
- Number of net new jobs generated: 206,000
- Number of building rehabilitations: 79,000
- Ratio of reinvestment into the community (the amount of new investment that occurred, on average, for every dollar a participating community spent to support the operation of its Main Street program, based on the average annual program costs reported to the National Trust's National Main Street Center by statewide and citywide Main Street programs): $39.22 reinvested for every $1 spent
- Average cost per job created: $1,878
- Average cost per business created in a Main Street district: $7,567[33]

Some Unresolved Issues

Housing and Gentrification

A call to action of special importance for local preservation was passed at the 1990 National Preservation Conference in Charleston, South Carolina. The "Charleston Principles," as they are known, call for the conservation of community heritage according to a step-by-step procedure. First, a community must identify the historic, architectural, and natural places that give it its own special character. Second, the preservation of historic places must be an integral part of planning for land use, economic development, housing, and transportation. Third, institutional, regulatory, and incentive mechanisms for preservation must be created, along with local leadership. Revitalization strategies that capitalize on the existing value of neighborhoods and provide well-designed, affordable housing without displacement must be developed. At every step of the process, local leaders must ensure that decisions on community growth respect the local heritage and enhance overall livability. The community must demand excellence in design and recognize cultural diversity.

These principles not only address today's most urgent planning issues, they amount to a major paradigmatic shift in local thinking about historic preservation over the last forty years. The application of the Charleston Principles to every community in the United States would not only advance preservation but also enhance quality of life, make communities more livable, instill public pride, and conserve natural and human resources.

The most obvious of all local problems is housing. In every city, some neighborhoods are in decline and others are being born anew. Ecologists tell us that these changing patterns of land use are part of a repeating cycle of invasion and succession.[34] People move from one section of the city to another as work, entertainment, and shopping locations change. As people move, real estate values in some neighborhoods decline as residents sell their properties or rent to populations that cannot afford more desirable locations. Neglect overtakes the area. Houses and businesses are abandoned. Later, a new cycle begins. Others looking for affordable and decent housing move in, followed by a second wave of people seeking for architectural distinction and possibly a sense of community. The neighborhood revives as absentee owners repair old buildings and cash in on the revived desirability of the area. Those who had previously lived there because it was the only place they could afford are forced out by sales or higher rents and move on. The neighborhood is said to have been gentrified, and preservation gets the blame. The issue of gentrification goes back to the 1950s.

Blaming preservation for gentrification is an oversimplification of a highly complex problem. Displacement and a lack of affordable housing are the result of market forces and uncaring owners, not the preservation of old buildings. The Charleston Principles require an all-out effort to stop the neglect of existing housing stock and eliminate slums. They call for decent, well-designed housing in both historic and new neighborhoods, made affordable through subsidies similar to those for business and industrial development. Gentrification is an almost inevitable consequence of neighborhood recycling, whether or not the reuse of old buildings is called "preservation." But the preservation movement has, for all practical purposes, officially adopted the cause of inner-city reuse and rehabilitation as an alternative to continued suburban development. Our real problem, then, is to deal specifically with the problem of affordable housing.

Preservation and Rural Areas

In thinking about local preservation, we tend to focus on the efforts and programs of cities and towns. But in our view, counties are as "local" as cities. Preservation in rural areas beyond the suburbs presents special challenges not easily dealt with.

In terms of their history and purpose, counties are very different entities than cities. American counties share certain physical characteristics. Unlike compact cities, they cover large, thinly populated land areas that make it difficult to provide public services. Relative to cities and towns, they tend to be poor in terms of property tax revenues and thus have smaller professional staffs available. Many of their inhabitants are by nature politically conservative, either by virtue of having migrated to rural areas to escape the constraints of urban living or possessing an independent, agrarian, self-reliant view of the world. Because there is typically much room for "growth" in rural areas, counties tend to shy away from extensive land-use regulation—including preservation. And because residents live at a distance from the county courthouse, they generally have no habit or tradition of going to a government office for a permit to do anything, much less a certificate of appropriateness.

The cultural resources to be found in rural areas are rarely aggregated in districts. Except for the increasingly rare small crossroads village, cultural resources tend to be individual landmarks, and only occasionally are they what might be called "high style." They are for the most part vernacular in character, with layered accretions of functional, agricultural accessory buildings scattered around the landscape. In fact, the principal cultural resources of many rural areas are more easily described as scenic and land-related than historical or architectural. They do not lend themselves as easily to definition, evaluation, and classification as do the subjects of traditional historic preservation programs. Although the NPS has recently devoted much attention to evaluating rural areas more systematically, landscapes do not lend themselves easily to the crisp definitions or classifications needed for fiscal subsidies or regulatory processes. Thus, they are less easily enfolded into traditional preservation programs. Precisely because they are somewhat atypical or nontraditional, rural areas are perhaps our best seed grounds for experimentation with such new preservation approaches as heritage areas and the transfer of development rights.[35] By their nature, rural areas might well be more creatively and effectively dealt with through local and state programs, locally devised, than by more standardized federally based approaches.

Balancing Property Rights with the Common Good

Private property rights interests, known sometimes as the "wise-use" movement, have attempted to federalize local land-use regulations through the Private Property Rights Implementation Act, first introduced in 1999, which passed the U.S. House of Representatives before dying in the Senate. Preservation interests are not a collateral casualty in these efforts; indeed, they are often cited as an example of why such legislation is needed. Preservationists have been successful to date in working with other interests to thwart the wise-use movement, but it can be expected that it will persist, perhaps giving more attention to the passage of similar legislation at the state level.

The Religious Land Use and Institutionalized Persons Act of 2000 has introduced an element of uncertainty for local governments in applying local zoning, including historic preservation ordinances, to religious properties. It is an ironic truth that our most constant enemies are those same interests widely assumed to be the enduring carriers of our best cultural traditions: governments at all levels, colleges and universities, and churches.

Demolition by Neglect

An increasing number of communities are beginning to address the deterioration of historic resources due to a deliberate lack of maintenance known as demolition by neglect. Severe deterioration can lead to findings by building officials that a property is a health or safety hazard, resulting in demolition as the result of local government processes that circumvent local preservation ordinances.

Successful ordinances dealing with the problem of demolition by neglect must recognize several fundamental legal principles. There must be legislative authority provided by state enabling legislation or "home rule" powers. They must ensure due process of law, both procedural and substantive. There must be safeguards to protect property owners from economic hardship and the risk that a court will find that there has been a regulatory taking of property without compensation. Furthermore, the ordinance must include standards to provide benchmarks and procedures for evaluation, open procedures regarding petition and action by the city, economic hardship provisions, methods of appeal, and specific enforcement mechanisms. The economic hardship provisions are especially important; they must contain clearly defined financial evaluation criteria to safeguard property owners from regulatory takings.[36] Cooperative partnerships with neighborhoods and local government agencies charged with enforcement must also be established and nurtured to administer such a program effectively.

New Directions for the Future

In 1996 Pratt Cassity, former executive director of the National Alliance of Preservation Commissions, wrote, "It is at the local level where we will see the next trend or encounter the next big obstacle in historic preservation."[37] His prediction has proven correct. As local preservation begins to master some of the traditional problems of acceptance, education, and institutionalization, other challenges arise such as the expansion of traditional preservation fields into new areas, the ever-quickening pace of development, and the constant need for updating tools and preservation methods.

The Recent Past

One of the most urgent and most difficult issues is the preservation of the recent past. Most people perceive that what is recent is not historic, a sentiment reflected in most historic resource surveys. The mere thought of considering an early- or mid-twentieth-century gas station, post office, bus station, school building, military base, or designed landscape as a cultural remnant worth preserving is sometimes rejected almost out of hand. Thus, the cultural heritage of the twentieth century, much of which is rapidly disappearing, is endangered.

Cultural Diversity

The preservation of diverse, ethnic cultures is a special concern at the local level, notwithstanding that it is widely accepted as imperative at the national level. Though the physical environment remains paramount in preservation, more attention needs to be given to the social environment. There are notable exceptions, of course—larger metropolitan areas are one—but small communities still concentrate their preservation efforts on the great events and individuals. As Antoinette Lee eloquently surmised, "Not all immigrant groups had an opportunity to express their heritage and aspirations for a new life in new buildings."[38] Consequently, minority and ethnic communities and neighborhoods are widely ignored. Although it may be more difficult to break through the minority race and class bias on the local front, it is, at the same time, probably the single most necessary change in the preservation battle. Inclusion of minority resources in historical surveys, representation in the composition of review boards, and welcomed involvement in the entire range of other preser-

San Antonio Farmers' Market exterior

San Antonio Farmers' Market interior

An architectural historian could doubtless provide a convincing description of the Barrio building in which this farmers' market is located. But many would argue that it is the intangible cultural heritage represented by the lifestyles associated with the activities of the market that are important to preserve. Distinctions between tangible and intangible cultural heritage are often subtle, and how to merge or coordinate programs for the preservation of both are important agenda items for the future. (Robert E. Stipe) vation-related activities are critical steps toward a more inclusive preservation movement.

Plugging into the Future

Myrick Howard writes: "The national preservation movement in the United States has always been stymied by the fundamental verity that, like politics, 'all preservation is local.'" As he sees it:

> The advent of new communications technologies and the attitudes of the young Americans who embrace it bode well for preservation in the foreseeable future. With tools like the internet, preservationists can share local experiences and start to function like a national movement. The experiences learned in saving a high school in Lincoln, Nebraska, can help preservationists save a high school in Maine or California. Today, when local preservationists encounter a specific problem that needs an immediate response, they can turn to their allies across the nation through new technologies for quick answers. Less and less must they feel isolated and alone.
>
> Also arising from the new technologies and the new businesses they have spawned is a new market for downtown buildings and industrial spaces. Throughout the country many downtown commercial and industrial districts are experiencing an exciting revival. Loft conversions of upper downtown floors are selling as quickly as they are announced. High-tech companies are seeking out large former industrial spaces for their offices, as young employees seek "funky" work spaces near where they live. Restaurants, coffee shops, bars, and other "third places" are springing up close by to provide convenient services and social outlets. Some experts are predicting as much as a 50% increase in the population of central cities in the next decade.
>
> The bountiful opportunities that new technology promises for preservation also present major challenges to local governments: the availability of funding for the acquisition and updating of technology, including networking, internet access, data storage, database compilation and manipulation, geographical information systems (GIS), global positioning systems (GPS), computer imaging, computer assisted design, and virtual reality. Gains in these areas will be incremental as local governments adopt these technologies, but the promise of better information management for preservation, particularly in the planning arena, presents great opportunity. Future preservationists versed in technology will make important contributions to the field. Preservationists can take advantage of the tools and analysis made pos-

sible by this technology at every level we work in, from monitoring individual properties to maintaining state or national cultural resource inventories.[39]

Huge gains have been made in computer software and hardware, but we are still far from the day when most interested citizens across the country can reasonably expect to access state and local databases of cultural resources, or when a prospective purchaser of a local property can look at a personal computer screen and layer the various local, state, and federal restrictions and opportunities that might be available. We noted earlier the urgent necessity for training programs for preservation commission members. Long-distance learning programs based on digital technology will inevitably have an important contribution to make here.

Conclusion

Local preservation has crossed the threshold into the twenty-first century with many accomplishments to celebrate. More people in rural, small-town, and urban America know about preservation than twenty years ago. More people have had direct, positive experiences with both the aesthetic and economic advantages that a preservation presence brings to a community. As the subject matter of preservation expands, more people will see that they, too, are connected to preservation and understand how fundamental those connections are. They will see that preservation is not just about saving a few grand old houses somewhere else, but it is right here, that it is about them and their families, what they hold dear, and where they call home.

During the last twenty years, people in more than 1,600 communities have had their lives touched by revitalized Main Streets. People have seen their towns and cities become Certified Local Governments, establish historic districts and commissions, and survey their historic resources. New technological tools and capabilities have had and will continue to have far-reaching analytic and educational applications. Though future political shifts and their associated impacts on the legislative and funding climate for local preservation cannot be known with certainty, the broader, more diverse constituency that local preservationists have built along with their state and federal counterparts should prove to be an asset. The National Trust's 2000 partnership initiative that will make money available to traditionally underserved small historic property and neighborhood markets, if successful, will go a great distance toward building an even broader preservation constituency.

In terms of a substantive vision, local preservation must continue to embrace and include; it must broaden its ethnic participation; it must continue to enlarge its focus in a comprehensive way. The key to preservation's future success in the high-stakes world of development, local government, and politics is to realize that preservation is infrastructure of the highest degree. Local preservationists, and their counterparts at state and national levels, must work toward validating the importance of historic preservation to a broad range of citizens and bringing them to an understanding of its importance in their daily lives.

Preservation Law and Public Policy
Balancing Priorities and Building an Ethic

On July 13, 1995, Tim Hutchison (R.-Ark.) rose in the U.S. House of Representatives to introduce an amendment to the U.S. Department of the Interior's appropriations bill that would eliminate the remaining $3.5 million in federal funding for the National Trust for Historic Preservation. In his speech, Hutchison was careful to say that the debate was not about historic preservation but was simply about eliminating a federal subsidy. The members of the House who stood up after him to speak for or against funding apparently had not listened to him, for they proceeded to debate the actual merits of the Trust's various activities from their points of view. Robert Goodlatte (R.-Va.), who followed Hutchison, argued that the National Trust should stick to acquiring individual historic sites like Montpelier, the home of James Madison; it should not become involved in "anti–free enterprise" activities such as opposing large-scale sprawl developments. David McIntosh (R.-Ind.) stated that historic preservation was an appropriate activity *so long as private property rights were protected*. According to Tom Delay (R.-Tex.), the Trust merely served as a slush fund for the wealthy and elite to oppose developments that offended their aesthetic tastes. Several congressmen mentioned the Trust's litigation program and expressed the opinion that the National Trust should not sue the federal government.

Those who opposed the amendment emphasized a dramatically different role for historic preservation. They stressed the importance of the Main Street program in revitalizing small-town main streets and the economic benefits of the rehabilitation tax credits to their communities. Karen McCarthy (D.-Mo.) pointed out the number of new jobs and rehabilitation tax dollars generated by historic preservation, ending with the plea: Do not abandon downtowns, do not abandon local communities, preserve funding for historic preservation. Richard Neal (D.-Mass.) told his colleagues that, as the mayor of Springfield, he had been sued by preservationists, but that in the end, he had to support historic preservation because its achievements far outweighed its shortcomings. Jack Kingston (R.-Ga.) noted that tourism was one of the top industries in many cities and that people went to tourist centers because of historic landmarks; historic preservation was an economic investment, not just something that was nice or aesthetically pleasing. Bruce Vento (D.-Minn.) argued that the National Trust should lobby and litigate and be an advocate in local land-use planning and zoning—that is how it saved historic places.

The House members were essentially debating the place of historic preservation in the United States, not just the activities of the National Trust. The issues they raised—whether the historic preservation movement should become involved in broader land-use issues and oppose sprawl-type development, whether preservation regulation impermissibly intruded on the rights of property owners, whether land-use decisions should be made only at the local level, whether preservation was justified economically, and whether the government should fund historic preservation—are the key issues facing the preservation movement today.

Several questions raised in the congressional debate go to the heart of the preservation movement and what historic preservation is about. Should preservation be limited to such important historic landmarks as presidential houses, or should it address broader issues of change in America? What resources should the movement attempt to protect and why? What is the justification for preservation as public policy?

Many other concerns raised in the debate are much broader than preservation as such. The "property rights" or "takings" controversy—the extent of the government's power to regulate private property for the public good—affects all government regulation, not just preservation regulation; it has already strongly affected the enactment and enforcement of preservation laws. Similarly, the continuing debate about how to draw the line between the right of individuals to the free exercise of religion and the ability of the government to regulate other activities has made the preservation of historic churches and synagogues controversial. Finally, the fiscal conservatism and smaller government movements of the 1980s and 1990s, which eventually led to the elimination of the National Trust's federal funding, and the shift of power from the federal government to the states, are forces that have influenced historic preservation policy in the past twenty years. Fiscal issues and the state-federal relationship will continue to do so in the foreseeable future.

The resolution of these questions will define the role and relevance of preservation in American society in the immediate future. Preservationists must therefore address them with intellectual vigor and strategic political thinking if they are to enact new pro-preservation laws, strengthen the enforcement of existing laws, and build public support for historic preservation.[1]

Preservation Law as a Reflection of Society's Values

Competing Values: Balancing Priorities

Preservation laws provide us with a measure of the strength of public support for preservation. Although laws are not a perfect reflection of society's values and do not represent the values of every individual in society, they do provide some indication of society's shared goals and priorities and the resources we value. At least since the enactment of the National Historic Preservation Act in 1966, the preservation of historic resources has been increasingly recognized as a beneficial societal goal and valid policy at all levels of government. Private preservation activities are encouraged by tax incentives, regulation of private activities that may harm historic resources is authorized by state and local laws, and many other federal, state, and local policies incorporate concerns about the preservation of historic resources. Although preservation is clearly sanctioned under law as a legitimate activity of government, and as a private activity to be encouraged, it is not usually viewed as a priority or even an important pursuit. For example, the statutes that protect historic resources from government action, such as Section 106 of NHPA, generally balance historic preservation against other government priorities. These are typically procedural laws that require government agencies to consider the effect of their actions on historic resources, but they do not dictate a pro-preservation result. NHPA does not *require* the federal government to preserve historic resources, only to consider them.[2]

Preservation fares even more poorly when it conflicts with other compelling interests, such as the fundamental protections for the individual included in the Bill of Rights. When preservation directly conflicts with the protection of free speech or the protection of the free exercise of religion, it is treated under the law as the lesser priority. Although these fundamental First Amendment protections are only rarely in direct conflict with historic preservation, our existing laws reflect society's judgment that preservation is less important than these fundamental values. In other words, the courts generally recognize preservation as a legitimate goal of government, but not a compelling one.[3]

In analyzing the strength of historic preservation laws and policies, perceptions are important. Though preservation is widely supported, there are problems with the way the public perceives preservation and preservation regulation.[4] As demonstrated by the congressional debate on National Trust funding, many individuals and elected politicians believe that preservation is anti-progress and elitist, that it is bad for the economy, that it does not produce jobs, that it is antibusiness, and that some of the historic resources it protects are not really worth preserving. Many even believe that, as an "aesthetic" regulation, preservation is simply a frivolous exercise of the "taste police." These perceptions weaken both the enactment and the enforcement of preservation laws. As a result, historic preservation ordinances are sometimes repealed, the boundaries of historic districts are shrunk, and owner consent provisions are inserted into local historic preservation ordinances, severely limiting their effectiveness. Debates over the relative importance of preservation are played out in town councils considering the designation of historic districts, in local historic district commission meetings in which applications for certificates of appropriateness are heard, and in state legislatures considering tax incentives or takings bills. They have also taken place in Congress when considering the Historic Homeownership Assistance Act and in state and federal courts reviewing the actions of local preservation commissions.

Strengthening the Preservation Ethic

Some of these negative perceptions of preservation are beginning to change as preservationists address them topic by topic. New studies demonstrate the tangible benefits of preservation to the economy; they reveal the hidden or unrecognized public subsidies for new development and for the destruction of historic or older resources. We are gaining a better understanding of the benefits, both quantitative and qualitative, of maintaining and preserving older neighborhoods.[5] As part of this shift, members of the general public, local politicians, investors, and developers are beginning to understand that the preservation of historic neighborhoods has quantifiable benefits in terms of investment, tax revenues, and high-quality job creation.

Although the preservation movement has done a good job of demonstrating the tangible value of preservation, it has not invested adequate financial, intellectual, or other resources in strengthening preservation as an ethic in recent years. Advocates often decry the fact that preservation has never become the broadly popular ethic that environmentalism has. But the truth is that the pub-

Teardown of 4407 Stanford Street, Chevy Chase, Maryland, before and after demolition and replacement of the first building. The neighborhood was proposed to be included in a local historic district, but following significant community objection it was never listed, resulting in numerous teardowns and the loss of historic streetscapes. (Julia Miller, National Trust for Historic Preservation)

lic does not perceive preservation to be as relevant to their daily lives as the natural environment. To strengthen the preservation ethic, the preservation movement must explore and articulate the real relevance of historic preservation from a broader societal point of view. Why should we preserve older and historic places? A society that is as wealthy as the United States in the early twenty-first century does not need to preserve from an economic point of view. We actually have the wealth to completely rebuild everything, however wasteful and unwise that might be.[6] Preservation as an ethical proposition is therefore a choice.

In developing a strategy to formulate a preservation ethic, a host of issues need to be explored. Part of this process should include an analysis of what our current legal tools protect, whether there is public support for those regulations, and how to strengthen that support. Are we overregulating certain resources? Are we failing to protect resources that should be preserved and that the public does care about? Are we adequately balancing preservation against the other concerns that society values? As a movement, preservation has been narrowly focused on buildings. But what of the other elements that contribute to our historic environments—gardens, landscapes, farmland, forests, trees, neon signs, or even the night sky?[7] Is the preservation movement encompassing and protecting all of the elements of our physical environment that are necessary to retain a sense of place? If preservation policy is to move forward, we must do a better job of identifying those resources that are important and build the public support required to protect them.

With Heritage So Rich included a finding that, if the preservation movement is to succeed, it must attempt to give a "sense of orientation to our society, using structures and objects of the past to establish values of time and place" (p. 207). To move up to the next level in public policy, the basic ethic of historic preservation—that preservation is good because those values of time and place are essential, necessary, and life-giving for our society—must grow. Until the general public believes in preservation as a basic value, preservation policy and preservation laws will continue to be outweighed by other priorities. Without neglecting the practical and financial rationales for historic preservation, we need to develop and encourage practitioners who can articulate the real "why" of preservation. As James Marston Fitch stated in the October 1999 issue of *Preservation*, "The greatest gift one can give the built environment is an enlightened and participatory public."

With this underlying need to build and articulate a stronger, more widely popular preservation ethic in mind, the remainder of this chapter examines preservation law and public policy with an eye to assessing the importance of preservation relative to other public priorities. The discussion centers on two themes: first, finding a proper balance between preservation as a goal of government and other competing government priorities; and second, finding the balance between the power of society to preserve historic resources for the public good and the rights of the individual, including property rights and religious liberty. In both of these areas, the relevance of preservation to people's daily lives is a key factor in determining the strength of the laws and policies.

Balancing Preservation with Other Government Policies and Priorities

Assessing and Controlling Specific Government Actions

From courthouse construction and highway funding to the siting of a new post office or the creation of a new zoning ordinance, government policies and actions have the potential to benefit or destroy historic resources. Over the past thirty years preservationists have primarily been involved in opposing and preventing the negative effects that can result from specific government actions. Only recently has the preservation community begun to analyze and attempt to change the underlying government policies that impact preservation.

In the mid-1960s, as a result of large-scale government programs, laws were passed at federal, state, and local levels to protect historic resources from potentially harmful government actions. The federal laws include the National Historic Preservation Act, Section 4(f) of the Department of Transportation Act, and the National Environmental Policy Act. These laws are covered in other chapters.

Two general trends in public policy shared by a number of laws have emerged since the early 1990s. One has been a greater delegation of decision making and authority to the states, and the other is the increasing recognition of diverse cultural groups. Under NHPA, more Section 106 cases are handled at the state level than ever before. Moreover, under NHPA and new procedures of the Advisory Council on Historic Preservation there is also greater recognition and involvement of Native American tribal groups.[8] The trend toward increased recognition of diverse cultural groups is also shown by the number of National Register listings representing the history of African Americans, Asian Americans, Native Americans, and, with the designation of the Stonewall Inn in 1999, gay Americans as well.

At the state level, laws protecting historic resources from destructive actions of the state itself are now far more common. Many of them are modeled on equivalent federal statutes and are similar to Section 106 of NHPA or Section 4(f) of the DOT Act. The diminutive terms by which many are known—for example, "little 106s" or "little 4(f)s"—belie their power, since state laws may impose an even higher standard than comparable federal law. In recent years, preservationists have relied more and more often on the provisions of these state laws in attempting to control projects affecting their communities.[9] They are an important legal hook to control state projects when there is no federal funding or other federal involvement to trigger the federal laws. These laws are also being used to try to control sprawl and sprawl developments.[10] In addition, some local governments have environmental review ordinances that provide protection for historic resources from local government actions.[11]

Again, however, whether federal, state, or local, the laws that control government actions are primarily procedural, even though, as John Fowler points out in Chapter 2, they can often achieve substantive results. Federal and state governments may formally establish preservation as official policy, but the implementation of that policy will always be balanced against other priorities. They generally require only that the government consider the effect of its actions on historic resources and that preservation interests be given an opportunity to comment, as in the federal law.

A few state laws go further and provide substantive protections for historic resources and actually require the state transportation or other agencies to choose a pro-preservation result unless "there is no prudent or feasible alternative," a standard comparable to the federal Section 4(f). Although the preservation community has become adept at the use of commenting procedures and the higher standard just mentioned, it must continue to advocate more substantive protections at both federal and state levels.

Changing Broader Government Policies to Support Historic Preservation

The more significant development in recent years has been a shift from simply trying to protect historic resources from *specific* government actions to a more active advocacy that changes broader policies. The new approach takes a comprehensive look at policies and laws that affect historic resources indirectly, steering investment, economic vitality, and development toward an overall preservation result and at the same time eliminating conflicting policies that undermine preservation and direct it away from older and historic areas. This broader, more comprehensive and positive approach to changing government policies has occurred at both federal and state levels.

At the federal level, an earlier executive order now codified in NHPA encourages the government to locate federal offices in historic buildings in traditional downtowns. In addition, two recent transportation funding bills—the Intermodal Surface Transportation Efficiency Act and its sequel, the Transportation Equity Act for the Twenty-first Century—have included substantial funding for "enhancements," including transportation-related historic preservation projects. These laws go beyond road construction and fund all forms of transportation. This flexibility permits the funding of mass-transit projects that may be more pro-preservation than road construction because they serve older areas rather than newer, dispersed communities. Related initiatives include a congressional bill providing communities with more opportunities to participate in decisions concerning the consolidation and relocation of postal facilities. The traditional U.S. Postal Service position has been that it can make these decisions without regard to local land-use laws, building codes, or the economic impact of the relocation on the community.[12]

A number of states, in cooperation with preservation organizations, have performed comprehensive reviews of their laws and policies to determine their effect on preservation. Many state laws are adverse to preservation. For example, state school construction policies may discourage or prevent the reuse of older school buildings. The distribution of state infrastructure funding for water and sewer projects may encourage development outside of older areas to the detriment of historic neighborhoods or commercial districts, and building code requirements may conflict with historic rehabilitation. The state audits serve a useful purpose in looking comprehensively at the larger body of state legislation. The National Trust has performed several such "audits" for individual states to analyze state laws and policies that affect historic preservation positively or negatively.[13]

Several states, such as Maryland through its Smart Growth and Neighborhood Conservation Initiative, have changed their policies to encourage local government to control growth and direct it to historic commercial and residential areas and to preserve farmland and open space. Maryland, for instance, encourages local government to provide state funding for infrastructure projects only for communities that have addressed these issues in their comprehensive plans. New Jersey and Maryland have revised their building codes to eliminate unnecessary obstacles to the rehabilitation of older buildings. All states should be encouraged to review their policies across the board to determine their impact on the preservation of older, historic communities.

Tax Policy

In recent years, tax incentives have become a principal tool for historic preservation. Despite the prevailing political mood of fiscal conservatism, antiprivate property regulation, and the general concern for property rights that prevailed in the late twentieth century, those same forces generally favored the use of tax incentives for preservation. Tax credits, of course, do not carry the same political baggage as regulatory controls. But here again, they are balanced against other government priorities, such as tax relief for other purposes. The federal rehabilitation tax credits have now been in effect for more than twenty-five years. Other forms of preservation tax incentives are rehabilitation deductions or credits against state income taxes and local property taxes, which may take the form of temporarily frozen property tax assessments, reduced property tax payments, or reduced assessments.[14]

Although the 1986 Tax Reform Act substantially undercut the rehabilitation tax credit, many have forgotten that the rehabilitation tax credit was one of the few to survive tax reform at all. Notwithstanding the initial dramatic decrease in tax credit projects immediately after 1986, the number of projects has steadily increased.

At the same time, state legislatures have become increasingly active, enacting a number of tax credits, property tax abatements, and other tax incentive programs in the 1990s.[15] These range from those that simply add an additional state income tax credit to the federal tax credit, to those that also offer an income tax credit for the rehabilitation of private residences. Congress has considered a tax credit for owners who rehabilitate their historic homes, which, if passed, could become one of the strongest incentives for historic preservation available.[16]

Government Funding for Historic Preservation

Throughout the 1980s and 1990s Congress and many state legislatures consistently sought to reduce government spending, particularly for domestic programs. As demonstrated by the debate over National Trust funding described at the outset of this chapter, preservation was in a sense targeted by Congress as an inappropriate use of federal money. With the perceived federal surpluses that began in the late 1990s, however, interest in funding for historic preservation and conservation began to resurface. The Save America's Treasures program, originally part of the Millennium celebration, which encourages private donations to historic preservation projects and provides federal grants to individual projects, has remained popular with Congress. With the expectation of a continuing federal budget surplus, preservationists began to advocate for full funding of the Historic Preservation Fund and other initiatives.[17] But hope for increased funding by the federal government faded after the tragic events of September 11, 2001.

Zoning and Planning

It has long been apparent that preservation of historic resources is virtually impossible unless preservation ordinances are closely coordinated with local planning and zoning regulations. Zoning laws can either encourage or undermine preservation activities. Since World War II, local government planning policies have generally emphasized new development. A growing number of communities throughout the country have tried in recent years to bring their planning, growth management, and historic preservation programs into better balance to achieve better coordination among them.

Several areas of coordination are particularly significant. First, historic preservation is increasingly mentioned in state legislation as a desirable—and in a few cases, mandatory—comprehensive plan element. Second, comprehensive plans and local land-use regulations generally are coming under greater scrutiny to ensure that the character and economic vitality of older historic areas are not threatened or undercut by new development or inappropriate density requirements.

The Sprawl Debate

The issue of using zoning and planning to direct investment and growth to older and historic areas raises the question of sprawl, a topic of popular discussion and much media attention at the turn of the century. The term "sprawl," as defined by many in the preservation community, captures a number of undesirable conditions: traffic jams, long commutes, allegedly characterless development, the dominance of chain stores and big-box retailers, the loss of

Mexican embassy, Washington, D.C. This scene makes clear that height and density regulations should always be examined to ensure that they are consistent with existing buildings. (Thompson Mayes, National Trust for Historic Preservation)

farmland and countryside, residential development separated from retail and work places, huge parking lots, automobile-centered development, and the loss of a sense of community.

The National Trust maintains that sprawl is a preservation issue and has taken a strong stand against it. But not all preservation organizations and preservationists, and certainly not all elected politicians—as demonstrated in the debate over National Trust funding—agree that there is a direct connection between sprawl and preservation, nor do they accept that sprawl is even a preservation issue.

Preservation organizations supporting the antisprawl argument cite a number of reasons. Sprawling developments use historically agricultural and forest land and destroy farmland and forest, resulting in the loss of scenic vistas, open space, and historic landscapes. Many residential and commercial developments use the same designs for buildings throughout the country and break down a traditional separation between town and countryside, thus destroying distinctive historic qualities that make each place unique and recognizable. Sprawling developments, if uncontrolled, lead to disinvestment in older neighborhoods and downtown main streets. In particular, big-box, chain retail enterprises drive historic commercial establishments out of business, leading to vacant buildings, the loss of the economic strength of the commercial core, and eventually demolition. The loss of independent local businesses is itself a preservation issue, as distinctive local businesses contribute to the character of older neighborhoods. The same is true of residential developments. If too many new residential developments are permitted, it is argued, the older residential neighborhoods lose their vitality, leading to vacancy, deterioration, and eventual demolition.

Critics of sprawl as a preservation issue argue to the contrary. Big-box retailers, they assert, are elitist in that they disfavor middle- and lower-income families attracted by lower prices, and obsolete, inefficient Main Street retail businesses have no inherent right to economic survival in a free market economy. They argue that families who choose the suburbs over central cities have every right to do so, and that restricting the amount of suburban housing reduces the housing choices available to minority and ethnic populations.

Witold Rybcynski has pointed out that many places we now choose to preserve were the suburbs of their time—trolley car or train line suburbs, or even automobile suburbs.[18] His argument is that most families prefer suburban living, and that preservationists should not expect all Americans to choose either an urban or a rural place to live in. Other critics, including dedicated preservationists, feel that their credibility as preservationists will be lost as the line between planning and preservation becomes blurred.

Finally, some critics have questioned the antisprawl movement's relationship to neotraditional town planning or the "new urbanism," which mimics certain aspects of earlier architectural detailing, street patterns, and urban development patterns and densities. But neotraditional town planning is a red herring in the discussion of sprawl and its relationship to preservation. From a strictly preservationist point of view, there is nothing inherently pro-preservation about neotraditional towns. Neotraditional towns may harm historic areas in the same way that sprawling developments do. It is flattering that traditional neighborhood development projects imitate older historic districts, but that should not obscure the reality that neotraditional towns are *not* old places. They cannot provide the sense of orientation to our society that truly old places, which use structures and objects of the past to establish values of time and place, do.[19] Preservation has the special advantage that it is grounded in the real and irreplaceable.

Responses to these concerns help to define the relationship between sprawl and preservation. The primary validity that preservation organizations bring to the sprawl issue is their concern for the inherent social value that historic resources give to any community. There are clear connections between sprawl and the loss of historic resources, whether farmland, Main Street commercial corridors, or older neighborhoods. But some sprawl issues do not directly impact historic resources. For example, preservationists should not blindly oppose big-box stores per se. Not all of them have a negative effect on historic preservation; indeed, there are appropriate places for such retail operations. Similarly, preservationists should not blindly oppose suburban development. Not all suburban development is harmful to historic resources and, in fact, may be necessary to take the pressure off attempts to demolish them.

Throughout this debate, the objective must be the preservation of older, historic resources—whether open spaces, forests, townscapes, buildings, or historic districts. Government policies that encourage preservation may be compatible with government policies that discourage sprawl, but they are not necessarily identical. Preservation, while sharing common cause with the antisprawl movement, must ensure that the policies of government are designed to encourage preservation activity.

Whether through policies that promote undue, inappropriate sprawl, planned highway projects through historic neighborhoods, or the construction of new courthouses, government actions and policies have a tremendous impact on preservation. Preservationists must therefore continue the work of protecting historic resources from destructive activities by government, while at the same time increasing their efforts to channel those broader government policies that adversely affect or insufficiently support historic preservation into a more positive, preservation-oriented stance.

Historic Preservation, Society, and Individual Rights

Embodied in the U.S. Constitution is a fundamental balance between the rights of the individual and the power of society, through government, to act for the public good. In the past fifteen years the tension between those competing values has intensified. Property rights advocates, who complain that their ability to use and change their property is being eroded by government regulation, and that this diminution of rights should not be allowed without compensation, have demanded a reexamination of the rights of property owners. Corporations and land developers have urged the repeal of regulations they consider burdensome. Members of the public raise concerns of fairness. Religious organizations assert the need for greater autonomy when faced with regulation.

On the other hand, environmentalists, neighborhood activists, and preservationists have sought more regulation by government to protect the environment and older and historic neighborhoods. These debates are broader than historic preservation. The primary areas of property rights, procedural due process, and religious liberty will continue to have a profound effect on historic preservation law and public policy.

Property Rights

In the past twenty years the debate over property rights in the United States has exploded into a full-scale public policy war. Anyone who has sat through local historic preservation commission meetings during this period has heard a property owner at one time or another say, "Are you trying to tell me what I can do with my own property?" or "That's an unconstitutional taking!" Both phrases are likely to strike terror in the hearts of the commission members.

Narrowly considered, the property rights debate is about the meaning of the "takings" clause of the Fifth Amendment of the Constitution. The meaning of the phrase, "nor shall private property be taken for public use without just compensation," is hotly debated, not just in the courts, which are the final arbiters of its meaning, but in state legislatures, Congress, law reviews, and the popular media.

Broadly speaking, the property rights debate is about how to maintain a balance between the rights of society and the rights of property owners—even about changing concepts of the nature of "property." We now generally accept that we have a right to clean air and clean water, and that any individual property owner's right to pollute must be subordinate to the greater right of society to preserve the environment. Some societies recognize a comparable right in the public to the preservation of society's cultural heritage. As applied to historic preservation, this debate is ultimately about the degree to which our society recognizes a right to the preservation of historic and cultural resources.

The property rights battle occurs in two principal arenas. For the past thirty years the courts have been the primary arena, as they interpret the meaning of the takings clause in the federal and state constitutions. But over the last ten years, property rights advocates have introduced bills in state legislatures and Congress that attempt to impose a standard that is more protective of property rights than those presently guaranteed by the courts.

Takings and the Courts

The concept of "takings" and "property rights" cannot be fully grasped without also understanding the way the Fifth Amendment has been interpreted by the courts. The leading U.S. Supreme Court decision interpreting the takings clause continues to be the 1978 historic preservation case, *Penn Central Transportation Co. et al. v. New York City Co. et al.*[20] In that case, the Court upheld the authority of the New York City Landmarks Commission to deny the owner of Grand Central Station the ability to build a fifty-five-story office tower atop the station, holding that whether a taking had occurred must, by its nature, be made on a case-by-case basis. The Court established a number of factors to be looked at in examining this issue, including the economic impact on the owner, the owner's "investment-backed expectations," the character of the government's action, and whether the action authorized a physical invasion by the government. The Court also established a rule that a court must examine the economic value of the parcel as a whole, not merely some distinctive aspect of it, such as air rights, that might be diminished by the regulation.

Because the New York landmarks law did not authorize a physical invasion of Grand Central Station, and because the owners were left with a reasonable economic use of their property—they could continue to operate it and lease office space within the station—the denial of a permit to build the office tower atop the station did not result in a taking of the property, said the Court.

Although the Supreme Court has consistently reaffirmed its holding in *Penn Central* since 1978, it has begun to reexamine the takings area and to clarify the basic rules established in *Penn Central*.[21] In 1980 the Court restated *Penn Central*'s three-part inquiry into a two-part test: a regulation will constitute a taking if it fails to substantially advance legitimate state interests or denies the claimant the economically viable use of his property.[22] Five years later the Court reaffirmed that a court will not review a takings claim until the regulatory agency, such as a historic preservation commission, has reached a final decision.[23] Two years after that it confirmed that a court considering a takings claim must look at the parcel as a whole, not just the part of the property that was regulated.[24]

The Supreme Court case most often cited by property rights advocates to support the contrary argument, that a historic preservation regulation may constitute a taking, is *Lucas v. South Carolina Coastal Council*.[25] That case involved the application of state coastal zone regulations to an unimproved beach front lot that prevented the owner from building a house. The Court held that where the application of a regulation denies the property owner *all* economically viable use of his or her property, the regulation would constitute a taking *unless there was a basis for the regulation in underlying state nuisance law*. In other cases, the Supreme Court has limited the manner in which local governments may require monetary or financial contributions from property owners requesting a permit. It has held that the exaction must bear a proportional relationship to the requested permit itself, and that if the local government attempts to impose an exaction that is more than proportional to the impact of the development, the regulation may result in a taking under the Fifth Amendment.[26]

Although these cases have clarified certain aspects of the takings issue, the basic rule of *Penn Central*, that the application of a government regulation to a parcel of property, in the absence of a physical invasion, constitutes a taking only if no beneficial, economically viable use of the property remains. Although the Supreme Court continues to review takings cases, as of this writing the Court has not fundamentally altered the *Penn Central* doctrine. Thus, takings claims brought under historic preservation ordinances will most likely be unsuccessful, because the building at issue almost always has some economically viable use. Courts are therefore, under the current constitutional scheme, likely to uphold preservation regulations against takings challenges.[27]

Legislative Efforts

The courts are only part of the story, however. Property rights advocates, dissatisfied with the response of the courts, have taken their arguments to the legislative branch. As of fall 2001, there was pending in Congress a property rights bill that would allow takings claims to bypass state courts and local zoning and land-use dispute resolution.[28] More than twenty similar property rights laws have been enacted by state legislatures.[29] These more draconian approaches would clearly have a chilling effect on the willingness of elected officials and government agencies to impose additional regulations, and their long-term impact on historic preservation programs remains to be seen.

Although they have generally prevailed against takings claims in the courts, preservationists have not always been as effective in countering the arguments of the property rights advocates in legislatures or in the popular media. Defenders of property rights depict property as a fundamental building block of American society—as do preservationists. The preservation community must become equally persuasive in the same political venues.

It must be remembered that rights to the free use of private property have always been balanced by collateral duties to society—to protect water, for example, and to avoid committing nuisances that adversely impact neighbors or the public. Arguments about where the proper balance between public and private interests lies have continued throughout U.S. history. Indeed, the traditional (conservative) view held by many property rights advocates has emphasized stewardship. This concept—shared by many religious denominations—has always maintained that the land must be respected, cared for, and preserved, and that its owners are simply stewards for future generations.

Procedural Due Process: Fairness

In balancing the rights of the individual and those of society, one of the chief protections for the individual is the procedural due process protections that derive from the Fifth and Fourteenth Amendments to the Constitution. The Fifth Amendment provides that a person shall not "be deprived of life, liberty, or property, without due process of law." Simply stated, due process protections have been interpreted to require notice to the public and, to affected property owners, an opportunity to be heard and the adjudication of rights by fair and unbiased decision makers.[30] Historic preservation commissions, as agencies of local government, are required to comply with the minimum due process requirements set forth under the U.S. and state constitutions. They must also comply with the specific requirements of state law, the local ordinance, and—most important—their bylaws or rules of procedure.[31]

There is an additional aspect of procedural due process that is based as much on policy and community relations as on law as such. Preservation commissions are too often perceived by property owners and the public as "taste police," whose judgments are essentially subjective. A commission's special—and most difficult—task is to apply specific criteria to the proposals set forth in each certificate of appropriateness. Dealing with the perception problem is largely a matter of carefully defining the design and preservation criteria contained in the ordinance, and of using the hearing process itself to educate rather than to frustrate property owners. When property owners understand that there are sound reasons underlying a commission's decisions, and that the decision-making process is consistent and disciplined, their frustration is less likely to become the subject of litigation or appeals. This is not simply a matter of procedural due process; it is also a matter of fundamental fairness and of good public policy.

Historic Preservation and Religious Properties

Just as the U.S. Constitution embodies a balance between the rights of the individual to property and the needs of society and requires that regulatory processes be unbiased and fair, so it seeks to balance the individual's ability to worship freely with the societal goal of treating all religions equally and avoiding religious intolerance. In the past twenty-five years religious groups have become increasingly involved in politics and public policy. Most of them have focused on promoting specific agendas related to their religious beliefs, including a vigorous assertion of the right of free exercise of religion under the Constitution. Some have strenuously resisted government regulation of their activities, including historic preservation, thereby producing a number of court cases applying constitutional principles to balance religious freedom with the protection of historic buildings.

The leading federal case involving the application of historic preservation regulations to a historic religious building involved St. Bartholomew's Church in New York City.[32] In that case the court of appeals upheld the denial of a permit to demolish a portion of the church complex, finding that there was no substantial burden on the free exercise of religion. The court relied in part on an earlier Supreme Court case unrelated to historic preservation, but which set forth an important principle: that government may not "substantially burden" the free exercise of religion unless it can establish that the burden is the "least restrictive means" of furthering a "compelling governmental interest," unless the regulation is a "neutral law of general applicability."[33] Usually, historic preservation ordinances, because they apply to everyone without regard to religion, are considered neutral laws of general applicability and thus fall within this exception.[34]

Dissatisfied with the standard set out by the courts, religious organizations lobbied Congress to establish a standard that would permit them to avoid government regulation more generally, including the avoidance of zoning and historic preservation regulation. In response, Congress, in 1993, passed the Religious Freedom Restoration Act, which sought to overturn that portion of the Supreme Court standard providing an exception for neutral laws of general applicability.[35] A case quickly arose testing the application of the law when the city of Boerne, Texas, sought to apply its historic preservation ordinance to the local Catholic church. The church resisted and sued the city, claiming a violation of the act. The case, *Flores v. City of Boerne*, eventually reached the Su-

St. Bartholomew's Church, Park Avenue, New York. A federal appeals court upheld the New York City Landmarks Commission's decision to deny the church's request to demolish the parish hall and replace it with an office tower. This case establishes a key legal precedent regarding the constitutional validity of government efforts to protect church-owned historic property under the First Amendment to the U.S. Constitution. (Paul Edmondson, National Trust for Historic Preservation)

preme Court, which found that Congress had overstepped its bounds in attempting to overturn the interpretation of the First Amendment stated by the Court and declared the law unconstitutional.[36] Although it was unclear how this law ultimately would have affected the protection of religious landmarks, preservationists had argued that preservation laws should not be interpreted to impose a "substantial" burden under the language of the act, and therefore preservation laws would remain unaffected by the law.

Undeterred by the *Boerne* decision, religious organizations have sought to enact comparable religious freedom acts in the state legislatures and a modified version of the Restoration Act in Congress. As of 2002, eleven state statutes have been enacted, one state constitution has been amended, and several other states are considering such proposals. In addition, President Bill Clinton signed into law the Religious Land Use and Institutionalized Persons Act of 2000, which specifically targets land-use regulation and historic preservation. It is virtually certain that this measure will be challenged on constitutional grounds.

As a result of this continuing debate, religious organizations are taking other initiatives to avoid the regulation of historic properties. Several local ordinances have incorporated exceptions for religious organizations, amounting to an "owner consent" provision. In Chicago, the ordinance was amended by the

St. Peter Catholic Church, Boerne, Texas. The application of historic preservation regulations to this church led the U.S. Supreme Court to overturn the federal Religious Freedom Restoration Act. (National Trust for Historic Preservation)

city council virtually without the knowledge of the preservation community, and the exception remains the law. At the state level, the California legislature amended its preservation enabling legislation in 1994 to exempt churches from historic preservation regulation.

It is likely that some religious organizations will continue to attempt to avoid historic preservation, land-use, and other regulations through court action and by pressing for legislative exemptions. Preservationists, in turn, must be prepared to respond. Although these two competing interests appear to be diametrically opposed from a legal perspective, there are encouraging signs that the two sides can work together to find common ground.[37]

Economic Hardship

In the preservation context, the tensions between the rights of the individual and the rights of society are presented most strongly in the implementation of local historic preservation ordinances. In recent years two of the most notable provisions included in local ordinances are economic hardship and demolition by neglect. Economic hardship provisions permit preservation commissions to address economic hardship as an administrative or quasi-judicial matter, even though in a substantive sense the takings issue is directly involved. In some ways, an economic hardship provision may be said to operate as a "safety valve" in those situations where literal application of the ordinance might arguably amount to a "taking." Hardship provisions generally provide for a variance or other relief in the rare instance where the owner is denied all viable economic use of the property. This avoids a takings challenge that could ultimately result in a claim of monetary damages or the invalidation of the ordinance.

The benefit of an economic hardship provision is that it allows a local commission to address certain limited economic hardships, thus avoiding the time and expense of an appeal to a trial court. The commission can evaluate the degree of hardship against specific criteria spelled out in the ordinance in a public hearing; this, in turn, provides the record that goes to court on appeal in case of a challenge. On appeal, the commission's findings of fact are generally binding as a matter of law, and there is no new hearing regarding the facts on which the decision was based.

It is important to note that economic hardship always focuses on the property itself and not on the owner's personal financial situation—a distinction most lay commission members fail to understand. Thus, the proverbial widow who can no longer afford to maintain her historic house does *not* have a claim of economic hardship simply because she cannot afford the house anymore. In most states, she has a valid claim of economic hardship only if the house, as designated, no longer has any economically viable use or can no longer provide a return on the property.

Although economic hardship provisions are increasingly included in historic preservation ordinances, they are not always well crafted, nor are they well understood by volunteer boards. Yet economic hardship provisions are an essential tool in tempering takings claims. They provide a mechanism for addressing the loss of economic viability in the preservation context, rather than in the heated, expensive, and prolonged context of subsequent litigation.

Demolition by Neglect

Occasionally, a property owner will attempt to get rid of a historic building simply by allowing the building to deteriorate to such a degree that it fails to meet occupancy codes or cannot be economically rehabilitated. Typically, a demolition by neglect provision will permit the local government to repair the property and impose a lien on it to recoup the cost of repairs. It is a most difficult area from both a legal and a practical standpoint, since it is almost impossible to prove intentional neglect on the part of the owner. Including affirmative maintenance obligations in the ordinance can assist in addressing the situation before the building is demolished.

Owner Consent and Owner Objection

Concerns over property owners' rights have also led in recent years to a growth in the number of "owner consent" or "owner objection" provisions added to local historic preservation ordinances. Owner consent provisions require the owner to consent to designation as a historic resource before a property may be designated or listed. Owner objection permits the owner to object to such designation. Many people take the position that historic preservation regulation is acceptable if individual property owners can opt out of the regulation if they do not wish to be regulated. Although this often appears to members of the public to be fair and logical, allowing property owners to opt out in this fashion undermines the effectiveness of the ordinance, which is based on the fundamental concept of the property's significance to the larger society, rather than the preferences of the current owner.

Owner consent provisions potentially undermine the legal basis for the ordinance.[38] The equal protection provisions of the Constitution require that all individuals similarly situated must be treated alike. Owner consent ensures an opposite result: that all historic properties will *not* be treated alike. Owner consent provisions may also constitute an unlawful delegation of legal authority from the local government to members of the public.[39] From a practical standpoint, the property owners who are most likely to demolish or harm a historic building are given the opportunity to opt out of the regulation. The growth in owner consent provisions in recent years represents a failure to take historic preservation regulation seriously as well as a failure of political support as a matter of public policy.

In addition to owner consent provisions, designations of historic resources are increasingly being challenged.[40] In some cities, the fight over district or landmark designation has led to the development of negotiated designations. To avoid a protracted legal battle, the preservation commission or local preservation organization will, for example, agree not to designate the property in exchange for review of the development project or other concessions. These ne-

gotiated designations ultimately pose the same legal problems as owner consent: they undermine both the substantive and the legal bases for the preservation ordinance.

Concluding Thoughts about Regulation

Preservationists must be conscious of both the political realities and the larger
goals of each community. The overarching goal should be to preserve historic
environments as living parts of our day-to-day lives. Finding a balance between
regulation that will achieve the preservation of the resource, while permitting
the community to function in modern life, all within the political restraints of
what a given community will tolerate, is a difficult and constant challenge. Ironically, many local commissions have the power to regulate the details of changes
to historic properties but do not have the ultimate power to prevent demolition. The unfortunate reality is that preservationists may spend three hours in
a public hearing debating the relative merits of real versus fake window mun-
tins in the context of a historic preservation ordinance that does not prohibit
demolition. In many situations, it may be preferable to focus on the preservation of the building rather than regulating all of its detail. Preservationists
should constantly examine and assess alternative options.

Private Preservation Protections:
Preservation Easements

Private restrictions on the use of property, imported as aspects of the ancient
common law of England, have been available for many years. However, preservation and conservation easements did not find extensive use in the United
States until the environmental movement was well established. Because they
are not government regulations, they often appeal to property owners as a means
of controlling the future use or conservation of property. And not least, under
the federal tax code and the income tax laws of many states, a tax deduction is
available for the donation of a qualified, perpetual preservation or conservation
easement to a nonprofit preservation organization or government entity.

Easements continue to be widely used and have become a primary tool of
many conservation organizations and preservation revolving funds (see Chapters 6, 7, and 10). They are also increasingly used to control sprawl. Many
communities have instituted programs to acquire easements over sensitive

National Union Building, F Street, Washington, D.C. This building (left), fully intact, is protected by a historic preservation easement held by the National Trust. In contrast, the buildings with only facades remaining were protected by the local preservation ordinance.
(Thompson Mayes, National Trust for Historic Preservation)

land, such as open space, farmland, and greenbelts. The owners of the property in these areas, who are often under intensive development pressure, are
thereby compensated for the development value of their land in exchange for
imposing a protective easement in perpetuity. Thus, easements are widely seen
as a fair solution because they do not impose the entire burden of preservation
or conservation costs on individual property owners. Easements are also particularly effective tools in communities that will not support comparable regulatory controls.

Balancing the Rights of the Individual
with the Rights of Society

Finding a good balance between achieving the goal of preserving our communities and protecting the rights of individuals will always be with us. The current hot spots of religious liberty and property rights have been issues since the

Grand Central Station, New York. In 1978 the U.S. Supreme Court upheld the authority of the New York City Landmarks Commission to deny an application to construct a contemporary office tower above the terminal. The decision validated local landmark laws and remains the lodestar of takings law under the Fifth and Fourteenth Amendments to the U.S. Constitution. (Paul Edmondson, National Trust for Historic Preservation)

creation of our country and will continue to be debated, legislated, and litigated. The level and intensity of the debate ebbs and flows with public opinion. Although historic preservation may never be recognized under the law as important a value as the fundamental constitutional protections discussed earlier, the extent to which the public believes preservation to be important affects, in turn, the treatment given by elected officials, administrators, politicians, and judges. In strengthening historic preservation as a policy, it is essential that we explain the purpose of regulation, that we treat people fairly and with respect, that we open our eyes to the resources valued by the public, and that we develop tools that will protect those resources.

Conclusion

In 1978 the late Justice William J. Brennan Jr., in the landmark *Penn Central Transportation Co. et al. v. New York City Co. et al.*, wrote:

> Over the past 50 years, all 50 States and over 500 municipalities have enacted laws to encourage or require the preservation of buildings and areas with historic or aesthetic importance. These nationwide legislative efforts have been precipitated by two concerns. The first is recognition that, in recent years, large numbers of historic structures, landmarks, and areas have been destroyed. The second is a widely shared belief that structures with special historic, cultural, or architectural significance enhance the quality of life for all. Not only do these buildings and their workmanship represent the lessons of the past and embody precious features of our heritage, they serve as examples of quality for today. "Historic conservation is but one aspect of the much larger problem, basically an environmental one, of enhancing—or perhaps developing for the first time—the quality of life for people."[41]

Today, nearly twenty-five years after *Penn Central*, historic preservation is widely viewed as an important element of our lives. Senator John Chaffee (R.-R.I.), addressing the 1999 Annual Preservation Conference of the National Trust, stated, "Preservation is not just about conserving brick and mortar, lintel and beam. It is about the quality of life, and the possibility of a bright future." Quoting novelist D. H. Lawrence, Chafee reminded us that "the spirit of place is a great reality."[42]

Although the preservation ethic is widely held, it is not yet strong enough to overcome opposing forces and priorities: competing claims on government funding, concerns about religious freedom and property rights, and the economic machine that supports sprawling new development over the rehabilitation of older communities. Nearly twenty years after *Penn Central*, during the 1995 debate over the funding for the National Trust, Representative Tom Delay continued to believe that "[Preservation] . . . is a luxury for a few, not a necessity for many."[43]

The primary challenge facing historic preservation today is to strengthen and build widespread understanding that preservation is essential to our quality of life and that it is, indeed, a "necessity for many" and not a "luxury for a few." It is only by building that ethic that laws and policies for historic preservation will be maintained and improved. We must therefore continue to promote, explain, teach, preach, and show that historic preservation provides, as stated in *With Heritage So Rich*, an essential "sense of orientation to our society, using structures and objects of the past to establish values of time and place."

2 New Directions since 1966

Preserving Important Landscapes

Historic landscape preservation came of age in the last quarter of the twentieth century. A movement that barely had a name in 1975 became codified and bureaucratized during the 1980s and 1990s, as preservation professionals developed criteria, guidelines, and standards for evaluating, nominating, and treating significant designed, vernacular, and rural landscapes. A number of nonprofit groups and organizations and government agencies at both the state and national levels began formal programs to incorporate landscape preservation into the larger preservation arena.

Building a Constituency for Landscape Preservation, 1975–2000

For most of the twentieth century, landscape preservation involved garden restoration projects. Early twentieth-century historic landscape projects, such as those sponsored by the Garden Club of Virginia at Stratford Hall or Kenmore, concentrated on planting plans intended to create a "historic feeling" in the vicinity of an important historic house, rather than to achieve strict historical authenticity. This practice was consistent with the accepted notion of the time that landscapes were significant primarily as the settings for important buildings and were not based on rigorous historical research or sophisticated archaeology. Prior to the 1980s, most private preservation efforts were intended to beautify historic grounds and gardens, and landscapes received little attention within federal preservation programs.

Despite the attention paid to architectural significance following passage of the 1966 act and the subsequent development of the Secretary of the Interior's Standards for Rehabilitation, the federal preservation program did not limit or exclude landscapes from receiving the same designations and protections afforded other significant resources. In fact, many landscapes were included

Tourists at Yosemite Valley, California. Popular tourist destinations such as Yosemite National Park face increased visitation pressures that threaten their inherent natural and cultural values. (Land and Community Associates, Charlottesville, Virginia)

within the boundaries of the early properties and districts listed in the National Register. Few landscapes were well documented, however, or specifically delineated as contributing landscape features. The inclusion of districts, and acceptance by the National Register of ridge lines, river banks, and fence and tree lines for historic district boundaries, set a precedent for recognizing landscape values even before the program considered the need for landscape evaluation criteria.

Major landscape projects such as those of Arthur Churchill at Colonial Williamsburg, Virginia, and Sturbridge Village in Massachusetts, initially planned and implemented in the early twentieth century, were more accurately characterized as Colonial Revival interpretations of colonial gardens. Both projects were conducted concurrently with major architectural restorations and reconstructions. Even when archaeological investigations were undertaken in conjunction with such projects, the primary purpose was to pinpoint building locations. Identifying character-defining landscape features such as historic plant material or the configurations of walks and fences was of minor or secondary importance. Ironically, these very landscape projects, derided by some individuals associated with the landscape preservation movement of the 1970s and 1980s, are now recognized as significant, early-twentieth-century designed landscapes worthy of study and preservation.

Although a number of historic battlefields, particularly Civil War sites administered by the National Park Service, received considerable attention at the time of the centennial observance of the war in the 1960s, they were largely regarded as historic scenes and not evaluated or treated as landscapes. The focus was on re-creating historic military sight lines and removing cultural features not directly associated with the 1860–65 period. In most instances, battlefield landscapes were not evaluated for their importance as historic farms, plantations, or villages, or for the natural landscape features that contributed to their temporary military uses. Associated military uses like encampment areas and military routes were not evaluated for their larger landscape significance, and preservation treatment was aimed primarily at places where the most intense fighting had occurred.

In the last three decades of the twentieth century landscapes came to be recognized in their own right as significant cultural resources. Frequently, these landscapes were associated with prominent personalities or events in history, but increasingly they began to be recognized as consequential designed or rural landscapes that possessed distinctive landscape features and qualities representative of a particular period, design, region, or landscape type.

This transition in perception, evaluation, and treatment began to occur in the 1970s as preservationists—both individuals and groups—began to address landscape issues as more than beautification and as more than preserving a historic setting. The National Trust for Historic Preservation, notably through its Rural Project, sponsored conferences and workshops, and the Association for Preservation Technology (APT), through a small group of members who used its meetings to develop an initial landscape network, played leadership roles in landscape preservation.

As landscape preservation moved into the mainstream of preservation activity, landscape values became critical to an understanding of battlefields, national and state parks, institutional grounds, urban parks, rural cemeteries, seashores and lakeshores, plantations, ranches, farms, and urban and suburban neighborhoods. By the end of the twentieth century, landscapes were no longer seen simply as settings for an event in history or a work of architecture, or something to be merely viewed and enjoyed from a car window or by strolling through a historic site. Landscape preservation is now as likely to apply to a tallgrass prairie reclamation or a regional viewshed protection plan as it is to restoring a colonial garden for a Virginia plantation or reconstructing a fence for a New England house.

An early preservation effort to address broad-ranging landscape concerns

South Manitou Lighthouse, Sleeping Bear Dunes National Lakeshore, Michigan. The NPS commissioned a joint historic structure and cultural landscape report to address both conservation technology and shoreline erosion issues that challenge the lighthouse. (Land and Community Associates, Charlottesville, Virginia)

occurred in 1975, when the Western Regional Office of the National Trust cosponsored a conference on conserving the historic and cultural landscape with the Trust for Public Land, the American Society of Planning Officials, and the Colorado State Historical Society. The conference, held in Denver, brought together planners, preservationists, and landscape architects to consider landscape preservation issues, many of which still remain a concern. The conference raised issues that would form the basis of landscape preservation efforts for the next two decades, including the need for landscape conservation guidelines and classifications based on natural systems and processes in addition to cultural values. Other concerns such as land-use policy and alarm over unplanned and inappropriate growth were also raised. These continue to polarize the American public in the wake of current concern about the loss of rural land and natural areas. The National Trust Rural Project led the way in mentoring and providing technical assistance to local citizens in organizing and advocating the preservation of rural landscapes. The project also recognized from the beginning that successful landscape preservation involved an understanding of natural systems.

About the time of the Denver conference, a small group of members of a relatively new Canadian-American organization, the Association for Preservation Technology, began talking among themselves about landscape preservation. Spurred on by landscape architect Thomas Kane, who then chaired the American Society of Landscape Architects (ASLA) committee on historic landscapes, the group met first at the Cleveland, Ohio, APT meeting in 1977. This group of about twenty architects, landscape architects, historians, and educators began an informal discussion of the role of landscapes in historic preservation. The next June the small group met in New Harmony, Indiana, where Kane was directing a landscape preservation project, and in the following year the group incorporated as the Alliance for Historic Landscape Preservation (AHLP) at a meeting held at the Clearing, landscape architect Jens Jensen's historic retreat in Wisconsin.

The AHLP immediately began to take a leadership role in landscape preservation in the United States and Canada, and an active interest in both designed and rural landscapes. Meeting annually at a historic landscape to discuss members' projects and research, the alliance began to publicly articulate the issues related to landscape preservation in both practice and scholarship. In 1980 it sponsored a historic landscape symposium and training session in Williamsburg that provided the first professional training course in North America specifically devoted to landscape preservation. Meeting at such landscapes as the Amana Colonies in Iowa, Skyland at Shenandoah National Park in Virginia, and the rural community of Cazenovia in New York, the early alliance meetings provided an informal forum for the exchange of ideas and a place to incubate new programs and initiatives for both designed and vernacular landscapes. What began as an emphasis on fences, walls, and small auxiliary structures such as gazebos and smokehouses gradually evolved into a more wide-ranging discussion of the landscape as an interrelated system of both natural and cultural resources.[1] In Cazenovia, the alliance concentrated on the National Trust Rural Project's demonstration projects in Cazenovia and Oley, Pennsylvania, which emphasized citizen involvement and the use of overlay mapping techniques and visual assessments.

In 1980 another group of concerned preservationists, both volunteers and professionals, formed the National Association of Olmsted Parks (NAOP). The NAOP organized to recognize and promote the preservation of the landscape design legacy of Frederick Law Olmsted and his firm, Olmsted and Vaux. By the 1970s many Olmsted urban parks had deteriorated and were overgrown with weeds, threatened by both neglect and park modernization. Citizen activists concerned about safe and pleasant parks joined with landscape architects, planners, and educators to restore Olmsted landscapes. The NAOP, which

Reenactment of the Battle of Cedar Mountain, Culpeper County, Virginia. Increased interest in Civil War sites has focused considerable attention on the need for land-use planning to protect these typically rural sites with significant war associations. (J. Timothy Keller, FASLA)

became politically active, began to explore legislative and other governmental approaches to landscape preservation. Its involvement was instrumental in alerting the National Register program of the need to designate and protect designed landscapes such as parks, institutional grounds, estates, and exemplary examples of urban and regional planning.

Meanwhile, the ASLA's historic landscape committee began to work within the profession of landscape architecture to promote awareness of historic landscapes and the need to designate and protect significant designed landscapes. The committee worked with landscape architects, the AHLP, the NAOP, and other groups to strengthen the attention and protection afforded landscapes within the federal program and to improve landscape architects' understanding of landscapes. The committee also sponsored workshops and training courses in conjunction with the ASLA annual meeting for landscape architects interested in learning more about landscape preservation.

The growing interest in historic landscapes heightened the awareness for scholarly investigations of landscapes and the need to collect and preserve historic plans, drawings, specifications, and other documentation associated with these landscapes. In 1979 the NPS established the Olmsted Archives at the Frederick Law Olmsted National Historic Site in Brookline, Massachusetts. The Olmsted Archives, which now has a collection of more than a million historical documents related to the Olmsted practice, provides researchers with access to historic documentation for Olmsted-designed landscapes. Over the years, landscape architect and historian researchers have created a broad base of information on both the Olmsted firm and other landscape architects and designers associated with them. Another archival and research repository at Wave Hill, New York, has become an important archive for historic landscape research. Wave Hill also sponsors historic landscape symposia and other events related to landscape preservation.

In 1975 only a few faculty members in landscape architecture at American colleges and universities included landscape preservation in their courses of study, and then generally only out of personal interest. Through their classroom lectures, papers delivered at professional and academic meetings and conferences, historical research, and applied projects, landscape architecture professors provided an initial linkage between the study and practice of landscape preservation in the 1970s and 1980s.[2] By the 1990s college and university courses in landscape preservation had become widespread.

Through the 1980s and 1990s the NPS undertook a landscape preservation initiative that built on the earlier work of the AHLP, the NAOP, and the ASLA. During that period, the National Park Service worked closely with those organizations and their representatives to develop and begin to implement a national agenda of increased understanding of landscape preservation and activity, now identified as its cultural landscape initiative. As a result of this initiative, the term "cultural landscape" is gradually gaining acceptance within the wider historic preservation community.

The Park Service began to offer landscape preservation training courses for NPS personnel, using such NPS sites as Cumberland Island, the Green Springs Rural Historic District in Virginia, and the Columbia River Gorge as cultural landscape laboratories. It also began to explore ways that it could address historic landscape issues in national parks.[3] The National Register followed through in the 1980s with the publication of technical bulletins offering guidance on the evaluation and nomination of eligible landscapes. These bulletins became part of a larger landscape initiative that has produced numerous publications, offers substantial technical assistance, and has placed historical landscape architects and cultural landscape specialists in NPS positions nationwide.[4] The Olmsted Center for Landscape Preservation at the Frederick Law Olmsted National Historic Site supports the NPS work by providing technical assistance in landscape research and undertaking projects at NPS properties. Cultural landscape reports (CLRs) have joined historic structure reports (HSRs) as standard preservation documents. The Park Service has established terminology and principles of practice that are generally considered the standard for landscape preservation work in the United States and that serve as models for several other nations as well. The recently established Marsh-Billings National Historical Park in Woodstock, Vermont, continues the NPS efforts in landscape preservation through establishment of the first national park to focus on the theme of conservation history and the changing nature of land stewardship in the United States.

Criteria for Landscape
Identification and Evaluation

One of the major obstacles to landscape preservation before the 1980s was the absence of criteria to guide informed documentation and evaluation of landscapes. Both historical researchers and historic resource surveyors in the field were looking for direction in approaching the new need to conduct landscape documentation and analysis in the late 1970s and early 1980s when there were few landscape preservation projects to serve as precedents.

Both the NPS and private practitioners directed much attention in the 1980s and 1990s to developing and testing various criteria to use in identifying and evaluating landscapes. Early landscape recordation projects such as the HABS/ HAER documentation of the Missouri Botanical Garden and the Meridian Hill Park in Washington, D.C., the first efforts to document landscapes separately from buildings, provided useful models for adapting and applying traditional architectural documentation and evaluation criteria to landscapes.[5]

Rural landscapes, however, presented somewhat different challenges in landscape documentation and analysis. Other than the guidance available for documenting historic districts as part of the National Register process, there was little precedent for documenting rural lands and communities. The district evaluation and recording process, although sometimes covering large land areas, was oriented toward architectural resources. Rural historic districts established by the late 1970s—among them, Goose Creek and Green Springs, Virginia— included individually prominent historic houses throughout their rural acreage. No criteria had been established to identify or evaluate significant landscape features, even though the rural landscape quite obviously contributed to the overall importance and integrity of these districts.

In the late 1970s a number of projects in the Midwest began to focus on the

Taro fields, Hawaii. The 1,000 Friends of Kauai undertook one of the first comprehensive historic landscapes inventories and used that information to develop a protection plan for its culturally and agriculturally significant taro fields. (Land and Community Associates, Charlottesville, Virginia)

role of the landscape in rural environments and on the urgent need for landscape criteria. Four projects, located in New Harmony, Indiana, the Amana Colonies in Iowa, Old World Wisconsin, and an NPS model rural project at Buffalo River National Historic Site in Arkansas, played a major role in increasing an awareness of the need for useful standards.

Private landscape architecture consulting firms working at New Harmony and the Amana Colonies began to develop survey forms, data sheets, and recording techniques. Each also created experimental techniques for evaluating landscape integrity. Since both New Harmony and the Amana Colonies had developed initially as religious communities based on communitarian values, each required a preservation master plan that not only was resource based, but also identified and preserved significant landscape features. Village layout, orchard and vineyard locations, historic fences, cemeteries, and other features were as important in representing their historic characters as preserving historic brickwork and architectural details.[6]

Subsequent discussion of these projects by the AHLP provoked comparisons with a very different type of landscape, one that required an extensive search for ethnic criteria that could be employed in research and documentation. The

Old World Wisconsin outdoor exhibit of historic farmsteads represented the multicultural heritage of Wisconsin's settlers. To create Old World Wisconsin required new guidelines in such areas as spatial organization, land use, and the interrelationships between landscape and buildings, as well as between plant material and historic landscape features.[7]

In 1980 the National Park Service began working on a cultural landscape project to investigate rural historic districts within the NPS and to identify the special characteristics of such districts.[8] This project developed an initial list of characteristics, which even though modified and reinterpreted over time, still provides the basis for defining cultural landscapes within the NPS. One of the lasting legacies of this project has been the development of a working vocabulary for landscape preservation. These key components of the vocabulary include overall patterns of landscape spatial organization, land use, response to natural features, circulation networks, boundary demarcations, vegetation, cluster arrangement, structures, small-scale elements, historical views, and other perceptual qualities.[9] By 1997 this new approach was recognized in a new NPS classification system, which included natural systems and features, spatial organization, land use, cultural traditions, cluster arrangements, circulation, topography, vegetation, buildings and structures, views and vistas, constructed water features, small-scale features, circulation, and archaeological sites.[10]

More important than the individual components, however, was the recognition of a fundamental interrelationship between the natural environment and cultural resources represented by these components.[11] These initial NPS efforts at identifying historic landscape criteria directed the previous emphasis away from the architectural and art history bias based on historical styles and periods. The 1984 publication, *Cultural Landscapes: Rural Historic Districts in the National Park System*, resulting from this work, by introducing a means of systematically categorizing and evaluating landscape components and features, provided the first available guidance for rural surveys and National Register nominations.[12]

By the late 1970s and early 1980s the National Register, encouraged by such groups as the AHLP, the NAOP, and the ASLA Open Committee on Historic Landscapes, began openly and seriously to consider ways to evaluate the significance and integrity of designed landscapes and to include them on their own merits in the National Register program. Although a number of historic landscapes had been listed in the register, most had been included because of their relationships to works of architecture or associations with historically prominent individuals. Developing criteria to use in assessing the significance of landscapes was a critical first step. But rather than create new categories and separate approaches for landscapes, the National Register chose to adapt existing guidelines to meet the special circumstances of this new resource. Its 1986 publication, *How to Document, Evaluate, and Nominate Designed Historic Landscapes*, covered college campuses, estate grounds, urban parks, and other designed landscapes. The criteria include the dynamic, seasonal, and other variable characteristics of landscapes not present in architecture, including maturity of plant species, loss of species, and the integrity of substitute plant material.[13]

Dealing with landscape change has continued to be an important aspect of NPS landscape preservation efforts and has been addressed in subsequent bulletins on the nature of rural historic districts, battlefields, and cemeteries. These bulletins are the primary resources that provide guidance to state historic preservation offices, the Advisory Council on Historic Preservation, and preservation and planning professionals engaged in evaluating landscape resources and determining landscape significance and integrity.

Through the remainder of the 1980s and the 1990s, the NPS continued to promote and nurture other publications contributing to the knowledge required to document and evaluate landscapes, including an initial reading list and a landscape preservation bibliography.[14] The subsequent publication of the two-volume *Pioneers of American Landscape Design* (1993 and 2000), which identified a number of nineteenth- and early-twentieth-century landscape architects, landscape gardeners, horticulturalists, writers, educators, and others and their work, provided the first readily available information to use in designed landscape historic contexts.

Concurrent with these efforts, another publication, *Presenting Nature: The Historic Landscape Design of the National Park Service, 1916–1942* (1993), explored both national and state park designs in rural and wilderness settings.[15] This study was intended to encourage nomination of park landscapes and to provide the basis for recognizing the significance of designed parks as well as the rustic architecture within their boundaries. Subsequently republished as *Building the National Parks: Historic Landscape Design and Construction* (1997), it provided the context for evaluating naturalistic landscape design and determining the relative significance and integrity of national, state, and community parks. A subsequent book, *Building the National Parks* (1998), also addressed historic park development in the United States and documented the value of parks for their cultural and historic significance in landscape design, as well as their natural wilderness value.[16]

Landscape architects, historians, and others in related disciplines have published scholarly books and articles on historic landscape designs and designers that contribute to a growing body of historic landscape research and writing that provides important contextual information used in evaluating the significance and integrity of landscapes.[17] Their work ranges from the earliest colonial gardens and settlements, to westward migration and urbanization, to popular contemporary and rural landscapes.

The heightened interest in landscape history and preservation throughout the profession has led to increased scholarly research on these topics among faculty and graduate students in most departments of landscape architecture. Authors have also begun to investigate the work of modern landscape architects of the twentieth century, such as Dan Kiley and James Rose. Interest in historic landscape research appears to be growing. The one hundredth anniversary meeting of the ASLA in 1997 included a large number of papers on historic landscapes and landscape preservation, and the APT published its second landscape preservation issue in recent years in 2000.

Although ethnic landscapes have been underrepresented in cultural landscape scholarship and documentation, the number of publications documenting African American landscapes is increasing. The National Park Service has undertaken a number of studies related to ethnographic landscapes and is contributing to the knowledge concerning Native American horticulture and uses of indigenous plants through ethnobotanical and other studies at various parks. Hawaiian landscapes such as the Hanalei Valley taro landscape and the effects of tourism on that landscape have been investigated for more than a decade. Other landscape architects and scholars are contributing to a growing interest in Asian, Hispanic, Eastern European, and other ethnic influences, both historically and in contemporary landscape adaptations associated with recent immigration and settlement trends.

Methodologies

Advances in the methodologies associated with landscape preservation have kept pace with changes in the ways landscapes are considered. Both innovative technologies and traditional methods of inquiry are used to document, analyze, and treat cultural landscapes. Through the 1970s and 1980s landscape architects, historians, architects, and preservation professionals debated the approaches needed to bring landscape preservation into mainstream preservation, and a number of methodological techniques have been developed and tested.

Much of the progress in the development of landscape preservation methods and techniques has been provided by the NPS. More than any of its other publications, the *Cultural Landscape Report*, as a parallel publication to the *Historic Structure Report*, has influenced methodological developments. In the 1990s the Park Service began to develop a new database of cultural landscape information through its cultural landscape inventory (CLI). This essentially preceded the development of a cultural landscape report. Designed as a management tool, the CLI combines identification of character-defining landscape features and landscape integrity evaluations for all NPS landscapes considered eligible for the National Register. Every NPS regional office has begun to participate in the CLI process. The information provides a basis for evaluating the effects of proposed park developments such as visitor centers, maintenance facilities, trails, and picnic and parking areas.[18]

Inventory and evaluation techniques have by now expanded beyond those addressed in the National Register bulletins to other NPS policies and publications, such as the *Guide to Cultural Landscape Reports*. This guide provides methodological guidance for the entire cultural landscape process from inventory through treatment recommendations. *The Secretary of the Interior's Standards for the Treatment of Historic Properties with Guidelines for the Treatment of Cultural Landscapes* outlines the official basis for making informed treatment decisions.[19] However, new techniques, methodologies, and approaches continue to develop as more landscape preservation projects proceed from evaluation through treatment.

The first HABS/HAER projects, which documented landscapes in the Missouri Botanical Garden, Meridian Hill Park, and Shenandoah National Park, relied on adapting the traditional measured drawing techniques developed for buildings.[20] But a major concern for the Missouri Botanical Garden documentation was how to identify plant material without overpowering the drawing with plant nomenclature and dimensions. The solution involved the use of abbreviated names and the combined identification of adjacent material of the same species to keep the drawing more legible. Because landscapes possess certain intangible and ephemeral qualities that do not express themselves easily in two-dimensional documentation, more text was included to address design intent, implementation, and other features that are not conveyed well in plans and elevations. The 1985 Meridian Hill pilot project in landscape documenta-

Plain Sect farm, Lancaster, Pennsylvania. For more than a decade the Pennsylvania Department of Transportation has explored strategies to meet ever-expanding transportation needs in the culturally distinctive Plain Sect agricultural landscape of Lancaster County. (Land and Community Associates, Charlottesville, Virginia)

tion also became a useful model because of the use of historic photographs and overlay drawings to delineate seasonal variations and detailed information on vegetation for the approximately twelve-acre urban site.[21]

Comparative analysis has become an important methodological tool in determining a landscape's period of significance and evaluating its integrity. A comparison of existing conditions with those of clearly defined and delineated historical periods has become a standard step in historic landscape documentation and analysis. Although the hand-drawn analyses used for Meridian Hill Park continue to be used, more sophisticated photographic and computer-assisted methods of investigation and analyses have also been developed for historic landscapes.

As in the case of architectural resources, photographic documentation is a decisive part of the inventory process. Aerial photography has become a valuable tool in recording and analyzing large-scale landscapes. For some landscapes, infrared photography has been used to provide even more information. An important part of the methodology for analyzing many landscapes is the comparison of early-twentieth-century aerial photographs with current photographs and other information to develop period plans and aid in evaluating integrity. Aerial photogrammetry to create CAD drawings as a landscape base and geographic information systems have begun to be used with greater frequency and will contribute to increased accuracy for recorded landscapes. GIS is now recognized as useful in analyzing and predicting landscape change. In numerous cases GIS has been employed in site inventory and analysis, concept initiation, and spatial diagramming for landscape preservation projects.

Global positioning systems (GPS) complement GIS in cultural landscape projects. Though certainly not limited to historic preservation and natural resource planning, GIS and GPS have become invaluable in these areas where efficient, economical, and accurate inventory and location of features are vital.

There are now a broader range of alternatives to replace plant materials that are damaged, diseased, dying, or missing from a site. The options include replacing vegetation with exact genetic duplicates, taxonomic replacements, or substitute plant materials that are similar in appearance to the original. The decision is influenced by the significance of the original plant material and its importance in the landscape. For example, genetic replacement has occurred at both the White House and the Adams National Historic Site because of the associations of specific plant material with the historic site. A number of sources exist for historic plant material replacement.[22]

Archaeological techniques used in cultural landscape studies have also advanced. Today they include a variety of options that range from written archaeological overviews, to traditional ground-penetrating investigations, to sonar, infrared, and satellite imagery of sites. Archaeology has been used to identify the location of buildings, structures, fences, walls, and other landscape features. The use of pollen, phytolith, and macrofloral analyses has been of particular value in providing information essential to identify historic vegetation. Pollen studies employed at Jamestown, Virginia, have identified certain plants that were extant historically while the presence of phytoliths, the mineral fossil casts of plants, has been used to indicate the specific locations of cropped fields at Thomas Jefferson's Monticello. Macrofloral research has also been used at Monticello to identify historic plant material where the buried seeds, fruit, and other remains of plant material have been found in charcoalified form.

Although the age of some existing plant material is well documented through contemporary descriptions, garden books, or construction documents, it is difficult to assess in many instances. Tree coring, which makes counting annual growth rings possible, has become recognized as an acceptable way of determining the age of healthy trees. Ring counting downed trees prior to removal or disintegration can provide a noninvasive technique for approximating the ages of similar sized trees of the same or similar species.

Specific methods and techniques have also been developed to deal with specialized landscapes such as battlefields, where earthworks may be present. Using case studies of both Revolutionary and Civil War battlefields in Virginia, the National Park Service in 1989 commissioned development of a manual to evaluate management practices for earthworks. The manual contained guidelines for managing vegetative cover, stabilization, and revegetation of damaged ground surfaces.[23] The NPS, in association with the Georgia Trust for Historic Preservation, has developed a revised handbook on sustainable earthworks management in both forested and open conditions. In the late winter of 2000 NPS personnel visited battlefields in France and engaged in a dialogue with international experts in battlefield preservation to consider significant terrain and battlefield characteristics.

Rural Landscapes: Issues Related to Identification and Evaluation

Although rural landscapes have received considerable attention in the last quarter of the twentieth century, they remain underrepresented on both the National Register of Historic Places and most state registers. By 1999 the National Register still listed fewer than one hundred rural historic districts even though large rural districts such as the entire township of Oley, Pennsylvania, and the several-thousand-acre Lake Landing historic district in Hyde County, North Carolina, had set the precedent for listing large rural districts. Both of these districts included substantial numbers of characteristic landscape resources, such as hedgerows, fencing, and drainage ditches, as well as architecturally significant buildings and structures. Despite the availability of the *National Register Bulletin Guidelines for Evaluating and Documenting Rural Historic Landscapes*, there remains a widespread perception among traditional preservationists and the public that rural landscapes are ordinary places. Although the constituencies for rural historic landscape identification and evaluation are growing as the issue of urban sprawl is seen by many as a preservation issue, rural areas still present major challenges in the most basic stages of preservation documentation and analysis.

The small number of current listings is directly related to the issues associated with identification and evaluation, not with the number of presumed eligible rural districts, which is assumed to be considerable. Although the National Register criteria and current listings clearly include resources that are characteristic as well as unique, it has been difficult to develop awareness even among state historic preservation offices that many rural landscapes meet historic district criteria. Many present listings include architecturally distinguished or early country houses on small parcels of land that do not correspond to either the existing or historic boundaries of the property during its period of significance. Many factors contribute to this. Rural counties and towns jurisdictions have limited budgets that cannot be stretched to fund historic resource surveys and therefore may be less likely to participate in government-funded programs such as the Certified Local Government program. When surveys are commissioned, they are more likely to include and emphasize well-known architectural resources rather than landscapes, which are considered by some surveyors to be simply open fields or woodlands without identifiable features and characteristics.

Rural surveys may take longer to complete than urban surveys if they focus on large and remote geographic areas. In addition to possessing a basic knowledge of architectural history, surveyors need to be aware of changes and innovations in agricultural technology, rural economic trends and demographics, indigenous plant material, crop patterns and production, and other information about rural life. There may be a lack of written documentation for rural properties since building permits and other resources are rarely found in urban areas. Photographic documentation may be hard to locate, especially if the owner has recently acquired the property and does not possess photographs of the land as it appeared in the past. But historic documentation such as land grants, homestead papers, and U.S. government land records relating to the government's nineteenth-century land surveys may be useful.

Surveyors may need access to specialized transportation, such as an off-the-road-vehicle, and local guides to locate abandoned roads and other potential resources. Some rural surveys may benefit from using a boat or canoe if areas along bodies of water are inaccessible by foot or car. Some surveys can only be accomplished by hiking or walking along trails or even by traveling by horseback. Sometimes it is difficult and time-consuming to secure permission to visit properties that cannot be seen from public rights-of-way.

The heightened, sometimes heated, debate over private property rights in the 1980s and 1990s has sometimes made it more difficult to document rural properties. Areas in which residents or owners oppose new residential or commercial development, activities such as mining or logging, or proposed transportation projects may require surveyors to rely on aerial photographs and other available sources where personal observations are not possible. Some residents of rural areas adjacent to federal lands, including national parks or national forests, fearing additional government land acquisition, are suspicious and even hostile to outsiders investigating an area.

Some property owners are hesitant to have their properties nominated to the National Register because they mistakenly believe that listing a property will require public access or restoration, or because they fear federal or state interference or limitations on the use of their property. Others who may be contemplating development in the future may prefer to divert attention away from their properties.

There are other problems that contribute to the underrepresentation of rural districts. Although the federal tax incentives for certified rehabilitation have served as a catalyst for registering urban districts, no comparable program exists for landscapes. Few farms have taken advantage of the tax incentives to restore agricultural buildings associated with income-producing activities, perhaps because of the low tax liability of many agricultural enterprises or possibly to avoid increased property taxes on improved structures.

Much of the documentation that has been accomplished in rural areas is associated with the environmental review process required for federally funded and licensed projects in which the survey is undertaken or contracted by a state or federal agency proposing projects like highway improvements, water impoundments, or correctional facilities. In such instances, the predisposition of the proposing agency is that historic resources do not exist, that they are few in number, and that boundaries can be drawn to identify an area where the proposed project can occur without affecting the historic resource. Landscape features are rarely identified and enumerated through this process unless there is an objection by the state historic preservation office, local citizens, or preservation advocacy groups. Citizen groups in West Virginia, for example, organized in the 1990s to advocate findings of eligibility for rural districts in areas likely to be affected by proposed transportation projects. But they found a distinct unwillingness on the part of Federal Highway Administration consultants to acknowledge the existence of rural districts. Instead, the FHWA approach was to acknowledge the significance of individual properties, leaving open corridors where new roadways could be constructed. Boundary delineation in rural historic districts has become an increasingly complicated and controversial step in the registration or eligibility process.

A factor contributing to the reluctance to affirm rural districts is the continued practice at both the state and federal levels of describing resources as contributing and noncontributing and the strong architectural bias inherent in such a system. Since features dating from a period that postdates the period of significance are listed as either contributing or noncontributing, a farm complex with a number of small but recently constructed auxiliary structures may not be evaluated as eligible even though the complex retains its larger historic landscape and many smaller features such as hedgerows, farm lanes, and woodlots. These features, although they may extend for miles or constitute a significant percentage of a property's total acreage, are each counted as a single resource if they are linked continuously. A several-mile perimeter fence and a ten-square-foot well house, for example, would each be counted as one resource.

Analysis and evaluation of rural properties have come under increased scrutiny, especially when they occur as part of an environmental review for a controversial project. Although urban neighborhoods and commercial districts routinely possess buildings that have been altered—sometimes with adjacent parking or redevelopment areas—they are often evaluated as contributing to the character of the area. It is not unusual for rural properties to be excluded from rural districts, however, if the principal residence possesses such revocable alterations as aluminum siding or an enclosed porch, even though the basic architectural form and domestic cluster are intact and recognizable. At the end of the twentieth century, there was a growing recognition that some rural properties are held to a higher standard than urban neighborhoods and commercial districts.

The extension of the interstate highway system throughout the United States, the upgrading of many secondary roads, and the construction of bypasses and connectors on former farmland have fractured a number of rural districts, contributing to the dilemma over how to delineate their boundaries. Where no interchanges exist and no additional development has occurred, there is no consensus on whether the highway becomes a de facto new boundary for any historic district or rural property. The historic property of Belvedere in Jefferson County, West Virginia, near the historic community of Charlestown, has been separated from a portion of its traditional acreage on the opposite side of the Route 340 bypass. The owner requesting a boundary reevaluation from the National Register was able to extend the size of the original register boundary, but not to include any land on the opposite side of the bypass although the original environmental impact study had determined that construction of the bypass would have no effect on the integrity of the property. Similarly in rural Greene County, Pennsylvania, near Chambersburg, two rural districts linked by historic associations and strong cultural traditions have been delineated simply because of the presence of I-81, despite the fact that both included areas of substantial, recent, suburban development. Dealing with the effects of vehicular transportation corridors in the evaluation process remains a distinct challenge in rural landscape identification and evaluation. The irony is that whereas proposed projects are often found to pose no effect on historic rural resources while they are in the planning stages, once built they almost always are considered intrusive and affect boundary determinations and evaluations of integrity.

Vegetation and land use present other complications in evaluating the integrity of rural properties and districts. Often there were several successive land uses during an extended period of significance; perhaps a field was alternately planted and left fallow and has since been allowed to evolve into woodland. The National Register has recently ruled that for the historic farms of Hopewell and Riverside adjacent to the Shenandoah River in West Virginia, woodland on formerly cropped land does not necessarily exclude the forested fields from their boundaries.

Continued urban encroachment and suburbanization can be expected to affect rural areas and their historic resources in two ways. Rural resources, such as agricultural outbuildings, schools and churches, graveyards, pecan groves and cedar allées, roadside farm stands, and peach and apple orchards, increasingly appeal to newcomers moving into traditional rural areas. Intrigued by the novelty of rural life, some are compelled to begin to research and document facets of rural life that many natives find commonplace. Finally, the reality that the rural landscape is changing rapidly is sure to lead to an increased recognition that once-characteristic features are becoming rare and endangered examples are worthy of documentation and perhaps preservation.

Special Problems and the Politics of Preserving Rural Cultural Resources

If inventorying and registering rural landscapes are challenging tasks, taking steps to plan for and protect them is even more formidable. Protecting rural landscapes is perhaps the most politicized aspect of historic preservation at the beginning of the twenty-first century. Efforts to protect rural land can rarely be separated from the local development process, state and local politics, or, for that matter, rural sociology and economics. Although many urban preservation programs were highly successful through the 1980s and 1990s as a result of federal tax and other incentives, finding a way to work with financial interests and developers to meet rural preservation goals has been extraordinarily difficult. Nor have rural preservation efforts in general been as sustained over long periods of time. The tendency has been for rural preservationists to organize over a single issue or individual site but fail to develop long-term strategies for rural land preservation. The exceptions have been well-financed rural and state preservation and conservation organizations like the Piedmont Environmental Council in Virginia, the Brandywine Conservancy in Pennsylvania, or 1,000 Friends of Oregon. These organizations have been politically active over long periods of time and have succeeded in enlisting the support of influential state and local public officials and citizens to help them achieve their goals.

The rapid rise in the value of farmland, or forest and wilderness lands, near urban centers and of waterfront land near scenic or recreational areas, has made much rural land attractive to investors and developers. Family lands once seen as an obligation of the current generation to maintain now have an unanticipated and unrealized monetary value that outstrips sentiment or long-term family attachments to it. Rising increases in the cost of farmland mean that fewer young farmers are likely to invest in agriculture with its annual risk of drought, floods, low economic return, and reduced government subsidies. The same financial realities motivate older farmers and their heirs to sell rural land for speculation, for development, or to pay off federal estate taxes, state inheritance taxes, or local property taxes based on the increased value of their land. Although there have been a number of individual success stories in rural preservation across the nation, the overall national trend remains toward development of rural areas near population centers and scenic attractions. At the same time nonmetropolitan counties, particularly in the Great Plains region, continue to lose population through out-migration to urban areas and other regions of the country and farm consolidation. Both trends result in increased losses of cultural landscape features through new development, expanded agricultural operations, or neglect and abandonment.

Increasingly, an alarming number of historic and cultural sites in once-rural areas, including many of our national parks, can be reached only by passing through unending stretches of scattered development and spreading suburbanization. Nicknamed "sprawl," this largely unplanned growth, responding to market forces and the public appetite for convenience and privacy, has begun to disturb public officials and citizens at all levels of government. During the Clinton administration, both the president and vice president spoke of Smart

Growth and the need to save open space in their speeches. A *Time* magazine feature article in the spring of 1999 reported that people in many communities were fighting back against sprawl. One farm family near Des Moines, Iowa, where residential and commercial development is expanding outward in all directions into prime farmland has resorted to placing Burma Shave–type signs critiquing the intruding suburbs. "It's not pretty" . . . "Save a farm" . . . "Build in the city," their signs proclaim to passing motorists. Even so, politicians who dare to do more than decry the wastefulness and tastelessness of sprawl by supporting restrictions on land development risk political ruin in the wake of the strong property rights battles of the last decade and a half. Legislators who support pro-development and road-building agendas are often more able to attract the support and campaign donations of pro-development business interests than conservation-minded candidates.

At the same time, there is a growing public awareness and even horror at unprecedented growth in formerly rural areas and the loss of the tangible reminders of the nation's agrarian past. The National Trust has taken its popular rural conservation handbook, *Saving America's Countryside*, through two editions. The handbook, a how-to volume that deals with grassroots civic action, cites numerous local examples of successful rural preservation strategies and case studies. Local groups mobilize, sometimes successfully, against the most identifiable symbols of this growth, symbols such as Wal-Mart and McDonald's, using sprawl as an effective sound bite. Others organize to protest tall communication towers or other highly visible projects. Most often, these battles are localized and can be characterized as "NIMBY" (Not in My Back Yard) opposition. Widespread attention to preserving rural landscapes, however, often occurs in response to a highly visible project, such as the abandoned Disney theme park project near historic Civil War sites in Virginia, that can attract national figures and outside funding in support of landscape preservation. Meanwhile, other less notorious development continues to occur on millions of acres of rural land, with only mild nostalgia and regret at a lost farmstead.

Many rural counties and townships experiencing unprecedented growth still have only basic government systems in place, often limited to a single county administrator with little or no professional planning staff. Many have no zoning and have never adopted uniform building codes. They are unprepared when a large project is proposed and have no legal mechanisms to control or mitigate the effects of development, even on local schools and roads, to say nothing of preserving the rural character of open land. Other rural communities located where growth is unlikely to occur have very different problems—for instance, seemingly attractive proposals for landfills, power plants, correctional facilities, and other uses that would most certainly meet opposition in more prosperous and scenic rural areas. In rural areas without prospects for other types of development, proposals like these are often seen as providing opportunities for economic development and jobs.

Sadly, most government programs favor rural development over rural preservation. Although the Department of Transportation programs ISTEA and TEA-21 (see Chapter 2) that are administered by state transportation departments have restored railroad depots and converted rail beds to pedestrian and cycling trails, most major transportation projects still threaten rural resources and rural land, opening undeveloped land for new residential and commercial development. These improved corridors divert traffic away from established commercial centers in small rural towns and away from traditional commercial rural crossroads.

Modern agriculture itself poses various threats to landscape preservation. Agricultural areas that remain viable often include new structures such as unsightly modern chicken houses and metal clad machine sheds that are necessary for modern agriculture. In addition, modern agricultural uses frequently conflict with nearby residential areas. The increased need for larger acreage promotes farm consolidation and the loss of traditional landscape features such as hedgerows and fence lines and even the characteristic farmhouse clusters of the American farmstead. Local property taxes on all buildings and structures also provide incentives, not for preservation of complexes of historic buildings, but for demolition by removing old and obsolete structures from the tax rolls. Similarly, new construction not only satisfies a farming operation's need for modern structures that will meet new technological requirements but also provides new opportunities for depreciation and other financial advantages over preservation.

A final failure of historic preservation to deal effectively with rural landscape preservation has been the inability and lack of vision to link rural land development with urban flight, blight, and decline. The urban–rural connection has been largely lost on the preservation and planning communities, which have focused on making new growth tasteful or compatible. The National Trust's infatuation with neotraditional design at Seaside and Kentlands, for example, makes little sense when Seaside spins off its own suburban development and when row houses in authentic urban neighborhoods, as in Baltimore, are still being demolished as unsafe eyesores.[24] Until preservationists understand that only extensive rehabilitation and even selective redevelopment in urban centers and deteriorating inner suburbs will begin to halt the continued development and despoliation of farmland and countryside, rural land protection is likely to continue to be a series of skirmishes and brushfires with successes concentrated primarily in well-off rural communities.

Scenic versus Cultural Resources

There is still no clear understanding or consensus within the preservation community concerning what distinguishes a cultural landscape from a scenic landscape. The issue is further confused by the distinction between natural and cultural resources. In addition, the very term "landscape" carries with it an implication of beauty that may affect findings of significance and integrity and provides an incentive to make a landscape appear more attractive than it was during its period of historical significance. Just as architectural preservationists have struggled for decades with those who might wish to make historic buildings appear even older than they are, so too do landscape preservationists contend with those who would improve on historic landscapes by cleaning them up and making them more beautiful than they were historically.

Some scenic resources have cultural value and significance, often related to their natural resource value or natural setting and features. National treasures, such as Yosemite and the Grand Canyon, are clearly natural and scenic resources. However, both also possess cultural value for their historic roles in land conservation and for their park designs and rustic architecture. The same is true for many state and local parks as well as parkways, estate grounds, and other designed landscapes that have been conceived to take advantage of views of notable natural features. With such landscapes, there is often a tendency to overlook their design elements and consider them from the standpoint of natural landscapes. The result is that design features are lost or altered without being evaluated for their significance and integrity. Conversely, there is a growing danger that the professional zeal to preserve documented landscapes will create conflicts between natural and cultural resource protection in places that were developed originally to support preservation or public enjoyment of natural landscapes or wilderness values.

Another issue relates to the aesthetic value of cultural landscapes and the effects of perceived ugliness on findings of significance and integrity. The issue of the aesthetic quality of setting and the areas adjacent to cultural landscapes is sometimes considered more important in evaluating integrity for landscapes than for architecture. For example, a state historic preservation officer recently found that a historic overlook lacked integrity because it was not a "pristine" view, since the municipal water tower in the county seat several miles distant was seen as part of the viewshed. Though aesthetics is an inherent quality of most designed landscapes and other works of design, it is not always credited as a characteristic of landscapes, particularly industrial and agricultural landscapes. Smokestacks, mining scars, and maintenance areas may actually be contributing landscape features, even though they are not beautiful by traditional norms.

What is worse, authentic qualities and features of historic landscapes are often removed or altered to make them more attractive, or new elements are added to make them look quaint or charming or to be economically viable. Main Street projects especially have encouraged facade rehabilitation for historic commercial buildings but largely ignored historic landscape values when developing urban design solutions for traditional downtowns. In fact, many approved projects—motivated by the financial incentives offered by federal tax credits—have included destructive new construction that destroyed or altered historic landscape features when projects expanded into adjacent gardens, playgrounds, schoolyards, or other landscapes to build additional income-producing space, provide parking, or offer other project amenities.[25]

Downtown streetscapes and urban parks have generally been considered amenity issues—important in attracting and pleasing shoppers and tourists—but not often regarded as historic landscapes. Most paradoxical of all is the fact that so many American preservationists have embraced the neotraditional town concept at the expense of rehabilitating the authentic traditional landscapes of old urban neighborhoods. The failure of historic townscape projects to take hold in the United States as they have in European cities, particularly in Great Britain, is perplexing.

The popular preservation movements of the 1970s—the back-to-the city efforts and Main Street revitalization projects—involved beautifying the landscape without a conscious recognition that it was as much a part of the historic character of an area as its architecture. While urban pioneers painstakingly restored Victorian row houses and glorified the virtues of urban neighborhoods, the issues they claimed as their own were more classic architectural issues of appropriate building preservation technology and design. Rear decks of wood and brick patios often replaced historic back stoops and small backyard gardens. Cobblestone and brick walks and alleys were designed for spaces that had never had any pavement more grand than unornamented concrete or asphalt.

Telephone lines were sent underground or to the rear parking areas although clearly visible in the early-twentieth-century photographs used in facade restorations. And lighting standards and benches, more grand than anything that ever existed historically, have been installed in numerous downtowns to create a false impression of a more prosperous and ornate commercial landscape than ever existed.

A recent challenge has been to develop cultural landscape design guidelines for the new *Brown v. Board of Education* National Historic Site in Topeka, Kansas, without attempting to beautify the neighborhood of the historically African American Monroe School beyond the character of the industrial/commercial/residential neighborhood that existed prior to the 1954 Supreme Court decision. The danger of overenhancing cultural landscapes is a pitfall that is difficult to avoid, since it is sometimes hard to distinguish between necessary visitor and resident amenities and false embellishments.

Tourism as an Opportunity and a Threat

Visitor destinations, such as the Monroe School of the *Brown v. Board of Education* National Historic Site neighborhood, illustrate both the opportunities and the threats that tourism presents for a cultural landscape. Tourism has long been regarded as a plus for historic preservation. Preserving a building or a landscape provides educational and recreational benefits that can justify the costs of acquisition, preservation treatment, and operation. The associated economic benefits of preservation also have been well documented by the National Trust and statewide preservation organizations such as the Preservation Alliance of Virginia. In rural or isolated areas, tourism-related preservation provides an enhanced economic base, jobs for unskilled and semiskilled workers, and opportunities for local entrepreneurs. In urban areas, tourism can help expand an economic base or compensate for a shift away from traditional industries and economies without destroying the resources associated with earlier historical periods.

Although cultural tourism or ecotourism may provide an alternative to loss of historic buildings and landscapes, the landscapes of tourism have also faced increased economic, visual, and social pressures that threaten their inherent natural and cultural values. In many communities, the result has been dramatically increased real estate values that have excluded many local people from buying property and that have presented the elderly and families not involved in tourism with increased property taxes and loss of traditional occupations. A significant number of traditional coastal communities where families have made their living on the water for generations have undergone a complete transition to a tourist-based economy in less than a generation. Now jet skis instead of crab pots can be found in Chesapeake Bay yards as well as abandoned work-boats unable to afford high-priced dock space eagerly claimed by pleasure craft. Similar scenarios occur in Vermont and Rocky Mountain landscapes where the development associated with the snow ski industry impinges on the landscape that supports tourism. In addition, the economic benefits of late-twentieth-century tourism were as likely to be realized by outside speculators or a few well-positioned local families in many tourist locales as by the entire community.

The edges and approaches of historic and scenic landscapes are especially vulnerable to commercial, second-home, and residential development. The landscape horror stories about the effects of tourism on culturally distinct communities such as the Lancaster County area of Pennsylvania are well known, but they continue to worsen as an affluent and increasingly suburban population seeks respite in rural areas.

In areas adjacent to historic sites or within historic communities, visitation may also create a secondary market for support industries such as lodging and eating establishments, gas and convenience stores, and the associated retail development of gift shops, apparel stores, and galleries. In addition, developers of outdoor recreational parks, second-home developments, retirement communities, and retail complexes are often attracted to such locales. Williamsburg, Virginia, for example, has been a magnet for such development: major discount shopping centers, an outdoor recreational theme park, and a water park appear near its edges, in addition to extensive residential development and a growing number of restaurants and hotels in nearby locations. Whether the traditional or scenic landscape that attracts visitors absorbs a new fast-food restaurant sited in a typical roadside strip or several of its historic houses are adapted as bed-and-breakfast inns, the cultural landscape changes as a result of increased tourism.

At the same time, however, tourism must be acknowledged as an effective incentive for preservation. It often motivates property owners and investors to appreciate and care for historic architectural and landscape resources, albeit with considerably altered landscape settings and surroundings.

Increasingly, visitors to historic sites comment on adjacent lands. The guest book at the entrance to the Homestead National Monument of America near

Beatrice, Nebraska, contains several visitor comments critical of adjacent sub-division development visible from trails through the monument. And yet that suburban development is the logical outgrowth of the Homestead Act that the monument symbolizes and commemorates. The monument's managers, through its general management plan and cultural landscape report process, are seeking interpretive solutions as alternatives to visual screening to encourage an under-standing of the history of land development in the United States and the asso-ciations between historic westward migration and contemporary land sub-division trends.

Many historic sites and historic communities have taken steps to define and protect their historic viewsheds. As early as 1971 historic Nantucket, Massa-chusetts, began to consider the significance of the entire island and not merely buildings. Both buildings and landscape were addressed in the 1978 design hand-book for its Historic District Commission. Two historic presidential homes, Monticello and Mount Vernon, undertook historic viewshed studies in the 1980s. At approximately the same time, many communities realized the impor-tance of their landscapes to tourism and quality of life and began to develop design guidelines. Among the best of this genre are *Change in the Connecticut River Valley: A Design Manual for Conservation and Development* and *The Town of Leesburg, Virginia, H-2 Corridor Design Guidelines*.[26]

Tourist visitation can easily overburden a historic landscape. It may neces-sitate such extensive rehabilitation measures as widening or straightening en-trance roads to accommodate tour buses, developing parking areas, or creating visitor facilities within historic boundaries. Public access can result in soil com-paction that threatens historic plant material, an increased potential for vandal-ism, or even the theft of small-scale features. Visitation may also increase the need for accessibility and require additional alterations and accommodations to meet the needs of all visitors when the historic materials, slope, or dimensions of garden paths and park trails cannot meet accessibility requirements.

Increasingly, large historic sites and state and national park landscapes that support tourism play a major role in open space and rural land protection. In Virginia's suburbanizing Henrico and Hanover Counties, sites designated as national battlefields may be the only remaining large parcels of undeveloped land in a region that once was almost entirely rural. The same may be true of the Shenandoah Valley, where battlefield protection is receiving national, state, and local attention. These battlefield landscapes may ultimately be appreciated as much for their open space value as for their historic associations as hallowed ground. Similarly, our lakeshores and seashores may represent the nation's last substantial areas of undeveloped coastline. Lighthouse stations in the Upper Great Lakes or on North Carolina's Outer Banks give an indication not only of historic light-saving operations and awe-inspiring vertical architecture but also glimpses of seaside life before ocean-view condominiums and sprawling triple-decked beach palaces were the predominant waterfront development pattern. Jimmy Carter's peanut farm in Plains, Georgia, which is being preserved by the NPS, may ultimately be one of a handful of surviving agrarian landscapes that represents everyday rural life in the South in the early twentieth century.

Another issue affecting historic landscapes attractive to tourists is the effect of preservation management. There is the risk that preserved landscapes that were once vital and dynamic may become static, since the process of preservation can create artifact and artifice out of places, systems, and even communities.[27] Places that no longer serve their original purpose, such as historic forts, decommissioned lighthouses, and presidential birthplaces, are preserved because of their value as artifacts with historic associations. In the 1970s Alvin Toffler predicted in his book *Future Shock* the need to set aside a few time warps: places that would reveal what life was like in the past. It may well be that the only places that can truly fill this role in the future will be the places where landscapes have been consciously and deliberately protected from development because of their economic potential as visitor destinations. Even so, thoughtful preservationists consider that managing a landscape may come at the price of losing the inherent historic character of places when landscape change is restricted and the daily activities, sights, sounds, and smells associated with them during their periods of significance no longer take place.

The Treatment of Cultural Landscapes: Technical and Procedural Issues

Having provided excellent guidance on documenting and evaluating landscapes, the NPS again took the lead in landscape preservation in 1989 by shifting the focus of its cultural landscape initiative to the *treatment* of cultural landscapes. Continuing its earlier policy of approaching landscapes in a manner parallel to that already in place for architecture, the Park Service began to develop a landscape preservation brief as part of its technical brief series and to adapt the Secretary's Standards as the basis for national guidelines for the treatment of cultural landscapes.

The resulting NPS publication, *Preservation Brief 36: Protecting Cultural*

Suburban development. Historic rural landscapes are especially vulnerable to suburban residential development. (J. Timothy Keller, FASLA)

Landscapes and Guidelines for the Treatment of Cultural Landscapes, provided the first professional guidance for planning, designing, and implementing landscape preservation projects.[28] The document, which appeared in an approved NPS publication in 1996 after having been available in draft form to many historic landscape professionals for several years, is applicable to diverse cultural landscapes, including both nationally significant designed works of landscape architecture and vernacular farmsteads. The guidelines articulate what is essential to protect, what can be removed or allowed to disappear, and how landscape change can be managed. They also provide a national basis for acknowledging that some landscapes can absorb little or no change at all, whereas others can absorb considerable change in specific places. They were intended to guide decisions about treating a wide variety of landscape features, from shuffleboard and horseshoe courts in urban parks, to bridle trails in rural battlefield parks, to roads and highways of the early automotive age. Highly illustrative, the guidelines have been instrumental in articulating appropriate approaches to decision making regarding cultural landscapes. The guidelines define preservation, rehabilitation, restoration, and reconstruction treatments for landscapes and provide examples of each. There is also guidance for each step of the process, from documentation through implementation to keeping maintenance and treatment records.

As might be expected, the most frequent application of these NPS publications to date has been in the preparation of cultural landscape reports (CLRs) for NPS properties. NPS managers, historical landscape architects, and their consultants have adhered to guidelines, models, and precedents for landscape preservation practice first disseminated in 1992. Examples from several CLRs that had been completed or were in progress during the development of the guidelines were included in the illustrations for the publication. Illustrations from completed or in-progress landscape treatment projects outside the NPS, such as garden reconstruction at Thomas Jefferson's Monticello, also appeared.

The treatment of vegetation has proven to be a major concern associated with the development of landscape treatment plans. The value of original vegetation is a complex issue that historical landscape architects, arborists, and cultural resource managers must consider at many historic sites. At Thomas Jefferson's Poplar Forest, his rural retreat in Bedford County, Virginia, the treatment and ultimately the fate of historic poplars dating from the period of Jefferson are still being considered and debated. Although these mature trees no longer represent the appearance they displayed when Jefferson was in residence, they represent a tangible link with the former president.[29] Some believe that there is a need to propagate new stock and to replace the trees as soon as possible, whereas others think that a phased replacement over time would be most appropriate.

Issues of mature vegetation and vegetation that no longer represent the period of significance confront managers at most historic sites. Large white oaks that witnessed the death and destruction of the Seven Days Battle at the Gaines Mill Unit of the Richmond National Battlefield Park were only saplings during that battle. At the battlefield and at similar sites the witness trees stand in silent testimony to the events of the past. Yet they create a false impression of a battlefield scene that was largely an open field in 1862, with low vegetation in riparian areas. At the Fort Larned National Historic Site near Larned, Kansas, the current pristine parade ground reflects a military grandeur absent when drilling soldiers trampled the native prairie on the western frontier to expose dry, dusty patches of bare earth. Even replanting the parade in buffalo grass will never replicate the worn appearance of the mid-nineteenth-century fort when daily drills were the rule. Only an intensive living history component could re-create the nineteenth-century character of the fort. At historic sites such as these, landscape managers must weigh authenticity and integrity of the landscape with visitor comfort and convenience and pragmatic maintenance needs. Other vegetative issues include the appropriate response to invasive exotic plant materials with historic associations to a site, such as the *poncira tri-foliata* that threatens the survival of significant indigenous plants at the Arkansas Post National Memorial in Gillett.

Methodological issues and philosophical questions regarding landscape preservation are intertwined with preservation treatment. At the new Tallgrass National Preserve in Chase County, Kansas, for example, both cultural and natural resource managers grapple with the conflicts inherent in continuing agricultural practices such as viable ranching with the need to protect the tallgrass prairie. One current proposal includes reintroducing the bison that predominated prior to Euro-American occupation of the site. Ranching is a historic land use related to the site's significance, but management practices oriented primarily to livestock operations have contributed to erosion of both natural riparian areas and watering ponds. But removing cattle altogether would have a dramatic visual effect on the cultural landscape. The reintroduction of bison would symbolize a visual return to the preranching period, produce visual incongruities and resource conflicts, and introduce a major visual change.

At some sites, original vegetation may affect the health or safety of landscape users or may have been an inappropriate choice for the site or its climate. The parking lot in an orchard at Curry Village in Yosemite National Park that was part of an Olmsted Brothers park design illustrates that point. The orchard has become a modern maintenance and safety hazard, attracting coyotes and bees to a heavily visited area. Hybrid, nonfruit-bearing species may be appropriate as a substitute for the original. At the Herbert Hoover National Historic Site in West Branch, Iowa, the decision was made after consultation with the original designer that substitute plant materials could be used at the Hoover gravesite because the existing yews and *arbor vitae* did not fulfill the intent of the original design. Consequently, the gravesite rehabilitation plan called for introducing substitute species that were better suited to the site and that would require less maintenance to produce the "fluffy, natural evergreen" appearance planned originally.[30]

Substitutions or changes from historical documentation may be appropriate for other reasons when planning landscape treatments. In our current litigious and safety-conscious climate, it would be dangerous to preserve or restore obsolete playground equipment that would not meet contemporary standards and codes in an unmonitored outdoor setting. Similarly, it would be inappropriate to reconstruct a floral swastika design that existed in an urban park in the 1920s.

Perhaps one of the most difficult judgments is determining treatments for

Lincoln Highway, Iowa. As the first transcontinental highway in the United States, Lincoln offered travelers the first automotive route between New York and California. Today both government agencies and private preservation organizations are documenting the highway's surviving historic features and exploring preservation planning strategies for a historic highway threatened by urban sprawl, modern highway standards, and the increased speed and scale of modern traffic. (Iowa State University Library, Special Collections Department)

landscape features that date from before or after the landscape's period of significance. Although there is currently considerable sentiment for preserving "layered" landscapes—that is, those that reflect the evolution or progression of a site through more than one period—treatment plans may vary in their approach to landscape features from different periods or that relate to different themes or contexts. The NPS has been criticized for its destruction of the twentieth-century grotto at Mission Nuestra Senora de la Purisima Concepcion in San Antonio because it did not relate to either the Spanish colonial period or the early-twentieth-century Colonial Revival restoration effort. The Texas Historical Commission objected because the grotto possessed local significance for its later period. In other parks, particularly Civil War battlefield parks, the NPS has been denounced for preserving resources that were developed after the period of significance.

Through the 1990s cultural landscape treatment increasingly has been considered as part of an overall resource protection and planning process. Cultural landscape reports for the Yosemite Valley of Yosemite National Park, for example, have had to consider sensitive and complex issues such as circulation

Mission San José, San Antonio Missions National Historical Park, Texas. The cultural land-scape report for this mission acknowledged the significance of twentieth-century Colonial Revival preservation efforts as well as its Spanish colonial heritage. (Land and Community Associates, Charlottesville, Virginia)

and transportation conflicts in the often-congested Yosemite Valley, as well as the philosophical question of natural versus cultural resource protection and interpretation.

At the turn of the twenty-first century, the *Guidelines for the Treatment of Cultural Landscapes* have been largely untested for applicability outside the realm of NPS property, historic park, and grounds restoration and rehabilitation projects funded by state and local governments and nonprofit preservation organizations. The applicability and compliance issues likely to arise as the guidelines are used in evaluating CDBG and TEA-21 enhancement projects will provide serious tests of their usefulness in a very different context. If the landscape guidelines are interpreted strictly by state historic preservation offices and the Advisory Council on Historic Preservation, their effects will be widespread and controversial. It is likely that the guidelines could have an even greater impact than the decades-old standards for historic buildings and structures. When federally funded civic improvements such as cobblestone alleys, brick sidewalks, and Victorian light standards are disallowed for a downtown revitalization project in a National Register historic district because they will create a false sense of history for a landscape that possessed concrete walks, gravel alleys, and early-twentieth-century lamps during its period of significance, the guidelines will be one of the most all-encompassing and far-reaching documents in the history of preservation in the United States.

Conclusion

Landscape features are sometimes fragile, transitory, and vulnerable. Yet, distinct, recognizable landscapes often endure for centuries with obvious layers reflecting decades or centuries of use. Almost unimagined technological innovations will make future preservation decision making even more complicated than at present, since there will be more and more possible alternatives for landscape preservation treatments. Only budget constraints and lack of documentation limit treatment options. However, preservationists need to be wise enough to understand that interpretations, attitudes, values, and perceptions change as time passes and new information becomes available.

Historic landscapes need not experience yet another physical change each time there is a perceptual or attitudinal change among historic preservation professionals. Landscape information can be imparted to visitors in a variety of ways; that is landscape interpretation's role. In many ways, twentieth-century landscape preservation was born of an ability and desire to experience and read the landscape and decipher and trace its transitions and continuities through time. The writings of J. B. Jackson, Kevin Lynch, Grady Clay, and others influenced late-twentieth-century landscape preservationists to observe, record, and analyze landscapes as products of their time and as tangible evidence of cultural traditions and adaptations. Despite these influences, landscape preservation to date has concentrated more on physical treatment than on landscape interpretation through planning treatments that have added a new layer to an already layered landscape or subtracted or modified layers considered insignificant. The extensive landscape documentation assembled for most sites remains archived or bound in reports, as yet not shared with the public. For a decade, landscape preservationists have been talking about landscape interpretation, but the challenge of effective and appropriate landscape interpretation still remains to be explored.

Eventually, the landscape treatments inspired by the landscape preservation initiatives of the late twentieth century will be recognizable as products of their time, just as clearly as the early-twentieth-century landscape restorations are now seen as part of a larger Colonial Revival movement. Their sources are well documented in the bureaucratized and linear process of the NPS cultural landscape initiative, although they were inspired and promoted initially by private sector practitioners and professors of landscape architecture and landscape history. Self-conscious and self-celebratory, the landscape preservation movement has inserted itself into historic preservation as an integral, but obvious, add-on set of concerns. No longer totally dominated by building bias, preservation has embraced the landscape. But integrating landscape preservation back into a larger historic preservation context, along with effective landscape interpretation, remains to be accomplished.

The Natural Environment

The eighteenth-century farm on which artist Andrew Wyeth painted more than a thousand scenes of southeastern Pennsylvania landscapes and rural life was acquired in late 1999 by the Brandywine River Conservancy, a private land trust, from its elderly owners through a creative estate-planning transaction. Other land conservation organizations across America have protected culturally significant rural and natural landscapes.

Recently, one of a few surviving historic covered bridges in North Carolina and its surrounding old-growth hardwood forest, mountain laurel, and stream, with remnant populations of rare aquatic species, were acquired, and the bridge was restored by two private land trusts. Other land trusts have protected many more historic landmarks and archaeological sites across the continent.

Thousands of acres of antebellum rice plantations and live oak–bordered historic roads near Charleston, South Carolina, with landscapes distinguished by maritime forests, salt marshes, and barrier island beaches, have been protected by the Low Country Open Land Trust. Likewise, other private land trusts have conserved many hundreds of historic farmsteads, plantations, ranches, and other features of America's cultural and natural heritage.

These are only a few of the many instances in which private land trusts have protected land enriched with both natural and cultural heritage resources. Hundreds of others could be cited: Native American archaeological sites; historic canals, mills, and industrial sites; battlefields; and historic roadways. Twenty-five years ago the boundaries between nonprofit historic preservation and land conservation organizations were clear. Now those lines are blurred and have often been eliminated completely. This chapter raises important issues about whether the agencies representing these closely related interests should engage and support one another in more formal ways, and how. However, any discussion of these issues must begin with a clear understanding of the history of the natural areas protection movement itself.

Braun Old Stone House, Rowan County, North Carolina. A donated conservation easement protects the 22-acre landscape of forest and meadow enveloping this 1766 farmstead. The historic landscape surrounding it was preserved by a permanent easement agreement between the local Rowan Museum and the Land Trust for Central North Carolina. (Staff photo, Land Trust for Central North Carolina)

Growth of Concern for Natural Environments

Public and private efforts to protect natural environments have vastly increased in the United States over the past thirty years. Since the original "Earth Day" public awakening in 1970, America has moved beyond placing full faith and primary reliance on government agencies to protect a relatively few and widely spaced, publicly owned, natural places such as parks and wildlife refuges. The advent of private land trusts and conservancies in America has seen the establishment of thousands of nature preserves and has fundamentally changed the natural resource conservation programs of government agencies at all levels. These private land conservation organizations are the products of an increased environmental consciousness and the widespread and deep financial support and activism of millions of people. The changes and accomplishments are the results of a pervasive shift in public awareness and concern for protecting natural environments.

In a span of less than ten years, beginning in the mid-1960s, landmark legislation for environmental protection marked an awakening comprehension by the general public and politicians that serious deterioration of environmental resources could be arrested only by fundamental changes in government policies and programs. That period saw the enactment by Congress of the first National Wilderness Preservation System (1964), the Eastern Wilderness Act (1975), the Land and Water Conservation Fund to finance acquisition of public lands for conservation and recreation (1964), the Endangered Species Preservation Acts (1966 and 1973), the Wild and Scenic Rivers Act (1968), the National Environmental Policy Act (1970), the National Forests Management Act (1976), the Clean Water Act (1973), and the Clean Air Act (1970). The Environmental Protection Agency was created by executive branch reorganization (1970), and state legislatures followed by enacting similar laws and initiating environmental protection programs at the state and local levels.

Nongovernmental Organizations

Because of differences in the nature of the resource, it is important to understand what nongovernmental organizations do and how they do it. Their organizational structure, problems, and methods are similar to those of historic preservation organizations. But there is one important difference. The methods and purposes of natural resource conservation organizations are based on science rather than culture.

Nongovernmental organizations operating on the national and international scale are largely responsible for the American public's awareness of and sensitivity to the values and fragility of natural environments. Revolutionary changes in media techniques and technology have made clear that the country's natural environments are in jeopardy and that public action is required for environmental protection. That lesson has been underscored repeatedly by environmental disasters: urban development in the wrong places, elimination of rural landscapes and natural habitats, fouling of streams and other water bodies, deterioration of air quality, public health threats from pollution, plummeting populations of once-common wildlife, and accelerating rates of extinction among native plant and animal species.

There is a widely perceived crisis that natural areas and undeveloped rural lands in general are threatened by the development activities of mankind throughout America and worldwide. Between widespread habitat destruction and the threatened extinction of thousands of animal and plant species, the public has come to realize, and to accept at the political level, that time for maintaining the integrity and existence of nature is running out. Consequently, there is a sense of urgency to protect places of nature and beloved green spaces before the opportunity is lost forever.

As has been the case with the historic preservation movement, perhaps the most influential factor in the rise of modern land conservation efforts in America has been the loss and destruction of the resource itself. Just as we have lost thousands of historic buildings, structures, and archaeological resources, so have we also eliminated vast numbers of the continent's native plant and animal species. Virtually every species eliminated from the United States since the Ice Age has been pushed into extinction by humans. These include more than 100,000 species of plants and animals. Of the approximately 200,000 total species of plants and animals of all classes believed present in the United States, about 20,900 are vascular plants (15,990), vertebrate animals (2,497), or "higher" invertebrate animals (2,410). Of this total, about 32 percent are presently considered at risk of extinction and 1 percent are presumed extinct.[1]

Whereas only 1 percent of America's flowering plants and vertebrate animal species vanished in the first three centuries of European occupation of the continent, now an estimated 16 percent (more than 4,500 species) are in immediate danger of extinction and another 15 percent are considered vulnerable to elimination. Altogether, one-third of the plant and animal species in the United States are now at risk.

Of the threats to survival of species, habitat destruction—not altogether unlike the destruction and loss of historic urban neighborhoods—is the most prevalent. It has attributed to the decline of at least 85 percent of all endangered plants and animals in the United States. The spread of nonnative or alien plant and animal species—again, comparable to the spread of corporate architecture to inappropriate locations—is a most serious threat. Other contributing disturbances to all populations, including our own human habitations, are air and water pollution from pesticides, fertilizers, overharvesting, and disease.

Three young sciences—conservation biology, landscape ecology, and restoration ecology—have provided new knowledge and perspectives that are dramatically changing efforts to protect and manage both natural and settled landscape areas. In the late 1980s through the 1990s, there was widespread realization that survival of rare and endangered species could not be accomplished simply by acquiring and saving relatively few and widely scattered nature preserves. We became aware of the consequences of ecological fragmentation. Instead, much more difficult and challenging design strategies had to be employed for protecting functioning natural ecosystems. Those strategies have to combine natural areas and areas of human habitation. Instead of setting aside relatively small or linear preserves, conservationists have shifted their approach to trying to protect and restore larger landscape areas that include both natural

Middleburg Plantation, Charleston, South Carolina. The Low Country Open Land Trust of Charleston protects this antebellum estate with a conservation easement that includes the oldest surviving plantation house in South Carolina (ca. 1699), a rice mill, commissary, stable, toll house, kitchen, slave cemetery, and historic rice fields along the Cooper River. (Staff photo by Cunningham, Low Country Open Land Trust)

communities and human settlements. As a sideline, one has to ask whether there are not parallels in the world of cultural resources.[2]

Private Organizations Dedicated to Environmental Protection

An astounding array of private, but publicly supported, organizations have led the campaign to build greater awareness of environmental issues and rally public responses. They number in the dozens at the national level, and each one attempts to carve out a distinct role for itself. Among them are The Nature Conservancy (TNC), the Sierra Club, the National Wildlife Federation, the World Wildlife Fund, the National Audubon Society, the Environmental Defense Fund, the Natural Resource Defense Council, the Defenders of Wildlife, the National Parks and Conservation Association, and the American Farmland Trust. Other citizen groups focus on and target specific issues of protecting and restoring clean water and air, pesticide control, wildlife populations, and hazardous waste control. Interestingly, the same proliferation of specialist groups has happened within the historic preservation movement.

Prior to the 1970s a few midwestern states, where native prairies and oak savannas had been nearly eliminated, pioneered some of the country's first state government-supported nature preserves programs. In New England numerous local townships had established land conservation committees and local nature preserves. Otherwise, efforts to save natural areas were primarily within the auspices of the National Park Service and state and occasional metropolitan park systems. A smattering of sanctuaries were owned and managed by local community groups, wildlife preservation organizations, universities, or private individual initiatives. Other public lands, such as recreational parks, wildlife refuges, and government-owned forests provided de facto conservation.

No single environmental organization has been more effective and influential in focusing public attention and rallying public support for the protection of America's ecological resources than The Nature Conservancy. That group rose to preeminence over the past thirty years, after creating an unparalleled alliance of scientists, business managers, and resource protection planners to build the world's most aggressive and accomplished land preservation program. TNC grew out of initiatives in 1951 by the Ecological Society of America to set aside remnant natural areas where ecological processes were as yet undisturbed. Under a new team of entrepreneurial administrators, TNC beginning in the early 1970s adopted land protection techniques first employed by private land conservancies in the New England states and launched an extraordinarily successful program to preserve the biological diversity of America.

TNC has engineered the protection of more than ten million acres of natural areas in North America and amassed a privately managed system of more than 1,400 nature sanctuaries across every state of the Union. Its programs are now financially supported by more than one million members. Over the 1990s TNC expanded its preservation programs to the full American hemisphere and, as the world's largest and most successful private land conservation organization, more recently moved into the Pacific and Asia.

TNC has emphasized land conservation as a science-based decision process, with its focus on preserving biological diversity and functioning natural ecosystems. Beginning in the mid-1970s, it began establishing biological resource inventories and protection planning programs on a state-by-state basis. Within fifteen years, every state in the United States, mostly funded by state governments, and many Canadian provinces and Latin American and Caribbean countries had instituted biological conservation data banks and natural heritage protection programs under TNC guidance.

Inventories of the biological diversity of each state have been "element"-based and specifically targeted at identifying and assessing each population of rare and endangered species on sites of wildlife concentrations and exemplary sites of natural community or ecosystem types. Each "element occurrence" of every vulnerable species and more than four thousand natural community types are recorded and periodically monitored. Cumulatively, tens of thousands of sites have been surveyed and monitored. In the 1980s TNC began building its own science capacity, stationing staff scientists in its own field offices throughout the country.

The Nature Conservancy's scientific emphasis is on interpreting data for conservation purposes, including preserve planning, management, and monitoring. In coordination with eighty-five state-based natural heritage programs and conservation data centers in other countries of the American hemisphere, TNC tracks the individual populations of species of imperiled plants and animals and exemplary occurrences of natural communities.[3] The advent of sophisticated computer systems and geographic information systems has provided the capacity to maintain these dynamic inventories. The power of this combined quantitative and qualitative inventory has a profound influence on public conservation actions. The large majority of natural area protection efforts are now based on rational decisions founded on scientific knowledge.

The influence of TNC and state natural heritage programs on the academic sector also has been far-reaching. Over the past thirty years the advent of "conservation science" has made it possible to incorporate better understanding of ecological processes in the design of nature preserve systems, implementation of conservation plans, and improvement of land management. Whole new scientific disciplines have come into play, such as fire ecology; control of exotic, nonnative species; restoration ecology; and biohydrology. This innovative, applied conservation science has been accelerated by its application in nature reserves acquired by TNC. Concepts such as "ecological viability"—how big a population of a certain species must be for its survival over the long term—are applied to the design of sustainable natural refuges.

Although TNC has captured a public image focused on virtually all natural places, it has for the past two decades concentrated on more scientifically rigorous standards of preserving "biological diversity." Most of its acquisitions are for critical habitats for endangered species and larger landscape units con-

Tennessee River Gorge. The Tennessee River Gorge Trust is protecting 26 miles of the river gorge downstream from Chattanooga and includes the 450-acre Williams Island, site of rich archaeological remains of Native American occupation since 14,000 BP. (Photo by Edward Schell, Tennessee Conservationists)

taining functional ecosystems. TNC owns and maintains more than 1,400 nature sanctuaries in the United States, exceeding 1,177,000 acres, but its preferred mode is to convince government agencies to acquire more land areas for parks, wildlife refuges, wilderness areas, and preserves. The conservancy has engineered the acquisition of more than 12 million acres for conveyance to government agencies.[4]

That trend in the United States has been augmented or reinforced by two other national groups—The Conservation Fund (TCF) and the Trust for Public Land (TPL)—each originating from TNC roots. Both of these organizations acquire parks and conservation land areas and transfer them into public ownership. However, TPL has assumed a more urban focus and encourages the integration of open spaces, outdoor recreational areas, and parks as integral parts of livable and healthy human communities. From 1972 to 2000 it helped protect more than 1.2 million acres in forty-five states—ranging from public recreational areas, to urban greenways, to urban neighborhood parks and gardens.

Sibley Farm, East Montpelier, Vermont. The Vermont Land Trust protected this historic farm by purchasing the nonfarm development rights. The Preservation Trust of Vermont furnished a historic rehabilitation preservation grant to repair the barn roof. (Vermont Land Trust, Mark McEathron)

TCF is more free lance in orientation and engages in a more eclectic range of land protection projects—again, almost always as a "land broker" for a public agency. Since 1985 TCF has been involved in protecting 3.2 million acres of land nationwide, ranging from river corridors, watersheds, and historic battlefields, to urban greenways, wildlife habitat areas, and managed forest lands. Both TCF and TPL attempt to integrate land conservation and economic development goals, such as nature-based tourism.[5]

The Rise of Land Trusts in the United States

Another national trend that has profoundly changed land conservation in America is the phenomenal increase in locally based land conservation groups, commonly referred to as "land trusts." Land trusts are nonprofit, tax-exempt organizations that conserve land primarily by acquiring land or interests in land through purchase or gift. They operate in a manner similar to a local historic house museum or complex, retaining ownership of the resource.

They are governed by local volunteer boards of directors, and most have relatively small professional staffs. They are financially supported by a cumulative total of an estimated one million individual members. Most are tax-exempt charities. Though many use the same conservation methods as TNC, they primarily focus on the environmental resources of greatest importance to local communities and their surrounding regions.

The number of land trusts surged in the 1980s and 1990s, when close to two-thirds of the present number were formed. Their forerunners have existed for some decades, but only in limited numbers and concentrated in the New England. Interestingly, the Trustees of Reservations in Massachusetts, incorporated in 1891 at the beginning of the American City Beautiful and the National Parks and Monuments movements, served as the model for the British National Trust for Places of Historic Interest and Natural Beauty, that nation's largest integrated historic preservation *and* land conservation organization.[6] Land trusts originating in the northeastern United States (where per capita income and threats to the relatively few remaining natural land areas were both high) were organized by the hundreds with private funds. They continue to play crucial roles in preserving natural areas and open space lands, and they have been copied in more recent years in other regions of the country.

The recent phenomenal growth of local, regional, and statewide land trusts represents an enthusiastic public response to perceived threats to environmental resources. Though only a few dozen existed prior to the 1970s, a 2000 survey by the Land Trust Alliance noted that more than 1,200 local and regional land trusts were then currently operating in every state, a number roughly comparable to local historic preservation organizations. Approximately two-thirds were formed as citizen initiatives between 1988 and 1998. Almost one million acres of the lands protected by land trusts were protected as public parks, greenways, and wildlife refuges through partnerships with public conservation agencies or conveyance of the land to government agencies.[7]

The large majority of America's land trusts are local in their coverage, but through economies of scale many of the most successful are regional or even statewide in scope. Land trusts covering states or large regions are the Montana Land Reliance, Iowa Natural Heritage Foundation, Colorado Open Lands, Chesapeake Bay Foundation, Society for Protection of New Hampshire Forests, Vermont Land Trust, Conservation Trust for North Carolina (CTNC), Minnesota Land Trust, New Jersey Conservation Foundation, and Virginia Outdoors Foundation. States with almost comprehensive coverage by local and regional land trusts include Connecticut, Maryland, Massachusetts, North Carolina, Pennsylvania, New Hampshire, and Vermont. That trend will grow elsewhere. The trend appears to parallel the growth in statewide historic preservation revolving funds.

Other land trusts specialize in particular conservation themes or specific natural resources. Examples are the Appalachian Trail Lands Trust, Civil War Trust, Southeastern Cave Conservancy, Rocky Mountain Elk Foundation, Ice Age Park and Trail Foundation, Save the Redwoods League, Pacific Forest Trust, and New England Forestry Foundation. Still others engage in land conservation actions of relatively wide scope but have a particular area of emphasis, such as the Scenic Hudson, Southern Appalachian Highlands Conservancy, Low Country Open Land Trust in South Carolina, Big Sur Land Trust, Maine Coast Heritage Trust, Potomac Conservancy, and Jackson Hole Land Trust.

Interestingly, an increasingly number of land trusts appear to concentrate on what they can do to affect the character of rural communities and countryside, protecting regional water quality and designing limited development with open space reservations, such as the Piedmont Environmental Council and Valley (Shenandoah) Conservation Council in Virginia, the Brandywine Conservancy and Natural Lands Trust in the greater Philadelphia region, the Peconic Land Trust on Long Island, and the Chesapeake Bay Foundation. It is in this area that there appears to be a complete overlap with the more recent interest expressed by the National Trust for Historic Preservation in Smart Growth.

The success of land trusts derives from Americans' willingness to donate dollars and land for environmental protection. Citizen activism and philanthropy are honored and encouraged in our culture, and it is no secret that Americans are great "joiners." Additionally, the philanthropic example set by wealthy citizens—most notably, John D. Rockefeller Jr., who acquired land for many units of the National Park System (as well as Williamsburg, Virginia) in the first half of the twentieth century—has broadened into widespread financial support by many Americans at all levels of giving.

Tools and Techniques

Aside from straightforward land purchases for preservation, the use of conservation easements—deed restrictions that specifically prohibit land uses detrimental to environmental resource protection in perpetuity—has become the most popular and effective method of protecting natural and open spaces. They are more widely used by land trusts than by government agencies or the national land conservancies. Of the almost 6.5 million acres protected by land trusts over time, nearly 2.6 million acres were protected by conservation easements. By the end of 2000 land trusts had secured more than 11,570 easement agreements with landowners. The increased use of conservation easements continues to accelerate, encouraged by federal and state laws that provide substantial reductions in federal and state income and estate and inheritance taxes, and sometimes local property taxes. These benefits came about largely through the intense, widespread lobbying efforts of the national Land Trust Alliance, the Piedmont Environmental Council of Virginia, and others in the late 1990s. It is noteworthy that the use of easements for land protection purposes is no different, as a technique, than the use of easements (by whatever legal name, technically speaking) for historic preservation purposes. In both cases the primary advantage is the easement, which is far more advantageous taxwise and less expensive cashwise, than the acquisition of the full fee simple title.

Conservation easements have been honed by land trusts as an alternative to acquisition of full property titles; in this respect, they are often more attractive to private property owners and local governments. Although land affected by the restrictions against intensive development may qualify for present-use property taxation, properties encumbered by easements still contribute to the local tax base and remain in private ownership. However, many land trusts prefer to own a fee simple interest in property because it is easier and less complicated to monitor than land under easement. Ownership of land encumbered by easement agreements is essentially divided. The private owner continues to enjoy possession and restricted use of the property under easement, but the organization holding the easement has permanent responsibility for surveillance and enforcement of the restrictions. Few land trusts have raised sufficient funds to monitor and enforce easements adequately, and the rate of violations will likely increase as land ownership passes on to a new generation of occupants.

America's land trusts will continue to grow in number, geographic coverage, strength, and achievements over the next several decades. The land trust movement is where the action and soul of landscape conservation will reside in the United States. It is through this grassroots initiative that we will see the greatest land conservation accomplishments over the next thirty years, at both the local community and the regional levels.

The Overlap of Natural and Cultural Resource Preservation

The land has shaped all of human culture, and people have shaped the land. In temperate North America, like most of the world, no land area has been un-

Ohio River/Erie Canal Towpath Trail. The Trust for Public Land has partnered with the NPS by securing numerous purchase options to protect the towpath for the Cuyahoga Valley National Recreation Area. (Photo by Tom Jones, TPL)

affected by centuries of use and impact by humans. All of America's landscapes hold the imprints of human occupation. Modern Americans are linked to their natural environments just as their historic predecessors were linked to the land before us. Consequently, all efforts to protect land areas, even when motivated by objectives to preserve pieces of the natural landscape and ecological resources, also serve to protect parts of our cultural heritage.

The ecologist and the amateur naturalist have both come to understand and to read the cultural history of the natural landscape. No natural area is so remote or so wild not to retain vestiges of human presence and change. *Every natural area that is preserved also saves a historic site*. Ecologists have largely discarded the notion that there truly existed any "forest primeval" since the settlement of America by humans. Enormous areas of the continent's forests and grasslands were essentially cultural landscapes that were profoundly shaped by human actions ever since forests reestablished themselves northward behind the retreating continental glaciers more than ten thousand years ago. The pre-European human population of America regularly set fire to millions of acres of grasslands and forest areas, and cleared other tens of thousands of acres for agriculture. The first European explorers and colonists found the remnants of these human-changed landscapes everywhere, even though the pestilence and pandemics unleashed by that European invasion had already exterminated most Native Americans. Some ethnohistorians estimate that the Native American

Pisgah Covered Bridge, North Carolina. One of only two surviving covered bridges in North Carolina, this structure was preserved by the local Land Trust for Central North Carolina and the Piedmont Land Conservancy through a land donation conservation easement and restoration. Other partners in this project were the North Carolina Zoological Park, the North Carolina Department of Transportation, and the land donor. (Land Trust for Central North Carolina)

population of North America collapsed from as many as twelve to eighteen million in the year 1500 to fewer than one million by the late 1700s, when the first waves of European settlers expanded westward beyond the Appalachians.[8]

The European colonists found vast portions of America's forests and prairies that still retained the open conditions maintained by frequent burning conducted by the original human occupants. Over the course of the past five hundred years and under the impact of ever-increasing human populations and technologies, the effects of humans have so completely influenced the American landscape that essentially no land area lacks human-induced disturbances and evidence of use.

Indeed, there is controversy among land preservationists as to what is the appropriate "place in time" in which nature preserves should be maintained—a problem that finds its parallel in the restoration of historic buildings. Even if the often ubiquitous invasions of exotic species of plants and animals that were imported by humans could somehow be contained, how can dynamic natural ecosystems be "managed" back to some prehuman natural condition? What would be the "proper" vegetative composition? What would be the appropriate "natural" community type? What would be the truly "natural" condition and appearance if unaffected by human use and climate changes?

Managers of public lands and private nature preserves wrestle with these questions in their decisions for ecosystem management, as do historic preservationists, who are often confronted with the question of which earlier period is the most important to preserve. In the real world, however, we must be content to arrest totally "unnatural" land uses and save those parts of the landscape that still exist in relatively natural conditions. The best that can be accomplished is to bring forests back within their historic range of conditions, and even that is a daunting challenge. Philosophically, the concept is not that much of a departure from the "adaptive use" espoused by the historic preservation community.

There has been continuing and contentious public debate over the validity of publicly declared wilderness areas—large-scale preserves of wild land in which all human influence is eliminated. These uninhabited areas, from which all earlier human settlements have been removed, are a unique cultural concept: that of the "original" natural garden or "forest primeval," outside of human history and time, that largely forbid human uses.[9] The concept of wilderness areas is one of inviolate natural areas as they might have appeared at the dawn of human civilization. But in reality, most wilderness areas bear some impacts of past human use and require substantial levels of human management to restore and maintain their natural ecosystems.[10] Nevertheless, the national wilderness system does provide a land bank of large-scale reserves that permit both nature preservation and the recovery of largely natural ecosystems. Designated wilderness areas may best be appreciated as large and essentially wild places, but in the same continuum with the smallest natural areas and urban green spaces, where nature also finds a home.[11] Therein is the essential truth best articulated by Henry Thoreau in declaring that "in Wildness is the preservation of the World," for *wild*ness (as opposed to wilderness) can be found anywhere, even in a city.[12]

Another pioneering conservationist, Aldo Leopold, observed that the love for and sense of sacredness in nature can be found most readily in those common places with which we are most familiar. In those truths are rooted the efforts by land conservationists to protect natural places wherever they can survive.[13] Is it, perhaps, the same underlying urge that tells us we must protect the original architectural and townscape set piece such as Williamsburg?

In most of the American landscape the legacy of human past lives on, both in us and in the land around us. We are linked to the land—past, present, and future. A better understanding of those connections will make us better stewards of the land.

Cultural Resources in Natural Settings: Common Ground

It is unlikely that there is a single "natural area" in North America that lacks signs of human culture and human imprints. Even if the flotsam and jetsam of twentieth-century human occupation and visitation could be removed, there seldom exists a natural landscape of any size that does not have some signs of human use and manipulation. In "reading the landscape," ecologists become historians. Everywhere in the natural landscapes are signs of human habitation: roads and trails, canals and mills, building sites, wells and fences, forest clearings and old field succession, bridges and fords, cemeteries and shrines, ruins and vestiges. Ecologists proficient in "reading" the human influences of even the most mature forest communities recognize that the composition and structure of those ecosystems have been fundamentally affected by past human use.[14] Like an autobiography, landscapes are a record of our human past. These landscapes and natural resources have been influenced by human settlement patterns, movements, economy, and leisure activities. Today they reflect both past and current values and activities, both good and bad.[15]

This is where the interests of private land trusts and historic preservationists converge. Until recently historic preservation efforts for the most part concentrated on protecting and restoring the built environment, principally the structures of human residence, commerce, and industry. Only in the 1980s did they begin to expand the concept of historic districts from urban to rural landscapes. Clearly, land trusts are protecting landscapes that are both naturally and culturally important. More often than not, protected natural areas and rural lands are part of the historic context for the human environment. Thus, rural historic districts are frequently the same kinds of landscapes that land trusts often focus on. As a result, land trusts are protecting cultural and historic resources in practically every one of their land protection projects.

Although the primary objectives of most land trusts are to preserve ecological resources and places of natural beauty, our projects extend to concurrently protecting the cultural resources present on the land. For example, the Conservation Trust for North Carolina has thus far protected more than 22,000 acres, primarily associated with its protection project for the Blue Ridge Parkway scenic and natural corridor. In every tract protected are the remnants of old homesteads and roads and trails. We find the ruins of homes and farms, evidence of past timbering operations, and traces of historic human uses everywhere. In many other places preserved by CTNC, functioning farmsteads and rural land uses are protected from being overwhelmed by modern urban and suburban development. The North Carolina Coastal Land Trust and the Low Country Open Land Trust in the Charleston, South Carolina, area are protecting natural areas and scenic country roadways associated with the historic plantations on the rivers and estuaries of the coastal region. The Research Triangle and Piedmont Land Conservancies in North Carolina are protecting natural forests along streams, in which are found historic canals and abandoned iron foundries and gristmills of eighteenth- and nineteenth-century communities, and the occasional National Register historic country home. The Land Trust for Central North Carolina is purposefully acquiring permanent conservation easements over historic farmlands and plantations along the Yadkin and Pee Dee Rivers and their tributaries, frequently enveloping National Register houses and archaeological sites.

These blended interests in natural and cultural resource preservation are increasingly replicated by other land trusts across America. The New Mexico Heritage Preservation Alliance works with a variety of environmental, farm, ranch, and land trusts. The Maryland Historical Trust and the Maryland Environmental Trust coordinate their work on easements and solicit joint gifts of protective easements. A regional preservation group, Adirondack Archiectural Heritage in New York, has recently received an award from the Adirondack Council, the chief conservation group for the Adirondack region. In Virginia, a dozen "Rural Heritage Districts" have been designated by the commonwealth's Board of Historic Resources. These areas are thought of as living landscapes that are both productive and culturally distinctive places. They vary from 1,100 to 25,000 acres. The rural character and beauty of all these districts derive from a blend of their natural and cultural landscape attributes. Their natural and pastoral scenes are at least as important as their historic structures to the character and beauty of the countryside.

Historically and culturally significant landscape areas are often nominated to the National Register of Historic Places out of combined conservation and preservation objectives. Some are very large landscapes; the Lake Landing historic district in northeastern North Carolina, for instance, exceeds thirty thousand acres.

Since political acceptance of land-use regulations based on the states' police power on any large scale in rural areas of the country is generally unlikely, to say the least, protection of the rural cultural and natural heritage can be accomplished in the long run only by employing long-term land-use management agreements with private property owners. That is precisely what conservation easements can do. Successful resource protection programs for large landscapes thus require a viable combination of economic incentives, public education, and voluntary conservation management agreements, along with such restrictions on incompatible development as are acceptable to the local communities. Clearly, long-term protection requires integrated, well-coordinated efforts not only by historic preservation and land conservation organizations, but by public agencies and local communities as well.

Overlapping Interests:
A Problem and an Opportunity

With increasing frequency, land trusts arrange and accept conservation easements on environmentally important properties that also possess, by the accepted norms, "historical" significance. By the same token, nonprofit or government historic preservation organizations often accept preservation easements on historic properties that also contain important natural resources and open space or scenic landscapes. Typically these are highly valued by the local community as a whole, but by separate constituencies within it. To the extent that a kind of separatist approach still exists—and it is improving here and there— the problem is a critical one, especially in rural areas where both important historic and environmental attributes overlap on the same tract of land.

The extent of the problem is revealed by looking at the content of the covenants or restrictions used by each type of organization.[16] Preservation organizations will normally provide very detailed restrictions regarding the use and treatment of historic buildings on the premises but deal only in a nominal way with respect to landscape values of a scenic or biotic character. The reverse will be true with respect to the typical conservation organization.

Without burdening the reader with too much legalese, the differences between the two types of protective agreements show up most sharply in the language of a 1979 North Carolina statute, the purpose of which was to do away legislatively with many of the old and complex common-law disabilities often employed by courts to invalidate restrictions on private property. In the statute, landscape and preservation restrictions are defined as:

> [Those dealing with] land or water areas predominately in natural, scenic, or open condition or in agricultural, horticultural, farming or forest use, to forbid or limit any or all (a) construction or placing of buildings, roads, signs, billboards or other advertising, utilities or other structures on or above the ground; (b) dumping or placing soil or other substance or material as landfill, or dumping or placing of trash, waste, unsightly or offensive materials; (c) removal or destruction of trees, shrubs, or other vegetation; (d) excavation, dredging or removal of loam, peat, gravel, soil, rock or other mineral

substance in such manner as to affect the surface; (e) surface use except for agricultural, farming, forest or outdoor recreational purposes or purposes permitting the land or water area to remain predominately in its natural condition; (f) activities detrimental to drainage, flood control, water conservation, erosion, control or soil conservation; or (g) other acts or uses detrimental to such retention of land or water areas.

In the statute, historic preservation restrictions are defined as:

[Those dealing with the] preservation of a structure or site historically significant for its architecture, archaeology, or historical associations, to forbid or limit any or all (a) alteration; (b) alterations in exterior or interior features of the structure; (c) changes in appearance or condition of the site; (d) uses not historically appropriate; or (e) other acts or uses supportive of or detrimental to appropriate preservation of the structure or site.[17]

The formats and legal implications of conservation and historic preservation easements can be, and often are, essentially the same. The substantive and procedural contents may also be the same. In fact, standard model easements were constructed and published as a cooperative project of the national Land Trust Alliance, the Trust for Public Land, and the National Trust for Historic Preservation.[18] The ideal easement will combine objectives for permanent protection of environmental and historic resources in a single agreement, as well as list prohibited property uses expressly designed to safeguard both land and buildings. In all other content and substance, the easement agreement can be the same.

In some cases, a single easement can be constructed for an environmentally and historically significant property and be simultaneously held and enforced jointly by a conservation land trust and historic preservation organization according to procedures mutually agreeable to both parties. In other situations, two parallel easements might be simultaneously designed and executed—one held by the conservation land trust and targeted on maintaining and protecting the land's natural resources and open space characteristics, and the other held by the historic preservation organization and specifically designed to protect the built structures of historic interest.

Experience tells us that many existing easement agreements do not comprehensively identify or protect all environmental and historical resources on the properties. Too often existing conservation easements make only vague reference to maintaining historic structures without any meaningful description or prescription. Similarly, many historic preservation easements generally call for the maintenance of woodlands, pastures, and fields, or other natural areas, but with no specificity and no precise documentation of their location, extent, or character in the "baseline" inventories of a property's natural resources. The reality is that these vague and useless generalities will prove basically unmeasurable and unenforceable in the future. Of course, these situations can be corrected and opportunities maximized by amending existing easements or by overlaying new easements on those properties, but in real life this is not often done.

There is hope for improvement. It is possible that landowners will be encouraged to accept these changes and increased specificity of property restrictions by provisions of federal (and some state) tax laws that now reward them with greater income, estate, inheritance, and gift tax reductions for an amended or extended easement agreement that is more definitive in its enumeration of prohibited and allowable uses.[19]

Traditionally—and probably still in the majority of such cases—organizations with overlapping interests in the same property will each go their own way. However, some land conservation and historic preservation organizations are beginning to coordinate their efforts to protect individual properties more comprehensively. The Maryland Historical Trust and the Maryland Environmental Trust work closely together and try to obtain gift easements on a joint basis. The Adirondack Architectural Heritage organization has received an award from the Adirondack Council, the region's primary conservation organization, for the AAH's work in protecting the Adirondack Great Camps and fire towers. The New Jersey Conservation Foundation holds detailed historic preservation easements, and there are doubtless other examples. The coordination and integration of conservation and preservation objectives should increase in the future, and this kind of organizational coordination is to be encouraged. Success will largely depend on both personal and institutional determination at local and regional levels. As a practical matter, such a goal cannot be legislated.

The use of private restrictions is, of course, a highly specialized area, much of it derived from English common law; each state will exhibit its own peculiarities regarding how they are drafted, when they may be enforced, and who has "standing" to make a legal claim. Here we are concerned only with the larger area of overlapping conservation and preservation interests of law, and the need for improved personal and institutional coordination between interests that continue, too often, to act independently of one another.

Heritage Landscapes and Heritage Conservation:
New Entrants in the Preservation Field

The initiation of a National Heritage Area program by the NPS in the 1980s represented an increased interest in urban cultural and industrial resource protection, and, in some instances, a convergence of interests between historic preservation and land conservation interests.

The first NHA designation came about almost by default, when the NPS resisted local, widespread political enthusiasm for designating the Illinois and Michigan Canal a unit of the National Park System. Instead, in 1984 Congress defined the industrial corridor along the canal as a National Heritage Corridor (NHC), a kind of hybrid park. Other similar designations followed: the Blackstone River Valley NHC (1986) and the Delaware and Lehigh Canal NHC (1988). The Southwestern Pennsylvania Heritage Commission, covering a nine-county region, was also identified in 1988. These first four designations spurred interest in other designations and caused the NPS to start thinking seriously about a formal NHA program backed by a rational designation process. By 1998 Congress had designated a total of seventeen NHAS, most recently the Automobile Heritage Area in Detroit.[20]

In the private sector, a National Coalition for Heritage Areas was formed in the early 1990s. Its purpose was to advocate federal legislation for the promotion and designation of heritage areas, and to develop a systematic process for designating and protecting distinctive environmental, cultural, and scenic resources on a larger geographic scale. Primary impetus for the coalition came from the National Trust and the Countryside Institute; the NPS provided staff support. The general concept was that in those designated landscapes, greater public and private investments could be focused on education, tourism, recreation, and other economic opportunities. The blend of resources and interest was thought to encourage partnerships among public agencies and civic and nonprofit organizations. Regional coalitions were created to advocate the designation of NHAS in fifty or more areas.

Today, the National Coalition has been replaced by an Alliance for National Heritage Areas, comprised of the NHAS that have been designated to date, and efforts to create a permanent program and system of National Heritage Areas continues. No legislation for such a system has yet been accepted by Congress. The most recent legislative effort (as of August 2002) is a National Heritage Areas Policy Act, introduced by Representative Lynn Hefley (R.-Colo.), which would establish NHAS as a continuing program of the federal government within the NPS. There are also bills pending in the House and Senate that would designate an additional thirty NHAs, in addition to eight proposed by the NPS awaiting action.[21]

The creation of such a permanent program would be a major step forward in an area of growing importance in historic preservation and the conservation of natural areas. Heritage areas, heritage tourism, and heritage resource development provide economic benefits to local communities while enhancing the historic qualities of the area.[22]

Interestingly, the concept is fairly similar to one put into effect by the Carter administration through the creation of a Heritage Conservation and Recreation Service, based on a programmatic arrangement said to have worked well in Georgia. Under it, these same programs were brought administratively and politically under one roof separate from the NPS. But the program was poorly administered, and the old order of things was reestablished by the Reagan administration. Georgia, of course, has enacted legislation that formally establishes processes for defining regionally important and geographically large-scale natural and historic areas, and these are incorporated into state-mandated comprehensive land-use planning.

Heritage areas have also been designated in various parts of the country by the states without benefit of federal designations. An emerging example is the initiative by the Uwharrie Lakes regional coalition of public agencies and private organizations in the western central piedmont region of North Carolina. Its purpose is to promote public awareness that protecting the region's environmental resources and natural beauty is critical to the local economy, especially that based on ecotourism. The cluster of national and state forests, wildlife refuges, historic sites, a state zoo, and a heavily forested corridor along the Yadkin–Pee Dee Rivers is now popularly seen as the state's "Central Park," bounded by the rapidly urbanizing Charlotte-Greensboro-Raleigh "Piedmont Crescent," which is expected to become the nation's fourth largest metropolitan area within the next fifteen years.

A related initiative of the NPS, also begun in the early 1990s, was encouragement for nominating rural historic landscapes to the National Register, discussed in greater detail in Chapters 2 and 6. Rural historic landscapes are broadly defined as geographic areas that have been used, or modified, by people and that possess distinctive combinations of cultural and environmental resources. Examples of historic landscapes include continuously used trails and roadways, battlefields, lumbering and mining communities, land areas used or

Brandy Station, Virginia. In 2000 the Civil War Preservation Trust acquired a 258-acre parcel that, when added to 500 acres acquired previously, preserves the core of the Brandy Station battlefield—the site of the largest cavalry battle ever fought in America. In the same year the trust added a 136-acre tract to the Manassas National Battlefield Park and a 245-acre farm in the core of the Malvern Hill area of the Richmond National battlefield. (Photo by Eric Long, courtesy of the NPS)

revered by Native Americans, public recreational and scenic parks, and agricultural rural communities.[23]

Registers of Natural Areas

In 1962 the NPS initiated, but soon "mothballed," a National Register of Natural Landmarks as an intended parallel to the National Register of Historic Places, basing its authority to do so on the Historic Sites Act of 1935. Unlike the National Register of Historic Places, the register of natural areas had no specific basis in law. For a short period, natural landmark areas were designated by an edict of the secretary of the interior under guidelines issued in 1963. But these areas were already protected for the most part by state and federal agencies.

The process of designating natural landmark areas began with an internal NPS determination that a site met criteria as a nationally significant natural area and was therefore eligible for registration. However, like National Historic Landmarks, the only consequence of designation was the formality of a letter to the owner requesting that he or she sign an agreement to preserve the important natural values. Signature of the voluntary agreement constituted the actual registry of the natural landmark.[24] The program atrophied in the late

1970s, when funding for its small staff ended, and it was effectively forgotten by the 1980s. Lack of congressional authorization and support was largely responsible for its failure.

Many states created their own programs for registering and dedicating important natural areas. This movement began in the Midwest in the mid-1960s and was adopted by other states in the 1970s and 1980s. Generally authorized by state legislatures through nature preserves acts, these programs created a two-tiered system of designating outstanding natural areas. They were based either on voluntary agreements and pledges between the states and private and public landowners, or on the creation of more restricted nature preserves protected by legally binding conservation agreements. Most of these state programs now appear to be moribund, but a few thrive—notably in Illinois and North Carolina, whose natural areas registry and nature preserve programs each include many hundreds of registered sites and preserves.[25]

Special Dilemmas in Preserving Nature

Private land trusts are engaged in protecting a wide variety of significant land resources. These include not only special natural areas and wildlife habitats, but also areas possessing outstanding scenic views, historic landscapes and sites, outdoor recreational areas, wetlands and watersheds, working farms, and forest lands. Land trusts also have to assess the practical feasibility of their objectives. The Nature Conservancy did this in the 1990s. After assessing the risks of acquiring and maintaining fragmented and dysfunctional natural ecosystems, it shifted its emphasis away from acquiring relatively small, remnant natural areas in favor of preserving whole landscape units of functioning natural ecosystems. Indeed, TNC transferred many of its previously acquired preserves to local and regional land trusts when it concluded that some preserves were too small and isolated to maintain the populations of the native species for which the land was acquired and thus did not serve its "global" biological preservation mission. Although those natural resources may have been of great importance at the local level, they no longer fit TNC's primary aim of preserving the best and most unique biological diverse resources from a global perspective. In some cases, smaller natural areas may be better utilized for preserving green spaces for the use and enjoyment of people, and for habitation by common resident and migratory wildlife, than as refuges for endangered species.

As a result of this philosophy, TNC has had to concentrate on preserving the earth's biological diversity and thus must frequently operate on a huge landscape scale and assemble multiple tract preserves. Many local and regional land trusts also engage in large-scale land protection projects, but they also are concerned about protecting a wide variety of land resources for public use and value. With increasing frequency, joint efforts are being undertaken by local land trusts and national conservation organizations to accomplish large-scale and complex protection projects. At the same time, land trusts often pursue smaller-scale land protection projects for a variety of reasons. Probably the majority of locally protected land resources are most often the places that people simply love and appreciate. They may not necessarily be "pristine" or "untouched." They are often more familiar and accessible to people, and often as much valued for their cultural benefits as they are for their natural or ecological attributes.

Are the functions of land trusts called into question by the new scientific rationale propounded by ecologists and conservation biologists that only large natural areas are truly functional and stable enough to maintain viable populations of native species and ecosystems? In that case, are land trusts more likely to save remnants of green space than ecologically functioning natural areas? If TNC's shift of focus is appropriate, does that indict the efforts of many land trusts as meaningless?

That dilemma has been considered by environmental historian William Cronon, who has observed that because nature is dynamic and changes just as human cultures do, no tract of land can be completely protected from the flow of time or from history and human interference. So the task of conserving nature is one of conserving "nature in time."[26]

A Question of Values

This returns the argument to the relationship between land valued for its natural and ecological importance and land valued for its cultural attributes. Like the historic preservation community, the natural preservation community faces basic issues related to significance, integrity, periodicity, and the like. Just as the preservation community must always confront the basic issue of which period a building is to be returned to when it is being preserved or restored, the conservation community must face comparable issues. Do we try to return land

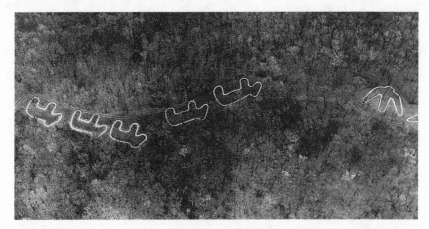

Effigy Mounds National Monument, Harper's Ferry, Iowa. The Iowa Natural Heritage Foundation has acquired more than 1,000 acres for addition to this monument and an adjacent state forest. Human heritage resources are frequently protected by private land trusts. (Photo by Al Zarling, Iowa Natural Heritage Foundation)

areas to their character and presumed appearance before the Native Americans were here? Or should we attempt to restore natural landscapes as they appeared when first encountered by European settlers? Do we try to create active human manipulation, such as regularly set fires that contributed to the open forests and grasslands that characterized much of temperate North America for millennia? What exactly is "natural" and how do we conserve and maintain "natural areas?" How far back should we go in restoring or preserving an old building or an entire neighborhood?

The role of land trusts is validated when we understand that we cannot stop the flow of history and the influence of humans on any part of our landscapes. Nature preserves must be designed and managed to accommodate the extremely dynamic human and natural systems of which they are a part. Neither land conservancies nor public agencies can simply purchase entire functional ecosystems, such as whole river valleys or mountain ranges or places like the Greater Yellowstone ecosystem. If we are going to protect entire functioning landscapes, we necessarily need to concern ourselves with human and cultural history as well as natural history. People will continue to live around and affect nature preserves. Historical and cultural forces will shape the way people use and manipulate those lands.

Notley's Landing, California. In 2001 the Big Sur Land Trust acquired the historic Notley's Landing along the renowned Big Sur coast. The property straddles scenic Highway 1 on the rugged coast about 11 miles south of Carmel and includes the site of the nineteenth-century Redwood timber shipping port and village. (Big Sur Land Trust)

Conservation and Preservation in the Real World

The land that makes up entire rural and natural landscapes will be owned by many: private individuals, corporations, government agencies, and land trusts. People will always be part of the natural systems and landscapes. Conservation on a larger, more comprehensive scale will require new and innovative strategies firmly based on an acknowledged ethic and a sense of responsibility toward living in some degree in a sustainable balance with nature. In addition, the behavior of landowners and human occupants will be shaped by a complex blend of regulations, ordinances, covenants and easements, cultural traditions, and sensitivity and goodwill. Landscape conservation will be impossible without new coalitions that recognize, in a balanced way, the importance of scientifically based natural and ecological principles and those that are culturally and historically determined.

Over the next decades land conservation programs will expand, in exciting and challenging ways, to influence land uses in and around nature preserves, as well as to save prime farmlands, working forest lands, watersheds and water supplies, and places of public recreation, scenic and natural beauty, and historic and cultural value. Success will require new and complex coalitions, new and blended methods, refinement and manipulation of real estate and tax laws, political and civic involvement, and legal tactics. New and flexible techniques—perhaps methods not even currently contemplated—will be needed. The critical question is how best can we bring such closely related interests together so that the efforts of each adds up to more than the sum of the parts?

Land conservationists, like historic preservationists, are being forced to move beyond the comparatively safe and nonconfrontational strategies of simply buying choice tracts of land to save it, whether as pristine natural landscapes or historic house museums. There is simply not enough money, public or private, for that approach to sustain itself. We will be contending with finding practical ways to influence human relationships with the land that are environmentally sustainable, culturally aware, and historically responsible. If we hope to influence human behavior on regional landscape scales, we have to base our strategies on what will affect people's behavior and what will motivate them to act responsibly toward the land and its nonhuman inhabitants. If in conserving whole landscapes with natural and culturally important resources, we can find ways to organize human communities and economies to protect the natural systems, historic sites, and places we hold dear, then we will have made profound advances in conserving both nature and people.

Again, as observed by Cronon, success in protecting the natural and human environment can be derived only by fostering a sense of love and respect for the land. That is a mission that local land trusts can best accomplish by using nature preserves to educate and remind the public of the special truths of their interconnections with the land. Out of that sense of love and respect for land as "home," which is best derived from firsthand familiarity, will come ever-greater public support for the work of land conservation and the preservation of cultural resources. The ultimate success of land trusts will be in sustaining and fostering human love for the land.[27]

Just as clearly, the interests of the land conservation movement and the historic preservation movement have at long last begun to converge—and, in some places, recognize that convergence and have begun to build on it. Though it may demand much of human nature to do so, it seems both important and timely to suggest that the executive and trustee custodians of national, state, and local historic preservation and conservation organizations should begin—however informally—to explore the ways in which their organizations can provide mutual support and reinforcement for one another's programs. Especially is this enhanced institutional collaboration needed as society at large, and, in turn, its legislative and judicial leadership, move toward increasingly conservative postures in which threats to both natural and cultural resources are on the rise.

Uncertain Destiny

The Changing Role of Archaeology in Historic Preservation

Archaeology is fundamentally different from other professions within historic preservation. The difference is essentially one of orientation. Historic preservation is concerned with the future of old buildings, neighborhoods, and landscapes—managing change—whereas archaeology is primarily interested in recovering and interpreting human behavior of the past. A historic preservationist looks at the main street of small-town America as a prime candidate for architectural rehabilitation and commercial revitalization, easements, architectural review boards, zoning regulations, and design guidelines, but the archaeologist is most interested in the town's backyards where the sheet middens, privies, and trash pits are a veritable gold mine of information about the community's history. Historic preservation exists on the rehabilitation and restoration of past places and landscapes, whereas American archaeology thrives on destruction of the past through excavation, analysis, and interpretation.

Archaeology is perhaps best understood as modern-day alchemy: turning base materials—soil and stone, bone and ceramic—into the gold of archaeological observation and interpretation. This analogy also captures the experimental and destructive nature of archaeology as a method of scientific inquiry about the past. Each excavation is an experiment in recovering past activities, one that, unlike the pure sciences, is not replicable. It is a truism that archaeology is an inherently destructive process, which justifies the profession's concern for record keeping. This fact alone distinguishes the archaeology from the rest of the preservation field. The archaeologist, unlike the historian, architectural historian, or other preservation professional, destroys nonrenewable resources to advance our understanding of the past.

For a true believer, it all begins with a reverence for the practitioner's medium: the archaeological record. Most archaeologists have a firm belief that the archaeological record presents special documentation of the past. The stories held within the earth are unique and democratic; that is, they represent all of a society—not just the learned—and illustrate most aspects of a culture, from the mundane to the ideological. The archaeological record is a three-dimensional jigsaw puzzle often rearranged by the passage of time that requires considerable training and thought to reconstruct a site's history: turning the trash into tales about the past.

American archaeology is primarily a hand-labor and handmade endeavor that borrows tools, technology, methods, and theory from other disciplines. Stratigraphic excavation techniques and the concept of superposition (older things are found below newer things) come from geology; theory is derived primarily from anthropology; and the principal excavation tool, the trowel, was adapted from the mason's tool kit. Practitioners typically build their own dry screens, water screens, and flotation tanks to separate artifacts from the soil, while at the same time using satellite imagery and sophisticated computer programs to help predict where archaeological sites will probably be found with statistical certainty across large, relatively unexplored landscapes. Yet despite all the models, computers, and technological advances, archaeology still relies on the lowly shovel test pit (a hand-dug, one–two-foot diameter excavation) to find sites.

In adapting to legislative and regulatory changes since the 1960s, American archaeology has developed conventional practices and language that is unique to this discipline within historic preservation. The phrases "Phase I, Phase II, and Phase III," "data recovery," and "mitigation" have distinct meanings in the profession. Although there is some regional variation, in the field of historic preservation there is a distinctive archaeological dialect, shaped by archaeological culture itself since the mid-1960s.

Like a guild, archaeology also has its own brand of apprentices, journeymen, and masters. Apprentices are the field-workers—archaeological technicians—the crews that provide the raw labor of excavation. Journeymen (more commonly women) are those who have passed through an educational apprenticeship and become field directors or crew chiefs, overseeing the labor of apprentices. Masters of archaeology are anointed by educational degrees (the M.A. or Ph.D.) as experts in the field or laboratory, with the ability to practice archaeological alchemy. Since World War II, as archaeology has progressed from primarily an avocation to a profession, the lines between professional and amateur have become more distinct and sometimes confrontational. This debate between avocational and professional archaeologist is not found, to the same degree, in other preservation fields.

Learning the Craft, 1960–1980

Like much of the country's culture, American archaeologists underwent a revolution in the 1960s. The "New Archaeology" of Lewis Binford and others—with its insistence that archaeology was anthropology or it was nothing—forever altered the discipline and its approach to the archaeological record.[1] American archaeologists increasingly adopted a scientific, positivist approach that shifted the focus of their work from the classification and description of resources to the development of testable research designs—asking questions that count and recognizing meaningful patterns in the archaeological record. The search for what came to be called "middle range theory," one that linked patterns revealed through excavation with associated human action, became the common and respected mission of archaeology. Entering academe in the 1960s, historical archaeology was particularly attracted to the idea of connecting archaeological patterns to those found in the documentary record.[2]

The New Archaeology promised great things during this period. With just the right research questions, methods, analysis, and interpretation, archaeologists thought they might develop lawlike principles of human behavior. Ultimately, this high purpose floundered as they discovered that revealing true meaning from a somewhat fickle archaeological record was full of difficulties. In a sense, the goal was unobtainable because of the unique nature of individual archaeological sites.

At the same time that archaeological method and theory was undergoing a shift in orientation, the historic preservation movement received its largest boost with the passage of the 1966 National Historic Preservation Act. The execution of Section 106 of NHPA—the "New Preservation"—changed, and was changed by, the practice of the New Archaeology.

Perhaps the most lasting impact of the archaeological paradigm shifts of the 1960s was the acceptance of scientific method by historic preservationists. This was a convenient and pragmatic choice for the profession. Within a huge universe of potential resources, the use of explicit research design, statistical sampling, and modeling helped planners, engineers, and other decision makers feel more comfortable with proposals for extensive archaeological projects. Representative sampling in particular was a necessary methodology in that it justified the conventional wisdom that survey and excavation revealed only a part of the archaeological record.

Today's language of archaeology reflects this wholesale use and influence of the positivist approach. The New Archaeology fundamentally shaped the way we identify, evaluate, and excavate sites across the country. Most state historic preservation offices have specific guidance for archaeological surveys that require explicit statements about field and laboratory methods. In one jurisdiction, for example, the maximum distance between survey excavations (usually small diameter shovel test pits) is defined as the smallest size of an archaeological site that could be considered eligible for the National Register of Historic Places.[3]

National Register Criterion D states that historic properties must have yielded or have the potential to yield important information about the past to be eligible for listing in the register. "Important information" is defined as data that address research questions developed about a particular archaeological site. Thus, to be eligible for the National Register, an archaeological site must meet two requirements: the property must have, or have had, information that can contribute to our understanding of human history or prehistory, and the information must be important.[4] As archaeologists adapted their craft to the new realities of NHPA and Section 106 compliance, there was a general assumption that the NPS established Criterion D specifically to address and accommodate archaeological sites.[5]

With the expansion of the historic preservation field following the 1966 act, American archaeologists had to relearn their craft. The profession spent much of this time developing its tool kit: laws and regulations, method and theory, and analysis and interpretation. As a discipline, historic preservation invented a variety of basic concepts and conventions—the idea of historic context and the National Register criteria, for example—that govern the way the endeavor operates. In a similar way, American archaeology adapted to the new regulatory world that came with the passage of NHPA and the National Environmental Policy Act in 1969. Many archaeologists were well placed to take advantage of NEPA because of their anthropological training in the culture-ecology school, which focused on the relationship between people and their environment. NEPA's regulatory umbrella and multidisciplinary approach to planning and decision making helps to accommodate archaeological resources within broader environmental management themes.

Another important trend in the 1970s was the rise of public archaeology programs. Founded in 1975, Virginia's Alexandria Archaeology is probably the best known and most successful of these programs. Sponsored by the city of Alexandria, Alexandria Archaeology has undertaken or overseen numerous excavations throughout the city, operated a publicly accessible museum in a revitalized downtown shopping area, and, since 1992, directed a local compliance program for development projects within areas of archaeological sensitivity. Alexandria Archaeology's long-term success has not been replicated in many other historic cities primarily because of the unique circumstances that led to its founding: a convergence of professional, political, and grassroots support during the height of urban renewal threats to architectural and archaeological resources; a focus on volunteers, community-based programs, and civic service rather than on compliance; and the personal charisma and political pragmatism of the core staff and program supporters. Its challenge will be to pass down this inheritance to the next generation of practitioners.

The archaeological tool kit was more complete in 1980 than in 1960. The profession had adopted with gusto new computing technology, adapted to the new regulatory environment, and started training a new generation of practitioners. By 1980 archaeologists generally shared a common language and understanding of the NHPA compliance process. Most practitioners knew the level of effort required for background research, fieldwork, analysis, reporting, and curation. The players—contractors and clients, SHPOs and FPOs, Native Americans and interested parties, the Advisory Council on Historic Preservation, and the National Park Service—and their roles were well established.

In some ways, however, the position of archaeology within the preservation field did not change much in the twenty years before 1980. Just as historical archaeology was labeled the "handmaiden of history," archaeology at times appeared to be an afterthought within historic preservation. The phrase "historic and archaeological sites" suggested that somehow archaeological properties were fundamentally different from historic sites—that they were not really historic in the same way as standing structures or buildings. Ironically, at the same time archaeologists came to dominate the cultural resource management (CRM) industry, both in the private sector and in government service, by taking advantage of emerging employment opportunities. The growing challenge in American archaeology is to demonstrate to the wider historic preservation field and to the general public that archaeological resources have value other than for research.[6]

Gunpowder Site, Maryland. American archaeology before the rise of the CRM industry was often conducted by volunteer groups led by professionally trained archaeologists with academic postings. Notice the experimental cylinder screen in the background of this excavation by the Archeological Society of Maryland in 1963. (John H. Sprinkle Sr.)

Archaeology Becomes a Business

Invented by the NPS and other federal agency archaeologists in the early 1970s, the phrase "cultural resource management" exists within the larger field of historic preservation and generally applies to all types of cultural resources, buildings, structures, landscapes, and archaeological sites.[7] In the twenty years since 1980, the CRM industry has strengthened its position as the dominant paradigm in American archaeology. By one estimate, at least 80 percent of all archaeology in the United States today is tied to CRM programs. Between two-thirds and three-quarters of the membership of the Society of American Archaeology participates in some aspect of the CRM industry.[8] The domination of CRM has had an impact on all aspects of the archaeological guild, from what projects are undertaken to the adoption of new technology. By 2000 there was no area of American archaeology that was not intimately tied to the CRM industry.

One aspect of the rise of CRM is the introduction of a business mentality to a formerly academic and avocational pursuit. Just as the archaeological guild adapted to the language and philosophy of historic preservation in the 1970s, the profession learned a new grammar of business practices and government

Ozette Site, Washington State. One of the enduring characteristics of American archaeology continues to be its experimental and experiential nature. Each site presents new challenges in recovering information about the past. In 1970 archaeologists used water to excavate fragile remains from mud-soaked soils at this site. (NPS, National Register of Historic Places)

procurement regulations in the 1980s and 1990s. Business has influenced all levels of the archaeological guild, from the senior managers through the lowliest field excavator. From masters to apprentices, the guild struggled to learn how to make the nature of archaeological research, excavation, analysis, and reporting understandable to civil engineers, planners, and NEPA specialists, as well as to regulators, clients, and agency sponsors jointly participating in the overall environmental compliance process. Today, in addition to understanding the technical field, the successful archaeologist must have extensive knowledge of labor laws; health, safety, and insurance issues; contracting and subcontracting practices; financial operations; and marketing.[9] The transformation of archaeology from avocation to profession to business enterprise walked hand in hand with the rise of CRM during the last twenty years.

In 1985 one of the fathers of the regulatory framework for CRM, Thomas F. King, reviewed the impact of historic preservation on archaeology and vice versa. American archaeology changed historic preservation by shaping the way federal agencies conducted preservation planning, bringing a disciplined approach to the process of identifying significant historic properties, and adapting anthropological concepts to the practice of preservation within diverse local, traditional, and ethnic communities. Regarding the impact of archaeology on preservation, King concluded: "Archaeologists bring with them the basic philosophy of their parent discipline, Anthropology, contributing to the idea that American preservation should address the histories, the artifacts, and the intangible cultural values of all of the nation's diverse ethnic and social groups. Archaeological emphasis on understanding the past in the context of larger physiographic regions and the natural environment supports the idea that preservation should take a broad, comprehensive view of its subject matter."[10]

Also in 1986, on the occasion of its fiftieth anniversary, the SAA took stock of the profession—its past accomplishments and future prospects. In a publication entitled *American Archaeology Past and Future*, the editors stated that the major problem facing American archaeology in the mid-1980s was methodological—the question of how we know what we know about the past. This worrisome issue has troubled practitioners since the paradigm shift of the 1960s toward the New Archaeology—a critical adoption of scientific methods in structuring research, excavation, analysis, and interpretation of the archaeological record.[11]

This review of a quarter-century of the New Archaeology focused on two substantive changes: the growth of cultural resources management as the primary mechanism for archaeological investigations, and the quantitative revolution brought by access to computers and other technological marvels for the collection and analysis of large sets of data. As a practical matter, the CRM industry has fully adopted the positivist approach to understanding the past— the faith that a structured research design, consistent methods, and quantitative analysis will reveal patterns that have historical meaning. Computers and other technologies—as the tools of science—require this structured thinking.

One impact of the New Archaeology and its challenges is the development of "archaeologies"—diverse new subfields that use some aspect or concept of the archaeological craft to portray a particular area of the past. Thus, in the last twenty years bioarchaeologists have begun the study of microscopic plant remains to aid the reconstruction of past landscapes and environments, while geoarchaeologists use the tools of prospectors and remote sensing to model strata and a history of deposition. Other subdisciplines, such as industrial archaeology and commercial archaeology, have adopted the term "archaeology" to symbolize their approach to the built environment.

This diversity is seen not only in what archaeologists call themselves, but in how they view the past and the accessibility of a real past. Assessing the future of American archaeology in 1985, the SAA presented three views on the impact and future of the New Archaeology. One vision focused on the "entanglement of history and ideology" and recommended that archaeologists must be up front about the inherent biases in their work: Was a real past actually knowable? Another view challenged years of attacks on the New Archaeology by focusing on the accomplishments that a scientific approach had brought to our understanding of the archaeological record. The third perspective reaffirmed that the archaeological record is a unique guide to a real past.[12]

Recognizing the importance of CRM in American archaeology, the SAA focused on the increasingly "public" nature of this endeavor and the responsibilities of the profession toward diverse public interests. It also provided a legislative context beyond NHPA to include the umbrella NEPA and its impact on cultural resource management. The argument was simple (and is still valid, since most of the funding for archaeology comes from public coffers): Archaeology must be responsive to the general public, primarily by making its work understandable and relevant. Archaeologists practicing within the CRM industry must balance the needs of the resources, the business, the client or sponsor of the investigations, and the public.[13]

Pointing to the enormous growth of the archaeological database generated by the CRM industry, the SAA was optimistic about the future of CRM and archaeology's role in it. Today we know a great deal more about where archaeological sites may be found, and, perhaps more important, we have more equal levels of information about where sites will *not* be found than we did during the mid-1970s. Our site inventories, many now stored in an electronic format as well as in our laboratories, are bursting with the by-products of extensive site surveys and excavations—again, all fueled by the growth of CRM.

The Rise of a Public Archaeology Perspective

In the last twenty years there have been three major impacts of CRM on American archaeology: the rise of a public archaeology perspective, a concern for professionalism, and the domination of procedures and process over the protection of properties by regulations. One concept frequently mentioned in the retrospectives of the last two decades is the idea that publicly funded archaeology must be responsible to a broader public.[14] Public support for archaeological programs has never been stronger at the local level, often because archaeologists have become somewhat more able to mobilize the public for political ends. Few large projects undertaken in the 1990s did not include some component for public education. The rise of public archaeological efforts occurred not only as a result of local government or house museum programs, but also as a consequence of the compliance required by NHPA. To paraphrase Louis Binford's New Archaeology precept: American archaeology is public or it is nothing!

In the beginning, public archaeology merely signified that archaeologists had to consider what to tell the public about their work as unexpected visitors encountered an excavation. Since then, simple signs indicating that an excavation was taking place have been replaced by detailed interpretive programs that include the extensive use of signs, pamphlets, scheduled tours, and report summaries designed for public consumption. As public programs have grown in number in cities and other jurisdictions across the country, archaeologists have become highly effective at telling archaeological stories to a public that supports their work.

But telling stories to the public is a double-edged sword. The subject matter is often complex—only an archaeologist can appreciate the need for understanding "how Archaic resource procurement practices are evidenced by mid-post glacial xerothermic adaptations to an estuarine environment." And, at times, information must be withheld from the public, especially when a site may contain human remains or artifacts that have monetary value on the antique or collector markets. In addition, there is often an inherent conflict between a client's desire for a less expensive and less noteworthy CRM project and the public's right to know about the history beneath their backyards.

Public archaeology in the early twenty-first century involves a variety of constituencies whose cultural and historical values differ from those of archaeologists. Various ethnic, religious, and racial groups have confronted practitioners with differing explanations and expectations for the buried past than those told by archaeology. Some groups have raised basic questions about who should have access to the past and who should be allowed to explore it. At sites where human remains may be found, many groups, especially Native Americans, have questioned the morality and legitimacy of any archaeological excavation whatever. Archaeologists, on the other hand, point to the vast quantities of scientific and interpretive data to be discovered from these precious resources. In the end, the archaeological guild must resolve these issues with all interested parties and the public prior to excavation.

Concerns for traditional practices and beliefs among Native Americans effectively caught the archaeological community unprepared to deal with living cultures. Talking to people, rather than talking about the artifacts they left behind, requires different skills and time frames for the decision-making processes in historic preservation. A common failure within the historic preservation movement was, and continues to be, the assumption that Native American and other traditional cultural issues fall exclusively within the discipline of archaeology. Much broader input is needed. A primary objective of the published NPS guidance on the inventory and evaluation of traditional cultural properties is to train practitioners in a variety of disciplines, such as ethnography, folklore, and traditional culture.[15]

Professionalism

Although the rise of public archaeology is one of the principal results of the CRM model, other changes include an increasing concern with professionalism within the archaeology guild. Thirty years ago the only credential an archaeologist needed was either a love for the endeavor or a traditional academic appointment. Today, with so few archaeologists working in the academy and so many more working in other venues, the guild has had to devise new approaches to recruiting, training, and credentialing new members, as well as overseeing standards of practice in a rapidly changing business environment.

From its beginnings, CRM has changed the way archaeologists are trained. In the late 1970s students graduating with a bachelor's degree in anthropology generally got field experience either from working with avocational groups or, more commonly, working under the direction of a university-based archaeologist. Around 1980 the employment picture for apprentices, journeymen, and masters changed. With growth in the CRM industry, the first archaeological programs were established in large environmental and engineering firms. For the first time, archaeologists could consider CRM a career, with competitive salaries, benefits, and retirement programs. Although archaeological field schools were still the primary avenue for obtaining basic skills, students could now be reasonably assured of finding gainful employment once they completed the requirements of a field school or received a master's degree.[16]

The first nationwide attempt to recognize professional archaeologists was the organization of the Society of Professional Archaeologists (SOPA) in 1976.[17] Despite the adoption of standards of practice, a grievance procedure, and other professional guidelines, SOPA membership was required in only a few jurisdictions. The society eventually failed as an organization and in 1998 became the

Registry of Professional Archaeologists (ROPA), which drew on the membership and financial support of the Archaeological Institute of America, the Society of American Archaeology, and the Society for Historical Archaeology.[18] Since the mid-1970s, a graduate degree in anthropology or a related field with specialization in archaeology has been the "union card" signifying one's status as a professional archaeologist. In the early 1980s the NPS codified this convention, equating professional qualifications with completing a graduate degree program. Most states have adopted these federal standards, and many state-level professional societies now require graduate training for membership.

Many professional challenges in archaeology in the last twenty years developed from the integration of a traditionally academic endeavor with a business and regulatory environment. Few archaeologists in the mid-1970s were concerned with issues such as ensuring health and safety training for workers on sites with potential hazardous materials; maintaining fair labor practices, pay, and per diem levels; and establishing a level playing field for archaeological contracting. Many traditional business practices have been good for the archaeology guild. Without CRM, archaeologists would probably not have had serious discussions about quality control, peer review, ethics, and responsibilities to the public, clients, and the profession. The business side of CRM also challenged the relevancy of traditional academically based archaeological associations. Seeing an obvious void in the guild, the American Cultural Resources Association (ACRA) was established in 1995 as the trade association for the CRM industry. Created in 1991, the Union of Archaeological Field Technicians (UFAT) became affiliated with the International Union of Operating Engineers of the AFL-CIO as Local Union 141 in 1995.[19] The principal conflict between these two organizations is defining the appropriate role and adequate compensation for the "archaeological technician" as a component in the CRM industry. There is no better evidence that CRM has transformed American archaeology from a discipline to an enterprise than the presence of both a union and a trade association.

Policy, Procedures, and Process

Laws, regulations, official policy, and technical guidance, whether imposed by government or as part of the business practice of a particular agency or firm, structure the way archaeology is practiced in the United States. American archaeologists, by necessity, have had to become masters of policy, procedure, and process. Good archaeology requires an explicit method, and cultural re-

Mount Vernon, Virginia. Mount Vernon illustrates the rise of the public archaeology paradigm. Each year more than a million visitors have the opportunity to interact with active excavations conducted across the estate, such as here at the South Grove trash midden in the early 1990s. (Mount Vernon Ladies Association)

source management demands a consistent regulatory compliance process. Archaeologists, with their love of jargon, were specially well adapted to carrying out the regulatory process created by NHPA.

The last twenty years have seen a transformation in the laws and regulations that affect the discipline. Every aspect of it has been altered as a result: who can be called a professional archaeologist, the issuance of permits for excavation on federal lands, and how collections are treated. Most of these changes occurred at the federal level via the National Park Service and the Advisory Council on Historic Preservation. Some change is the result of state action or, rarely, that of a local government.

The three principal laws governing the practice of archaeology in the United States are the National Historic Preservation Act of 1966, the Archaeological Resources Protection Act of 1979, and the Native American Graves Protection and Repatriation Act of 1990 (see Chapter 2). Archaeologists are especially concerned with Sections 106 and 110 of NHPA. In the CRM industry Section 106, for example, is a sacred text, one that knowledgeable practitioners learn to recite from memory. That it took the Advisory Council more than five years to shepherd the most recent revisions to 36 CFR Part 800 through the regulatory review process is ample evidence of the complexity of CRM today.

ARPA and its amendments established procedures for permitting excavations on federally controlled lands and instituted penalties for illegal excavations, vandalism, and, most recently, the transport of illegally obtained archaeological materials across state lines. It opened up new avenues of resource management and expanded the audience for the protection of archaeological resources.

NAGPRA details the rights of Native Americans and other groups with respect to the treatment, repatriation, and disposition of "human remains, funerary objects, sacred objects, and objects of cultural patrimony."[20] Consultation regarding NAGPRA-related issues, whether the inventory and repatriation of objects in museum collections or the circumstances surrounding the excavation of human remains on federal or tribal lands, has required a high level of contact, cooperation, and consultation between Native Americans and the archaeological community. In practice, the impact of NAGPRA goes beyond federally recognized tribes. Many federal agencies apply NAGPRA-like conditions to archaeological projects affecting human remains and sacred or funerary objects associated with state-recognized tribes. In addition, most agencies sponsoring archaeological projects on nonfederal or nontribal lands will conduct NAGPRA-like consultations with any federally recognized tribe that has an interest in the site.

Although changes initiated by NHPA, ARPA, and NAGPRA significantly shaped American archaeological processes, other laws and regulations have also had an impact. In 1990 the guild addressed its stewardship responsibilities through regulations dealing with the "Curation of Federally Owned and Administered Archaeological Collections" (36 CFR Part 79) and guidance of the 1987 Abandoned Shipwreck Act, which transferred the title for all abandoned shipwrecks to the states in an attempt to provide further protection from looting.

Few persons outside of the archaeology guild understand how extensively Sections 106 and 110 regulate the way archaeology is practiced in the United States. The culture of the individual agency responsible for compliance with NHPA also critically shapes the practice of preservation as it applies to archaeological properties. Equally important is the interaction of NHPA with other national priorities such as defense, transportation, clean water, wetlands, and flood plain management. Three examples will demonstrate the impact of these regulations.

For many years, American archaeologists accepted the false notion that excavation of an archaeological site prior to work on a federal project was not, in

Section 106 language, an "adverse effect."[21] The "research exception" to the criteria of adverse effect was developed as a regulatory shortcut, so that archaeological sites would not hold up the review of projects in situations where potential impact could not be determined during early project planning. Specifically, the "no adverse effect through data recovery" regulation was particularly useful to transportation planners, who also had to contend with Section 4(f) of the 1966 U.S. Department of Transportation Act. Under this program, however, sites regarded as important only for their scientific information are exempted from additional consideration.

The real effect of the research exception was that consideration of archaeological resources could be avoided until other environmental and political factors had been taken into account. Delaying concern for the archaeological record meant that major decisions about where to site a new school or how to align a proposed highway were difficult to change in light of later archaeological discoveries. Project sponsors soon concluded that, except in rare instances—as when human remains were involved—archaeological resources would not influence overall planning decisions. Unlike other threatened resources such as wetlands or endangered species, it became conventional wisdom that the presence of National Register–eligible archaeological sites would not stop a project from going forward.

Despite a strong conservation ethic, the archaeology guild went along with this "no adverse effect" fiction because it also funded large-scale excavations on temporally and geographically diverse archaeological sites. In theory, the purpose of project planning was to identify potential sites early on, so that adverse effects to significant sites would be avoided through project redesign or other measures. Many archaeologists were disturbed by the all-too-frequent happenstance that a successful project (from a conservation standpoint) that had avoided an archaeological site later turned sour because subsequent developments not subject to NHPA compliance destroyed sites located nearby. Archaeologists thus quickly came to believe that it was better to destroy sites through excavation than to avoid them and see them blitzed by later developments.

Defining the boundaries between potential impact areas and those beyond the scope of NHPA compliance also presented regulatory challenges. The Advisory Council's definition of the "area of potential effects" (APE) was sometimes sufficiently vague (or perhaps insufficiently enforced) as to produce considerable argument within the guild. Without uniform national guidance, SHPOs and project sponsors developed conventions that sometimes differed from area to area and from project to project. If federal funds were to be used to provide additional highway lanes and a new interchange for a proposed theme park, should the theme park development area itself be included in the APE? Should the borrow pits used to generate fill dirt for a development project be so designated?

Defining the APE was extremely important for archaeological projects because it established the area endangered both by the proposed project itself and by the archaeologists. Linear corridors were especially vexing. Constrained by a narrow APE, archaeologists frequently encountered hints of potentially significant resources at the edges of these projects but were denied access to the rest of the site.[22]

Another, more general, boundary issue has an impact on archaeological practice. That is the boundary between compliance with NHPA and NEPA.[23] As explained in Chapter 2, NEPA and NHPA are individual laws implemented by different regulations; even the vocabulary is distinct and somewhat confusing. NEPA is concerned with "significant impacts to the human environment," whereas NHPA covers "adverse effects to significant historic properties." Often NEPA and NHPA practitioners borrow terms of art, as when archaeologists use the phrase "segmenting the project." Segmenting a project—that is, dividing up a complex proposal into smaller parts to hide cumulative effects to the environment —is illegal under NEPA. But until the most recent Advisory Council regulations governing Section 106 were issued, NHPA made no reference to segmentation.

As a project-planning and decision-making tool, NEPA compliance drives a broad-based environmental review process for many federal undertakings that includes consideration of archaeological resources as environmental values. Agency project planners, faced with the need to gather relatively expensive archaeological information, often delayed NHPA compliance. Many environmental assessments and environmental impact statements contained the sentence: "Compliance with Section 106 of the National Historic Preservation Act will be completed when a preferred project alternative has been selected." Through the use of this tactic, numerous archaeological sites have been excavated—and hence destroyed—under the Advisory Council's research exception, because identification and evaluation were delayed until after other environmental laws were complied with, development sites selected, and project plans finalized.

In the early 1980s excavations at an inundated mill site in Maryland were stopped because regulators thought that the fieldwork might jeopardize an Army Corps of Engineers wetlands permit granted under the Clean Water Act. More recently, the Federal Emergency Management Agency sponsored extensive data recovery excavations at the site of a well-documented archaeological

Thomas Jefferson's Poplar Forest, near Lynchburg, Virginia. In the last twenty-five years archaeologists have moved from conducting excavations in support of building restoration projects to programs that seek to understand past lifeways and landscapes. (Photo by Mark Thompson, *Lynchburg News and Advocate*)

village site in Georgia, because project planners thought that redesign of a roadway might require revisiting previously completed environmental reviews.

Legislative and regulatory changes within the last twenty years point to a number of current issues in American archaeology: resource identification and protection, curation, and consideration of public values. The proliferation of laws, regulations, and guidance related to archaeology within the broader field of historic preservation is clear evidence that the CRM industry dominates archaeological practice.

As a result of the explosion of CRM-based work, the literature of archaeology has grown tremendously in the last two decades. The diversity and accessibility of this literature reflects the nature of the profession today. For guidance, most states have standard procedures that require a minimum level of effort for archaeological studies—in fieldwork, background research, laboratory analysis, curation, and reporting. Often these standards mimic the relevant federal regulations. Using these standards, the CRM industry has generated vast quantities of "gray literature," a term that somehow denigrates the hard work and professionalism required to produce it. Popular versions of long technical reports are often required as part of the compliance process, so that many public-oriented versions have been funded in recent decades.

The NPS and other federal agencies regularly publish materials on archaeology. *Common Ground* is a quarterly magazine that focuses on issues of national, state, and local significance while reporting on the progress in repatriation in NAGPRA and ARPA criminal cases.[24] *Common Ground* and its companion work, *CRM: Cultural Resource Management*, as well as other federally sponsored periodicals, illustrate how multiple public values are now considered within the American archaeological guild.

Uncertain Destiny: Issues for the Future

Because it is perceived as beholden to an inherently destructive practice, the American archaeological guild is often viewed as the black sheep of the historic preservation movement. An archaeological record or report does not easily contribute to livable communities, Main Street programs, antisprawl campaigns, or any other mainstream historic preservation initiative. At times during the last twenty years the marriage of archaeology and preservation was tense, especially in environments where fiscal resources were constrained.

Within the historic preservation movement archaeology is treated as the "A-word," which often gives it token representation. For example, not one of the one hundred accomplishments and failures listed in the fiftieth anniversary issue of the National Trust relate to archaeological sites. Other Trust "anniversary" publications have continued to show minimal acceptance or interest in archaeology as an aspect of historic preservation. Thus, the greatest challenge for the archaeological community will be to reestablish and strengthen its relationship with the larger historic preservation movement.[25]

The problem is that archaeologists love the archaeological record. They continue to believe that material culture found in the ground is a revelation about history. Buried stuff—if you can tease out its mysteries—has true meaning about the past. Archaeologists live and breathe data—because the archaeological record is an elusive, sexy, democratic past—not one generated by clerks, accountants, or politicians, but by the folks. American archaeologists entered the field because of the romance and mystery of the archaeological record. For most archaeologists, the excitement is in discovery—excavation and field-work—not in revisiting previously excavated materials or places. Beyond its relationship within the historic preservation community, the future of American archaeology lies in how well it adapts to new technology and how well it manages the crisis in curation and a declining resource base.

Technology

By nature and by necessity, archaeologists have adapted the technological marvels of global positioning satellite systems, ground-penetrating radar (GPR), and geographic information systems to their everyday practice. Remote sensing, total station transits, laser levels, digital cameras, digital site reports, and computer-resident databases have brought technological complexity to the work of archaeological investigation. At times, archaeological publications read like computer technology trade magazines.[26]

Technology's real promise and true power appears at its best when incorporated into the archaeological discovery and interpretation process. It is easy to envision a time when archaeological surveys, guided by computer-based predictive models, are ground-truthed using a hand-held GPS system with pull-down menus that also provide the template for showing where individual excavations are to be made, what soils will be encountered, and what artifacts will be recovered. Such data collection methods, tied to a computer-resident, spatial data base, would improve the ability to identify sites and understand the patterns within sites.

With computers came databases, which fostered the archaeologist's love for statistics and pattern recognition. Databases became much more than tools for manipulating archaeological collections. In the last twenty years it has become much easier to manage large sets of site data, even at the national level. Today, the National Archaeological Database (NADB) lists over 240,000 site reports from across the country, while the National Register Information System (NRIS) provides access to about 5,000 National Register listings of archaeological sites in the United States. At the state level, it was the CRM industry that funded efforts to digitize site information for individual jurisdictions. Many states have received funds from the DOT or other federal agencies to support the development of computer resident data and geographic information. Increasingly, this information at the state and national levels is accessible through the World Wide Web.[27]

In many ways technology has invaded archaeological research and laboratory analysis to an even greater extent than excavation processes. The ability to manipulate larger and larger sets of data from multiple sites is contrasted with the inability to reach a consensus on how to describe and catalog the things we find in the ground. Only in the last few years have the federal regulators been able to enforce standard language and protocols as more and more state agencies begin to digitize information contained in archaeological site files. The inherent particularism of archaeology makes it difficult for the profession to take full advantage of borrowed technology.

Archaeology has been slow to arrive at a consensus on technological issues, because to do so would require a disciplined standardization of archaeological method. Few research areas have a strict protocol for conducting basic research in the field or in the laboratory. To illustrate, there is no standard for estimating the minimum number of vessels in an assemblage. One school of thought counts only distinctive rim shards; another counts bases. It is natural that archaeologists tend to retain their particularism and individualism when confronted with scientific advances. They do things as they were taught in graduate school or in field school. Archaeology is hampered in this respect, because its experiments and excavations are not, as in other sciences, replicable, since every site is at some level unique.

Technology has also invaded archaeological publications. One of the most impressive studies of recent date was entitled *Excavating Occaneechi Town: Archaeology of an Eighteenth-Century Indian Village in North Carolina* (1998). Published by the University of North Carolina Press, this CD-ROM is both a comprehensive site report and a dynamic teaching tool combined in a unique format. *Excavating Occaneechi Town* not only presents most of the raw data from several years of excavations, it also provides links between the excavation (photographs and line drawings) and the artifacts found within individual features.[28]

Over the last decade a new technological revolution—perhaps equal in its impact to radio carbon and other absolute dating techniques—has emerged in American archaeology: the exploration of DNA evidence contained in the archaeological record. Most DNA studies in the New World have focused on the timing of the arrival of humans from Asia, a story of international significance tied to the diffusion of people across the globe. Other work has focused on local issues, such as determining the genetic relationship of individuals in a graveyard or a tomb. As noted in a recent review of the emerging field, the extent of DNA analysis, a collaborative effort between microbiologists and archaeologists, will remain limited in the near future because of the time and costs associated with the work. In addition, because a principal source of new information includes human remains, further studies must involve consideration of issues concerning Native Americans and other interested parties.[29]

The full benefit of the technological revolution is yet to be realized. Advanced technology helps to organize and synthesize the archaeological record, while combating the particularism of CRM and the site-centric nature of archaeology. But the technological revolution has penetrated archaeology only to a limited extent. Good field and lab work still requires careful observation with attention to detail. Archaeology is still an experimental science—the investigator has to see things in the ground or recognize patterns in the laboratory. Technology has helped archaeologists in their often-desperate search for pattern —any pattern—in the archaeological record. Our theoretical and practical need for a patterned past makes use of the computer, laser, and other tools too tempting. Ironically, as of the turn of the century, some archaeological technology continued to be handmade—flotation machines, water screens, and mechanical dry screens. Not surprisingly, then, a certain level of experimentation and craftsmanship continues to be found in field and laboratory work.

The Curation Crisis

The future of American archaeology lies both in field records and in the condition of archaeological collections. The profession will be judged by the quality of its records and how well it keeps the artifacts. There is a general consensus within the guild that archaeological sites do not exist unless a descriptive report has been prepared, the raw data presented, and the records and artifacts made available for further analysis. The CRM industry has created a curation crisis: too many artifacts, records, and the like with too few custodians to care for them. By a 1994 estimate, the collections of the NPS alone numbered over fifty-seven million archaeological artifacts.[30] On many sites, the majority of archaeological samples are never processed, analyzed, or interpreted. Both in the field and in the laboratory, what to save and what to toss is a perennial, if often ignored, question. To paraphrase Tom King—"culture's clutter" needs extensive caring for as we approach the twenty-first century.[31]

Archaeological guild members are basically either field people or lab people. Unfortunately, laboratory specialists are rarely in charge of projects, and they bear the brunt of reduced resources and cutbacks. Coming at the end of the archaeological process, laboratory analysis, conservation, and curation are often

Archaeology project in downtown
Philadelphia

Archaeology project in Washington, D.C.

Urban archaeology has challenged the profession in any number of ways, from designing
and implementing complex research projects to the logistics of mounting excavations where
issues relating to health and safety and hazardous materials are present. These excavations
in Philadelphia and Washington, D.C., were conducted as part of CRM projects. (Courtesy of
The Louis Berger Group, Inc.)

forgotten. To most of the public, archaeology means excavation. The laboratory phase is invisible and not as exciting. In public archaeological programs, the emphasis on education means that "public programs" are equated with active excavations, not laboratory analysis and conservation. Increasingly, laboratories are mere stops on the standard tour of archaeological institutions and museums. In Virginia, three different sites offer a view into the laboratory: the city-sponsored Alexandria Archaeology, a house museum; Thomas Jefferson's Poplar Forest; and the Virginia Department of Historic Resources, the commonwealth's primary repository for archaeological collections.

In addition to producing a wealth of archaeological artifacts and associated records, the CRM industry also has an impact on the curation crisis in several other ways. First, a consulting firm must formulate research questions long before the true research potential of a site is known. A research design created at the completion of fieldwork adequate to determine National Register–eligibility of a particular site may not fully prepare the archaeologist for what will be found during Phase III data recovery excavations. In urban and other deeply buried sites, where the window on the site is usually small and narrow, further excavations can reveal whole areas of analysis that were not expected or fiscally planned for. For instance, a site thought to contain significant information on the production of stone tools during the Archaic period may also yield data on subsistence practices that were unknown at the time excavation was started. Sponsors of archaeological studies in the compliance world do not generally favor requests for additional funding as new discoveries are made in the field. Moreover, agencies following a compliance process will rarely support the reanalysis of previously excavated materials.

Second, laboratory work and curation are often afterthoughts in compliance projects. In graduate school, archaeologists are taught that they should budget three days of background research, laboratory processing, cataloging, analysis, and reporting for every day of excavation. But few compliance budgets consider this conventional wisdom. State historic preservation offices bear the burden of maintaining these collections, many without the ability to charge for permanent curation and conservation. Here again, as with the rest of the NHPA compliance system, the emphasis is on completing excavations, compiling reports, and obtaining necessary agency reviews. By the time a collection is submitted to a repository for permanent curation, the project and the regulatory process have long since been completed.

A Declining Resource Base

How many sites are left—and how many of them are important—is a difficult question to answer. What the archaeological community should do about this declining and irretrievable resource base is even more perplexing. The fact is that sites will always be threatened by development, and the need for archaeological salvage or rescue programs is readily apparent. Who will take the lead in mandating site preservation? Where are the tools for helping communities to preserve sites? Why should we preserve sites? Why should we preserve sites if their value is solely to obtain information about the past?

Archaeological sites contribute to a community's well-being, historical awareness, and quality of life in ways that are different from other types of historic properties. Across the country, there are few tax credit or incentive programs to assist in the protection of archaeological sites. Unlike farmland preservation, which enjoys extensive support in rapidly developing areas, a landowner cannot sell his development rights for property that includes archaeological resources in exchange for a tax credit or cash payment. True preservation of irreplaceable resources, as demonstrated by the Archaeological Conservancy since its establishment in 1980, only comes with ownership, either in whole or through easements.[32]

The pace of destruction of archaeological sites is matched by the pace of suburban, urban, and industrial development. Despite the thousands of NHPA compliance projects that identify archaeological sites as a result of a federal undertaking, thousands more projects are without the benefit of federal, state, or local oversight. The rate of site destruction is also measured by the growth of the CRM industry. If the archaeological community decides that some sites are worth saving without excavation, who will say what sites are worthy of this level of protection? Are there some sites too precious to dig today? Again, the American archaeological guild must provide answers to these questions if it is to be a vital force in the historic preservation movement of the twenty-first century.

Hand in hand with the bulldozer and the tracked excavator that destroy archaeological sites are the perpetrators of "time crime." These are the looters who destroy archaeological sites for fun and profit. Often operating in the shadows of legitimacy, or out in the open as members of local associations, treasure hunters, and individuals with metal detectors—a distinction the participants suggest is important—hundreds of individuals are out in farm fields and woodlands every weekend collecting materials from both recorded and unknown sites. There is no adequate way to measure the impact of these individuals and groups on the archaeological record. In some cases, metal-detecting clubs have successfully partnered with professional archaeologists to identify and record locations of archaeological sites. However, one has only to look at the flagrant and frequent violation of ARPA provisions by "pot hunters" to estimate what the country has lost for all time.[33]

Laws relating to illegal or unauthorized excavation on archaeological sites are found in every state and locality. From criminal trespass to violation of sepulcher, law enforcement agencies have any number of ways to investigate archaeological crimes. In most states legislation restricts the excavation of human remains on public and private lands. Some states have a permit system that governs archaeological excavations on state lands. But laws are only as effective as their enforcement. In an ironic turn of events, a recent ARPA investigation had targeted a local amateur archaeological group in the mid-Atlantic region. Assisted by state police, the investigation revealed that the group had excavated Native American human remains without the required state permits and then transported the remains across state lines. Several weeks later, the same state police allowed a local high school teacher to excavate the remains of a Civil War soldier without obtaining a required permit. Clearly, if archaeological resources are to receive the legal protection they deserve, education is the message and the medium for both the archaeological and law enforcement communities.

Conclusion

Where will the American archaeological guild be in twenty years? A recent review of archaeological programs in Virginia identified "leadership and vision" as the primary unmet need within the commonwealth's many archaeological communities. Who will lead the next generation of archaeologists? Will it be the regulators who operate the CRM system, the academics who train the practitioners, or the business leaders working within the CRM paradigm? As federal and state agencies react to the new world of NHPA compliance, with greater emphasis on SHPO and federal agency agreement, how will power shift in American archaeology?

The simple answer to these questions is to follow the money. It is obvious that state and federal agencies with significant fiscal resources that can act as sponsors will be the de facto leaders in American archaeology in the decades to come. In most states, efforts by SHPOs to place archaeological site information

in a computer resident format floundered for many years until the financial resources of another state agency—typically the Department of Transportation
—were brought to bear on the problem. Clearly, the guild must be creative in
its attempts to leverage financial commitments from companion agencies, outside partners, and others. As in all endeavors, however, creativity has its risks.

In the early years of the twenty-first century, American archaeological al-
chemists are in a strong position to shape their uncertain destiny. The archaeological community must first strengthen its presence within the wider world
of historic preservation, which means that individual archaeologists must participate in the preservationists' agenda. Archaeology's most productive contribution to preservation is its ability to excite the general public about the past
and to develop constituencies through public education at individual sites or
within communities. Fostering broader public support for preservation makes
archaeological programs more relevant to mainstream preservation issues and
programs, and strengthens the links between the two endeavors. Within historic preservation, archaeologists must enhance and expand the public archaeology paradigm—that archaeological resources are rare and threatened, unique
and nonrenewable. Public archaeology means that there is a common responsibility for resources, one that must be shared by the wider world of historic
preservation.

Internally, the guild's future is assured if it fosters the leadership and vision
that expands public appreciation and understanding of the multiple values of
the archaeological record, ensures the highest professional standards in all archaeological work, and adheres to existing laws and regulations while improving the quality of guidance. History will judge us by what sites we choose to
study, how well we excavate them, the records we keep, and the artifacts we cu-
rate for the next generation.

Private Sector Involvement
in Historic Preservation

In 1973 the American Institute of Architects (AIA) published a full-page adver-
tisement featuring Boston's 1867 Old City Hall with a caption that read, "The
Most Promising Trend in Modern Architecture." At the time, Old City Hall
and Ghiradelli Square in San Francisco were two of a handful of successful
commercial adaptive use projects nationally. Although teasing at the time, the
AIA ad proved to profoundly predictive of the shift that was about to occur in
real estate development and historic preservation.

Within a thirty-year period, the number of adaptive use and commercial rehabilitation projects has grown from a few high-risk, hard-fought ventures undertaken by developers who had both the resources and the passion to chance
an uncertain market response into a multibillion-dollar business in which nearly
every real estate entity participates. The realization that making economic use
of historic buildings is an effective preservation solution and, frequently, a
financially and politically constructive way to create housing, offices, industrial
space, and so forth has caused preservation and real estate interests to find
common ground. The National Park Service and the Internal Revenue Service
(IRS), both agencies responsible for administering investment tax credits for rehabilitation, estimate that more than $21 billion has been invested in historic
properties since the passage of the first investment tax credit program in 1976.

The growth of private sector involvement and investment in historic preservation has occurred in parallel with a changing cultural ethos toward urban life
and historical continuity in the United States. This shift in the cultural climate
has been reinforced by favorable public policy initiatives, tax incentives, funding programs, innovative development projects, and a positive market response.

The preservation movement itself has turned increasingly from a regulatory
approach to more of a market-driven reality. Although the use of regulatory
tools such as landmark and historic district ordinances and environmental
quality legislation will remain the backbone of protecting historic properties

and districts, preservationists are working at the state and local levels to establish incentives that encourage market-based development. Typically, preservation incentives ranging from funding programs to tax breaks help to offset the risk and development costs associated with property conversion and rehabilitation.

The Smart Growth movement is having an impact by pushing the market toward existing neighborhoods and the reuse of historic buildings. The past twenty-five years have witnessed a dramatic shift from a suburban development ethic to one that is increasingly focused on the revitalization of the historic centers of our communities. Small-town main streets have been repositioned as viable commercial centers. City-defining bank buildings, hotels, government buildings, and office buildings have been recycled for contemporary variations of the same use or adapted for new uses. Inner-city neighborhoods are being reclaimed as stable centers of affordable housing, historic industrial properties have been renovated for contemporary industrial use, and institutional buildings of all types have been reused for every variation of commercial, residential, and continued institutional purposes.

The revitalization of neighborhoods, urban districts, and key landmark properties requires distinct approaches to their accomplishment. However, there are fundamental development elements that have been essential to the success of the private sector's investment in historic preservation. These have included:

- Private sector initiatives
- Determination that there is a market that will buy, rent, or invest in the historic property or area
- Involvement of experienced developers and lenders in the development process
- Public policy on the federal, state, and local levels that supports the reuse of historic properties
- Tax incentives and public funding programs that mitigate the financial risk associated with historic property development and finance the "gap" between available private financing and project costs
- Public-private partnerships in areawide and specific property development

A balanced pattern of development between new construction and the reuse of historic properties relies on the sophistication and constructive interaction between key groups in the development process—developers, government agencies, community groups, and preservation organizations. This chapter considers some of the primary components of the development process in the context of the principal concerns of the private sector involved in historic preservation.

The Development Team

The real estate developer, with the investment team, is the focal point of the development process. The developer is defined as the one who assembles property, capital, and human resources to construct an improvement for use by a third party with no preset constraints on risk or financial return.[1] The developer creates a team of people to work on the project. This team includes a real estate broker for the acquisition and marketing of the finished product, the lender and/or equity investor, the construction company (contractor) and subcontractors, and the property manager or operator. In return for being the first to provide capital or seed money, assembling the critical components of land, capital, and labor, rehabilitating the building, and marketing the space to a (third party) user, the developer is last in line to receive a financial return from the project. The developer is thus the critical risk taker in the development process.

There are a number of different types of developers, and they classify themselves by land use (e.g., a retail, residential, office, or hotel developer) as a speculative or nonspeculative developer, a fee developer, a merchant builder, or a developer willing to undertake public-private ventures. Each of these classifications has an inherent understood range of risk that the developer is willing to undertake. Within each of these general classifications, a corps of experienced preservation developers has emerged. These include both for-profit and nonprofit development groups.

The Development Process

The development process has four basic phases: predevelopment, construction, marketing and leasing/sales, and management or disposition of asset. The successful completion of these stages can mean the difference between a successful property development or a stalled project. Undertaking the risk of investment or development in historic property, the developer/investor will have three primary concerns that will determine whether he or she will assume the risk. Issues of timing, clarity, and closure are first-level criteria that every investor must assess in calculating the degree of risk inherent in the project. Assessing these factors allows the investor to qualitatively and quantitatively ascertain risk in terms of degree of support or opposition, probability of success, and investment required to complete the review and development process effectively.

Timing

Real estate wisdom used to be that the three main ingredients for project success were location, location, and location. Although that adage still applies, the more important ingredients in today's competitive markets are timing, timing, and timing. An investor's primary interest is the speed and certainty with which the real estate product can be brought to market. The timely completion of a project can mean the difference between full rent up and laggard sales. The timely financing of a project can mean the difference between favorable interest rates or those that will make a project's capital structure infeasible. Since many of the major capital markets are aligned with national or international capital markets, financing can be available with attractive interest rates in one financial quarter and be reduced to a trickle in the next, depending on stock market conditions, national market supply-and-demand trends, or a wide range of external factors totally beyond the control of the developer. Disruption or impediments to completing the project approval process, construction process, or marketing of a project can significantly affect the profitability anticipated by a developer and project investors. The developer will make every effort throughout the financial, legal, and political process to ensure that a project moves smoothly and efficiently through the system.

Clarity

The real estate investor will be most interested in historic property opportunities where there is certainty within the development process. Communities that have resolved the key issues of zoning (such as densities, land use, and growth direction) and that are clear about market realities can offer the historic property investor the most valuable development incentive: that of certainty of direction and process. Such clarity can mean the difference between months of time the developer must spend in community meetings working out fundamental growth and development directions to get his or her single project through the approval process. Without clarity, projects can become embroiled in adversarial community debates or lengthy litigation. Communities as diverse as Seattle, Washington, and Savannah, Georgia, have illustrated the economic benefits of establishing a clear, specific development framework through their community planning process so that developers can understand from the outset what is allowable and what will be unwelcome. Without such a framework, each project review becomes an ad hoc, time-intensive exercise to establish the foundation for project development. This can significantly erode the potential profit from the project and discourage broad-based investment interest in historic property development.

In addition to a clear development climate for historic preservation-oriented development, an investor will look for collateral conditions that will assist the project. These include adequate parking, high levels of public safety, and positive environmental conditions to avoid the time and costs associated with legal challenges or remediation; quality schools; infrastructure repair; the availability of zoning variances; land assembly and tax incentives, and low-income housing tax credits.

Closure

Developers and successful advocates for historic preservation have learned that the most effective means of creating a reasonable development climate is to ensure project closure. Closure means that once it has successfully completed community and regulatory reviews, the project can proceed. Difficult problems occur when a challenge is brought late in the review process or after the process has been completed. A challenge can be made in the form of public protest, adverse publicity, or a legal challenge. The developer and public officials must make every effort to identify project concerns early in the development process and to resolve these. Successful preservation advocates have learned that they are taken seriously over time when they are able to clearly articulate project and community goals early in the process, work constructively to develop compatible solutions, and, once negotiations are concluded, resist further modifications.

Project Risk Control

Private sector involvement in historic preservation relies on the developer's ability to control or pin down as many elements in the development process as possible. This control allows the investor to contain project risk to the greatest extent possible within a process that is full of inherent, multifaceted risks. Project risk is defined as "uncertainty or variability or the possibility of a loss. Risk is the possibility that returns from an investment will be greater or less than forecast. Diversification of investments provides some protection against risk."[2] Project risks entail:

- Regulatory risk: tax law changes, rent control, zoning, and other restrictions imposed by government that could adversely affect the profitability of investments.
- Construction risk: all factors associated with the building and renovating process—the more complex the project design, construction process, or use, the greater the risk. It can also include the volatility of labor markets in terms of pricing, labor shortages, and strikes. Most failures in renovation projects are the result of underpricing the cost of construction, inadequate contingency funds, and contractors who are inexperienced in renovation, adaptive use, and restoration.
- Financing risk: risk of loss due to the use of debt financing, which increases as the amount of debt on a real estate investment increases. The risk depends

on the extent of prior claims of lenders on income and proceeds on liquidation of the investment.

- Political risk: occurs in the context of seeking the necessary support and approvals from elected officials, agency departments, and local stakeholders. It is significantly reduced for projects in communities where the public and private sectors have worked cooperatively to assess market conditions, developed a consensus regarding development goals and standards, established financing mechanisms, removed institutional disincentives to private redevelopment, changed zoning codes, and authorized government loans and subsidies. Without basic agreement in these areas, political risks can lead to stalled projects, litigation, and default.[3]
- Market risk: a property may be subject to a higher mortgage interest rate than the overall market rate. In the real property leasing market, a long-term lease may lock the owner into low rents. Rents, vacancies, or operating expenses may vary from projected amounts. Finally, within the real estate market there is the risk that resale proceeds may be less than anticipated.
- An act of God: an unpreventable destructive occurrence in the natural world—for example, earthquakes, floods, hurricanes, lightning, and tornadoes. A contract can protect a buyer by including a provision that allows the buyer to default if the property is damaged by an act of God. Insurance can offer protection against certain risks. Owners can insure buildings against risk of loss caused by fires, storms, and other hazards by taking out a hazard insurance policy.[4]
- Timing: local market demand is critical to support the reuse of architecturally or structurally desirable buildings. Changes in local and regional growth patterns can affect project viability. Many regions of the country and locations within cities experience differences in the rate of growth due to changes in demand, population changes, and similar factors. Project success can depend on accurately assessing and anticipating market demand, financing availability, and the market reception to the proposed use.

Private sector interest in historic preservation projects is based on the expectation of reasonable financial return for the substantial risk involved. Each of these areas of risk possess a wide range of elements that alone or in combination can spell the difference between success and limited returns.

Predevelopment planning will assess the extent of these risks along with the actions that could mitigate risks or turn them to the advantage of the project. From a developer's perspective, the ideal situation is one in which the develop-

Spring Street artists lofts, Los Angeles. Former office buildings are being adapted for live-work office space using tax and zoning incentives. (Photo by John C. Lewis, J. Paul Getty Trust, Getty Conservation Institute)

ment climate favors preservation-oriented development and where the public and private sectors have preorganized reviews and approvals, project assistance, and incentives to help offset risks.

Development Incentives

The most successful development projects in the country are those that have strong local support and incentives. Public policy initiatives have taken the form of tax and funding incentives for investing in historic properties, favorable zoning and building and safety regulations, and a community planning process that addresses community concerns. Typically, these are accompanied by companion disincentives to discourage the destruction or substantial alteration of historic resources. In several cities representing a wide range of cultural resources such as Pittsburgh, Pennsylvania, Charleston, South Carolina, and Seattle, Washington, there has been a carefully crafted link between the public and private sector at the local level and through local, state, and federal programs.

Zoning and Land Use

Favorable zoning ordinances can facilitate development in a variety of ways. When density allowances are compatible with the scale of existing buildings, redevelopment pressure on historic buildings is reduced. The financial return from new construction is placed on a par with a preservation development project.

Several cities have adopted adaptive use ordinances that adjust parking requirements to existing conditions and allow use categories to reinforce the mixed-use character of the area. This can allow the developer to proceed with a project on an as-of-right basis, without incurring the time and cost of a lengthy public approval process for a variance or conditional use permit.

Historic District Zoning and Landmark Designation

Designation as a landmark or a historic district (for large areas of cities) clearly establishes the protection and development direction for properties. Designated landmark properties and properties within designated historic districts are essentially prequalified for incentives created to encourage historic preservation. For commercial property developers, all designated landmarks and contributing properties within a historic district are eligible for the Investment Tax Credit for Rehabilitation.

Tax Incentives

Tax Increment Financing. Tax increment financing (TIF) is a mechanism authorized by many states to help local governments fund areas designated for redevelopment. This tool has been used in Main Street revitalization programs, urban redevelopment project areas, and Business Improvement Districts, as well as for individual properties by cities nationwide to encourage development in distressed areas. Depending on the state enabling legislation, TIF can be used to pay for physical improvements in a historic area such as new sidewalks, the undergrounding of utilities, and a parking garage. TIF may also be employed to provide incentives for development (grants and loans) and to cover the administrative costs of a downtown revitalization program.

Tax increment financing is a legally authorized process associated with local property tax programs. At the outset of a program, the community assesses the local property values within the TIF district. The sum of these values becomes the baseline. To the extent that tax revenues generated as a result of the local revitalization program exceed the baseline, they can be plowed back into the improvement program itself instead of reverting to the city's general fund rev-

Knoxville, Tennessee, Mall, 1962. Downtown began to fight back as customers moved to the suburbs after World War II. Knoxville embarked on this early downtown project in the early 1960s as the Main Street model of its day (although not called that). It protected shoppers from the rain but did little for the architectural character of the area. (Robert E. Stipe)

Louisville, Kentucky, Galleria, 1972. The downtown Galleria opened ten years after the Knoxville Mall. It is still attractive and economically viable. (Robert E. Stipe)

enues. Alternatively, the local government may decide to issue bonds to pay for the revitalization activities. The extra taxes generated through revitalization are used to pay off the bonds.

Another approach is to freeze property taxes during the development process (sometimes extending through the early years of a completed project) and give the developer an additional financial cushion to make a project financially viable until market conditions improve.

Federal Investment Tax Credits for Rehabilitation. Federal tax policy has had the most profound effect in attracting private investors and reclaiming historic properties for contemporary purposes. The creation of the Investment Tax Credit for Rehabilitation in 1981 initially established a generous, 25 percent tax incentive for investors in historic properties rehabilitated for contemporary, commercial purposes. Prior to the enactment of the tax credit legislation, historic properties were considered uneconomic resources due to the greater development and construction risks. In commercial centers, historic properties competed with the development potential of high-rise construction. With a lower buildable and rentable area and the extreme difficulty of obtaining financing for conversion or renovation, there was a tremendous loss of valuable historic resources.

The Investment Tax Credit (ITC) was introduced to provide additional economic support sufficient to attract private investment for the reuse of historic buildings. Conceptually modeled after the tax credit incentives available to investors in affordable housing, Congress recognized the desired social and economic benefits of extending or re-creating a productive use for historic and older buildings. The preceding three decades of urban renewal programs had caused widespread economic disruption and the destruction and destabilization of neighborhoods and center-city areas.

At the outset, the ITC provided a 25 percent tax credit, straight-line depreciation, and no limitations on the use of the credits by investors. Although federal tax policy changed in 1986 to reduce the amount of the credit to 20 percent and to restrict the use of the credit to qualified investors based on the IRS passive loss rules, the tax credit continues to be one of the most compelling economic incentives for investing in historic properties. Very simply, it considers nearly all of a project's development and construction costs to be qualified rehabilitation expenditures. Twenty percent of the value of those expenditures can be packaged as a tax credit and used by the developer or sold to an entity needing tax losses, generating, in most cases, the equity needed to obtain financing for the project.

The tax credits are available to the investor in the year in which the rehabilitated property is placed in service; that is, when the property is open for tenants to occupy. The depreciable basis for the property is reduced by the full amount of the credit in the year it is deducted. If a rehabilitation investment tax credit is taken and the property is disposed of in the first five years after the rehabilitated building was placed into service, some of the credit will be recaptured. The amount of recapture is a percentage of the original tax credit. For example, if a property is sold one full year after it was placed into service, it is subject to 100 percent recapture, after two years 80 percent, after three years 60 percent, and so forth. The federal tax incentives have worked in partnership with a range of other federal, state, and local incentives that have been developed to address local conditions and to further appeal to the investor.

Low-Income Housing Tax Credits. Rehabilitation tax credits have been used extensively in association with low-income housing tax credits to develop affordable housing within rehabilitated historic structures. Owners of residential rental property providing low-income housing are eligible to claim a credit annually for a period of ten years. The annual credit has a maximum rate of 9 percent for new construction and rehabilitation and a maximum rate of 4 percent for the acquisition cost of existing housing. To qualify, projects must meet explicit construction expenditure minimums, and income levels for renters must meet federal guidelines. When used in association with rehabilitation tax credits, the potential to raise cash equity in a project increases substantially.

State Tax Credits. More than fifteen states offer some form of tax credit for investments in rehabilitation and efforts are under way to do so in many others. In thirteen of these states, credits are available for both income-producing properties and historic homes. Five states (Missouri, West Virginia, Maryland, Virginia, and North Carolina) have received the most attention because their tax credit statutes do not place a dollar cap on the credit and work well on large-scale projects that also qualify for federal rehabilitation and affordable housing credits. Missouri, Maryland, and Virginia provide a 30 percent credit for income and owner-occupied properties; North Carolina has a 20 percent credit for income-producing buildings and a 25 percent credit for homeowners.[5]

These state tax credits generate highly meaningful amounts of project equity when used in combination with the federal tax credits. Typically, the com-

St. Andrews Bungalow Court, Hollywood, California, before renovation (Photo by Richard Barron, architect)

St. Andrews Bungalow Court after renovation (Photo by John C. Lewis)

St. Andrews Bungalow Court is a group of sixteen residential units grouped around a land-scaped courtyard dating from the early 1990s. The developer used federal low-income housing and rehabilitation incentives combined with California's Mills Act (a local preservation property tax incentive) to bring a completely derelict neighborhood back to life. (J. Paul Getty Trust, Getty Conservation Institute) bined federal-state historic tax credit investment should raise about 1.5 times the amount of the federal-only investment. The value of the tax credits can produce all of the equity required for a rehabilitation project, in some cases creating more than 20 percent of the financing required for a project. However, a number of issues make the state historic rehabilitation tax credits more difficult to place than federal credits. These include the generally lower income tax rates at the state level (7 percent, compared to the top federal corporate tax bracket of 39 percent) and heavy discounts on state credits due to the impact of state tax payments on corporations' federal tax liability. In the latter case, a reduction in state corporate tax liability means an increase in federal taxable income. The state tax credits are discounted to offset this increase. While federal tax credits typically are priced at approximately 85–95 percent of value, state tax credits are valued at 50–60 percent.

St. Louis, Missouri, provides one of the best illustrations of the importance of state ITCs. Investment in rehabilitation projects almost came to a halt after introduction of the passive loss rules as part of the Federal Tax Reform Act of 1986. As St. Louis continued to lose population, deferred maintenance and demolition thwarted all efforts on behalf of preservation and revitalization. With passage in 1988 of a 25 percent transferable credit toward eligible rehabilitation costs for both residential and commercial projects, twenty new rehabilitation projects were started in downtown St. Louis. The heart of the revitalization effort is Cupples Station, a historic railroad freight depot featuring ten buildings on twelve acres. The combined federal and state tax credits will produce $50 million in equity for the $250 million project.

Other planned rehabilitation projects will reinforce the Cupples Station venture. Also using the state and federal tax incentives, they include a 1,081-room Marriott Renaissance Hotel involving the rehabilitation of two historic hotels and a dozen loft building housing conversions in the old garment district.

Homeowner Tax Credits. Presently the 20 percent federal tax credit for rehabilitation is limited to income-producing properties, which excludes owner-occupied homes. There have been numerous attempts to establish a homeowner tax credit program to encourage rehabilitation of private homes, recognizing the hundreds of thousands of homes in big-city and small-town neighborhoods that are in need of rehabilitation. The neighborhoods tend to be among the oldest and most architecturally distinctive in their communities. Buyers or owners of homes in state or federally designated historic neighborhoods could receive up

Los Angeles bungalow, Genesee Street. State and city legislation can create incentives providing tax relief to owners of historic properties in exchange for agreements to maintain their properties. (Photo by John C. Lewis, Getty Conservation Institute)

to 20 percent of their renovation expenses back in the form of tax credits, up to $40,000 per home. Alternatively, the credit could be used to reduce mortgage interest rates far below prevailing market levels. A restoration that cost $50,000 would generate a $10,000 credit. Efforts to win passage of such a credit have not yet succeeded in Congress.

Real Estate Development Feasibility Analysis

Analysis of project feasibility for a rehabilitation project is complex and multidimensional. The political, economic, and physical conditions must be accurately assessed in terms of time and financial and human resources that need to be expended to create a viable project. The first step should be to gauge the local government's political will. Any project, no matter how perfect, may fail if it encounters strong resistance from City Hall. The city of San Francisco, for instance, sued to return a rehabilitated hotel to its former use as a low-income residential building. Lodging rooms designated for residential use could not be

Hotel Oakland, Oakland, California. Federal income tax credits have stimulated significant investment in the rehabilitation of historic properties nationwide. Projects numbering in the tens of thousands have ranged from small commercial and residential rental properties to the conversion of the landmark Hotel Oakland to provide housing for the elderly. (Advisory Council on Historic Preservation)

converted to tourist use without a wholly discretionary conditional-use permit. No matter how beneficial the new hotel's use, the city took a dim view of removing affordable housing units from circulation.

Clearly gauging government reaction to a proposed reuse can be critical to the timing, cost, and ultimate success of a project. The investor must then tie up the property with a long enough contingency period to complete all necessary due diligence. Can the property be made to meet current Americans with Disability Act requirements as well as environmental, zoning, and building code specifications? Is insurance available to protect against the unknown? Must the property be subdivided before its use can be changed? Does it need a zoning change or a conditional-use permit to accommodate the new use? Must tenants be relocated (and are there rent-control or relocation ordinances governing how much notice must be given and the payments necessary to get tenants to vacate)? Are there commercial leases that can be terminated or bought out?

Once the project's physical and political issues have been analyzed, it is important to consider the public and private sources of funds available for the conversion and the time and resources required to obtain them. Properly assessing each of these factors and the risk and potential cost to the project during the planning phase allows the developer to structure adequate time and financing for project development.

Financing Preservation Projects

Financing adaptive use projects remains the most challenging part of the development process. This is true for any investment or development project. However, lenders tend to be more cautious and conservative with rehabilitation projects due to the perception that this real estate product has more variables in construction, marketing, and returns than the more standardized, new construction counterparts in any of the land uses (e.g., commercial office, retail, and residential)

The National Trust for Historic Preservation, the NPS, and many state and local organizations have devoted extensive resources to documenting and promoting the economic benefits of historic preservation. These organizations and state and local government entities have also developed a panoply of incentives, funding resources, and subsidies. These can cover the gaps or financial shortfalls that must be dealt with when conventional lenders or market conditions do not adequately cover the financial requirements of a particular investment.

For the private sector to succeed in historic preservation, investors have used a range of financing approaches. Preservation investors may be credited with a willingness to be more creative in assembling the financing for a project. Such financing can range from consortium financing, public–private partnerships, the use of ITCs, limited partnerships or syndications, and the transfer of development rights. To accomplish transactions of greater complexity, it is important to fully understand the basic principles of real estate and real property, and the assumptions and conventions that lenders and other investors will use in making investment decisions.

Legal Considerations

Legal considerations ultimately affect the expected benefits and risk associated with investing in or financing a real estate venture. In a free market economy when transactions involving a specific good or service occur repetitively, various institutional and legal arrangements evolve to standardize and facilitate such activities. Financing real estate is no exception to this rule. Because of the economic magnitude and social importance of real estate, the protocols are significant.

When the acquisition or development of residential or commercial properties is financed, the nature of the borrower's interest in the property, which is generally used as security for a loan, must be identified and acceptable to the lender who is being asked to advance funds for the project. Because there are so many different types of interests in real estate that can be conveyed or used as collateral for lending, our legal system insists that any conveyance must be in writing and in the form of a contract to be valid.

Property Rights. When financing or investing in real estate, U.S. law offers ways for the investor to be creative and apportion these various interests among various parties. Property rights refer to the right of a person to possess, use, enjoy, and dispose of his or her property. The value of a parcel of real estate is the total price that individuals are willing to pay for the flow of benefits associated with all of those rights. One does not have to be an owner to have rights to some of those benefits. For example, if you rent office space, you have the right to exclusive use of the office premises for a period of time. The value of a building can be improved by the extent to which the rights, that is, leases, are extended and the relative harmony in which respective rights are held. Conversely, potential conflicts may affect the value or price individuals are willing to pay for an interest in real estate and, ultimately, the value of a property.

The Taking Issue. A central issue of preservation law is the diminution or "taking" of property rights as a result of landmark designation under state and local laws. Owners have contended that the restrictions imposed on designated property restricted their freedom to use it beneficially and thereby reduced its market value. Fortunately, both public policy and case law have deflected this argument. (See Chapter 5.) The law accepts that communities have the right to plan and regulate land use, as in zoning, and that the preparation of a historic resources survey along with a preservation plan will tend to foreclose owners' charges of "spot zoning" or designations that are arbitrary, capricious, and confiscatory.

Transfer of Development Rights. Some communities and developers have used highly sophisticated real estate conveyancing techniques to carry out economic- and market-based preservation solutions. The transfer of development rights and the donation or sale of preservation easements are two examples of how one can use the "bundle of rights" that are said to represent property "ownership" to generate revenue or tax savings achieving a preservation objective.

"Development rights" are, simply, the unused space that a property owner has the "right" to use under current zoning but, for whatever reasons, is unable to use. This unused space has value in the real estate market and can be bought, sold, or transferred from one owner to another. The transfer of these unused development rights effectively protects a landmark property by maximizing the financial return from the property as the result of the transfer or sale. In municipalities that have authorized this technique (New York, Chicago, Denver, and Los Angeles), there are designated receiving zones to which the unused air rights may be conveyed. Most states that have authorized the use of this technique also require that all or a substantial portion of the proceeds from the sale of air rights be used to repair, rehabilitate, or maintain the landmark property from which the rights were carved out.

To be effective, development rights transfers require, among other things, a strong, bullish real estate market, an absolute commitment on the part of the local government to the implementation of a land-use plan, and a fairly sophisticated local planning program not often found, as a practical matter, in smaller cities and towns.[6]

Preservation Easements. A similar conveyance of property rights to create a preservation solution and economic advantage is the sale or donation of a preservation easement to a preservation organization that commits to maintain, supervise, and enforce the easement in perpetuity. Property owners in many states are allowed to donate a preservation easement to a qualified tax-exempt organization and thereby receive certain tax advantages. Most preservation easements convey the right to protect the facade of a building, the entire exterior, or, in some cases, significant interior spaces or elements.

A preservation easement is similar to other types of easements in that it represents "the right, privilege or interest that one party has in the land of another."[7] The recipient must be a qualified preservation organization that has the capacity to enforce the provisions of the easement. Recognizing that the obligation to conduct an annual inspection of the easement property and enforce its maintenance has financial consequences, many recipient organizations also require the contribution of a maintenance fund or endowment to cover the organizational costs. For the donor of an easement to receive the authorized tax benefits, the easement must be given in perpetuity.

The tax benefits of easement donation can include a charitable contribution deduction for federal and state income tax purposes and a reduction in the assessed value of the property for local property tax purposes. A qualified, experienced appraiser must undertake the valuation of an easement donation.

The development of preservation tools based on the idea that owners should be compensated through tax benefits for rights given, sold, or received is growing. This tendency will continue to bring historic preservation efforts more into the mainstream of conventional real estate practice. Developers and investors understand and take advantage of these advantages in other types of real estate development and investment transactions. Like the investment tax credit and other state and locally based programs, these "carrots" can attract a powerful range of resources to achieve preservation objectives.

The Mortgage Instrument. A mortgage is another example of rights enjoyed by nonowners. The mortgage holder has rights in the property, which are pledged as security for a loan. The lender's secured interest is the right to repossess or sell the property if the borrower defaults on the loan. Typically, a promissory note is signed concurrently with the mortgage. The promissory note establishes the obligation to repay the loan according to the terms and conditions of the mortgage. The note is secured by the mortgage.

This highly simplified description of real property is the core of a complex, creative field of putting deals together. Real estate developers, attorneys, investors, and lenders constantly work together to maximize the economic return from real estate projects while creating space for homes, businesses, and institutions.

Financial and Investment Considerations

When making an investment decision, investors are often faced with many properties from which to choose. Most experienced investors will also assess the risk of a real estate undertaking relative to other investment alternatives. The economic return on a property needs to be better than what could be realized from mortgage interest rates; otherwise, the investor is better off being a lender rather than an investor. Properly assessing the financial feasibility of a project and its projected return is critical to successful development and is the basis on which lenders and prospective investors will consider participation in a project.

In conventional real estate terms, the financial feasibility of a project is determined by the extent to which its projected income from operations justifies the investment of debt and/or equity capital. In today's market, for example, a developer seeking a 12 percent return should be willing to invest $100 million to create a project capable of generating an annual operating income, after expenses, of $12 million. Such assessments of financial feasibility are routinely conducted by or for potential lenders and investors.

Investing in historic properties frequently requires investors to use conventional analytic tools of market and financial analysis in concert with their own best judgment about trends, risk, and the speed with which a reasonable return can be expected. It is important to keep in mind that a property's historic and cultural value may be greater than its market value, and its investment value may be different still. Early investors in buildings in commercial historic districts such as Denver's Larimer Square, Boston's Faneuil Hall Marketplace, or Seattle's Pioneer Square, as well as many other ground-floor opportunities across the country, realized significantly favorable returns over time. The favorable economics were due to low acquisition costs, reasonable financing rates, favorable market response, an upturn in the general market, and, frequently, long-term ownership of the property. In many of these cases, conventional real estate analysis and risk assessment might have discouraged the investment. Real estate analysis has become more sophisticated, lenders have more experience with historic property investment and rehabilitation tax incentives, and public response has created a demand for historic property renovation.

Motivations. Investors who invest their money in real estate have four primary motivations:

- First, they feel that the market demand for space is sufficiently strong that, after the collection of rents and the payment of operating expenses, net income will be produced.
- Second, they anticipate selling the property at some future time and believe that the combination of market strength and an inflationary environment will contribute to a favorable return.
- Third, they want a diversified portfolio of investments to insulate them from market fluctuations in any one area.
- Fourth, they continue to find the preferential tax treatment historically associated with real estate investments to be a strong inducement, although this has been a somewhat less significant motivator since the Tax Reform Act of 1986.

Taking these motivations into account, investors use a range of analytic tools to evaluate a property's investment potential. These also help to answer other important questions: Should the property be purchased? How long should it be held? How should it be financed? What are the tax implications of owning it? How risky is it? Some measures that are used to screen an investment are the price per square foot, the capitalization rate, the equity dividend rate, and debt coverage ratios.

Cash Flow. The income from a particular property will depend on several factors, including expected market rents, expenses associated with its operation, and the nature of any leases on the property. Net operating income (NOI) is one component of an investor's return on a property before it is sold.

Debt Financing. Investors usually pay for a property by combining their own money (equity) with a loan (debt): that is, purchase price = debt + equity. Subtracting debt service (loan payments) from NOI results in before-tax cash flow from operations. This is also referred to as the equity dividend because it represents the cash flow that an investor will actually receive each year, analogous to a dividend on common stocks. When considering an investment, an equity investor will use the equity dividend rate as a test of reasonableness. This rate is established by dividing the equity dividend in the first year by the initial equity investment.

Internal Rate of Return. The internal rate of return (IRR) provides a way of measuring a return on an investment over the entire investment period, expressed as a compound rate of interest. An investor determines the IRR by finding the discount rate, which equates the present value of the future cash inflows with the initial cash outflow. This reveals the yield (before-tax) that the investor may expect to earn on equity over the investment period. Like the other tests of reasonableness, the investor compares the IRR with that of other real estate investments with similar risk characteristics. It should also be compared with the effective interest cost of any mortgage financing that could be obtained to buy the property.

Capitalization Rates. Another preliminary test of reasonableness of the property's purchase price is the ratio of the first-year NOI to the asking price. This is referred to as the "capitalization rate" or "cap rate." It is not a rate of return on investment (like an IRR) because it does not consider future income from operations and resale of the property at the end of the holding period. It does, however, represent a benchmark from which to look for comparability or significant deviations. For example, if the capitalization rates were in the range of 15 percent for most similar properties as compared to 10 percent for our property, this would probably indicate that the asking price for the property we are considering may be too high relative to what other investors have recently paid for comparable properties.

Public-Private Partnerships

According to the Urban Land Institute, over $50 billion has been invested in projects characterized as public-private partnerships. Of these, a majority involved the rehabilitation of existing buildings. A substantial percentage of the rehabilitation projects were in urban redevelopment areas.[8]

Public-private partnerships provide a mechanism for increasing investment in rehabilitation projects by making high-risk projects feasible. For example, the costs of downtown rehabilitation projects are typically higher and rents are lower than in suburban locations. Although this economic condition has changed in some notable markets such as New York, Boston, San Francisco, and Seattle, where office rents substantially exceed those in suburban locations, in some urban markets the costs of rehabilitation work may exceed those for comparable new construction.

Public and private sector roles in redevelopment have become more clear over the past twenty-five years. The role of local government is to define public rehabilitation priorities, to provide financial support needed to bridge the financial feasibility gap, and to provide loan-packaging services to assist private sponsors in utilizing public financial tools.

The private partner's role is to underwrite, construct, and operate the project. The private sponsors assume the financial risk and the elected officials assume the political risk. The primary responsibility for built environment decisions rests with elected public officials and private developers, since they are in control of the project financing. Public officials are thus fiduciaries to voters and private developers are fiduciaries to lenders and equity investors.

In many communities, the public sector has initiated and funded projects and implemented strategies to create an infrastructure that the private sector would not or could not fund. These projects and strategies can significantly strengthen the market conditions and environment for private sector development. Some of them have included:

- pedestrian improvements
- public transit improvements
- urban renewal services, such as property acquisition and redevelopment for

housing, hotels, office construction, convention centers, sports stadiums, research centers, business incubators, farmers' markets, parking structures, and government facilities
• sponsorship of art and cultural centers
• marketing and promotional activities

Successful public-private partnerships rely on a number of factors that span issues of human dynamics, financial capacity, market conditions, and project management. The public sector is increasingly performing roles that were previously the domain of private investors to better establish their position as full partners rather than merely as financial intermediaries. Many redevelopment agencies are now undertaking sophisticated market and financial feasibility studies, carefully shaping project design and development guidelines, and assigning financial and development responsibility to the private sector to mitigate impacts on public infrastructure, services, and the environment.

As development expands in existing neighborhoods and commercial centers, it is expected that public-private partnerships will increase markedly. Almost all real estate products have their own conventions in terms of financial structure and accustomed subsidies from the public sector. Partnership structures will reflect the dynamic nature of the private capital markets, public funding and tax incentives, and the political climate. The preservation professional will need to keep abreast of this critical area to maximize the public and private benefit from these development partnerships.

Institutional Sources of Project Funds

Mortgage and Equity Financing Sources. Mortgage loans constitute the largest source of private credit in the United States. Historically, mortgage credit comprises about 25 percent of the long-term uses of credit in our economy. This far exceeds credit usage by corporations, state and local governments, and consumers.

The availability of mortgage funds is highly cyclical and depends on interest rates. This cyclical pattern has caused numerous problems in residential markets for households seeking financing for house purchases, as well as for developers who need money to finance their projects. Lenders can also face serious problems when they experience an imbalance between the cost of funds and their return on assets. Two contributors to this pattern of imbalance are a general decrease in the amount of savings by households and the increasing amount of savings invested directly in other investments, such as stocks, bonds, and real assets, which offer yields that are expected to keep pace with inflation.

Mortgage funds may be found in:

- depository-type institutions, include savings and loan associations, commercial banks, and mutual savings banks offering a variety of deposit accounts
- pension funds
- real estate investment trusts (REITS)

Life insurance, pension, and retirement sources are thought of as "contractual" companies that typically provide retirement and death benefits to individuals and require a contractual commitment of savings over a long time. Specialized mortgage market intermediaries include mortgage companies, REITS, and federally related agencies that restrict their investment activities primarily to the mortgage market. Most of the funds they use do not come from savers, but from investors.

Commercial Banks. Commercial banks have the largest deposit base of all institutions. By far, the largest amount of construction funding for commercial real estate projects originates from commercial banks, followed by mortgage bankers. Commercial banks are also the most important construction lenders for multifamily developments, as well as a valuable source of funding for the origination of long-term or permanent loans. Historically, commercial banks and life insurance companies have been the largest originators of long-term loans for commercial real estate projects.

Pension Funds. One of the most significant developments in the flow of funds into real estate has been the entry of pension funds as lenders and investors, primarily because of their large and rapidly expanding pool of assets. Equity investment in real estate by pension funds is by far the most popular way to achieve high returns and optimal diversification effects for their portfolios. Participation in a project is usually accomplished by (1) direct investment, (2) use of an investment adviser to help with direct investment or establish a separate investment account on behalf of the pension plan, or (3) investment in a real estate fund commingled with other pension funds. A number of pension funds, most notably the California State Teachers Retirement Fund, have a dedicated pool of assets assigned to Smart Growth and rehabilitation projects. The availability of such a significant dedicated funding commitment will be highly influential in directing investment to central-city areas.

Real Estate Investment Trusts. The other prominent source of funds and investment in real estate is the REIT. The two principal types of trusts are equity trusts and mortgage trusts. The difference between the assets held by an equity trust and those held by a mortgage trust is fairly obvious. The equity trust acquires a direct property interest, whereas the mortgage trust purchases mortgage obligations and thus becomes a creditor with mortgage liens given priority over equity holders.

The equity-oriented REIT gives investors an opportunity to invest funds in a diversified portfolio of real estate under professional management; this provides better liquidity than would be the case if a property were acquired outright. REITs typically own and manage portfolios of properties, and pass rental income through to shareholders via dividends. (Federal tax law requires that 90 percent of their profits be returned to investors annually.) Given their relatively high dividend yields, REITs are favored by investors looking for more secure investments in a volatile market. Although many REITs such as Arden Realty have a considerable percentage of their portfolio assets in renovated office buildings, a REIT exclusively dedicated to adaptive use projects does not yet exist.

Syndication. A real estate syndicate is a group of investors who have combined their financial resources with the expertise of a real estate professional for the common purpose of carrying out a real estate project. Syndication offers smaller investors the opportunity to invest in ventures that would otherwise be beyond their financial and management capabilities. Syndicators benefit from the fees they receive for their services and the interest they may retain in a syndicated property. Syndication employing the limited partnership structure has been the usual method to attract investors to preservation projects using the rehabilitation investment tax credit. Most states limit participation to relatively wealthy individuals.

Financing preservation projects is heavily dependent on all of these sources of capital. As capital markets are progressively linked to the performance of Wall Street and the interest rate manipulations of the open market committee of the Federal Reserve Board, investors in historic properties will, like investors in other real estate, learn to adjust to an uncertain business environment. It will increasingly be an environment in which capital flows and investor-required rates of return change instantaneously, and in which markets are buffeted by factors unrelated to underlying industry and market fundamentals.

Conclusions: Some Major Public Policy Issues

Smart Growth: Opportunities and Limitations

The Smart Growth movement has been championed by the historic preservation community as a panacea for sprawl and a catalyst for urban revitalization. Smart Growth has two primary tenets: (1) better planning of how we use our land, and (2) greater use or reuse of older neighborhoods, towns, and downtowns. The National Trust has given particular emphasis to uniting conservation and preservation goals in order to achieve environmental and economic harmony. The Urban Land Institute has made Smart Growth one of the primary elements of its educational and advisory programs.

Smart Growth has assumed a status akin to motherhood and apple pie. After all, smart growth is so obviously better than dumb growth. That the pro-, moderate-, and slow-growth factions within the various land-use communities have embraced Smart Growth may be attributable to its vagueness. The pro-growth movement continues to endorse the idea that few limits be imposed on the pace, scale, and location of new development. But it also wants to take advantage of the infrastructure of existing areas in order to build buildings of greater density. Pro-growth enthusiasts see Smart Growth as a new market opportunity, especially where local ordinances do not proscribe high-rise development or suburban development models in urban settings. The moderate-growth advocates believe in the revitalization of core areas and bringing growth to the center of cities but not with the attendant gentrification. They believe in more mass transit and higher densities, especially at former edge locations, but are having a difficult time persuading communities to go along with their utopian visions. The slow-growth movement is trying to limit the outward expansion of the city by advocating mass transit, higher density, and revitalization of inner-core areas with new development. It, too, is having limited success.

As most communities realize, it is almost impossible to control or manage growth on a regional basis. Growth is largely dependent on location, past investment, and the economic activities that support or generate further growth.

Old Union Depot, St. Paul, Minnesota, before renovation

Old Union Depot after renovation

Possibly the most successful and extensive urban design and renovation project in the United States has been developed by the public sector and through public-private partnerships over twenty years by the Lowertown Redevelopment Corporation of St. Paul. It consists of an imaginative mix of high-rise apartments, condominium towers, historic buildings, offices, retail shops, and the city's most beautiful urban park. Shown here are before and after pictures of the Old Union Depot, which stood empty for more than a decade until it was restored recently as an elegant in-town restaurant. Through public-private partnerships, Lowertown has attracted investment of more than $400 million and created thousands of jobs for the local economy. (Courtesy of the Lowertown Redevelopment Corporation, St. Paul, Minnesota)

When one locality attempts to limit growth, it typically shifts to another community. Numerous attempts to address growth issues of traffic congestion, concentrated poverty in inner cities, and even business growth have been frustrated due to the regional nature of economic and land-use activities. The only reasonably successful growth management effort of the federal government has been in the area of air pollution.

The Smart Growth movement needs to address the complex social, economic, and political questions associated with its advocacy of highly integrated uses, lower densities, mass transit, and stringent limitations on development in outlying areas. In highly developed urban areas like New York, Chicago, and San Francisco, historic development patterns of mixed-use, pedestrian, and public transit–based movement of people and established concentrations of retail and commercial activities have allowed those cities to create a dynamic urban environment. After decades of languishing in the second half of the twentieth century, these cities, among others like them, are experiencing a tremendous revitalization based on the reinvigoration of their cultural institutions; the expansion of the housing stock, primarily through adaptive use and higher density development; and business growth in these urban environments. Their health has also been interdependent on the development of many towns and suburbs over the past 150 years.

Smart Growth tenets may provide the answer to urban and economic development so long as they offer a balanced approach. Land conservation and urban revitalization need to be well grounded in demographics, a match between supply and demand, and the reality of development that is market-driven. Preservationists in such metropolitan markets will have to concede higher density development in selected areas to accommodate demands for housing and office space. Similarly, preservationists will need to work for incentives that are compatible with real estate industry practices to stimulate investment in historic properties and the urban infrastructure that supports them.

The impact of technological change through advances in telecommunications and computer technology is not yet fully discernible. The assumed preference of advanced technology companies and their employees for more urbanized locations and historic buildings has been a significant boon in many communities. The broader impact of technology on the workplace, and on the character and role of our cities, will be one of the more important future challenges for the preservation community.

Development Quality and Design Quality

The federal Secretary's Standards have been the requisite guidelines for rehabilitation work since passage of the Tax Reform Act of 1976. These guidelines have a marked economic impact because they must be met to qualify a project for the Investment Tax Credit for Rehabilitation. The standards are premised on the notion that "less is more." Less change in the historic fabric will produce a more authentic as well as more enduring and cost-effective design quality. While meeting the secretary of interior's valuable guidelines for creating and measuring preservation and design quality, architects and developers have expressed frustration over the essentially conservative nature of the standards and the frequently subjective reviews by staff of state historic preservation offices and the NPS itself. The debate centers on the issue of design integrity. Should the architecture of historic buildings prevail over advances and concepts in contemporary design?

The simple answer would be that if the preservation agency is authorizing and "paying" in toto for the work through rehabilitation tax credits, the preservation approach should dominate. However, all buildings are layered in the sense that they were created over time, and each layer or time period contributes distinctive design elements—a sequential history, as it were. The Secretary's Standards lean strongly toward preserving the stylistic elements of a single historical period—in effect, denying, rather than promoting, history. As a matter of public policy, this approach to preservation makes little sense.

The basic precept of preservation that less is more has proven to have a salutary effect on individual historic buildings, as well as in historic districts where architectural changes in a wide range of buildings and uses are subject to review. Precedent and experience have demonstrated that certain trends in architecture or the enthusiasm of owners do not always stand the test of time. The exposed brick walls and oak trim of early rehabilitation projects look, at best, quaintly dated. This is especially true when contrasted with more sophisticated work premised on retaining original architectural features and adding new elements only when necessary—when the elements may be reversible or when the new materials invoke the style, tone, or proportions of the original property.

Similarly, when contemporary buildings are juxtaposed with historic buildings, the results can be exciting and reinvigorate both buildings as well as the area in which they are located. The I. M. Pei–designed addition to McKim Mead and White's Boston Public Library in the Back Bay is an excellent example of the power of this architectural-historical dynamic. There are numerous other illustrations as more and more architects and preservationists seek to adapt public policy to this dynamic "strike point" between old and new architectural designs and development.

Not only are the architectural and environmental effects positive, but the economic effects are also compelling. Studies of the economic contribution of historic preservation conducted in New Jersey and Texas from 1994 to 1999 found that historic designation and design review requirements were associated with higher property values in all of the CLGs studied.[9] In the Texas cities, property designations had a statistically significant positive effect on property values, averaging between 5 and 20 percent. The economists found that in dollar terms (dollar value change per housing unit), historic designation was associated with average increases in housing values ranging between approximately $3,000 and $19,000.[10]

As communities recognize the relationship between design quality, architectural stability, and economics, we can expect that the role of design review will increase. With increased experience, there will be greater sophistication, trust, and flexibility in the design and development process. Communities, designers, and developers will recognize that they have a common purpose in creating projects that have high design standards and commensurate economic potential.

Who Pays for Historic Preservation:
Are Subsidies Necessary? Are They Forever?

Throughout the last half century, a fundamental premise of urban development was that economic activity required economic stimulus. Shortly after the establishment of the U.S. Department of Housing and Urban Development in 1949, Congress passed advanced legislation that led to a next half century of property development dominated by a range of federal programs addressing urban and economic development. There are few communities in the United States that did not participate or rely on funding from the programs of HUD, the Economic Development Administration of the U.S. Department of Commerce, the Small Business Administration, and the DOT, among others. Despite substantially reduced funding levels and prescriptive policy mandates, public subsidies still play a meaningful role in most projects undertaken in urban areas, mature suburbs, and rural communities.

The issue of whether historic subsidies are still necessary is a legitimate public policy concern. On the one hand, it can easily be argued that since other forms of development benefiting economic development receive public support, historic preservation should also. In fact, historic preservation may be better able to justify public subsidies because of the greater economic multipliers.

Recent studies of the economic impact of historic preservation have demonstrated that the costs of public tax and funding subsidies to historic preservation are more than offset by the enhanced tax revenues resulting from the public investment. Economic effects are specified with respect to jobs, income, wealth, and taxes. The economic benefits studies of 1994–99 in New Jersey and Texas found that statewide historic rehabilitation investments were a superior economic catalyst compared with other economic development investments. In New Jersey, for example, every $1 million invested in nonresidential historic rehabilitation created 38.3 jobs nationally and 19.3 jobs in the state. By comparison, $1 million invested in new nonresidential construction was found to generate only 36.1 jobs nationally and 16.7 jobs in the state.

A collateral question is whether—given that preservation is now sufficiently well established and investor returns are so favorable—subsidies are no longer needed. Many investors feel that the high returns from historic preservation investment in a favorable market are justified by the substantial risks and uncertainties involved. In an emerging real estate market, where an insufficient critical mass of successful projects has been established, special preservation incentives are regarded as essential for generating interest on the part of the investment community.

Most investors and economists contend that the development interest in historic properties would not occur but for the incentives that are available. If federal, state, and local incentives were diminished or eliminated, they believe, interest in historic properties would return to the limited levels existing before passage of the first investment tax incentives in the Tax Reform Act of 1976. There is a widespread perception that the front-end costs associated with site acquisition, more complex financing, unforeseeable construction issues, marketing, and, most important, the reduced rentable area in smaller buildings, mitigate against equal treatment of historic properties with other real estate products.

The cultural and social value of historic preservation tax incentives has had a highly beneficial effect on most communities. No longer regarded as the special domain of history buffs or the academic community, preservation has been accepted as a major political and economic issue. The growth of heritage tourism, the rebirth of Main Street and historic commercial centers, and the increased value of properly rehabilitated historic properties have been powerful persuaders.

The issue of subsidies for preservation takes on far broader importance in the field of housing and economic development generally and the important social and economic benefits that it has provided. With a strong economy, favorable financing rates, and clear local regulation, it is apparent that the private sector, acting alone, can frequently create a product that meets community goals, one that the public sector cannot provide. This is especially true in the case of affordable housing. Developers and public agencies alike agree that the administrative costs of housing subsidies drive up development costs to a level that exceeds development costs for luxury housing. Justification for the continuation of housing subsidies is based on the argument that the development community would not build low- and moderate-income housing unless the construction and operating subsidies were in place. Because of the relatively simple administrative procedures for federal and state preservation tax incentives and the available grants and loans, the overhead cost attributable to preservation programs is modest by comparison.

The general feeling of the preservation community at this time is that unless and until there is a sustained, strong market in historic neighborhoods and commercial centers and conventional new development is unsubsidized, it makes limited economic, public policy, or cultural sense to reduce the subsidies that have spawned and supported the preservation of our historic resources to date. Indeed, given the fundamental economic disparity between new buildings at higher densities than are attainable with historic buildings, present subsidies may be an absolute requirement for historic preservation to succeed.

Nonprofits in the American Preservation Movement

A bold group of patriotic ladies in antebellum Virginia took a preservation crisis into their own hands and gave birth to a movement that to this day is largely dependent on organized citizen action. Chartered in 1858, the Mount Vernon Ladies Association became a model for private preservation approaches in the United States. Today, we would refer to this association as a private nonprofit organization and its efforts to save Mount Vernon would be viewed as distinctly American.

A Distinctly American Beginning

From the days of de Tocqueville's visit to the United States to our own times, Americans have been viewed as joiners and organizers, mostly relying on the private sector rather than government for solutions to problems. In the 1830s and 1840s citizens were establishing private academies and colleges in one small town after another, and those with the means were financing new private hospitals and cultural institutions. The motivation was civic betterment, not tax savings or financial remuneration. To be sure, public institutions were also being formed, but local residents were often found taking matters into their own hands. For every public university, for every public opera house, there were dozens, if not hundreds, of private ones paid for by public subscription.

Any examination of historic preservation in the United States must recognize the monumental importance of nonprofit institutions in preserving the nation's heritage. After private property owners, private nonprofit organizations have played the largest role in the preservation of historic properties. When one surveys great American preservation success stories, whether the preservation of the great houses of Charleston, South Carolina, the commercial strand of Galveston, Texas, the illustrious buildings of Frank Lloyd Wright, or the industrial heritage of the steel industry in Pennsylvania, one usually finds a nonprofit organization at center stage—organizing, educating, raising private funds, lobbying, cajoling, undertaking real estate transactions, and whatever else it takes to succeed.

What Is a "Nonprofit"?

At the outset, we need a sentence or two about the nature of nonprofit organizations simply because most people are unfamiliar with the term. Essentially, nonprofits are just like other business organizations, but with several important exceptions. One is that any "profits" after expenses are not distributed to the owners of the business but are used to further the charitable or public purposes of the organization. A second important difference is that unlike ordinary businesses, nonprofits do not pay income tax on their "profits," and gifts to the organization are tax-deductible to the donor.

Nonprofit organizations are also complex entities that reflect the personalities of their founders, their directors, and, where applicable, their staffs. Like families, they may operate smoothly, providing tremendous service to the constituents they serve, or they may be utterly dysfunctional, mired in internal conflict and the politics of personality. They may be constantly struggling with finances or affluent with endowment support. Nonprofit preservation organizations in America cover a spectrum from highly regimented tax-exempt corporations to loose confederations of interested citizens.

Incorporating a nonprofit historic preservation organization takes only a few hours, generally requiring the registration of an organizational charter and by-laws with the appropriate local or state authorities. The documents are essentially legal boilerplate, and almost any lawyer can generate them quickly. The more difficult step is to create an effective board of directors and adopt a viable mission.

Like other corporations, a nonprofit is governed by a board of directors or trustees, who bear legal and financial responsibility for the actions of the organization. Being nonprofit does not mean that the organization cannot make money on transactions; rather, it signifies that no board members may profit directly from the organization's activities. There are no stockholders. The organization may hire staff and pay competitive salaries, but those salaries are subject to scrutiny by government officials and the general public. Property owners may benefit from the work of a nonprofit (such as through the adoption of tax incentives advocated by the organization or through the increase of property values resulting from its work), but board members who so benefit must be careful to avoid conflicts of interest, real or perceived.

Following incorporation, a nonprofit must apply to the IRS for what is called "501(c)(3)" status, through which contributions to the organization are tax-deductible. Obtaining tax-exempt status is a tedious process that takes months and sometimes years. The IRS requires a multiyear plan for the organization, including details about its mission, directors, planned activities, and projected budgets. But once 501(c)(3) status is received, donors may contribute (money, stock, property, etc.) to the organization and deduct the value of the gifts from their federal income taxes; nonprofits may obtain other advantages such as local property tax exemptions and sales tax refunds from state and local governments as well. Private foundations, as well as most state and local governments, will not grant funds to a nonprofit organization unless it has 501(c)(3) status.

Although 501(c)(3) status provides many benefits, it also imposes limitations. The finances of the organization are open to public scrutiny. Legislative advocacy is limited to a modest percentage of the organization's budget and program. Many aspects of the organization's operations must be reported annually to the IRS on a form that dwarfs an individual's Form 1040. For all its limitations, however, the benefits of 501(c)(3) status usually far outweigh the costs and inconveniences, especially in the field of historic preservation, where the preservation of buildings and sites is an expensive and long-term proposition.

Many historic preservation organizations have operated for years without staff, often boasting of what they have achieved without "bureaucracy." And yet, it is a rare organization that can achieve sustained effectiveness without reaching a point where paid employees execute the day-to-day responsibilities. Since the 1960s, especially as more women enter the workforce, volunteers who can commit long hours every week have become rare.

When a historic preservation organization becomes large enough to hire staff, achieving organizational balance between directors and staff is difficult. Generally, the board of directors or trustees is responsible for establishing policy and overseeing the organization's financial health (budget administration and fund-raising), and the staff is charged with implementing policy. The line between the responsibilities of the board and staff is a fine one and is often the source of internal conflict. Many nonprofit executives have left organizations because of disagreements over their respective roles. Many organizational development consultants have found employment trying to sort out board/staff relationships in preservation (as well as other) nonprofit organizations.

The National Trust has published a number of titles in its information series about the creation, growth, and management of nonprofit preservation organizations. A complete set of the Organizational Development booklets is available through the National Trust website, ‹www.nthp.org›.

The Historical Role of Nonprofits
in Historic Preservation

An American institution still unknown to most cultures, nonprofit organizations have played an important part in the preservation of America's heritage. In addition to the Mount Vernon Ladies Association, some of the earliest nonprofit preservation societies included the Association for the Preservation of Virginia Antiquities, established in 1889, and the Society for the Preservation of New England Antiquities, founded in 1910. Here and there, similar groups assembled at the local level; for example, in 1918 the Cupola House Ladies Association was formed in the tiny town of Edenton, North Carolina, to save the remains of a 1757 house whose interior woodwork had been purchased and removed by the Brooklyn Museum of Art. Usually the goal of these organizations was to acquire an especially early or significant endangered building—generally a house—and restore it for museum use.

The restoration of Colonial Williamsburg, first financed in 1926 through the nonprofit Colonial Williamsburg Foundation, created a passion for preservation among many Americans, including wealthy industrialists. One outdoor museum, Greenfield Village at Dearborn, Michigan, was funded by Henry Ford, and another, Sturbridge Village, Massachusetts, was conceived in the 1930s by Albert Wells, owner of the American Optical Company. Winterthur Museum, a decorative arts museum in Wilmington, Delaware, which opened in 1951, grew out of a collection by Henry Francis du Pont. In the historic district of Newport, Rhode Island, dozens of houses were purchased and restored by an organization created and funded by Doris Duke, daughter of wealthy tobacconist James B. Duke.

The restoration of Colonial Williamsburg and its counterparts coincided with the advent of the automobile vacation. Many middle-class families probably took their first extended car trip to visit one of these restored historic vil-

Farmer's Museum, Cooperstown, New York. Part of a working farm since 1813, when it was owned by James Fenimore Cooper, the Farmer's Museum opened its doors to the public in 1944. The museum complex includes structures dating from 1790 to 1845 relocated from other towns in central New York. Illustrated are the cultivation of hops (once a major agricultural product of the region), the church, and the apothecary. (J. Myrick Howard)

lages. The impact was widespread and long-lasting. From the 1920s to the present day, new suburban houses have proclaimed to be "exact replicas" of specific Williamsburg or James River houses—complete with two-car garages.

A potent array of nonprofit preservation organizations was founded in the mid-1920s and through the 1930s. Some were spin-offs from garden clubs that were very fashionable for wealthy ladies and those with social aspirations. Automobile touring had become immensely popular, and clubs used auto tours to promote visitation of historic gardens and houses. The Garden Club of Virginia in 1929 sponsored a two-week garden tour, an elaborate auto journey to the state's great plantation houses and gardens of the eighteenth and nineteenth centuries. The proceeds from its annual Garden Week were used to restore the grounds of early museum houses, such as Kenmore in Fredericksburg and Stratford Hall, the birthplace of General Robert E. Lee.

Transportation and communications advances between the wars enabled national meetings of patriotic, cultural, and garden organizations, and these, in turn, nourished interest in historic preservation across the nation. Attendees of the national meetings of the Daughters of the American Revolution and the National Society of the Colonial Dames of America went home inspired.

Eventually the Colonial Dames became the largest private steward of historic houses in America.[1] Within years of the first Virginia Garden Week, Garden Weeks were common along the East Coast. Garden club after garden club published books in the 1930s about historic homes and gardens. Even the similarity of names for local events and organizations reflected the national cross-fertilization. But it was not until 1949 that preservationists had a national nonprofit organization of their own, the National Trust for Historic Preservation.[2]

The 1950s and 1960s were demoralizing for preservationists nationwide. The Internal Revenue Code provided incentives for demolition and new construction but offered none for rehabilitation. Federal housing programs simultaneously offered cheap mortgages for new suburban neighborhoods and dictated the redlining of older neighborhoods. Millions of federal dollars poured into urban redevelopment, cutting swaths of destruction through older areas in cities. Interstate highway construction opened up vast new lands. Cities were abandoned by middle-class whites, and fiery race riots in the late 1960s, high crime rates, and poor schools further encouraged escape to the suburbs.[3] During those decades, most preservation nonprofits were fortunate to survive. Progress, not preservation, was the national obsession. Meanwhile, many women who had populated the movement in the 1920s and 1930s passed from the scene.

In the late 1960s and early 1970s a whole new breed of preservation nonprofits came into existence, driven by a new breed of preservationists. These new groups were often intent on saving major public landmarks and whole neighborhoods, not just fine early houses. Reflecting the activist spirit of the times, and bolstered by the National Historic Preservation Act of 1966 and the creation of the National Register of Historic Places, a new generation of activists took to the streets to save local heritage.

Preservationists rallied around endangered public buildings (such as Boston's Old City Hall, saved from demolition by Historic Boston, and New York City's Pennsylvania Station, which was lost), important collections of commercial structures (such as the cast-iron storefronts of Louisville, Kentucky, and the Strand in Galveston), and hundreds of historic residential districts (from Beaufort, North Carolina, to Kansas City, Missouri, to Pasadena, California). Massive highway projects, such as those in San Francisco and Boston that would have cut through the heart of their cities, were stopped, sometimes in midcourse. Even the organizational names changed. Organizational monikers like "Don't Tear It Down, Inc." in the District of Columbia and "Stop H-3" in Hawaii replaced the earlier, more genteel nonprofit "Antiquities" societies.

Preservationists interested in saving houses shifted their emphasis from museum houses, which were sometimes eschewed as expensive and irrelevant relics, to whole neighborhoods needing to be reclaimed from the ravages of disinvestment. Candlelight Christmas tours showed off the rich architectural detailing of freshly restored homes to thousands of intrigued onlookers, while collecting dollars for the sponsoring nonprofit organizations.

A bevy of new nonprofits, both local and statewide, were incorporated in the 1970s, and several older organizations were substantially reorganized, reflecting the new preservation interests. For the first time, local preservation efforts became professionalized as nonprofits began to hire individuals with degrees in business, planning, marketing, or law. Often an organization's first goal was to advocate the designation of local landmarks and the establishment of local historic districts, providing for the first time real protection for thousands of historic buildings. These new or renewed nonprofit organizations pushed public agencies to undertake local surveys and inventories, many of which were then privately published. Statewide conferences were instituted, providing a new network for preservationists. Newsletters were printed and distributed.

Preservation revolving funds were created, emulating the successes of the Historic Charleston Foundation's groundbreaking fund. A newer wave of revolving funds, such as the Historic Savannah Foundation and the Pittsburgh History and Landmarks Foundation, took on whole blocks of houses, such as Marshall Row in Savannah, or ambitious commercial ventures, such as Station Square in Pittsburgh, an adaptive mixed use of a railroad complex. North Carolina created the first statewide revolving fund.

As the 1970s progressed and into the 1980s, many American cities experienced the beginnings of rebirth. The 1973 Arab oil embargo, which disproportionately drove up the costs of new construction and made commuting from the suburbs more expensive, and new federal tax incentives for income-producing rehabilitation again changed the role of preservation nonprofits. Nonprofit organizations teamed up with developers, realtors, and accountants to produce workshops about the economics of historic real estate development. The energy virtues of older buildings, long demonized as energy hogs, were extolled in preservation publications and conferences.

At the urging of nonprofit groups, local and state governments, previously antagonists, were becoming advocates for neighborhoods and protectors of historic resources. Preservationists talked about expanding tax bases and enhancing property values in cities that had experienced the opposite for at least two decades. Citizens who gained leadership experience in nonprofit preservation organizations often later ran for office.

In light of increasing property values in older neighborhoods, a number of nonprofit preservation organizations turned their energies to the creation of affordable housing. The Pittsburgh History and Landmarks Foundation worked extensively in several working-class neighborhoods, while a spin-off Savannah organization was established to develop affordable housing in the city's Victorian district. Preservation-minded developers, often working with nonprofit preservation groups or community development corporations, learned how to combine the incentives for affordable housing with the incentives for historic rehabilitation, and thousands of new affordable housing units were created under the rehabilitation tax credit program.[4] In the 1990s, as organizations matured and grants for bricks-and-mortar projects became more difficult to obtain,[5] attention turned to documenting the tangible achievements of preservation. State and local nonprofit organizations and the National Trust for Historic Preservation commissioned economic impact studies to quantify the impact of historic preservation on job creation, private investment, tax revenues, and other measures of economic development. Studies documenting the acceleration in property values in historic residential and commercial districts and the net tax revenues gained from existing neighborhoods helped set the stage for preservation organizations to take a leadership role in the Smart Growth movement of the late 1990s.[6]

The Patchwork Quilt of Organizations

In some fields, an organizational chart can be drawn of the national, statewide, and local nonprofits showing logical boundaries and hierarchical relationships. From the National Audubon Society to the American Diabetes Association, the common prototype is the national nonprofit organization with state and local chapters. Policy decisions, and even some operational mandates, are made nationally, and the state and local organizations follow in concert, not always without complaint. This has not been so in preservation.

Historic preservation is about place. It is fundamentally local in its orientation. Most people care intensely about the historic properties in their own backyard and may not have generic or broad preservation interests. So the organizational structure of the nation's preservation movement is not linear and hierarchical. It is more like a patchwork quilt. Many local nonprofit preservation organizations, and some statewide organizations, long predate the National Trust and are loath to give up what they regard as traditionally local pre-

Los Angeles theater. A primary focus of the nonprofit Los Angeles Conservancy is the preservation of the city's extensive Art Deco heritage, such as this theater on Wiltshire Boulevard in Hollywood. Each Saturday the group sponsors an Art Deco walking tour. The conservancy also works to save historic buildings and neighborhoods throughout the city through advocacy, education, and property intervention. (J. Myrick Howard)

Kamphoefner House, Raleigh, North Carolina. Several of Raleigh's Modernist houses from the late 1940s and 1950s, designed by faculty members of North Carolina State University's then new School of Design, have been listed in the National Register. These houses are small by today's standards and are situated on sizable suburban tracts with substantial development value for infill. Without protection through private preservation easements, their future is uncertain. (Bryan Hoffman)

rogatives. Similarly, many statewides are relative newcomers, newer than their local counterparts. Trying to retrofit the movement with a nationally coordinated program with state and local chapters of the National Trust would be an exercise in futility, and it would risk sapping the movement's vitality.

Elemental to the historic preservation movement is the widespread recognition that each place is different. By the same token, each nonprofit is distinctive. Many cities and states would benefit from having a well-financed and sophisticated nonprofit preservation organization. Unfortunately, this is not the case. Most preservation nonprofits have limited resources and must choose how to ration their resources to best meet local needs. Preservation is a generalist's dream field, attracting a wide variety of interests and motivations. Just as a cafeteria line offers a diner hundred of choices, preservation offers a nonprofit organization a seemingly endless array of potential programs. The prudent diner will choose a few well-balanced items from the cafeteria's many offerings, and so must the smart nonprofit organization. Without deep pockets, few organizations can sustain a wide variety of programs.

The National Trust for Historic Preservation

Among American nonprofits, the story of organizational structure in preservation begins with the National Trust. Chartered by Congress in 1949, the Trust is regarded as the leader of the private historic preservation movement. Presently it has more than 250,000 members, a staff numbering more than 300, an annual operating budget of $40 million, and a collection of twenty historic sites open to the public. For more than fifty years, the National Trust has faced some of the same challenges encountered by many local and statewide preservation nonprofits.

The National Trust started with a staff of four, and by 1952 its membership had grown to five hundred. Its annual conference provided the opportunity for like-minded citizens to gather and learn. Its first two decades were marked by the donation of several prominent houses to open as museums. Many of these properties were contributed with only modest endowment support, so funding for their operation and upkeep had to be found.

In 1966, along with representatives of the National Park Service and private citizens, the National Trust helped frame the National Historic Preservation Act, which expanded the National Register of Historic Places and created the Advisory Council on Historic Preservation. The 1966 act helped convert the federal government from foe to frequent ally of historic preservation, and over the next two decades many state legislatures enacted preservation programs. Congress also provided the National Trust with federal funding, allowing it to expand greatly beyond its previous size.

In 1969 the Trust established the Preservation Services Fund (PSF), a program of small matching grants to nonprofit organizations, universities, and public agencies. One of the Trust's most valuable programs, PSF has long provided the modest planning funds necessary to save many endangered structures and to jump-start numerous valuable preservation initiatives. Often, all a local preservation crisis needed was the funding to hire a preservation-minded engineer or a fund-raising consultant. PSFs provided that kind of early start-up funding, and by bestowing the Trust's imprimatur on the effort, such grants gave projects credibility.

In 1970 the National Trust filed its first amicus brief in court to save historic properties through litigation. Since then, it has been involved in more than 130 court cases, including the 1978 *Penn Central Transportation Co. v. City of New York*, widely regarded as preservation's most important ruling. The National Trust Legal Defense Fund's team of staff attorneys and associates works with local preservation advocates across the nation to encourage government agencies and others to protect historic sites, neighborhoods, and landscapes— whether through litigation, public advocacy, or mediation. Since 1982, the Law Department of the National Trust has published the authoritative *Preservation Law Reporter* to provide up-to-date information to attorneys and other preservation professionals about developments in the law.

The year 1971 saw the creation of a National Preservation Loan Fund to help local and statewide preservation organizations save endangered properties. The fund provides below-market-rate loans of up to $150,000 to nonprofit organizations and public agencies to assist in preserving properties listed in or eligible for listing in the National Register of Historic Places. Funds may be used to create or expand local and statewide preservation revolving funds for site acquisition or rehabilitation work. By 1999 the fund had committed more than $15 million in low-interest loans.

During the remainder of the 1970s and into the early 1980s the National Trust sponsored a wide variety of new programs reflecting the energy and spirit found among preservationists after the Bicentennial. Each year's conference seemed to mark the announcement of yet another new initiative or program. A few faded away by the next year, but many have helped shape the modern preservation movement.

The advent of the Main Street program in 1977 (started as a National Trust pilot project in the Midwest) and the subsequent creation of the National Main Street Center by the National Trust in 1980 had a momentous impact on preservation nationwide. Based on four simple principles, the Main Street program had its origin in five demonstration states and spread to more than forty, growing from 30 cities and towns to more than 1,400 in 1999. Not a government grant program, Main Street taught local business and political leaders how to use their historical and architectural assets to rebuild their downtowns. Many towns established a nonprofit downtown organization to manage their programs, and in each town a Main Street manager was hired. A vast number of new entry-level jobs for professionals interested in preservation were created, and hundreds of new preservation-oriented nonprofits were launched. Significantly, a national network of private downtown development practitioners was organized—with annual meetings, training programs, and state networks.

In 1982 the National Trust announced a challenge grant program to encourage the creation of new statewide nonprofit preservation organizations and the strengthening of existing ones. The challenge grants helped several organizations hire their first staff or undertake their first major membership drives. At the time, only about a dozen statewide organizations were professionally staffed, many of which were relatively new. But the program disappeared shortly after it was announced, and many of its gains proved short-lived. More than a decade elapsed before the strengthening of statewide nonprofits became a sustained priority for the National Trust.

Another evolving component of the National Trust's program has been its operation of museum properties (now twenty in number), spread across the United States. Early on, these properties provided the Trust with its initial visibility and vitality. Then in the 1980s, as other programs came to the fore, their relative prominence seemed to wane. Indeed, some younger preservationists viewed the museums as an anachronistic holdover from the days when society women dominated preservation. With the growth of heritage as a leading sector in the tourism industry, these properties have once again emerged as useful economic development and membership recruitment models. Increasingly, preservationists are recognizing that museums are often the general public's entryway into historic preservation, and that these resources should receive attention. In fact, the National Trust has added new properties to fill voids in its collection, such as the Lower East Side Tenement Museum in New York City, added in 1998.

In 1988 the National Trust promulgated its first list of the nation's "Eleven

Most Endangered Historic Places." This and successor lists have helped focus attention on the preservation movement nationwide by reintroducing the newsworthy drama that sometimes accompanies historic preservation: Will the property be saved at the eleventh hour? Usually the lists have highlighted individual properties, but they have also been used to spotlight trends and types of endangered properties. Listing the entire state of Vermont as an endangered property in 1993 provided a high-profile way to portray the impact of sprawl and big-box retailers. The 2000 listing of historic neighborhood schools brought national attention to a commonplace building type often in jeopardy.

Reflecting the broadening of the preservation movement in the 1980s and 1990s, the National Trust added a number of financial services programs to encourage preservation efforts in middle-, low-, and mixed-income historic districts or to assist in the development of affordable housing. Created in 1982, the Inner-City Ventures Fund provides low-interest loans on flexible terms for projects that reuse historic properties for affordable housing, community facilities, and retail and office space in low- and mixed-income neighborhoods. In 1994 the Trust launched the Community Partners Program (CPP), a neighborhood initiative to promote the use of historic preservation to revitalize America's historic urban neighborhoods. Designed as a grassroots planning model, CPP creates partnerships between community development and historic preservation groups to demonstrate the effectiveness of preservation-based community development. It has relied on demonstration programs that can be replicated on a site-by-site basis depending on staff resources and funding availability.

Because it must rely on private support and earned income, especially since 1995, when Congress started scaling back its funds, the Trust's newest financial services programs are more entrepreneurial in character, charging fees for services to for-profit and nonprofit developers of historic real estate. Heritage Property Investors (HPI), a fee-for-service program, provides developers of historic rehabilitation tax credit projects and historic/low-income housing tax credit projects with access to corporate equity investors. HPI offers developers preservation technical assistance and can also arrange financing.

Throughout the 1990s the National Trust became a stronger, more strategic organization. Ironically, the total withdrawal of congressional funding in 1998 may in the long run prove to be beneficial, as it has forced the Trust to enhance its private resources through an Independence Fund, more precisely define its mission and message, and focus on how it can best contribute to preservation nationally.

One step toward these goals has been an extensive review of the Trust's relationship with statewide nonprofit preservation organizations. Beginning with a 1993 task force, the Trust has considered how to organize the national movement to best use its limited resources. Taking a page from national environmental organizations, members of the task force agreed that emphasis should be placed on building the capacity of statewide nonprofit preservation groups. The ideal national preservation movement was envisioned as a decentralized one operating primarily at the local and state levels, with the National Trust serving as a broad umbrella for advocacy, communications, public relations, financial resources, and technical assistance.

One recommendation of this task force was that the National Trust first build a network of strong, independent statewide organizations. This conclusion was strategic as well as practical. By concentrating on statewide organizations, the Trust has taken significant steps to establish a nationwide network of capable nonprofits from every state. Strong statewide organizations will thus be better positioned to build more and stronger local preservation organizations.

So far, the accomplishments of the program bode well. Almost every state now has a statewide preservation organization. From 1994 to 1999, with financial and organizational assistance from the National Trust, the number of professionally staffed statewide groups increased from seventeen to thirty-six. A few groups have staffs of ten or more. The Trust has entered into several pilot projects with statewides to test ways of improving technical support for local preservation and of improving public policy for preservation at the state level. The lines between the Trust and the statewides have sometimes been blurred through cooperative ventures in which technical assistance is provided for the Trust by an employee of the statewide organization, rather than by an employee of the Trust's own regional office. The lines will be further blurred as an agreement reached in 2000 to coordinate fund-raising between the Trust and statewides is implemented. The ultimate success of this new level of coordination and cooperation is likely to depend on the outcome of these fund-raising efforts. The relationship will be shaped by whether statewide organizations, many of which are financially marginal, perceive the Trust as a competitor for limited dollars or as an ally in the attempt to increase funding for historic preservation.

The future of the preservation movement will be significantly shaped by this program. If the new statewide preservation organizations can be sustained over the long term, the movement will be stronger and better able to respond to local needs.

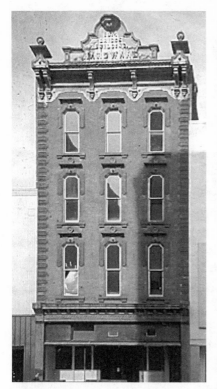

Briggs Hardware, Raleigh, North Carolina, before renovation

Briggs Hardware after renovation

Vacant, deteriorating, and located on an unsuccessful 1970s downtown mall, the 1874 Briggs Hardware Building was purchased and renovated by a partnership between a private foundation and a nonprofit preservation group. This "early skyscraper" serves as headquarters for these two organizations, as well as other nonprofits. Its renovation has been a catalyst for additional rehabilitation projects in the vicinity. (Patti Smith/Preservation North Carolina)

Statewide Preservation Nonprofits

America's statewide preservation organizations themselves are as varied as the members of an extended family. Some focus on public policy and advocacy, others emphasize technical assistance and public education, and still others feature real estate work. Even within these broad categories, the differences in organizational personality are striking. A few examples will demonstrate the variety.

Vermont

For many years, one full-time professional staffed the Preservation Trust of Vermont, founded in 1981. It has no members, eschewing the inevitable expansion of record keeping and support staff that a membership program would require. Until 1998, it also avoided property ownership and management as complicating. The Vermont trust has stuck doggedly to its well-defined role as enabler of the efforts of other groups and individuals to preserve and use the state's historic architectural resources, its cultural landscape, and the fabric of its communities. By encouraging others to do good preservation work, the Preservation Trust has made a huge difference in the state's quality of life. For many years it has administered a grants program for historic preservation, subgranting funds received from several private foundations. The Vermont trust has worked closely with environmental groups, land trusts, and the Vermont Housing and Conservation Board, which has the goals of "creating affordable housing, conserving agricultural and recreational lands, natural areas and historic properties."[7]

The Preservation Trust of Vermont has become an outspoken advocate for better land-use plannning and the state's most potent opponent of sprawl. In 1993 it succeeded in getting the entire state of Vermont named as one of the National Trust's "Eleven Most Endangered Historic Places." Recently, the Preservation Trust has added a technical assistance "circuit rider" representing both the statewide and the National Trust.

In 1997 the Vermont organization was offered a real estate opportunity too good to pass up: the donation of the Grand Isle Lake House, the last remaining turn-of-the-century hotel on Lake Champlain. After examining its willingness to take on the ownership and management of historic real estate, the board of the Preservation Trust concluded that the chance to preserve a major landmark had great merit. The trust raised funds for the hotel's rehabilitation, oversaw its renovation, and contracted its management out to a sympathetic private entity. Besides preserving the structure and protecting nearly a half mile of shoreline along the lake, the project will provide a stream of income for the organization. There have been other benefits. On weekends the inn is usually booked for special events, and on weekdays it is available at special rates for retreats for other Vermont nonprofit organizations. Both private and nonprofit use of the Grand Isle Lake House builds greater awareness of the mission and work of the Preservation Trust.

Indiana

Quite different in character from the Vermont organization, the Historic Land-marks Foundation of Indiana (Indiana Landmarks) is the largest of the state-wides. It was blessed with a substantial gift from philanthropist Eli Lilly in the 1970s that now stands as an endowment of more than $45 million, producing more than $2 million annually for operating support. With more than six thou-sand members, Indiana Landmarks has numerous regional offices around the state, operates a revolving fund, supervises and publishes county inventories of sites of historic and architectural significance (under contract from the state historic preservation office), and operates historic houses that are open to the public. Indiana Landmarks also serves as the local preservation organization for Indianapolis, the state capital.

The foundation has centered much of its efforts on service and support for local preservation and historical organizations. This statewide has created a council of local organizations, bringing them together to learn from each other and to provide guidance for the statewide's programs. Its revolving fund offers special grants and low-interest loans to local groups seeking to save community landmarks. Indiana Landmarks, like the Preservation Trust of Vermont, cre-ated the position of a "circuit rider" in cooperation with the National Trust, to provide field services and technical assistance on behalf of both organizations in southern Indiana and northern Kentucky, making it the first statewide to cross state boundaries in the delivery of services. Through a variety of educa-tional programs, the organization has also made concerted efforts to foster in-terest in preservation among African Americans.

Unlike Vermont's organization, Indiana Landmarks has a large staff and ag-gressive membership and resource development programs. Like Vermont, In-diana has enjoyed stable executive leadership for more than two decades. And, like Vermont, Indiana Landmarks has become involved in a major real estate development project, the West Baden Lakes, a huge and handsome vacant landmark hotel in a remote setting. Indiana Landmarks, offered the property and a substantial grant toward its stabilization, knew that without its direct in-tervention the remarkable early-twentieth-century landmark would be lost. For several years, the organization has been preparing the hotel for eventual private rehabilitation. At the beginning of 2000, the property was being mar-keted for $32 million. The hotel has become an icon for the foundation, which has featured it on tours and in publications.

Indiana Landmarks and some local groups publish lists of endangered properties annually. Like the National Trust's "Eleven Most Endangered" list, the Indiana lists are used to call public attention not only to specific buildings and districts, but also to types of endangered landmarks. Ownership and operation of museum houses, more common among local organizations, are rare among statewides, but Landmarks and a handful of other statewide organizations believe that museums play an important role in introducing the general public to preservation issues for the first time and an essential role in dealing with larger preservation issues.

With its substantial endowment and seasoned leadership, Indiana Landmarks has become the benchmark organization to which many others look as a mentor. Its broad range of activities substantiate the importance of building a significant endowment, which provides the organization with the financial stability to excel.

North Carolina

The evolution of North Carolina's statewide organization, Preservation North Carolina, is in many ways representative of the movement at large. Following the 1939 publication of *Old Homes and Gardens of North Carolina* by the Garden Club of North Carolina, the North Carolina Society for the Preservation of Antiquities (Antiquities Society) was founded. Its board was a who's who of North Carolina women, including the wives of some of the most prominent political figures and business leaders in the state.

The Antiquities Society played a tremendous role in aiding new local historical museum groups. Each year it collected a monetary offering and gave the funds to a deserving local presrevation project. Many major local museums throughout North Carolina owe a debt of gratitude to the society for financial assistance and public recognition at a time when sources of funding for restoration were limited.

In the 1950s and 1960s the vision of the Antiquities Society must have seemed feeble and irrelevant. Responding to the destruction caused by federal programs, the society created a Minuteman committee to alert its membership to sites that were destined for the bulldozer. But except for raising its voice, the society was powerless to do anything. As the 1960s progressed, the makeup of the society began to change. Increasingly, wealthy older members were replaced by young activists. Unfortunately, however, the society was not endowed by any of its founders.

In 1973 the Antiquities Society decided that the time had come to reorganize. A new, more modern name, the Historic Preservation Society of North Carolina, Inc., was adopted; the size of the board of directors was reduced, and its meetings were made more frequent. An annual conference and periodic newsletter was instituted, and a bold new program was conceived to counter the demolition of the state's resources. A new statewide revolving fund, patterned on the work of the Historic Savannah Foundation, was established.[8] The philosophy behind the revolving fund was that the best way to control property is to buy it. These moves infused new energy into the society.

Professional staff was hired, for the first time in four decades. The character of the organization and its membership changed quickly. In 1976 at its first annual conference, participants were as likely to be in their twenties and thirties as in their sixties or seventies; the number of males and females was nearly equal. Its fund-raising requirements also changed. An organization that had operated for years on a few thousand dollars annually (including the grants it had made to local museums) now needed hundreds of thousands of dollars to purchase endangered properties, operate programs, and pay staff. In 1984 the society and the revolving fund merged to create the Historic Preservation Foundation of North Carolina, Inc., or Preservation North Carolina (PNC), as it is presently called.

Although PNC operates a variety of programs, including public education, awards, and advocacy, it is best known for its endangered properties program (as the revolving fund is now known), which by the end of 1999 had placed more than 450 historic properties under its protective covenants or easements.[9] The types of real estate in which the properties program has become involved have evolved from rural late-eighteenth- and early-nineteenth-century houses to commercial buildings (working with the North Carolina Main Street Program), to schools, and most recently to large industrial buildings and associated worker housing. The organization has even placed easements on important Modernist houses of the 1950s. In an entrepreneurial spirit, PNC has used gifts of real estate to build the endowment that its founders never funded. The organization has grown to sixteen full-time staff members in six locations across the state.

Other Statewides

Most other statewide organizations are considerably smaller or younger and support at best a small staff of one or two professionals. Most hold an annual conference, produce some form of periodic newsletter, and conduct an awards program. Beyond these activities, their programs range widely. The California Preservation Foundation has produced a large and profitable annual statewide conference and advocated policy initiatives concerning regionally important issues such as seismic retrofitting for historic structures. Preservation Texas has brought special attention to the rehabilitation needs of the state's many fine historic courthouses.

By the end of the 1990s dozens of statewide preservation organizations had been coaxed into existence or goaded into a higher level of operation by the National Trust's Statewide Initiatives Program.[10] Statewides such as those in Mississippi, Alabama, Oklahoma, West Virginia, and Delaware hired professional staff—in many cases, graduates of historic preservation master's programs—and expanded their programs well beyond what volunteers alone could achieve. One of the basic tenets of the Statewide Initiatives Program is that a capable full-time professional staff is essential to operating a successful statewide program.

Some preservationists have complained that the National Trust has emphasized its work with statewide organizations at the expense of local groups. However, as the Trust and its allies learn more about how to build sustainable and effective statewide organizations, the lessons learned can be applied locally. In turn, the strengthened statewide organizations themselves can be partners in building local partners. Others have questioned the implications of the Statewide Initiatives Program for the Trust's own regional offices. Currently when a local preservationist needs assistance or expertise, he or she is likely to turn to one of the National Trust's regional offices, which are closer to local preservation activities than its headquarters. But when the nation is blanketed with effective statewide preservation organizations, what will be the role of the regional offices? Until then, the regional offices provide statewide and local preservation organizations with one of their best allies for the provision of field services.

Local Nonprofit Preservation Organizations

Local preservation groups are the backbone of the preservation movement. They have thrived for decades without concerted organizational support from the National Trust or other national or statewide organizations, and many of them predate the Trust. Like their statewide counterparts, they vary greatly in structure, organization, goals, and resources. Some local nonprofit preservation organizations have been so successful that they have literally helped shape their cities and towns. The nonprofit revolving funds in Charleston, Savannah, Galveston, and Pittsburgh, each in operation for thirty years or more, have preserved large areas of architectural importance and attracted massive economic investment and recognition for their cities. Local organizations have published thousands of books and newsletters about preservation, hosted innumerable festivals, conducted tours and other special events to call attention to their historic resources and educated children, local citizens, and tourists by the thousands.

Many local groups can trace their roots to an effort to save a specific threatened landmark—a landmark now operated as a museum by the organization that saved it. But most organizations have moved away from their museum origins to undertake a variety of educational, advocacy, technical assistance, and financial assistance programs. A look at several local preservation organizations demonstrates the variety.

The Historic Charleston Foundation, founded in 1947, is well known and respected for protecting and promoting the heritage of one of the nation's best-loved historic cities. Until recently the foundation had no membership. Revenue for its extensive programs comes from museum admissions (it owns and operates three restored house museums), revolving fund transactions (it pioneered the revolving fund and holds easements and covenants on nearly two hundred properties), and annual house and garden tours. The foundation is actually Charleston's "newer" organization, having been established by younger activists who split off from the older Preservation Society of Charleston formed in 1920 as the Society for the Preservation of Old Dwelling Houses.

The Galveston Historical Foundation is Texas's oldest historic preservation organization. This group cleverly used preservation easements to stimulate the revitalization of Galveston's historic commercial district, the Strand; each easement stipulated that the purchase proceeds for the easement would be invested in the restoration of the protected building facade. The organization's annual festival, Dickens on the Strand, draws hundreds of thousands and raises funds for its operations. In addition to maintaining more traditional museums, the organization has restored and operates a schooner as a tourist site, promoting the city's maritime heritage. Most recently the Galveston Historical Foundation has partnered with the federal government to restore the 1861 Galveston

Custom House, a building housing only six government employees and deteriorating badly. The federal government has leased the building to the foundation, which will restore it with private funds and move into it.

Organized in 1956, the Providence [Rhode Island] Preservation Society (PPS) devoted its first decades to the revitalization of College Hill, the oldest neighborhood in the city. At a time when the federal urban redevelopment program was destroying thousands of historic resources, Providence used urban renewal funds to develop a preservation plan for College Hill. This pioneering demonstration study inventoried the area's architectural and historic resources and outlined strategies for encouraging public and private investment in the neighborhood.

The PPS has worked with these planning programs for decades; as a result, Providence has undertaken some of the nation's finest civic design and downtown revitalization initiatives. The Preservation Society is engaged in heritage tourism and in educational programs that inform citizens about Providence's rich architectural heritage. It reaches into the elementary schools to teach three thousand students per year. In 1980 the society spun off the PPS Revolving Fund as a separate but closely associated organization. Using low-interest loans, this highly regarded revolving fund has been very successful in stimulating the revitalization of deteriorated neighborhoods.

On a smaller scale is the Historic Salisbury Foundation, which protects the heritage of a North Carolina town of twenty-four thousand. Founded in 1973, when a fine Richardsonian Romanesque church was destroyed for a bank parking lot, the foundation has maintained a sophisticated mix of programs. Its museum properties include a historic home and a roller mill. Working cooperatively with the city government and a local Main Street program, the foundation operates a revolving fund that has helped revitalize several neighborhoods and the downtown commercial district. After years of frustrating negotiations with two railroads, it managed to acquire a vacant and vandalized railroad depot and restored it as a mixed-use public facility. Its October Tour of Homes draws thousands to the town and helps pay for the foundation's programs. The Salisbury Foundation's political strength became apparent when its president was elected mayor.

One common thread among the most successful local preservation organizations is passionate and visionary leadership. Analysis of these organizations will quickly identify a small cadre of leaders. Whether as staff or volunteer, these individuals have remained committed for decades to preserving their heritage.

To this day, many local preservation groups maintain a wide variety of interests. Some members are devoted to a museum and the social events associated with it—while other supporters are more involved in preserving neighborhoods, downtowns, landscapes, and distinctive architectural landmarks. Those interests may now include working-class homes, Modernist architecture, and the gaudy signs of 1960s highway strip development—a far cry from the vision of the groups' founders. Keeping these interests in the same tent is truly a challenge.

Affinity Groups: Many Interests, Many Groups

Through the years nonprofit affinity groups have sprung up to advance the interests of specialized preservation interests. The list is long and varied. Some groups are interested in particular types of architecture: the Victorian Society in America, Friends of Art Deco, Friends of Cast Iron Architecture, League of Historic American Theatre Buildings, and Society for the Preservation of Industrial Archaeology—to name just a few. Other groups organize around special career interests: the Vernacular Architecture Forum, Society of Architectural Historians (SAH), and National Council on Public History. Still others pursue professional and organizational issues: the National Council of Preservation Executives, National Alliance of Historic Preservation Commissions, and National Association of Statewide Preservation Organizations. Minority groups have their own organizations, for both personal support and professional strength, such as the African American Heritage Preservation Foundation and the Organization of Lesbian Architects and Designers.

These varied groups have their own meetings, activities (ranging from conferences to dances), and newsletters. Usually they provide networks for people with similar concerns who wish to meet and learn from others and promote their interests. Often they have been associated with an individual or small group of individuals who helped found them. The test of their viability has often come when the founders fade away and the organizations fall into the hands of a new generation of leaders.

Preservation Action, founded in 1974 as a voice to lobby in Congress, has an impressive record of achievement. Created at a time when it was awkward for the National Trust to take controversial stands since it was receiving appropriations from Congress, PA energized preservationists to go to Capitol Hill to meet with their elected officials. PA conducted workshops on how to lobby effectively, guidance that strengthened preservationists on state legislative matters as well. One of PA's biggest challenges has been financial. Because it is a lobbying organization, membership dues are not tax-deductible as charitable contributions, making it more challenging to broaden the financial base of PA.

Partners for Sacred Places, based in Philadelphia, has the formidable mission of building bridges between the preservation and religious communities. With a profusion of redundant churches and temples in cities in the Northeast and Midwest and, conversely, with rapidly expanding religious institutions in the South and Southwest, Partners for Sacred Places attempts to bring parties with very different goals to the same table. Partners has had to avoid being too identified with either community because of the distrust often found between them. Its board of directors has a mix of clergy and preservationists, and its funding has come from foundations with a special interest in religious and social affairs.

The most productive affinity groups have generally been those that work in concert with other preservation groups, making the case for their specialties while remaining part of the larger preservation movement.

Revolving Funds: Risks and Opportunities

One of the most effective tools in the nonprofit arsenal for protecting historic properties is the revolving fund. With a revolving fund, an organization becomes directly engaged in the business of preservation in the real estate market. Successfully operating a revolving fund provides perhaps the ultimate organizational challenge and the greatest rewards.

Typically, revolving funds are categorized as either acquisition/resale funds or lending funds. An acquisition/resale revolving fund usually purchases troublesome historic properties and resells them to sympathetic purchasers with preservation restrictions (requiring rehabilitation; prohibiting demolition; limiting alterations, the cutting of large trees, subdivision, etc.). A lending fund, known as a revolving loan fund, commonly makes loans on favorable terms to persons or businesses for the purchase or rehabilitation of important structures; as the loans are repaid, new loans are made, recycling the same funds.

The Historic Charleston Foundation, Historic Savannah Foundation, Pittsburgh History and Landmarks Foundation, and Historic Galveston Foundation, among others, have pioneered acquisition/resale revolving funds with enormous success. Entire neighborhoods of derelict structures have been revived by private purchasers, returning millions of dollars to local tax bases and creating a lucrative market for heritage tourism. The organizations themselves have become local economic and political powerhouses. The Historic Salisbury Foundation has demonstrated the benefits of a revolving fund in a smaller town, reselling more than eighty structures in a city of twenty-four thousand. On a statewide level Preservation North Carolina has operated an acquisition/ resale fund for a quarter-century, protecting more than 450 properties with a combined current market value of over $80 million. Most of its properties have been located in rural areas or in small towns.

In recent years acquisition/resale funds have been used for more diverse purposes. Once the province of simply saving important landmarks, these funds now help produce affordable housing and encourage neighborhood diversity. Since the 1960s Pittsburgh History and Landmarks has worked with the local housing authority, foundations, and housing nonprofits to encourage the rehabilitation of buildings in the historic Manchester neighborhood by existing residents for use by existing residents, making the revolving fund a tool to revitalize an urban neighborhood while minimizing the displacement of low-income inhabitants. It has done so primarily with private sector support.

The Providence Preservation Society created one of the nation's finest revolving loan funds in 1980. Technically the PPS Revolving Fund is a separate nonprofit corporation, but the two boards are interconnected and work closely together. The Providence fund uses CDBG funds administered by the city of Providence to buy and renovate troublesome properties in moderate-income neighborhoods, reselling them with favorable financing for qualified purchasers. The revolving fund has been able to work as a stabilizing influence in transitional urban neighborhoods. The statewide nonprofits in Indiana and Utah have each operated similar loan funds in their capital cities.

One of the attractions of a revolving fund to donors is that funding is reused many times. However, because it is dealing with properties that have been bypassed by the private real estate market, revolving funds usually lose money on each transaction after administrative costs are factored in. Thus, revolving funds need constant financial replenishment to sustain their level of capitalization. Involvement with troubled real estate and the need for constant fundraising at a much higher level often engenders organizational timidity for many preservation nonprofits, making them hesitant to stick their toe into the revolving fund waters.

Preservation professionals who have long been working with revolving funds have expressed disappointment among themselves that more revolving funds were not created in the 1980s and 1990s. In the conservation movement, land trusts have proliferated across the country in these two decades, finding millions of dollars of funding and replicating many features of a preservation revolving fund. Yet in the preservation movement, few new revolving funds have emerged. Over the 1980s and 1990s the National Trust has provided several forums for revolving fund specialists to convene. Many organizations invited to the first forum, held in Hartford, Connecticut, in early 1980, are the same ones represented at revolving fund workshops conducted at recent National Trust annual conferences. The workshops are immensely popular and well attended, the audiences are engaged and enthusiastic, but from one year to the next, one senses that few new revolving funds are actually being created.

Why haven't revolving funds multiplied in recent years at the same rate as their sister organizations, land trusts? Many nonprofits are averse to risk, and the thought of acquiring vacant downtown buildings or crack houses in declining neighborhoods can easily cause organizational heartburn. The cost of operating a revolving fund is much higher than the cost of sponsoring a conference or publishing a newsletter. A revolving fund also needs highly specialized personnel, whether volunteer or paid. Many preservation organizations are run by generalists, but a revolving fund needs personnel knowledgeable about real estate, law, and finance. Few if any preservation degree or certificate programs offer in-depth training in these subjects.

Another reason that revolving funds have not proliferated may be that in most communities few high-style, high-profile buildings are threatened, leaving revolving funds to work with properties that are of less interest to the general public. In the 1960s, when Historic Boston was attempting to save the Old City Hall, it received both local adoration and widespread national acclaim. On the other hand, efforts to preserve a textile mill or a Victorian row house or a rural house built by an African American craftsman may inspire only the most ardent preservationists, despite the economic development or social value of such resources.

Many preservationists believe that an organization must raise hundreds of thousands of dollars before it can start a revolving fund program. Year after year, revolving fund experts are asked at National Trust meetings, "How much money is needed for a revolving fund?" The answer is that real estate expertise, operating expenses, and an organizational commitment to work directly with real property are more important than a large pot of capital. In fact, very little capital is needed. Many revolving funds use inexpensive property options to carry out their transactions. By acquiring only an option, the fund can find a buyer for the property before it obligates itself to an outright purchase. When a buyer is found, the revolving fund's purchase can take place on the same day as its sale, sometimes in a double closing. When a buyer cannot be found, the fund can walk away from the property and go to work on another one, having lost nothing but the cost of acquiring and administering the option and promoting it.

When a large amount of capital is unavailable, the revolving fund may choose to operate with borrowed funds, which eases the problem of raising capital. For example, a line of credit from a friendly bank can make capital available on short notice for property acquisition or development. It will typically be easier to raise $8,000 to pay for a year's interest on borrowed funds than to raise $100,000 in capital, and the organization may be able to leverage its assets by borrowing to achieve even greater results. Sometimes a preservation organization can find individuals or groups willing to lend it funds at very favorable rates for revolving fund work. Using borrowed funds, of course, adds risk, and this requires sound overall financial management to maintain a sound credit rating.

One of the best ways to capitalize a revolving fund is through gifts of real estate. After years of operation, several established revolving funds have received gifts of historic properties valued at millions of dollars. In 1995 Preservation North Carolina, after two decades of revolving fund operation, received a historic textile mill and mill village with fifty-seven houses as a donation. The donor had closed the plant as unprofitable; the gift solved public relations and real estate management problems for the corporate donor in addition to serving preservation interests. The sale of the property, worth over $2 million, has helped establish and endow a regional office for PNC. It has also garnered tremendous publicity and enthusiasm among preservationists. To have raised a similar amount through traditional fund-raising efforts would have taken years of effort.

Preservation Easements:
Obligations in Perpetuity

Since 1969, federal (and often state) income tax laws have allowed a charitable deduction for the donation of preservation easements on historic properties. A preservation easement is a set of legally binding restrictions that are voluntarily placed on a property by its owner. The restrictions often include limitations on demolition and new construction, affirmative obligations for rehabilitation or maintenance, provisions for the retention of important landscape features, and prohibitions on subdivision and other forms of development. A nonprofit organization or government agency is named in the document as the holder of the easement, thereby having the right and the obligation to enforce its provisions. If the easement meets certain specifications dictated by the IRS, an owner may deduct the amount by which the easement is determined to have reduced the property's value.[11] An easement may also have important ramifications for additional forms of taxation, such as local property taxes and federal estate and state inheritance taxes. Among environmental organizations, conservation easements are similarly used for the protection of natural sites and farmland.

Many preservation easements have been donated on downtown properties, where the historic buildings are considerably smaller than the modern buildings being constructed nearby. Often, the monetary value of the land has far exceeded the value of the buildings situated thereon. Sometimes, easements have been placed only on the front facades of downtown structures, leading to the oft-used term "facade easements." Easements on strategically placed properties can stop large redevelopment projects that otherwise would have leveled numerous older buildings to make way for huge new behemoths.

Holding easements carries with it substantial legal responsibilities for a nonprofit organization. Since an income tax deduction is often central to the language, timing, and valuation of the easement, the nonprofit recipient must take its enforcement responsibilities seriously or risk scrutiny and possible penalties from the IRS. Therefore, making the decision to hold easements is not to be taken lightly.

In the late 1970s and early 1980s the use of easements as preservation incentives gained wide popularity. Developers sought to use easements to increase the profitability of preservation projects, and shrewd property owners used them to reduce taxes. A number of urban preservation organizations (e.g., the LaFont Preservation Trust in Washington, D.C.) were created for the primary purpose of accepting and administering easements. Other organizations, local and statewide, added easement holding to their catalog of activities. Many of these easement-holding preservation organizations realized a financial bonanza by charging fees for accepting preservation easements. Fees for administering easements were often based on the size of the charitable deductions, which in some cases were large. Some far-sighted groups used these fees to build endowments to provide for future legal fees anticipated in the enforcement of

Edenton Mill housing before renovation

Edenton Mill Village (after renovation)

After closing the unprofitable Edenton Cotton Mill in 1995, Unifi, Inc., a large textile manu-
facturer, donated the mill and surrounding mill village to Preservation North Carolina for redevelopment through its revolving fund. The gift of fifty-seven houses (mostly vacant) and
the empty mill provided a sizable charitable deduction for the corporation and presented
a considerable opportunity for the nonprofit organization. PNC commissioned a master
plan, undertook extensive infrastructure improvements, subdivided the property, and sold
the houses and mill with extensive preservation covenants. Six years later, the renovated
village contributed substantially to the local tax base and to heritage tourism efforts.
(J. Myrick Howard)

Loray Mill, Gastonia, North Carolina (postcard). The preservation of the 1901 National Regis-ter Loray Mill, donated to Preservation North Carolina by Firestone, is perhaps PNC's most ambitious revolving fund project. A deadly strike that took place at Loray in 1929 strongly colors local opinion about whether the mill should be saved. According to current plans, the massive mill will be renovated for residential, office, retail, and civic uses. (J. Myrick Howard)

easements. Others, less prudent, used the fees to cover current operating costs.

As the number of easement donations climbed, the IRS weighed in with doubts, and the valuation of easements came under scrutiny. Many easements were determined to have little monetary value. Deductions were denied, and stiff penalties were added for overvaluation. Now, if a nonprofit preservation group agrees to accept an easement for which the donor took a charitable de-duction, the group is obligated to provide continuous monitoring and docu-mentation of the property. By the end of the 1980s the number of easement do-nations had fallen, and preservation organizations were less likely to look at the administration of an easement program as a financial windfall. Nonetheless, easements remain one of the most important tools in a nonprofit's arsenal.

Organizational Issues for the Future

Nonprofit preservation groups have waxed and waned, come and gone, their successes and failures often turning on the actions of a handful of dedicated people. In those communities where preservation has been a meaningful force,

Interior of Coolmore House, near Tarboro, North Carolina. Built immediately before the Civil War, Coolmore Plantation, with its main house and five outbuildings, is noted for its extraordinary collection of intact decorative paint, original furnishings, and family documentation of the house's construction and plantation operations. Preservation North Carolina is working to conserve the house and its collections in preparation for its eventual opening as a heritage tourism site. Many local nonprofits, a few statewides, and the National Trust operate museum sites as a central part of their mission. (Tim Buchman)

the names of a few individuals usually come to the fore. Often these activists have been preservation advocates for decades, at first as lonely voices against the tide and eventually as respected and admired community leaders, sometimes as distinguished political officeholders.

Where strong continuous leadership has not emerged, preservation has seldom taken root. That leadership requirement is especially true for nonprofit organizations. A scan of the panoply of nonprofits in the United States will quickly equate the most successful organizations with a few key people whose service tends to have been long and continuous.

One of the most discouraging trends in historic preservation in the 1980s and early 1990s was the movement's endless turnover of nonprofit professional staff. Whether at the National Trust, statewides, or local organizations, every year's meetings seemed to be characterized by new faces and new ideas—and little or no continuity of staff. Many professionals left the field after a couple of years; others hopped from organization to organization. This personnel turnover, which has since seemed to slow, raised questions about the viability of working for a nonprofit historic preservation organization. In many cases individuals simply made bad professional choices; in others, the problem has been low pay and excessive stress. It seems clear that the new university programs in historic preservation must pay more attention to motivation and essential personal skills at the time decisions are made to accept or reject a student applicant. The problem of staff continuity is a serious one, since a change in management every few years means that an organization has to constantly reinvent itself. It needs to be emphasized that the impact of constant turnover is especially discouraging to prospective donors.

The financial future of most nonprofit preservation organizations will be determined by their success in attracting planned gifts, such as bequests and charitable trusts. Only in that way can they obtain donations large enough to build substantial endowments, thereby creating long-term stability and security. Donors need to have absolute confidence in a nonprofit group before they designate it as the beneficiary of a major gift. High staff turnover establishes a pattern that virtually guarantees that few preservation nonprofits will ever reach the high plateau enjoyed by well-endowed organizations in other fields of interest.

Preservation groups will lead a hand-to-mouth existence unless they invest in their staff for the long term. All too often, board members say they cannot pay competitive salaries or provide benefits found elsewhere in the marketplace. Most professionals entering careers in the nonprofit realm know that they will not get rich. They have chosen to accept gratification from their labor as one form of compensation. But if they find that their jobs do not provide gratification, then they will move on.

The issue is more than just salary and benefits. Having a close, trusting, collegial relationship with board members can be one form of compensation for an executive. Having board and staff roles clearly defined and respected is another. Numerous capable nonprofit executives have quit because of micromanagement by officers or board members, unpleasant internal organizational politics, or inappropriate communications between board and staff.

Another nonprofit organizational necessity is having a clear agreement on mission and goals. A preservation organization has a choice among dozens of potential activities such as newsletters, conferences, awards, advocacy, grants programs, technical assistance to owners of historic properties, revolving fund, and development of affordable housing. But to be successful, a nonprofit must choose only a few of these, stick to these choices, and do them well. It should try to strike a healthy balance among its choices and budget. Once those choices have been made, there are real and practical limits for reconsidering and reorienting them.

A nonprofit organization evolves over time. Its goals change, its board members are replaced, and its financial status rarely remains static. Dealing with change is particularly difficult for a nonprofit preservation organization because preservation groups, by their very nature, are involved in long-term projects. Some obligations will be "in perpetuity," which is a long, long time. Sooner or later most groups will face challenging organizational questions: How does one deal with obligations that were assumed years earlier and now seem incidental to current goals? Or, how does one deal with an important founder or benefactor who is no longer in full agreement with the organization's programs? Paying attention to the organizational well-being of the nonprofit group and recognizing the dynamics of organizational maturation is key.

One of the greatest challenges for preservation nonprofits today is to position themselves as known relevant players in community discussions about their future. Literally and figuratively, the preservation movement has to a large degree changed from restoration and rehabilitation to maintenance—important but infinitely less gratifying. The community exhilaration experienced in stopping the bulldozers from destroying the most prominent historic building in town is seldom found today. Often those key buildings and sites have already been protected and preserved. Finding the money to sympathetically rewire the old courthouse for computers, though essential to the building's survival, is not nearly as exciting as saving it from demolition. Here, the role of the preservationist changes from community visionary to restoration technician.

Furthermore, like much of the nonprofit world, the preservation movement has evolved from a volunteer-based to a staff-driven crusade. In many communities, the executive staff represents the face of preservation. An organization must monitor the organizational persona projected by its staff within the community from which it derives its support.

Volunteers are still essential to preservation nonprofits, and, contrary to popular belief, Americans are spending more hours than ever doing volunteer work. But the identity of the typical volunteer has changed, due to the changing demographics of the American workforce and retirement practices. The volunteer of the future is as likely to be a computer-savvy "Generation Xer" as an older retiree or a member of the local woman's club. The nature of volunteerism has also changed. More often, volunteers want to accomplish a specific task, without long-term commitments. Standing committees will be replaced by time-limited task forces. Luncheon meetings will be switched to breakfast, evening, or weekend times. Preservation organizations need to look for programs that will appeal to the new volunteer. Although the national Christmas-in-April program, which uses volunteers to rehabilitate houses for the disadvantaged, would not classify itself as a "preservation" program, many of its local chapters have demonstrated that enormous volunteer energy can be unleashed for preservation when coupled with community-based goals.

Preservation organizations must build their financial resources to a point where they can take care of the urgently needed but unexciting "maintenance" of ongoing operations. Then, they can turn their attention to programs and activities that are most relevant to the community. At present, one can count on one hand the number of preservation organizations nationwide that are well endowed. For this movement to thrive in the future, that number must increase a hundredfold or more, especially as the country experiences a massive generational transfer of wealth.

Another challenge will be for historic preservation to find a way to boldly communicate its message to the public. The message of preservation is compelling: environmentally, socially, culturally, and economically. Nevertheless, this message is too seldom heard outside the preservation community, unlike the message of home builders, developers, and other interests not always friendly to preservation.

Changes in technology will also continue to challenge the movement. The advances in computer technology since the early 1980s and the arrival of the Internet are two examples of how technology has altered the playing field of nonprofit preservation organizations. Many groups have seen their record keeping evolve in short order from index cards to computer databases; a decade ago no one would have predicted the role of the Internet in soliciting memberships or selling historic properties. The changes promise to be even quicker in the future, and the organizations that keep up with these changes will have a distinct competitive edge.

One of the most urgent tasks for nonprofits is to develop stronger alliances with the environmental and conservation movements. Environmentalists sound more and more like they are taking lessons from preservationists—talking about sprawl (long a preservation concern) and setting up land trusts (which resemble revolving funds). Coming from the environmental community, that message is getting much greater political and philanthropic support than ever before.

America's demographics are changing, and wise organizations will consider the ramifications. As noted elsewhere, by the middle of the twenty-first century whites will no longer be the majority in the United States. Nonprofits that ignore the ascendancy of people of color do so at their peril. The demographics of the American family are also changing, and nontraditional families—gays and lesbians, single parents—are becoming increasingly common. Nonprofit groups that recognize these changes and welcome diversity among their staff, board, and membership will reap advantages.

Policy Issues for the Future

Although preservation nonprofits generally succeed on the basis of their local leadership and support, the role of federal and state governments, the health of the economy, and other external forces will also shape their future. The intergenerational transfer of wealth anticipated in the first decades of the twenty-first century presents an unequaled opportunity for preservation organizations to build their endowments. Over the next half-century more than $41 trillion will be transferred on the death of Americans who have experienced unprecedented wealth accumulation, and tax laws strongly encourage planned charitable giving to avoid huge federal estate and state inheritance taxes.[12] Organizations that encourage their members to make bequests, charitable remainder trusts, and other forms of planned giving will build a sustained base for future generations of preservationists.[13] Partnering with community foundations—the country's fastest-growing form of philanthropy—will provide opportunities for nonprofit preservation organizations to build endowments protected from invasion or incompetent investment.

The overall success of nonprofits in the preservation movement will to a large degree be determined by their success in finding funding in both the private and public sectors. Sometimes "funding" means incentives for the private rehabilitation of historic buildings. In the states that have adopted progressive incentives for historic rehabilitation, savvy statewide and local nonprofit groups have been able to parlay interest in those incentives and the preservation successes spawned by them into new organizational energy, new partnerships, new memberships, and new sources of financial support.[14] The creation of a national tax incentive for the rehabilitation of owner-occupied historic homes would energize nonprofits nationwide.

Sometimes "funding" means direct financial support for nonprofits. The availability of federal, state, and local government grant programs for historic preservation has a direct impact on nonprofits—for both operations and special projects. In other cases, funding is indirect. Certainly the continuation of federal and state tax laws permitting deductible charitable donations will be of

John Brown House, Providence. The house, donated in 1941 to the Rhode Island Historical Society, was used as a library before the society removed its collections, then restored and furnished it for public visitation. As in many communities, the local preservation society was spun off from the local historical society in recognition of the differing interests of the two groups. (J. Myrick Howard)

great importance to nonprofits. The adoption of a flat tax without provision for charitable deductions would deal a blow to all nonprofits, taking away any financial incentive to be charitable. The elimination of federal estate and state inheritance taxes would be especially detrimental to planned giving efforts, through which charities receive their largest donations.

Funding, private or public, for nonprofit partners in the preservation world will have an impact. In these early years of the new century, the National Trust is conducting a comprehensive capital campaign with a goal exceeding $100 million. The National Trust and most of its statewide nonprofit partners have agreed to coordinate fund-raising, sharing donor information and occasionally soliciting funds for joint projects. One of the Trust's fund-raising goals is to obtain money to continue and expand its Statewide Partners program. Meeting that goal will have a direct impact on statewide organizations nationwide.

For years, many local and statewide preservationists have dreamed that the

National Trust might someday build a substantial capital fund for preservation. Until recently the Trust has had $15 million available for loans to organizations, but with interest rates generally low and stable, its cumbersome loan process is unappealing, and $15 million in capital does not go far nationally. A large national loan fund for preservation would encourage local and statewide organizations to venture more aggressively with revolving funds, a seriously underused tool. A newly announced equity fund for historic rehabilitation tax credit projects, sponsored by one of the nation's largest banks, is promising.[15]

Changes in federal or state funding for public historic preservation efforts, such as by the National Register and the state historic preservation offices, will be important to the nonprofit sector, even though the professional cultures found in public and nonprofit preservation work are undeniably different and probably inescapable. Whether at the local, state, or national level, public preservation agencies and their nonprofit counterparts are seldom close allies, even though their work is complementary. Their roles are very different. Public agencies are involved in documentation and evaluation of historic resources, and their part in resource protection is generally regulatory. Nonprofit agencies must be more entrepreneurial as they look for revenue sources in addition to mission-related accomplishments. In their quest for members and funding, they must seek out every opportunity for visibility. Public agencies complain that nonprofits sometimes compromise their preservation ethics too easily. On the other hand, nonprofits bemoan rigid public employees or programs that do not appear to understand the realities of the public marketplace.

Despite the occasional mutual sniping, most nonprofits recognize the importance of the work of their public counterparts and will lobby for funding for their programs, and vice versa. Preservation nonprofits would suffer badly if funding for public preservation programs were eliminated or reduced.

Nonprofit and public agencies need to chart a concerted strategy to deal with institutional and governmental impediments to the rehabilitation of historic buildings and neighborhoods. When government agencies and the secondary mortgage markets adopt rules that make rehabilitation unduly difficult, preservation nonprofits need to join together as advocates for common sense. Over the last two decades, preservation has been stymied by several environmental hazards du jour, whether asbestos, underground oil tanks, radon, or, most recently, lead-based paint. With each of these, the regulatory response has been disproportionate to the problem, resulting in the expenditure of millions of dollars to mitigate exaggerated hazards and leaving thousands of buildings unrenovated because of excessive cost estimates. Sometimes, a political re-

Sacred Heart Church, Augusta, Georgia. This splendid 1900 edifice, noted for its brickwork and imported stained glass windows, was closed in 1971 after many parishioners left downtown for the suburbs. It sat vacant for more than a decade until a nonprofit organization purchased and renovated the building as a cultural center. The former sanctuary is used for concerts, festivals, and lectures and may be rented for special events such as weddings and parties. (J. Myrick Howard)

Shell Station, Winston-Salem, North Carolina. The restored 1930s gas station serves as Preservation North Carolina's regional office for northwestern part of the state.

sponse has been necessary to reach reasonable solutions, as with brownfields regulations.[16] The preservation community needs to recognize the potential damage of these alleged hazards in the private real estate market earlier than in the past, and the nonprofit sector needs to take the leadership in making sure that the movement is not set back by unreasonably disproportionate regulations and fears.[17]

The National Trust has challenged the preservation movement to consider how best to allocate the work of historic preservation between the Trust, statewides, and local nonprofits so that each is doing its job effectively and efficiently. It does not make sense for a national organization to engage in local preservation battles when the Trust can most appropriately concern itself with national issues that affect every preservationist. To the contrary, local nonprofit organizations cannot take on the nation's secondary mortgage market or HUD's lead-based paint rules and win.

Preservation nonprofits have made great contributions to historic preservation in the United States. It seems clear that given their work in the private sector, where most preservation happens, their role in the larger movement will continue to grow. As they begin to genuinely coordinate their preservation activities, nonprofit organizations and government agencies—notwithstanding their sometime differences in mission and points of view—have the potential to build a true national movement, one where preservation continues to be local but the search for local solutions becomes national. With an eye on changing technology and its impact on people, and with enlightened creativity in advocacy and fund-raising, America's nonprofit preservation groups can make even mightier strides in advancing their cause well into the next century.

Historic Preservation in a Global Context
An International Perspective

In the last thirty years the world has become smaller as the result of faster, cheaper telecommunications, air travel, the Internet, and other modern technologies. It will surprise many to realize the extent to which we have already begun to borrow, reshape, and use some of the preservation tools and procedures of other nations. By the same token, it is reasonable to assume that the reverse is true—that some American approaches to preservation will find increasing application in the programs of various other countries. But in considering these possibilities, we must remember that precise analogies between American preservation practices and those of other countries are extremely difficult to draw because of differences in legal systems, government structures, economic conditions, cultural traditions, and the like. Political contexts and attitudes about historic preservation—what it is, how it should be accomplished—differ widely among nations. Having said that, however, at a very general level some commonalities do exist.

Virtually all countries in which property is privately owned have adopted some system for inventorying, listing, and protecting individual landmark buildings and historic areas against inappropriate new construction, additions, and demolition. But within this system, differences can be significant. For example, with the exception of a few federal states such as the United States, Germany, Austria, and Switzerland, most parliamentary democracies do not have an intermediate, sovereign, state-level government. In most countries, local regulatory authority over historic buildings is shared directly with a national government ministry; in these countries, unlike the American system, the central government may often intervene or override decisions of the local government, sometimes even without notice to the property owner.

As in the United States, most countries rate or grade buildings according to their importance or significance. Most countries, too, compensate owners or provide other relief when regulations become too burdensome. Restoration and rehabilitation grants to private owners are also common. Unlike the United States, however, most countries have no hesitation about subsidizing the preservation of churches. (Church governing authorities may themselves have separate preservation systems in effect.) Almost everywhere the adaptive use of historic buildings is the order of the day, but moving buildings as a device to "save" them, as we so often do in the United States, is now almost unheard of.

Our accepted time frame for listing most buildings as "historic" is fifty years. The British have recently moved theirs up to thirty if they are outstanding. Federal and state governments in the United States have found it politically expedient to finance preservation by credits against income tax (and, to a lesser extent, direct grants), but the British rely increasingly on the proceeds of a national lottery, and, in the case of some extremely important properties, through adjustments in death duties (i.e., estate taxes) that allow the heirs to remain on the premises for a time. Increasingly, we accept as professional preservationists the holders of certificates or degrees from university preservation programs. Other countries tend to be much more conservative, relying entirely on licensed architects or individuals with university doctorates in art, art history, architectural history, or archaeology.

Most significantly, and unlike the United States, there is a pronounced tendency in other countries to integrate preservation-related regulatory efforts with routine building, land use, and growth management strategies, and to integrate building and landscape preservation with the day-to-day administration of planning programs. "Planning" in most foreign venues is taken much more seriously than in the United States, where the continuing disconnect between planning and zoning in most states leaves much more room for slippage between good intentions and what happens on the ground. Planning control in other countries may cover an even broader spectrum of values. In Britain, for example, many legally designated, closely restricted large Areas of Outstanding Natural Beauty (AONBs) are created primarily on the basis of aesthetics and scenic qualities alone under the various countryside acts. In these areas, historical and cultural attributes are indeed important, but only of secondary interest.

Moving still further away from preoccupation with monuments as such, the British Town and Country Planning (Amendment) Act of 1962 authorized local governments to create Conservation Areas, defined as "area[s] of special architectural or historic interest the character or appearance of which it is desirable to preserve or enhance."[1] Highly successful in placing special emphasis on overall neighborhood character and appearance, rather than mere collections of listed buildings, this approach to preservation is beginning to make a dent in America as a modification of the traditional historic district.[2] The British Conservation Areas also served as the model for the Washington Charter for the Preservation of Historic Towns, adopted in 1994 by the U.S. National Committee of the International Council on Monuments and Sites (US/ICOMOS).[3]

In many foreign countries, garden and landscape preservation, designed and vernacular, in both urban and rural areas, has been regarded as no less important than saving buildings. But in the United States, that kind of integrated effort is still in an early, formative stage. It has been said that if one wishes to see the future of planning, historic preservation, and growth management in America, one needs only to look at the current state of British practice, which generally remains two decades ahead of our own, as it has since the Town and Country Planning Act of 1949.[4]

Some countries in Western Europe have developed a special concept of "protecting the homeland" or *heimat*—a German word that is not easily translated into English—through national membership organizations devoted to the preservation of folkways—the intangible cultural heritage—as well as embracing a traditional concern for architectural and a broad range of cultural resources. Bond Heemschut (the Netherlands), Schweizer Heimatschutz (Switzerland), and Deutscher Heimatbund (Germany) are prominent membership organizations whose programs have lessons for the United States as we devote increasing attention to diverse ethnic cultural traditions and to the concept of "heritage," as distinct from history as such. Architecture and "place" are important components of their programs. America would come close to having the equivalent of these organizations if the National Trust for Historic Preservation were to merge its programs with those of the American Folklife Center in the Library of Congress.

Even diversity in languages, always a problem with respect to technical terms in preservation and related fields, is being dealt with creatively. In 2001 the International Federation of Landscape Architects (IFLA) published—both in book form and as a CD-ROM—a 1,065-page glossary of 10,000 preservation and planning-related technical terms in American English, British English, German, French, and Spanish, a project that took a twelve-member international committee twenty-three years to complete.[5]

Just as we are sometimes able to import ideas from other countries, our own are there for the taking in appropriate situations. For instance, in the former Soviet satellite nations, such as Slovakia, where property confiscated by Communist governments in the 1940s is being returned to private ownership, there are obvious opportunities for the export of the American concept of the revolving fund, rehabilitation tax credits, easements, and the like.[6] The recent work of a U.S. preservation consultant in promoting the creation of a bilingual, visitor's Internet website for the Novgorod Museum and Novgorod City in Russia, where that technology is still somewhat new, is notable.[7] Unfortunately, however, as this chapter points out later, the opportunities for systematic evaluation and exchange of U.S. policies and program concepts with most other countries are still limited.

There is insufficient space in an essay such as this to do more than hint at the number and scope of increasingly diverse and fungible aspects of preservation-conservation practices that can be transferred from one country to another as the world grows smaller. Cultural diffusion is, after all, a constant phenomenon within as well as without nations.[8] Sadly, one finds increasing numbers of highway strip businesses—billboards and used car lots—throughout Europe, a French Disney World, and the ubiquitous McDonald's hamburger emporiums everywhere.

The Institutional Setting

Interesting as such comparisons may be, the starting point in obtaining both perspective and a working knowledge of details about preservation in other countries is to understand the programs and institutional settings of U.S. organizations with an interest in foreign preservation activities. There are a surprising number of venues and institutional frameworks, public and private, within which exchanges of preservation knowledge and practice can and do take place. For the most part, the international program interests of these U.S. organizations are fairly narrow, and they tend to operate more or less independently of one another. Thus, the principal point of entry to the international preservation scene is to familiarize oneself with the programs and interests of U.S. organizations with international connections and objectives, and to become familiar with what they do and how they are organized. The remainder of this chapter provides an American audience with a road map to the formal structures that presently exist.

A cautionary note is in order. Notwithstanding the number and range of interests of these organizations, and despite today's unprecedented opportunities to exchange information, interest among some American historic preservation professionals in the international dimension of historic preservation has waned. This may be due to highly specialized job functions in historic preservation, where success is measured by the number of projects reviewed and processed, the number of approvals or rejections issued, and the number of statistics compiled into reports. In light of the nature of much of historic preservation work, professional staff members may wonder about the relevance of ideas from abroad to day-to-day activities in the United States. They may even question the merit of participating in cooperative international ventures when there are few direct and immediate results that can be observed in this country. The absence or rarity of long-term planning for historic preservation is part of the overall pattern that contributes to the lack of appreciation of its international dimension.

Similar to the truism that understanding a foreign language helps us understand our own native language better, making greater connections between the United States and foreign preservation practices helps us understand our own preservation system better and thus contributes to a better vision of where it should go in the future. Foreign preservation practices provide important lessons that can advance our own field, particularly in areas such as land-use planning, the management of change, and the role of cultural conservation within a larger society that is primarily concerned with education, housing, transportation, recreation, and the alleviation of poverty. Again, the potential for beneficial foreign influences is not a one-way street. Many countries can learn much from our own historic preservation programs, including our emphasis on the private, profit-making sector and accommodating cultural diversity in cultural heritage work.

A Historical Perspective

In previous years, the United States has not been hesitant to turn to foreign experience for inspiration and models to improve its national preservation program. Twice in the twentieth century, the nation turned to Europe for precedents, concepts, and approaches. The first of these initiatives, in the mid-1930s, focused on the national level. The second, in the mid-1960s, dramatically expanded the national program and significantly set the stage for the transformation of the nation's state and local preservation programs.

The federal Historic Sites Act of 1935 was preceded by an extensive tour of Europe by J. Thomas Schneider, a lawyer retained by the U.S. Department of the Interior to examine a number of European systems for whatever transfer value they might have for the United States. The Rockefeller family, which contributed heavily to preservation and conservation of important historic and natural places throughout the nation and abroad, funded his study. Schneider's findings and recommendations were published in a report to the secretary of the interior in the same year.[9] The outcome of the report was Congress's passage of the 1935 act. It reinforced the role of the federal government and its National Park Service in the preservation of historic places and the need for federal preservation activities to extend beyond the boundaries of national park units.

Thirty years later, in the mid-sixties, a similar process was followed to address the dramatic changes in the landscape caused by federally funded development projects. This time, a large, influential contingent of members of Congress, federal cabinet officers, a state governor, senior federal government officials, and leading private citizens led the investigation. This Special Committee on Historic Preservation, commonly referred to as the Rains Committee (named for Alabama's Congressman Albert Rains, who served as the chair), was organized under the auspices of the U.S. Conference of Mayors and funded by the Ford Foundation. Its extensive European tour in 1965 focused on national and urban historic preservation examples then in place or under development.

The committee's final report took the form of a book, *With Heritage So Rich*, that purposefully targeted each member of the U.S. Senate and House of Representatives.[10] It found a receptive audience in Congress, and the result was passage of the National Historic Preservation Act of 1966. The foreign experience played a major role in the formulation of the committee's recommendations.

To show how the U.S. preservation program was, is, or is not relating to international efforts, we briefly look first at the international public sector and then at the private sector. As U.S. participation in the public sector has declined, the more limited roles of the private sector have assumed greater significance.

The Public Sector

To gain some understanding of the shift from a leading American role in the 1960s to a greatly reduced role by the 1990s, we must consider the work of the United Nations Educational, Scientific, and Cultural Organization (UNESCO), the Convention Concerning the Protection of the World Cultural and Natural Heritage (World Heritage Convention), the U.S. Departments of the Interior and State, and the international financial institutions.

In addition to the two major pieces of historic preservation legislation, the

1935 Historic Sites Act and the 1966 NHPA, the United States benefited from the development of other cultural heritage programs in the post–World War II era. A key development was the establishment of the United Nations (UN), intended to foster international understanding and the settlement of disputes by an international body. As the UN evolved, it created a number of specialized entities to address specific subjects on a global basis. One such organization was UNESCO, of which the United States was a driving force in founding, leadership, and financial support. UNESCO's Cultural Heritage Division became a strategic link between U.S. and foreign historic preservation programs. A major connection was UNESCO's subsequent role in encouraging and facilitating the founding of a number of international organizations and programs that brought together specialized interests from around the world. These included the International Centre for Study and Conservation of Cultural Property in Rome (1959), the International Council on Monuments and Sites (1964), and the World Heritage Convention (1972).[11]

The high point of America's effective engagement in UNESCO's historic preservation programs spanned the period from the early 1950s through the early 1980s. The United States not only paid its annual membership dues; it was also well represented and served by senior professional staff. Leading U.S. preservation professionals participated in a host of significant conferences and working groups. During this time, the United States contributed both technically and financially to international campaigns to preserve threatened sites. American preservation interests were also represented on the U.S. National Commission for UNESCO.

As an internationalist, Richard M. Nixon provided significant leadership of the last major international preservation achievement at the federal level. During his presidency, the United States was the first country to ratify the World Heritage Convention. After Nixon left office and following the brief Ford administration, the U.S. government rapidly de-emphasized and significantly disengaged from international preservation. Jimmy Carter's short-lived and poorly conceived Heritage Conservation and Recreation Service was the first step backward. A fatal blow came in 1984, when the United States withdrew completely from UNESCO under Ronald Reagan. Dissatisfaction with the size of the UNESCO budget, the staff, and the managerial style of UNESCO director-general Amadou-Mahtar M'Bow were among the justifications for this retreat. The United Kingdom also withdrew its membership, but has since rejoined. The Reagan administration's stated commitment that U.S. dues to UNESCO would be reallocated to support domestic entities engaged in international sci-

Abu Simbel, Nubia, Egypt. The temple complex, relocated from the lake created by the Nile River's Aswan High Dam, was part of the first UNESCO International Safeguarding Campaign that began in 1960 and concluded in 1980. It was partially funded by a large U.S. grant-in-aid that represented a pioneering use of foreign funds held by the United States for historic preservation. Egypt and other countries were allowed to buy surplus U.S. food with their local currency rather than U.S. dollars, and these funds could thereafter be used for other agreed-upon development projects within the purchasing country. President John F. Kennedy authorized the use of "Food for Peace" funds in Egypt to help rescue and preserve this site. (Russell V. Keune)

entific, educational, and cultural programs never happened. Nothing changed in this respect under the senior Bush or Clinton administrations.

The ascendancy of the conservative private property rights agenda in Congress and the Reagan administration contributed to crippling the U.S. nomination of qualified National Historic Landmarks such as the Savannah, Georgia, Historic District to the World Heritage List. Beginning in 1996 under Bill Clinton, legislation has been repeatedly introduced in Congress to place restrictions on the nomination of qualified NHLs, private and public, to the World Heritage List. Though none of the bills have passed, these efforts have had a chilling effect on the U.S. role in preparing and submitting nominations. Thus, as the World Heritage List of historic cities grows and with a new international Organization of World Heritage Cities chartered and headquartered in Canada, the United States continues to sit on the sidelines. The presence of American entries on the World Heritage List demonstrates not only support for the convention, but also an international commitment by the U.S. government to ensure the preservation and protection of such sites.

In pursuing regulatory reform and budget reductions under Reagan and the senior Bush, the federal Advisory Council on Historic Preservation was for all practical purposes divested of its international role, with the single exception of participation in the Rome Centre. It was not restored during the Clinton administration, and what happens next remains to be seen, although George W. Bush announced in 2002 his intention that the United States would return to membership in UNESCO.

The leading UN agency financially supporting international historic preservation studies and projects is the United Nations Development Program (UNDP). In the senior Bush and Clinton administrations, the United States became the largest debtor UN member state, resulting in a continuing loss of influence within UN programs.

Seen in its entirety, the American position in international preservation efforts is both limited and precarious. With the exception of the statutory authority for U.S. membership in the Rome Centre and the ratification by Congress of the World Heritage Convention, the lack of essential legal authority is seen as a serious problem by those who support the U.S. government's involvement in international historic preservation affairs. Absent such a foundation, the occasional supportive efforts of individual federal officials tend to have a short life span.

Senior federal political appointees may bring strong historic preservation backgrounds and personal interest to their positions. Often, they may wish to see this interest used in an international arena by the programs they administer. In the past America's most significant participation in international programs has been due to the leadership of short-term, non–civil servant political appointees. In the future, preservationists must seize the moment to encourage and facilitate such interests while supportive individuals are in high-level, decision-making positions; once they depart, the success rate for the continuation of an initiative tends to be very limited. Within the Department of the Interior's Office of the Secretary, David Hale's staunch support of the World Heritage Convention placed the United States in a leadership position. As the associate director for Educational and Cultural Affairs, Dr. William P. Glade embraced and broadened the role of the United States Information Agency (USIA) in historic preservation.

Previously, the federal government was a prominent supplier of professional staff for both long- and short-term assignments to international preservation organizations and programs. For example, UNESCO's Cultural Heritage Division and the ICOMOS Secretariat, both in Paris, France, and the Rome Centre's teaching faculty were all staffed by U.S. government professionals. But that era ended when America withdrew as a member, federal funding was reduced, and senior administrators were unwilling to commit resources to international programs.

Like many federal agencies, the NPS maintains an international office and program. The Office of International Affairs hosts delegations of international visitors interested in the American national park system and in programs that address cultural, natural, and recreational resources beyond park boundaries. The NPS also administers U.S. participation in the World Heritage Convention and other international accords. Though several NPS cultural resources staff members are individually active in international conferences and organizations and lend their expertise to preservation issues abroad, flat funding for cultural resources and historic preservation programs over the past decade has been reduced and has limited the attention given to international efforts.

Few American preservationists view the U.S. State Department as engaged in historic preservation. Traditionally, however, it has been financially responsible for American membership in international preservation organizations and attends to international treaties concerning historic preservation. Actually, the State Department's Bureau of Educational and Cultural Affairs (BECA), formerly known as the USIA, has the greatest potential for involvement in preservation. It is well known and respected outside the United States for its excellent work in communicating a wide variety of American values and information. Yet it is little known or understood in the United States.

With rare exceptions, most international historic preservation initiatives supported by BECA must originate with our foreign embassies. Foreign preservationists and their public and private organizations in any foreign country must deal directly—and actively—with the American cultural attaché in a given U.S. embassy. Unfortunately, many senior BECA officials do not readily understand the broad contemporary sweep of historic preservation in America and do not see it as their cultural responsibility. The situation is improving slightly, but only here and there, and more on an individual basis rather than as State Department policy. Ironically, international cultural exchanges related to painting, music, sculpture, theater, dance, archaeology, architecture, museum exhibits, and literature are usually more readily understood and supported. The one State Department project best known to American citizens is the Fulbright Program. A number of leading U.S. preservationists have been awarded Fulbright scholarships for research or teaching abroad, and foreign nationals have occasionally received Fulbright scholarships to come to the United States for the same purpose. A national commission in each country establishes the eligible themes under which candidates may apply.

On the brighter side, BECA's International Visitors Program regularly supports and organizes visits to the United States for a variety of preservation professionals—individually and in groups. Curators, agency and museum administrators, architects, archaeologists, historians, planners, and the like have participated. In 1993, for example, a delegation of nine architects, city planners, and public agency administrators from the Caribbean and Central and South America visited six southern U.S. cities for two weeks to learn how they created and administered urban historic districts. The foreign participants are selected by the BECA staff in the country of origin based on established criteria related to the specific International Visitors Program.

The newest BECA program is the Ambassador's Fund for Cultural Preservation. Established in 2001, it is intended to help less-developed countries preserve their cultural heritage. The $1 million annual fund is competitively distributed in the form of grants to specific projects in sixty-one eligible countries.

The Voice of America's TV broadcast system, World Net, has prepared very effective programs broadcast to a number of countries dealing with American preservation information and techniques. With the assistance of US/ICOMOS, it has produced a number of international TV programs on topics such as urban archaeology, historic district regulations, and new developments in U.S. preservation programs.

Among the more ambitious of BECA's international historic preservation initiatives was a series of regional conferences held throughout the developing world. The first of two such conferences was held in 1991 in Hawaii for fifteen countries from Southeast Asia; the second was conducted in 1993 in Cairo for fifteen nations from the Middle East and North Africa.[12] Intended to bring together the leading figures from both public and private historic preservation organizations, a weeklong series of preplanned seminars allowed regional officials to share their preservation policies, laws, regulations, programs, and financing. However, as is so often the case, with the departure of the political appointee who spearheaded the initiative, the series ended and no other conferences were held.

To prevent the illegal importation of cultural property into the United States, BECA also administers the 1970 international Convention on the Means of Prohibiting and Preventing the Illegal Import and Transfer of Ownership of Cultural Property.

The State Department's Office of Overseas Buildings Operations does have a significant role in international preservation based on the important historical architectural presence of the United States in many countries. Our inventory of some 150 historic buildings and properties throughout the world is employed in the service of international diplomacy. It includes embassy buildings, ambassador's residences and grounds, and cultural centers. But compared with other federal agencies, the State Department was slow and unenthusiastic about meeting the intent and requirements of the 1966 NHPA. Although the department has completed an inventory of its holdings, it is only now, more than thirty-five years following passage of the 1966 legislation, coming into compliance with the requirements of the act. It has recently established a Cultural Resources Committee and a Secretary of State's Register of Culturally Significant Property.[13]

Many U.S. embassies were designed in the 1960s by some of the most renowned American architects of that time. They do not yet meet the National Register criteria and face an uncertain future. The U.S. embassy in Accra, Ghana, designed by the late Harry Weese, FAIA, and considered by Ghanaian architects to be the most elegant contemporary building in the country, was abandoned by the U.S. government as being an unsecure facility; the current U.S. embassy is among the most undistinguished buildings in Accra. Other comparable situations exist around the world.

The U.S. Agency for International Development (USAID), which administers most of our foreign aid, has occasionally supported foreign historic preservation programs. However, based on my experience, this support is not an easy sell given USAID's existing policies and programs. Aid related to preservation often needs the "muscle" of an interested U.S. ambassador or the understanding and support of a foreign USAID mission director. Interestingly, historic preservation stands a better chance when it is part of a larger environmental or economic development program. But overall, it is absolutely essential as a practical matter that there exist a supportive and influential in-country preservation constituency.

In Jordan and Guatemala, USAID has supported the planning, development, and expansion of national park systems, including historic resources. USAID has also supported the preservation and interpretation of World Heritage sites in Ghana as part of a national tourism development program. Egypt has also received $15 million in USAID dollars to finance the Egyptian Antiquities Project

San'a, Yemen. One of the finest surviving historic urban complexes on the Arabian Peninsula, this historic city is entered on the World Heritage List and is one of UNESCO's International Heritage Campaigns. Concerned that the United States was the only major Western country having diplomatic relations with Yemen that was not supporting a preservation project in this campaign, the U.S. ambassador to Yemen attempted to enlist federal support for a specific major building, a seventeenth-century caravanserai. His efforts were ultimately thwarted by U.S. foreign policy decisions resulting from the war with Iraq. (Russell V. Keune)

of the American Research Center in Cairo. Finally, the agency has retained a consultant to explore how it might become more supportive of and involved with sites on the World Heritage List in developing countries. We await the outcome of these more preservation-supportive events.

International Financial Institutions

Following World War II the United States helped found the World Bank and the Inter-American Development Bank to assist developing countries; these are worldwide and regional financial institutions headquartered in Washington, D.C. An African Development Bank is based in Nairobi, Kenya, and an Asian Development Bank is headquartered in Manila, the Philippines. The United States has official delegations representing its interests in each bank.

Of the four, the World Bank has been the most active in lending to foreign historic preservation projects. Recent World Bank preservation studies have been completed for such ancient cities as Lahore, Pakistan; Fez, Morocco; and Ninbo, China. When measured against its several thousand loans, however, preservation-related projects are still few in number—thirty-four, according to a September 1998 directory.

The senior leadership of the World Bank has generally supported the idea that the bank should play a more active role in financing historic preservation projects. But in fact, preservation is not a current priority of the bank's governing board. Bank loans proposed or requested by member states are developed and prioritized within the borrowing country. Thus, the borrowing country itself must be a vocal proponent of preservation. An enthusiastic U.S. preservation organization cannot originate a bank-funded project in a foreign country unless it is proposed by the member state. Preservationists in foreign countries do not customarily deal with their national Ministry of Finance, and therefore they are not closely connected to their own country's internationally financed development programs. It is a discouraging picture. UNESCO and ICOMOS could, if they wished to do so, provide programs to train their members in various developing countries to reach out to decision makers within their national governments who originate international preservation project lending proposals. Sadly, they have not done so.

On a brighter note, the World Bank has recently convened two international conferences related to historic preservation. "Culture in Sustainable Development" was the theme of a 1998 program and a traveling exhibition, and "Preserving the Architecture of Historic Cities and Sacred Places" was addressed in a 1999 forum, both held in Washington, D.C.[14]

The potential role of international lending organizations to support a broad array of preservation programs in developing countries is indeed substantial. The current $41 million loan by the Inter-American Development Bank to Ecuador's Empressa del Centro Historico de Quito is a significant prototype that could be applied to World Heritage cities throughout Central and South America and the Caribbean. Likewise, the World Bank's $41.1 million loan for a diversity of urban preservation initiatives in St. Petersburg, Russia, is an important precedent. In partnership with other international preservation organizations, these could be major facilitators in transferring knowledge, technology, and financing mechanisms. However, it is a role that has yet to be developed. Clearly, this is a worthwhile objective. But the American preservation community must convince these institutions—and the official U.S. representative, the U.S. Department of the Treasury—of the importance of reforming existing bank policies and priorities. Such a task will at the very least be a daunting one.

The Private Sector

As the role of the federal government shriveled, the international role of private organizations within the American preservation movement expanded significantly. For examples, we will look briefly at private nonprofit organizations, a regional trade organization, a corporation, and a foundation.

For many years, the National Trust was a leader in linking the U.S. movement with preservation activities abroad. Between 1949 and 1980 it maintained close ties with other national trusts throughout the world and assisted in the formation of new foreign organizations such as the National Trust of the Philippines, Heritage Canada, and regional trusts in Australia. An International Relations Committee of the board of trustees monitored related international preservation developments. It was represented in the U.S. delegations that formed ICOMOS in Vienna in 1969, it participated in exchange programs with the British and Australian National Trusts, and it was a leader in the important 1973 international conference on "Preservation and Conservation: Principles and Practices."[15]

The library of the National Trust collected international publications and resources and provided personal and organizational contacts with foreign organizations and individuals. Most significantly, it served as the staff secretariat for both the Rains Committee and US/ICOMOS. With the American National Association of Counties and the British Civic Trust for the Northwest, it conducted a series of workshops in Manchester, England, for Virginia preservationists. Building on the example of the British Civic Trusts, the workshop led directly to the establishment of the highly successful Virginia Piedmont Environmental Council, which periodically continues its exchange with British counterparts. In the late 1970s, however, as a result of a round of internal strategic planning, the Trust's board of trustees and management chose to abandon its international role in order to concentrate on what it considered to be pressing domestic concerns.

With the support and urging of UNESCO, a new nongovernmental organization, designed to attract the top preservation professionals of UNESCO member states, formed in 1965. Named the International Council on Monuments and Sites, it was headquartered in Paris. The United States was a founding member, and an American, Robert Garvey Jr., then executive director of the National Trust, was elected as one of the first three vice presidents. The new ICOMOS network played a key part in the preliminary plans leading to passage of the 1966 NHPA. Though it is impossible to describe all of the many roles of ICOMOS in this text, the council stands out as the principal point of access to international preservation efforts for American practitioners, and a few of its programs merit comment here.

One of ICOMOS's major contributions over the years has been to write and promulgate internationally so-called charters that present basic philosophies and principles covering a broad array of preservation subjects. As of August 2001, its work was divided into twenty-one major topics—for example, earthen structures, wood, historic towns, cultural tourism, and legislation. US/ICOMOS leadership has been especially strong on the council's Specialized Committee on Cultural Tourism, which published a site manager's handbook on coping with tourism at world heritage cultural sites.[16] Each of the 109 ICOMOS national committees participates in several such specialized committees on a national basis. Representatives of these committees meet every three years in a General Assembly. ICOMOS is supported financially by dues from individual members, subventions from member states, and grants and contracts from other agencies and foundations.

US/ICOMOS, formed immediately after the creation of the parent body in 1964 and headquartered in Washington, D.C., is a membership organization for professional preservationists. US/ICOMOS conducts an annual symposium, publishes a newsletter, organizes occasional foreign tours, and collaborates with the NPS on domestic World Heritage Convention programs. From time to time it also administers private grants to foreign preservation projects, such as the restoration of the Arneri Palace in Croatia and the USAID program in Ghana. In the mid-1980s it supported the publication of a series of monographs describing preservation programs in fourteen foreign countries and several occasional papers on technical topics.

US/ICOMOS's best-known and most successful program sends approximately thirty American students and beginning professionals abroad for a summer learning experience and brings an equivalent number of foreign students to the United States. Most of the incoming foreign students are placed with documentation teams of the Historic American Buildings Survey and the Historic American Engineering Record. American students abroad work for a variety of public and private preservation organizations.

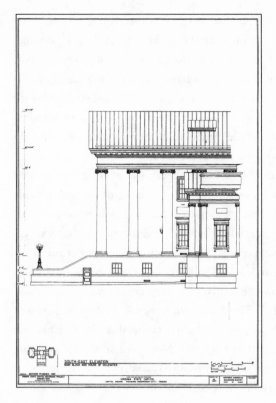

HABS drawing of the Virginia capitol, Richmond. This depiction of the southeast elevation is representative of the architectural measured drawings prepared by international summer interns employed by the Historic American Buildings Survey of the NPS in collaboration with US/ICOMOS. This 1989 drawing was prepared by Gerhard Pfundner, an architectural student from Germany. (US/ICOMOS and HABS)

In 1965, when Venice, Italy, was seriously threatened by flood waters, the World Monuments Fund (WMF) was created to support the preservation and restoration of significant sites in that city. Since then, WMF has evolved into an international membership organization operating out of New York City with affiliate organizations in five other countries. Among its services, it provides foreign lectures and tours, financial support for site-specific preservation projects, and a variety of seminar and training programs. It maintains a reference center, produces a newsletter and publications, and presents an annual Hadrian Award for distinguished international achievement in historic preservation. WMF also undertakes studies on broad international themes—for instance, a Jewish Heritage Program—and recently initiated the World Monuments Watch, which identifies and publishes a list of the world's one hundred most endangered sites with financial support from the American Express Company (AMEX). In addition, WMF provides grants to assist specific sites included on the most endangered list.

The Pacific Asian Tourism Association (PATA) is the leading international trade association for tourism throughout the Pacific Rim and Asia. National government tourism ministries, airlines, cruise ship lines, hotel chains, credit card companies, travel publications, travel agencies, and a host of other organizations related to tourism in this part of the world are members. Although there are many such organizations, PATA is unique in that it has committed itself to a major international historic preservation program that relies heavily on American preservationists for advice and assistance.

In the late 1970s a number of PATA leaders became increasingly concerned about the impact of a growing tourism economy on many of the region's cultural, historical, and architectural resources. The result was the creation of PATA's first Heritage Committee, which turned for assistance to the U.S. National Trust for Historic Preservation. There followed a number of major regional conferences throughout Asia—Thailand, Nepal, and the Philippines—to bring together leaders from the tourism industry, government officials, and experienced preservationists.[17] These, in turn, were followed by country and site-specific technical assistance teams to help PATA members develop historic preservation programs. Macau, the Philippines, Singapore, India, and the Cook Islands were among the diverse sites that received assistance.

Tourism and historic preservation are closely linked. American Express (AMEX), a prominent U.S. corporation with a strong international focus, supports and nurtures this linkage. Working through a separate corporate foundation, it has significantly expanded its role in recent years. AMEX has a record of seeking out and working collaboratively with American international preservation organizations such as US/ICOMOS and WMF.

To stimulate local historic preservation initiatives throughout the Caribbean basin, AMEX supported a multiyear international preservation awards program as part of the Christopher Columbus Quincentenary. To encourage preservation action by national governments throughout Southeast Asia, it supported the preparation and distribution of a major book, *Trails to Tropical Treasures: A Tour of ASEAN's Cultural Heritage*,[18] and most recently funded the five-year, $5 million WMF program, World Monuments Watch. Grants-in-aid support the preservation of individual properties drawn from the one hundred listed on the Monuments Watch. The international vision and extensive commitment of AMEX serve as a model for other corporations engaged in international tourism.

A few American philanthropic foundations and trusts have been generous supporters of international historic preservation efforts. Foundation grants are

The Church of St. Paul, Macau. This Portuguese colony is the oldest European missionary and trading center in Asia. It was the subject of a heritage tourism study sponsored by the Heritage Committee of the Pacific Area Tourism Authority in which U.S. preservation professionals took part. The seventeenth-century church ruins are among the colony's primary historic resources. (Russell V. Keune)

Chinatown, Singapore. Singapore's Ministry of Tourism and its Urban Development Authority invited the Heritage Committee of the Pacific Area Tourism Authority to undertake a design workshop focused on the potential of preserving and adapting Singapore's historic Chinese core as both a functioning business and residential area and a tourist destination. The area was later designated as a protected historic district and has been successfully preserved. U.S. preservation professionals were members of the design team. (Russell V. Keune)

key elements in most of the international programs undertaken by U.S. organizations. Private funding often partially supports American preservationists invited to participate in important international conferences or meetings.

Among the leading U.S. private funding sources for international programs and projects is the Getty Trust's Grants Program. Since 1984 Getty has had a specific category supporting the conservation of architectural heritage, both for the identification and planning of actual projects and for implementation. Representative grants include $54,000 to the St. Lucia National Trust for the Pigeon Island National Landmark and $150,000 for the Postepowa Synagogue in Cracow, Poland. In addition, the Getty Trust supports specialized training and research programs in conservation, such as the conservation of earthen structures and the economics of heritage conservation. The Kress Foundation has a distinguished record in supporting the participation of qualified Americans in preservation courses and conferences outside the United States.

International Educational Opportunities and Conferences

The last thirty years have seen an expanding number of educational opportunities for American students and preservation professionals outside the United States. Government-supported international organizations, such as ICCROM, train professionals in specific disciplines such as archaeology, architectural conservation, and the conservation of stone. The student selection process is highly competitive and requires recommendations from the American member, the Advisory Council on Historic Preservation. Professionals from the United States have occasionally served on the ICCROM faculty.

International nongovernmental organizations such as ICOMOS also offer specialized training courses available to American preservation professionals. A well-established example is the course on wood preservation and conservation offered by the ICOMOS International Specialized Committee on Wood and the ICOMOS Norwegian National Committee.

Most American university degree-granting programs in historic preservation and related fields, such as landscape architecture and architecture, have by now established working partnerships that provide international educational experiences for their students as a regular part of their degree programs. Two notable examples are the historic preservation programs in the University of Florida's Department of Architecture and the University of Hawaii's Depart-

Brimstone Hill, St. Kitts, West Indies. This large eighteenth-century British fortification is an ongoing preservation project. It was one of the historic preservation programs honored in the Caribbean Preservation Awards Program sponsored by the American Express Company as part of the Christopher Columbus Quincentennial. (Russell V. Keune)

ment of American Studies. The Florida program focuses on historic preservation in the Caribbean, and the Hawaii program reaches out to the entire Pacific rim. These programs include actual on-site, short-term class studies in foreign countries. Abroad, excellent postgraduate preservation courses are offered by the Institute of Advanced Architectural Studies at the University of York, England, and Academia Istropolitana Nova (Institute for Advanced Studies) in Svaty Jur, Slovakia.[19]

International Conferences

The vehicle that offers some dimension of international historic preservation to the largest number of people in the American preservation community is the international conference, of which literally dozens are conducted each year around the world. The real value of these get-togethers is not only the narrow technical topics or broader themes they address, but also the opportunities they provide to meet preservationists from other countries with shared professional interests.

International conferences take several traditional forms. Private, nongovernmental organizations (NGOs) hold one worldwide "congress" or "general assembly" every few years. Most of them are in Europe, but the ease of international air travel now allows them to be located anywhere in the world. Recent ICOMOS general assemblies were held in the United States (1987), Switzerland (1990), Sri Lanka (1993), Bulgaria (1996), and Mexico (1999). Such events usually are thematic and are preceded by an open call for papers to be submitted by members. For those invited to make a presentation, such meetings represent a significant opportunity to appear before an international audience and to have the paper published in conference proceedings.

The domestic arms of international organizations, such as US/ICOMOS, have annual meetings and conferences that are open to members and guests. Many of them invite foreign speakers. Because they are more readily and economically accessible than a foreign event, they also provide excellent opportunities to meet and associate with a diverse array of foreign preservation professionals.

From time to time domestic and international organizations will hold major conferences on a special topic. An example is the first World Conference on Cultural Parks, sponsored by the NPS, US/ICOMOS, and other international organizations in 1984 at Mesa Verde National Park, Colorado. These events tend to be by invitation only.

Creating International Standards

The most influential and longest-lasting U.S. historic preservation role abroad has been the American contribution to the formulation of international preservation standards and guidelines. These documents, which take the form of "charters," "recommendations," and "standards," are widely acknowledged as "best preservation practices." Although each country adapts the charters to accommodate its own preservation traditions and laws, they can be applied to any country in the world. Such documents are prepared in two international arenas: government-to-government within UNESCO, and nongovernment-to-nongovernment within organizations such as ICOMOS. The United States remains active in the promulgation of ICOMOS standards, whereas it sits on the sidelines with respect to UNESCO.

A classic example of a government-to-government process is UNESCO's 1976 "Recommendation Concerning the Safeguarding and Contemporary Role of

Historic Areas," more commonly known as the Historic Towns Charter. A four-member delegation of experienced American preservationists—the United States was a dues-paying member of UNESCO then—was invited by the State Department to participate in a weeklong conference in Warsaw, Poland. The purpose of the conference was to draft, debate, and adopt this first international charter. The American contribution to the charter, which drew on local, state, and federal preservation practices, was highly significant. The opportunity to meet face-to-face with experts from other parts of the world and compare the U.S. experience with that in other countries was especially rewarding and in subtle ways played a part in later American legislation and practice. A most interesting aspect of the conference was the occasion it offered to establish personal friendships with preservation experts from countries with which the United States then had no diplomatic relationships or other contacts.

A second important government-to-government example is American leadership in drafting the criteria for the new World Heritage List procedures in 1976. Again, U.S. involvement and leadership opportunities of this kind have greatly diminished in the face of the more recent conservative political climate in Congress.

Access to International Information

Published information about international preservation programs can still be difficult to find. When it is available in written form, it is likely housed in the specialized library collections of international organizations. Obviously, most U.S. preservationists cannot travel to Paris to visit UNESCO, the International Council on Museums, or ICOMOS libraries—or "Documentation Centres," as they are known internationally). The most valuable collection of international preservation documents is located at the ICOMOS Documentation Centre in Paris, although major collections exist at the Institute of Advanced Architectural Studies at York University in England, the Rome Centre, and Academia Istropolitana Nova in Slovakia.

In the United States, smaller collections can be found in the professional offices and libraries of such organizations as US/ICOMOS, the American Institute of Architects, the international office of the NPS, and, more recently, the Getty Conservation Institute in Los Angeles. Some are also located in the libraries of university departments with historic preservation programs. The Internet is a major source of information on international preservation. Today, all of the major international preservation organizations have websites and many are hyperlinked.

Among publications, the domestic newsletters and other publications of international preservation organizations are excellent sources of current news and feature articles. One of the best is the bimonthly US/ICOMOS newsletter. The Getty Conservation Institute's *Conservation*, published three times a year, primarily highlights the institute's domestic and international programs. The World Monuments Fund publishes a member newsletter, *Milestones*, and the NPS's *CRM* (Cultural Resources Management) occasionally devotes an entire issue to international topics. American preservationists interested in international programs should also note the availability of the *ICCROM Newsletter*, UNESCO's biweekly *World Heritage News*, and the *World Heritage Newsletter*.

Areas for Exploration

At one level, the transfer of preservation techniques from one country to another can be easily accomplished. For example, in the remote town of Banska Stiavnica, Slovakia, a car approaching the historic town center will be stopped by a small man wearing a change machine and a ticket dispenser standing in the middle of the street. To proceed farther, one has the option of paying the gentleman twenty-five cents and buying a ticket authorizing entry to the town center —a simple solution to maintaining both historic character and a pedestrian-friendly atmosphere. Or, we could greatly improve the administration of our local historic districts, for example, by following Dutch or Scottish examples: the city of Amsterdam provides free architectural advice to property owners contemplating changes or additions to buildings, and the Edinburgh, Scotland, New Town Conservation Committee's insurance program for homeowners provides free annual property inspections—an early warning system of needed improvements and essential repair work. Luxembourg maintains a national registry of individuals with special crafts skills. These are fairly simple, obvious approaches.

At another level, however, the transfer of ideas becomes more complex. Looking abroad, American preservation since 1966 represents a rich and diverse bundle of theory, practice, and experience worth sharing with an international audience. At the heart of American experience is the role of the private sector—as volunteer, advocate, activist, fund-raiser, committee worker, docent, board member, and leader. The scope and scale of private-sector volunteer accomplishment in the United States is, frankly, not presently widespread in much of the world, but many aspects of it will have increasing and substantial transfer value to other countries as time goes on.

The American preservation system has been especially creative in developing imaginative funding techniques. Our traditional approach to financing historic preservation endeavors relies heavily on personal private investment, donations, government grants-in-aid, and philanthropic support, reinforced by the availability of revolving funds, below-market interest rate loans, tax incentives, and easement programs. Many of the newer techniques are unknown abroad, and all have potential application to other countries notwithstanding differences in government structures and legal systems. This is especially true for the new democracies that have emerged from the dissolution of the Soviet Union, where the restitution of private property to the heirs of owners from whom it was confiscated by former Communist governments is under way. The American experience will doubtless have wider application as countries in South America and Southeast Asia move away from command economies to more democratic, market-dominated ones.

In many countries, historic preservation is the primary responsibility of the national government, and the role of local governments is very limited. In countries where local responsibility for environmental regulation is increasing and local control is growing relative to central governments, the experience of American local and state governments has much to offer, especially for landmark regulation and the protection of historic neighborhoods. Preserving old neighborhoods is a complex affair requiring the preservation community to reach out to the design professions, local governments and their bureaucracies, and nonprofit organizations to create new levels of cooperation and coordinated programming. That we have yet to establish a solidly integrated relationship between landmark and historic district regulation on the one hand and the larger set of traditional zoning and land-use controls on the other is clear. We have not, in fact, established good connections between planning objectives per se and the growth management techniques needed to accomplish those objectives. The situation in most other developed countries is just the opposite: the regulations and the plan are one, and historic preservation controls are an integral part of the whole. This area is worth careful study on this side of the pond, especially as many state and local governments are, for the first time, seriously exploring the possibilities of Smart Growth.

There is a special advantage to be gained by a close examination of the British approach to preserving historically important natural landscapes, a relatively new concern in the United States since 1966. It seems obvious that there will be few future opportunities to create new publicly owned national parks in the United States. In Britain, however, national parks are located on privately owned land to which the general public has generous access in exchange for strict regulation of buildings and land and have easy access to maintenance grants for the upkeep of private buildings and landscape. As compensation, property owners are relieved of tort liability to visitors for accidents occurring on their grounds. This approach to preserving rural landscapes is reinforced by the designation of dozens of Areas of Outstanding Natural Beauty through the various Countryside Acts. Such approaches have obvious transfer value to the United States, especially as the concept of state- and federally designated heritage areas becomes a reality.

University degree and certificate programs in a variety of disciplines have become a well-established component of the American preservation movement. Starting with a small core group of academic programs in the late 1960s, the United States now can point to a number of university academic programs related to historic preservation. Many of these programs can be emulated by other countries.

Motivated by the 1976 federal tax incentives, the United States has promulgated a sophisticated, clearly articulated approach to the adaptive use of historic buildings through specific norms called the Secretary's Standards. Here, a caution is in order. Though, arguably, these standards may have transfer value to other countries, we must acknowledge that basic historic preservation philosophy will vary greatly from one culture to another. In Japan, no one thinks twice about repairing damaged or worn-out pieces of a historic temple with replacement parts; in fact, some listed historic buildings have no original materials—in other words, they consist entirely of replacement parts. But for that, they are deemed no less worthy of veneration as cultural icons. In the United States, such an approach would be a direct violation of the Secretary's Standards.

Recommendations for the Future

Given the progress of our domestic historic preservation, it is past time to resume our former role in matters related to international preservation. It is urgent that we strengthen our authority to do so. A number of specific tasks need to be accomplished.

Cape Coast Castle, Cape Coast, Ghana. Built by a European trading company, the castle played a significant role in the African slave trade. It is one of a series of fortifications on the Ghanaian coast entered on the World Heritage List and received financial support for its preservation and interpretation by the USAID. The project was one element of a major international tourism program focused on historical and natural resources developed by the government of Ghana. US/ICOMOS and the Smithsonian Institution representatives were part of the team of advisers working with USAID and the Ghanaian Museums and Monuments Board. (Russell V. Keune)

The federal government must reengage itself with the international organizations working in historic preservation. We should rejoin UNESCO. In doing so we must return qualified, experienced professionals to the staff of the Cultural Heritage Division. We must once again be an active contributor to international forums preparing international treaties, charters, and recommendations. Above all, the United States should participate both financially and professionally in UNESCO International Safeguarding Campaigns to preserve and conserve sites on the World Heritage List. This is an especially important task in developing countries. Qualified American professional firms and individuals should once again become eligible to compete for UNESCO and UNDP international historic preservation contracts.

To reestablish our standing within the parent organization, specifically the UNDP, we must pay our outstanding dues and assessments owed to the United Nations. Again, we should support its preservation programs in developing countries.

University of Virginia Academical Village, Charlottesville. The original village was founded and designed by Thomas Jefferson. It is one of the few nonfederal properties in the United States that have been entered on the World Heritage List. (Russell V. Keune)

The U.S. Senate should ratify the thirty-five-year-old international "Convention for the Protection of Cultural Property in the Event of Armed Conflict." Inasmuch as the federal government participated in its preparation following World War II and seventy other countries have ratified the convention, the failure of the United States to ratify after all these years is an embarrassment to our standing in the international preservation community.

Congress should amend its legislation on historic preservation to authorize the expansion of appropriate domestic programs into the international arena. The nomination of qualified American National Historic Landmarks to the World Heritage List should be reactivated, preferably without unanimous owner consent.

The application of Section 106 of NHPA should be expanded to apply to "American foreign-aid programs as they may affect World Heritage Sites and other officially designated historic properties in recipient countries."

There should be a careful review of the USAID and BECA programs to determine how preservation components might be strengthened. The Departments of the Interior (including the NPS) and HUD must be given clear legislative authority to engage in international historic preservation activities when such activities are appropriate extensions of their domestic missions.

The enormous technical and financial resources of the world's multilateral lending organizations—the World Bank, Asian Development Bank, African Development Bank, and Inter-American Development Bank—must be encouraged to support economically viable historic preservation projects in the borrowing member countries whenever possible. Government and nongovernment representatives to each of these organizations must henceforth forcefully advocate that historic preservation elements be included in the technical support and lending programs of these international institutions.

The United States has a wealth of contemporary historic preservation literature that merits translation into foreign languages, including laws, regulations, guidelines, standards, and technology in many preservation-related fields. Such translations could encourage and support preservation efforts in other countries. Spanish, French, and Mandarin translations would reach large segments of those seeking such information, especially in the developing world. The US/ICOMOS series of publications, "Preservation in Other Countries," should be reinstated, and the publications programs of the WMF should be endowed and supported.

International preservation programs in the United States, both from a substantive and an institutional standpoint, become the victims of insular thinking within and without the historic preservation community. To some extent this is inevitable, given that public concern with events outside our borders tends to be limited to peacemaking, poverty, AIDS-related health, and international trade. It is both surprising and disappointing, given the shrinking of borders through communications and travel, that the American travel and financial communities have not assumed leadership positions in promoting historic preservation. The ideas that the preservation of cultural resources is a frill relative to other public goods and that "charity begins at home" are deeply entrenched in our economic and political systems. Increasingly conservative thinking about private property has repeatedly led Congress to place disqualifying restrictions on the nomination of internationally important landmarks to the World Heritage List. All of the organizations described earlier in this chapter—the National Trust, Interior Department and NPS, USIA, State Department, WMF, US/ICOMOS and ICOMOS, PATA, the Getty Trust, and others—focus their international efforts on narrow organizational goals; none of them are specially oriented to dealing collaboratively with the problems identified in this chapter.

Taken together, these attitudes and their consequences send a signal to other countries that America is not serious about preservation and reinforce the popular notion here and abroad that we are a young country with nothing much worth preserving. Our international connections are thus tenuous and hang too often and too strongly on the personal interest of transient, high-level government appointees and civil servants; that, in turn, makes our involvement in international preservation activities a matter of chance. A variety of special initiatives to surmount these fundamental limitations would seem to be important.

3 The Human Face of Preservation

The Social and Ethnic Dimensions
of Historic Preservation

Few other topics so perfectly capture the essence of "a richer heritage" than the social and ethnic dimensions of historic preservation. Today, the preservation field embraces the heritage of numerous cultural groups that made their mark on the American landscape. Surveys are conducted of the historic properties associated with diverse communities. Historic properties in ethnic neighborhoods are enjoying a longer life through historic rehabilitation. The stories of diverse groups are being interpreted for community residents and visitors alike.

Historical studies of diverse groups are yielding an unfolding tapestry of ethnic heritage. The popular media provides frequent reports about the unearthing of ethnic and minority history in archaeological investigations, archival research, and even DNA test results. The "recent past" provides a rich trove of possibilities as the nation explores themes such as the desegregation of the public schools and public facilities. And events of today will take on significance as they fade into the past. New groups continue to arrive at the country's shores and are making their own marks on the face of the nation.

The authors of the essays contained in *With Heritage So Rich* could not have imagined that the historic preservation field would incorporate such a broad story into the narrative of the nation's heritage. When one reads this seminal work of 1966 through the lens of today's social history, there is hardly a mention of social or ethnic history. This oversight is due in part to the nature of historical study in the mid-1960s. The "new social history" was not yet a presence in the history courses that were taught in colleges and universities and pursued in graduate studies. The focus of history instruction was on military and political events and zeroed in on the achievements of national figures, usually European American men. In addition, architects of the mid-1960s played a major role in the development of the legislation, and their focus was on high-style architecture.

Early Efforts at Ethnic Preservation

It may surprise many preservationists that Congress undertook some of the earliest "official" attempts to preserve African American history. In 1943, in the midst of World War II, Congress added the George Washington Carver National Monument in Diamond, Missouri, to the National Park System. This may have been an acknowledgment of the sacrifices that African Americans were making to the war effort. In 1956, as the civil rights movement was gaining momentum across the South, the Booker T. Washington National Monument in Hardy, Virginia, was added to the NPS. Both Carver and Washington represented moderate figures in African American history. In 1962 the NPS assumed responsibility for the Frederick Douglass House in Washington, D.C., the home of the noted civil rights leader, orator, and presidential adviser. With this acquisition, Congress began to speed up the process of adding important sites associated with ethnic history in America's urban centers. Later, ethnic historic sites were acquired in remote places as well.

Despite these actions of Congress, *With Heritage So Rich* virtually ignores ethnic groups and minority personages. Nevertheless, the legislation that followed the publication laid the groundwork for a broad historic preservation movement that eventually embraced these groups and their prominent figures. Though ethnicity was unstated, the 1966 act represented a reaction to the massive urban renewal and transportation projects of the 1950s and 1960s that had wiped out urban neighborhoods where ethnic groups had made their homes. The policy direction of the report pointed toward preserving whole districts of historic buildings and focusing on historic properties of local and state importance, as well as nationally significant properties. Unknowingly, this laid a foundation for the unprecedented preservation activities of minority and ethnic groups.

It is difficult to pinpoint the earliest ethnic historic preservation activities outside the boundaries of the NPS. African Americans preserved their family and community history through a variety of means. They had maintained historic sites like the Frederick Douglass House before such properties were added to the NPS. Public schools were named in honor of African American leaders. Church records and family mementos constituted an important way to preserve memories of the past. Individuals and organizations maintained their communities' lore. Storytelling was a crucial means of passing down history from one generation to another. The same could be said about the cultural heritage of other ethnic groups that settled and built the nation.

One of the first ethnic efforts to receive the attention of the established historic preservation field was Project Weeksville, which began in 1968 in the Bedford-Stuyvesant section of Brooklyn, New York. The discovery of the historic Hunterfly Road and subsequent archaeological investigations in the area led to the establishment of the Society for the Preservation of Weeksville and Bedford-Stuyvesant History. Today the society continues to use the preserved remains of the historic neighborhood to educate neighborhood children about the richness of their heritage in Brooklyn and nationwide. The society's work also serves as a focal point for the surrounding dynamic multiethnic community.

The society's founder and president, Joan Maynard, became a national figure in the historic preservation field. She sat on the board of trustees of the National Trust for Historic Preservation and later was a recipient of its prestigious Louise du Pont Crowinshield Award. As a result of her national prominence, Maynard became a spokesperson for the value of preserving African American historic places throughout the nation.

Carl Westmoreland of Mount Auburn, Cincinnati, was another early leader in diverse historic preservation activities. Mount Auburn developed in the nineteenth century with large suburban villas occupied by the city's elite. By the 1960s the neighborhood had become largely African American, and its residents organized to resist urban renewal plans promoted by the city and its business establishment. Westmoreland spoke for the Mount Auburn Good Housing Foundation, which undertook housing improvements through the purchase and management of buildings and the designation of the area as a historic district. The Mount Auburn leaders viewed preserving buildings as one component in community revitalization, along with education and social services.

Westmoreland's role in neighborhood revitalization took him to the annual meeting of the National Trust in 1971; he was the only African American there. Later, Westmoreland became a trustee of the National Trust and a spokesperson for similar opportunities in inner-city neighborhoods. Concern for the multiple dimensions of neighborhoods led to many community preservation efforts nationwide, which tied historic preservation to other neighborhood services. Such efforts in urban areas helped to combat the impression that preservation caused displacement of low-income residents.

As the nation entered the Bicentennial era, many organizations and agencies developed historically related publications and programs to commemorate the two hundredth anniversary of the Declaration of Independence. In 1972 the NPS funded a survey of black historic sites to increase the number of National Historic Landmarks related to black history. As a result, additional landmarks were designated, including schools, residences, commercial areas, neighborhoods, and communities. This survey was followed in 1979 by studies of several dozen ethnic communities that could be used as a basis for Historic Landmark nominations. One such study on the "War in the Pacific" led to the designation of the Manzanar War Relocation Center in Lone Pine, California, as a National Historic Landmark.

From its establishment in 1966, the National Register captured an increasingly diverse record of officially recognized historic places. As early as 1973, it listed Bear Butte, in South Dakota, a purely natural formation, based on its significance to the cultural identity of nearby Indian tribes. As the nominating authorities—state historic preservation offices, federal preservation offices, and later tribal preservation offices (TPOs)—included more and more buildings, sites, and historic districts associated with the history of Native Americans (Chapter 13), African Americans, Hispanics, Asians, and other ethnic groups, the National Register began to reflect the diversity of the nation. The register's listing and its associated benefits provided a meaningful way for this history to be validated in the historic preservation movement.

While the NPS was expanding its National Historic Landmarks designations and National Register listings, the Smithsonian Institution undertook the memorable *A Nation of Nations* exhibit at the Museum of History and Technology (now the National Museum of American History). A critically acclaimed display, it clearly defined the United States as a nation of immigrants, which was a source of its unique character and strength.

The capstone of the 1970s was the publication in 1976 of Alex Haley's book *Roots*, which was followed by an immensely popular television series by the same name. The book traced one black man's family through five generations based on research in Africa and the United States. Haley used the methods already well known to oral historians and genealogists but elicited unprecedented public appreciation for the results of his research. *Roots* set into motion increased public and scholarly interest in African American genealogy and local history, which continues to this day.

In the 1980s many government agencies and private organizations reached out to diverse communities. Publications such as Carole Merritt's *Historic Black Resources: A Handbook for the Identification, Documentation, and Evaluation of Historic African-American Properties in Georgia* (1984), produced by the Georgia State Historic Preservation Office, are an indication of the preservation establishment's activities in this area.[1] Surveys like the ones of German-Russian folk architecture in South Dakota, social institutions of the black community in Columbia, Missouri, and ethnic and racial minority settlement in Arkansas became commonplace.

To facilitate increased minority involvement in historic preservation, several state historic preservation offices formed affiliated committees. In 1984 the Alabama Historical Commission established the Black Heritage Council to advise the commission and to undertake its own projects. In the late 1980s the Georgia State Historic Preservation Office organized a Minority Heritage Preservation Committee and later a Minority Preservation Network.

The 1983 publication *Cultural Conservation: The Protection of the Cultural Heritage of the United States* was a benchmark in acknowledging that not all of the nation's cultural heritage fell into the neat categories of building, structure, district, site, or object.[2] Many groups valued intangible resources, such as crafts, rituals, and language, to maintain their cultural identity. Although there was no immediate legislative or programmatic outcome of this report, it remains a landmark publication in the effort to embrace all expressions of cultural identity, not just those that fall under the "built environment" umbrella.

Shifting Populations, Shifting Values in the 1990s

In the 1990s cultural diversity in historic preservation activities reached a new plateau, one that now enriches much of the field and promises to transform it in the new century. Whereas the framers of much of national historic preservation legislation came from the ranks of the white-dominated establishment, it is likely that future laws will bear the strong mark of the increasingly diverse national population and the preservationists that emerge from it. Increasingly, Congress is passing measures to establish programs that emphasize America's diverse cultural groups, such as the Underground Railroad Preservation and Education Initiative, preservation grants to Historically Black Colleges and Universities, and Tribal Preservation Program grants. These programs reflect the growing political power of minority groups.

The National Preservation Conference in 1991, which was held in San Francisco in commemoration of the twenty-fifth anniversary of the National Historic Preservation Act, served as the forerunner to the new emphasis on diversity. The conference organizers acknowledged that the agenda set out in 1966 had been largely achieved. The conference proceedings were planned to develop new directions that could carry the historic preservation field through

Lookerman House, Delaware State University, Dover. This building is the recipient of funding for the rehabilitation of historic buildings on the campuses of historically black colleges and universities. Delaware State is the first HBCU to establish an M.A. program in historic preservation. (Antoinette J. Lee)

the remainder of the decade and into the next century. Speakers like David McCullough and Henry Cisneros emphasized the important demographic changes that had taken place nationwide and the need for the historic preservation field to incorporate the concerns of diverse peoples.[3]

During the conference, participants placed cultural diversity high on the list of major challenges to the field. Increased diversity would focus attention on the types of resources protected, the range of communities served, the demographics of the community activists and professional ranks of the field, and the imperative to work with the rising generation of young people who would someday be the nation's leaders. The wrap-up speakers challenged the audience to invite disparate peoples to the next conference so that the audience would be more diverse.

Pursuing this issue, the 1992 National Preservation Conference, held in Miami, Florida, featured "Cultural Diversity" as its theme. But it was not enough to announce a subject and organize sessions around it. More needed to be done to change the demographics of the attendees. Fortunately, the Getty Foundation contacted the National Trust and offered to fund scholarships to attract more diverse attendees. The scholarships worked. For many longtime conference participants, the Miami meeting will remain a milestone in the evolution of the National Preservation Conference. Getty's support for the diversity

New Florida Bakery, Little Haiti, Miami. The bakery's painted sign illustrates the cultural heritage of the nation's newer immigrant groups. (Charles Kelley)

scholarships continued for several years and then was augmented and supplanted by funding sources from the other foundations, the NPS, and local organizations.

The scholarship program was enormously successful in diversifying the attendance at National Trust meetings. People who had never previously been to the annual gatherings found supportive networks and now viewed attendance at the conference as mandatory, with or without scholarship support. Prospective participants now take it for granted that the conference will include diversity sessions, field trips, and receptions. Although the diversity scholarship program transformed the attendance, the term "diversity scholarship" was deemed to be patronizing. Many diverse people attended the conference without scholarship support. In addition, young people and students, regardless of ethnic background, received scholarships. In 1999 the program was renamed the Emerging Preservation Leaders Scholarship Program.[4]

The increased presence of diverse participants and speakers led many longtime preservationists to acknowledge that they had learned as much, if not more, from this newer group. In many cases, the newer attendees had long been involved in neighborhood and community improvement activities but had just not called them "historic preservation." As they found kindred spirits at national conferences, they pronounced themselves to be "preservationists."

Despite the growing diversity at National Preservation Conferences, a similar transformation did not occur in the professional ranks of the field. The historians, archaeologists, historical architects, organization executives, and other professionals have, with a few exceptions, remained remarkably unchanged in ethnic makeup. There are several reasons for this. The first is that many academic programs that feed new employees into these positions are not themselves ethnically diverse. The second is that preservation remains a little-known and esoteric profession. To many young people considering an occupation, careers in law, medicine, computer science, and teaching are much more familiar and predictable. The third is that historic preservation still carries an air of "elitism" that derives from the pre-1970 era. What can be done about the paucity of diverse professionals will be addressed later in this chapter.

Social/Ethnic Preservation Activities in the 1990s

For much of the 1990s, the historic preservation field witnessed a growing and confident diverse community of grassroots activists and a broadened scope of historic preservation that incorporated the cultural heritage of many diverse groups. The stage was set for several projects and organizations that became major players in the field. Despite their success, however, several faced significant resistance. Many diverse leaders believed that ethnic cultural values had a long way to go before they were acknowledged and accommodated by the established historic preservation field.

One of the test cases was the town of Eatonville, near the sprawling theme parks of Orlando, Florida. In the late 1980s Eatonville, with a population of 2,500, faced the possibility that a highway-widening project would decimate its community. The town—established in 1887 by African Americans who discovered refuge from racism through self-government—found its salvation in its historical roots. Eatonville also drew strength from its most famous resident, Zora Neale Hurston, who introduced countless numbers of readers to her town through her writings. The Association to Preserve the Eatonville Community (PEC), after its organization in 1987, set about raising the town's presence in the historic preservation community. However, a National Register nomination for Eatonville languished in the register's pipeline because preservation professionals believed that the town did not possess sufficient importance to merit listing. After years of frustration, the old guard changed and the National Register nomination finally was approved in early 1998. Eatonville became a Certified Local Government and benefits from a local historic preservation board. The PEC-sponsored annual festival, "Zora," celebrating Hurston, Eatonville, and African American culture, attracts thousands of people.[5]

The formation of the National Association for African American Historic Preservation (NAAAHP) in 1995 reflected the need to focus on African American heritage free from the agendas of existing organizations. NAAAHP was "born of the good efforts initiated . . . by the National Trust for Historic Preservation as they seek to expand their ranks to include the built history of all Americans."[6] At the National Preservation Conference, the Trust's scholarship program brought together "preservationists-of-color" who wanted to take primary responsibility for improving their own communities. The "most effective and respected preservation efforts in African American communities must come from within those communities."[7] For a number of years, NAAAHP has sponsored conferences, published a newsletter, and maintained an Internet website.

The African Burial Ground case in New York City seemed to vindicate the "separatist" approach that NAAAHP espoused. The African Burial Ground, a municipal cemetery used between the late 1600s and 1796, came into being because Africans in America were not permitted to bury their dead in church cemeteries. The cemetery provided a "rare setting in which the enslaved could assert their humanity and respect their own culture."[8] By the end of the eighteenth century, it was estimated that thousands of Africans had been buried there. Over the years, development projects turned over and disturbed portions of the site. In 1991 the U.S. General Services Administration planned to construct a new federal office building on a section of the cemetery. Under the provisions of the 1966 NHPA, archaeological surveys and excavations were conducted prior to construction. Without adequate public consultation, GSA removed more than four hundred burials, while African Americans in the city held protests at the cemetery's edge.

In the end, one-third of the city block planned for construction was used solely for memorialization and the main part of the federal building was allowed to proceed. With funds provided by the federal government, Howard University in Washington, D.C., has performed research on the excavated remains, a process that will conclude with reburial and memorialization. The Howard University team examined several aspects of the remains, including the variety of African burial customs and the physical manifestations of life

Snoma Finnish Cemetery, Snoma County, South Dakota. This historic site, which is associated with the state's Finnish settlement, is listed in the National Register. (South Dakota
State Historic Preservation Office)

under slavery where premature mortality was high. Most important, the studied remains testify to the preservation of African culture through burial rituals
and symbols.

The outpouring of public emotion over the fate of the African Burial
Ground left much of the historic preservation establishment in New York City
observing a level of passion that was rare in the day-to-day proceedings of
preservation activities. In response to this phenomenon, the Municipal Art Society of New York conducted a study and subsequent conference, "History
Happened Here: A Plan for Saving New York City's Historically and Culturally Significant Sites." Dated November 1996, the study acknowledged that for
many New Yorkers, "historic preservation is—and should be—based on architectural beauty and significance. . . . These values are not wrong, but they
are too narrow."[9] The report and conference featured historians of the city who
viewed historic places as "living texts" that embodied history regardless of architectural merit. The report called for action at all levels of government. Among
its findings was the need for a more diverse staff in the New York City Landmarks Commission, including experts in urban anthropology and folklore.

In contrast with NAAAHP and related organizations that believed in shaping
their own preservation destiny, other African American preservation communities formed alliances across geographic boundaries to encourage new state

and local organizations and to exchange information. In 1995 the Southeast Regional African American Preservation Alliance (SRAAPA) was established to encourage the preservation of African American sites and culture and lend support to African American preservation groups in southeastern states and communities. It held its first conference in Birmingham, Alabama, in 1999.[10] Because SRAAPA's original members are closely allied with state historic preservation office programs, the organization tends to work most closely with the historic preservation establishment. This close relationship is evident in its sponsorship of programs and receptions at the National Trust's National Preservation Conferences in Savannah (1998) and Washington, D.C. (1999).

While the African American community pioneered some of the most creative approaches to preserving its cultural heritage, other ethnic groups made significant advances as well. The addition of Manzanar National Historic Site at Manzanar Station, California, to the National Park System in 1992 raised the specter of interpreting a painful chapter in the nation's history. Manzanar was one of ten relocation camps that incarcerated people of Japanese ancestry during World War II. One of the site's major activities is hosting the annual pilgrimage by people who resided at the camp and those descended from former residents.

Another property of interest to Asian Americans is Angel Island Immigration Station in San Francisco Bay, considered the Ellis Island of the Pacific region. This was where thousands of immigrants from Asian nations came before setting foot on the mainland of the United States. Nearly forgotten a decade ago, Angel Island's role in Asian American history was rediscovered by state park rangers who noticed Chinese messages engraved in the walls of the surviving buildings. In 1997 the property was designated a National Historic Landmark, and in 1998 Congress appropriated $100,000 to study the feasibility of making this major West Coast immigration center a museum of Asian American immigration history.

Latinos and Hispanics were the subject of additional explorations of cultural heritage. A conference on "Latinos in Historic Districts: Whose History? Whose Neighborhood?" was held in Philadephia and Lancaster, Pennsylvania, in November 1997 to increase the dialogue between the Latino and the historic preservation communities. The locations mystified many professionals, who believed that few, if any, Latinos lived in Pennsylvania. This perception led to a Latino population that was largely alienated from the historic preservation

Chinatown, San Francisco. Like Chinatowns throughout the nation, this section of the city is distinctive for its signage and newer additions to historic buildings. This "ephemeral" and recent cultural heritage challenge established historic preservation criteria. (Antoinette J. Lee)

establishment in Philadelphia. Latino leaders wondered why their community was obliged to preserve the historic properties that had been built by other cultural groups. The Latinos in Philadelphia wished to add balconies, establish courtyards, and make other modifications to buildings in the historic neighborhoods that were under the protection of local preservation ordinances. By contrast, in the smaller city of Lancaster the preservation and government establishment had carefully worked out accommodations with the Latino community that provided ways for residents to incorporate their cultural imprint on historic buildings while adhering to local ordinances.

Among ethnic groups, African Americans have had the greatest involvement in the established historic preservation programs, which can be attributed to their greater participation in the political life of the nation. This comfort level translates into involvement in a broad range of political activities, including preserving their cultural heritage. Other ethnic groups—including Asian Americans, Hispanics and Latinos (especially the recent arrivals), and Native Hawaiians—have been less involved in established preservation programs.

This can be a factor of their lesser involvement in broad political activities. However, it should not be assumed that these groups are not interested or active in preservation. Rather, they tend to rely on their own communities and families to maintain cultural identity. In addition, they may view established programs as unresponsive or even irrelevant to their preservation concerns.

Problems of Multicultural Documentation and Preservation

As the historic preservation field evaluates, preserves, and interprets an increasing number of diverse and ethnic historic properties, the question arises: How qualified are preservation professionals in managing the historic preservation process for the groups they purport to represent? Even today, in the early twenty-first century, the composition of the historic preservation field is predominantly European American. Some practitioners believe that professional decisions are "objective" and therefore as applicable to one group's heritage as they are to another. Many members of ethnic groups resist the notion that such objectivity is possible and want to manage their own cultural heritage. For example, surveys of cultural resources often fall into two major categories: architectural and archaeological. Where does ethnic and social history fall when the surviving historic properties are neither architectural nor archaeological sites? Many ethnic groups think that their cultural heritage is thus undervalued when left to preservation professionals.

As envisioned and developed by the preservationists of the post-1966 era, the standards and criteria at all levels of government serve as the threshold for determining significance, for evaluating treatments, and for guiding interpretation. These standards and criteria also are general statements that are then applied by the preservation professionals who administer government programs. How standards and criteria are interpreted is where diverse individuals are likely to find fault. Whereas one generation of government officials may determine that a property does not meet the standards and criteria, the next generation of bureaucrats will make a different determination.

It is not surprising, then, that many diverse individuals and organizations perceive that their cultural heritage is being underestimated by the "professional elite" who have little, if any, experience with diverse cultures. This perception has limited the interest of ethnic communities in supporting the historic preservation programs of all levels of government.

Engaging the diverse population in cultural programs and institutions is imperative if these programs and institutions are to survive into the next century. This need is recognized by private foundations that are now funding efforts to diversify museums, historical societies, and cultural institutions. Diversifying these organizations and agencies means diversifying programming, diversifying attendance and public supporters, and diversifying professional staff.

These changes will not take place quickly. Programming is the easiest to change. Program changes bring in new participants and adherents. Diversifying staffing is the most difficult because of the advanced education required and the tendency of young minority individuals to pursue more traditional careers.

Diversifying cultural institutions is a particularly relevant topic for the NPS, which administers over 380 national park areas. While numerous national parks are natural wonders, many more smaller areas interpret various aspects of America's history. Many parks and programs have been oriented to white, middle-class Americans simply because of tradition. In January 1999 the National Parks and Conservation Association held a conference on "America's Parks, America's People: A Mosaic in Motion, Breaking Barriers of Race and Diversity in Our National Parks." This gathering "explored the challenges to greater participation of diverse populations in our national parks, while dispelling the myth that these communities do not care about our parks and public lands."[11] One of the outcomes was the recognition that the NPS needed to work more closely with diverse community groups that were interested in national parks and the opportunities they provided.

The efforts of the NPS and its partnership organizations to reach out to diverse populations is a template being repeated at all levels of government, where public support is paramount to the continued survival of government cultural heritage programs. Involved in this mission are the Smithsonian Institution, state historic preservation officers, local governments programs, and countless museums across the nation.

Despite these advances, the prospects of diversifying the preservation profession remain dim. Few, if any, minority or ethnic students are enrolled in the major undergraduate and graduate programs that train young people for careers in the field. With this reality in mind, in late 1998 the NPS established the Cultural Resources Diversity Initiative to change the demographics of the historic preservation profession over the next decade or two. The new approach involved targeting undergraduate students and providing them with internships in cultural resources programs at the NPS and, eventually, in preservation offices at all levels of government and in the private sector. Looking for diverse students in traditional graduate programs in historic preservation usually is fruitless because career decisions are made at an earlier stage. The initiative also developed methods of maintaining regular communication with professors at diverse colleges and universities and with diverse organizations. New training opportunities are being developed to deliver preservation services to currently underserved diverse communities.

A more diverse preservation profession will likely hold different views of what is worth preserving, how heritage should be preserved, and who should be involved in interpreting the past. The conference, "Sites of Memory: Landscapes of Race and Ideology," held at the University of Virginia's School of Architecture in March 1999, gave a glimpse of the future. Organized by Professor Craig Evan Barton of the regular architecture faculty, this meeting explored the "soundscapes" of jazz culture in 1930s Chicago and the effects of seeing African and Africa-descended people on the landscape. As the introduction to the conference paper abstracts stated, "Much of the black cultural landscape . . . was shaped by spaces 'designed' by appropriation, custom, or use. As a result such critical components of the physical past have remained outside the analytic view of historians and designers. Often obscured over the course of time, these larger cultural landscapes, defined by customs and events as much as by specific buildings, and represented in text, image, and music, offer invaluable insights to the memory of place."[12] The conference constituted a major attempt to articulate the principle that diverse groups and individuals see the landscape differently.

Interpreting Multiracial Historic Properties: Whose History?

As the historians, ethnographers, and other professionals involved in historic preservation have documented and protected the places important to diverse groups, they have uncovered broader stories that might be related to the public. For example, at Thomas Jefferson's home at Monticello, property staff and community leaders expanded the interpretation of Jefferson. No longer a man living on an isolated mountaintop, Jefferson is now seen as part of a large population of slaves and servants, as well as family members, who lived on the plantation and contributed to its development and maintenance. The recent publicity over DNA tests suggested that Jefferson could have fathered at least one child with his slave, Sally Hemmings. The findings and the public's reaction to them raise important issues about the relationship between masters and their slaves, one that keeps historic properties like Monticello in the front pages of the national media.

The need to expand the interpretation of historic properties to incorporate the stories of women and diverse groups is an imperative that extends to nearly all units of the National Park System, state historic sites, local historic properties, and privately operated historic house museums. The telling of "untold stories" is in keeping with the nature of historical research as it unearths new findings that are relevant to American life. For instance, the NPS administers many Civil War battlefields. Until a decade ago, much of the interpretation at the battlefields focused on battle maneuvers and military leaders. Little was said about why the Civil War was fought because of the great reluctance to address the "S" word, or slavery. When reinterpreted, Civil War battlefields appeal to more than military history buffs and living history reenactors. They also attract individuals interested in the history of slavery and in the lives of ordinary people caught up in the war.

Another theme that is gaining a good deal of attention from preservation professionals and the public is the life of enslaved and free African Americans in the colonial and antebellum periods. Archaeologists are uncovering artifacts and practices that are derived directly from Africa. Among them, burial practices indicate that slaves resisted their owners' attempts to strip them of their traditional culture.

In the interpretation of slave life during the colonial period, the Colonial Williamsburg Foundation is far ahead of any other historic property. Starting in the mid-1980s with large investments in research and interpretive planning, Colonial Williamsburg initially focused on slave life at Carter's Grove, a plantation removed from the main part of the colonial capital city. Slave quarters were reconstructed as places where slave life could be depicted by black interpreters. Also in the 1980s, "living history" actors walked throughout the town and engaged visitors in spontaneous discussions about everyday life in Williamsburg. In 1994 the first slave auction was staged in the colonial city, an event that attracted the national media for its brutality. In 1999 actors played out additional painful displays of slave life in the town of Williamsburg itself, thereby weaving the story of slavery into the everyday life of the city.[13]

The efforts of Monticello, Colonial Williamsburg, and a growing number of historic house museums and outdoor historic villages are responding to growing numbers of preservation professionals and members of the general public who are interested in presenting history as it happened. The interpretive mes-

Booker T. Washington National Monument, Hardy, Virginia. Acquired by the NPS in 1956, this memorial is one of the nation's earliest historic places to commemorate African American history. Today, it serves as an outdoor museum that illustrates rural life when Washington lived as a slave on the property. (NPS)

sages are far removed from the genteel views of colonial life and of the nation's founding fathers typical of the pre-1970 era. Clearly, these interpretive programs generate a good deal of controversy and mixed responses from observers.

The story of the desegregation of public schools and public facilities, particularly in the South, attracts tourists from around the nation and the world. Historic photographs of the young black men and women who integrated the lunch counters in Greensboro, North Carolina, now form the centerpiece of tourism advertisements intended to draw tourists to the state. Interpretive stories about the nation's diverse past captivate visitors, regardless of race, and are popular themes for heritage tourism programs.

Multiculturalism: Pluribus or Unum?

The themes, methods, legislation, and programs that drive the historic preservation field in the United States are unique in the world. Few other national programs have invested so much in the tragedies and triumphs of its diverse groups. Even the United Kingdom's heritage preservation and conservation

Puerto Rican housing, Lancaster, Pennsylvania

Puerto Rican housing, Lancaster, Pennsylvania

The Spanish American Civic Association (SACA) Development Corporation of Lancaster has re-habilitated many historic buildings and sold them to members of the Puerto Rican commu-nity. By working closely with local government officials, the SACA Development Corporation has succeeded in meeting the Secretary of the Interior's Standards for Rehabilitation, while adding its own layer of Latino heritage and culture to the historic community of Lancaster. The sculptures at the entrance to the SACA Development Corporation headquarters and the paint colors used in the rehabilitated buildings are some of the Latino cultural expressions that can be found in the neighborhood. (Antoinette J. Lee) programs, which provided so much sustenance for U.S. historic preservation in the 1960s, now seem narrowly focused on architectural and classical archaeological values. When asked why Britain did not preserve historic places associated with the ethnic groups that today comprise that nation's people, the response would be, "The United Kingdom never had a civil rights movement."

Few nations have had such wrenching experiences with race and ethnicity as has the United States, and few have exhibited such a strong interest in preserving and interpreting places associated with this subject. Thus, the United States will lead the world in tackling such sensitive topics in its national historic preservation program. As the diaspora of people from all over the world settle in new countries because of free will or wars and conflicts, many more countries will host newcomers and will thus integrate new cultures into their existing ones. Many more countries will need to commemorate these places of entry and settlement and will look to the United States for models.

However successful America has been in integrating the story of race and ethnicity into cultural heritage programs, many lingering questions remain. How much will be enough? How many more groups must be studied, documented, and interpreted? How many more stories can be told of any one historic site or outdoor village? How many diverse professionals will be needed to counter deficiencies in the interpretation of standards and criteria? Should diverse professionals be expected to undertake primarily diverse projects? The United States has not yet provided answers to these questions.

The larger question facing the historic preservation field is the long-term effect of this emphasis on diversity. Will it lead to a greater appreciation and acceptance of diverse groups, or will it lead to resentments and alienation? Will these efforts knit the nation together into a coherent whole, or will they lead to the unraveling of national unity? Monolithic and singular norms of cultural heritage programs obviously did not reach the nation's diverse cultures, forcing them to develop their own programs and approaches. But how many approaches can the nation sponsor and still contribute to a sense of national identity, in addition to group identity?

Many cynics in the field view the current emphasis on diversity as a passing fad. They are waiting for certain individuals to step down as the top executive of an agency or organization in order to return to historic preservation as it used to be—aesthetically pleasing architecture that reflects the heritage of the European dominant culture. This assumption ignores the sheer momentum of demographic change that is sweeping the nation, with reverberations around the world. In a matter of years, the majority will be a minority in the United

States. Soon the country will have more citizens of Hispanic and Latino heritage than African Americans. The number of Asians is also on the rise. The groups' second and third generations often marry outside of their ethnic group. Their offspring will form the base of an increasingly multiracial society. More than any other force, even beyond that of financial resources or regulatory advances, race and ethnicity will shape the cultural heritage programs of the United States in the next century.

Native Americans and Historic Preservation

It will surprise many to realize that since the earliest historic preservation activities in the United States, Native American heritage has been an integral part of the nation's preservation effort. The principal work has been done by naturalists, community leaders, amateur historians, and archaeologists. For the most part, the effort has focused on Native American archaeological sites and historic places where Euro-American and Indian engaged in frequent, face-to-face, violent encounters.

Despite widespread interest in historic places associated with Native Americans, the dominant culture determined the extent and significance of Native American heritage to be preserved. In fact, until the early 1990s Indian tribes played little, if any, role in determining what should be preserved and how it should be preserved within the established administrative structures. Instead, many tribes and individuals worked to protect their cultural heritage outside of the established national programs.

The Euro-American approach to Native American cultural heritage largely paralleled American society's view of Native Americans. It also reflected the federal government's overall Indian policy, one that evolved from attempts to force Indians to relinquish their distinctive culture and assimilate into the dominant society. Now the policy prescribes self-determination for Native American people and tribal groups.

By the 1990s the role of Native Americans had become more prominent in the national historic preservation program. Today, dozens of recognized tribal historic preservation officers are conducting their own preservation activities as full and equal partners with federal agencies, state historic preservation offices, local governments, and the private sector. They are defining what is important to them and how this heritage will be preserved and interpreted.

Belatedly, many preservationists now recognize that Native Americans have protected their historic and cultural places from time immemorial. Native

American cultural heritage extends beyond places eligible for inclusion in the National Register of Historic Places to encompass distinctive ways of life, oral traditions, rituals, language, and other intangible forms. Greater understanding of tribal priorities is opening other doors as the preservation establishment seeks to more effectively integrate the cultural heritage of the nation's other diverse ethnic groups.

This chapter examines the history of the national historic preservation program and the place of Native Americans in it. Because the early history of American Indians can only be understood in context, this review focuses on how these preservation efforts were a direct reflection of the attitudes toward American Indians, as well as how those efforts both reflected and supported federal Indian policy. As these attitudes and policies evolved, so too did Native American involvement in historic preservation. Thus, this chapter also describes these historical efforts and the attitudes that supported them.

The development of American Indian historic preservation programs since 1966 continues to reflect the changing nature of historic preservation, changes in attitudes toward distinctive cultural groups and populations, and the recent evolution of federal Indian policy. All of these are explored as part of the development of contemporary Native American preservation activities.

Early Preservation of Native American Historic Places

Native American places figure in historic preservation from the early nineteenth century. Charles Hosmer relates that one of the earliest identifiable historic preservation activities in the United States involved efforts in 1847 to preserve the "Old Indian House" in Deerfield, Massachusetts. Local preservationists deemed this property to be important because it was the last building that survived the Indian "massacre" of 1704.[1]

In the eighteenth and nineteenth centuries, amateur naturalists were interested in Native American archaeological sites. They mapped sites, collected artifacts from them, and conducted excavations.[2] Archaeological investigations of Native American sites continued throughout the nineteenth century and moved along with the westward expansion of Euro-American settlement.

These early archaeological studies were motivated by more than mere curiosity. From a very early date, the origin of ancient archaeological sites was the focus of a heated debate that had critical public policy implications. The central bone of contention was whether or not these sites were in fact of Indian origin. A significant body of scholarly and public opinion held that the archaeological sites were not Native American—that they were evidence of other (that is, non–North American Indian) ancient peoples. This school of thought held that the sites were evidence of a "higher" civilization than was possessed by any of the contemporary Indians with whom the colonists were in contact. The "higher" civilizations included those of Mesoamerica, Vikings, Egyptians, the Lost Tribes of Israel, Irish monks—virtually any people but the ancestors of contemporary North American Indians.

The focus of this thinking was the question of the Mound Builders, the name given to the people who had constructed the spectacular archaeological mound complexes of the Old Northwest (Ohio, Indiana, and Illinois) and the mid-South. To the Mound Builder theorists, it was obvious that the Mound Builders could not have been Indians. Other scholars believed that archaeological evidence clearly indicated that the sites were directly related to Native Americans. In this view, the archaeological sites were evidence of earlier Indian civilizations and that Mound Builders were the ancestors of modern Indians.

The controversy—the Mound Builder debate—lasted through much of the nineteenth century. By the 1880s rigorous research demonstrated beyond any reasonable doubt that ancient archaeological sites were indeed the remains of earlier Indian societies. This position was universally accepted in the scholarly community, but in the eyes of the general public and some in the public policy community, the "non-Indian origin" position continued to hold sway. Indeed, a few proponents of the "non-Indian origin" position even today attribute these sites to extraterrestrials.

The Mound Builder debate was much more than merely a scholarly interpretive disagreement. It formed the basis for federal Indian policy. This policy was justified by the answer to the question, What happened to the Mound Builders? If the Mound Builders were not the ancestors of contemporary Indians, the most obvious explanation was that the ancestors of the contemporary Native Americans had displaced the Mound Builders. Not only is the question neatly answered, but the answer provided a rationalization to justify the Euro-American displacement of the Native Americans and the appropriation of their lands at the same time.[3]

When Euro-American settlers reached the southwestern United States in significant numbers and began encountering the cliff dwellings and other monumental ruins of the region, the Mound Builder controversy had been largely laid to rest. There was never disagreement about the Indian origin of the archaeological sites in this region.

Because the Southwest is extremely arid, these sites were much better preserved than those in the humid, wetter eastern and midwestern United States. The marvelous state of these ruins spawned a virtual artifact mining industry in the ancient sites.[4] Archaeologists "discovered" and excavated many of the most famous ruins in the Southwest, including the cliff dwellings in what is now Mesa Verde National Historical Park.[5] The looters who worked in Mesa Verde were so systematic, thorough, and energetic that some of the sites now incorporated into the national park have never yielded a single loose artifact.

By the late nineteenth century, there was widespread concern about the level of destruction resulting from these activities. This led to the creation of the first national park at Casa Grande, a monumental ruin near Chandler, Arizona, in 1889. In 1906 Congress passed the Antiquities Act to provide broader protection to sites in the region.[6]

The attempts to preserve the Old Indian House, the Mound Builder debate, establishment of Casa Grande, and the passage of the Antiquities Act typified Native American involvement in historic preservation until the end of the twentieth century. Although there was never any real question about the association of contemporary Native Americans and the ruins of the Southwest, preservation efforts were based on the values ascribed to those sites by non-Indians. Consideration of American Indian interests in the sites would not be given until the late 1980s.

Native Americans were implicated in whatever it was that made the place historic, but it was not the history or the perspective of the Native Americans. These places were reminders of whether Euro-Americans and Native Americans had had encounters, and what was important was the Euro-American experience of those encounters.

This history might have been worthy of little more than a footnote in this chapter, except that this expropriation of culture and memory continues today. One example is the recent controversy over the proper disposition of the Paleo-Indian remains that have come to be known as "Kennewick Man."[7] Some archaeologists now argue that Paleo-Indians were so ancient that it is wrong to think of them as "Indian." They offer as an alternative the concept described by the neologism "Paleo-American." Since it is wrong to think of these ancient remains as "Indian," it is also wrong to think of the "Paleo-

Americans" as in any way ancestral to contemporary Native Americans.[8] One of the foremost proponents of this position asserts that he is in possession of DNA evidence that links the Paleo-Americans to the contemporary inhabitants of the Iberian peninsula who reached North America by raft.

The real purpose of the Paleo-American argument is political, not historical or scientific. It provides a basis for claiming that contemporary Native Americans cannot be "culturally affiliated" with ancient remains.[9] Accordingly, no modern tribe can properly argue that it is culturally affiliated with Paleo-Americans. Such remains, therefore, should not be repatriated and reinterred. Instead, they should be curated and made available for archaeologists to study in perpetuity. Thus, at the beginning of the twenty-first century, archaeologists, who in the nineteenth century were instrumental in demonstrating that the Mound Builders were Native Americans, are now aggressively seeking to use the Paleo-American argument to expropriate the most ancient American Indian human remains from Native American heritage.

Tribal Sovereignty

The fundamental nature of the relationship between the federal government and Indian tribes, as well as part of the intense Native American interest in historic preservation, rests on the concept of tribal sovereignty. From the time of first contact, European powers dealt with the tribes that they were encountering as sovereign nations. The ideal that each group of peoples constituted a nation was deeply rooted in European history, going back to the earliest Greek writings about the relations among peoples. All identifiable societies—the civilized, the barbarian, and the savage—were conceived of as nations. This concept was brought to the New World.

Tribal sovereignty means that Indian tribes were nations exercising self-governance over the members of the tribe and the lands that they occupied. They could have a "foreign policy," engage in war, negotiate treaties, police their members, and regulate commerce. Accordingly, relations between the colonial powers (and later the United States) and tribes were governed by principles of international law. England accepted this concept as the basis for its relations with the Indians, and when the colonies liberated themselves, they continued to acknowledge this principle.

As European settlement expanded across the continent, tribes become incorporated into the colonies and later into the United States. Tribal sovereignty became increasingly complex, especially with respect to its practical applications as tribes became nations within a larger and powerful nation.

In 1831 the U.S. Supreme Court recognized the sovereign status of tribes, as well as the complex status of the relationship. Writing for the Court, Chief Justice John Marshall stated that "Indian tribes have been consistently recognized, first by the European powers, later by the United States, as distinct, independent political communities qualified to exercise powers of self-government, not by virtue of delegation of power from [a plenary sovereign], but rather by reason of their original tribal sovereignty." In Marshall's formulation, tribes were "domestic, dependent sovereigns." Marshall expressly turned aside the notion that conquest or incorporation into the United States terminated tribal sovereignty, stating that the "settled doctrine of the law of nations is, that a weaker power does not surrender independence—its right to self-government, by associating with a stronger, taking its protection. A weak State, in order to provide for its safety, may place itself under the protection of one more powerful, without stripping itself of the right of government, and ceasing to be a state."[10]

Sovereignty is important to a consideration of tribal preservation activities because sovereignty, rather than the national historic preservation program, provides the basis and justification for most, if not all, tribal preservation activities—even when a tribe has decided to participate in the national program. Sovereignty is also inextricably tied to the reasons tribes engage in preservation activities in the first place.

Tribal Involvement in Historic Preservation Activities

From time immemorial all tribes have protected their culturally and historically significant places by methods rooted in their cultures. Every Indian tribe used traditional cultural methods to protect their places of religious and cultural importance. For most tribes, the method of protecting such places was secrecy. The locations of culturally significant places were closely held secrets. Only a handful of the most knowledgeable religious and cultural leaders knew their locations. Information about such places was revealed only to individuals who needed to know about them and who had attained the level of cultural knowledge necessary to dealing with them appropriately. This ensured that members of the tribe who did not know how to interact with these places appropriately could not damage them and that enemies who might wish to defile or desecrate them could not do so.[11]

In the late nineteenth and early twentieth centuries, scholars and naturalists studied Native Americans. Such study had become the established domain of anthropology. These students of American Indian culture often gained the trust of the communities they were studying, sometimes living in them for years. Occasionally, they were initiated into the more esoteric aspects of traditional culture. In several instances, these scholars actually became accepted as practitioners and "priests." Many of them left "their" Native American communities and published what they had learned, including whatever secret cultural information they had accumulated. But numerous tribes have strict proscriptions against writing and reading information of this sort. Furthermore, this information was not generally circulating within the communities themselves. Its publication was and is widely viewed among Native Americans as the purloining of their cultural heritage and a betrayal of trust.

From 1850 to 1930 the federal government had a de facto policy of desecrating sacred sites. This was partly an effort to dominate and intimidate the tribes to make them more amendable to government control. It also was thought to promote assimilation in the same way that prohibiting Native American ceremonies and sacred dances did. If traditional forms of religion were outlawed, the government assumed that Christianity would fill the void.

Occasionally, even before the enactment of the National Historic Preservation Act in 1966, tribes sought to halt federal undertakings that would damage or destroy important sacred places by going to federal court. In these cases, they argued that the destruction of sacred places would do irreparable harm to their traditional religious practices. As part of these proceedings, tribes revealed what was traditionally secret or confidential information about places to lend credibility to the claim that it was central to their religious practices. But as the tribes never prevailed in such suits, they were unable to protect the important cultural and religious places. Moreover, tribal traditionalists were forced to violate proscriptions against revealing the information required to support the suit. Taken together, these experiences powerfully reinforced the need to strictly guard this kind of information and maintain it within the narrowest circle of individuals consistent with traditional beliefs.

The enactment of federal environmental planning laws in the late 1960s and early 1970s gave the tribes a new set of tools, but they were generally reluctant to use them systematically. Memories of deliberate desecration and destruction of traditional religious and cultural places as a matter of federal policy and dis-

Tuba City Boarding School, Navajo Nation. The 1931 Collegiate Gothic classroom building at this boarding school complex would have fit in better on the campus of an eastern prep school or college than in the high desert of the western Navajo Nation. The architecture bears no relationship to native building traditions of the region. The entire Tuba City Boarding School complex, built between 1911 and 1931, was an architectural expression of the federal government's assimilation policy. (Photo by Colleen Hamilton, from the collection of the Navajo Nation Historic Preservation Department)

Rainbow Bridge, Lake Powell. This Navajo sacred place is partially flooded, even at lowered water levels, by Lake Powell, a man-made lake created by Glen Canyon Dam on the Colorado River. Glen Canyon Dam was completed after the Navajo Nation lost its First Amendment lawsuit in federal court to prevent the flooding of Rainbow Bridge. (Photo by Richard M. Begay, from the collection of the Navajo Nation Historic Preservation Department)

Woodruff Butte, north-central Arizona. The butte is a sacred place to at least three tribes. The FHWA staunchly refused to take into account effects to Woodruff Butte from its use as a material source area for federal highway projects, even after being repeatedly notified of its importance to the tribes and its potential eligibility for inclusion in the National Register. (Photo by Peter T. Noyes, from the collection of the Navajo Nation Historic Preservation Department)

trust of scholars who came seeking this information ran deep. With some no-table exceptions, tribal elders elected to withhold information. In some instances, they openly stated that destruction of tribal sacred places was preferable to in-appropriate revelation of information about them. In other instances, they with-held information in the hope that the project would not harm traditional reli-gious and cultural places. Sometimes this strategy worked: the places were preserved, and cultural prescriptions and proscription were observed. In those instances where it became obvious that an important place was about to be badly damaged or destroyed, tribes occasionally provided information. Often, this came too late and the place was damaged or destroyed anyway.

Many contemporary tribal preservation programs have their roots in tribal history and archaeological programs that began during the 1950s in response to the establishment of the Indian Land Claims Commission. In 1948 Con-gress authorized tribes to seek compensation for tribal lands expropriated in the eighteenth and nineteenth centuries.[12] To provide a factual basis for a claim, Indian tribes were required to document the maximum extent of their tribal territory at the time when their lands were taken.[13] This involved histor-ical research, archaeological survey and analysis, and the recording of oral his-tories and oral traditions relevant to the places that could help support a tribal claim. Some tribes turned the documentation efforts over to their attorneys and the consultants and experts they hired. Other tribes developed tribal programs to gather the essential data. In many cases, tribal archaeological programs, tribal oral history programs, and tribal museums developed from these early efforts.

Tribal programs got a further boost with the enactment of the Archaeological and Historic Preservation Act (Moss-Bennett) in 1974. Moss-Bennett made the cost of archaeological data recovery allowable cost for all federal agencies and all federal projects. It provided the funding authority necessary to underwrite mitigation activities required as an outcome of efforts to comply with Section 106 of the 1966 NHPA. Tribal archaeological programs that had begun as a land claims activity now began to provide services to federal agencies seeking to satisfy the requirements of the act. In addition, several tribes that had not previously had archaeological programs established tribal programs or tribal enterprises to provide these services.[14] Some of these organizations restricted themselves almost entirely to the tribe's reservation; other tribes provided archaeological services across a broader area but generally limited activities as a matter of practice (if not necessarily of policy) to their traditional lands.

The American Indian Religious Freedom Act and the Archaeological Resources Protection Act

The American Indian Religious Freedom Act (AIRFA) requires federal agencies to consider the impact of their activities on Native American religious practices. Although AIRFA was passed by both houses of Congress in 1978, it is really an expression of the sense of the Congress. No procedures, regulations, or rights of redress were developed. The Supreme Court held that AIRFA does impose a requirement for agencies to consult with tribes, but it declined to suggest how an agency might meet this requirement. Consequently, AIRFA has no identifiable impact on protecting places that tribes deem to be most important to them.

The Archaeological Resources Protection Act was passed in 1979 as a response to a federal court ruling that found the Antiquities Act of 1906 to be unconstitutionally vague.[15] To eliminate this fault, ARPA provides a comprehensive laundry list of archaeological resources.[16] In more serious or repeated violations, it is a felony to damage, collect, excavate, or remove archaeological resources from federal or Indian lands except under the authority of a duly issued

ARPA permit.[17] It prohibits interstate trafficking in archaeological resources. Violations may be subject to both civil and criminal penalties.

Importantly, ARPA expressly acknowledges tribal interest in the preservation of archaeological resources and that this interest may well go beyond merely viewing archaeological sites as sources of historical and scientific data. ARPA recognizes that tribes own any and all archaeological resources located on tribal lands. Therefore, ARPA permits on tribal lands are subject to tribal approval, conditions, and stipulations. ARPA specifies no standards and sets no limitations on tribal stipulations.

On its passage, ARPA provided two important precedents. First, it specifically acknowledged that tribes exercise both sovereignty and dominion over the archaeological resources on their land. And second, it was the first cultural resource management law that expressly required that tribes be consulted when a federal action—for example, issuance of an ARPA permit—may affect a place of religious and cultural significance to the tribes.

The National Historic Preservation Act

The National Historic Preservation Act was passed in 1966 as a result of a growing recognition that federal projects (e.g., urban renewal, transportation, and other public works) were undermining the fabric of communities across the nation, including buildings, sites, structures, and districts that were of historical or architectural importance. NHPA was the culmination of over a century of preservation activities, and it created a process for considering the impact of federal undertakings on historically significant places.

The preservation movement historically has been most concerned with individual places or groups of resources that form an identifiable entity. Historic preservation began by setting aside such places to commemorate the individuals and events from which they derived their historical significance. NHPA assumes that historic properties are discrete places that can stand alone on the basis of their historical importance. Likewise, the process NHPA created to consider the effects of federal undertakings on historic properties shares this place and object orientation. For management and preservation purposes, historic properties are, with few exceptions, dealt with as places essentially isolated from their surroundings. Historic properties are points in space, with only the most attenuated connection with their environment. Accordingly, they can be managed to a large degree without consideration of their surroundings, except when those surroundings impact on the historic property or when a federal undertaking may affect the historic property.

When NHPA became law in 1966, it made no mention of Native Americans. In 1980 major amendments to NHPA were enacted, and references to Native Americans were sprinkled throughout the act. It is evident on even a cursory reading of the 1980 amendments that these references were largely an afterthought. Except for providing for direct grants to Indian tribes for preservation projects, the 1980 amendments did not assign Native Americans and tribes any real role in the national preservation partnership.

In 1992 NHPA was again substantially amended. The 1992 amendments finally gave Indian tribes a substantive role in the national preservation partnership: Indian tribes are now provided the opportunity to become full partners or to participate at whatever level meets their sovereign needs. The "Indian provisions" are found in Section 101(d) of NHPA, which enables tribes to establish tribal historic preservation officers when they can do so (on application to and approval by the secretary of the interior). Section 101(d)(2) authorizes tribes to assume any or all of the functions of state historic preservation officers on Indian lands.[18] To assume these functions, the chief governing authority of the tribe must request them, the tribe must appoint a THPO, and the THPO must develop and submit a plan that describes the functions that the tribe proposes to assume, the means of performing those functions, what functions will be left for the SHPO or the secretary of the interior to continue performing, and the means by which the traditional religious and cultural authorities of the tribe will be consulted on matters pertinent to them.[19]

The secretary of the interior must review the plan and consult with the affected SHPOs and any other Indian tribe whose ancestral sites may now be located on the lands of the tribe requesting assumption.[20] If the secretary concludes that the tribe is fully capable of performing the functions requested, the plan must be approved. Although SHPOs are required to perform the entire list of functions listed in Section 101(b)(2), in recognition of their status as sovereign nations, tribes can request any, all, or none of the SHPO functions.

Although the 1992 amendments authorized tribes to assume SHPO functions beginning in 1992, NPS staff stated that it would not consider approving a substitution agreement until it had developed and published regulations governing the substitution process. Over the next several years, the NPS developed and circulated for comment several drafts of such regulations. However, the drafts had not yet been published for public comment in the Federal Register as of June 2001.[21]

When it became evident that the regulations would not be issued in a timely fashion, the NPS accepted substitution plans. Several tribes submitted plans to assume some or all of the SHPO functions on their tribal lands. In 1996 the NPS approved the plans of fifteen tribes. As of June 2001, the total was twenty-seven.[22] A number of other tribes are currently in various stages of initiating or considering development of substitution plans.

The tribes that have obtained approval as well as the tribes seeking approval are doing so because the tribal government has determined that performing SHPO functions is in the best interests of the tribes. The reasons underlying the determination by each tribe varies. But all of the tribes involved so far have shared a common belief that assumption of SHPO functions is an important confirmation of tribal sovereignty and that a tribal agency better reflects the interests of the tribe in preserving its cultural heritage.

In a critically important provision of the 1992 amendments, places of "traditional religious and cultural significance" to an Indian tribe may be eligible for inclusion in the National Register. Federal officials are also required to consult with Indian tribes whenever an undertaking over which it has jurisdiction may affect places of "religious or cultural significance" to the tribe.

Finally, Section 101(d)(5) authorizes tribes to prepare tribal regulations to govern the federal review procedure required in Section 106 of NHPA. Such regulations must be presented to the Advisory Council on Historic Preservation. If the Advisory Council approves them, the tribal regulations can substitute for the federal regulations that govern the process. So far, only the Narragansett Indian Tribe of Rhode Island has had its regulations approved.

Tribal Preservation Programs in the 1990s

The participation of American Indian tribes in the national historic preservation program is an exercise of their sovereign powers. By the early 1980s a number of tribal archaeological programs began to move beyond the realm of conventional archaeological services provider into resource management activities that are more normally the purview of historic preservation organizations or agencies. Some tribes, for example, began issuing archaeological permits on behalf of their tribes, initiated preservation planning programs, prepared preservation ordinances, generally advised federal agencies, especially the Bureau of

Indian Affairs, on preservation matters. Given the limited funds available to finance tribal government programs, using revenues generated by tribal archaeological programs was often the only way to support these kinds of activities.

By 1985 the Navajo Nation realized that it could not expect to operate a successful archaeological services program while simultaneously engaging in management activities. Sooner or later, one or both functions would suffer. Consequently, in 1986 the Navajo Nation established its Historic Preservation Department, which remained the only tribal program solely devoted to historic preservation until after 1992.

Patricia Parker's *Keepers of the Treasures*, a report published by the NPS in 1990, was based on a series of consultations with individual Native Americans and tribal representatives as well as the responses to a survey of all tribes. This was the first attempt to assess the preservation needs of Indian tribes, Native Americans, Alaska Natives, and Native Hawaiians.[23]

Although now over a decade old, the *Keepers* report remains an essential source of information on the historic preservation needs of Native Americans. It provides a strong justification for the tribal historic preservation grant program and develops the blueprint for addressing the wide range of needs identified in the report. According to the report, in 1990 seventy-four tribes were engaged in some form of historic preservation. These activities included protecting traditional cultural places, researching traditional history, operating tribal archaeological programs, providing oversight to outsider archaeological programs, operating museums or cultural centers, surveying and recording historic properties, maintaining tribal registers of historic properties, issuing permits, consulting with the SHPO, and so forth. Not all tribes reported conducting all activities. All tribes had plans to expand their programs if funds were available to them.

In the federal budget for fiscal year 1990, Congress appropriated $500,000 to the Historic Preservation Fund for direct grants to Indian tribes for historic preservation projects. This was the first time Congress had made an appropriation for this purpose, even though the authority for such grants had been enacted in 1980s. The appropriation was made in response to a request from the Navajo Nation and was the direct result of the efforts of a single member of Congress, who proposed the appropriation and worked to add it to the Interior Department's budget. The tribal grants are now allocated to assist the work of THPOs. The grants also support historic preservation projects of all tribes on a competitive basis. The grants are applied to standard historic preservation activities, such as survey and inventory of historic places. Further, they support

Museum staff, Navajo Nation. Alfred Yazzie, a respected chanter, traditional healer, and elder, and other chanters examine a museum collection to determine which items the Navajo Nation should claim as artifacts of cultural patrimony for repatriation under NAGPRA. (Photo by Timothy Begay, from the collection of the Navajo Nation Historic Preservation Department)

oral histories and intangible heritage and ethnobotany studies, projects that extend beyond the standard activities of many government preservation programs.

Also in 1990 Congress passed the Native American Graves Protection and Repatriation Act. Enactment of NAGPRA was the culmination of over two decades of effort by Native Americans to obtain the return of skeletal remains of their ancestors, several hundred thousand of which were kept in museum collections as scientific specimens. NAGPRA also provided for the repatriation of items of cultural patrimony. Museums often argued that they had a property right in these "specimens" that superseded any human right Native Americans might have had to repatriate their ancestors and rebury them. Some museums even argued this position when the remains in question were those of a known individual and when the remains were obtained by what was indisputably grave robbing. Congress had unsuccessfully attempted to deal with this matter throughout the 1980s, but it was not until the conclusion of a year-long "national dialogue" among representatives of Native American communities, archaeologists and physical anthropologists, and museums that sufficient consensus emerged for the bill to move through Congress.

After the enactment of NAGPRA, a number of tribes established some means to coordinate activities under the act. Like more general preservation activities, this could be anything from an informal committee of interested and concerned tribal members, to a formal committee or a committee of council delegates, to a NAGPRA coordinator or even a tribal officer. This function was occasionally assigned to a tribal archaeological program; more often it was not. Many tribes provided for no coordination of NAGPRA activities, relying instead on dealing with each required consultation on an as-needed basis.

In addition to providing for the return of human remains and items of cultural patrimony in museums and federal agencies, NAGPRA also requires these entities to engage in consultation with Indian tribes about repatriation. Such consultations often lead to increased understanding among the parties—one of the most positive outcomes of the program. Equally important, NAGPRA requires federal agencies to consult with tribes regarding the treatment of human remains that were either disinterred by an archaeological project or discovered or exposed. The habit of free and open consultation between federal agency and tribal government on these issues has set the stage for government-to-government consultations on the preservation and management of tribal historic properties on federal lands.

Unfortunately, efforts on the part of some archaeologists to control the determination of what is to become of Kennewick Man or the "Ancient One," together with collateral efforts such as the "Clovis and Beyond" conference and the Society of American Archaeology's unilateral support for wholesale revisions of NAGPRA, has reversed many gains of the 1990s.[24] In some areas, relations between Native Americans and archaeologists have deteriorated dramatically. Long-term estrangement seems inevitable if archaeologists do not revise their position. Relationships with federal agencies also are degenerating markedly in some areas.

In the summer of 1997 the fifteen approved THPOs met in Salt Lake City, Utah, and agreed in principle to form a national organization. Subsequently, the tribes approved articles of incorporation for the National Association of Tribal Historic Preservation Officers (NATHPO), with its national office located in Washington, D.C. The purpose of NATHPO is to promote the preservation, maintenance, and revitalization of the culture and traditions of the native people of the United States.

Tribal Preservation Programs in the Twenty-first Century

When Congress enacted the 1992 NHPA amendments to create a formal place in the national historic preservation partnership for tribal governments and recognized as a matter of law places of "religious and cultural importance," it continued one of the strongest trends in historic preservation activities. The trajectory of historic preservation has been one of increasing inclusiveness. By the 1970s preservationists were beginning to include places associated with individuals and events important to ethnic groups and minority communities. Finally, a place at the table was made for Native Americans, Alaska Natives, and Native Hawaiians, and places of importance in the history of their cultures were added to the list of places worthy of preservation.

The development of the Native American historic preservation program addressed the real, identified needs of the indigenous people, as opposed to what the dominant culture thought the native peoples wanted or needed. The tribal program reflects tribal emphasis on Indian tribes as "living cultures," whose priorities include not only physical historic places, but also the full range of tangible and intangible culture. This template can be applied to the nation's other cultural groups as the national historic preservation program seeks to include them in the historic preservation field.

The long-term future of preservation lies in the protection of cultural landscapes. Anthropologists working in environmental planning have demonstrated that essentially all of the inhabited land in the nation looks the way it does because of human-environmental interaction. This is as true in Boston, Massachusetts, as it is in the desert of the Great Basin. Preservation is increasingly becoming a matter of planning for natural and historic values that contribute to the quality of life in a community. Preservation has been and will increasingly become a way for people to voice their desires for the kind of community they want to live in.

Native Americans tend to think of their reservations as living landscapes and their communities as living cultures. This means that dealing with these issues will be worked out first on tribal lands, and the results can be applied to future efforts. The whole nation, concerned about the quality of the physical and social environments, can embrace the results. Addressing native cultural heritage will be one of the ways that tribal preservation programs will lead the historic preservation field in the twenty-first century.

Folklife, Intangible Heritage, and the Promise and Perils of Cultural Cooperation

Taking the long view, we may regard all preservation activities as arising from a deep cultural impulse spurring people to take conscious actions to maintain or revitalize their cultural creations and traditions. From this vantage point there is a deep relationship among such diverse activities as the preservation of Mount Vernon, the contemporary revival of Appalachian oldtime string-band music, the nomination process for the National Register of Historic Places, a religious revitalization movement among Native Americans, and a Nevada buckaroo's living-room museum of traditional cowboy gear. Each reflects a conscious effort to preserve culture—to countervail the forces of neglect, erosion, and decay in our cultural life.

If all these activities may appropriately be called "preservation," then it is useful to consider what we usually call "historic preservation" side by side with these other forms of the preservation impulse. Historic preservation, in this light, may be seen as one important facet of a many-faceted cultural process. A complementary facet is the field of folklore and folklife, which is sometimes referred to by the historic preservation community as "intangible culture." Considering all facets of the preservation impulse together, we realize that cultural preservation has manifested itself in a number of separate but kindred forms throughout the twentieth and early twenty-first centuries. Each epicenter of preservation activity has broadened its focus in the course of time, and the broadening has led to a convergence among them, inviting us to consider them together in future preservation efforts.

Folklore and Folklife as a Preservation Field

Many people in the field of historic preservation today describe folklore and folklife using the term "intangible cultural resources." It is true that for many decades folklore research focused on verbal and musical traditions, which are intangible expressions of culture. But in recent decades, folklorists in both the academy and public programs have documented, preserved, celebrated, and theorized about material culture very extensively and systematically, making the equation of folklore and folklife with intangible culture quite problematic. This terminological problem will be revisited for analysis later in this chapter. For present purposes, it points to the need for both fields to acquaint themselves better with each other. Thus, in a book focusing on historic preservation, a few pages seem appropriate to introduce folklore and folklife as a discipline and network in the United States.

The field of folklore and folklife studies has a history stretching well back into the nineteenth century in the United States and earlier in Europe. When English writer William J. Thoms coined the term "folklore" in 1846, providing what he regarded as a considerable improvement over such phrases as "popular antiquities," similar terms had already come into being in German and other European languages.[1] In the United Kingdom, folklore was seen as representing either regional and ethnic identities or preindustrial cultural "roots." But in much of Europe, folklore became deeply associated with ethnic aspirations for nationhood. For example, the publication of the Finnish epic *Kalevala* (1835), assembled by Elias Loennrot from his own field documentation of epic Finnish songs, became a cultural landmark spurring the sociopolitical movement that led to the creation of Finland as a separate nation. Similarly, the research into German folk songs by Johann Gottfried von Herder in the eighteenth century, and into folktales by Jacob and Wilhelm Grimm in the early nineteenth century, contributed to the consolidation of a sense of nationhood in nineteenth-century Germany and, more ominously, was retrospectively cited in justification of state nationalism by the Nazis in the twentieth century.[2]

Folklore studies developed in a different way in the United States—closer in concept to the British Isles than to the rest of Europe, yet distinctive as well. A continental country, united by a constitution and integrated commerce, would inevitably come to see folklore, not as a key to unlocking national identity, but as a key to articulating subnational variety. Folklore would illuminate the variety and the spirituality of American ethnic and regional identity, while national institutions, interstate commerce, and public education all strengthened a growing national unity.

Thus the Pennsylvania German customs delineated in John Fanning Watson's *Annals of Philadelphia and Pennsylvania in the Olden Time* (1830) and the American Indian traditions described in Henry Rowe Schoolcraft's *Algic Researches* (1839) derive their interest from their cultural particularity, not their national applicability. *Slave Songs of the United States*, published by Allen, Ware, and Garrison in the wake of the Civil War (1867), offered a clarion call not for national unity but on behalf of the unquenchable human spirit of America's African American slaves.[3] From travel journals to local color writers to fiddle tune collections to hex signs on Pennsylvania German barns, folklore in America has articulated differentiated spiritual identities, whether ethnic, regional, religious, or occupational, within a vast and diverse continental country.

Folklore itself, as grassroots cultural expression, is, of course, always present wherever humans cultivate life with passion, devotion, and flair. But as a professional field, folklore studies did not emerge in America until the later nineteenth century. Its development closely parallels the development of anthropology, archaeology, historic preservation, and other professional fields during that era. In a sense, all these fields were closely allied in the period of their inception. Many leading scholars of the later nineteenth century ranged comfortably through multiple areas of research, so one encounters today many of the same names on the rosters of different organizations. And the wide-ranging scholarship of that generation was matched by a serious, unequivocal commitment to social activism; research and social action were seen as logically and comfortably complementary.[4]

There is no better example of the confident breadth of intellectual vision and action in the later nineteenth century than John Wesley Powell, a Civil War major and a pioneer in western American geology, American Indian linguistics, and various other fields. Powell was aggressive in espousing ideas and causes with members of Congress, and he became the founding director of the Bureau of American Ethnology in 1879 as well as an early director of the U.S. Geological Survey. Folklorists, anthropologists, archaeologists, and geologists today all look to him as a distinguished leader from the dawn of their disciplines, and the Bureau of American Ethnology he founded is an early landmark in the involvement of the federal government with cultural research, documentation, and preservation.[5]

A review of the publications and archival collections of the Bureau of American Ethnology quickly reveals the intellectual scope of that era. The photographs and manuscripts composing part of the bureau's documentary legacy repose in the National Anthropological Archives at the Smithsonian Institution. Another part of that legacy, the collections of wax cylinder sound recordings of American Indian music made by Alice Fletcher, Frances Densmore, Omaha Indian Francis LaFlesche, and other pioneering ethnographers, now resides in the American Folklife Center at the Library of Congress. Today the collections receive heavy use from researchers, including a steady stream of American Indians pursuing evidences of their own cultural history. It is tempting to attribute the administrative separation of these closely related ethnographic collections to the quirks of bureaucratic history in Washington, D.C. But a better explanation lies in the progressive differentiation and isolation of disciplines in the twentieth century. That professional specialization ushered in an era spanning much of the century during which each of these fields cultivated its own garden, and contact and cross-fertilization were very limited.

A key event in the professional development of folklore in America was the founding of the American Folklore Society in 1888. A similar organization, called simply the Folk-Lore Society, had been formed in London in 1877. The first issue of the American society's journal, the *Journal of American Folklore*, provides a significant statement of purpose, penned by editor William Wells Newell.[6] It articulates clearly the goal of the society: to explore, document, and publish evidences of the survival of older folk traditions resident in the United States. Newell names as likely targets not only the rural British American population but also African Americans, American Indians, and other repositories of ethnic traditions such as the German, Spanish, and French settlements in various regions of the country. The domain of folklore in America, the article implies, is maintained within various regional and ethnic groups at the subnational level, and the traditions thus revealed are not likely to demonstrate American unity so much as to reveal comparative variety and links with the people and traditions of other continents.

Throughout the early history of the American Folklore Society, its members oscillated in their interdisciplinary allegiances between literary studies and anthropology. The society's central preoccupations in its first half century tended to be the collection and analysis of verbal and musical genres of cultural expression—folktales, riddles, proverbs, legends, ballads, folk songs, and the like. Many members were active documentarians of various folk genres in the field. Most were affiliated with universities and colleges around the country; this sometimes inclined them to a regional focus in their fieldwork and even led to

Frances Densmore records Mountain Chief with an Edison phonograph for the Bureau of American Ethnology, Washington, D.C., 1916. (Photo courtesy of Prints and Photographs Division, Library of Congress)

friendly rivalries about which state or region could produce the most evidence of the older stratum of tales or ballads.

From the beginning, American folklorists included American Indian culture within their sphere of interest. Occasionally in America, and more persistently in Europe and elsewhere, there were efforts to distinguish "folk culture," operating within or at the margins of contemporary Western civilization, and "primitive culture," supposedly operating outside the sphere of a larger civilization. There was also a tendency to allocate the study of cultures outside the Western domain to anthropology, whereas other disciplines dealt with culture in the context of Western civilization. Such distinctions have proved more illuminating about Western civilization itself than about the cultural groups and traditions that were the objects of attention. But in fact, American folklore studies included American Indian culture from the outset and continue to do so today.

Members of the American Folklore Society in the first half of the twentieth century maintained connections with two cultural outposts within the federal government: the older Bureau of American Ethnology at the Smithsonian and a newer office, the Archive of American Folk Song, which was established within the Music Division of the Library of Congress in 1928. The Archive of Amer-

Charles Todd records the voices of Mr. and Mrs. Frank Pipkin on a Presto disc recorder from the Library of Congress at the Farm Security Administration camp in Shafter, California. John Steinbeck also visited this camp, and it has been said that Mrs. Pipkin was his model for "Ma Joad" in *The Grapes of Wrath*. (Photo by Robert Hemmig, from the Charles Todd Migrant Labor Collection, American Folklife Center, Library of Congress)

ican Folk Song had a halcyon period in the 1930s and early 1940s, when Texan John Lomax and his son Alan were, respectively, honorary curator and assistant-in-charge. The tenure of the Lomaxes coincided with the New Deal era, when active cultural programming was carried out under the auspices of various agencies of the Works Progress Administration (WPA). The archive staff during this period not only made celebrated forays into the field to document regional traditions, but also lent documentary equipment to various WPA-sponsored initiatives and to local and regional documentarians. Through these activities the archive became a major epicenter of cultural preservation in the New Deal era.

Thanks to the Lomaxes' folk song publications, documentary radio programming, and a pioneering published series of documentary sound recordings launched in 1942, the Archive of American Folk Song became a nationally famous collection of field recordings and manuscripts of folk music, folklore, and oral history. When the war came, the archive adjusted its mission and program to suit the times; with further adjustments, it survived the postwar down-sizing of government in the late 1940s. With each generation it has expanded its collections and its cultural domain. It is now part of the American Folklife Center within the Library of Congress and has been renamed the Archive of Folk Culture, reflecting its broadened cultural purview. Its collections number over 1.5 million items in every documentary medium from every continent, including not only musical and verbal traditions but also extensive documentation of material culture and cultural landscape.[7]

After World War II the epicenter of folklore studies shifted from Washington, D.C., to the academy. Indiana University began offering a Ph.D. program in folklore studies in 1949, and the University of Pennsylvania's program dates from 1962–63. Several ethnomusicology graduate programs also developed in the 1960s. Meanwhile, the Bureau of American Ethnology was being reorganized within the Smithsonian Institution, and the lone outpost of folklore and ethnomusicology was the understaffed Archive of Folk Song at the Library of Congress.

The inauguration of the Smithsonian Institution's Festival of American Folklife in 1967 signaled the emergence of a new era for folklore and folklife studies in the later twentieth century.[8] The Smithsonian's festival revived a tradition of professionally organized folk festivals that had flourished in the 1930s. A few festivals reflecting the earlier era of folk festival experimentation survived into the 1960s—notably the National Folk Festival, which alternated between Washington-based periods and periods of presentation in other sites around the country, and a few regional festivals such as the Kutztown Festival in Pennsylvania. But the new impetus toward folk festivals began with the Newport Folk Festival, and the chief organizer of that festival, Ralph Rinzler, brought his experience and ideas to the National Mall in Washington, D.C.

The Smithsonian festival provided a fresh arena in which a new generation of budding folklorists could participate and a fresh model to emulate. Many of the new folklorists were freshly minted products of graduate folklore and ethnomusicology programs at such institutions as Indiana University, the University of Pennsylvania, Cooperstown Graduate Programs, Wesleyan, the University of Texas, the University of North Carolina, Western Kentucky, and the University of California at Los Angeles. Others, galvanized by the experience of the festival, sought graduate training at these and other places. Soon many of them were moving into positions in what was variously called "applied folklore," "public-sector folklore," or simply "public folklore." By the end of the century, folklorists occupied positions in many local, state, and regional arts

Timber raising on the National Mall, Washington, D.C. Rudy Christian and Arron Sturgis, members of the Timber Framers Guild, raise an eighteenth-century-style carriage house as part of the "Masters of the Building Arts" program at the 2001 Smithsonian Folklife Festival. (Photo by Michael Carrier, courtesy of the Center for Folklife and Cultural Heritage, Smithsonian Institution)

councils, historical societies, museums, and other cultural agencies and institutions. As an index of the changing state of folklore and folklife studies in the last quarter of the century, the wing of the American Folklore Society devoted to public folklore grew to a size comparable to the older academic wing.

The creation of new programs within the federal government accelerated the growth of public folklore as a domain of professional activity. The National Endowment for the Arts began a grant-giving program in folk arts in 1974, fostering a network of state and regional programs addressing folk arts and cultural heritage. In 1976 Congress passed the American Folklife Preservation Act (Public Law 94-201), creating the American Folklife Center within the Library of Congress. The new center launched a series of field documentary projects that prominently featured material culture and cultural landscape. The field projects led to publications, exhibitions, conferences, and dissemination efforts in various media. The center absorbed and expanded the long-standing Archive of Folk Song, which was renamed the Archive of Folk Culture and grew by leaps and bounds. By the year 2000 a number of its multiformat archival collections were fully available online through the World Wide Web.

During the same period, the Smithsonian's Festival of American Folklife

Agnes Vanderburg, a member of the Flathead tribe in Montana, explains her method for baking wild camas roots to folklorist Kay Young during a summer class on tribal cultural traditions she offered to community youth in 1979. (Photo by Michael Crummett for the American Folklife Center, Library of Congress)

became a traditional component of Washington's annual cultural fare, and the annual festival generated a larger Center for Folklife and Cultural Heritage, including Smithsonian Folkways Records, which maintained and expanded the documentary record releases developed since World War II in the private sector by Folkways Records. The National Park Service also reflected the growing interest in folklore and folklife. Many newer parks, such as Lowell National Historical Park, in Lowell, Massachusetts, highlighted living grassroots culture as a central theme. Other parks developed annual folk festivals or included living cultural presentations as a key component of their daily interpretive programming. And cultural professionals throughout the NPS—both in the parks proper and within the historic preservation network—revealed a growing concern for and sensitivity to fostering and featuring "living culture."

Convergences

If the early twentieth century was a period of professional specialization and decreasing communication across disciplinary borders, the later twentieth and early twenty-first centuries have showed signs of reviving cross-disciplinary communication and collaboration. In part, the cross-disciplinary stirrings reveal a blurring of disciplinary boundaries in the American academy. In part, they are a natural result of the expanding scope of the work of all the various disciplines.[9]

The historic preservation movement steadily expanded its purview as the twentieth century unfolded. There was a broadening of the view of what should be preserved, and a no-less-important expansion of the contexts within which to regard the objects to be preserved. The broadening process could, for example, expand the focus from individual buildings to clusters and ensembles of buildings, then to districts, towns, and even regions. Or it could expand from the gems of high architecture to ordinary buildings in various folk and popular styles. Buildings could be examined not only as evidence of history, but also as exemplars of form and craft. Historical interpretation could include not only political events and the lives of notables but social history and the lives and creativity of the unsung and forgotten as well.

The expansion of the purview of historic preservation was paralleled by the broadening of the field of archaeology, which had become linked to historic preservation not only by federal law and governmental activities but also by the logic of coherent fieldwork. Sites that need preservation above the ground often need simultaneous archaeological attention beneath the ground. What is more, as archaeologists expanded their own purview by researching recent historical sites as well as prehistoric sites, their work naturally linked more with the work of architectural historians and preservationists.[10]

Archaeology has maintained powerful intellectual links with anthropology, and anthropology in the American academy has included a profound commitment to research into the history and culture of Native American communities. Further, the Department of the Interior, which became the locus for federal efforts regarding historic preservation, has also been for more than a century the locus for anthropological research and cultural programming regarding American Indian communities. Anthropology, like folklore studies, has tended to balance historical with present-day perspectives and to insist on attention to "living culture." In the second half of the twentieth century, there was a rapid expansion of the attention of American anthropologists beyond Native American and foreign cultures into other arenas of contemporary culture. Through both the alliance with archaeology and the extension of historic preservation concerns to native peoples, anthropological perspectives began to find their way into the historic preservation movement, which had originally been dominated by the academic disciplines of history and architectural history.[11]

Finally, the field of folklore studies broadened its purview in the second half of the twentieth century to a point where it overlapped with all these other disciplines. It had reflected a strong preservation impulse since its founding in America, and it likewise had a history of interdisciplinary connections. In its underlying concept, folklore has to do with artistic forms and human performances of all sorts, but in practice the network of folklorists originally concentrated on verbal and musical traditions—those expressive forms that anthropologists and historic preservationists came to refer to as "intangible culture." But by the second half of the twentieth century, a strong movement arose within the folklore network to add material culture to the intellectual repertory of folklorists.

In Pennsylvania, an organization of scholars and devotees of Pennsylvania German culture, led by Alfred Shoemaker, Don Yoder, and J. William Frey, imported the European concept of "folklife" (*folkliv* in Swedish; *volksleben* or *volkskunde* in German) as a way of incorporating material culture and a "way of life" into their studies.[12] Their journal, founded under the title *Pennsylvania Dutchman*, was changed in 1958 to *Pennsylvania Folklife*, which seems to be the earliest prominent institutional use of the word "folklife" in English. The term was adopted by the Department of Folklore and Folklife at the University of Pennsylvania in 1968, at the urging of faculty member Don Yoder, who had been one of the original Pennsylvania importers of the word. In 1964 Lewis Jones launched a program in American Folk Culture as one of the graduate programs sponsored by the New York Historical Association at Cooperstown, intertwining with its graduate program in museum studies. Indiana University's Folklore Institute included a professor, Warren Roberts, who specialized in material culture. A younger generation of folklorists, led by Henry Glassie and inspired by the pioneering work of cultural geographer Fred Kniffen, forged new directions in the study of folk architecture and material culture in the 1960s and 1970s.

Developments in public programming by folklorists echoed the expansion of academic folklorists into material culture. The Smithsonian Institution's Festival of American Folklife, first presented on the National Mall in Washington, D.C., in 1967, included from the beginning a strong crafts and material culture component. Its founder, Ralph Rinzler, was devoted to both folk music and folk crafts, and a generation of folklorists influenced by the Smithsonian's festival model developed public programs that included material culture on an equal footing with music, dance, and verbal traditions.

When the Pennsylvania Folklife Society imported the word "folklife" into American English, they did not envision the term as denoting material culture alone. Rather, they construed folklife studies as a broad and encompassing discipline, including both material and "spiritual" culture. A Latinate equivalent term is "regional ethnology." But there was a tendency, both in Europe and in the United States, for folklife studies to concentrate on and be loosely equated with material culture. Nevertheless, the Smithsonian's Festival of American Folklife from the beginning used the term in the broadest sense, including performing arts, verbal traditions, material culture, and a wide variety of cultural skills. Inspired by the visible success of this festival on the National Mall, Congress adopted the new term "folklife" in the legislation creating the American Folklife Center, and the word, like the older companion "folklore," came gradually to be used as an all-encompassing term for the entire range of cultural expressions studied by the field, or for the field itself.

The definition of "folklife" embedded in the American Folklife Preservation Act reveals the comprehensive view of the field envisioned by folklorists by the 1970s and remains a useful definition today:

> "American folklife" means the traditional expressive culture shared within the various groups in the United States: familial, ethnic, occupational, religious, regional; expressive culture includes a wide range of creative and symbolic forms such as custom, belief, technical skill, language, literature, art, architecture, music, play, dance, drama, ritual, pageantry, handicraft; these expressions are mainly learned orally, by imitation, or in performance, and are generally maintained without benefit of formal instruction or institutional direction. (Public Law 94-201, Section 3[1])

This definition was crafted by folklorist Archie Green, whose labors over several years led to passage of the American Folklife Preservation Act in 1976. Since then, the definition has influenced cultural legislation in several states and some foreign countries as well.

Cultural Conservation and Common Cause

As the various preservation networks broadened their purviews, they began to encounter one another more frequently and insistently. Historic preservationists, whose attentions were focused on buildings and material culture, inevitably began reflecting more on the relationship of material culture to other facets of culture. Archaeologists began researching recent historical sites and including within their scope of work the built environment above ground. Anthropologists expanded beyond their early focus on native and foreign cultures. And folklorists added material culture to their repertory while rapidly expanding public programming that focused on cultural preservation and presentation at the grass roots. Increasingly, it seemed to make sense for these overlapping movements to begin making common cause.

A legislative event in 1980 presented a golden opportunity to facilitate common cause among all the preservation networks. The National Historic Preservation Act amendments of 1980 contained the following mandate:

> The Secretary [of the Department of Interior], in cooperation with the American Folklife Center of the Library of Congress shall . . . submit a report to the President and the Congress on preserving and conserving the intangible elements of our cultural heritage such as arts, skills, folklife, and folkways. . . . This report shall include recommendations for legislative and administrative actions by the Federal Government in order to preserve, conserve, and encourage the continuation of the diverse traditional prehistoric, historic, ethnic, and folk cultural traditions that underlie and are a living expression of our American heritage. (Title III, Section 502)

When the act became law, the American Folklife Center and the NPS jointly undertook the preparation of the required report by assembling a multidisciplinary panel of experts and hiring a project coordinator, Ormond Loomis, to manage an elaborate process of deliberation and consultation and to draft the report. The resulting policy report was published in 1983 under the title *Cultural Conservation: The Protection of Cultural Heritage in the United States.*

The essence of the report is nicely summarized in the report itself: "Cultural conservation is a concept for organizing the profusion of private and public efforts that deal with traditional community cultural life. It envisions cultural preservation and encouragement as two faces of the same coin. Preservation involves planning, documentation, and maintenance; and encouragement involves publication, public events, and educational programs."[13] Thus cultural conservation becomes an overarching term embracing all the facets of the cultural enterprise: "In application, cultural conservation means a systematic, coordinated approach to the protection of cultural heritage."[14] In other words, the report proposes cultural conservation as an umbrella term under which all

Folklorist Elaine Thatcher interviews Sal Putiri while he makes a Christmas log from sphagnum moss and evergreens during the American Folklife Center's Pinelands Folklife Project in the Pinelands National Reserve, southern New Jersey, 1983. (Photo by Sue Samuelson for the American Folklife Center, Library of Congress)

the various preservation networks can work together. It also includes consideration of a domain not usually considered with cultural preservation issues: natural conservation, the environment, and ecology.

The American Folklife Center was already experimenting with interdisciplinary teams for its fieldwork projects before the issuance of the *Cultural Conservation* report. For example, its Paradise Valley Folklife Project in northern Nevada (1978–80) utilized not only folklorists and ethnomusicologists but a cultural anthropologist specializing in Basque cultural studies, a western historian of material culture, and a small archaeological team, led by historical archaeologist James Deetz, who explored the site of a now-abandoned Chinese community in the valley.

When the *Cultural Conservation* report was published, the American Folklife Center resolved to continue and expand this pattern of interdisciplinary experimentation. It undertook a project in Utah, the Grouse Creek Cultural Survey, which experimented successfully with new sorts of collaboration among the disciplines of folklore, history, and architectural history, as the report had recommended.[15] The Utah State Historic Preservation Office shared with the folklorists in the state a desire to explore and document the community of Grouse Creek in northwestern Utah—a culturally intriguing example, as the study later demonstrated, because Grouse Creek lies along a major cultural boundary separating Mormon traditions to the east from buckaroo ranching traditions to the west. The team was convened in the summer of 1985, and their labors eventually led to publication of *The Grouse Creek Cultural Survey: Integrating Folklife and Historic Preservation Field Research* (1988), which both presents the survey findings and delineates how an interdisciplinary team expanded and clarified the findings.

The center also explored the linkages between cultural and natural conservation through a field project in the Pinelands National Reserve of southern New Jersey. The Pinelands Folklife Project considered the living cultural traditions of a large region of South Jersey, the Pine Barrens. The legislation creating the national reserve had established a regional planning commission to manage the conservation of the ecology of the Pine Barrens—including the remarkable aquifer that underlies the region—and its ecological, archaeological, historical, and architectural features had been extensively documented. The Pinelands Folklife Project added to the planning equation the key missing ingredient: the living cultural traditions of present-day inhabitants, who are the very people whom regional planners must consult. The project also explored and highlighted the inseparable interconnectedness between the region's ecology and its cultural traditions. The final report of the project, *One Space, Many Places: Folklife and Land Use in New Jersey's Pinelands National Reserve* (1986), contains the results of the cultural survey and recommendations for a planning process that will include local people and local culture.[16]

Mary Hufford, the folklife specialist at the American Folklife Center who coordinated the Pinelands Folklife Project, continued the exploration of folklife, ecology, and cultural planning by coordinating two projects in southern West Virginia in the 1990s. The first documented the living cultural traditions in and around New River Gorge National River and provided a report on the possibility of a cultural center in the park. The second explored in great detail the culture of the inhabitants of the hollows along Coal River and its tributaries. The latter project emphasized the profound relationship between the culture of local communities and the Appalachian forest and watershed. It also illuminated the many ways in which the forest acted as a cultural "commons," cultivated for generations by the local community for sustenance and serving as the central spiritual touchstone and knowledge base for the local culture of the region.[17]

Interdisciplinary initiatives appeared at the state level as well. In several states, such as Utah, Kentucky, and Maryland, the state historic preservation office engaged folklorists to work on projects. In Florida, the employment of folklorists in a state historic preservation office led to such results as the successful National Register nomination of the historic African American town of Eatonville, just outside Orlando. Eatonville is not only a place of continuing viability but also a symbol of identity and accomplishment to African Americans everywhere; moreover, it is the hometown of legendary writer and folklorist Zora Neale Hurston. But it is a town where the existing buildings, conventionally appraised, provided an inadequate measure of the community's values or the township's cultural significance.

The American Folklife Center's efforts to follow up on the recommendations and the spirit of the *Cultural Conservation* report were complemented by the efforts of others. Indeed, a series of conferences and experimental projects around the country in the 1980s can be characterized as ripples from the original report. These efforts culminated in a 1990 conference at the Library of Congress on "Cultural Conservation: Reconfiguring the Cultural Mission." The conference was avowedly multidisciplinary. Coordinator Mary Hufford managed it together with a panel of experts from various disciplines and agencies, and representatives of numerous disciplines and professions attended. Natural conservation occupied a larger place than it had in the *Cultural Conservation* report, where it was present but somewhat recessive. Environmental and heritage planning, which tend by the nature of planning to be interdisciplinary in perspective, were more in evidence than before. The word "heritage" had come more to the fore, as it continued to do in the cultural realm during the 1990s. The book arising from the 1990 conference was entitled *Conserving Culture: A New Discourse on Heritage* (1994). Its three large subsections—"Conserving History," "Protecting Biocultural Diversity," and "Encouraging Folklife" —suggest the contours that had begun to evolve in the discourse on cultural conservation.[18]

Heritage Areas and Sense of Place

Both historic preservation and folklife, as preservation strategies, tap into a larger cultural phenomenon in the body politic, sometimes referred to as "sense of place." The term has been on the ascent in the intellectual discourse of the past quarter century. There is a growing literature on sense of place, beginning with a seminal volume on the subject, Yi Fu Tuan's *Space and Place: The Perspective of Experience* (1977).[19] But though the preservation systems implemented by the various professional networks have always given some attention to the value of place, the importance of sense of place at the regional level has not been well tapped as the basis for a cultural strategy. Then a cultural program based on regional sense of place arose in the 1980s and 1990s from an interesting quarter.

Whereas the 1960s and 1970s had been a watershed period for cultural legislation, the 1980s and 1990s did not seem auspicious years for new regulations. Until the mid-1990s, when the budgetary tide began reversing course, it was a time of rising federal deficits and increasing rhetoric about reducing the size and scope of the federal government's domestic programs. Though Secretary of the Interior James Watt forwarded the *Cultural Conservation* report to the president and Congress, the Department of the Interior did not push for further legislation based on the recommendations of the report. It was left to mid-level administrators and adventuresome professionals around the country to experiment with some of the many recommendations contained in the report. The American Folklife Center pushed ahead with its own experimental projects, and there were some responsive developments among state historic preservation offices, arts councils, and historical societies. But for the most part, things remained the same in the Washington cultural infrastructure and in the networks of state cultural agencies tied into that federal infrastructure.

Curiously, though, one arena emerged in the 1980s and 1990s as the focus of active congressional attention, while all other cultural arenas were under budgetary or ideological pressure. Congress has always been the source of major initiatives in the cultural realm. Now, through the time-honored technique of earmarking special projects in omnibus appropriations bills, lawmakers began to explore the idea of "heritage corridors," creating several in Pennsylvania and in other eastern states.

These new heritage areas were literally unauthorized, in the technical sense that the programs thus constituted had no authority deriving from legislation originating in the congressional authorizing committees. Rather, they were creatures of the Appropriations Committees, added at the urging of various members of Congress who wanted such programs in their state or district. Thus the newly funded heritage areas generated some consternation in professional networks and in the NPS, which was generally charged with managing the day-to-day implementation of what Congress had envisioned. The NPS had its own funding priorities and naturally feared that new parks and parklike initiatives would drain away the resources needed for the better administration of existing parks. The term "park barrel" began appearing in newspaper features and crept into the cultural lexicon.

But to a rising generation of planners in the NPS and a rising generation of local advocates around the country, the new heritage corridors provided an intriguing opportunity for a fresh approach to the cultural mission. Heritage areas were deeply rooted in the same sense of place that had underlain much of the historic preservation legislation over the past century. Further, they avoided the enormous costs of land acquisition, and they offered the possibility of a new cooperative relationship between the NPS and local communities, instead of the older acquire-and-control strategy so deeply entrenched in the administrative mentality of the Park Service.

Heritage areas as a phenomenon in fact offered many potential cultural and social benefits. The corridor concept fueled a grassroots process of regional planning among communities more accustomed to competing than working together. They focused local community members on identifying and protecting the full panoply of their cultural resources as unique assets for both community development and cultural tourism. They encouraged comprehensive regional assessments that merged or treated in tandem the older categories such as historic buildings, folklife, archaeological resources, and natural resources. They also embraced comfortably, under the capacious rubric of "heritage," the historic resources that had been the focus of some of the older cultural networks, the living cultural resources that had been the focus of others, and the natural resources of the region. "Heritage" began to fill an important conceptual need, uniting in one term the totality of resources within a region.

The heritage corridor idea quickly took hold in the Mid-Atlantic region and expanded into the Northeast, Southeast, and Midwest. A new organization, the National Coalition for Heritage Areas, convened national conferences and lobbied for broader congressional and public support. Older and better-established organizations like the National Trust for Historic Preservation began lending their support. Ultimately, the senior administrators of the NPS shifted their strategy from resistance to leadership, arguing that well-crafted national legislation providing rational and coherent standards for future development was far better than futile resistance to the crazy quilt of heritage areas that had sprung up. Although no such legislation passed in the 1990s, due primarily to opposition from property rights groups, the idea continued to percolate, and an analogous concept—the American Heritage Rivers initiative—arose with support from the Clinton administration. By the end of the decade the Alliance for National Heritage Areas formed to promote and connect the work of the existing congressionally created heritage areas.[20]

Some people have seen the 1980s and 1990s as a period of marking time for many of the older preservation networks. For two decades there were no significant legislative or budgetary advances for these networks at the federal and state levels. But during this period the heritage area movement arose from congressional initiatives and gradually became a national movement with deepening support in the administration and in the national cultural community. The movement accomplished organically some of the deeper underlying recommendations of the *Cultural Conservation* report. Fundamentally, it provided a new approach that, unhampered by the systems and strictures of the older professional networks and legal frameworks, offered the possibility of managing regional resources in a holistic, organic, professionally broad, and administratively cooperative way. Time will tell how fully and how well the heritage area movement realizes that historic possibility.

Some Terminological Considerations

As different networks move toward working together, one of the most tenacious impediments is terminology. Anthropologists are sometimes uncomfortable with the term "folklore." Architectural specialists may feel a discomfort at calling above-ground research "archaeology." Historians occasionally worry about the validity of "oral history" and are not always comfortable with the relationship between "history" and "story." In general, people from any cultural arena view their own arena expansively and adjacent arenas narrowly.

The term "intangible culture" was probably devised in an effort to reach out beyond the customary domain of archaeologists and historic preservation professionals.[21] Since the buildings or pots that architectural historians and archaeologists deal with so extensively are tangible manifestations of culture, the preservation community have come to refer to the stories, music, dance, and other cultural elements that they encountered as "intangible culture" or "intangible elements of culture." They add the adjective for intangible culture but do not use the adjective "tangible" in the more familiar domain of material culture where their own work is concentrated. Similarly, folklorists use "material culture" (borrowed from anthropology) but never refer to "immaterial" or "intangible" culture, which is the domain more central to their historical mission.

One might conclude that we all append adjectives to describe domains with which we are less familiar. From the point of view of an architectural historian or an archaeologist, it is understandable that tangible cultural elements would be the chief focus of attention, and that other elements would come to be described collectively as "intangible." Indeed, the phrase "intangible cultural heritage" has now achieved the distinction of being used in official descriptions of culture by UNESCO. But an old truism about definitions cautions against defining things by saying what they are not. Calling elements of culture "intangible" is problematic, because instead of describing the salient features of these elements, it simply names a category to which they do not belong.

Ultimately, the "tangible–intangible" terminology is conceptually confusing as well. The word "culture" is a verbal noun (Latin *cultura*) describing not an object but a process or activity. Its meaning, in its root sense, is "the process of cultivation" or "that which is cultivated," and it originally referred to the process of food cultivation. Thus culture itself is intangible, comprising a mental and spiritual system established and nurtured by human society for its better perpetuation and fulfillment. Stories, riddles, songs, dances, pots, quilts, or buildings might better be described, not as culture, but as "expressions of culture." At the level of cultural expressions, one may distinguish between tangible expressions (a pot, quilt, or building) and intangible expressions (a story, riddle, or song). But still there remain categorical problems: a dance or a meal seem tangible, yet their form is fleeting, making them performances more than artifacts. And even the most concrete artifacts gradually change over time.

It is interesting to reflect that documentation of any cultural expression creates a tangible analog to the original expression, fixing the expression in a form where it can be preserved more effectively or shared more widely. Copyright law, which has always focused on intangible cultural expressions such as verbal and musical creations, has long recognized the importance of fixing an expression in some analog form. Writing, sound recording, still photography, videotape, and motion picture film all have the effect of fixing cultural performances in a preservable, verifiable, and sharable medium. They make cultural expressions, whether intangible or tangible in their original form, tangible in a new fixed form analogous to the original creative work.

Other Impediments to Cultural Cooperation

Cooperation is easy to advocate but not always so easy to implement. Many impediments lie in the way of the goal of getting the various preservation networks to work together. The paragraphs above cited terminological impediments, and those below cite some additional barriers. To them may be added the general impediment to all change—inertia, which in the case of human networks inclines individuals to stay within the patterns of contact and behavior that have proven successful, or at least comfortingly familiar, in the past.

One impediment to cooperation between the historic preservation and folklife networks is the differing cultural strategies developed by the two networks. The historic preservation network has placed much of its energy in a national strategy of preliminary selection, documentation, evaluation, and final designation. The Historic American Buildings Survey in the 1930s experimented with documenting whole communities, and state historic preservation offices in recent decades have carried out survey work that strives to be comprehensive within the area surveyed. But overall there has been an inclination to ration resources and emphasize what are judged to be the most worthy or the most endangered historic resources. The larger strategy of the National Register, despite the great broadening of its focus in recent decades, implies a stamp of distinctiveness and superior quality. Indeed, much of its popularity and effectiveness as a tool of local preservation and planning derives from this sense of professional evaluation leading to the conferral of a national imprimatur.

The public folklore and folklife network, on the other hand, has pursued strategies that diffuse and blur special recognition. Working from a beachhead established largely in the arts network during the 1970s and 1980s, folklorists have tended to favor small grants to local individuals and organizations to stimulate cultural activity at the grass roots. Grants are culturally stimulative but time-bound, conferring no formal or permanent imprimatur on the recipients. Similarly, festivals, publications, and other public programs confer temporary spotlights but stop short of permanent designation.

Another barrier to cooperation is conceptual. Historic preservationists tend to look at their work as fundamentally historical—that is, focused on the past. Much energy is expended on issues such as the amount of modification a building can undergo and still maintain its "integrity" or the number of years required to pass before a building can be eligible for consideration as a historic building. The context woven around the built environment is past-oriented, and the citizens of the present are viewed almost as bystanders for whom the past is explicated, or as an educative context for which the history is interpreted.

Further, history is cast in a periodic mold. The past tends to be viewed episodically, through a prism of periods, so that one works one's way back through the Great Depression to the Roaring Twenties, or forward from the Early Republic into the era of Jacksonian Democracy. The reliance on periodicity is even more pronounced in architectural history, which tends to view buildings as describable through a series of terms designating the styles of successive eras.

Folklorists and cultural anthropologists tend, on the other hand, to work from a conceptual model that might be described as the "living culture model." In this way of approaching the subject, people in the present are the focus, and the past is a context for the present. Culture is a living, organic phenomenon, and history is important as a way of understanding the present, or as an interpretation of the past by the present. "History" is seen, not as a body of events in the past that can be sifted in the present to establish the realities of fact and motive, but as a narrative in the present that offers an explanation or interpretation of the past. "History," in other words, is "story" writ large.

A major bureaucratic barrier to cooperation has arisen because the federal agencies managing aspects of the cultural mission have created, in the decades since the spate of cultural legislation in the mid-1960s, separate networks of cultural agencies at the state level. The network of state historic preservation offices is funded by, and thus connected to, the National Park Service. State arts councils are connected to the National Endowment for the Arts. State humanities councils are connected to the National Endowment for the Humanities. Interestingly, some state governments have pursued the idea of connecting these autonomous cultural agencies more effectively to each other. Some state historic preservation offices are lodged within the older and larger state historical societies—themselves the product of a significant earlier cultural movement in America. Other states have grouped several cultural agencies into a larger cultural department. But there is often less motive and inclination to cooperate, less sense of cultural common cause, at the federal than at the state level. The federal agencies, with their funds and clout, thus have drifted paradoxically toward a role that seeks to preserve provincialism and narrowness of cultural mission at the state level.

Trends Favoring Cultural Cooperation

Despite these and other impediments, the ideal of cooperation in the cultural realm now encounters certain trends that work in its favor. The first boon to cooperation is the tendency of Congress to favor cooperative efforts and to dream up new initiatives without regard to professional specialization or disciplinary autonomy. The *Cultural Conservation* report itself is a fine example of the former, and the heritage area legislation is a dramatic example of the latter. The second boon is a pronounced trend within the White House beginning in the late 1990s to exert leadership in the cultural realm. The White House Millennium grants, managed through the Department of the Interior but ultimately involving all the cultural agencies of the federal government, may prove an augury of an era of greater White House leadership in the cultural realm. Such executive branch leadership, like congressional leadership, will by its nature tend to favor and encourage cultural inclusiveness and interagency cooperation.

Certain larger cultural trends in the civilization have also had an impact on all of the preservation networks. One is the reshaping of academic programs and departments, which has rapidly undermined the established academic order of the mid-twentieth century and substituted a more fluid and avowedly interdisciplinary order. This trend has had its virtues and defects, but it certainly has fostered an environment of experimentation in many professional fields. That tenor within the academy is now spreading into the professional fields working on various aspects of cultural conservation, often countervailing the conservative scope and mission of the federal cultural agencies.

Other societal trends also have had an impact on the professional networks of preservation and conservation. The societal motive of cultural inclusion has pushed all the cultural networks toward greater focus on the cultural life of minorities, women, and the poor. Further, by extension, the ideal of inclusion has led in educational and cultural networks to a great deal of discussion about multiculturalism and related ideas. Despite popular usage, culture and group are not coterminous concepts; individuals as well as communities are multicultural, and culture both expresses the values of groups and is constantly shared across group lines. Nevertheless, the concepts of group, community, and culture are obviously closely connected, and the nation's larger concerns about these domains of identity have facilitated valuable cooperative work across disciplinary lines in the fields of cultural preservation.

At another societal level, there has been a sharp increase in awards programs in America since the 1980s. The televised awards ceremonies of the entertainment industry, which have become a national preoccupation, are echoed by a number of more modest programs sponsored by the preservation and folklife communities at the state and national levels. Perhaps the most significant of these is the National Heritage Fellowships, a program developed by the Folk Arts Program of the National Endowment for the Arts. Begun as an annual awards ceremony in 1982, the program honors each year about fifteen artists as exemplars of various folk art forms currently practiced in America. The art forms range from music to dance to crafts, and the regional and ethnic distribution is very broad, from Native American to the most recent immigrants.[22]

Despite the great visibility of the National Heritage Fellowships program each fall in Washington, D.C., the program is not widely known around the country, except, of course, within the folklore and folklife network. Anthropologists, historic preservationists, and others in the cultural world sometimes propose—in the spirit of brainstorming—that we explore instituting in the United States a living national treasures program comparable to the internationally prominent Japanese cultural program by that name. In fact, the National Heritage Fellowships comprise just such a program. It does not go by the precise name of the Japanese program, and, as suits its American character, it is somewhat less formal in the expectations imposed on its recipients to pass their art along to the younger generation. Still, without fanfare we have indeed instituted a living national treasures program in America.

One value shared by historic preservationists and folklorists is a devotion to documentation as a culturally powerful tool. Both fields realized early in the twentieth century that the emergence of multiple documentary media was a culturally important development. Still photography, sound recordings, and motion pictures not only transformed cultural research but also, as they became democratized, began to assume a central role in the contemporary cultural process itself. Thus documentary initiatives directed at aspects of American culture could not only serve the purposes of documentary preservation, but could also be used in public education to inculcate a preservation sensibility in local communities and the citizenry at large.

Since the end of the nineteenth century, Americans have used new technologies for cultural documentation and dissemination almost as fast as the technologies have been invented. Since the 1930s, the federal government has sponsored significant programs for broad national documentation of culture. The Historic American Buildings Survey and the Archive of American Folk Song flourished in this era; so did a number of WPA arts-related projects and the photographic unit of the Farm Security Administration.[23] Thus the history of commitment to documentation by all the fields under the rubric of cultural conservation provides a useful basis for comparative research and even collaborative documentation in the future.

Phong Nguyen receives the National Heritage Fellowship. The Vietnamese musician and scholar and First Lady Hillary Rodham Clinton hold the 1997 award as Jane Alexander, Chair of the National Endowment for the Arts, looks on. (Photo courtesy of the National Endowment for the Arts)

Prospects

The multidisciplinary field projects and World Wide Web presentations of the American Folklife Center in the past quarter-century point the way toward future professional efforts that use documentation and dissemination for a larger educational purpose. Other initiatives, such as the small community-oriented grants of the Fund for Folk Culture or the Keepers of the Treasures program of the NPS for native communities, suggest the need to train local community members to use documentation more effectively themselves in their own cultural programming.[24] As the new century unfolds, documents and documentation are likely to prove even more central to cultural programming, both by cultural professionals and at the community level.

Equally significant is a strong trend among all the disciplines and networks involved in aspects of cultural conservation toward community-oriented programming. A generation ago the ideal of community cultural programming was galvanized by the American Revolutionary Bicentennial celebrations, which, as they arose and evolved, took on a pronounced grassroots character. Since that period in the 1970s, the professional fields have progressively deepened their commitment to making community development and encouragement the keystone of their work. Whereas "professional" and "community" once seemed to represent opposing values, increasingly all professional networks have embraced the credo of supporting community values. In this arena, folklorists and cultural anthropologists have a great deal of experience to offer, both in untangling what "community" means and in implementing a variety of cultural programs that can support and nourish community values. In the context of seeking to build programs on the base of community values, professional networks will find it easier, it may be hoped, to work fruitfully together.

In the context of working together, the *Cultural Conservation* report provides an array of recommendations that, nearly a generation after they were drafted, seem invitingly doable as the twenty-first century begins. Further, the report's useful categorization of the "profusion of private and public efforts" seems absolutely relevant a generation later. A number of the recommendations have been experimented with consciously; others appear to be happening through a kind of unconscious volition, thanks to larger trends in society. It is not unreasonable to hope for more progress in the coming decades on the report's recommendations.

In an era of economic prosperity, cultural innovation seems to be a normal consequence of the introduction of new technologies. A century's experience with new technologies teaches us that any technologies that are widely diffused and democratized will quickly be adapted to community cultural purposes. The current crop of new technologies appears to permit people to connect with one another in innovative ways, and that characteristic already holds promise of exciting cultural applications. We can only speculate about where it will all lead, but we know from past experience that the innovation will not be as inimical to community culture as the bystanders of the time fear. Indeed, cultural innovation arising from the grass roots will lead quickly to new means and modes of cultural conservation.

Historic Preservation in the
Twenty-first Century

Where Do We Go from Here?

The United States now has in place a historic preservation program that is the equal of any in the world. The state and local programs of the pre-1966 era, if not entirely a thing of the past, have been largely replaced by the federal, state, and local partnership created in the sixties. We owe a tremendous debt to those individuals who created the 1966 National Historic Preservation Act and sold it to Congress, as well as to those who came before them.[1]

But no system or, indeed, the larger context in which it operates is stable indefinitely. Times change, values and fashion change. Preservationists come and go, and over time even generational changes occur in thinking about preservation. Although the basic preservation-conservation process described in Chapter 1 remains much as it always has, some aspects of the field—especially those having to do with significance, integrity, and treatment—are moving targets. Challenges to the concept of what is worth preserving and to whom it is important have been forthcoming with an ever-stronger voice since the early 1980s, and the beginning of the twenty-first century seems an opportune time to reexamine our traditional ways of doing things. This chapter reviews our strengths as a movement, as well as those circumstances that give us difficulty and that work against us. It ends with some personal observations about how we might become more effective preservationists and the new directions we might take.

We Have Come a Long Way

The basic philosophy underlying the new preservation of the 1960s and 1970s was not really new. It built upon then-current ways of doing things and continued to focus on historical events in which the major players were, as someone irreverently put it, dead white guys of European descent. It placed strong emphasis on protecting the physical reality of buildings, structures, objects, and places whose underlying values were associated primarily with Euro-centered, art-oriented, Renaissance traditions. Most preservation advocates, both before and immediately following the 1966 act, comprised a rather narrow segment of society. They were white, upper-middle-class individuals. The strategic posture of the preservation movement was then, as it sometimes is now, mostly crisis-oriented and essentially defensive in nature.

Happily, even though we were not then prepared to take full advantage of it, the 1966 act also recognized that historic preservation might serve an important purpose in the daily lives of people and communities. But then, as now, established ways of doing things were slow to change, and the early thrust of the program remained on history, buildings, structures, and the artifactual content of our environment. Only during the last two decades has there been a significant redirection of American preservation to an emerging emphasis on *both* physical and social community building, and on more inclusive and diverse aspects of history, culture, and heritage.

These changes in emphasis have been a response to changes in the U.S. economy, changes in thinking about the environment, energy shortages, demographic change and desegregation, diversity, and the growing impact of the Internet and computer-based technology. Views about whose history is important and why, especially about the preservation of racial, ethnic, and folk cultures, have changed radically.

Conceiving a new, national, partnership approach to preservation in 1966 was not all that difficult. In one sense, the drafters of the 1966 legislation were simply adding building blocks to an existing structure and called it a "Register." But in expanding the content of that register and adding consequences to that content, they were starting almost from scratch. The machinery they envisioned was simple, inclusive, and elegant. The concept of a National Register of Historic Places and a relatively mild protective process that did not unduly restrict the owners of historic properties was accepted without much question or fanfare. However, the processes, agencies, and organizations that have grown from this simple premise have been many and much more complex. Seemingly toothless review and comment processes once thought to be merely pro forma have, over time, become substantive in that, more often than not, they have led to compromise and agreements that do, in fact, afford a degree of protection for the resource. As John Fowler points out in Chapter 2, the "no-build" option is rare.

The post-1966 partnership goes beyond governments. The National Trust for Historic Preservation has provided a rich menu of innovative, even aggressive, approaches to preservation including major initiatives in property stewardship, Main Street programs, inner-city and housing ventures, rural and landscape preservation, maritime preservation, adaptive use, and minority involvement in preservation, finance, and stewardship. The National Conference of State Historic Preservation Officers, Preservation Action, and the National Trust together have provided a strong voice in national and state legislatures, as well as support to the states. State and local nonprofit organizations have grown in numbers and effectiveness, increasingly in more formal partnership agreements with SHPOs, statewides, and the National Trust. Local governments, again as a result of the 1966 act and its amendments, have significantly expanded preservation efforts. All these have been joined by literally thousands of national, state, and local groups concerned with specialized aspects of preservation and conservation-related activities.

At the project level, success has been on our side. Where private market investor expectations—or even the often uneconomic but proud ambitions of tens of thousands of private owners—have been met, tens of thousands of urban and rural preservation projects have been completed in the last twenty years. Preservation success stories are legion.

It seems important to emphasize at the outset the tremendous leap of progress we have made since 1966 for two reasons. One is that many among today's younger generation of preservationists are unfamiliar with the overwhelmingly important contribution made by the 1966 act. The second is that an older generation that has grown up with it tends to overlook how far we have come since those early days. The system created by Carl Feiss, Bob Garvey, Gordon Gray, Laurence Henderson, Albert Rains, and others has worked splendidly over the years, and a moment of appreciation and remembrance is in order.

Despite our obvious success, much remains to be done. One distinctive characteristic of the American preservation movement has been its constant and ebullient spirit of optimism. We are on track to winning as many battles as we lose, and we take great pride in winning and telling others about it. Our success stories give us bragging rights to the public, help us to enlist others in our cause, and reinforce our belief that what we do is important. We have earned the right to be optimistic.

While mulling over success stories, however, we tend at the same time to undervalue the lessons that emerge from the difficulties encountered along the way.[2] It goes against human and corporate nature to talk openly about mistakes and failed efforts, but there is much to be learned from looking at what went wrong when we did lose, if for no reason other than to avoid having to face the same result twice. This chapter attempts to look in a balanced way at both our strengths and weaknesses as a movement. If it is not always a pleasant story with a happy ending, it is a necessary one.

Some Unresolved Difficulties beyond Our Control

Money

Our principal problem centers on money. Preservation, vis-à-vis *new construction*, is expensive and almost always requires subsidies in one form or another. Direct federal (and much state) government funding for preservation at all levels has been inadequate from the beginning. Federal funding in inflation-adjusted dollars has actually been declining for many years. The long-hoped-for reliable source of income that comes from a permanently funded Historic Preservation Fund built on revenues from offshore oil drilling has yet to be approved by Congress. A philosophy that uses revenue from one depleted resource to shore up another is both ethically sound and rational. But removing preservation funding from the congressional appropriations process may never happen, since Congress has an understandable reluctance to give up its annual decision-making authority.[3]

Preservation has enjoyed much bipartisan support in Congress over the years, but, as John Fowler suggests in Chapter 2, that support is a mile wide and an inch deep. As for appropriations from general revenues, neither Republicans nor Democrats have given their unstinting support to full preservation funding, many feeling that the states should bear the primary burden. To make matters worse, state budget analysts, who usually have the first—and often the last—word over state appropriations, respond that state funds are not needed in any case, since the 1966 historic preservation program is essentially a federal program. Thus, from a funding standpoint, preservation is caught in a frustrating, revolving-door situation. And state legislatures, like Congress, can usually find higher-priority expenditure items with which to complete their annual or biennial budgets. At the local level, funding for preservation is spotty, tending toward generosity or stinginess, depending on the prevailing political climate and available funds.

As noted many times in earlier chapters, back-door subsidies through federal, state, and local tax incentives of one kind or another have had a spectacular effect on preservation activity. However, public administration theorists, opponents of preservation, and conservative thinkers generally continue to argue that, as a matter of public policy, tax incentives are essentially undemocratic, off-budget approaches that deprive elected representatives of the opportunity to make politically acceptable spending choices out in the open and subject to public scrutiny. A less frequently heard argument is that all activities subsidized in this way become more subject to the vagaries of the market itself and the momentary state of the economy.

The argument for preservation tax subsidies is that they are needed to provide a level playing field, not unlike those enjoyed by steel, oil, agriculture, and hundreds of other industries and businesses—although preservationists rarely draw such comparisons. We like to think that our claim to public support stands on higher moral ground, but, again, that depends on whom one is talking to. The real issue is whether we can nudge our claim to public support to a position closer to the head of the line. Existing preservation subsidies in the form of grants, loans, tax concessions, and the like have indeed helped level the playing field. Those of us who support preservation view these government subsidies as a public good, but our opponents see them as just another kind of pork, no different from any other special interest. Public sector budget analysts, who wield more authority than most people are aware, view them as revenue lost to the government.

The economics of preservation tell us that it can rarely be wholly public or wholly private, and that of necessity it will almost always be dependent on government support of one kind or another. Public support thus places preservation squarely in the political arena. We preservationists should not kid ourselves. Historic preservation as a widely popular public goal is not, and probably never will be, a highly valued public priority. Law enforcement, drugs, education, welfare, homeland defense, and many other items place much higher on the public agenda. Even within the environmental movement, of which most preservationists consider themselves to be a part, clean air and water, the protection of endangered plant and animal species, and the preservation of farmland and open space receive significantly higher support among the public and politicians at all levels.

Politics

In political terms, historic preservation, despite the fact that congressional support is usually bipartisan, is assumed by many to be a liberal cause. To this extent, it will always be anathema to conservative political interests, for which cutting government expenditures and reducing government control over private property are fundamentally important goals. Preservation initiatives at every level of government will thus be won or lost according to the balance of liberal-conservative political authority in national, state, and (less often) local political forums. Of course, this is not to say that business interests that profit from preservation-related activities will not support us.

The rising tide of conservative government, beginning with the Reagan administration in the eighties and the Republican-controlled Congress in the nineties, has not been propitious for preservation. The National Historic Preservation Fund has never been fully funded and the Advisory Council on Historic Preservation and the National Trust have seen their appropriations deeply cut or lost altogether in the last decade. The Trust has made a significant fiscal comeback, however, through an ambitious program of private giving, its early involvement with the Save America's Treasures program, and a renewed focus on direct funding for buildings as such. "Takings" bills restricting the regulatory authority of state and local governments have been passed in the U.S. House of Representatives and in twenty-two state legislatures, and one with good prospects for passage made significant progress in the last Congress. In that Congress, and in a number of states, Religious Freedom Restoration Acts have come close to freeing churches from local land-use and preservation controls. The Historic Homeowners Tax Credit initiative has languished in five successive sessions of Congress. Individual landmark and district enrollment in the National Register has remained subject to an owners' veto since 1980, and federal law now prohibits the nomination of American historic landmarks of international significance to the UNESCO World Heritage List without specific congressional authority.

Also of concern, the U.S. Supreme Court has shown a reawakened interest in the Fifth Amendment takings issue after many decades of benign silence in this area. Several of its recent decisions show a distinct tendency to return issues related to government control over private property to the states, which, under state constitutions, will almost inevitably take a more restrictive view of government authority.

At the local government level, it is no secret that many voters and their representatives continue as a matter of personal philosophy to favor growth, development, jobs, and "progress." In a free market society, where competition and other factors limit the ability of individual businesses to raise prices at will over those of competitors, the main road to increasing profits is to increase the turnover of goods and services—and this, in turn, will favor an increase in the number of customers. Thus, "growth is good," and activities and programs that appear to restrict growth "are bad." Indeed, a preoccupation with growth, progress, and the future has been deeply embedded in the American soul since the founding of the Republic. It is not surprising that preservation, which is explicitly tied to a historic past, does not arouse widespread public or political enthusiasm.

These issues are not unrelated to the personal value systems held by many Americans. As a preservation activist and the former chair of a local historic district commission, I am acutely aware that district and landmark regulations —indeed, private property restrictions in whatever form—are stubbornly opposed as a matter of principle by those who prefer freedom in the use of private property. These feelings have dominated many issues for centuries, and there is no reason to believe that they will disappear any time soon or that preservation will be exempt from them. It is a continuing tug-of-war inevitably tied to fundamental political beliefs about free markets and personal freedom from government restrictions.

The Federal Partnership

Finally, we must acknowledge the existence of fundamental philosophical divisions between and among the different levels of government within our federal system. The national government, through the Department of the Interior and the Advisory Council, are essentially responsible for defining the basic philosophy and operating procedures that undergird what we do. Since much of the funding for the national preservation program, which includes the salaries of many state preservation staff members, comes from Washington, the states are often viewed by state and federal officials alike, and the public, as branch offices of a federal program. An underlying goal of the federal agencies is to see that program standards are strictly adhered to.

Most state governments, on the other hand, tend to be strongly oriented toward growth, economic development, and progress. (There are exceptions, of course.) State historic preservation officers are appointed by the governor in each state, which means that they must serve two masters and often find themselves reaching for an unhappy compromise between two conflicting objectives. We have seen a number of instances where SHPOs were fired for taking strongly preservation-oriented stands that conflicted with state economic development opportunities.

Within almost all state governments, historic preservation offices tend to be weak relative to the politically powerful, giant state agencies that deal with transportation, public works, educational facilities, prisons, the environment, and fiscal policy. As a result, SHPOs are often forced to compromise preservation objectives when confronted by more powerful state agencies, influential state legislators, and favored political appointees and patrons.[4]

Within the Preservation Movement

The above array of external problems lies largely beyond the control of the preservation movement. They are forces with which we must contend simply because they are there and about which little can be done in the short run. But we also need to acknowledge the existence of some intrinsic problems that lie within the preservation movement itself—indeed, within all of us.

The first is the human tendency of individuals and organizations to resist change, to hang on to existing ways of doing things. In the world of physics, it is called momentum, the tendency of an object in motion to continue moving in the same direction, absent some stronger outside directional influence. Change comes hard to both individuals and organizations.

The second is the intrinsic tension inherent in partnership arrangements, where decision making among nominally equal partners can be difficult. A high-level NPS official responsible for preservation programs once said to me, "The attitude of the states is just send us your money and don't tell us what to do with it." Some state officials still feel disappointed that the recommendations of a 1994 study that held promise of devolving more programmatic independence to the states did not reach its full potential.[5] For somewhat the same reasons it is difficult for state preservation offices to cede full program independence to certified local governments—especially when resources to assist them to do a better job are wholly inadequate, or when it would be embarrassing to decertify one that marginally fails to meet federal requirements. At the lower level of the partnership, local governments sometimes chafe at what they perceive as state "supervision" over presumably local affairs.

A third problem is the difficulty that all of us encounter in the daily rush of events to take a long-term view. For example, most of us are pleased that tribal preservation programs and offices now have a recognized place at the preservation table. For the moment, budgets are modest, tribal jurisdiction beyond the reservation is largely consultative, and there are relatively few tribal preservation programs. Looking far ahead, however, the day will surely come when there is the potential for the creation of 250 or more tribal preservation offices and officers, but no more than 50 at the state level.

Administrative Structure

At the national level, the national historic preservation program remains a third- or fourth-tier priority within the U.S. Department of the Interior and the National Park Service, which has been historic preservation's home base since 1916. The NPS is but one of Interior's many statutory responsibilities. Within the Park Service itself, historic preservation is but a part of the larger NPS mandate to manage its lands, maintain scenic resources, and promote recreational opportunities for park visitors. Among preservation personnel, some note a significant "age gap" between younger and older preservation professionals. Older ones cleave to long-established preservation doctrine and procedures, while those of younger age appear to be more willing to reach out with new ideas about what is worth preserving and to embrace new procedures and alliances. In the last several decades, new programs related to regional heritage tourism, rivers and trails, recreation and like activities—all of which are closely related in one way or another to historic preservation—have arisen to compete for internal resources with the more well-established National Register programs. In some respects they are the price of success and changing concepts of what is worth preserving, as the broader concept of heritage, the preservation of place, and a wider, more inclusive range of associative values begin to take hold.[6]

There is a second institutional friction within the preservation movement that needs to be addressed, and that is between government interests and those of the increasingly important state and local nonprofit revolving fund organizations. Government programs based on the 1966 act have very high preservation standards, as defined by the Secretary of the Interior's Standards for Rehabilitation—standards that must be strictly followed if preservation tax credits are to be realized. The federal-state preservation partnership properly takes a relatively uncompromising, protective view of those standards when reviewing applications for tax credits or preservation grants-in-aid.

On the other hand, preservation revolving funds make markets by focusing on the adaptive potential of historic buildings and must, by their nature, be more accommodating in dealing with building fabric as a means of "doing the deal" to keep old buildings standing and in use. State and local revolving funds may be forgiven for needing to bend the standards from time to time. Revolving fund executives, who typically operate on tight budgets and independently of government funding (but who nonetheless indirectly depend on it), and who must raise their operating funds in a less certain or secure financial environment, may also be forgiven for expressing a certain amount of jealously toward the security enjoyed by their state- and federal-level civil service partners and resentment of their regulatory authority.

One growing problem within the preservation movement is the sheer proliferation of organizations that serve narrow and sometimes competing interests. Organizations established to preserve particular types of historic resources, from Civil War battlefields to building types such as theaters, churches, railroad depots, gas stations, and commercial strips, have mushroomed since 1980.[7] At the local level, large metropolitan areas like Washington, San Francisco, and New York City may each have hundreds of nonprofit entities with responsibility for an individual landmark building or house museum, each operating independently.

Presently there are probably more than ten thousand national, state, and local nongovernmental preservation and historical organizations, each of which has an important specialized role. This proliferation and fragmentation of interests and leadership not only can lead to competition for membership and funding that tends to fragment the movement, but also narrow or unnecessarily compartmentalize the horizons of individual preservationists. In such a climate, long-term thinking about the future of preservation becomes more difficult. As interests narrow and organizations multiply, it is probably inevitable that they reach out to one another only when there is a momentary convergence of financial or political interests, but more often go their own way when there is not.

A related problem stems from the overlapping responsibilities of organizations with fundamentally different purposes. As Charles Roe points out in Chapter 7, there is a significant overlap between land conservation organizations and historic preservation nonprofits serving preservation and conservation interests through the acquisition of ownership interests, each having some property responsibility of the other, but neither quite fulfilling the purposes of the other organization.

In the 1960s and 1970s the membership growth curve of historic preservation organizations was relatively steep. Now, for whatever reasons, that curve is tending to flatten. Part of the problem has been the rapid growth since 1966 of a professional class of preservationists. The grassroots, activist preservationists whose passions drove the movement forty years ago have to a significant extent been replaced by experts from national and state preservation offices and the better-staffed preservation nonprofit organizations. Citizen preservation partisans who would once have marched angrily on city hall or chained themselves to the pillars of a threatened building (as a few actually did) now tend to look to the growing number of professional preservationists for solutions. Today, the direct and immediate response to a preservation crisis is more likely to be a telephone call or fax to the state historic preservation office, a regional office of the National Trust, or a statewide nonprofit with the expectation that "they" will handle it.[8]

Many feel that current preservation philosophy is still too narrowly focused on architecture as the dominant associative value. Much of this interest is a holdover from earlier federal preservation programs, such as the 1935 Historic Sites Act, the basic thrust of which was continued and broadened in the 1966 legislation. This and the federal-state-local partnership that has since emerged from it has created substantial federal and state preservation bureaucracies trained or at least habituated to continue this tradition. The movement's emphasis on the preservation of physical remains and its staffing patterns and procedures have meant that our national program and its state partners tend to be slow and cautious in picking up on new ideas. For example, current NPS programs for the preservation of designed and vernacular landscapes took a decade or more from the time they were first advanced in the 1970s to achieve an active, accepted place in the Park Service's permanent, ongoing programs. Diversity initiatives that might have been undertaken as early as the civil rights movement of the 1950s and 1960s have gathered real strength only in the last two decades. A coordinated, holistic approach to broader "heritage" preservation opportunities, momentarily of interest during the Carter administration, especially those involving natural, intangible, and vernacular resources, is only now carving out an accepted place in the larger scheme of things. Grafting new concerns onto the existing system and opening it up to new ideas and people tends to be a slow and haphazard process in any large organization. This caution has been reinforced to some extent by our sometimes uneven reliance on the fifty-year rule.

An alleged overemphasis on buildings, structures, and objects, as well as a continued focus on the historical for history's sake, has caused a long-simmering disagreement about who is an officially "qualified" preservationist to bubble up to the surface. Some argue that relative to local citizens who are not professionally certified, too many important preservation decisions are made by professionals. National Register review procedures, enforcement of the Secretary's Standards for tax credit purposes, CLG requirements, and other processes, taken together, make clear that the national preservation machinery remains largely in the grip of historians and architectural historians who hold specified professional and academic qualifications. Among those frustrated by a 1998 determination that they were "unqualified" are planners, cultural anthropologists, ethnologists, folklorists, agricultural economists, cultural geographers, and others from related disciplines essential to preservation endeavors. The cohort of occupational groups that feel somewhat marginalized might be expected to grow as the concept of what is worth preserving continues to expand.[9]

If there is a predominant voice that speaks on behalf of a national historic preservation movement and policy, it is the National Trust. There have been few if any significant new ideas or programs in American preservation during the last half-century that it has not sponsored or in which it has not been directly involved. While not losing sight of the importance of the movement's traditional core values grounded in architecture and history, the Trust has pushed for an expanded view of the movement in ways and at a rate that government and government-related institutions cannot match.[10]

In the last few years many preservation organizations and public programs have come together to support funding issues and opportunities. The National Trust now works closely with thirty-one statewide preservation organizations in thirty states through its Statewide Partners program, and through its Office of Statewide and Local Partnerships, it has also begun a new effort to strengthen collaboration with the myriad of local organizations across the country. Both Preservation Action and the NCSHPO have also collaborated with the Trust and the statewides in many efforts to strengthen preservation programs and initiatives. But the raising of many voices and the normal forces of institutional competition and allegiance still have the potential to dilute the position of historic preservation in American life.

Is It Time to Rethink Basic Associative Values?

The original nineteenth-century preservation paradigm, reaffirmed in the 1935 and 1966 acts, has been gradually expanded over the last two decades to include a broader range of social and environmental values and the concept that preservation offers opportunities for a better life for all Americans. Operationally, however, the focus remains on material culture. In many respects, material culture—history as represented in buildings, districts, and landscapes —is the strength of our national program. The challenge is to demonstrate the relationship between material culture—a building, a group of buildings, a landscape, a structure, an archaeological site—with the larger set of intangible social and environmental values we seek to portray and preserve. The best programs do account for intangible, local community values in the way they administer their survey and registration programs. But are the finite, descriptive emphases on material culture found in the Venice Charter, or in the National Register criteria or the Secretary's Standards, the best way to describe the totality or range of values we seek to promote? How do we move beyond the traditional ways of defining who we are and what we do, and how do we explain these persuasively to a larger public?

Of course, clinging to accustomed boundaries offers significant economic and political advantages. History, architecture, and archaeology, even when embellished with the post-1976 values of diversity and inclusiveness, energy conservation, economic benefits, tourism, and the like, are limited goals—specific targets, as it were. This is the easy road. The objectives are clear and subject to long-established procedures and norms. A preservation infrastructure centered on the National Register is in place. Obviously, it is easier to administer a program based on a known and precisely defined set of resources and procedures. If the preservation movement does not save old buildings and neighborhoods, no one else will. But does heavy reliance on National Register values tend to choke out or subordinate other important aspects of a heritage? Clearly, to some extent it does.

Not many average citizens would oppose saving old buildings as a matter of general principle, but experience gives rise to doubts that historic preservation as a larger goal enters the public mind very often. When active support for preservation does surface, it is typically addressed to specific buildings. Years of involvement have convinced me that only a small percentage of the general public cares at all for preservation as an important public value. Even within the larger community of environmental interests, we remain at the bottom of the stack in terms of popular support.

Henry Ford's famous quotation that "History is bunk" probably still reflects widespread popular sentiment in America today.[11] American history is no longer the presence in public education that it once was. In attempting to enlarge our base of support, we have tended in recent decades to latch on to more popular themes as they catch the attention of the public. As a 1995 state preservation plan put it: "[Preservation] includes tourism, economic development, open space protection, heritage education, rehabilitation of historic buildings, community conservation, affordable housing, neo-traditional planning, sustainable development, downtown revitalization, cultural celebration, archeology, design and craftsmanship."[12] Others would add energy conservation, the avoidance of pollution and global warming, and the preservation of everything that is irreplaceable. Now one must ask whether preservation in America is becoming *too* inclusive, with something for everyone. If viewed only in its traditional way of saving old buildings, it will not gain much support. The difficulty is that preservation regarded in this modern, more inclusive iteration, while perhaps attracting attention, may begin to appear as a crusade to "save everything"—which is also unlikely to build widespread popular support.

Elsewhere in the world, the concept of historic preservation moved beyond history and architecture a long time ago. The 1972 Convention for the Protection of the World Cultural and Natural Heritage, adopted in Paris by UNESCO, spoke of a need to protect a larger "cultural heritage," defined as:

> monuments, architectural works, works of monumental sculpture and painting, elements or structures of an archaeological nature, inscriptions, cave dwellings and combinations of features, which are of outstanding universal value from the point of view of history, art or science:
>
> . . . groups of separate or connected buildings which, because of their architecture, their homogeneity or their place in the landscape . . .
>
> . . . works of man or the combined works of nature and of man, . . . of outstanding universal value from the historical, aesthetic, ethnological or anthropological points of view.

Article 2 of the convention did not hesitate to include the natural environment as well, defined as

> natural features consisting of physical and biological formations or groups of such formations . . .;
>
> . . . [the] habitat of threatened species of animals and . . .
>
> . . . natural sites or precisely delineated natural areas of outstanding . . . value from the point of view of science, conservation or natural beauty.[13]

This wider range of associative values was proposed to include not only history and architecture, but art, science, aesthetics, ethnology, anthropology, conservation, and natural beauty as well. But here again, these are values primarily of interest to scholars and well-educated, sensitive members of a well-off, privileged upper middle class.

Believing the time had come to focus less on scholarly pursuits and more on a means of improving the human condition, North Carolina preservationists in the mid-1980s attempted to redefine preservation's core associative values to those that have the improvement of the human environment and the daily lives of the average citizen as their primary purpose. The definition of areas to be preserved was to be derived from its end result rather than its content: [To be preserved were those areas that] "possess form, character, and visual qualities derived from arrangements or combinations of topography, vegetation, space, scenic vistas, architecture, appurtenant features, distinctive natural habitats, natural formations, or places of natural or cultural significance, *that create an image of stability, comfort, local identity, and livable atmosphere*" (italics added).[14] This new emphasis was to be less concerned with artifactual content than with ambiance and the preservation of place.

That this new—and to many, radical—place-oriented philosophy was not adopted as law does not lessen its importance as a paradigm that goes beyond cultural values of primary importance to scholars and professionals. In this new scheme, history and architecture remain as important, respected values, but they become shared values in a larger context that emphasizes human purposes—that sense of "stability, comfort, local identity, and livable atmosphere." Sigfried Gideon and Sir Bannister Fletcher thus give way to new theories of place and place making advanced by Kevin Lynch, Christopher Alexander, Alfred Eide Parr, Mary Hufford, Delores Hayden, and others who in recent years have considered the preservation of place as important as the preservation of buildings.[15]

Heritage Areas

In Chapter 11 Russell Keune mentions the existence of German, Dutch, and Swiss citizen organizations that have managed to merge a concern for historic buildings with more traditional folkways and with landscape, aesthetic, and scenic values.[16] In many respects, they represent a European version of the increasingly popular American concept of heritage corridors, rivers, and areas, of which twenty-three have already been created in the United States by Congress and another thirty by the states in recent years. These foreign organizations date back to the early nineteenth century, and their widespread popular support is largely based on the more inclusive nature of their overall mission and the public perception that they serve human rather than scholarly interests.

There may be significant advantages in moving on to such a broader context.

Place theory is built on a much more inclusive range of associative values than those enumerated in the National Register criteria, notwithstanding it is in name a register of "Places." It emphasizes the qualitative aspects of growth and provides a logical point of entry for those primarily interested in growth management and sustainable development. It is overtly tied to recreation, tourism, and economic growth and progress. The concept is not hindered by crisply elaborated federal standards or necessarily by state-local regulatory processes with actual or perceived limitations on the use of private property. And both its outlook and the processes that drive it are essentially local in orientation rather than state or national. Place theory does not count numbers or calculate the percentage of "contributing" or "noncontributing" buildings. The associative values on which it is built value equally the vernacular with high style and the intangible with the tangible. Underlying all is an emphasis on local initiative and cooperation.

The new heritage areas (a local version of which might be a variant of the emergent "conservation" areas described in earlier chapters) would in all cases be reinforced by our existing, post-1966 historic preservation programs and laws. Traditional historic preservation approaches would have an important part to play, but the role of traditional preservation programs would be supportive rather than central. Most important, a programmatic move in this direction would inevitably attract a much broader base of public and political support, heretofore lacking, and would facilitate a much closer identification with the larger environmental protection movement. Most likely, it would also facilitate new opportunities for cross-connections and program coordination among neighboring political jurisdictions and related existing environmental protection programs. It would easily lend itself to a closer programmatic identification with the intangible cultural heritage and with the more recent diversity initiatives, while at the same time retaining the participation of scholarly and established professional interests on an as-needed basis.

The downside to such an approach is that some of the values and interests inherent in the concept of heritage areas are difficult to measure, to describe, and to quantify. It is easier to identify contributing buildings in a National Register historic district nomination and to speak of them in terms of tried-and-true historic styles than to identify, catalog, and register the components of a townscape or landscape, or to assess character, legibility, and accustomed comfort, as described a few pages back and in Chapter 6. The tasks of evaluation, registration, and the administration of subsidies in various forms become increasingly difficult as the traditional focus on buildings and other artifacts is diluted with more aesthetically and environmentally based elements such as ambiance, spatial structure, the larger context, place, and "culture." However, the reality is that since 1966 we have become quite competent at saving historic carpentry, but we remain relatively incompetent at saving historic context.

It is important to emphasize here that our existing historic preservation system and processes are not rendered less useful as a new and potentially more popular paradigm comes to the fore. It is essential that historic preservation programs—national, state, and local—and the institutions that presently promote and manage them, be protected, supported, and advanced in every way possible. Preservation as we have come to know it can support the concept of heritage, but conceptually and for practical purposes, each of the two approaches must be regarded as distinctive and separate, each supportive of the other.

Growth Management

A related issue is whether the current preservation paradigm has been extended too far, too fast into the field of growth management. It is one thing for the preservation movement to serve as the curator of past traditions and artifacts whose importance or value have stood the test of time. It is quite another for the movement to advocate the past as a model for the future, or even to attempt to influence patterns of future growth.[17] "Williamsburging" Main Street, architecturally speaking, enjoyed wide popularity in the 1940s and 1950s, but the style eventually fell out of favor in the early 1960s, to be replaced with the imitative model of the new suburban shopping center promoted by the Urban Land Institute. Presently the pre–World War I era "Main Street look" is favored. But increasingly in design circles, one hears the criticism, "You've seen one Main Street, you've seen them all."[18] The Seaside, Sun City, and so-called traditional neighborhood developments (TNDs) have already been criticized by many designers. These developments are not new and, in my opinion, are often not even a good imitation of the old. From a design standpoint, the issue is not entirely unrelated to the arguments heard over "facadism" a decade or so ago. And from a political perspective, the antisprawl movement is also the subject of increasing public controversy in many local venues where business and traditional real estate interests hold sway.[19] Thus is raised a larger issue: Where does "historic preservation" end? What are its proper boundaries?

Where Does Preservation End?

The traditional underpinnings of the American preservation movement have broadened markedly since 1980, again led by the National Trust. This expansion of the movement to encompass a wider range of social, economic, diversity, and environmental goals is long overdue and is now generally accepted by the preservation community. For the future, however, we should probably think long and hard about how much of this broadened support should be identified with the preservation movement as such. This is especially true with respect to issues directly related to planning, growth management, sprawl, the new urbanism, and traditional neighborhood development.

We have made great gains in fulfilling our traditional role as preservationists. Local regulatory controls over privately owned cultural resources through historic district and landmark regulations are now widespread, and any lingering doubts in some states about their constitutionality died with *Penn Central* in 1978. An array of federal and state environmental review processes are in place to slow down the harmful impacts that might otherwise be caused by government projects. And a number of federal, state, and local front- and back-door public subsidies for preservation through direct appropriations and tax incentives are prevalent at all levels of government. These gains are closely related in one way or another to programs that have grown from NHPA.

Changing Motives

As long ago as the early 1960s the preservation movement sought to demonstrate its relevance to the quality of urban life in its reaction to the harmful effects of highway building, gentrification, urban redevelopment, and the like. Preservation was promoted as an effective counter to the destruction of central cities. In the mid-1970s, following the Arab oil embargo, many sought to relate preservation to the goal of energy efficiency on the grounds that the reuse of old buildings and materials was more energy-efficient than new construction, and that inner-city preservation could be an effective counter to the problem of exploding suburbs. With the emergence of the civil rights movement in the 1950s and hoping to reduce the stigma of elitism with which preservation had long been associated, the movement embraced the goal of inclusiveness early on. Since approximately 1975, diversity has also come into its own as a preservation imperative.

This new populist interest has led, perhaps not coincidentally, to a celebration of the vernacular. In the 1980s there emerged a special concern for a broader kind of "heritage" preservation and a corresponding need for strong ties to the growing popular goals of tourism, recreation, and economic development. Responding to these changes, the national historic preservation program was administratively relocated for a brief time during the Carter administration to a semi-independent Heritage Conservation and Recreation Service. When the heritage paradigm resurfaced in the 1990s, the National Trust replaced its old logo—visualized since 1949 by a marble column with an American eagle perched on top—with a new one combining natural landscape elements, a town center, buildings, open space, and a new slogan: "Protecting the Irreplaceable."

This broadened view of the field of historic preservation has led the movement to confront issues normally regarded as the province of the planning profession and into the arena of local growth management politics. Many of us are now directly involved as combatants fighting such issues as suburban sprawl, big-box retailing, traffic congestion, the decline of Main Street, and the loss of farmland and open space. In some places we devote as much energy to Smart Growth, the "new urbanism," "sustainability," and antisprawl as we do to the saving of old buildings. Following the lead of the National Trust, preservationists and their partners have moved beyond the advocacy of established programs of neighborhood preservation and housing to confront sprawl and the destruction of the rural countryside.[20]

The impact on traditional downtowns and Main Streets from big-box retailing as practiced by Wal-Mart, K-Mart, CVS, Target, and other "killer category" retail operations has also engaged the attention of the preservation community. Preservationists are concerned about the demolition of buildings that anchor downtown historic districts and the negative effects on small retail businesses that have been the foundation stores of Main Street America for many decades; they are concerned that these operations consume large areas of land and alter the character of suburban and rural areas. But retailing has changed in recent years, and the computerized methods of just-in-time inventory control, low overhead, quick turnover approaches to the sale of a wide variety of consumer goods, pharmaceuticals, and construction materials at significantly reduced prices has opened consumer markets to segments of the population that cannot afford the higher costs associated with more traditional retailing. Low unit profit margins requiring large inventories and the need for huge accumulations of retail goods at one location have reinforced the need of retailers for larger sites on cheaper rural land closer to suburban customers. Indeed, conservatives would say that no business, including one on Main Street, has an inherent right to economic survival. Nevertheless, big-box retailing is indeed a threat to Main Street in much the same sense that the automobile was a threat to the shop selling buggy whips. Discussions of this issue to date have tended to over-simplify a vastly more complex economic and social phenomenon.

Preservationists are concerned about losing good, useful, architecturally appealing central-city buildings. The central city and its older buildings and neighborhoods are clearly important, both to those who live there and to the larger community. But so are the post–World War II suburbs, even those that sprawl; to value one over the other forecloses the opportunity to explore the possibility of achieving a good life for both the city *and* its suburbs.[21] In many respects, the controversy defines a dilemma—often ignored by partisans on both sides—that places us in a clear conflict with the very historic patterns of development that most preservationists would like to preserve. Many of today's National Register historic residential neighborhoods were the sprawling suburbs of yesterday, and to many preservationists the suburban strip development has long been a revered part of the American scene.[22]

Unquestionably, urban and rural environments that preserve some past traditions are better than those that do not. But just as change is a constant in all societies, what kind of change is better and what is worse in a free market society will always be the subject of intense debate.

It is apparent that we must engage simultaneously in inner-city revitalization and better defining the limits of suburbanization. The preservation community needs to recognize that direct, active involvement with issues related to environmental protection, growth management, and land-use planning, though achieving societal ends, also has the potential to seriously jeopardize the identity and effectiveness of the historic preservation movement itself. If the preservation community takes inflexible stands in opposition to big-box retailing and promotes preservation as an either-or alternative to sprawl, it will not only confront powerful and well-organized construction, investment, and real estate interests whose political strength is well established, it will also run the risk of losing the support of an equally powerful (and numerically greater) compromise-minded segment of its customary constituency. On the other hand, if it concentrates on the rehabilitation of older neighborhoods and the landmark buildings such as schools and churches that anchor them, finding acceptable design compromises on the new forms of retailing and on the revitalization of downtowns, demonstrating their benefits to the public, it can make a difference.

But we must be careful not to oversimplify. The growth patterns that presently disturb environmentalists and preservationists alike have emerged from historical patterns that are inextricably interwoven with cultural and historic places that have long been an important focus of the preservation movement. Whether a hangover from the deeply ingrained nineteenth-century notion of Manifest Destiny or the offspring of the General Motors Futurama of the 1939 New York World's Fair, the Great American Dream of a home in the suburbs and a new car in the garage is no less powerful than ever and will remain deeply embedded in American culture for generations to come. Economic, social, and educational stratification among the population as a whole is not going to disappear. Telecommuting, long-distance learning, dot.com shopping, and a deeply felt internal resistance to change on the part of individuals will all have an impact. The events of September 11, 2001, have already generated discussion about the future of central cities.[23] Because these issues involve deeply held values of the preservation community and confront American values and historical patterns of development, they deserve more substantive—and more balanced and disciplined—debate than they have received to date.

Changing Imperatives for Preservation

Beyond question, in the last two decades the American preservation movement has made serious, sustained, and successful efforts to become much more inclusive of human values. Congress has chosen to recognize American Indian and Hawaiian tribal interests in sacred lands and to protect ancestral human tribal remains, hitherto widely regarded as artifacts of scientific interest primarily to archaeologists or paleontologists. Following the lead of the National Trust, the NPS, and many states, initiatives that recognize the diverse contributions to American tradition of ethnic and minority populations are increasing.

Recently, the gay and lesbian community, which preservationists have long quietly acknowledged as active and substantively important participants in the preservation movement—especially in places like Key West, New York, Washington, D.C., New Orleans, Baltimore, and San Francisco—have sought public acknowledgment of their special contribution. Places important to the gay and lesbian movement have been entered in the National Register.[24] The acceptance of diversity and the move beyond a strongly traditional Eurocentric view of preservation is one of the movement's most notable changes in the last two decades. There are now hundreds of National Register properties and many districts with strong ethnic identities. But as time passes and presently obvious ethnic identities are shadowed by the passage of time, the question becomes one of whether the places they inhabit have lost their significance when all that remains is a street pattern and a few old buildings long ago identified as ethnically significant.

By what criteria do we save or preserve these places? Which ones? Who decides? Antoinette Lee has raised important questions beyond even these in Chapter 12: "How much [diversity] will be enough? How many more groups must be studied, documented, and interpreted? . . . The larger question facing the historic preservation field is the long-term effect of this emphasis on diversity. Will it lead to a greater appreciation and acceptance of diverse groups, or will it lead to resentments and alienation? Will these efforts knit the nation together into a coherent whole, or will they lead to the unraveling of national unity?"[25] These are issues that we skip over at our peril as a society.

We can only speculate about the answers. Since the mid-nineteenth century cultural separatism and physical segregation have tended slowly to be replaced by differences related more to class than race, but the advocates of diversity continue to remind us that today's white majority will be reduced to minority status by 2050. However, general principles of human ecology, the accelerating speed with which cultural diffusion is already taking place throughout the world, and the long-term tendency of disparate populations toward cultural, ethnic, and racial homogeneity suggest that the problem may eventually solve itself. For most of us, this is too easy an answer to an immediate and complex problem, and one to which we would take profound and loud objection.

The questions of how to deal with situations in which one historical tradition conflicts with another, or where jurisdictions overlap, and whose history is the more important, have also been raised. Indian tribes, legally recognized as sovereign states, have demanded and received commenting responsibilities and a seat at the Section 106 table regarding sacred places that lie beyond the boundaries of reservations and within the traditional jurisdiction of state governments. With the passage of NAGPRA, controversies over which tribe is to have the ownership of human remains of uncertain origin for burial purposes have already arisen. If in time there are more than 250 tribal preservation offices and 50 state offices, that numerical imbalance alone may inevitably produce conflicts with the states. Whether the preservation movement can indulge the luxury of facing the problem later, when it may be intractable, is highly questionable.

Changing Venues, or Who Can
Do Preservation Best?

Though the effect of the 1966 act was to create an expanded federal responsibility to provide assistance to what traditionally had been primarily a local and state responsibility, there has been a pronounced tendency since 1980 in the opposite direction: to shift responsibility for preservation back down from federal to state and local governments. One reason for that shift has been the result of periodic reductions in federal funding, placing increased fiscal and administrative responsibility on the states. Another has been the resentment still occasionally heard in private conversations in state historic preservation offices about complex and detailed federal program reviews and requirements, referred to by state offices as "bean counting." An additional push in this downward direction occurred with the 1980 NHPA amendments, which created CLGs that continue to lay claim to 10 percent of all federal appropriations to the states. In 1994 an NPS performance review proposed to delegate to the states yet more authority related to National Register nominations and tax act administrative decisions—authority earlier wielded by its regional and Washington offices. Good intentions notwithstanding, some SHPOs and state historic preservation office staff members will privately argue that the NPS continues to micromanage state and local programs.

These periodic shifts in levels of responsibility relate to a larger question: Who should do what in preservation? Or, who can do preservation best? In our society it is axiomatic that the "best" government is the one that is closest to the people. The federal establishment in Washington, D.C., is a long way from most local jurisdictions, occasional district appearances notwithstanding, and federal officials are widely perceived as inaccessible. State governments are closer, but the ordinary citizen's representative on the city council is, in many instances, just a phone call or a block away. As many believe, preservation, like all politics, is local.

Perhaps this is the place to say, parenthetically, that it is time to look beyond government. Our present way of thinking about preservation has evolved largely from the way in which government programs have been conceived and carried out over the years, supplemented by support agencies like the National Trust that have filled many gaps. Presently, however, our preservation policies are, like our national arts policies, fragmented by "discipline, generation, ethnicity, and geography."[26] Is it time for new approaches and new organizations—

larger than and independent from existing institutions—to play a leadership role in dealing with the issues raised so far?

Two Fundamental Elements of Local Preservation

Two aspects of this phenomenon are of special importance. One is the continuing divide between local preservation efforts in the volunteer and nonprofit sectors; the other is the heavy reliance of most local public efforts on the regulation of private property.

There is no easy way to generalize about the work of the volunteer programs carried out by local preservation organizations, except to say that they remain the heart and soul of the preservation movement. A growing number, especially in large metropolitan areas, carry on first-rate educational programs, operate successful revolving funds, have merged low- and middle-income housing goals with those of preservation, and carry considerable political clout. Pittsburgh, Sacramento, and Savannah are excellent models. Hundreds more could be cited.

At the opposite extreme, many local preservation groups, particularly in small towns, still amount to little more than social clubs, focused strongly on such activities as Christmas candlelight and historic trolley tours or the maintenance of a historic house or two and their period furnishings. In terms of programs and accomplishments, most local associations are somewhere in between. National and state preservation programs tend to exist separately from these activities, but if there has been significant improvement in the work of these local groups over the last dozen years, much of the credit goes to the educational programs of a few strong statewides, the National Trust's Statewide Partners program, and some state historic preservation offices, especially through the networks encouraged by the CLG program.

Notwithstanding the growth of CLGs since 1980, of which there are now almost 1,300, and the widespread success of Main Street programs, most medium-size, nonmetropolitan local governments continue to assign a low priority to historic preservation as one of the many programs for which they are responsible. Typically, preservation remains on a level with the arts and similar programs. It thus tends to be isolated not only from day-to-day operations in city hall, but isolated as well from planning and growth management operations of a fiscal and regulatory nature. Though a growing number of states specifically authorize the inclusion of a preservation element in the local comprehensive plan, only a few actually require one. And current wisdom notwithstanding, an even smaller number of states actually require a binding connection between the comprehensive plan and the zoning ordinance, which is the ultimate arbiter of location, density, and land-use patterns. Public buildings such as schools, post offices, and many other facilities continue to fall victim to parking lots, new offices, and other forms of private development.[27] Thus, the burden of proof that something is worth preserving is still carried by the preservation-conservation community, and the task of "making preservation real" at the local level is still carried by the volunteer and local nonprofit sector.

Local Governments and Regulation

Local citizens play an extremely important role in one aspect of preservation at the local government level, however, and that is in the regulatory area involving the administration of historic district and landmarks ordinances. In concept and procedure, we have not moved much beyond the first Charleston ordinance of 1931, the thrust of which is to require, under the cover of the states' police power, a special permit for the construction, change, demolition, or moving of buildings. As Thompson Mayes points out in Chapter 5, we have made tremendous progress in the courts and state legislatures, and the number of regulatory commissions, now numbering approximately 2,500, has approximately doubled each decade since the first ordinance was passed in 1931. The regulation of landscape elements is beginning to take hold, but indefinite delays of demolition and demolition by neglect and the control of interiors are still approached timidly, if at all, by most local jurisdictions.

For better or worse, the American political and legal tradition assigns this function through legislation to local boards and commissions that typically must carry out their duties in a quasi-judicial fashion in evidentiary hearings, whether they understand the implications of this or not. These boards and commissions must conduct themselves much like a court, and this requires a level of procedural conduct and ritual of which relatively few lay bodies are capable. Though the performance of these boards and commissions is clearly better than a decade or so ago, thanks to the training programs and technical publications of the National Alliance of Preservation Commissions, the National Trust, some statewides, and SHPOs, there is still much room for improvement.[28]

Regulatory approaches presently available (as well as the environmental review processes of national and state governments) deal poorly with several serious problems. One problem that demands special attention is how we are to go about refocusing the attention of local regulatory commissions on the *tout ensemble*. Most local commissions deal reasonably well with the preservation of architectural character and detailing, but poorly with issues related to a building's relationship to its larger environment. Closely related to this is the distressing tendency of many local commissions to use some combination of the National Register criteria and the Secretary's Standards as design guidelines, rather than those specially derived from the overall character of each local district.

An equally difficult but little discussed aspect of this problem is that such boards are essentially reactive. Except for the few that operate—or have close ties to—revolving funds, the authority of the commission does not come into play until the individual property owner wishes to do something. How to reposition our preservation regulatory bodies so they can more easily play a more proactive role in dealing with larger environmental design issues remains an unsolved problem.

How Do We Prepare for the Next Twenty Years?

A major step toward fulfilling the goals of the 1966 legislation is to recognize that times have changed and to accept that the preservation movement must change with them. It is perhaps time to question what we are doing, why we are doing it, and whether our current approach is the most effective use of limited resources. Is it time for a new paradigm for the preservation movement? If so, it is important to recognize that if, or as, the paradigm changes, so will the list of our supporters (and detractors) and the political context in which we work. Institutional interests and players will move up, others will move down. The movement will gain some new supporters and inevitably lose some old ones.

It seems beyond question that the future direction of the American preservation movement will depend to some extent on the emergent physical form of our cities and towns. Nonprofits and the private sector have already had a significant impact on the physical form of central cities through large-scale projects, such as Lowertown in St. Paul, Minnesota; the Inner Harbor in Baltimore, Maryland; the reuse of economically obsolete mill villages in Edenton, Burlington, and Gastonia in North Carolina; and many other places. The housing market for inner-city living among certain segments of the population, as well as a continuing strong consumer demand for suburban housing, shows few

signs of significant change. The preservation movement, as such, will doubtless have some impact on established patterns of housing preference. But the
centrifugal forces that have flung cities outward during the last one hundred
years are no less powerful than ever. In this age of exploding computer and remote communications technology, and an economy based largely on rubber-
tired transportation, it is hard to imagine that countervailing economic or technological centripetal forces will pull us back to a more compact, physical form
of development.[29]

Where Do We Stand?

The 1966 legislation has served us well. In all, more than a million buildings
have come under its protective wing, and billions of dollars have been spent on
various kinds of preservation work. This does not begin to include the private
sector activities of the many individuals and families who do not know the difference between the National Trust and the National Register, or who even
think in terms of "official" preservation programs or policies when they begin
to fix up an old house or undertake a loft conversion. Preservation in America
has become a major industry, thanks to public television's *This Old House* and
the emergence of the do-it-yourself industry supported by the likes of Home
Depot, The Paint Doctor, and similar private sector support businesses and organizations. The annual Restoration and Renovation Conference has become a
major event. Many homeowners who are fixing up an older residence or retrofitting an old barn would probably be startled to learn that they are engaged in
something called "historic preservation"—whether or not the result complies
with the Secretary's Standards.

For all its success, however, historic preservation is not yet regarded as a
mainstream public priority. It remains badly underfunded at all levels of government, and the administrative placement of the national program in the federal government leaves much to be desired. The growth of the preservation
movement has left us with a number of challenges that must be addressed.

Public Support

Public support and, in turn, political support will in the long run come only in
response to more energetic and sustained efforts at public education. Conser-

vation values can be taught as early as kindergarten and in one form or another must be continued throughout the school years. Recognizing this fact, heritage educational programs, largely through state and local nonprofit organizations, have proliferated in recent years.[30] The NPS has recently developed a "Teaching with Historic Places" program and, hoping to develop a useful national model, has begun a new local project in Louisiana through the National Center for Preservation Training and Technology. There is, however, no reliable data on the effectiveness of the various state and local preservation educational programs. Although the National Trust and many statewides have produced excellent materials for both in- and out-of-school use, there are literally hundreds of public interest claimants for curricular time and competition for classroom time is stiff. As most of the educational materials that cross our desks illustrate, we continue to address much of our effort to other preservationists —a sort of preaching to the choir. Preservation should be ready for prime-time, network television, but it is never to be found there.

A preservationist friend recently posed this question: "How can preservation become part of a popular cause that is ingrained in every American?" My response was that it is probably unrealistic, or even naive, to think that preservation in its present posture can or needs to be a popular cause ingrained in every American. The question we ought to be asking ourselves is whether or not the relatively small minority of people who do care about preservation can become more effective. For the most part we are still playing defense, a posture in which few games are won. The question is, can we get ahead of the curve in terms of political effectiveness, with a clear focus on specifically defined objectives, and thereby be poised to make strategically and politically opportunistic moves ahead of the opposition forces? It is not necessary to have "every American" on board. In all decision-making venues—Congress, state legislatures, local councils, the courts, even preservation commissions—a plurality of one vote provides a sufficient majority to carry the day.

Our most visible efforts tend to be sporadic and crisis-oriented. The "most endangered" lists published annually by the National Trust, statewides, and local groups are highly effective. But to some they come across as reactive, eleventh-hour pleas for help; to others, by emphasizing the most endangered, they mislead them into thinking that those not listed are unimportant. Anniversaries like the American Revolution Bicentennial, the Millennium Year, and Preservation Week are episodic or one-time events.[31] They speak to preservationists, but they leave little in the way of a lasting impression on the larger public.[32] The joinder of many preservation interests in a coordinated educational effort on a continuing basis, focused on the larger preservation ethic rather than on individual organizations or threatened resources, might be a step in the right direction. Programs tailored and targeted to commercial, prime-time TV viewers would reach a much larger audience than a three-hour special on public television.[33] Here, once again, is an area where larger institutional backing that reaches beyond existing preservation organizations could be of immeasurable help.

Expanding the Boundaries: Heritage Areas

Looking at preservation from a consumer standpoint, we proposed earlier that public interest in preservation might be enhanced by concentrating on results such as "comfort and stability" rather than the preservation artifacts. Perhaps the heritage area programs, under consideration by Congress and a growing number of states, along with the rivers and trails programs of the NPS, are as well or better positioned to build public enthusiasm than traditional historic preservation programs.[34] Although history and architecture will always be important to the preservation of place, many other values are involved. Indeed, "historic preservation" may no longer be a useful phrase to describe what we do.

It is useful to recollect that the National Register as incorporated into the NHPA in 1966 was a National Register of Historic *Places*. A more clearly articulated place-based theory of preservation may be as appropriate for the new century as the focus on architecture and history was forty years ago.[35]

Are there disadvantages to such a new approach? Of course. Few governments, especially local governments, are intellectually or professionally ready to deal politically or administratively with such concepts as "stability" and "accustomed comfort." Even fewer are prepared to cooperate in the cross-jurisdictional boundaries that are inevitably involved with heritage areas. New professional and academic interests will have to be integrated as partners into a new way of thinking about preservation—a daunting task given the likely response of entrenched academic and professional interests. Inevitably, preservation and conservation efforts based on the notion of heritage areas will be drawn into politically difficult planning controversies. Worse, established communities—bureaucratic, nonprofit, and others—will see their authority and prestige diluted or diminished. Sharing does not come easily.

It is perhaps at the local level that place theory, with its emphasis on a broad range of unfamiliar, more subjective and fragile associative values, will find it most difficult to advance to "design guidelines" capable of interpretation by lay commissions or governmental bodies. Commissions will have to feel as comfortable with larger urban and rural development patterns and design concepts as they now (in theory, at least) do with history and architecture. Their outlook and capabilities will have to be much broader, both in the composition of their membership and in the way they think. This will, in turn, call for new thinking by their state and national support agencies. Their responsibilities will extend well beyond the regulatory role of today's preservation commissions to provide design, advisory, and coordinating services, as well as planning counsel. New players in the design and allied arts—landscape architects, urban geographers, conservationists, environmental psychologists, economists, and others—will be required. The preservation of place and heritage will require adventurous thinking about which professions are needed to help manage the process, while at the same time providing a better balance of from-the-bottom-up citizen input.

To be effective, heritage areas will need to be integrated into the day-to-day activities of and closely associated with the private and nonprofit sectors. One model for such an agency may be the British local planning authorities that have responsibility for advising and implementing the conservation area schemes called for by Britain's 1961 Conservation Area legislation. The implementation of the conservation of "place" as a new associative value will also call for entirely new, less regulatory approaches to controlling what gets built and what does not. One senses that we are inevitably moving in this direction.[36]

The Future of a National Program

If it is time to move beyond the 1966 legislation, then we must explore how this might be done and what its impact might be on the present system to which we are by now habituated. The goals outlined in *With Heritage So Rich* were right for their time and have been implemented with great success. It is now almost four decades later, however, and the philosophical context of preservation is much changed and changing. It is a different time.

In Chapter 2, John Fowler projects a rather neutral prospect for the growth of federal programs in historic preservation. This may be inevitable in view of the political and administrative context of the program, but perhaps it also provides an opportunity. Given the present emphasis on the celebration of many diverse cultures—racial, ethnic, and tribal—and the variety of specialized preservation interests described in earlier chapters, plus the sheer geographic size of the United States, perhaps it will be the states, tribes, and local governments that become the principal sources of innovation in preservation thinking. If two heads are better than one, as the saying goes, then perhaps 50-plus state governments, 250 tribes, and 20,000 local governments are more likely to devise useful, innovative approaches to local conservation and preservation than one in a national capital many miles distant.

This suggests a relative increase in federal support for state programs, but less federal involvement in defining their content and administration. There may be an increasingly important role for the expanded or supplemental use by states of state registers. If, as many argue, real preservation happens at the local level, the argument for unrestricted block grant funding at both state and local government levels is greatly strengthened.

Building on Existing Programs

As we have said, if the preservation movement is to survive and grow, existing programs, specifically the National Register program, must be protected. Though the criteria for the entry of properties, districts, objects, and sites are fairly specific, as are the exceptions—and the exceptions to the exceptions—they are reasonably broad and inclusive. But the nomination process itself can be eccentric in application. There are several problem areas that must be monitored.

For example, according to the criteria, buildings that have been moved from their original sites are ineligible for the National Register. But the issue of how far they can be moved and retain the quality of integrity may be differently interpreted by National Register Advisory Committees, SHPOs, and the NPS. A collateral issue is the siting of moved buildings, which is supposed to be sensitive to the siting at a new location. These are judgment calls, often subjective, and often made by individuals who have little or no experience or training in site design or landscape assessment, which are highly specialized fields.

It is also not unusual for there to be a rush to judgment on the grounds that entry onto the National Register will save a building from a proposed highway, or that favorable tax incentives make it a prime candidate for preservation, or that it is under option by a known preservationist who has sufficient resources to complete an outstanding building restoration. Experience tells us that state or local political pressures are also sometimes a factor in advancing a nomination. These factors are not properly National Register criteria, but in a real-world setting, such conduct is as understandable as it is inevitable. The danger is that failure to play by the rules at every level of the nomination process will in time undercut confidence in it.

A second problem in protecting the integrity of the National Register has been the failure to obtain from Congress a stable and predictable level of financial support for the larger program. As the demand for Section 106 and related environmental reviews grows at an exponential rate, in addition to the demand for staff review and monitoring of federal and state tax credit projects, the number of qualified state staff diminishes as the result of budget cuts at the very time the workload increases. Inevitably a backload of applications will develop, or the process will become so badly administered that it will lose credibility. Both possibilities have the potential for an unwelcome political backlash against preservation.

There remains in the minds of some the unresolved question whether properties of local significance should be a concern of the national government. One important underlying rationale for expanding the National Register through the 1966 act was the widely accepted concept that the nation's history is nothing more or less than the sum of its state and local history. For the purposes of environmental review of federal projects and the receipt of federal income tax benefits, the inclusion of properties of local significance is essential. But whether uniform national criteria for designation should be used for state register purposes or local regulatory actions, as is often now the case, is highly debatable. Except for federal actions involving Section 106 or NEPA, some practitioners still feel that locally significant properties are more properly recognized and dealt with at the state or local level, and by the nonprofit and private sectors, than by the federal government. A necessary distinction, not often made, is the difference between a mechanism for determining what makes properties significant, to whom, and why, and decisions about whether or not they will be preserved.

When this chapter was first written, there was hope that the Historic Preservation Fund might eventually be fully funded and that the need for annual appropriations by Congress could be avoided. But after a mild economic downturn and after the events of September 11, 2001, the outcome of recurrent efforts to find a source of permanent, reliable funding is still very much in question. Many state historic preservation office positions are federally funded and, as a result of the ups and downs of the annual appropriations process, now have fewer staff members than in 1980 despite the added responsibilities thrust on them since then.

A third problem is an innate tendency toward turf protection by those who presently administer or participate in the administration of the American preservation system. At the beginning, the program was dominated by historians, architectural historians, and archaeologists. Academic historians looked down on it, although through the years the profession has assumed a coequal if not a dominant place in the program, largely as the result of a continuing drive of the national program leadership to build coherent historic themes into all National Register nominations. Given the much broadened content of the program since 1980, it seems reasonable that a more inclusive list of professional and academic specialties would be qualified to participate in it directly.

A fourth, final, and very serious problem is the organizational position of the national preservation program within the Department of the Interior. It should be independent of, and equal to, the National Park Service itself, which still remains its administrative "parent," often indifferent to historic preservation. A truly national program of consequence would be represented at the assistant secretary level and not tied administratively to NPS interests, which are not always friendly to it.

For a brief time during the Carter administration a measure of program independence from the NPS was established through an administratively created Heritage Conservation and Recreation Service. But that experiment put preservation in bed with strongly entrenched, more powerful public recreation interests and did not provide a substantive basis for preservation. The experiment was unsuccessful from a leadership standpoint, and President Ronald Reagan restored the original organizational scheme, placing the preservation program back under the NPS where it remains today. Administratively it exists within a "cultural resources partnership," but many argue that preservation should stand on its own feet within the Department of the Interior.

Administrative structures can work for or against preservation. The ambiguous position of preservation, which remains far below the secretarial level, is somewhat analogous to the declining prestige of preservation at the state level following the wave of state government reorganizations in the early 1970s. The purpose of these reorganizations—the earlier equivalent of today's "reinventing government"—was to reduce the number of independent agencies reporting to the governor and to place them under a more direct line of political control. After reorganization, historic and preservation interests that had formerly enjoyed direct access to the governor found themselves administratively aligned with other state agencies such as state libraries, art museums, symphonies, travel, recreation, tourism interests, and natural resources. State preservation programs came under the thumb of politically appointed secretaries whose primary interests might or might not have anything to do with preservation.

The National Register has been reasonably accommodating in accepting new values such as post–World War II suburbs, designed and vernacular landscapes, more recent contemporary buildings, commercial and industrial archaeology—but sometimes slower to act than might be desirable. One alternative would be to fund the use of state registers based on criteria specifically appropriate to and defined by a given state. However, that blurs the relationship of state and local history to the larger history of the nation and dilutes the value given to these resources as part of the whole. Such an approach also poses the problem of overlap, duplication, and confusion among property owners who face varying consequences when individual properties are subject to more than one designation. Even the basic distinctions between National Register historic districts and local zoning historic districts are more than most property owners can reasonably comprehend.

It is not a question of whether a national program should be dominated by Washington, D.C., but rather how the federal leadership and responsibility for maintaining standards and criteria will be exerted. Day-to-day irritations and program disruptions follow frequent changes in the national organization chart, personal conflict among individuals in a given office, conflicts between Washington and its regional offices, and, to a lesser extent, a generation gap between conservative, old-line preservationists and a more liberal and experimentally minded younger generation.

The feeling of most SHPOs is that without the federal program, state legislatures would cut them adrift financially; they thus prefer to operate within the shell of a federal program. The question then becomes whether the states should be restricted or limited by the directives of a federally funded, uniform national program or whether they should be free agents to develop programs specifically targeted to local or indigenous state and local heritage resources. At the local level, it is no secret that occasionally CLG programs barely or only nominally meet the federal standards required to qualify for 10 percent pass-through federal funding, but they continue in operation either because of the flexibility and sympathy of SHPOs for the special role of local programs or because of the potential embarrassment and political problems that would result from decertifying them. A few local governments feel that given the paperwork involved with becoming certified and maintaining that status, the 10 percent funding is simply not worth the trouble. Most, however, find their place in a state preservation network with special access to state programs to be of sufficient benefit.

Given our governmental structure, the problem then is how to provide incentives and encouragement for the state and local governments to do preservation their way, while at the same time maintaining the integrity of the National Register programs. There is also a reverse issue resulting in an unfortunate tendency for state and local governments to play follow the leader and use national guidelines and standards in local situations for which they are inappropriate or of little use. It is not unusual to see National Register criteria used for the designation of local landmarks or the establishment of local zoning historic districts. But these standards are often unsuitable for the designation of districts or for the review of permits within locally designated historic districts. This is especially true with respect to the larger environmental context, which is a central purpose of local regulation, but for which the national criteria are of little or no use.[37]

This is *not* to suggest that funding for the federal program and the National Register, as the framework of an established national program, should be reduced. Though the states may sometimes chafe under federal procedures, they also welcome the protective framework of the national program. However, given the long-standing tendency of federal program administrators to tell state, local, and tribal governments what to do and how to do it, coupled with the dominance of federal programs (and, in turn, state programs) by a chosen few "acceptable" professions, it is not unreasonable to believe that fresh thinking about the future boundaries of what we now call preservation might more readily come at state, local, and tribal government levels.

As the sovereign units of government in our federal system, states already inherently possess all the needed tools for preservation. Most states have "little NEPAs" and state equivalents of Section 106 for environmental review. They have broad discretion to provide financial incentives through front-door, direct appropriations for state and local programs, and in increasing numbers they are providing state or local back-door financial support for preservation through state and local property and income taxes.

Even more important, the states hold the ultimate key to protecting cultural or place-based resources: the power to regulate private property through their retained police power. As Thompson Mayes notes in Chapter 5, the U.S. Supreme Court has recently shown an increasing tendency to look to the states for the resolution of land-use disputes, and each state has its own constitutional equivalents regarding religious freedom, Due Process, and Equal Protection.

None of this speculation diminishes the role of the National Trust, Preservation Action, or the National Conference of State Historic Preservation Officers. It does perhaps suggest somewhat greater emphasis on resources devoted to the Trust's regional offices, and it may strengthen the hand of the Trust's state-based Board of Advisers and its statewide partners in devising and advising on program parameters. Preservation Action and the National Trust will always be needed to lobby Congress on matters of national importance, and the role of nonprofit statewides, as political players at state and local levels, will in some cases be greatly increased. Preservation, as has been noted in several chapters, is very much a political game. The role of NCSHPO, if it can successfully advocate for local governments as well as it does for states themselves, becomes ever more important. The National Alliance of Preservation Commissions, which serves local interests almost exclusively, will require vastly increased resources for a vastly increased presence. Its training "camps" for local preservation commissions have already proven themselves many times over.

Thinking about the Future

Among many questions that remain are those of a new paradigm for preservation and the need to broaden its associative values. Others include preservation's relationship to the environmental movement and its organization at national, state, and local levels. Do we need to reconsider the level at which properties of local significance can be dealt with more creatively and flexibly? Should there be an attempt to raise historic preservation to a higher level of public consciousness and if so, how? What is preservation's value to and place in contemporary life? If such values as "accustomed comfort" and "stability" are goals that have meaning to a broader public whose support we need to attract, how do we define them in ways that are administratively useful and usable in legal, administrative, and fiscal terms? Where, how, and to what extent can we better merge our interests with those concerned with the natural environment and the intangible cultural heritage?

Unfortunately, there is presently no single forum within the preservation community, entirely free from the weight of its own institutional mission, able to undertake the broader, balanced assessment of larger issues that transcend the boundaries of the historic preservation movement as we have come to know it. How do we break out—indeed, reach out—to form the kinds of partnerships and build the enduring, respected political and economic strength so desperately needed in and by a rapidly changing society? Like it or not, recognized or not, we are an essential component of the American search for the "good life." How do we put aside narrow institutional and organizational interests to consider new strategies and goals appropriate to a new age of explosive growth for which we are presently ill prepared? What is needed goes far beyond a national conference or an additional ad hoc coordinating committee.

It is impossible to overstate the boost to the American preservation movement provided by the 1966 act. It has been wildly successful even beyond the imagining of its original sponsors. That we have come this far in little more than three decades is difficult for older preservationists to comprehend. But it is also difficult to predict what lies ahead for preservation in political venues. In many respects, the burden of proof still lies on those of us who would preserve anything, and we continue to lose important resources every day. Many of our most important current legislative initiatives remain unfulfilled as of this writing, and, indeed, most of these efforts are still defensive rather than offensive in nature. "Bigger is better" and "progress" still prevail as a national ethic.

In facing the future, our problem is as much internal as it is external. We are still confronted by major issues about the changing nature of the preservation movement itself, the rapid growth of specialized preservation professionals and institutions, demographic change, the uncertain direction of future urban development and suburban settlement—to say nothing of the technological revolution and the ultimate consequences of the environmental movement.

An emerging issue of similar importance is how we define ourselves. Much of what we are has been serendipitous, the result of a historical accretion of traditional ways of thinking about our mission—doing more of the same, as it were. Increasingly, there is a need to accommodate—perhaps "assimilate" would be a better word—the growing number of special interests and organizations mentioned earlier that cluster around and later join together with the established preservation community to fight a common enemy. In many venues we are viewed by much of the world as a club of romantics locked into an old building mentality. In others, we are increasingly perceived as impractical environmental partisans who are dangerously close to wanting to "save everything." Regardless of which view prevails, we bear a burden of proof that is unreasonably heavy.

Perhaps our greatest need is for some mechanism or procedure by which the preservation movement in America can look more deliberately and objectively at itself and the larger world that surrounds its work—a process by which an increasingly broad variety of preservation and conservation-related interests can come together and seek agreement among themselves regarding who fits where. Given that preservation and preservation support organizations continue to grow to accommodate an increasingly broader ranges of interests, clarity of purpose and message can only help in political venues and public educational efforts.

"Historic" preservation is perceived by many as no longer adequately descriptive of what we do and who we are. What we are trying to preserve, and for whom, is increasingly the subject of conferences and publications in which new voices are heard. Place theory has become important not only among an increasing number of traditional preservationists, but also among those concerned with the protection of intangible cultural heritage and with many in the design professions. Roles are changing. Some professional interests are uncertain of their place in the larger scheme of things. Historical archaeologists specially concerned with building preservation seem clearly to be part of the preservation movement. But other branches of that field are uncertain whether or not they are really part of it, or whether they wish even to be associated with it. Indeed, some preservationists feel that archaeology, now having its own base of fiscal, public, and political support and the field known as "cultural resource management," should go its own independent way. Those especially concerned with intangible cultural resources are clearly part of a larger heritage preservation effort, but their relationship to the historic preservation movement is uncertain and bureaucratically separate. Those concerned with diversity and the preservation of racial and ethnic identity have begun to play a much more important role in both the preservation and conservation worlds, but the future of this aspect of the field is unclear.

What *is* clear is that as the boundaries of the preservation field expand and become more inclusive, they also become fuzzier—professionally, institutionally, and intellectually—and in the public mind the movement begins to take on a "save everything" mentality. As it embraces what is called "Smart Growth," the boundaries between preservation and environmental planning also become less well defined. "Protecting the Irreplaceable" is without question a noble goal, and the National Trust is to be commended for moving so energetically and enthusiastically beyond the earlier conceptual boundaries of the preservation movement. However, without a clear, guiding statement of policy in the form of a commonly understood, carefully articulated, and widely agreed-upon philosophy that identifies just what is irreplaceable, the movement begins to fragment and to dissolve into a loose coalition of sometimes mutually reinforcing, but sometimes competing or conflicting, special interests.

An example is the clear and unyielding difference of values between those concerned with preservation of the built and natural environments, even within the same environmental institution, as Charles Roe (Chapter 7) and the Kellers (Chapter 6) have observed. At this writing, important National Register buildings on Cumberland Island in Georgia, presumably prized and certified by the traditional historic preservation community, are succumbing to a contrary philosophy propounded by wilderness interests also domiciled within and beyond the Department of the Interior that all traces of human occupation and use should be removed from the island and that it should in time revert to a "natural," wilderness state. The buildings must go. Examples of such conflict, even within the same federal agency, are legion and may be expected to appear with increasing frequency as the boundaries of the preservation-conservation movement are shifted outward. By the same token, it is entirely reasonable that a Native American cultural tradition that relies on the hunting of whales for both cultural and economic reasons should be privileged to do so; it is also entirely reasonable that others with an equal claim to environmental betterment should oppose the killing of whales.

The motivations for historic preservation, as we presently define it, are as wide as the human imagination. An important aspect of the American cultural tradition is the ease, speed, and enthusiasm with which special interests are organized—in preservation as well as other fields of endeavor. Americans have always been "joiners." The problem with such a fragmentation of interests is an old one: How many special interests and organizations, each with a stake in obtaining and hanging on to needed resources and political support, can stand under the same umbrella and stay dry?

The heart of the problem has been our failure or inability to create an independent institution that can look at larger, long-term issues in a critical, disciplined way. We need both the will and a mechanism by which the preservation movement can catch its breath, step back, and take a broader look at itself, in the end producing a document—perhaps in the nature of a charter—that outlines or defines who we are and the content and boundaries of the movement to which we subscribe.

One senses that we are on the verge of trying to be too many things to too many constituencies, and that our purpose needs to be more deliberately and precisely drawn. In our present situation, long-standing National Register criteria and the Secretary's Standards, while helpful in this respect, are at the same time too narrowly drawn in others. A document more closely related to the UNESCO declarations described earlier could perhaps more accurately say what we are truly about. But where do values like "accustomed comfort," "livability," and "local identity" fit in? The authors of Chapter 4, Linda Cofresi and Rosetta Radtke, have asserted that the public does not support preservation as it should because it does not see itself getting what it needs from it. Would embracing "comfort, livability, and local identity," perhaps factored in through heritage area programs, local conservation districts, or some other means, make a difference in this respect?

We need to create an institutional mechanism, perhaps in the form of a think tank or foundation, that can look at these issues without the blinders or the baggage of their own institutional interests—whether we are talking about the NPS, the National Trust, the Advisory Council; specialized organizations such as NCSHPO, NCPE, APT, SAH, TPOS, and statewide nonprofits; or the professional interests of public historians, architectural historians, architects, landscape architects and historians, planners, lawyers, anthropologists, ethnologists, and many others. Somehow we need to create an institution that can "rise above it all" and look at larger, long-term issues in imaginative and constructive ways. Above all, it must be a bottom-up, consumer-oriented structure rather than a top-down aggregation of national organizational interests. Otherwise, we will continue to talk to ourselves rather than engaging a world that needs us.

There is presently no single institution or publication that can deal with these larger issues. The National Trust's *Forum Journal* and the National Park Service's *CRM*, the best and most comprehensive of preservation journals, mostly deal with highly specialized or technical issues. We have had some success over the years in addressing some of these larger issues with the Trust's Williamsburg seminars in 1963, 1968, and 1988; with 1966-based "anniversary" celebrations in 1976 and 1986; and with such annual policy-oriented meetings as the Trust's recent conferences in San Francisco and Charleston. But these attempts at defining a long-term future tend to have little immediate or direct impact on institutional change.[38]

On occasion, individual organizations can deal effectively with larger issues. The late 1990s seminars on preservation values, sponsored by the National Council on Preservation Education, and the 2000 DOT conference on integrity are excellent examples of "big thinking."[39] But for the most part, helpful as they are in presenting and debating issues, the results of these meetings and celebrations tend to remain on library shelves as temporal catalogs or lists of problems, rather than blueprints or road maps or useful solutions to problems. As instruments for defining and providing incentives for institutional change, they are less than useful. These efforts may be the best we can do as a movement, but one hopes for more.

What Is to Be Done?

The preservation movement in the United States, for all its success, is growing in an ad hoc, arguably disorderly, manner. Internal and external institutional frictions persist, notwithstanding occasional attempts to reinvent and smooth out the way we do things. There is excellent coordination and cooperation on some issues, such as lobbying and program coordination, but there is some real friction between and among levels of government, and between the controllers of the purse and those who receive the funds. If we are to speak in political forums with a stronger voice, there must not only be stronger public support, but also a more unified and consistent vision of where we are going and what we stand for. The Secretary's Standards and the National Register criteria are no longer enough.

Interestingly, the solution may lie in fields having nothing to do with preservation. Perhaps the most useful approach—beyond suggestions for yet one more Williamsburg or Pocantico conference of high-level preservationists, or even yet another volume of collected essays—is to be found in the thoughts of George F. Kennan, America's most distinguished twentieth-century foreign service officer. His book, *Around the Cragged Hill: A Personal and Political Philosophy* (1993), about the difficulty of dealing with comparable problems related to defining America's foreign policy during the early years of the Cold War, holds some good advice for the preservation movement.[40] The issues he encountered in attempting to develop coherent, long-term foreign policy goals were very similar to those facing the preservation movement today. Kennan proposed a new kind of exploratory policy commission:

> To have any serious effect on . . . policy and action, a commission giving this sort of outside advisory assistance . . . would have to have a number of characteristics that the *ad hoc* commission simply does not have: among them, *greater permanency, a wider spectrum of responsibility, an ability to relate recommendations in one field to those in another, and, above all, a general prestige that would lend to its findings and conclusions weight and endurance in the public eye and would compel serious attention to them on the part of governmental policy makers, executive and legislative* (italics added).[41]

Kennan goes beyond this to elaborate criteria for forming such a commission and making it operational. One of the principles he proposes applies with special force to the preservation movement:

"Membership would have to be drawn exclusively from persons outside the active establishment . . . devoid not only of any existing official position but of any current political connections or ambitions. The commission would have to be purely advisory to established institutions and not be empowered to substitute its judgment. . . ." It would require the sanction of the preservation community and be established by it, and membership would have to be by higher authority to give it the authority and prestige it would need. "It would need, as an institution, a permanent financial base in the nature of an endowment. Finally, it would occupy itself only with long-term questions of . . . [preservation] policy or philosophy, restricting itself to the identification of principles and directions of action, and refraining at all times from any involvement with the implementations of any suggestions it offered."

It is tempting to add that such a group of individuals should have, essentially, a local orientation (rather than a state or national one) and be concerned primarily with the impact of heritage preservation on the consumers of its programs rather than the purveyors of it.

It is easy to dismiss such a suggestion as "pie in the sky," but such is the degree of fragmentation, specialization, and diversity of narrow interests in the preservation and conservation movements in the year 2002 that an independent, outside critique by disinterested individuals free to take a long-term look at where we are and where we are headed would be useful. In 1966 the need was to put a national program in place. Now the need is less for legislation than it is for imagination, initiative, coordination, and a general coming together. No single existing organization is capable of doing this free from the limitations of its own self-interest and its place in the existing order. One would think that the academic component of the preservation movement, with its traditional freedom from the hustle-bustle of daily involvement, could accomplish this, but academic remoteness from the real world is also a problem.[42] It is especially important to note that academic communities carry their own special brand of partisan baggage.

Much of preservation's future depends on how we wish to be known. There is nothing wrong with joining the many planner-environmentalists opposed to sprawl, big-box retailing, or promoting environmental sustainability. Some of the outcomes advanced by this recent movement will be socially, economically, and aesthetically beneficent for preservation. However, the more closely identified we become with these and related trends, the closer we come to losing our identity as the keepers of cultural tradition. I believe that history "is," and that not only one day will the lifeways and artifacts of today be seen as part of a larger tradition worth saving, but that they already have a valued place in securing our present life environment. The greatest risk, over time, is that the preservation community will, in using past themes to create future environments, meet itself coming and going, and that we will be too quick to judge that which is worthy of preservation and that which is not—or, worse, that we will succumb to historical fakery. There must be an acceptance of change, for without change there is no such thing as tradition to preserve.

Notes

Prologue

1. From Robert E. Stipe, "Why Preserve?," *Preservation News* (July 1972). Interestingly, the closing paragraphs were severely criticized by a number of my colleagues, who saw in them "a radical idea," "way ahead of its time," that "might drag preservation into the controversial field of urban planning." However, some of these words later found their way into Justice Brennan's majority opinion in *Penn Central Transportation Co. et al. v. New York City Co. et al.* and were widely seen as reinforcing the philosophical underpinnings of the majority opinion. See Chapter 5.

Introduction

1. Brown Morton III, "What Do We Preserve and Why?," in *The American Mosaic: Preserving a Nation's Heritage*, ed. Robert E. Stipe and Antoinette J. Lee (Washington, D.C.: US/ICOMOS, 1987), 150.

2. Ibid., 152.

3. Ibid.

4. William J. Murtagh, *Keeping Time: The History and Theory of Preservation in America* (New York: Sterling Publishing Co., 1988), 32–33.

5. Morton, "What Do We Preserve?," 155–56.

6. George B. Tobey Jr., *A History of Landscape Architecture: The Relationship of People to Environment* (New York: American Elsevier Publishing Co., 1973), 162–65.

7. Morton, "What Do We Preserve?," 156.

8. Michael Holleran, *Boston's "Changeful Times": Origins of Preservation and Planning in America* (Baltimore: Johns Hopkins University Press, 1998), 216–17.

9. David R. Goldfield and Blaine A. Brownell, *Urban America: A History* (Boston: Houghton Mifflin, 1990), 275–76.

10. Murtagh, *Keeping Time*, 53.

11. Ibid.

12. Ibid., 57.

13. Charles B. Hosmer Jr., *Preservation Comes of Age: From Williamsburg to the National Trust, 1926–1949*, 2 vols. (Charlottesville: University Press of Virginia, for Preservation Press, 1981), 1:19–22.

14. Ibid., 1:243, 296.

15. Cheryl Hargrave, "Authenticity: The Essential Ingredient for Heritage Tourism," *Forum Journal* 13 (Summer 1999): 39.

16. Ibid., 15, 25–26.

17. Norman Tyler, *Historic Preservation* (New York: Norton, 2000), 38.

18. Hosmer, *Preservation Comes of Age*, 75.

19. Walter Muir Whitehill, "Promoted to Glory," in *WHSR*, 43.

20. J. Myrick Howard, "Where the Action Is: Preservation and Local Governments," in Stipe and Lee, *The American Mosaic*, 115.

21. Eugenie Ladner Birch and Douglass Roby, "The Planner and the Preservationist: An Uneasy Alliance," in *Controversies in Preservation: Understanding the Preservation Movement Today*, ed. Pamela Thurber (Washington, D.C.: NTHP, 1985), 39.

22. *The New Encyclopedia Britannica*, 15th ed., s.v. "Great Depression."

23. Tyler, *Historic Preservation*, 40–41.

24. Murtagh, *Keeping Time*, 55–57.

25. Hosmer, *Preservation Comes of Age*, 825.

26. Elizabeth D. Mulloy, *The History of the National Trust for Historic Preservation, 1963–1973* (Washington, D.C.: Preservation Press, 1976), 10–11.

27. Ibid., 19–20.

28. ACHP, *Twenty Years of the National Historic Preservation Act: Report to the President and the Congress of the United States, 1986* (Washington, D.C.: ACHP, 1986), 16–17.

29. Howard, "Where the Action Is," 127–28.

30. Ibid., 122.

31. Ibid., 123.

32. Patricia Poore and Clem Labine, eds., *The Old-House Journal New Compendium* (Garden City, N.J.: Doubleday, 1983), 3.

33. Birch and Roby, "The Planner and the Preservationist," 203.

34. Kim Keister, "Main Street Makes Good," *Historic Preservation News* 42 (September–October 1990): 46.

35. Robert E. Stipe, Introduction to *New Directions in Rural Preservation*, ed. Stipe (Washington, D.C.: HCRS, U.S. Department of the Interior, 1980), xi.

36. Ormond H. Loomis, coordinator, *Cultural Conservation: The Protection of Cultural Heritage in the United States: A Study* (Washington, D.C.: American Folklife Center, Library of Congress, in cooperation with the NPS, 1983), 7.

37. ACHP, *Twenty Years of the National Historic Preservation Act*, 23, 28.

38. Howard, "Where the Action Is," 126, 135.

39. Murtagh, *Keeping Time*, 76

40. "Future Brightens for St. Louis's Landmark Warehouses," *Preservation News* 30 (August 1990): 41.

41. Donald Dworsky, "A National Perspective," in *Preservation: Toward an Ethic in the 1980s* (Washington, D.C.: Preservation Press, NTHP, 1980), 95.

42. John M. Fowler, "The Federal Government as Standard Bearer," in Stipe and Lee, *The American Mosaic*, 68.

43. Robert Stanton, "The National Park Service: A Partner in Preservation," *Historic Preservation Forum* 14 (Winter 1999): 24.

44. Howard, "Where the Action Is," 135–36.

45. "The Landmark Designation," *Preservation News* 30 (February 1990): 11.

46. "Victory in St. Bartholomew's Case," *Preservation News* 30 (October 1990): 1.

47. Mark Severin, "Rescue Expected for Walden," *Preservation News* 30 (October 1990): 3.

48. "States Chosen for Tourism Project," *Preservation News* 30 (May 1990): 16.

49. "'Something Spectacular': Kemp Dedicates New Orleans' Housing Rehab," *Preservation News* 30 (March 1900): 1.

50. "Portal to America Opens Again," *Preservation News* 30 (November 1990): 17.

51. "Teaching with Historic Places," *Social Education* 2 (September 1992): 312.

52. Elizabeth Hightower, "Walking the Walk," *Preservation News* 49 (September–October 1997): 20–22.

53. "Scenic Byway Plan Advances," *Preservation News* 30 (January 1990): 2.

54. "Penna. Canals Named Heritage Corridor," *Preservation News* 30 (March 1990): 6.

55. Constance Beaumont, "States Boost Protection from Their Own Actions," *Preservation News* 29 (August 1989): 8.

56. "Rhode Island Report," *Preservation News* 29 (August 1989): 11.

57. Peter States, "Seattle CAP's Growth," *Preservation News* 29 (July 1989): 1.

58. "Charleston Charms Preservationists," *Historic Preservation News* 30 (December 1990): 8.

59. Ibid.

60. Antoinette J. Lee, ed., *Past Meets Future: Saving America's Historic Environments* (Washington, D.C.: Preservation Press, 1992).

61. James Oberstar, "ISTEA: A Bill for the American Community," *Historic Preservation Forum* 11 (Fall 1996): 9.

62. Richard Moe, "On the Move," *Preservation* 50 (November–December 1998): 6.

63. Lee, *Past Meets Future*, 192.

64. Roger D. Stone, "Support Grows for Slow Growth," *Preservation* 51 (January 1999): 12.

Chapter 1

1. Robert E. Stipe and Antoinette J. Lee, eds., *The American Mosaic: Preserving a Nation's Heritage* (Washington, D.C.: US/ICOMOS, 1987), 3.

2. Ibid., 11.

3. This is, of course, something of an oversimplification. American preservation has always been the beneficiary of individuals, organizations, and institutions to whom financial reward is a secondary consideration. We refer, of course, to those who take pride in a restored home, a house museum, a public building, or similar enterprise.

4. Stipe and Lee, *The American Mosaic*, 11.

Chapter 2

1. *WHSR.*

2. Public Law 89-665, 80 Stat. 915 (1966). The act has been amended numerous times, with substantial changes in 1980 and 1992.

3. The authorities of the secretary are spelled out in Section 101 of the act (16 U.S.C. sec. 470a). Section 301(11) delegates those responsibilities to the director.

4. The external historic preservation program is currently divided into nine elements and lodged in the National Center for Cultural Resource Stewardship and Partnerships, answering to an associate director. The *American Indian Liaison Office* provides technical assistance and services to Indian tribes and promotes communication between the NPS and the tribal community. The *Archaeology and Ethnography Program* carries out the NPS role in archaeology, including administration of ARPA, which regulates excavation on public lands; providing technical assistance under the Archaeological and Historic Preservation Act of 1974; implementing NAGPRA; developing the National Archaeological Database; and pursuing general coordination and public understanding of the federal archaeological program.

Heritage Preservation Services manages the programs central to the partnership between the federal government and the other players in the national historic preservation program. Key functions include management of the NHPA grants program; assistance to federal agencies in meeting their NHPA obligations, training and educational aid; coordination of the partnerships with state, tribal, and local governments; administration of the federal historic preservation tax incentive program; provision of technical preservation advice and guidance; and coordination of special programs to protect historic battlefields, promote historic landscape preservation, assist the preservation of National Historic Landmarks, encourage cultural resources diversity, and transfer surplus federal historic properties. The HABS and HAER are long-standing NPS programs to document significant examples of American architecture and engineering. The *Museum Management Program* is responsible for the more than 71 million objects in over 300 park museums.

The *NCPTT* advances preservation research and technology and supports training and education in the field. The *National Center for Recreation and Conservation* embraces a group of programs that promote the protection of natural and cultural areas. Some programs, such as the Land and Water Conservation Fund and the Wild and Scenic Rivers Program, are primarily oriented toward natural resources, while others, like the National Heritage Areas, American Heritage Rivers, and the Rivers, Trails, and Conservation Programs, bring together cultural and natural interests. The *National Register, History, and Education Program* contains the core function of maintaining the National Register and other NPS programs associated with the identification of historic properties, such as the National Historic Landmarks Survey, National Maritime Initiative, and Park History Program. It also houses the NPS initiatives to promote public understanding of historic properties, such as the Teaching with Historic Places Program. The *Park Historic Structures and Cultural Landscapes Program* focuses on the protection of resources within units of the NPS, advancing research, planning, and stewardship.

5. Public Law 101-601, 104 Stat. 3048, 25 U.S.C. secs. 3001–13.

6. Information on these programs can be found at the NPS website, ‹www.nps. gov›.

7. A recent example is the historically black colleges and universities grants program, mandated by Congress in annual appropriations bills for the past several years and included in the administration's own budget requests.

8. Title II of NHPA creates the ACHP, specifies its membership and authorities, and establishes its administrative structure. 16 U.S.C. secs. 470i–v.

9. An excellent example of this kind of effort is the ACHP's recent report on federal stewardship of historic properties. Titled *Caring for the Past, Managing for the Future: Federal Stewardship and America's Historic Legacy*, the report details the need of managing federally owned historic properties and offers recommendations to improve their care. See ‹www.achp.gov›.

10. See generally *WHSR*.

11. The full National Register criteria are published at 36 C.F.R. sec. 60.4. Information on the application of the criteria and the administration of the process can be found at ‹www.cr.nps.gov/places.htm›.

12. The NPS does not publish a list of National Register properties but does maintain the NRIS. This computerized database is accessible at ‹www.cr.nps.gov/nr/research›.

13. Executive Order 11593, "Protection and Enhancement of the Cultural Environment," May 15, 1971. Relevant codifications in NHPA are found in Section 110 (16 U.S.C. sec. 470h–2).

14. See generally GSA, *Held in Public Trust* (Washington, D.C.: GPO, 1998). The GSA prepared this excellent report to set forth a strategy for using its historic buildings.

15. An example is Army Regulation AR 4-200, which establishes procedures for army installations to follow when proposed actions will affect historic properties.

16. Resistance by Procter and Gamble to the designation of its historic plant reversed a decision by the NPS to list the complex on the National Register in 1979 and fomented legislative changes in the designation process. In 2002 this was echoed in an effort by the pipeline industry to exempt historic pipeline from the NHPA. An administrative compromise was reached.

17. 16 U.S.C. sec. 470f.

18. A compendium of federal court decisions can be found on the ACHP's website at ‹www.achp.gov›.

19. There are a few rare exceptions, such as federal regulation of surface mining activity under the Surface Mining Control and Reclamation Act, which specifically includes impact on historic properties as a basis for denial of a federal mining permit. See 30 U.S.C. sec. 1272(e).

20. The only recent exercise of the power of eminent domain for preservation purposes was acquisition of threatened lands at the Manassas National Battlefield Park to thwart intrusive commercial development in 1987.

21. Though any federal action is technically covered by the definition of "undertaking," the reality is that the more tenuous the federal nexus, the less likely an agency will take its Section 106 duties seriously.

22. Section 101(d)(6) of NHPA (16 U.S.C. sec. 470a[d][6]), added in 1992, directs federal agencies to consult with Indian tribes that attach religious and cultural significance to historic properties affected by an undertaking. The 1992 amendments authorize tribes to have THPOs who will assume the duties of SHPOs on tribal lands, including the SHPO role in the Section 106 process. Where the Section 106 rules require agencies to consult with SHPOs, they also require consultation with THPOs when the undertaking is on or affects tribal lands.

23. The formalities of National Register listing do become important when qualifying for federal historic preservation tax credits or HPF grants.

24. The specific criteria for adverse effects are found in the Section 106 regulations at 36 C.F.R. sec. 800.5(a)(1).

25. The track record on ACHP comments is mixed. Most often agencies follow ACHP advice that urges further consideration of alternatives and proceed to develop additional mitigation. But they have resisted recommendations to scrap a project.

26. 16 U.S.C. sec. 470h–2(f); 42 U.S.C. sec. 4231 et seq.; 49 U.S.C. sec. 303(f).

27. 42 U.S.C. sec. 4331(b)(4).

28. The regulations of each agency that guide the conduct of this evaluation generally conform to governmentwide regulations issued by the Council on Environmental Quality, a small agency located within the executive office of the president.

29. Probably the most controversial highway project that has been thwarted (though not yet killed) is the proposed 710 Freeway in Pasadena, Calif. Massive impact on historic properties laid the basis for successful court challenges that have so far prevented the final approval of construction.

30. 16 U.S.C. sec. 470a(e)(1).

31. Interestingly, Congress has taken a strong interest in maintaining the SAT program. This is undoubtedly due to the fact that a sizable proportion of these funds are earmarked by members for projects advanced by their constituents.

32. For example, the administration in FY 2000 sought $15.5 million for HBCUs out of an overall HPF request of $80 million. In the 106th Congress, a bill was introduced to provide similar earmarked funds for colleges and universities historically limited to women. It did not pass.

33. See generally 16 U.S.C. sec. 470a(d).

34. Public Law 106-208, 114 Stat. 318, sec. 5(a)(2).

35. H.R. 701, 107th Cong., 1st sess. (2001).

36. 16 U.S.C. sec. 470d.

37. 16 U.S.C. sec. 470a(e)(3).

38. The initial incentives changed the depreciation rules, allowing a choice between accelerated depreciation for new construction or five-year amortization of rehabilitation expenses. As a disincentive, new replacement structures built on the site of demolished historic buildings were limited to straight-line depreciation. The objective was to level the playing field for historic rehabilitation and new construction, although the disincentive to demolition perhaps tipped the scales a bit more toward preservation.

39. The limitation added in 1986 was to subject the incentives to passive loss rules (requiring active participation of the taxpayer in the project to reap the full benefit of the credit), which effectively curtailed the syndication of larger historic rehabilitation projects. Designed to curb unwarranted tax shelters, the passive loss rules regrettably met their objective as far as the historic preservation credit was concerned.

40. For comprehensive information on the current tax incentive program, see the NPS website, ‹www.nps.gov›.

41. The NPS posts statistics on the tax program on its website and periodically issues a report.

42. ACHP, *Federal Tax Law and Historic Preservation* (Washington, D.C.: ACHP, 1983).

43. The Secretary's Standards and NPS "Guidelines" can be found on the NPS website at ‹www2.cr.nps.gov/tps/tax/rehabstandards.htm›.

44. Valuation of easements for tax purposes has impeded the use of this provision over the years. Normally, the value is defined as the difference in the fair market value of the historic property before and after the easement is granted. This assumes that a property with a preservation easement would be of less value than one without. The IRS has questioned whether this is true for historic buildings, since their value derives in part from the continued existence of their historic features.

45. 42 U.S.C. sec. 5300. Subsequent HUD programs to promote affordable housing also have been used to support rehabilitation of historic residential properties. See the HOME Partnerships Program (42 U.S.C. sec. 12701) and HOPE, authorized by the Housing Opportunity Program Extension Act (42 U.S.C. sec. 12870).

46. Public Law 102-240. Its provisions are scattered in Titles 23 and 49 of the U.S. Code. The transportation enhancements are found at 23 U.S.C. sec. 133.

47. Public Law 105-178.

48. 16 U.S.C. sec. 469a.

49. These include the Martin Luther King Jr. National Historic Site, Atlanta, Ga.; Minuteman National Park, Lexington and Concord, Mass.; Lowell National Urban Historical Park, Massachusetts; Canyon de Chelly National Monument, New Mexico; Women's Rights National Historical Park, Seneca Falls, N.Y.; Eugene O'Neill National Historic Site, Martinez, Calif.; Vietnam Veterans Memorial, Washington, D.C.; and Chesapeake and Ohio Canal National Historical Park, Md. Likewise, they cover the entire United States from Hawaii Volcanoes National Park and Wrangell-St. Elias National Park in Alaska to Acadia National Park in Maine and Everglades National Park in Florida, as well as sites in Puerto Rico and the Virgin Islands.

50. See ACHP, *Caring for the Past, Managing for the Future.*

51. Executive Order 11593, "Preservation and Enhancement of the Cultural Environment," May 13, 1971. The *Federal Register* can be accessed at ‹www.nara.gov/fedreg/›.

52. "The Secretary of the Interior's Standards and Guidelines for Federal Agency Historic Preservation Programs Pursuant to the National Historic Preservation Act," 63 *Federal Register* 20495.

53. 33 C.F.R. Part 325, App. C.

54. Executive Order 13006, "Locating Federal Facilities on Historic Properties in Our Nation's Central Cities," May 21, 1996. The provisions of this executive order have been substantially incorporated into NHPA in amendments passed in 2000. See 16 U.S.C. sec. 470h–2(a)(1), as amended by Section 4 of Public Law 106–208.

55. 16 U.S.C. sec. 470h–3.

56. 16 U.S.C. sec. 431.

57. The two designations, both in Arizona—Agua Fria, north of Phoenix, and Grand Canyon–Parashant, bordering the North Rim of the Grand Canyon—affected 1,085,000 acres of federally owned public land and caused a significant outcry in Congress. A legislative response to limit the ability of the president to desig-

nate national monuments without congressional consent was introduced but failed to pass. The Bush administration is reviewing the national monument designation process.

58. 16 U.S.C. sec. 470aa. The permit system is implemented through uniform regulations that were issued by the Tennessee Valley Authority and the Departments of Agriculture, Defense, and Interior, respectively. 18 C.F.R. sec. 1312.1 et seq., 36 C.F.R. sec. 296.1 et seq., 32 C.F.R. 229.1 et seq., and 43 C.F.R. 7.1 et seq.

59. 25 U.S.C. sec. 3001. The regulations are found at 43 C.F.R. Part 10.

Chapter 3

1. See Elizabeth A. Lyon, "The States: Preservation in the Middle," in *The American Mosaic: Preserving a Nation's Heritage*, ed. Robert E. Stipe and Antoinette J. Lee (Washington, D.C.: US/ICOMOS, 1987); Charles B. Hosmer Jr., *Presence of the Past: The History of the Preservation Movement in the United States before Williamsburg* (New York: G. P. Putnam's Sons, 1965); and Charles B. Hosmer Jr., *Preservation Comes of Age: From Williamsburg to the National Trust, 1926–1949*, 2 vols. (Charlottesville: University Press of Virginia for Preservation Press, 1981).

2. Lyon, "The States: Preservation in the Middle," 87; Charles R. McGimsey III, *Public Archeology* (New York: Seminar Press, 1972). For the early history of NHPA, see James A. Glass, *The Beginnings of a New National Historic Preservation Program, 1957–1969* (Nashville, Tenn.: American Association for State and Local History, 1990).

3. See Timothy J. Crimmins, ed., *Proceedings of the Southeastern Conference on the National Register as a Planning Tool* (Atlanta: Georgia State University and the Georgia Department of Natural Resources, 1978).

4. NCSHPO, *Compendium of Policy Resolutions, 1969–1990* (Washington, D.C.: NCSHPO, 1991), 55, 58, 62–63.

5. See Chapter 2.

6. States with established archaeological surveys, like Arkansas, New Mexico, and other western states, were associated with universities and have tended to retain separate identities. Most other states responded to mandates under state and federal law to incorporate archaeological programs directly into their state preservation offices.

7. The new job market created by these requirements eventually spurred the development of graduate historic preservation degree programs across the country from which many state staff are now hired. See John C. Waters, "Master of Historic Preservation Programs: Flooding the Market or Filling a Niche?," *Preservation Forum* 11, no. 3 (Spring 1997): 1–7; Fritz Pannekeok, "The Rise of the Heritage Priesthood or the Decline of Community Based Heritage," *Preservation Forum* 12, no. 3 (Spring 1998): 4–10; DeTeel Patterson Tiller, "The Role of the Professional in Preservation Today," *Forum Journal* 13, no. 3 (Spring 1999): 4–6.

8. NPS, Heritage Preservation Services, *State Historic Preservation Activities: Funded by the Historic Preservation Fund, 1987–1997* (Washington, D.C.: NPS, 1998); NCSHPO, Information Sheet to all SHPOs, *Historic Preservation Fund, Fiscal Year 2002* (Washington, D.C.: NCSHPO, September 26, 2001).

9. David L. S. Brook and Elizabeth A. Lyon, "*A Richer Heritage*: Survey of the

States, April–July 1999," National Trust Library, Special Collections, University of Maryland; Elizabeth Morton, *Partnerships for Preservation: State Historic Preservation Offices and Statewide Nonprofits* (Washington, D.C.: NTHP, 1997), 30–31.

10. Funding for state staff positions related to environmental review has come from state departments of transportation, housing, and finance agencies, the federal Office of Surface Mining, and private utility companies, all of which must comply with Section 106. At least five states have been able to contract with other agencies for preservation program activities of mutual benefit, such as surveys, National Register evaluations, and emergency services following disasters.

11. NPS, *Government Performance and Results Act: Properties Designated and Protected by CLGs under Local Law* (Washington, D.C.: NPS, March 17, 1999); Judith Bittner, "NCSHPO 1995 Planning Session: Summary of SHPO Responses for Issues/Recommendations" (memorandum to colleagues, November 2–3, 1994).

12. Brook and Lyon, "*A Richer Heritage*: Survey" (Utah).

13. In Minnesota, for example, cooperative projects include a preservation plan with the Mille Lacs tribe that provides for cross-training of THPO and SHPO staff and a joint traditional cultural properties pilot project with the Leech Lake tribe.

14. In only one state, Rhode Island, the nation's smallest in land area, was there an articulated goal of a complete aboveground historic property survey. This was accomplished by 1996, when the SHPO announced the publication of the final community survey, for Jamestown; he noted that included in these surveys was a full historic context as well as the detailed fieldwork. NPS, "Significant Preservation Accomplishments," End-of-the-Year Report, 1996, on file with State, Tribal, and Local Programs, Heritage Preservation Services, National Center for Cultural Resources, NPS.

15. Judith E. Bittner, "States Take Preservation beyond NHPA," *CRM* (*A Model Partnership: 30th Anniversary of the National Historic Preservation Act*) 19, no. 6 (1996): 19–20.

16. NPS, *Historic Preservation Fund: State Outlay, Effort, and Products, 1980–1984* (Washington, D.C.: Interagency Resource Division, NPS, 1982, 1984); NPS, Heritage Preservation Services, *State Historic Preservation Activities*. From a collective average in 1985 of 300,000 properties per year, the annual numbers since 1987 have ranged between 131,000 and 209,000.

17. NPS, "Significant Preservation Accomplishments," 1996–98, on file with State, Tribal, and Local Programs, Heritage Preservation Services, National Center for Cultural Resources, NPS; Franco Ruffini, "Online Data Access Survey," Ohio State Historic Preservation Office, December 7, 2001.

18. Betsy Chittenden, *A Profile of the National Register of Historic Places* (Washington, D.C.: NTHP, 1984).

19. NPS, Heritage Preservation Services, *State Historic Preservation Activities: Funded by the Historic Preservation Fund* (Washington, D.C.: NPS, 1987–97). FY 2000 figures are cited in NPS, *The National Historic Preservation Program: The Historic Preservation Fund Grant Program at a Glance* (Washington, D.C.: NPS, March 2002).

20. NPS, *Government Performance and Results Act*. Thirty-five states are represented in this survey. "State Legislative Activity," *NCSHPO News*, August 1989, 7.

21. See, e.g., Amy Worden and Elizabeth Calvit, "Preserving the History of the Cold War," *CRM* 16, no. 6 (1993): 28–30; Rustin Quaide, "Documenting the Cold War: Investigating Available Resources," *CRM* 22, no. 9 (1999): 45–47.

22. NPS, "Significant Preservation Accomplishments," End-of-the-Year Reports, 1996.

23. NCSHPO, *Historic Preservation Fund*; NPS, *State Historic Preservation Activities*; NPS, *The National Historic Preservation Program*.

24. Brenda Barrett, "A Framework for Creative Mitigation," *CRM* (*In the Public Interest: Creative Approaches to Section 106 Compliance*) 22, no. 3 (1999): 27–30; Brook and Lyon, "*A Richer Heritage*: Survey" (Minnesota and Colorado).

25. "State Legislative Activity," *NCSHPO News*, June 1989, 4; NCSHPO and National Conference of State Legislators legislation database updated annually, ‹www.ncsl.org/programs/arts/statehist.html›.

26. Lyon, "The States: Preservation in the Middle," 95–96.

27. NPS, "Impact of the Emergency Jobs Act of 1983," briefing sheet dated December 14, 1993, on file with State, Tribal, and Local Programs, Heritage Preservation Services, National Center for Cultural Resources, NPS.

28. Bittner, "States Take Preservation beyond NHPA," 19–20.

29. Ibid. In many states, the HPF grants program barely functioned, as Bittner stated. See also "Significant Preservation Accomplishments," End-of-the-Year Reports, 1996–98, where states like Nevada and Hawaii indicate severe problems because of the reduced level of federal support. Compounding the problem, state support also fell off, as the NPS indicated in 1991, noting that thirty-four states had lost staff in that period due both to lower federal funding levels and state budget cuts.

30. NPS, *Government Performance and Results Act*.

31. NPS, *Federal Tax Incentives for Rehabilitating Historic Buildings: Statistical Report and Analysis for Fiscal Year 2002* (Washington, D.C.: NPS, February 2002); NTHP, "Historic Rehabilitation Tax Credits: Today and Tomorrow," *Forum News* 8, no. 3 (January–February 2002): 1–2, 6.

32. For a bibliography that includes recent state publications and a link to the National Trust Library collections bibliography of state publications there, see NCPTT website, ‹www.ncptt.nps.gov›.

33. Center for Historic Preservation, Middle Tennessee University, *Focus on 2000: A Heritage Education Perspective* (Murfreesboro: NCPTT, 1997).

34. Bittner, "States Take Preservation beyond NHPA," 19–20.

35. Theodore W. Hild, "Preservation Commentary: 'The Vision Thing,'" *NCSHPO News*, September 1993, 4.

36. NCSHPO Listserv survey, 1999.

37. One of the most unusual state-level funding success stories was the creation of the Alabama Cultural Resources Preservation Trust Fund. Its annual $700,000 allotment for preservation projects came from the settlement of a Section 106 case in which the Federal Energy Regulatory Commission fined the Transcontinental Gas Pipeline Company $8.5 million for illegally proceeding with a 125-mile pipeline through ten counties. The interest from the settlement principal supports the Alabama grants program. "Alabama Inaugurates Major Trust Fund," *NCSHPO News*, May 1994, 4.

38. NCSHPO and National Conference of State Legislators legislation database; NTHP, "Historic Rehabilitation Tax Credits," 1–2, 6.

39. NPS, "Significant Preservation Accomplishments" (Kentucky, Ohio, New Hampshire, New Jersey), 1996–98. For North Carolina's archaeological facility, see *Forty-Sixth Biennial Report, 1994–1996* (Raleigh: Division of Archives and History, North Carolina Department of Cultural Resources, 1997), 4.

40. Alison Barr, *Destination Preservation: Putting TEA-21 to Work for Historic Preservation* (Washington, D.C.: Preservation Action, 1999).

41. Susan Langley, Maryland State Historic Preservation Office, e-mail to David Brook regarding *U-1105*, August 30, 1999.

42. NCSHPO, Information Sheet to all SHPOs, *Senate Subcommittee Increases Legacy Funding to $50 Million* (Washington, D.C.: NCSHPO, July 1994); "U.S. Navy Shipwreck Preservation Efforts," *NCSHPO News*, February 1995, 6.

43. For community preservation in the context of state programs, see Elizabeth A. Lyon, "Partnerships in Community Preservation," in Antoinette J. Lee and David M. Brook, eds., *A Model Partnership* (Washington, D.C.: NPS, 1996), 21–24. See also NPS, "Significant Preservation Accomplishments," 1996–98.

44. NCSHPO minutes, 1991, NCSHPO office, Washington, D.C., and most SHPO offices; Judith Bittner, "Summary of SHPO Responses and Issue Recommendations for the NCSHPO 1995 Planning Session" (memorandum to colleagues, November 21, 1994).

45. David L. S. Brook, "From Dreams to Process to Dreams: State Historic Preservation Programs in North Carolina, 1970–1990" (graduate study research paper, Raleigh, December 10, 1991), 59–60; Robert A. Caro, *The Years of Lyndon Johnson: The Path to Power* (New York: Vintage Books, 1983), 315.

46. Beginning in the early 1980s, when a new administration touted a "new federalism," many reports and discussions within the preservation community have pointed to the national historic preservation system as a model for this concept. See NCSHPO minutes for this period and ACHP, *Report of the Task Force on Federalism and Preservation* (Washington, D.C.: ACHP, 1982).

47. NPS, *Historic Preservation Fund Grants Manual* (Washington, D.C.: NPS, 1997); Eric Hertfelder, "The National Park Service and Historic Preservation: Historic Preservation beyond Smokey the Bear," *Public Historian* 9 (Spring 1987): 138–39.

48. The minutes of the NCSHPO from 1979 to the present detail the many issues that have been addressed. See esp. National Register discussion minutes, June 25, 1989, and NCSHPO, *Compendium of Policy Resolutions: 1969–1990* (see n. 4 above), which records the actions of these meetings through 1990.

49. Hertfelder, "Smokey the Bear," 136–39. Mention was made of a survey of the states that concluded that the program was "severely over administered" in "National Conference Elects Officers and Directors," *NCSHPO News*, April 1991, 1.

50. "Preservation Technology and Training Projects and Grants: 1994–1999 in Review," *NCPTT Notes*, no. 34 (Fall supp., 1999).

51. Historic Preservation Performance Review Committee, NPS Advisory Board, *National Performance Review of the Historic Preservation Fund Partnerships* (Washington, D.C.: NPS and NCSHPO, March 6, 1994).

52. Ibid., 7. Read twice and with care, this bit of federal government double-talk could be interpreted to mean just the opposite—that, in fact, the states serve as nothing more or less than branch offices of the federal program administrators.

53. "FY '91 Appropriation for Historic Preservation" (*Preservation Action*, one-page flyer, typed, undated, discussing presidential budget requests); Hertfelder, "Smokey the Bear," 139, quoting the secretary of the interior in the secretary's "Twentieth Anniversary Report on the NHPA."

54. Hertfelder, "Smokey the Bear," 139–40.

55. Noted in NPS, "Fact Sheets" (March 1998); Brook and Lyon, "*A Richer Heritage*: Survey," in which Virginia's SHPO in 1999 reported that the 30 percent increase in the office's federal allocation had failed to keep pace with incremental increases in staff salaries and increasing operational costs.

56. NCSHPO, "2002 Work Plan," November 11, 2001.

57. David Brook, "From the Administrator's Desk," *North Carolina Historic Preservation Office Newsletter*, Summer 1993, 7–8; "Vento Holds Hearing on NHPA Amendments," *NCSHPO News*, May 7, 1992; "HR 4849 Changes Eligibility Process," *NCSHPO/ALERT!*, April 21, 1992, 1–2 (includes *Congressional Record* text of Governor George Allen's speech supporting local government vetoes).

58. John S. Salmon (historian, Virginia Department of Historic Resources, Richmond) to David Brook, September 9, 1999; John E. Wells (architectural historian, Virginia Department of Historic Resources, Richmond), e-mail to David Brook, September 22, 1999.

59. Salmon to Brook and Wells to Brook; "National Trust Opposes Disney's America," *NCSHPO News*, May 13, 1994, 4–5, enclosing copy of quoted letter of Richard Moe (president, National Trust) to Michael Eisner (chairman, Walt Disney Co.), May 2, 1994; "Bumpers Hearing on Disney," *NCSHPO News*, July 5, 1994, 2.

60. NPS, "Significant Preservation Accomplishments" (Virginia, 1996, 3–4, and 1997, 2); Virginia Department of Historic Resources, *Financial Impact of Historic Designation*, 1992, S. Doc. 23.

61. Brook and Lyon, "*A Richer Heritage*: Survey" (Minnesota).

62. Ibid. (Minnesota, Alaska, New York, Vermont).

63. NPS, "Significant Preservation Accomplishments" (Illinois, 1996, 1).

64. "New Life for Georgia Mills: Preservation Revives Economic Cornerstones," *The Rambler* (newsletter of the Georgia Trust for Historic Preservation), Spring 1998, 6–7; Elizabeth A. Lyon, letter to the editor, *The Rambler*, March 1999.

65. "Flood Relief and Historic Preservation," *NCSHPO News*, August 1993, 1.

66. *After the Flood: Rebuilding Communities through Historic Preservation* (Atlanta: Historic Preservation Division, Georgia Department of Natural Resources, September 1997); Britta Bloomberg, "Lessons Learned in Disaster Recovery," *Minnesota Preservation Planner* 9, no. 3 (Summer 1998): 1–2; Bloomberg, "Recovery Underway at St. Peter," *Minnesota Preservation Planner* 10 (Winter 1999): 1–2; Ken Story, "Disaster Relief, Recovery, and Historic Preservation: Arkansas and Its 38 Tornados," *CRM* 22, no. 5 (1999): 10–11; NPS, "Significant Preservation Accomplishments," 1996–98, wherein several states describe disaster relief activities.

67. "Georgia Affordable Housing Workshop," *NCSHPO News*, March 14, 1995, 2; *Community Conservation and Affordable Housing in Georgia: An Agenda for the Future*

(Atlanta: Historic Preservation Division, Georgia Department of Natural Resources, 1995).

68. NPS, "Significant Preservation Accomplishments," Nebraska State Historical Society, 1996, 3; "Legacy at Work," North Carolina State Historic Preservation Office, *Annual Report, 1997–1998* (Winter 1998): 9.

69. Cathryn H. Slater, "The Advisory Council on Historic Preservation at 30," *CRM* 19, no. 6 (1996): 12.

70. Lynne Sebastian, "A Response to the 'Public Benefit of Mitigation' Workshop," minutes, NCSHPO annual meeting, Washington, D.C., 1995, located in NCSHPO office, Washington, D.C., and most SHPO offices. Dr. Sebastian was the New Mexico SHPO.

71. David McCullough, "A Sense of Time and Place," in Antoinette J. Lee, ed., *Past Meets Future: Saving America's Environments* (Washington, D.C.: Preservation Press, 1992), 29–34.

72. Antoinette J. Lee, "Discovering Old Cultures in the New World: The Role of Ethnicity," in Stipe and Lee, *The American Mosaic*; Elizabeth A. Lyon, *Cultural and Ethnic Diversity in Historic Preservation* (Washington, D.C.: NTHP, 1992); Patricia L. Parker, *Keepers of the Treasures: Protecting Historic Properties and Cultural Traditions on Indian Lands: A Report on Tribal Preservation Funding Needs Submitted to Congress by the National Park Service, United States Department of the Interior* (Washington, D.C.: NPS, 1990); Antoinette J. Lee, ed., "Cultural Diversity and Historic Preservation," *CRM* 15, no. 7 (1992): 47–48; Robert L. Spude, ed., "Exploring Hispanic History and Culture: A Dynamic Field," *CRM* 20, no. 11 (1997): 3–64; Michael A. Tomlin, ed., *Preservation of What? For Whom?: A Critical Look at Historical Significance* (Ithaca, N.Y.: National Council for Preservation Education, 1998).

73. A sample survey in 1999 confirmed that the percentages of minority staff identified in the 1990 report, especially in the professions, are virtually identical—12 percent of total and 5 percent professional. NCSHPO report, 1999, NCSHPO office, Washington, D.C., and most SHPO offices.

74. For similar conclusions about the profession generally, see Antoinette J. Lee, "Diversifying the Cultural Resources Profession," *CRM* 22, no. 8 (1999): 47–48.

75. "From Paper Files to Digital Databases: Modernizing the State Historic Preservation Office Historic Resource Inventory," 1999, a report of the Cultural Resources GIS Facility, HABS/HAER/HALS Division, NPS.

76. Cultural Resources Work Group Subcommittee on Cultural and Demographic Data, Federal Geographic Data Committee, minutes, January 7, 1999, Cultural Resources GIS Facility, ibid.

77. NCSHPO and National Conference of State Legislatures, State Preservation Legislation Database, ‹www.ncsl.org/programs/arts/statehist.htm›.

78. NCSHPO e-mail listserv for SHPOs and their staffs (inquiries and responses on a variety of technical topics), 1998–99; "Preservation Technology and Training Projects and Grants: 1994–1998 in Review," *NCPTT Notes*, Fall supp., 1999.

79. De Seve Economics Associates, Inc., *Economic Impacts of Development: Tax Incentives for Certified Rehabilitation under the Economic Recovery Tax Act of 1981* (Troy: New York State Office of Parks, Recreation, and Historic Preservation, 1983); Shlaes and Co., *Economic Benefits from Rehabilitation of Historic Buildings in Illinois* (Chi-

cago: Illinois Department of Preservation, 1984), and *Economic Benefits from Rehabilitation of Certified Historic Structures in Texas* (Chicago: Texas Historical Commission, 1985).

80. NPS, *Federal Tax Incentives for Rehabilitating Historic Buildings*; University of Rhode Island Intergovernmental Policy Analysis Program, *The Economic Effect of the Rhode Island Historical Preservation Commission Programs, 1971–1993* (Providence: Rhode Island Historical Preservation Commission, July 1993); Edward F. Sanderson, "Economic Effects of Historic Preservation in Rhode Island," *Preservation Forum* 9, no. 1 (1994): 22–27; Donovan D. Rypkema, *Virginia's Economy and Historic Preservation: The Impact of Preservation on Jobs, Business, and Community* (Staunton: Preservation Alliance of Virginia, 1995).

81. Center for Urban Policy Research, *Economic Impacts of Historic Preservation* (Trenton: Task Force on New Jersey History, 1997); New Jersey Historic Trust, *Partners in Prosperity: The Economic Benefits of Historic Preservation in New Jersey* (Trenton: New Jersey Historic Trust, 1998). The principal investigators for the research study, David Listokin and Michael L. Lahr, subsequently held a seminar at the Brookings Institution in 1998 under the auspices of the NCPTT, where invited economic experts discussed the model and ways it could be used and in 2000, with the NCPTT, produced a computer software program that can be used to assess the economic impact from various historic preservation activities on local, state, and federal economies.

82. Richard Moe and Carter Wilkie, *Changing Places: Rebuilding Community in an Age of Sprawl* (New York: Henry Holt and Co., 1997), is a good general reference and contains some specific case studies, particularly in Oregon, Maryland, and a few other states. NPS, "Significant Preservation Accomplishments" (Rhode Island and Michigan), 1997–98; Mark R. Edwards, "The Future . . . ," *Georgia Historical Quarterly* (Spring 1999): 126–29.

83. NPS, "Significant Preservation Accomplishments" (Delaware), 1996. For an example of a state planning law, see *General Statutes of North Carolina*, 1999, H.R. 168, Ratified Bill, Part 16, Department of Commerce, Section 16.7(a).

84. Morton, *Partnerships for Preservation*.

85. The funding authorization for the HPF from offshore oil leases expired in 1997 and was not reauthorized until May 22, 2000.

86. Donovan D. Rypkema, *The Value of Historic Preservation in Maryland* (Baltimore: Preservation Maryland, 1999), 16.

Chapter 4

Because no single individual can keep up with preservation efforts among the more than twenty thousand local governments in the United States, this chapter has necessarily had to be something of a cooperative effort. The authors of this chapter wish to acknowledge the special assistance of John Fowler, Elizabeth Lyon, David Brook, Tom Mayes, and Myrick Howard in detailing certain aspects of local government preservation practice. We would like to express our special thanks to Bob Stipe for the use of some of his previously published work in the area of preservation planning.

1. Robert E. Stipe and Antoinette J. Lee, eds., *The American Mosaic: Preserving a Nation's Heritage* (Washington, D.C.: US/ICOMOS, 1987), 276.

2. See Donovan Rypkema, "Rethinking Economic Values," in *Past Meets Future: Saving America's Historic Environments*, ed. Antoinette J. Lee (Washington, D.C.: Preservation Press, 1992). See also Chapter 1.

3. Stipe and Lee, *The American Mosaic*, 5–7.

4. See Lea, introduction to this book.

5. *WATCH [Waterbury Action to Conserve Our Heritage, Inc.] v. Harris*, 603 F.2d 310 (2d Cir. 1979), *cert. denied*, 444 U.S. 995 (1979).

6. Thompson Mayes (unpublished essay, 2001).

7. Ibid.

8. The executive director of the NACP recently submitted a list of large- and medium-size "best regulated" local governments to the National Trust's listserv (Internet chat room). It included San Antonio, Dallas, Seattle, Salt Lake City, Santa Fe, and Fort Collins (Colo.) in the West; Chicago, Milwaukee, and Madison in the Midwest; and Providence, Charleston, Lexington, Louisville, Boston, Portland, Charlotte, and Asheville in the East.

9. Martha Hagedorn-Krass, "History at the Crossroads," *Kansas Preservation* (Cultural Resources Division, Kansas State Historical Society) 21, no. 4 (July–August 1999).

10. See John Fowler (unpublished essay, 2001).

11. See David Brook and Elizabeth Lyon (unpublished essay, 2001).

12. Peter H. Brink and H. Grant Dehart, "Findings and Recommendations," in Lee, *Past Meets Future*, 16.

13. See Chapter 15.

14. *Opinion of the Justices to the Senate*, 333 Mass. 773, 128 N.E. 2d 557 (1955).

15. Historic Preservation Division, Georgia Department of Natural Resources, *New Vision: The Preservation Plan for Georgia's Heritage, 1995* (Atlanta: Historic Preservation Division, Georgia Department of Natural Resources, 1995), 36.

16. In the mid-1990s there were 22,415 municipal and county governments in the United States. U.S. Department of Commerce, *1997 Census of Governments: Volume 1, Government Organization* (Washington, D.C.: U.S. Department of Commerce, 1997).

17. The reader may wish to consult the NAPC, which maintains a collection of design guidelines from throughout the United States.

18. The best works for lay people in this area are Bradford J. White and Paul W. Edmondson, *Procedural Due Process in Plain English* (Washington, D.C.: NTHP, 1994), and Christopher Duerksen and Richard J. Roddewig, *Takings Law in Plain English* (Washington, D.C.: Clarion Associates for the American Resources Institute, 1994). Also an excellent reference is Julia H. Miller, *A Layperson's Guide to Historic Preservation Law: A Survey of Federal, State, and Local Laws Governing Historic Resource Protection* (Washington, D.C.: NTHP, 1997, 2000).

19. Historic Preservation Division, Georgia Department of Natural Resources, *New Vision*, 37.

20. The reference here is to the term "Comprehensive Plan" as city planners use

it, not the "comprehensive plan" referred to in zoning enabling legislation, which is quite different.

21. Robert E. Stipe, "On Preservation Plans and Planning," *Alliance Review* (January–February 2001): 1–4, and (March–April 2001): 4–5, 15.

22. Richard Moe and Carter Wilkie, *Changing Places: Rebuilding Community in the Age of Sprawl* (New York: Henry Holt and Co.), 1997. See also Constance Beaumont, *Smart States, Better Communities: How State Governments Can Help Citizens Preserve Their Communities* (Washington, D.C.: NTHP, 1996).

23. Politics, public policy, and law come together in the striking case studies contained in Richard F. Babcock and Charles L. Siemon, *The Zoning Game Revisited* (Boston: Oelseschlager, Gunn and Hain in association with the Lincoln Institute of Land Policy, 1985).

24. Stipe and Lee, *The American Mosaic*, 273.

25. Robert E. Stipe, "Conservation Areas: A New Approach to an Old Problem" (local preservation issues paper on conservation districts, Interagency Resources Division, NPS, 1994). See also "Use It or Lose It," *Dollars & Sense of Historic Preservation*, reprinted from *Building Renovation* (Spring 1995).

26. Mayes (unpublished essay, 2001).

27. Richard W. Longstreth, *History on the Line: Testimony in the Cause of Preservation* (Ithaca, N.Y.: Historic Urban Plans, 1998), ix.

28. "Creative Teaching with Historic Places," *CRM* 23, no. 8 (2000).

29. See ‹www.nthp.org›.

30. Keynote speech by Richard Moe (President, NTHP), Fifty-fourth National Preservation Conference, Los Angeles, 2000.

31. Jon C. Tearford, *The Rough Road to Renaissance: Urban Revitalization in America, 1940–1985* (Baltimore: Johns Hopkins University Press, 1990), 253.

32. See ‹www.mainst.org/AboutMainStreet/msapproach.htm›.

33. "The 2000 National Reinvestment Statistics," as reported at ‹www.mainstreet.org/AboutMainStreet/numbers.htm›.

34. Norman Tyler, *Historic Preservation: An Introduction to Its History, Principles, and Practice* (New York: Norton, 1994, 2000), 55–56.

35. John J. Costonis, *Space Adrift: Landmark Preservation and the Marketplace* (Urbana: University of Illinois Press, 1974). Development rights transfers have been the subject of considerable experimentation. See "A Review of Transferable Development Rights (TDR) Programs in the United States," *Preservation Law Reporter* 16 (April–June 1997): 1067–74.

36. Julia Miller, "Assessing Economic Hardship Claims under Historic Preservation Ordinances," *Preservation Law Reporter* 18 (April–June 1999). See also Dan Becker, "Establishing a Demolition by Neglect Ordinance," *Alliance Review* (February–March 1999): 1–2, 15.

37. Pratt Cassity, "Still Local after All These Years," *CRM* 19, no. 6 (1966): 25–29.

38. Antoinette J. Lee, ed., *Past Meets Future: Preserving America's Historic Environments* (Washington, D.C.: Preservation Press, 1992).

39. Myrick Howard (unpublished essay, 2002). See also Deidre McCarthy, "Ap-

plying GIS Technology to Preservation Planning," *Forum Journal* 15, no. 4 (Summer 2001): 41–48.

Chapter 5

The author would like to acknowledge the contributions of time and information from his colleagues in the law and public policy department of the National Trust, particularly Julia Hatch Miller, editor of the *Preservation Law Reporter*, without whom this chapter could not have been completed.

1. Although the amendment to eliminate funding was defeated that day (July 13, 1995), the National Trust had already made the decision to phase out its direct appropriation from Congress. It now operates without the subsidy, which allows it to take more aggressive positions on preservation issues.

2. This fact is at odds with the widely held but incorrect public perception that listing in the National Register ensures that a privately owned building cannot be demolished.

3. To date, no court has held that historic preservation meets the higher standard of being a "*compelling* governmental purpose" (italics added) as opposed to simply a *legitimate* governmental purpose. See Laura S. Nelson, "Remove Not the Ancient Landmark: Legal Protection for Historic Religious Properties in an Age of Religious Freedom Legislation," *Cardozo Law Review* 21 (December 1999): 721, 760.

4. See Constance E. Beaumont, "Historic Preservation in Wisconsin: An Assessment of Issues and Opportunities" (report prepared for the State Historical Society of Wisconsin, May 1993), 17.

5. See, e.g., *Partners in Prosperity: The Economic Benefits of Historic Preservation in New Jersey* (1998); *Historic Preservation and the Economy of the Commonwealth: Kentucky's Past at Work for Kentucky's Future* (1997); *Virginia's Economy and Historic Preservation* (1995); *The Economic Benefits of Preserving Community Character* (1991); and *Economic Impact of Historic District Designation* (1990)—reprinted as a series, *Dollars & Sense of Historic Preservation*, by the National Trust for Historic Preservation, 1996–98.

6. The problem of too much wealth in the absence of a preservation ethic has resulted in teardowns—individuals buying older houses in established neighborhoods and tearing them down to build new and significantly larger houses. It has also led to the reintroduction of massive urban renewal projects that call for the demolition of whole neighborhoods.

7. The New Mexico Heritage Preservation Alliance has listed the night sky as one of its "most endangered" places.

8. For the impact of these regulations, see "Advisory Council Issues: New Section 106 Regulations," *Preservation Law Reporter* 18, no. 1 (January–March 1999): 1088, and "Five-Step Summary of the Revised Section 106 Procedures," *Preservation Law Reporter* 18, no. 2 (April–June 1999): 1092. The recently revised Section 106 regulations not only are an attempt to simplify the Section 106 process but also are, to some

extent, representative of the "smaller government" initiatives of the early 1990s mentioned earlier.

9. See *National Trust for Historic Preservation v. City of Albuquerque*, 874 P.2d 798 (1994), interpreting New Mexico's state 4(f)-type law.

10. See *Beattystown Community Council v. Department of Environmental Protection*, 712 A.2d 1170 (N.J. App. Div., June 22, 1998).

11. See New York City Environmental Quality Act, Section 25–318 of the Administrative Code of New York City.

12. Executive Order 13006, "Locating Federal Facilities on Historic Properties in Our Nation's Central Cities." But see 40 U.S.C. sec. 619, which requires all federal agencies, including the U.S. Postal Service, to give "due consideration" to local laws.

13. *Virginia Policies That Contribute to Sprawl: An Agenda for Change* (Washington, D.C.: NTHP, 2001); *Historic Preservation in Wisconsin: An Assessment of Issues and Opportunities* (Washington, D.C.: NTHP, 1993).

14. For a chart of tax incentives, see Constance Beaumont, *Smart States, Better Communities: How State Governments Can Help Citizens Preserve Their Communities* (Washington, D.C.: NTHP, 1996), 114–23.

15. See Md. Code Ann., sec. 5-801, and N.C. Gen. Stat., secs. 105–29.35 et seq.

16. The *Historic Homeownership Assistance Act*, H.R. 1172, S.61A, would create a 20 percent federal income tax credit toward the rehabilitation of housing stock in deteriorating neighborhoods. 106th Cong., 2d sess. March 17, 1999, 2000.

17. The *Conservation and Reinvestment Act of 1999 (CARA)*, H.R. 701, would provide a permanent authorization of $100 million per year for the HPF.

18. *Wall Street Journal*, May 25, 1999.

19. A new development named "Riverside," near Atlanta, has actually created a fictional history for the community, which is being used as a marketing tool.

20. *Penn Central Transportation Co. et al. v. New York City Co. et al.*, 438 U.S. 104 (1978).

21. For a summary of recent court decisions, see "Supreme Court Takings Cases at a Glance," *Preservation Law Reporter* 18 (April–June 1999): 1059. For an excellent summary of the meaning of the takings clause, see *Takings Law in Plain English* (Clarion Associates, Inc., 1998).

22. *Agins v. City of Tiburon*, 447 U.S. 255 (1980).

23. *Williamson County Regional Planning Commission v. Hamilton Bank*, 473 U.S. 172 (1985).

24. *Keystone Bituminous Coal Ass'n v. DeBenedictis*, 480 U.S. 470 (1987).

25. *Lucas v. South Carolina Coastal Council*, 112 S. Ct. 2886 (1992).

26. *Nollan v. California Coastal Commission*, 483 U.S. 825 (1987); *Dolan v. City of Tigard*, 114 S. Ct. 2309 (1994). These and other cases raise a host of highly complex issues that go beyond the scope of this book.

27. Jerold S. Kayden, "Historic Preservation and the New Takings Cases: Landmarks Preserved," *Fordham Law Journal* 6, no. 3 (1995), reprinted in *Preservation Law Reporter* 14, no. 12 (December 1995): 1235. See also *Palazzolo v. Rhode Island*, No. 99-2047 (U.S., June 29, 2001).

28. See S. 1412, *The Private Property Rights Act of 2001*, 107th Cong., 1st sess., September 10, 2001.

29. These acts are generally of two types. One requires an assessment of the economic impact of the regulation, indicating specifically the extent to which it will lower the value of the property being regulated. The other calls for outright compensation for reduced property values resulting from the regulation. Florida's compensation statute is described in Bert J. Harris Jr., "Private Property Rights Protection Act," sec. 70.001, Florida Statutes, 1995.

30. Bradford J. White and Paul W. Edmondson, *Procedural Due Process in Plain English* (Washington, D.C.: NTHP, 1994).

31. See *Metropolitan Baptist Church v. District of Columbia*, 718 A.2d 119 (D.C. App. 1998).

32. *Rector, Wardens, and Members of the Vestry of St. Bartholomew's Church v. City of New York*, 914 F.2d 348 (2d Cir. 1990), *cert. denied*, 499 U.S. 905 (1991).

33. *Employment Division v. Smith*, 494 U.S. 872 (1990).

34. Courts in Washington State have decided a series of cases holding that the mere designation of historic buildings owned by religious organizations is a violation of the state constitution's guarantee of religious freedom, including a designation that does not impose any regulatory controls. See *First Covenant Church v. City of Seattle*, 840 P.2d 174 (1992).

35. 42 U.S.C. sec. 2000bb, et seq.

36. *Flores v. City of Boerne*, 117 S. Ct. 2157 (1997).

37. For a comprehensive article on regulating historic religious properties, see Nelson, "Remove Not the Ancient Landmark." A number of preservation organizations have specific programs to encourage the preservation of historic religious buildings—e.g., Partners for Sacred Places in Philadelphia and Inspired Partnerships in Chicago.

38. See Christopher D. Bowers, "Is Owner Consent Objectionable?," *Alliance Review* (May–June 1997). See also Chapter 2 on the National Register owner consent provisions included in the 1980 amendments.

39. See Julia H. Miller, "Owner Consent Provisions in Historic Preservation Ordinances: Are They Legal?," *Preservation Law Reporter* 10 (February 1991): 1019.

40. In one of the most highly watched cases during the 1990s, the Pennsylvania Supreme Court initially struck down the designation of a historic theater, holding that the mere designation constituted a "taking" of property. The court subsequently reversed itself in *United Artists Theater Circuit v. City of Philadelphia*, 635 A.2d 612 (Pa. 1993).

41. *Penn Central Transportation Co. et al. v. New York City Co. et al.*, 438 U.S. 104, 107–8 (1978). Quotation from Robert Stipe, "Why Preserve?" (paper presented at the Conference on Preservation Law, Washington, D.C., May 1, 1971). Quotation also from Gilbert, introduction to "Precedents for the Future," 36 *Law and Contemporary Problems*, 311, 312, 1971, quoting paper by Stipe above, 6–7.

42. *Congressional Record*, November 4, 1999, S13922.

43. *Congressional Record*, 104th Cong., 1st sess., July 13, 1995, vol. 141, no. 113, H. 6988.

Chapter 6

1. Robert Harvey, professor of landscape architecture at Iowa State, observed that in the early days of AHLP, preservationists were looking primarily at "things in the landscape" and not necessarily at the landscape as a whole. Landscape Preservation Panel, Association for Preservation Technology Annual Meeting, October 1998, Williamsburg, Va.

2. Among the landscape architecture faculty members who incorporated landscape preservation into their lectures, seminars, and studio classes were William Tishler, University of Wisconsin; Robert Harvey, Iowa State University; Robert Melnick, first at Kansas State University, then at the University of Oregon; Suzanne Turner, Louisiana State; and George Curry, State University of New York at Syracuse.

3. Hugh Miller, a founding member of the AHLP and then chief historical architect of the NPS, saw landscapes as a way to address the many cultural values of rural and wilderness parks that had not been addressed adequately in the past. Landscape architect and professor Robert Melnick, while on academic leave, worked with Miller in developing the initial criteria to use in evaluating significant landscapes within the NPS.

4. Through the 1980s and 1990s landscape architects and cultural landscape specialists such as Charles Birnbaum, Ethan Carr, Shaun Eyring, Kathy Gilbert, Mary Hughes, Katy Lacy, Lucy Lawliss, Linda McClelland, Lauren Meier, Nora Mitchell, Robert Page, and Sherda Williams joined the NPS and directed or undertook the first cultural landscape reports; they also began to develop standards and guidelines and other technical information related to the documentation, management, and treatment of cultural landscapes for the NPS.

5. These used the HABS/HAER approach to documenting works of architecture and engineering in recording designed landscapes. Since the founder of HABS/HAER, the late Charles Peterson, had been trained as a landscape architect, HABS/HAER documentation had always included site plans and related information. John A. Burns, ed., *Recording Historic Structures: Historic American Buildings Survey/Historic American Engineering Record* (Washington, D.C.: AIA Press, 1989), 206.

6. Kane and Caruth, of Mount Kisko, N.Y., developed a master plan for New Harmony; Land and Community Associates of Charlottesville, Va., developed a master plan for the Amana Colonies. Both plans addressed landscape preservation for the historic communities.

7. The research was directed by landscape architect and University of Wisconsin professor William Tishler.

8. Robert Melnick directed this pioneering effort with the support of NPS chief historical architect Hugh C. Miller.

9. Robert Z. Melnick, with Daniel Sponn and Emma Jane Saxe, *Cultural Landscapes: Rural Historic Districts in the National Park System* (Washington, D.C.: Park Historic Architecture Division, CRM, NPS, 1984), 18.

10. Robert R. Page, Cathy A. Gilbert, and Susan A. Dolan, *A Guide to Cultural Landscape Reports: Contents, Process, and Techniques* (Washington, D.C.: Park Historic Structures and Cultural Landscapes Program, Cultural Resource Stewardship and Partnerships, NPS); Robert R. Page, *Cultural Landscapes Inventory Professional Procedures Guide* (Washington, D.C.: NPS, 1998).

11. Melnick brought an essential understanding of natural systems to the generally accepted National Register criteria.

12. Other concurrent and complementary efforts in landscape preservation during this period included Patricia O'Donnell, "A Preservationist's Glossary," *Landscape Architecture* 77, no. 4 (July–August 1987): 96–98, and Ian Firth's work with biotic cultural resources in the southeastern United States for the NPS that was concurrent with Melnick's work.

13. Development and publication of this bulletin occurred under the direct guidance of then acting keeper of the National Register, Carol Shull, and Linda McClelland, of the National Register staff. Written by J. Timothy Keller and Genevieve P. Keller, the bulletin built on the earlier work of several landscape preservation professionals, particularly that of Thomas Kane and Robert Melnick. In commissioning the first bulletin, Carol Shull advised the Kellers, who were experienced in nominating historic districts with significant historic and architectural resources, to develop criteria consistent with those used for evaluating buildings and structures and a parallel process for evaluation and nomination to avoid separate criteria and processes for landscapes.

14. These initial publications by NPS historical landscape architects Lauren Meier and Charles Birnbaum were helpful in directing researchers to works that would establish appropriate historic contexts for landscapes.

15. Author Linda Flint McClelland, of the National Register staff, expanded on work that grew out of her initial involvement in evaluating rural historic districts.

16. Following publication in 1998, the author extended the studies in park design into the late 1950s and early 1960s with research and documentation of the NPS Mission 66 park planning and design implementation. Ethan Carr, *Wilderness by Design: Landscape Architecture and the National Park Service* (Lincoln: University of Nebraska Press, 1998).

17. Scholars, theorists, and authors Charles Beveridge, William Cronon, J. B. Jackson, David Lowenthall, and John Stilgoe, to name only a few, in addition to the standard textbook source, Norman Newton, have provided a basis for landscape historical research and theory. An increasing number of scholarly and critical works related to cultural landscape studies have been published over the last decade, and many more are in progress.

18. David Uschold, Nancy J. Brown, ASLA, and Robert Page, ASLA, "More Than a Database: NPS's Cultural Landscape Inventory Improves Resource Stewardship" (proceedings of the ASLA annual meeting, Washington, D.C., 1999), 356–58.

19. Page, Gilbert, and Dolan, *Guide to Cultural Landscape Reports.*

20. Burns, *Recording Historic Structures*, 164–65, 206–19.

21. Large-format photography and a historical narrative supplemented the twenty-five drawings of the site.

22. "Historic Plant Material Sources," *Landscape Lines Bulletin 4*, 1998 (published by the Park Historic Structures and Cultural Landscapes Program, NPS).

23. The Philadelphia firm of Andropogon Associates developed the initial Earthworks Landscape Management Manual for the NPS.

24. Although it is likely that future generations may find such places significant cultural landscapes because of what they reveal about the late twentieth century, it

may be more appropriate to regard them as influenced by the historic preservation movement than as a solution to the effects of sprawl and rural development on historic preservation goals.

25. Although this may sound critical of the Main Street program, it actually is not. Without the earlier designation of urban commercial districts, it would have been a huge leap to the concept of rural historic districts. Main Street projects were actually nudging us a step in the direction of landscape preservation by encouraging holistic thinking—at least of a district as a distinct geographic area with diverse resources and multiple features and often lacking a single individually outstanding resource.

26. Robert D. Yaro, Randall G. Arendt, Harry L. Dodson, and Elizabeth Brabec, *Change in the Connecticut River Valley: A Design Manual for Conservation and Development* (North Amherst: Center for Rural Massachusetts, 1988). The *H-2 Corridor Design Guidelines* were developed by Land and Community Associates of Charlottesville, Va., in 1989 and adopted by the town of Leesburg in 1990.

27. The 1998 thirtieth anniversary meeting of the Association for Preservation Technology in Williamsburg, Va., had a session on the landscape as artifact.

28. The guidelines were initiated by the chief of the Technical Preservation Services Branch of the Preservation Assistance Division of NPS, Ward Jandl, a historical architect, and NPS landscape architect Lauren Meier in 1989; they were further developed, expanded, and completed by landscape architects Charles Birnbaum and Christine Capella Peters from 1992 to 1996. Birnbaum, as coordinator of the NPS Cultural Landscape Initiative, worked closely with the AHLP, state historic preservation offices, practicing landscape architects, and departments of landscape architecture to complete the guidelines.

29. At a 1999 meeting of Poplar Forest's landscape advisory panel, Peter Hatch of Monticello's Thomas Jefferson Memorial Foundation observed that he felt a reverence for the trees because of that historic association.

30. According to William Wagner, FAIA, the original designer, "The important thing is for it to look like that last drawing I made. How you get there, I think, is not important." Wagner to the authors, Iowa State University, 1996.

Chapter 7

1. TNC and Association for Biodiversity Information, *Precious Heritage: The Status of Biodiversity in the United States* (New York: Oxford University Press, 2000), 93–118.

2. Michael Soulé and Gary Lease, eds., *Reinventing Nature?: Responses to Postmodern Deconstruction* (Washington, D.C.: Island Press, 1995); Reed F. Noss, "Protecting Natural Areas in Fragmented Landscapes," *Natural Areas Journal* 7, no. 1 (January 1987): 2–13; David S. Wilcove, "From Fragmentation to Extinction," *Natural Areas Journal* 7, no. 1 (January 1987): 23–29.

3. See TNC website, ‹www.tnc.org›.

4. Ibid.

5. For more information, see the websites of TPL, ‹www.tpl.org›, and TCF, ‹www.conservationfund.org›.

6. Robin Fedden, *The Continuing Purpose: A History of the National Trust, Its Aims*

and Work (London: Longmans, Green, 1968). The British National Trust was incorporated in 1895. Lands held by the trust are inalienable and cannot be used for any other purpose, or even taken by the government for public use, except by a special act of Parliament.

7. Land Trust Alliance, *1998 National Directory of Conservation Land Trusts* (Washington, D.C.: The Alliance, 1998). See also its website, ‹www.lta.org›, for a national directory to all land trusts.

8. W. M. Denevan, "The Pristine Myth: The Landscape of the Americas in 1492," *Annals of the Association of American Geographers* 82, no. 4 (1992): 369–85.

9. William Cronon, "The Trouble with Wilderness; Or, Getting Back to the Wrong Nature," in *Uncommon Ground: Rethinking the Human Place in Nature*, ed. William Cronon (New York: Norton, 1996), 69–90.

10. John C. Hendee et al., *Wilderness Management*, Forest Service, U.S. Department of Agriculture Miscellaneous Publication 1365 (Washington, D.C.: GPO, 1978).

11. John Brinckerhoff Jackson, "Beyond Wilderness," in *A Sense of Place, a Sense of Time* (New Haven, Conn.: Yale University Press, 1994), 71–91.

12. Henry David Thoreau, "Walking," in *The Works of Thoreau*, ed. Henry S. Canby (Boston: Houghton Mifflin, 1937), 672.

13. Aldo Leopold, *A Sand County Almanac, with Other Essays on Conservation from Round River* (New York: Oxford University Press, 1966).

14. May Theilgaard Watts, *Reading the Landscape of America*, 2d ed. (New York: Collier McMillan, 1975).

15. Pierce F. Lewis, "Axioms for Reading the Landscape: Some Guides to the American Scene," in *The Interpretation of Ordinary Landscapes: Geographical Essays*, ed. D. W. Meinig (New York: Oxford University Press, 1979).

16. The terms "covenant" and "restriction" are used here in a generic sense to refer to any type of private land-use control implemented through recorded instruments, whether called "deed restrictions," "covenants," "restrictions," "agreements," or similar terms.

17. *General Statutes of North Carolina*, chap. 121, sec. 35.

18. Janet Diehl and Thomas S. Barrett, *The Conservation Easement Handbook: Managing Land Conservation and Historic Preservation Easement Programs* (Alexandria, Va.: Land Trust Exchange, 1988); Thomas S. Barrett and Stefan Nagel, *Model Conservation Easement and Model Historic Preservation Easement* (Washington, D.C.: Land Trust Alliance, 1996). These books may be ordered from the Land Trust Alliance website, ‹www.lta.org›.

19. Sec. 508 of the 1997 Taxpayer Relief Act, as clarified in 1998 and codified as U.S.C. 2031(c).

20. NTHP, *Regional Heritage Areas: Approaches to Sustainable Development*, Information Series 2188 (Washington, D.C.: NTHP, n.d.): Samuel N. Stokes, with A. Elizabeth Watson and Shelley S. Mastran, *Saving America's Countryside: A Guide to Rural Conservation*, 2d ed. (Baltimore: Johns Hopkins University Press for the NTHP, 1997), 289–300; Shelley S. Mastran (preservation consultant), interview with author, Falls Church, Va., July 26, 1999.

21. Internet Bulletin, August 1, 2002, from Brenda Barrett, National Coordinator for Heritage Areas, and telephone interview, October 16, 2002.

22. NCSHPO, *Weekly Legislative Update for SHPOS*, May 18, 2001.

23. *Guidelines for Evaluating and Documenting Rural Historic Landscapes*, National Register of Historic Places Bulletin 30 (Washington, D.C.: NPS, 1992).

24. *Federal Activities*, vol. 1 of *Preserving Our Natural Heritage*, prepared for the U.S. Department of the Interior, NPS, Office of the Chief Scientist, by TNC (Washington, D.C.: GPO, 1977).

25. Philip Hoose, *Building an Ark: Tools for the Preservation of Natural Diversity through Land Protection* (Covelo, Calif.: Island Press for TNC, 1981); Sam Pearsall, "Public Dedication of Nature Preserves," *Natural Areas Association Journal* 4, no. 1 (1984): 11–23.

26. William Cronon, "Conserving Nature in Time" (opening plenary address to the National Land Trust Rally, University of Wisconsin, Madison, October 1998).

27. Ibid.

Chapter 8

1. For a description of the New Archaeology and its impact on the profession, see Gordon R. Wiley and Jeremy A. Sabloff, *A History of American Archaeology*, 3d ed. (New York: W. H. Freeman and Co., 1993).

2. In the 1960s historical archaeology established itself as a unique subfield within anthropology. Many pre-1960s excavations on sites from the historic period were directed by architects in support of planned restoration or reconstruction programs.

3. In its statewide guidance, the Virginia SHPO defines an archaeological site as "the physical remains of any area of human activity greater than 50 years of age for which a boundary can be established." Virginia Department of Historic Resources, *Guidelines for Archaeological Investigations in Virginia* (Richmond: Virginia Department of Historic Resources, 1996).

4. Jan Townsend, John H. Sprinkle Jr., and John Knoerl, *Guidelines for Evaluating and Registering Historical Archaeological Sites and Districts*, National Register Bulletin 36 (Washington, D.C.: NPS, 1993), 23.

5. Jan E. Townsend, "Archeology and the National Register," *CRM* 18, no. 6 (1995 supp.): 1–4.

6. Robert L. Schuyler, *Historical Archaeology: A Guide to Substantive and Theoretical Contributions* (New York: Baywood Publishing, 1978); Ivor Noel Hume, "Archaeology: Handmaiden to History," *North Carolina Historical Review* 41 (April 1964): 214–25.

7. Joseph Schuldenrein, "Changing Career Paths and the Training of Professional Archaeologists: Observations from the Barnard College Forum, Part 1 and 2," *SAA Bulletin* 16, no. 1 (January 1998): 31–33, and 16, no. 3 (May 1998): 26–29.

8. Ruthann Knudson, "Contemporary Cultural Resource Management," in *American Archaeology Past and Future: A Celebration of the Society for American Archaeology, 1935–1985*, ed. David J. Meltzer, Don D. Fowler, and Jeremy A. Sabloff (Washington, D.C.: Smithsonian Institution Press, 1986), 395–414.

9. Charles M. Niquette, "Hard Hat Archaeology," *SAA Bulletin* 15, no. 3 (May 1997): 15–17.

10. Thomas F. King, "Beneath the American Mosaic: The Place of Archaeology,"

in *The American Mosaic: Preserving a Nation's Heritage*, ed. Robert E. Stipe and Antoinette J. Lee (Washington, D.C.: US/ICOMOS, 1987), 264.

11. See David J. Meltzer, Don D. Fowler, and Jeremy A. Sabloff, eds., *American Archaeology Past and Future: A Celebration of the Society for American Archaeology, 1935–1985* (Washington, D.C.: Smithsonian Institution Press, 1986).

12. Mark P. Leone, "Symbolic, Structural, and Critical Archaeology" (415–38), Patty Jo Watson, "Archaeological Interpretation, 1985" (439–58), and Lewis R. Binford, "In Pursuit of the Future" (459–79), ibid.

13. Knudson, "Contemporary Cultural Resource Management," 395–413.

14. See Daniel Haas, ed., "Reaching the Public," *Common Ground: Archaeology and Ethnography in the Public Interest* 3, no. 1 (Spring 1998), and Ronald M. Greenberg, ed., "Archaeology and the Federal Government," *CRM* 17, no. 6 (1994): 1–36.

15. Patricia L. Parker and Thomas F. King, *Guidelines for Evaluating and Documenting Traditional Cultural Properties*, National Register Bulletin 38 (Washington, D.C.: NPS, 1990); Patricia L. Parker, ed., "America's Tribal Cultures—a Renaissance in the 1990s," *CRM* 14, no. 5 (1991); Robert S. Grumet, ed., "Working Together to Preserve the Past," *CRM* 18, no. 7 (1995): 1–32.

16. Jason J. Gonzalez and Eden A. Welker, "Field Schools: The First Experience," *SAA Bulletin* 16, no. 2 (January 1998): 6–7; Barbara J. Mills, "The Archaeological Field School in the 1990s: Collaboration in Research and Training," *SAA Bulletin* 14, no. 3 (November 1996): 18–20.

17. *1998 Directory of Certified Professional Archaeologists, Florida* (N.p., Fla.: Society of Professional Archaeologists, 1998).

18. *The Register of Professional Archaeologists, 1999–2000 Directory* (N.p.: The Register, 1999). See Bill Lipe and Vin Steponaitis, "SAA to Promote Professional Standards through ROPA Sponsorship," *SAA Bulletin* 16, no. 2 (March 1998): 1, 16–17.

19. *UFAT Handbook* (N.p.: UFAT Membership Committee, 1997); W. Kevin Pape, "Emerging Crises in CRM Archaeology," *SAA Bulletin* 13, no. 2 (March–May 1995): 24–26.

20. Francis P. McMannamon, "Native American Graves Protection and Repatriation Act (NAGPRA)," in *Archaeological Method and Theory: An Encyclopedia*, ed. Linda Ellis (New York: Garland Publishing, 2000).

21. John H. Sprinkle Jr., "Do Archaeologists Dig, Destroy, and Discriminate?: The Historical Significance and Value of Archaeological Sites," in *Preservation of What? For Whom?: A Critical Look at Historical Significance*, ed. Michael A. Tomlin (Ithaca, N.Y.: NCPE, 1998), 169–80.

22. Defining which areas are subject to archaeological investigation depends on which stage of research is under way. Relatively narrow (300 feet wide) highway corridor studies often yield numerous archaeological sites that are only partially contained within the study area. For example, a proposed road improvement project in New York identified a prehistoric archaeological site along the edge of a suggested road cut. Survey of the site was limited to the small field included in the project's area of potential effect. Since it was not possible to conduct a proper assessment of the resource's National Register eligibility, further study was recommended. The second stage of work defined the site's boundary, which was well beyond the area of the proposed improvements, and found that the site contained important information about

the prehistory of that region. Yet the project was found to have no adverse effect on the site because the area within the APE did not include significant archaeological remains. If the APE did include important assemblages, then the mitigation of the adverse effect (an excavation to recover the archaeological data) would have been confined to the APE. Complicating this picture is the fact that APEs frequently change during the course of a project.

23. Tim Church, "Ecosystem Management and CRM: Do We Have a Role?," *SAA Bulletin* 15, no. 2 (March 1997): 25–26.

24. Formerly known as *Federal Archaeology Report* (1988–94) and *Federal Archaeology* (1994–96), *Common Ground* has been published with the subtitle *Archaeology and Ethnography in the Public Interest*, reflecting the growth of the public archaeology paradigm.

25. *Preservation* (magazine of the NTHP) 51 (September–October 1999); Donna Seifert, "Bricks and Mortar, Cups and Saucers: Bits and Pieces of the Past," *National Trust Forum Journal* 14 (Fall 1999): 45–47.

26. A small sampling of recent publications on the application of modern technology to archaeological fieldwork includes John W. Rick, "Total Stations in Archaeology," *SAA Bulletin* 14, no. 4 (September 1996): 24–27; Thegn L. Ladefoged, Michael W. Graves, Blaze V. O'Connor, and Robin Chapin, "Integration of Global Positioning Systems into Archaeological Field Research: A Case Study from North Kohala, Hawaii Island," *SAA Bulletin* 16, no. 1 (January 1998): 23–27; Robert G. Whitlam, "Cyberstaking Archaeological Sites: Using Electronic Marker Systems (EMS) for a Site Datum and Monitoring Station," *SAA Bulletin* 16, no. 2 (March 1998): 12–15; and John Rick, "Digital Still Cameras and Archaeology," *SAA Bulletin* 17, no. 3 (May 1999): 37–41.

27. Diane Vogt-O'Connor, ed., "Cultural Resources and the World Wide Web," *CRM* 18, no. 9 (1995): 1–36.

28. R. P. Stephen Davis Jr., Patrick C. Livingood, Trawick Ward, and Vincas P. Steponaitis, eds., *Excavating Occaneechi Town: Archaeology of an Eighteenth-Century Indian Village in North Carolina* (Chapel Hill: University of North Carolina Press, 1998).

29. For a review of DNA research, see Tabitha M. Powledge and Mark Rose, "The Greate DNA Hunt: Part II, Colonizing the Americas," *Archaeology* 49, no. 5 (September–October 1996): 36–47; Brenda Smiley, "Fingerprinting the Dead," *Archaeology* 49, no. 6 (November–December 1996): 66; and Peter Forster, Roslind Harding, Antonio Torroni, and Hans-Jurgen Bandelt, "Origin and Evolution of Native American mtDNA Variation: A Reappraisal," *American Journal of Human Genetics* 59 (1996): 935–45.

30. S. Terry Childs, "Caring for Collections," *CRM* 17, no. 6 (1994): 11.

31. Thomas F. King, Patricia Parker Hickman, and Gary Berg, *Anthropology in Historic Preservation: Caring for Culture's Clutter* (New York: Academic Press, 1977).

32. The Archaeological Conservancy now owns more than 175 sites across the country. See Carol Carnett, *Legal Background of Archaeological Resources Protection*, Technical Brief 11 (Washington, D.C.: NPS, 1991); Susan L. Henry, *Protecting Archeological Sites on Private Lands* (Washington, D.C.: NPS, 1993); Robert Thorne, *Developing an Archaeological Site Conservation Database* (Washington, D.C.: NPS,

1996); and Carol L. Carnett, *A Survey of State Statutes Protecting Archaeological Resources* (Washington, D.C.: NPS, 1995).

33. The NPS publication *Common Ground* is a good source of information on the status of ARPA investigations. See also Robert D. Hicks, "Time Crime." *FBI Law Enforcement Bulletin* 66 (July 1997): 1–12, and "A Time Crime: Summary of Federal and Virginia Laws: Theft of/Vandalism to Historic, Archaeological Resources" (paper presented at the Virginia Association of Museums Annual Meeting, Williamsburg, Va., March 1998).

Chapter 9

1. Jack C. Harris and Jack P. Friedman, *Barron's Real Estate Handbook* (New York: Barron's Educational Services, 1984), 75.

2. Ibid., 242.

3. William H. Hudnut III, "A Catalyst for Redevelopment," *Urban Land* 58 (November–December 1999): 70.

4. Harris and Friedman, *Barron's Real Estate Handbook*, 242.

5. David Listokin and Michael L. Lahr, "Economic Impacts of Preservation in New Jersey and Texas," *Forum Journal* 14 (Spring 2000): 58.

6. John Costonis, *Space Adrift: Landmark Preservation and the Marketplace* (Urbana: University of Illinois Press, 1974). See also Robert Lane, "Transfer of Development Rights for Balanced Development," *Land Lines* (newsletter of the Lincoln Institute of Land Policy) 10 (March 1998).

7. Lisa Burcham, "Urban Revitalization: When Rehab Grows Up," *Forum Journal* 14 (Spring 2000): 27–37.

8. Urban Land Institute, *Public-Private Partnerships Conference Brochure*, Spring 2000.

9. Listokin and Lahr, "Economic Impacts," 57–64.

10. Ibid.

Chapter 10

1. The National Society of the Colonial Dames of America owns and operates forty-two museum properties; in addition, it operates and manages forty-five museum properties owned by other organizations.

2. Elizabeth D. Mulloy, *The History of the National Trust for Historic Preservation* (Washington, D.C.: Preservation Press, 1976); Charles B. Hosmer Jr., *Preservation Comes of Age: From Williamsburg to the National Trust, 1926–1949*, 2 vols. (Charlottesville: University Press of Virginia for Preservation Press, 1981).

3. Both Ray Suarez, *The Old Neighborhood: What We Lost in the Great Suburban Migration, 1966–1999* (New York: Free Press, 1999), and Thomas W. Hanchett, *Sorting Out the New South City: Race, Class, and Urban Development in Charlotte, 1875–1975* (Chapel Hill: University of North Carolina Press, 1998), document the pivotal role of race in the abandonment of central-city neighborhoods after World War II.

4. According to the NPS, the historic rehabilitation tax credits have been used in combination with the affordable housing tax credits to create more than 30,000

affordable housing units in historic buildings. This combination of incentives has had the salutary benefit of preserving a number of important buildings that had few alternative adaptive uses, maintaining economic diversity in historic districts and downtowns, and dispelling the elitist image of historic preservation.

5. In the 1970s bricks-and-mortar funding could be obtained through grants from the NPS as well as from corporations and foundations. However, many foundations have eliminated bricks-and-mortar projects from eligible activities, whether for preservation or other purposes. Some foundations that gave for the restoration of museum properties in the 1960s and 1970s even eliminated historic preservation from their areas of interest to avoid having to fund the ongoing costs of museum repair and operation. Their prohibitions on funding historic preservation have often stayed in place, despite the evolution of the preservation movement into environmental, affordable housing, and economic development alliances. Corporate giving is now more closely tied to corporate communications than ever, supporting projects that enhance sales or boost the corporate image in the community. Preservation often runs counter to the short-term interests of many businesses.

6. Studies of the economic impact of historic preservation have been commissioned by the statewides in Virginia, Indiana, North Carolina, and New Jersey, among others. These studies have shown that preservation has succeeded admirably in adding to local tax bases with relatively little public investment.

7. Quoted from ‹www.vhcb.org/›.

8. The separately incorporated North Carolina revolving fund was initially turned down for tax-exempt status in 1977 by the IRS, which did not find the fund to be sufficiently different from a for-profit real estate entity. The fund appealed the ruling, and the resulting ruling paved the way for the creation of other statewide and local revolving funds as well as legitimizing the National Trust's own revolving fund. The IRS ruling limited the North Carolina fund to working with properties on or eligible for the National Register and required the fund to place preservation deed restrictions on all properties it sold to ensure their proper rehabilitation, maintenance, and public access.

9. After operating a revolving fund for nearly a quarter of a century, PNC recently opted to change the name of its real estate program to the "Endangered Properties Program." All too often, PNC's donors, as well as nonprofit groups seeking to emulate the revolving fund program, would mistakenly focus on the need for capital in the revolving fund, rather than the need for revenue to operate the program. The name "Endangered Properties Program" is more descriptive, and it highlights the programmatic nature of the activity. PNC also renamed the fund the "Endangered Properties Fund" after donors repeatedly confused the revolving fund with the endowment fund.

10. In 1993 the National Trust established a task force to examine the organizational structure of the historic preservation movement in America. After looking at the structures of other national movements, the task force recommended that the movement would benefit from the strengthening of independent, but cooperative, statewide and local groups. One of its most carefully examined issues was how the National Trust should work with local organizations during a period of intense commitment to building new and stronger statewide organizations.

11. The Tax Reform Act of 1969 and subsequent IRS regulations required that a preservation easement be made "in perpetuity" in order for the owner to take a charitable deduction for its donation.

12. In 1999 Boston College researchers Paul Schervish and John Havens published a study, *Millionaires and the Millennium: New Estimates of the Forthcoming Wealth Transfer and the Prospects for a Golden Age of Philanthropy* (Boston: Boston College, 1999), on the intergeneration transfer of wealth and its implications for charitable giving. They estimated that between 1998 and 2052, $41 trillion to $136 trillion would transfer between generations, with charitable bequests ranging from $6 to $25 trillion.

13. Planned giving is an organization's best tool for obtaining large donations and building an endowment, and nonprofit organizations must look creatively for additional prospects for these gifts. For example, gay men and women constitute a demographic group worth targeting. Frequently members of two-income, childless households and, in many cases, owners of historic houses, gays and lesbians are excellent prospects. With a creative fund-raising strategy, a preservation nonprofit might consider sponsoring planned giving informational programs targeted to the legal and financial needs of single individuals. Such a creative strategy, though causing discomfort for some, would also highlight the diversity of the preservation movement.

14. An example of finding new sources of financial support is provided by the New York Landmarks Conservancy's Professional Circle. The organization has created a special membership category for businesses and professionals engaged in the preservation of New York. In exchange for contributions from those professionals or their businesses, the conservancy promotes the Professional Circle on its website and in other publications, providing a benefit to its contributors. Visitors to the website can get the names and addresses of preservation-related businesses in New York, while the conservancy obtains increased financial support from those who benefit from its work. The program has been a financial success.

15. In 2000 Bank of America and the NTHP announced the creation of a $25 million nationwide historic tax credit fund that would target its equity investments toward the revitalization of small neighborhood properties.

16. Brownfields are abandoned, usually contaminated, urban industrial sites ripe for cleanup and recycling for new, contemporary uses.

17. In the 1980s every advocate for preservation was touched by the asbestos scare. The public heard over and over how old buildings had asbestos and how it cost a fortune to get rid of the fireproofing material. Newspaper, magazines, and TV newscasts showed workers suited up to look like astronauts venturing into basements to remove asbestos pipe wrap. Deals to renovate historic buildings were killed by asbestos-removal costs. Federal housing agencies and secondary mortgage lenders required asbestos removal before loans could be made. A decade later, research showed that asbestos was not nearly as harmful as originally thought. Cynics would say that the asbestos scare made tons of money for environmental laboratories and contractors who specialized in asbestos removal—as well as for new homebuilders. Asbestos—like previous concerns, such as underground oil tanks and basements with radon—set preservation efforts back by years.

The current scare is lead paint. As with asbestos, common sense has been thrown to the wind by public agencies and the secondary mortgage market. Every person who has reached adulthood by the publication date of this book grew up with lead paint. Health agencies are requiring the removal of lead paint from areas completely out of the reach of toddlers to minimize the risk of their licking or eating it. Reasonable mitigation efforts have been rejected in favor of total lead removal, a prodigious expense. Continued inflexibility about lead paint will lead to problems for owners of all homes and businesses built before 1970. New homebuilders and environmental specialists will have a field day, and historic buildings will again be deemed unsafe in the public eye. If preservationists are faced with the hazard du jour when trying to obtain a loan or a building permit, our older buildings and areas will languish. Preservationists must get their message out to the public, to federal agencies such as HUD, and to secondary mortgage purchasers like Fannie Mae.

Chapter 11

1. Antoinette J. Lee, "Conservation Areas in British Towns" (report prepared for the Washington, D.C., Branch, English-Speaking Union of the United States, January 27, 1977, revised March 18, 1977).

2. Robert E. Stipe, "Conservation Areas: A New Approach to an Old Problem," *Local Preservation* (Washington, D.C.: Interagency Resources Division, NPS) (July 1993): 3–8.

3. US/ICOMOS, ‹www.usicomos/org›.

4. Robert E. Stipe, *County Planning: How the English Do It* (Washington, D.C.: NTHP and National Association of Counties, 1972).

5. Klaus-Jürgen Evert, ed., *Lexikon Landschafts und Stadtplanung* (New York and Berlin: Springer-Verlag, 2001).

6. Robert E. Stipe, telephone interview with author, July 18, 2000.

7. See ‹www.novgorod-museum.ru›. Foreign guidebooks to museums and historic sites are fairly common. This bilingual website was designed to reach an American audience in lieu of a printed guidebook, which would have been more difficult to bring to market in the United States.

8. Douglas H. Swaim, "Global Markets, Global Culture?," *Business Ethics Forum* 4, no. 1 (1991): 30–35.

9. J. Thomas Schneider, "Report to the Secretary of the Interior on the Preservation of Historic Sites and Buildings" (Washington, D.C.: U.S. Department of the Interior, 1935).

10. *WHSR.*

11. Russell V. Keune, ed., *The Historic Preservation Yearbook, 1984–1985*, 1st ed. (Bethesda, Md.: Adler and Adler, 1984).

12. Margaret G. H. MacLean, ed., *Cultural Heritage in Asia and the Pacific: Conservation and Policy* (Marina del Ray, Calif.: Getty Conservation Institute, 1993).

13. *Acquisition and Preservation of Historically, Architecturally, or Culturally Significant Property Overseas*, Foreign Building Operations Policy and Procedures Directive RE005 (Washington, D.C.: Department of State, 2000).

14. Ismail Serageldin and Joan Martin-Brown, *Culture in Sustainable Development:*

Investing in Cultural and Natural Endowments (Washington, D.C.: The World Bank, 1999).

15. Sharon Timmons, ed., *Preservation and Conservation: Principles and Practices* (Washington, D.C.: Preservation Press, 1976).

16. ICOMOS International Specialized Committee on Cultural Tourism, *Tourism at World Heritage Cultural Sites: The Site Manager's Handbook* (Columbo, Sri Lanka: ICOMOS, 1993).

17. Hisashi B. Sugaya and Lisa Lange, *Proceedings from the Third International Tourism and Heritage Conservation Conference* (San Francisco: Pacific Area Travel Association, 1984).

18. World Monuments Fund and US/ICOMOS, *Trails to Tropical Treasures: A Tour of ASEAN's Cultural Heritage* (New York: World Monuments Fund, 1992).

19. The Slovakia course at Svaty Jur is targeted to students from the former Soviet Union satellite countries but is taught in English and welcomes students from the United States.

Chapter 12

1. Carole Merritt, *Historic Black Resources: A Handbook for the Identification, Documentation, and Evaluation of Historic African-American Properties in Georgia* (Atlanta: Historic Preservation Section, Georgia Department of Natural Resources, 1984).

2. Ormond H. Loomis, coordinator, *Cultural Conservation: The Protection of Cultural Heritage in the United States: A Study* (Washington, D.C.: American Folklife Center, Library of Congress, in cooperation with the NPS, 1983).

3. Antoinette J. Lee, ed., *Past Meets Future: Saving America's Historic Environments* (Washington, D.C.: Preservation Press, 1992).

4. Sierra Neal and Jonathan Sanchez, "Helping Grassroots Preservationists Emerge in the Field," *CRM* 22, no. 8 (1999): 41–44.

5. N. Y. Nathiri, "Heritage, History, and Hurston: Celebrated Author/Folklorist Establishes a Place for Eatonville within the Preservation Movement," *CRM* 22, no. 8 (1999): 6–8.

6. "NAAAHP History," NAAAHP, Indianapolis, Ind., n.d.

7. "Information Sheet," NAAAHP, n.d.

8. Michael L. Blakey, "The New York African Burial Ground Project: An Examination of Enslaved Lives, a Construction of Ancestral Ties" (briefing delivered before the Subcommission on Prevention of Discrimination and Protection of Minorities, Commission on Human Rights, United Nations, Palais des Nations, Geneva, Switzerland, August 19, 1997), 2.

9. Ned Kaufman, "History Happened Here: A Plan for Saving New York City's Historically and Culturally Significant Sites" (discussion draft, Municipal Art Society of New York, November 1996), 6.

10. Louretta Wimberly, "Making a Difference, Making It Happen," *CRM* 22, no. 8 (1999): 28–30.

11. National Parks and Conservation Association, "America's Parks, America's

People: A Mosaic in Motion, Breaking Barriers of Race and Diversity in Our National Parks" (conference highlights, San Francisco, July 1999), 2.

12. Craig Evan Barton, "Sites of Memory: Thematic Statement" (paper abstract presented at the "Sites of Memory: Landscapes of Race and Ideology" symposium, University of Virginia, School of Architecture, Campbell Hall, Charlottesville, March 25–27, 1999), 3.

13. For a comprehensive discussion of Colonial Williamsburg's evolving interpretive program, see Cary Carson, "Colonial Williamsburg and the Practice of Interpretive Planning in American History Museums," *Public Historian* 20 (Summer 1998): 11–51.

Chapter 13

1. Charles B. Hosmer Jr., *The Presence of the Past: A History of the Preservation Movement in the United States before Williamsburg* (New York: G. P. Putnam's Sons, 1965), 33–34.

2. Thomas Jefferson's excavations of a burial mound set a standard for fieldwork and publication of results that would not be consistently surpassed by professional archaeologists until well into the twentieth century.

3. That this was a policy question rather than a legitimate scientific issue is apparent when it is recalled that the entire argument revolved around the idea that the mound sites were abandoned at the time Europeans first arrived in the Americas. However, the Spanish encountered and wrote extensively about the mound-building tribes in the southeastern United States. The debate ignored these eyewitness accounts of the contemporary tribes building and living in mound villages throughout the region.

4. Today, this kind of work is considered to be looting. But this was the way that much of archaeology was carried out in the nineteenth and early twentieth centuries worldwide. Until well into the twentieth century, archaeology was mainly concerned with collecting artifacts for display at museums or for providing museums with collections. It was not, for the most part, about scientific reconstruction of cultural histories or past ways of life.

5. Museums made it a standard practice to purchase interesting artifacts from "freelance" archaeologists. The work of freelancers led to the wholesale excavation of sites in the Southwest. In some cases, the freelancers simply dug haphazardly in sites looking for salable artifacts. Other freelancers were more careful, keeping relatively accurate notes and excavating according to acceptable methods. Whereas the condition of sites after excavation by either method was very different, substantial destruction of the archaeological record occurred. The Indians of the region knew of all of these sites and often willingly led the miners to them (probably to keep them away from their own communities). The use of the word "discovery" is deeply offensive to most Native Americans because it is used in the context of European acts of discovery. Nevertheless, the miners are routinely credited with discovering these sites. Later, the sites were often rediscovered by archaeologists.

6. The Antiquities Act prohibited the excavation of archaeological sites on federal

and Indian lands without the authority of a permit issued by the Smithsonian Institution and later the secretary of the interior. It set a fine of $100 for the removal of archaeological or paleontological materials without a permit. Although this may seem to be a laughably small amount, it was a substantial sum of money in 1906. In the 1970s the fine was increased to $500, which is what it remains today. The Antiquities Act also authorized the president to set aside national monuments from the public domain. This authority has been exercised throughout the twentieth century to establish national monuments both for archaeological remains and for natural areas. Despite objections from some lawmakers in Congress, this authority remains federal law. Since its enactment, it has been used by all but three presidents. Most recently, President Bill Clinton created new national monuments under its authority.

7. Paleo-Indian refers to both the people and the time period of the earliest archaeological cultures in the Americas. Conventionally, the Paleo-Indian era dates from approximately 12,000 to 8,000 years ago. In the United States, the most famous Paleo-Indian archaeological cultures are known as Clovis and Folsom, after the sites where the defining artifacts were first discovered by archaeologists.

8. No one has seriously argued that the Paleo-Indians/Paleo-Americans had no descendants. The logic of the Paleo-American proponents requires a complete population replacement of the Paleo-Americans by some ancestral Native American population during the Archaic Period (the period that began approximately 8,000 years ago) and the rise of agriculture-dependent societies.

9. "Cultural affiliation," a term used in NAGPRA, is the principal basis for determining which Indian tribe has the right to claim and determine final disposition of Native American human remains excavated or discovered on federal lands.

10. *Cherokee Nation v. Georgia*, 30 U.S. (6 Pet.), 1 (1831).

11. The need to keep this information confidential is illustrated by Navajo beliefs. Sacred places are considered part of curing ceremonies. Navajo chanters believe that inappropriately speaking of such places may rob the chant of its power, diminishing the chanter's ability to heal the sick and bring individuals back into the harmony that is central to the Navajo Way.

12. Congress authorized compensation in very limited circumstances in which a tribe could demonstrate that it had not been adequately compensated for the taking of its lands by nontribal members. To sustain a claim, the tribe was required to prove that it had never been compensated or that any compensation it had received had been "unconscionably" low. In addition, the tribe had to show the extent of its tribal lands at the time when the claim was being made.

13. The date of the "taking" often was set to coincide with the date of the establishment of the reservation, often long after substantial reductions in tribal territories had begun.

14. A tribal enterprise is a special sort of business. It is essentially the tribe itself "doing business as" a corporate entity. Enterprises are unique to Indian tribes and are common throughout Indian country. They can be found anywhere a tribe is conducting business.

15. The United States sought to convict an individual who had stolen Hopi ceremonial masks and attempted to sell them. Apparently of recent manufacture, the

Hopi masks were made for and used in ceremonies, then disposed of on the Hopi tribal lands. The Court held that it was impossible to know when a person might be violating the Antiquities Act because it provides no definition of "antiquity." Since the looting and trafficking in archaeological materials was now more vigorous than in the early twentieth century, a new legal tool was needed to protect archaeological remains.

16. According to ARPA, archaeological resources refer to "any material remains of past human life or activities which are of archaeological interest, as determined under uniform regulations promulgated to this Act. Such regulations containing such determination shall include, but not be limited to: pottery, basketry, bottles, weapons, weapon projectiles, tools, structures or portions of structures, pit houses, rock paintings, rock carvings, intaglios, graves, human skeletal remains, or [a] portion of [a] piece of any of the foregoing items . . . that is at least 100 years old."

17. Whether an ARPA violation is charged as a misdemeanor or a felony depends on the severity of the incident. Second violations are always felonies.

18. NHPA's definition of "Indian lands" is problematical. Indian lands are all lands "within the exterior boundaries of an Indian reservation and all dependent Indian communities." Some tribes define the exterior boundaries of their reservations differently, claiming more (often substantially more) land than the federal government acknowledges. Such claims have sometimes been upheld in court. In addition, as tribal employees THPOs are obligated to comply with tribal ordinances, policies, etc. Such boundaries cannot simply be dismissed or ignored.

19. Likewise, "dependent Indian community" cannot be defined administratively but only in courts of law. It is common for immediately adjacent sections of land to be found "dependent," while the neighboring section is not held to be.

20. Who is to perform functions in disputed areas? Answering this question inevitably will lead to substantial conflicts between SHPOs, who are state officials, and THPOs, who as tribal officials must support the tribe's sovereignty. The definitions must rely on the sincere efforts and goodwill of THPOs and SHPOs or, failing these, congressional action. The act's use of "chief governing authority" is slightly problematic. It is used as a gloss for "tribal council," which can go by a variety of different names. On occasion, NPS has interpreted this to refer to the chief executive officer of the tribe, usually the council chairman, president, or governor. But the phrase indicates the legislative, rather than executive, nature of the "authority." NHPA designates the secretary of the interior as the reviewing and approving authority. Like virtually all of the secretary's historic preservation responsibilities, approval authority has been delegated to the director of the NPS.

21. Adopting regulations is governed by the Administrative Procedure Act, which requires that draft regulations be published for public comment. Each public comment must be analyzed and responded to in some form and the regulations revised, taking into account the comments received. Then the agency must publish the rule in final form for effect. There can, and often is, a time lag of months, often years, between publication in draft and publication for effect.

22. The twenty-seven tribes with THPOs are the Catawba Indian Nation, Cheyenne River Sioux Tribe, Chippewa Indians of Wisconsin, Confederated Tribes of the Colville Reservation, Confederated Salish and Kootenai Tribes of the Flathead

Nation, Confederated Tribes of the Warm Springs Reservation, Confederated Tribes of the Umatilla Reservation, Eastern Band of Cherokee Indians, Hualapai Tribe, Lac Courte Oreilles Band of Lake Superior, Lac du Flambeau Band of Lake Superior Chippewa Indians, Leech Lake Band of Chippewa Indians, Makah Tribe, Menominee Indian Tribe of Wisconsin, Mescalero Apache Tribe, Mille Lacs Band of Ojibwe Indians, Narragansett Indian Tribe, Navajo Nation, Poarch Bank of Creek Indians, Seneca Nation of Indians, Skokomish Indian Tribe, Spokane Tribe of Indians, Standing Rock Sioux Tribe, Tunica-Biloxi Indians of Louisiana, Wampanoag Tribe of Gay Head, White Mountain Apache Tribe, and Yurok Tribe.

23. Patricia L. Parker, *Keepers of the Treasures: Protecting Historic Properties and Cultural Traditions on Indian Lands: A Report on Tribal Preservation Funding Needs Submitted to Congress by the National Park Service, United States Department of the Interior* (Washington, D.C.: NPS, 1990). Two common misapprehensions about tribal governments are that (1) they receive lavish support from the federal treasury and (2) they are awash in casino profits. With respect to the first, the federal government spends approximately $4 billion on reservations and levees about $4 billion in federal taxes. Regarding casino profits, many tribes do not own casinos. In fact, most casinos make little or no profit; fewer than a dozen tribes have significant casino revenues. With the exception of a dozen tribes, no tribes have the revenues required to operate government programs to meet the life-and-death needs of its members.

24. Dean B. Suagee, "Keepers of the Native Treasures," in Antoinette J. Lee, ed., *Past Meets Future: Saving America's Historic Environments* (Washington, D.C.: Preservation Press, 1992), 189–95.

Chapter 14

1. Thoms proposed the term in an 1846 letter to the *Athenaeum*, reproduced in Alan Dundes, *The Study of Folklore* (Englewood Cliffs, N.J.: Prentice-Hall, 1965), 4–6.

2. For the development of folklore studies in Europe, see Regina Bendix, *In Search of Authenticity: The Formation of Folklore Studies* (Madison: University of Wisconsin Press, 1997).

3. William Francis Allen, Charles Pickard Ware, and Lucy McKim Garrison, *Slave Songs of the United States* (New York: A. Simpson and Co., 1867).

4. For the history of American folklore studies, see Simon J. Bronner, *American Folklore Studies: An Intellectual History* (Lawrence: University Press of Kansas, 1986), and Rosemary Levy Zumwalt, *American Folklore Scholarship: A Dialogue of Dissent* (Bloomington: Indiana University Press, 1988).

5. See Archie Green, introduction to *Folklife and the Federal Government: A Guide to Activities, Resources, Funds, and Services*, comp. Linda C. Coe (Washington, D.C.: American Folklife Center, Library of Congress, 1977), 1–9.

6. "On the Field and Work of a Journal of American Folk-lore," *Journal of American Folklore* 1 (April–June 1888): 3–7. Franz Boas and Francis James Child assisted Newell in drafting this statement. See Roger D. Abrahams, "Rough Sincerities: William Wells Newell and the Discovery of Folklore in Late-Nineteenth-Century America," in *Folk Roots, New Roots: Folklore in American Life*, ed. Jane S. Becker and

Barbara Franco (Lexington, Mass.: Museum of Our National Heritage, 1988), 61–75.

7. For a history of the archive before it became a part of the American Folklife Center, see Peter Thomas Bartis, *A History of the Archive of Folk Song at the Library of Congress: The First Fifty Years: A Dissertation in Folklore and Folklife* (Ann Arbor, Mich.: University Microfilms International, 1982). For a history of the center and the archive from 1976 to 1996, see Alan Jabbour, "The American Folklife Center: A Twenty-Year Retrospective," *Folklife Center News* 18 (Winter–Spring 1996): 3–19, and (Summer–Fall 1996): 3–23.

8. A history of the Smithsonian Institution's Folklife Festival, originally named the Festival of American Folklife, may be found in Richard Kurin, *Smithsonian Folklife Festival: Culture of, by, and for the People* (Washington, D.C.: Center for Folklife and Cultural Heritage, Smithsonian Institution, 1998).

9. See Alan Jabbour, "Some Reflections on Intangible Resources," in *Rescue Archeology: Papers from the First New World Conference on Rescue Archeology*, ed. Rex L. Wilson and Gloria Loyola (Washington, D.C.: Preservation Press, 1982), 251–56. The changes and continuities within the American Folklore Society are also discussed in Alan Jabbour, "On the Values of American Folklorists," *Journal of American Folklore* 102 (July–September 1989): 292–98, delivered on the occasion of the one hundredth anniversary of the society.

10. Henry Glassie, "Archaeology and Folklore: Common Anxieties, Common Hopes," in *Historic Archeology and the Importance of Material Things*, ed. Leland Ferguson, Special Publications Series 2 (Lansing, Mich.: Society for Historical Archaeology, 1977), 23–35.

11. See, esp., Thomas F. King, Patricia Parker Hickman, and Gary Berg, *Anthropology in Historic Preservation: Caring for Culture's Clutter* (New York: Academic Press, 1977); Patricia L. Parker and Thomas F. King, *Guidelines for Evaluating and Documenting Traditional Cultural Properties*, National Register Bulletin 38 (Washington, D.C.: NPS, 1990).

12. See Don Yoder, "The Folklife Studies Movement," *Pennsylvania Folklife* 13 (July 1963): 43–56.

13. Ormond H. Loomis, coordinator, *Cultural Conservation: The Protection of Cultural Heritage in the United States: A Study* (Washington, D.C.: American Folklife Center, Library of Congress, in cooperation with the NPS, 1983), iv.

14. Ibid.

15. Thomas Carter and Carl Fleischhauer, *The Grouse Creek Cultural Survey: Integrating Folklife and Historic Preservation Field Research*, Publication 13 (Washington, D.C.: American Folklife Center, Library of Congress, 1988).

16. Mary Hufford, *One Space, Many Places: Folklife and Land Use in New Jersey's Pinelands National Reserve*, Publication 15 (Washington, D.C.: American Folklife Center, Library of Congress, 1986).

17. See Robin Fanslow and Mary Hufford, *Tending the Commons: Folklife and Landscape in Southern West Virginia* (online presentation, American Memory, Library of Congress, Washington, D.C., 2000), ⟨http://memory/loc.gov/ammem/cmnshtml/cmnshome.html⟩.

18. Mary Hufford, ed., *Conserving Culture: A New Discourse on Heritage* (Urbana:

University of Illinois Press, 1994). On connections between folklife and environmental planning, see also Hufford, "Stalking the Native View: The Protection of Folklife in Natural Habitats," in *The Conservation of Culture: Folklorists and the Public Sector*, ed. Burt Feintuch (Lexington: University Press of Kentucky, 1988).

19. Yi Fu Tuan, *Space and Place: The Perspective of Experience* (Minneapolis: University of Minnesota Press, 1977).

20. A list of eighteen federally designated heritage areas, along with the year of designation for each of them and some discussion of their legislative history and programmatic potential, may be found in Judy Hart, "Planning for and Preserving Cultural Resources through National Heritage Areas," *CRM* 23, no. 7 (2000): 29–32.

21. Alan Jabbour and Howard W. Marshall, "Folklife and Cultural Preservation," in *New Directions in Rural Preservation*, ed. Robert E. Stipe, Publication 45 (Washington, D.C.: HCRS, U.S. Department of the Interior, 1980), 43–49; Jabbour, "Some Reflections on Intangible Resources," 251–56.

22. The printed program for the September 2000 awards ceremony, *The National Heritage Fellowships 2000*, contains a list of the 248 fellows over the nineteen years of the National Heritage Fellowships. In addition to ethnic and geographic sweep, there is surprising variety in what is regarded as an art—including, for example, the Japanese tea ceremony and Puerto Rican hammock weaving.

23. On the WPA and documentary projects, see William F. McDonald, *Federal Relief Administration and the Arts: The Origins and Administrative History of the Arts Projects of the Works Progress Administration* (Columbus: Ohio State University Press, 1969). Roy Stryker's famous photographic unit actually moved from the Resettlement Administration to the Farm Security Administration, then, after the outbreak of World War II, to the Office of War Information. See Carl Fleischhauer and Beverly W. Brannan, eds., *Documenting America, 1935–1943* (Berkeley: University of California Press, 1988).

24. *The Fund for Folk Culture: Seven-Year Annual Report* (Santa Fe, N.Mex.: The Fund for Folk Culture, 1997); Patricia L. Parker, *Keepers of the Treasures: Protecting Historic Properties and Cultural Traditions on Indian Lands: A Report on Tribal Preservation Funding Needs Submitted to Congress by the National Park Service, United States Department of the Interior* (Washington, D.C.: NPS, 1990).

Chapter 15

1. *WHSR*.

2. See *CRM*, the bimonthly magazine of the Cultural Resource program of the NPS, and *Preservation*, the monthly magazine of the National Trust.

3. The HPF as such goes back to 1966, and discussion about the use of revenues from offshore oil leases as a potential source of permanent funding free from the annual appropriations process began in the late 1970s. A legislative proposal for such funding was put forth in Congress for the first time in 1998 but did not pass. The amounts actually appropriated by Congress have never reached the levels authorized.

4. Examples include New Mexico, Ohio, North Carolina, and Illinois. The practice was also confirmed by my personal experience as North Carolina SHPO (1974–75). In a classic confrontation of this kind, an emissary ostensibly speaking on behalf

of the governor's office made it quite clear that I would be replaced as SHPO if I did not act in accordance with state, rather than federal, policy.

5. NPS Advisory Board, *National Performance Review of the Historic Fund Partnerships* (Washington, D.C.: NPS, March 6, 1994).

6. These new programs are reminiscent of the concept that gave rise to the HCRS, which was preservation's home base within the Interior Department during the Carter administration.

7. Examples include the Civil War Trust and state Civil War Commissions in many states, the Association for Commercial Archaeology, the Vernacular Architecture Forum, Partners for Sacred Places, the League of Historic American Theaters, black heritage councils and committees in the southern states, railroad historical societies, and organizations to preserve rural resources. A glance at successive issues of the National Trust's *Forum News* calendar of events confirms the existence of many and varied preservation-related organizations.

8. See Chapter 4.

9. Note that the SHPO is not required to have any particular qualifications for the job. For a recent discussion of the issue of professionals versus citizens, see Fritz Pannekoek, "The Rise of Heritage Priesthood," in *Preservation of What? For Whom?*, ed. Michael A. Tomlin (Ithaca, N.Y.: NCPE, 1998), and DeTeel Patterson Tiller, "The Role of the Professional in Preservation Today," letter to the editor, *Preservation Forum* 13 (Spring 1999): 4–6.

10. The broad, inclusive sweep of the National Trust's current philosophy of "protecting the irreplaceable" is not new. It had its origins thirty years ago in the controversial report of a 1972 special study committee comprised of trustees and national leaders in historic preservation. Elizabeth D. Mulloy, *The History of the National Trust for Historic Preservation, 1963–73* (Washington, D.C.: Preservation Press, 1976), app. 22–23. The broader concepts were further elaborated in *Preservation: Toward an Ethic in the 1980s: Goals from a National Preservation Conference Held in Williamsburg, Virginia, during March 1979* (Washington D.C.: Preservation Press, 1980). However, credit for serious programmatic engagement by the Trust in these then new and somewhat controversial activities must reside largely with fairly recent National Trust Boards of Trustees and the splendid executive management of the Trust's president, Richard Moe, and his staff.

11. John Hope Franklin, professor emeritus of history at Duke University, speaking at a conference of NPS employees in St. Louis, Mo., in September 2000, noted that 78 percent of America's colleges no longer require students to take any courses in American history, and that 66 percent of recent college graduates polled incorrectly identified Ulysses S. Grant (rather than George Washington) as commander of the Revolutionary American forces at the decisive Battle of Yorktown. A May 2001 article in the *Wall Street Journal* indicated that graduates of three prominent Ivy League universities failed to score higher than 30 percent on basic U.S. history questions.

12. *New Vision: The Preservation Plan for Georgia's Heritage* (Atlanta: Historic Preservation Division, Georgia Department of Natural Resources, 1995), 33–34.

13. Russell Keune, ed. *The Historic Preservation Yearbook* (Bethesda, Md.: Adler and Adler, 1984).

14. Legislative Research Commission on Historic Preservation, Report to the 1989 General Assembly of North Carolina, 1989 sess., Legislative Proposal 7.

15. The core reference volumes advocating this approach are Ervin H. Zube, Robert O. Brush, and Julius Gy. Fabos, *Landscape Assessment: Values, Perceptions, and Resources* (Stroudsburg, Pa.: Dowden, Hutchinson, and Ross, distributed by Halsted Press, 1975), and Arnold Friedmann, Craig Zimring, and Ervin H. Zube, *Environmental Design Evaluation* (New York: Plenum Press, 1978). See also Dolores Hayden, *The Power of Place: Urban Landscapes as Public History* (Cambridge: MIT Press, 1995); J. B. Jackson, *Discovering the Vernacular Landscape* (New Haven, Conn.: Yale University Press, 1984); Richard C. Smardon, James F. Palmer, and John P. Felleman, *Foundations for Visual Project Analysis* (New York: John Wiley, 1986); Roy R. Worskett, *The Character of Towns: An Approach to Conservation* (London: Architectural Press, 1969); Kevin Lynch, *Managing the Sense of a Region* (Cambridge: MIT Press, 1976), and *What Time Is This Place?* (Cambridge: MIT Press, 1976); Robert Yarow, *Dealing with Change in the Connecticut River Valley: A Design Manual for Conservation and Development* (Cambridge, Mass.: Lincoln Institute of Land Policy, 1988); Stephen Kaplan and Rachel Kaplan, *Cognition and Environment: Functioning in an Uncertain World* (New York: Praeger, 1982); Ian Laurie, "Aesthetic Factors in Visual Evaluation," in Zube, Brush, and Fabos, *Landscape Assessment*, 4–9; Robert O. Brush, "Perceived Quality of Scenic and Recreational Environments: Some Methodological Issues," in *Perceiving Environmental Quality: Research and Applications*, ed. Kenneth H. Craik and Ervin H. Zube (New York: Plenum Press, 1976); J. B. Jackson, "The Historic American Landscape," in Zube, Brush, and Fabos, *Landscape Assessment*, 166–80; and Robert E. Stipe, *Perception and Environment: Foundations of Urban Design* (Chapel Hill: Institute of Government, University of North Carolina, 1965).

16. Margaret Thomas Will, *Federal Republic of Germany, Switzerland, Austria*, vol. 2 of *Historic Preservation in Foreign Countries*, ed. Robert E. Stipe (Washington, D.C.: US/ICOMOS, 1984), 55–58.

17. Tomlin, *Preservation of What? For Whom?* and "Multiple Views, Multiple Meanings" (proceedings of a National Council on Preservation Education Conference, Goucher College, Baltimore, March 1999); Getty Conservation Institute, *Values and Heritage Conservation* (Los Angeles: J. Paul Getty Trust, 2000).

18. This is a bit harsh. Main Street projects, by and large, are an excellent example of "place making": preserving good buildings while at the same time creating environments in which a primary objective is "stability, comfort, local identity, and livable atmosphere." Legislative Research Commission on Historic Preservation, Report to the 1989 General Assembly of North Carolina, 1989 sess., Legislative Proposal 7.

19. In a public hearing at which I spoke on behalf of pending antisprawl and Smart Growth measures, I was confronted by an opponent who asked, "Who elected you . . . do-good, liberal, historic preservationist-planners to tell the rest of us where and how to live?" In the heat of the last presidential election, conservative voices argued that such measures were also a civil rights issue on the grounds that African Americans and Hispanic Americans would be excluded from owning a home "anywhere in America—including its suburban communities." Jim Nicholson, "Free Market Environmentalism," *Rising Tide* 6 (Fall 1999): 12–14.

20. Richard Moe and Carter Wilkie, in *Changing Places: Rebuilding Community in*

an Age of Sprawl (New York: Henry Holt, 1997), describe cases where these issues have been confronted and present a number of alternatives.

21. Grady Clay, *Close-Up: How to Read the American City* (Chicago: University of Chicago Press, 1973), 35–37.

22. Robert Venturi, Steven Izenour, and Denise Scott Brown, *Learning from Las Vegas: The Forgotten Symbolism of Architectural Form* (Cambridge: MIT Press, 1977).

23. The arguments for and against sprawl that came to the fore in the 1990s, and the primacy of the automobile as the principal means of transportation, are stated in Joel Garreau's 1991 work, *Edge City*, and in a prescient 1973 essay to the same effect by Grady Clay. Antisprawl arguments to the contrary appear in the rather more emotional arguments presented in James Howard Kunstler's *Geography of Nowhere*. See Garreau, *Edge City: Life on the New Frontier* (New York: Doubleday, 1991); Clay, *Close-Up*; and Kunstler, *The Geography of Nowhere: The Rise and Decline of America's Man-Made Landscape* (New York: Simon and Schuster, 1993). See also Randall O'Toole, *The Vanishing Automobile and Other Urban Myths: How Smart Growth Will Harm American Cities* (Bandon, Oreg.: Thoreau Institute, 2001), and Dowell Myers and Alicia Kitsuse, "The Debate over Future Density of Development: An Interpretive Review" (working paper, Lincoln Institute of Land Policy, Cambridge, Mass., 1999).

24. Dwight L. Young, "Out in Front," *Preservation Magazine* 51 (November–December 1999): 54.

25. Interestingly, the underlying issue was often paraphrased during the 2000 election campaign: "Will we have a continent or a country?"

26. Gigi Bradford, Michael Gary, and Glenn Wallach, eds., *The Politics of Culture: Policy Perspectives for Individuals, Institutions, and Communities* (New York: New Press, 2000). The relevance of this entire work, which deals with national arts policies, to historic preservation, especially the essay by Margaret Jane Wyszomirski, "Policy Communities and Policy Influence: Securing a Government Role in Cultural Policy for the Twenty-First Century" (pp. 94–107), is simply astounding.

27. Robert E. Stipe, "On Preservation Plans and Planning," *Alliance Review* (February–March 2001): 1–4, and (April–May 2001): 4–5, 15. Maryland was the first state to require a tight connection between preservation, the comprehensive plan, and the zoning ordinance, an approach that is still very much a minority rule. A few early experiments with this approach are falling victim to the public's displeasure, as in the case of Portland, Oreg., where voters in a special referendum in November 2001 overturned planned growth boundaries.

28. Bradford J. White and Paul W. Edmondson, *Procedural Due Process in Plain English* (Washington, D.C.: NTHP, 1994); Robert E. Stipe, "A Letter to George: How to Keep the Preservation Commission out of Court and Avoid Being Sued," *Alliance Review* (Spring 1993): 1–9.

29. The impact of the events of September 11, 2001, on the future of the central city in light of public perceptions about their future vis-à-vis the suburbs and more remote locations for business, industry, and dwelling has been the subject of widespread speculation. Steven Brill, in a *Newsweek* article of January 21, 2002, quotes investor Warren Buffett: "This could slowly but surely lead to the de-urbanization of America and the closing of any iconic buildings as the result of overwhelming cost in-

creases for central-city property insurance." Sue Shellenbarger, "Telework Is on the Rise, But It Isn't Just Done from Home Anymore," *Wall Street Journal*, January 22, 2002.

30. Caneta Hankins, principal author, "Focus on 2000: A Heritage Education Perspective" (report prepared by the Center for Historic Preservation, Middle Tennessee State University for the National Center for Preservation Technology and Training, Natchitoches, La., October 1997).

31. Save America's Treasures was originally proposed as a onetime program outside the continuing NPS historic preservation program, but it provided direct grants for many worthy projects, the first of its kind since 1976. The Bush administration proposed to drop SAT from the FY 2001–2 budget, but it has been reinstated, thanks, it is said, to the efforts of First Lady Laura Bush. It shows early signs of becoming a permanent program. Whether a second federally supported program outside or beyond the mainstream 1966 program is supportive, competitive, or merely duplicative is not often discussed.

32. On several occasions over the years, I have asked my graduate students in a Community Design Policy seminar whether they were aware that this was Preservation Week. In most cases, an average of one or two of twenty-five students were familiar with it. The occasional graduate student in architecture, landscape architecture, or public administration would ask, "What is historic preservation?" or "Preservation of what?" But students in my Historic Preservation seminar would invariably be familiar with Preservation Week.

33. Notably, however, the National Trust's 2001 list of most endangered historic properties was featured not only on the History Channel, but also on CNN's *Inside Politics* and *Headline News*.

34. Both are administratively located within a National Center for Cultural Resources Stewardship and Partnership Programs in the NPS. It can be argued that we have progressed backward to the Carter administration's experiment with the HCRS. Many will argue that historic preservation needs a separate, higher-level, more prestigious place on Interior's organizational chart. But it should also be remembered that programs located at higher levels in the administrative hierarchy of national and state governments are also more visible and therefore more vulnerable politically.

35. Robert E. Stipe, introduction to *Carolina Dwelling: Towards Preservation of Place: In Celebration of the North Carolina Vernacular Landscape*, ed. Douglas Swaim (Raleigh: School of Design, North Carolina State University, 1978).

36. Seth M. Low, "Cultural Conservation of Place," in *Conserving Culture: A New Discourse on Heritage*, ed. Mary Hufford (Urbana: University of Illinois Press, 1994).

37. This raises an interesting question for the future of heritage areas, with their presumed reliance or emphasis on local initiative and control. Sponsored and initiated by both Congress and the states to date, federal government assistance can be characterized as helpful as the concept takes root. But in the real world, such "help" or aid eventually becomes "guidance," and "guidance" tends to evolve over time into "standards," which in turn become a precondition to the receipt of federal assistance. Backers of the concept of heritage areas would be well advised to give thought to a seemingly inevitable tendency toward the eventual bureaucratization of such programs.

38. The best of the publications addressing this issue in recent years is Antoinette J. Lee, ed., *Past Meets Future: Saving America's Historic Environments* (Washington, D.C.: Preservation Press, 1992).

39. Tomlin, *Preservation of What?*

40. George F. Kennan, *Around the Cragged Hill: A Personal and Political Philosophy* (New York: Norton, 1993). Especially important works in a discussion of this topic are John W. Gardner, *Self Renewal: The Individual and the Innovative Society* (New York: Norton, 1995), and Peter F. Drucker, *The New Realities in Government and Politics, in Economics and Business, in Society and World View* (New York: Harper and Row, 1989).

41. Kennan, *Around the Cragged Hill*, 236.

42. See J. Mark Schuster, with John De Monchaux and Charles A. Riley II, eds., *Preserving the Built Heritage: Tools for Implementation* (Hanover, N.H.: University Press of New England, 1997). In 1966 many hoped that the ACHP, then known as the "President's Advisory Council," would embark on a role similar to that advocated by Kennan for the foreign service. But the council's status as an "insider" preservation agency and the mandate of Section 106 made this impossible.

Contributors

David L. S. Brook holds a J.D. degree from the Ohio State University College of Law and an M.A. in history from North Carolina State University. He served as SHPO of Ohio, Assistant Regional Director for Cultural Programs of the U.S. Department of the Interior, and Executive Director of the Louisville–Jefferson County, Kentucky, Preservation Alliance. Presently he is the Deputy SHPO for North Carolina and administers the state's historic preservation program. In 1989 he won North Carolina's top award for professional achievement in historic preservation.

Lina Cofresi is an independent scholar. Her M.A. and Ph.D. degrees are from Vanderbilt University, and she is a graduate of the landscape architecture and historic preservation program at the University of Georgia. An active preservationist, she served as Chair of the Franklin County, North Carolina, Historic Properties Commission. She has written extensively on historic landscapes and gardens of the coastal South, as well as on Savannah's historic squares, and is a contributor to the NPS series, *Pioneers of American Landscape Design*.

Alan Downer received his Ph.D. in applied anthropology from the University of Missouri–Columbia and has directed the Navajo Nation Historic Preservation Department for the past twelve years. Before assuming leadership of the Navajo preservation program, he was the Senior Archaeologist in the Western Division of Project Review for the ACHP. He was a founding member of Keepers of the Treasures, Inc., and presently serves as General Chairman of the National Association of Tribal Historic Preservation Officers.

John M. Fowler is a graduate of Princeton University and Yale Law School and has served in numerous capacities at the ACHP, where he has been Executive Director since 1997. He has been the Chair of US/ICOMOS and served on the board of trustees of the National Center for Preservation Law. He has lectured on preservation law at American University, Columbia, Harvard, Yale, and the University of Pennsylvania. He is the author of numerous articles on historic preservation law and environmental protection.

J. Myrick Howard has been President of Preservation North Carolina, one of the nation's largest and most prestigious preservation revolving funds, since 1978. A native of Durham, North Carolina, he attended Brown University and the University of North Carolina at Chapel Hill, where he received graduate degrees in law and regional planning. He is a member of the North Carolina bar. In 1983 he received North Carolina's highest award for professional practitioners in historic preservation. He serves on the Board of Trustees of the National Trust as Chairman of the Statewide and Local Partners.

Kathryn Welch Howe is the Founding Principal of KWH, a Los Angeles preservation and real estate development planning firm. A graduate of Vassar College, she was a Vice President of Goldman, Sachs and Co., New York, and Vice President for Regional Programs of the National Trust. She was the lead planning and development consultant for a number of major U.S. preservation projects. Presently she is developing a historic resource survey for Los Angeles in conjunction with the Getty Conservation Institute.

Alan Jabbour is the retired Director of the American Folklife Center at the Library of Congress. He holds a Ph.D. in English literature and folklore from Duke University. A specialist in American folk music, he has written extensively on folk music, folklore, and cultural policy. A former President of the American Folklore Society and Founding Chair of the Fund for Folk Culture, he has served on the boards of several cultural organizations, including the Humanities Council of Washington, D.C.

Genevieve P. Keller and J. Timothy Keller, FASLA, are Founding Principals of Land and Community Associates of Charlottesville, Virginia, and hold graduate degrees from the University of Virginia. Genevieve is an architectural historian. Tim is Professor and Chair of Landscape Architecture at Iowa State University. Since 1975, the Kellers, as private consultants, have completed a broad range of landscape conservation and preservation projects and coauthored many publications in the field, including National Register Bulletin 18 on the preservation of historic landscapes and *Saving America's Countryside* (1989). They were the recipients of Loeb Fellowships at the Harvard Graduate School of Design in 1991–92.

Russell V. Keune earned an M.A. degree in architecture from the University of Illinois and is a Fellow of US/ICOMOS and the American Institute of Architects. He is a former Vice President of the National Trust, where he managed the core preservation programs. He served as the Director of International Relations for the American Institute of Architects from 1993 until his recent retirement. He has worked on international preservation and planning projects in Singapore, Macao, the Philippines, Ghana, Yemen, and Yugoslavia.

Diane Lea is an active preservationist. She has served as President of the Chapel Hill, North Carolina, Preservation Society and as a trustee of Preservation North Carolina, Inc. As Vice President of a Raleigh, North Carolina, planning firm, she has advised communities on developing historic district ordinances and neighborhood design guidelines. She has published many scholarly and popular articles on preservation and historic architecture and has been a contributing editor for preservation in regional newspapers and magazines. She currently specializes in historic property marketing.

Antoinette J. Lee holds a doctorate in American civilization from George Washington University. She works as a historian in the cultural resources program of the NPS and teaches in the graduate preservation program at Goucher College. Her book, *Ar-*

chitects to the Nation: The Rise and Decline of the Supervising Architect's Office, was published by the Oxford University Press in 2000. In 1989 she prepared the World Heritage nomination for the University of Virginia and Monticello. She is the author, editor, and coeditor of a number of books on historic preservation.

Elizabeth A. Lyon received a Ph.D. from Emory University and was for many years the SHPO for Georgia. She has served the American preservation movement in many capacities, including as an officer, board member, and committee chair for the NCSHPO. In 1994 she was appointed by the Secretary of the Interior to the Board of the National Center for Preservation Technology and Training and elected to serve as its Chair. She has published numerous articles on community preservation and cultural diversity.

Thompson Mayes received a J.D. degree from the University of North Carolina at Chapel Hill and is a member of the North Carolina and District of Columbia Bars. He is Deputy General Counsel for the National Trust, specializing in both corporate and preservation law, and is the Trust's principal lawyer for corporate law matters relating to its twenty historic sites. He also teaches historic preservation law at the University of Maryland. He is the author of several articles relating to shipwreck protection and National Historic Landmarks.

Rosetta Radtke is an avid preservationist and design planner for the town of Apex, North Carolina. She completed her graduate studies in preservation and landscape architecture at the University of Georgia. Active locally, she served as Chair of the Franklin County, North Carolina, Historic Properties Commission. She has written extensively on historic landscapes and gardens of the coastal South and is a contributor to the NPS series, *Pioneers of American Landscape Design*. She is currently working on a major article about Savannah's historic squares.

Charles E. Roe holds M.A. degrees in American history and environment (Indiana University) and regional planning (the University of North Carolina at Chapel Hill). He has worked for HUD, the Environmental Protection Agency, and the NPS. From 1976 to 1991 he directed the North Carolina Natural Heritage Program, whose mission is to identify and protect important natural areas and critical habitats. He was the Executive Director of the Conservation Trust for North Carolina from 1983 to 2002 and is presently the President of Land Savers, Inc., a Raleigh, North Carolina, consulting firm.

John H. Sprinkle Jr. currently serves as Supervisory Historian for the NPS's National Historic Landmarks Survey. He holds a master's degree in anthropology and a doctorate in history from the College of William and Mary. The author of many articles on historic preservation practice, he is the editor of *The Archaeology of Nineteenth-Century Virginia* (1999). He serves on the Virginia Commission on Virginia Archaeology and the National Council on Public History. He is a registered professional archaeologist.

Robert E. Stipe holds degrees in economics and law from Duke University and a graduate degree in regional planning from the University of North Carolina. He was Professor of Public Law and Government at the University of North Carolina at

Chapel Hill (1957–74) and Professor of Design at North Carolina State University (1976–2001). He was a Senior Fulbright Research Fellow at London University in 1968–69 and served briefly as North Carolina SHPO in the mid-1970s. He received the Secretary of the Interior's Distinguished Service Award in 1978 and the National Trust's Louise du Pont Crowninshield Award in 1989. He is Trustee Emeritus of the National Trust.

Index

Abandoned Shipwreck Act (1987), 266
Academia Istropolitana Nova (Institute for Advanced Studies, Svaty Jur, Slovakia), 373, 375, 525 (n. 19)
Academic programs: in landscape preservation, 193; in archaeology, 264; in historic preservation, 344, 502 (n. 7); in folklore, 429, 433; interdisciplinary, 445. *See also* Historic preservation, education for; Historic preservation, professional training for
Accra, Ghana: U.S. embassy in, 364
Adams National Historic Site, 201
Adaptive use, 10; for historic properties, 237, 459; growth of projects in, 279; ordinances on, 287; REITs for, 304; under Secretary's Standards, 378
Adirondack Architectural Heritage, 239, 242
Administrative Procedure Act, 528 (n. 21)
Adverse effects: under Section 106, 48–49, 53, 500 (n. 24); mitigation of, 63, 66, 520 (n. 2); through excavation, 266–67; research exception to, 267, 268
Advisory Council on Historic Preservation (ACHP), 36, 38–41; creation of, 11, 499 (n. 8); makeup of, 38–39; oversight by, 39; implementation of NHPA, 39–40; in Section 106 processes, 45, 47–51, 536 (n. 42); evaluation criteria of, 48; formal comments of, 49, 500 (n. 25); in Section 110f processes, 50; standards used by, 62; on mitigation funding, 66; as coordinating body, 77; state involvement in, 82; funding for, 92, 455; rewriting of regulations, 92; Review and Compliance program of, 105–10; affordable housing guidelines of, 108–9; use of landscape guidelines, 197, 220; role in archaeology, 257, 265, 268; on areas of potential effects, 267–68; role of National Trust in,

322; international role of, 361; tribal regulations, 417
African American Heritage Preservation Foundation, 335
African Americans: historic places of, 12, 16, 198, 386, 387, 438; cultural recognition of, 163; preservation of cultural history, 386; National Historic Landmarks of, 387–88; genealogy of, 388; preservation activities of, 392–97; slaves, 400; folklore of, 426
African Burial Ground (New York, N.Y.), 393–94
African Development Bank, 365, 381
Agriculture: and landscape preservation, 209
Air pollution, 226
Alabama Historical Commission, 389
Alaska Natives: historic places of, 421
Alexander, Christopher, 465
Alexandria Archaeology (Virginia), 257, 275
Algic Researches (Schoolcraft), 425
Allen, James, 7
Alliance for Historic Landscapes Preservation (AHLP), 191, 192, 195, 196
Alliance for National Heritage Areas, 243, 440
Amana Colonies (Iowa), 191, 195, 514 (n. 6)
Ambassador's Fund for Cultural Preservation (BECA), 363
American Anthropology Past and Future (SAA), 260
American Association for State and Local History, 13
American Cultural Resources Association (ACRA), 264
American Express Company: support of preservation, 369, 370
American Folklife Center (Library of Con-

gress), 426, 429, 430, 434; report on intangible culture, 435; multidisciplinary projects of, 436–37, 447; experimental projects of, 439

American Folklife Preservation Act (1976), 430, 434

American Folklore Society, 426, 427, 430; changes within, 530 (n. 9)

American Heritage Rivers, 37, 440

American Indian Religious Freedom Act (1978), 414–15

American Institute of Architects (AIA), 279; library of, 375

The American Mosaic, 140

American National Association of Counties, 367

American Research Center (Cairo), 366

American Scenic and Historic Preservation Society (New York), 4

American Society of Landscape Architects (ASLA), 191; historic landscape initiatives of, 192, 198; Open Committee on Historic Landscapes, 196

American Society of Planning Officials, 190

Americans with Disability Act, 294

"America's Parks, America's People" (conference, 1999), 398

Angel Island Immigration Station (San Francisco Bay), 395

Animal species: extinction of, 225, 226

Annals of Philadelphia and Pennsylvania in Olden Times (Watson), 425

Annapolis, Md.: historic district of, 7

Anthropology: influence on archaeology, 254, 255, 260, 432–33, 518 (n. 2); study of Native Americans, 411; and environmental planning, 421

Antietam Battlefield, 69

Antiquities, popular, 424

Antiquities Act (1906), 5, 74, 414, 526 (n. 6); Department of Interior's role in, 37

Appleton, William Sumner, 4

Archaeological and Historic Preservation Act of 1974 (Moss-Bennett), 66, 407–8, 414

Archaeological Conservancy, 520 (n. 32)

Archaeological Institute of America, 264

Archaeological record, 253–54; impact of looting on, 277

Archaeological Resources Protection Act (ARPA), 74, 265, 414–15, 521 (n. 33); as management device, 75–76; violation of, 414, 528 (n. 17); administration of, 498 (n. 4); definition of resources, 528 (n. 16)

Archaeological sites, Native American, 5; under National Park Service, 37; effect of development on, 41; destruction of, 54, 276; data recovery for, 66, 93, 414; on U.S. public lands, 70, 526 (n. 6); under Antiquities Act, 74; excavation permits for, 74–75, 501 (n. 58), 527 (n. 6); protection of, 74–76; in historic landscapes, 188; land trusts for, 223; identification of, 254; in National Register, 256; inventories of, 261; legitimacy of excavation at, 262–63; looting of, 276–77, 408, 526 (n. 4); amateur interest in, 406; of Mound Builders, 407–8, 526 (n. 3); of Southwest, 408; Paleo-Indian remains in, 408–9, 527 (n. 7); definition of, 518 (n. 3); in highway corridors, 519 (n. 22)

Archaeology: federal programs in, 82; destructive nature of, 253; recovery of human behavior through, 253; role in historic preservation, 253–78, 432; anthropological theory in, 254, 255, 260, 432–33, 518 (n. 2); data recovery in, 254, 414; mitigation in, 254; phases of, 254; superimposition in, 254; techniques of, 254; professional, 254–55, 258, 263–64, 278; middle range theory in, 255, 256; New, 255, 256, 260, 261; positivist approach to, 255, 256; methodology of, 255–56; public programs in, 257; technology in, 257, 260, 271–72, 520 (n. 26); as a business, 258–61, 263, 264; subfields of, 260; public values and, 261–63, 270; interpretive programs in, 262; academically based, 264; federal standards for, 264; practice of, 264–70; literature of, 269–70, 272; DNA evidence in, 272, 520 (n. 29); particularism in, 272; site-centric nature of, 273; curation crisis in, 273–76; laboratory phase of, 275; resource base for, 276–77; amateur, 277, 406; funding for, 277; public paradigm of, 278; of built environment, 435; aboveground, 441; role of NPS in, 498 (n. 4). *See also* Excavations

Archaeology Week, 97

Architecture: as art, xiv, 30, 123; colonial revival, 3, 6, 317, 467; vernacular, 131, 216, 388; rustic, 197; landscape, 198, 514

Bureau of Indian Affairs, 417–18
Bureau of Outdoor Recreation (BOR), 14
Burnham, Daniel H., 4
Bush, Laura, 535 (n. 31)
Bush administration (first): UNESCO during, 360
Bush administration (second), 69; UNESCO during, 361; and national monuments, 502 (n. 57); "Save America's Treasures" program under, 535 (n. 31)
Businesses, local: demolition of, 168–69
Business Improvement Districts, 287

California: religious property of, 177
California Preservation Foundation, 332
Candlelight Christmas tours, 319
Capital: for commercial rehabilitation, 304
Caribbean basin: preservation initiatives in, 370, 373
Caring for the Past, Managing for the Future (ACHP), 499 (n. 9)
Carter, Jimmy, 215, 359
Carter administration, 14, 244, 469
Casa Grande (Chandler, Ariz.), 408
Casino Reinvestment and Development Authority (New Jersey), 113
Casinos: tribal revenues from, 529 (n. 23)
Cassity, Pratt, 152
Center for Folklife and Cultural Heritage (Smithsonian Institution), 431
Central Park (New York, N.Y.), 3
Certified Local Governments (CLGS), 14, 155, 393; preservation programs of, 83–84, 85–86; in state programs, 85, 458; certification process of, 86; grants by, 94; aid to local resources, 99; decentralization under, 121; local governments in, 125; matching grants under, 127–28; educational programs of, 135; planning through, 140; landscape programs of, 203; property values in, 309; devolution of authority to, 458; requirements for, 462; federal appropriations for, 473, 484; growth of, 474
Certified rehabilitation, 61
Chafee, Charles, 18
Chaffee, John, 183
Change in the Connecticut River Valley: A Design Manual, 516 (n. 26)
Charitable contributions, 347, 523 (nn. 12–13); under Tax Reform Act of 1976, 62

Charleston, S.C.: historic district of, 7–8, 20, 475; rice plantations of, 223; Society for the Preservation of Old Dwelling Houses, 333
Charleston Principles, 18, 148
Chicago, Ill.: Columbian Exposition (1893), 4; religious property of, 176–77; Inspired Partnerships, 513 (n.37)
Christopher Columbus Quincentennery, 370
Churchill, Arthur, 188
Cisneros, Henry, 390
Cities: sovereignty of, 28; in preservation movement, 118; planned, 141; archaeological programs in, 257; white flight from, 318
Cities, inner: historic neighborhoods in, 387; historic buildings in, 470; urban renewal in, 470, 476; role of nonprofits in, 476; role of private sector in, 476
City Beautiful movement, 4–5, 232
Civic centers, 4
Civilian Conservation Corps (CCC), 8
Civil rights movement, 461, 468; sites of, 90, 386
Civil War: historic sites of, 110
Civil War battlefields, 67; urban encroachment on, 68–69, 208; protection of, 105, 214, 217; evolution of, 219; interpretation at, 400
Civil War Commissions, 532 (n. 7)
Civil War Trust, 233, 532 (n. 7)
Clark, Stephen, 6
Clay, Grady, 221, 534 (n. 23)
Clean Air Act (1990), 225
Clean Water Act (1973), 225
Cliff dwellings, 408
Clinton, Bill, 73, 176, 527 (n. 6)
Clinton administration, 78, 207–8; UNESCO during, 360; ACHP during, 361; American Heritage Rivers under, 440
Closure: in commercial rehabilitation, 284
"Clovis and Beyond" (conference), 420
Coal River (W.Va.), 437
Coastline, undeveloped, 215
Code of Federal Regulations, 27
Cofresi, Lina, 490
College Hill (Providence, R.I.), 334
Colonial Revival movement, 221–22, 317
Colonial Williamsburg, 5–6; landscapes of, 188; landscape symposium (1980), 191;

development around, 213; National Trust seminars at, 490

Colonial Williamsburg Foundation, 316; interpretive programs of, 400, 526 (n. 13)

Colorado State Historical Society, 190

Columbian Exposition (Chicago, 1893), 4

Committee on Historic Preservation, 10

Common Ground (NPS journal), 270, 521 (n. 33)

Common law, English, 242

Communities: in preservation movement, 1, 117, 144; development activities of, 92; ethnic, 152; political context of, 180; natural resources of, 232; commercial redevelopment in, 283; effect of federal development on, 415; quality of life in, 421; culture of, 445, 448; master plans for, 514 (n. 5). *See also* Local governments; Neighborhoods, historic

Community Development Block Grants (CDBGS), 41, 63–64, 337; and affordable housing, 109

Community Partners Program (CPP), 325

Computer imaging, 154

Conservancies: establishment of, 224

Conservation (Getty Conservation Institute), 376

Conservation, natural, 438

Conservation and Reinvestment Act (proposed), 58–59, 126

Conservation Areas (Great Britain), 354–55

Conservation biology, 226

The Conservation Fund, 230; as land broker, 231

Conservation Trust for North Carolina, 238

Conservatism: fiscal, 158, 166; in U.S. Congress, 375; effect on historic preservation, 455

Conserving Culture: A New Discourse on Heritage (1994), 438

Constituency building, 128–29, 130

Construction projects, federal: and Section 106, 46

Convention for the Protection of Cultural Property in the Event of Armed Conflict, 380

Convention for the Protection of the World Cultural and Natural Heritage. *See* World Heritage Convention

Convention on the Means of Prohibiting and Preventing the Illegal Import and Transfer of Ownership of Cultural Property, 363–64

Corps of Engineers: permits from, 40

Council on Environmental Quality, 500 (n. 28)

Counties: preservation in, 149–50; growth in, 208

Countryside Institute, 243

Covenants, 240, 517 (n. 16)

Covered bridges, 223

CRM: Cultural Resource Management (journal), 270, 376

Cronon, William, 247, 250

Cultural affiliation, 409, 527 (n. 9)

Cultural conservation: in foreign venues, 357; of New Deal era, 428; and natural conservation, 437; community-oriented, 447

"Cultural Conservation: Reconfiguring the Cultural Mission" (conference, 1990), 438

Cultural Conservation: The Protection of Cultural Heritage of the United States (1983), 389, 435–36, 439, 441; natural conservation in, 438; cross-disciplinary aspects of, 444–45; recommendations in, 448

Cultural cooperation: impediments to, 442–44; trends favoring, 444–46

Cultural Coordinating Council (Virginia), 106

Cultural diversity: in historic preservation, 16, 152, 163, 389, 390

Cultural heritage: intangible, 13, 442, 466; local preservation of, 125; as societal right, 171; of Western Europe, 355; ethnic, 386–89; professional preservationists in, 397–98; multicultural, 397–99, 403–4; support for programs in, 398; in World Heritage Convention, 464. *See also* Landscapes, cultural; National Heritage Areas

—Native American: recognition of, 164; Euro-American approach to, 405; secrets of, 410–11, 413. *See also* Sacred sites, Native American

Cultural Landscape Report (NPS), 199

Cultural landscape reports (CLRS), 193, 217, 219

Cultural property: illegal importation of, 363; repatriation of, 419–20

Cultural resource management (CRM): rural, 150; growth of, 258, 259, 260, 261; public nature of, 261; public archaeology under, 263; regulatory compliance process for, 264–65, 269, 275, 277; particularism of, 273; and historic preservation, 488

Cultural resource management industry: archaeologists in, 257, 258; Society of American Archaeology in, 258; databases of, 261; growth of, 263; technicians in, 264; under Section 106, 265–66; domination of archaeological practice, 269; digitization funding from, 271; destruction of archaeological sites, 276

Cultural resources: databases of, 155; landscapes as, 189; and historic landscapes, 196; rural, 206–10; *versus* scenic resources, 210–12; and natural resources, 234–42, 247; role of land trusts in, 248; biotic, 515 (n. 12)

Cultural Resources Diversity Initiative (NPS), 398

Culture: homogeneity in, xiv, 24; living, 411, 431, 432, 444; material, 424, 433, 434, 435, 462–63; expressive, 434; terminology of, 441–42; as process, 442; inclusiveness in, 445; innovation in, 448; separatism in, 471

—intangible, 423, 433, 441–42; and material culture, 435, 463

"Culture in Sustainable Development" (conference, 1998), 366

Cumberland Island (Georgia), 489

Cunningham, Ann Pamela, viii, 2, 20

Cupola House Ladies Association (Edenton, N.C.), 316

Cupples Station (St. Louis, Mo.), 292

"Curation of Federally Owned and Administered Archaeological Collections" (36 CFR Part 79), 266

Curry Village (Yosemite National Park), 218

Databases: archaeological, 37, 271–72, 277–78; from surveys, 87; of cultural resources, 155

Daughters of the American Revolution, 2, 317

Decision-making: in historic preservation system, 29–32; under Section 106, 46, 47–48

Deerfield Village (Mass.), 6–7

Deetz, James, 436

Delaware and Lehigh Navigation Canal National Heritage Corridor, 16–17, 243

Delaware State Historic Preservation Office, 114

Delay, Tom, 157, 183

Demolition: regulation of, 122; local responses to, 130; Saturday-night, 143; by neglect, 151, 178–79, 475; of local businesses, 168–69; prevention of, 180; tax incentives for, 318; in historic districts, 469; of National Register properties, 511 (n. 2)

Demonstration Cities, 120

Densmore, Frances, 426

Desegregation, racial: interpretive programs in, 401

Deterioration: protection from, 32

Determination of Eligibility (DOE), 88

De Tocqueville, Alexis, 313

Deutscher Heimatbund (Germany), 355

Developers: in commercial rehabilitation, 281–82; work with nonprofits, 320; use of easements, 340

Development: federally supported, 40–41, 309, 358; mitigation of, 208–9; and urban decay, 209–10; threat to wildlife, 225; phases of, 282; incentives for, 286–93; feasibility analysis for, 293–305; transfer of rights in, 296–97, 510 (n. 35); quality of, 308–9. *See also* Private sector; Rehabilitation, commercial

Disasters: under Review and Compliance program, 108; environmental, 225

Disney theme park (proposed), 106, 208

DNA: in archaeology, 272, 520 (n. 29)

Documentation: of historic landscapes, 194, 199–200; of cultural landscapes, 198, 199; of plant material, 201–2; in folklore, 446; technology for, 446; in historic preservation, 446, 447

Documentation programs: federal, 8; of National Trust, 295; of ICOMOS, 375. *See also* Historic American Buildings Survey; Historic American Engineering Record

Due process, 138, 174, 485

Duke, Doris, 316

Du Pont, Henry Francis, 316

Earthworks Landscape Management Manual (NPS), 515 (n. 3)

Easements, preservation, 180–81, 339–42, 356, 377; deductions for, 62–63, 340, 342; use by land trusts, 233–34, 240–42; effect on property owners, 234, 239; model, 241; gift, 242, 339, 342; tax incentives for, 242; donation of, 297–98, 523 (n. 11); definition of, 339–40; enforcement of, 340, 342; "facade," 340; valuation of, 501 (n. 44); under Tax Reform Act of 1976, 523 (n. 11)

Eastern Wilderness Act (1975), 225

Eatonville, Fla., 392–93, 438

Ecological Society of America, 228

Ecology: restoration, 226; viability in, 229

Economic Recovery Tax Act (1981), 12, 15, 60

Ecosystems: in landscape preservation, 190; element occurrence in, 229; management of, 236; preservation of, 246; of small areas, 247

Ecotourism, 212, 244

Edinburgh (Scotland), New Town Conservation Committee, 376

Egyptian Antiquities Project, 364

"Eleven Most Endangered Historic Places," 324–25, 328, 330, 478

Eliot, Charles, 3

Ellis Island (New York), 16

E-mail, 112; in preservation programs, 111

Emergency Jobs Act (1983), 93

Emerging Preservation Leaders Scholarship Program, 391

Eminent domain: federal exercise of, 46, 499 (n. 20)

Empressa del Centro Historico de Quito (Ecuador), 366

Endangered Species Preservation Acts (1966, 1973), 225

Endowments: income from, 34

Environment, built, 141, 162, 301, 489; archaeology of, 435; past orientation of, 443

Environment, natural: protections for, 223, 224–25; public awareness of, 225; preservation techniques for, 233–34; chronological issues in, 236, 247; registers of, 245–46; small, 247. See also Landscapes, natural

Environment, urban: deterioration of, xv, 10, 146; open space in, 3; expressways in, 123; investment in, 304. See also Cities; Neighborhoods, historic; Urban renewal

Environmental assessment: federal, 51, 52; review process, 107; in land management system, 139; of historic landscapes, 204, 205

Environmental impact statement (EIS), 51

Environmental protection: legislation for, 224; nongovernment organizations for, 225–31; techniques for, 233–34; grass roots initiatives in, 234; and historic preservation, 240–42, 250, 349, 351, 486, 488–89; heritage, 243–45; coalitions for, 249, 250; sustainability in, 492

Environmental Protection Agency, 225

Equal Protection and Due Process, 138

Ethnic groups: heritage of, xv, 12, 23–24, 152; historic places of, 385, 386, 420; identity of, 424; folklore of, 426; contributions to American society, 471; cultural places of, 471. See also Historic preservation, ethnic

Ethnohistory, 235

Ethnology, regional, 434

Ethnomusicology, 429

Europe: homeland protection in, 355; folklore studies in, 529 (n. 2)

Excavating Occaneechi Town (1998), 272

Excavation: permits for, 74–75, 501 (n. 58), 527 (n. 6)

Excavations: stratigraphic techniques in, 254; adverse effects through, 266–67; boundary issues in, 268; under FEMA, 268–69; unauthorized, 277; Thomas Jefferson's, 526 (n. 2). See also Archaeology

Executive Order 11593, 12, 43, 71

Executive Order 13006, 73, 501 (n. 54)

Facadism, 467

Faneuil Hall (Boston, Mass.), 13, 299

Farmer's Museum (Cooperstown, N.Y.), 6

Farmland: loss of, 469

Farm Security Administration: photographic unit of, 446

Farmsteads: historic, 206, 238; vernacular, 216

Federal agencies: historic preservation programs of, 41–47, 71, 79, 163; under Section 106, 47–48, 52; under NEPA, 51–52; under Section 4(f), 53; preservation officers of, 72; property-managing, 72; cultural resource professionals of, 73; conveyance of land to, 232; archaeological data recovery by, 414; relations with

Native Americans, 420, 499 (n. 22); cultural mission of, 444; enforcement of standards, 457

Federal aid: loss of, 27; grants, 55–59; to state historic preservation programs, 93–94, 482, 504 (n. 45); for historic preservation, 157–58, 159, 166–67, 183, 323, 349, 457–58, 473. *See also* Funding, institutional; Grants; Loans; Tax incentives

Federal courthouses: preservation of, 70

Federal Emergency Management Administration (FEMA), 108; excavations under, 268–69

Federal government: documentation programs of, 8; preservation program of, 19, 41–47, 54–67, 79, 163; in preservation system, 24, 26–29, 35–79, 257; structure of, 24–29, 34; as derivative, 26, 28; as sovereign, 26, 28; regulatory authority of, 27; management of historic properties, 67–77; stewardship by, 74, 76–78; private partnerships of, 77, 78; budget deficits of, 79; as limited, 105, 512 (n. 8); partnership with state historic preservation programs, 114, 145, 325–26, 348, 451, 457–58, 459–60, 498 (n. 4), 506 (n. 52); influence on local historic preservation, 119–21; partnerships with local groups, 120–21, 123, 125–28, 451; volunteers in, 130; funding for historic preservation, 157–58, 159, 166–67, 183, 323, 349, 457–58, 473; budget surpluses of, 167; role in international preservation, 379; Indian policy of, 405, 407, 409–11; devolution of authority to states, 458; tribal appropriations of, 529 (n. 23). *See also* United States

Federal Highway Administration (FHWA): and Section 4(f), 53; standards of, 107; and rural landscape preservation, 204

Federalism: new, 26, 27, 101, 505 (n. 46); in federal preservation program, 79

Federal preservation officer (FPO), 72; role in archaeology, 257

Festival markets, 13, 146

Festival of American Folklife (Smithsonian Institution), 429, 430–31, 433

Financial aid. *See* Federal aid; Funding, institutional; Grants; Loans; Tax incentives

Financial institutions, international, 358, 365–67, 381

Fitch, James Marston, 162

Fletcher, Alice, 426

Fletcher, Sir Bannister, 465

Flores v. City of Boerne, 175–76

Florida: *Historic Schools Reuse* booklet, 95; compensation statutes of, 513 (n. 29)

Flynt, Charles, 6

Folklife: as intangible culture, 423; as preservation field, 424, 429, 430–31; European concept of, 433; and environmental planning, 531 (n. 18)

Folklore: as intangible culture, 423; material culture in, 424, 433, 434, 435, 441; European, 424, 529 (n. 2); as preservation field, 424–30; of slaves, 425; professional development of, 426; applied, 429; public, 429, 430, 443; cross-disciplinary studies in, 433; public programming in, 433–34; documentation in, 446

Ford, Henry, 6, 316, 463

Foreign policy: long-term goals of, 491

Forests: of Colonial era, 236

Fort Larned National Historic Site (Larned, Kans.), 217

Forum Journal (National Trust), 490

Forum News (National Trust), 532 (n. 7)

Fowler, John, 452, 454, 480

Franklin, John Hope, 532 (n. 11)

Frederick Douglass House (Washington, D.C.), 386

Frederick Law Olmsted National Historic Site, (Brookline, Mass.), 192–93

Frey, J. William, 433

Fulbright Program, 362–63

Fund for Folk Culture (NPS), 447

Funding, institutional, 302–5; "backdoor," 33–34, 454, 468; bricks-and-mortar, 61, 522 (n. 5); from commercial banks, 303; mortgages, 303; from pension funds, 303–4; corporate, 522 (n. 5). *See also* Federal aid; Grants; Loans; Tax incentives

Future Shock (Toffler), 215

Galesburg, Ill.: Main Street program of, 146

Galveston Historical Foundation, 333–34, 336

Garden Clubs: of Virginia, 187; of North Carolina, 330

Gardens, colonial, 198

Garden Weeks, 318; of Virginia, 317

Herder, Johann Gottfried von, 424
Heritage area. *See* National Heritage Area (NHA)
Heritage Conservation and Recreation Service (HCRS), 14, 359, 469, 483; administration of, 244; premise for, 532 (n. 6)
Heritage corridors, 17, 243, 439, 465
Heritage educational programs, 478; of nonprofit organizations, 97
Heritage Property Investors (HPI), 325
Highways: scenic, 16–17; federal construction of, 40; historic, 64; under Review and Compliance program, 107; prevention of, 318, 500 (n. 28). *See also* United States Department of Transportation
Highway strip development, 335
Highway Trust Fund, 16
Hillsborough, N.C.: 141
Historically black colleges and universities (HBCUs), 498 (n. 7); funding for, 56, 500 (n. 32)
Historic American Buildings Survey (HABS), 8, 30, 92, 446; under National Park Service, 36–37; landscape recordation projects of, 194, 199; exchange students in, 368; comprehensiveness of, 443; documentation programs of, 498 (n. 4), 514 (n. 5)
Historic American Engineering Record (HAER), 37, 92; landscape recordation projects of, 194, 199; exchange students in, 368; documentation programs of, 498 (n. 4), 514 (n. 5)
Historic Black Resources (Merritt), 388
Historic Boston (organization), 318, 338
Historic Charleston Foundation: revolving fund of, 319, 333, 336
Historic districts: of New Orleans, 7, 16, 120; of Charleston, 7–8, 20; ordinances governing, 28, 135, 140, 160, 279, 475; enabling acts for, 81, 131–32, 135; local, 118–19; commissions on, 133, 134, 135, 160; in comprehensive planning, 138; flexibility for, 141; zoning for, 287; administration of, 376; African American, 387; demolition in, 469; National Register criteria for, 485; economic diversity in, 522 (n. 4)
—rural, 194, 238, 515 (n. 15), 516 (n. 25); NPS work with, 196; on National Register, 202; boundary delineation in, 204

Historic Homeownership Assistance Act, 160, 512 (n. 16)
Historic Homeowners Tax Credit, 455
Historic house museums, 1–4, 6; in National Trust, 9; in 1990s, 17; of statewide nonprofits, 330; interpretive programs of, 400–401
Historic Landmarks Foundation of Indiana, 329–30
Historic preservation: economics of, ix, 455; effect of tax policies on, ix; global context of, ix, 353–82; Native American role in, ix, 405–21; nonprofit organizations in, ix, 313–51; private sector in, ix, 159, 167, 279–311, 453, 477; importance to society, xiii, xiv; public opinion on, xiii, 120, 160, 182; reasons for, xiii–xv; in quality of life, xv; *tout ensemble* concept of, 7, 140–42; during Great Depression, 8; in postwar era, 8–10, 19; adaptive use in, 10, 237, 459; and growth management, 11; state initiatives for, 11, 97–100; during Bicentennial, 12; as mainstream activity, 12–15; in rural areas, 13, 149–50, 189, 191; cultural diversity in, 16, 152, 389; in 1990s, 17–19, 392–97, 417–20; as business, 19; future directions for, 19–20, 476–77, 480–81, 486–91; education for, 23, 115, 144–46, 372–73, 478–79; basic values of, 23–24; effect of market economy on, 32–34, 79, 105, 118, 377, 456–57; as market phenomenon, 32–34; maintenance cost of, 33–34; coalitions in, 35–36; federal players in, 36–41; tax incentives for, 37, 59–63, 166, 454–55; review and comment processes in, 45, 46, 48, 417, 452; conflict with government processes, 46; under Section 4(f), 52–54; federal funding for, 54–67, 157–58, 159, 166–67, 183, 323, 349, 455, 457–58, 473; state funding for, 57, 97–98, 349, 454, 485, 504 (n. 37); under Internal Revenue Code, 59; political support for, 78; citizen constituency of, 83; public outreach in, 96–97; in disaster relief plans, 108; technical information on, 112; economic impact of, 113, 115, 123, 144, 508 (n. 81); and environmental protection, 119, 240–42, 250, 349, 351, 486, 488–89; in urban renewal, 120; decentralization of, 121; regulatory approaches to, 122; public participation in, 128–29,

144–46; of interiors, 134; comprehensive planning in, 136–40; local politics in, 142–44; community support for, 144; *versus* "progress," 145; long-distance learning in, 155; as infrastructure, 156; and property rights, 157–58, 163; as public policy, 158, 182–83; conflict of rights in, 159; as legitimate governmental purpose, 159, 511 (n. 3); societal values in, 159–63, 170–80, 184, 381, 385–404, 462; priorities in, 159–70; economic benefits of, 160, 212, 295, 522 (n. 6); as ethic, 160, 162, 511 (n. 6); negative perceptions of, 160, 161–63; as governmental goal, 163; and governmental priorities, 163–70; comprehensiveness of, 164–66; effect of sprawl on, 168–70; and religious liberty, 171, 181–83; and religious properties, 175–77, 336, 513 (nn. 34–37); revolving funds for, 180, 319, 355–56, 377; and quality of life, 183; role of landscapes in, 191, 222; role of land trusts in, 238; and conservation interests, 240–42; role of archaeology in, 253–78, 432; scientific method in, 255–56; market-based development and, 280; subsidies for, 309–11; overhead costs for, 312; socioeconomic benefits of, 312; state conferences on, 319; impact on job creation, 320; university programs in, 344, 502 (n. 7); institutional impediments to, 349; political context of, 353, 455–57, 476, 486; British, 354–55, 367, 378–79, 401, 403; models for former Soviet countries, 355–56, 525 (n. 19); international exchanges in, 356; specialization in, 356–57; long-term planning in, 357; foreign models for, 357–58; literature of, 381; and demographic change, 389–92; social/ethnic activities in, 392–97; multicultural, 397–401; interpretative programs in, 399–401, 432; diversity in, 401–4, 468, 471, 480–81, 487–88; tribal involvement in, 410–14; inclusiveness in, 420, 421, 463–64, 468; cross-disciplinary programs in, 431–34; cooperation among programs, 434–38; and folklife networks, 442–44; periodicity in, 443–44; documentation in, 446, 447; generational changes in, 451, 453, 459; partnership approach to, 451, 452; philosophy of, 451; Euro-centric, 451–52, 471; and

community building, 452; crisis-oriented, 452, 478; in daily life, 452; failures of, 453–54; public support for, 455, 457, 463, 468, 477–79, 486, 490; administrative structures of, 459–62; environmental values in, 462; associative values of, 462–67; basis of support for, 466; traditional, 466; boundaries of, 467–68, 486; changing motives in, 468–71; compromises in, 470; changing imperatives for, 471–72; changing venues for, 473–74; leadership in, 473–74; do-it-yourself, 477; "save everything" mentality in, 478, 488; local character of, 482; motivations for, 489; impact on consumers, 492; new federalism in, 504 (n. 46); influence on cultural landscapes, 515 (n. 24); elitism in, 522 (n. 4); corporate giving to, 522 (n. 5)
—ethnic, 195, 198, 392–97; early efforts at, 386–89
—international, 353–82; national governments in, 353, 377; planning in, 354, 357; cultural conservation in, 357; influence on U.S. programs, 357–58; U.S. participation in, 358–65; State Department support of, 362; inventories in, 364; World Bank funding for, 366; private sector in, 366–72; philanthropic support of, 370, 372; conferences on, 372, 373–74; educational opportunities in, 372–73; standards for, 374–75; access to information on, 375–76; local governments in, 377; recommendations for future, 378–82; role of federal government in, 379
Historic Preservation (journal), 9–10
Historic Preservation Foundation of North Carolina, Inc., 331
Historic Preservation Fund (HPF), 55–57, 455; appropriations for, 15, 55–57, 85, 104, 121, 167, 454, 482, 512 (n. 17), 531 (n. 13); grants to National Trust, 58; for Native Americans, 58, 418–19; bricks-and-mortar grants by, 61; beneficiaries of, 62; state use of, 94, 504 (n. 29); reauthorization of, 114; local funding under, 126
Historic preservation movement: communities in, 1, 117; grass roots in, 1, 128–29, 130, 460–61; early roots of, 1–4; impact of NTHP on, 10; socioeconomic aspects of, 18; "back-door" assistance to,

Investment, private: tax incentives for, 107–8, 289–90; in historic properties, 283, 310; risk in, 284–85, 294, 298, 310; financing for, 295–96; motivation for, 299–300; public partnerships in, 301
Investment Tax Credits (ITCS), 287, 289–90; and Secretary's Standards, 308

Jackson, J. B., 221
James Rouse Company, 146
Jamestown, Va., 6; pollen studies at, 201
Jandl, Ward, 516 (n. 28)
Japan: preservation standards in, 378; living national treasure program, 446
Jefferson, Thomas, 217, 399–400; excavations by, 526 (n. 2)
Jensen, Jens, 191
Jewish Heritage Program, 369
Johnson, Lyndon B., 35
Jones, Lewis, 433
Jordan: national parks of, 364
Journal of American Folklore, 426

Kalevala (epic), 424
Kane, Thomas, 191, 515 (n. 13)
Keepers of the Treasures (Parker), 418
Keller, Genevieve P. and J. Timothy, 489, 515 (n. 13)
Kenmore Association, 3, 187
Kennan, George F.: *Around the Cragged Hill*, 491–92
Kennewick Man, 408, 420
Keune, Russell, 465
Kiley, Dan, 198
King, Thomas F., 259–60, 273
Kingston, Jack, 157
Kniffen, Fred, 433
Kunstler, James Howard: *Geography of Nowhere*, 534 (n. 23)

Ladies Heritage Association, 3
LaFlesche, Francis, 426
LaFont Preservation Trust (Washington, D.C.), 340
Lahr, Michael L., 508 (n. 81)
Lake Landing historic district (Hyde County, N.C.), 202, 239
Land and Water Conservation Fund (NCPTT), 37, 225, 498 (n. 4)
Land conservation: science-based, 228; demographics in, 307; and nonprofit preservation organizations, 460

Land management, 139; Native Americans and, 54, 76; by private owners, 239
Landmarks: ordinances governing, 28, 132, 135, 279; regulation of, 132; commissions on, 133, 135, 143; legislation for, 172; natural, 245–46; in commercial redevelopment, 287, 296; local, 485. *See also* National Historic Landmarks
Landscape design: naturalistic, 197; historic, 198
Landscape preservation, viii–ix, 187–222, 514 (n. 2); in West, 3; rural, 131, 187, 202–6; private, 187; diversity in, 189; and growth management, 190; guidelines for, 190, 220; in higher education, 193; in Midwest, 194–95; master plans for, 195, 514 (n. 6); and mainstream preservation, 198; methodologies in, 198–202; use of GPS in, 201; environmental review process in, 204, 205; effect of interstate system on, 205–6; land use in, 206; plant material in, 206; political aspects of, 206–10; effect of out-migration on, 207; agricultural threats to, 209; and tourism, 212–15; in historic preservation context, 222
Landscapes: built, viii, 187; designed, viii, 187, 197, 461; as art, xiv; role in historic preservation, 191; cultural, 193, 514 (nn. 3–4); ecology of, 226; heritage, 243–45; vernacular, 461; regulation of, 475; historical research on, 515 (n. 17); as artifacts, 516 (n. 27)
—cultural: criteria for, 196; documentation of, 198, 199; databases of, 199; methodological guidance for, 199; inventory of, 199, 200; archaeological techniques in, 201; aesthetic value of, 210–11; technical issues in, 215–21; in planning processes, 219–20; in National Register, 239; influence of historic preservation on, 515 (n. 24)
—historic: in federal programs, 187; recreation of, 187; in archaeological investigations, 188; in National Register, 188, 192, 244–45; as cultural resources, 189; scholarly investigation of, 192; in National Park system, 193; documentation of, 194, 199–200; identification criteria for, 194–98; ethnic, 195, 198; classification systems for, 196; spatial organization of, 196; criteria for, 196–97; African American, 198; ethnographic studies in,

198; research into, 198; comparative analysis of, 200; aerial photography of, 200–201, 204; tax incentives for, 204; environmental review process for, 204, 205; urban encroachment on, 206; beautification of, 210, 211–12; authenticity in, 210–11, 217–18; effect of tourism on, 212–15; substitutions in, 218; evolution of, 219; layered, 219, 221; interpretation of, 221; of early twentieth century, 221–22

—natural: cultural resources on, 234–42, 247; pre-Colombian, 235, 248; human presence in, 235–36, 237–38, 248, 249, 250; conservation strategies for, 250; British approach to, 378. *See also* Environment, natural

—rural, 187, 194, 198; evaluation of, 202–6; surveys of, 203; property rights in, 203–4; long-term strategies for, 207; development of, 207–9

Land Trust Alliance, 232, 234, 241

Land Trust for Central North Carolina, 239

Land trusts: state, 232; proliferation of, 338

—private, 223, 246–47; establishment of, 224; volunteers in, 231; rise of, 231–33; regional, 232; specialized, 232–33; and rural communities, 233; use of easements, 233–34, 240; and historic preservation, 238; and national organizations, 247; and cultural resources, 248

Land use: invasion and succession in, 149; rural, 150, 206; history of, 214; ranching, 218; "unnatural," 236; restrictions on, 240–41, 517 (n. 16); conservation programs in, 249; in commercial redevelopment, 286–87; global context of, 354; Supreme Court decisions on, 485

Land-use planning, 167; local, 118; projections in, 136–37; in commercial redevelopment, 296; in foreign venues, 357. *See also* Planning

Land-use regulations: local, 28, 114; landscapes in, 190; political acceptance of, 239

Larimer Square (Denver, Colo.), 299

Latin America: historic preservation in, 366, 395–96

"Latinos in Historic Districts" (conference, 1997), 395–96

Lawrence, D. H., 183

Lead paint: removal of, 351, 523 (n. 17)

Lee, Antoinette, 152, 471

Lee, Charles, 145

Lee, Ronald F., 9

Legislation: religious freedom, 176; environmental, 224, 240–41, 279, 411; for heritage areas, 243–44, 445; cultural, 439

—preservation, 441; enabling, 81, 131–32, 135, 151; on property rights, 157–58, 171, 173–74; and public policy, 157–85; societal values in, 159–63; public support for, 162; state, 164; Supreme Court on, 183; foreign influences in, 357–58

Library of Congress: American Folklife Center, 426, 429, 430, 434, 435, 436, 439, 447; Archive of American Folksong, 427, 429, 430, 446; Archive of Folk Culture, 429, 430

Lighthouses: leasing of, 73–74

Lilly, Eli, 329

Listokin, David, 508 (n. 81)

Loans, 33, 323, 455; from revolving funds, 336

Local governments: derivative power of, 28; police power of, 28; block grants to, 64; state assistance to, 86, 458; fiscal incentives of, 117; under NHPA, 119; aesthetic regulations of, 122, 131–32, 160; in historic preservation system, 126; partnerships with neighborhoods, 151; infrastructure projects of, 165; natural heritage programs of, 229; rehabilitation projects of, 293–94, 301; transfer of development rights, 297; preservation advocacy by, 319; in international preservation, 377; regulatory functions of, 468, 475–76; preservation priorities of, 474; preservation incentives for, 485. *See also* Certified Local Governments; Historic preservation programs, local

Loennrot, Elias, 424

Lomax, Alan, 428

Lomax, John, 428

Long Island Parkway, 107

Loomis, Ormond, 435

Looting: of archaeological artifacts, 276–77, 408, 526 (n. 4), 528 (n. 15)

Low Country Land Trust, 223

Low Country Open Space Trust, 238

Lowell National Historical Park (Lowell, Mass.), 431

Lower East Side Tenement Museum (New York, N.Y.), 324
Lowertown (St. Paul, Minn.), 476
Lucas v. South Carolina Coastal Council, 172–73
Lynch, Kevin, 221, 465
Lyon, Elizabeth, 126

Madison, Ind.: Main Street program of, 146–47
Main Street programs, 13, 14, 20, 113, 145, 146–48, 155, 453; volunteers in, 130; four-point approach of, 147; economic results of, 147–48; congressional debate on, 157; authenticity in, 211; tax increment financing for, 287; origin of, 324; of North Carolina, 331; success of, 474; holistic approach to, 516 (n. 25); "place making" in, 533 (n. 18)
Manassas National Battlefield Park, 69, 105, 499 (n. 20)
Manzanar National Historic Site (California), 395
Manzanar War Relocation Center (Lone Pine, Calif.), 388
Maritime preservation, 13, 37
Market economy: effect on historic preservation, 32–34, 79, 105, 118, 377, 456–57; real estate in, 33, 34; effect on affordable housing, 149; local business in, 169
Markets, financial, 304–5
Marshall, John, 410
Marshall Row (Savannah, Ga.), 319
Marsh-Billings National Historical Park (Woodstock, Vt.), 194
Maryland: Smart Growth program, 113–14, 165; building codes of, 166; preservation planning in, 534 (n. 27)
Maryland Environmental Trust, 239, 242
Maryland Historical Trust, 239; gift easements to, 242
Mason, Billy, 16
Mayes, Thompson, 141–42, 475, 485
Maynard, Joan, 387
M'Bow, Amadou-Mahtar, 359
McCarthy, Karen, 157
McClellan, Linda Flint, 515 (n. 15)
McCullough, David, 110, 390
McIntosh, David, 157
McKim, Mead and White (firm), 308
Media: in preservation education, 96–97;

in constituency building, 128; historic properties in, 535 (n. 33)
Meier, Lauren, 515 (n. 14), 516 (n. 28)
Melnick, Robert, 514 (nn. 3–8), 515 (nn. 11–13)
Memoranda of agreement (under Section 106), 49–50, 106, 107
Meridian Hill Park (Washington, D.C.), 194, 199–20, 515 (n. 21)
Merritt, Carole: *Historic Black Resources*, 388
Mesa Verde National Historical Park, 408
Midwest: landscape preservation projects in, 194–95; natural resources of, 228
Milestones (World Monuments Fund), 376
Miller, Hugh, 514 (n. 3)
Millionaires and the Millenium (Schervish and Havens), 523 (n. 12)
Minnesota: tribal programs in, 503 (n. 13)
Minorities: in nonprofit organizations, 346–47; preservation activities of, 386, 389, 507 (n. 73); preservation training for, 398, 399; historic places of, 420; cultural life of, 445; contributions to American society, 471
Minority Preservation Network (Georgia), 389
Mission Nuestra Senora de la Purisima Concepcion (San Antonio, Tex.), 219
Missouri Botanical Garden, 194, 199
Model Cities program, 120
Moe, Richard, 146, 532 (n. 10)
Monroe School (Topeka, Kans.), 212
Monticello, 399; pollen studies at, 201; viewshed of, 214; garden reconstruction at, 217; multicultural interpretation at, 399–400
Mortgages: for commercial rehabilitation, 298, 302–3; sources of, 303
Mound Builders, 407–8, 409; Spanish encounters with, 526 (n. 3)
Mount Auburn Good Housing Foundation (Cincinnati, Ohio), 387
Mount Vernon, viii, 2; viewshed of, 214
Mount Vernon Ladies Association, 2–3, 20, 313, 316
Moynihan, Daniel Patrick, 18
Multiculturalism: in cultural heritage, 397–99, 403–4; in historic preservation, 397–404; in private sector, 398
Municipal Art Society of New York, 394
Museums: restoration of, 522 (n. 5); for-

eign guidebooks to, 524 (n. 7); artifacts in, 526 (nn. 4–5). *See also* Historic house museums

Nantucket, Mass.: viewshed of, 214
Naragansett Indian Tribe (Rhode Island), 417
National Alliance of Preservation Commissions (NAPC), 122, 335; educational initiatives of, 130, 136; guidelines of, 132–33; training programs of, 475, 486
National Anthropological Archives, 426
National Archaeological Database (NADB), 37, 271
National Association for African American Historic Preservation (NAAAHP), 393, 394
National Association of Olmsted Parks (NAOP), 191–92, 196
National Association of Statewide Preservation Organizations, 335
National Association of Tribal Historic Preservation Officers (NATHPO), 420
National Center for Cultural Resource Stewardship and Partnerships (NPS), 498 (n. 4), 535 (n. 34)
National Center for Preservation Technology and Training (NCPTT), 37–38, 84, 103, 111, 478; Wild and Scenic Rivers Program, 37, 498 (n. 4); grants from, 112; state surveys by, 112; "Teaching with Historic Places" program, 145, 478, 498 (n. 4); agenda of, 498 (n. 4); Land and Water Conservation Fund, 498 (n. 4); National Historic Landmarks Survey, 498 (n. 4); National Register, History, and Education Program, 498 (n. 4); Park History Program, 498 (n. 4); Brookings Institution seminar (1998), 508 (n. 81)
National Center for Recreation and Conservation (NPS), 498 (n. 4)
National Coalition for Heritage Areas, 440
National Conference of State Historic Preservation Officers (NCSHPO), 83, 92, 115, 453; in ACHP, 38–39; committee structure of, 99; negotiation with NPS, 102–3; survey (1990), 110; minority representation in, 111; collaboration with National Trust, 462; advocacy by, 486
National Conference of State Legislatures (NCSL), 112

National Council for Historic Sites and Buildings, 9
National Council of Preservation Educators, 111
National Council of Preservation Executives, 335
National Council on Preservation Education (NCPE), 490–91
National Council on Public History, 335
National Endowment for the Arts, 55; preservation funding of, 66–67; Folk Arts program of, 430, 445–46
National Endowment for the Humanities, 67
National Environmental Policy Act (NEPA, 1969), 50, 163, 225; federal agencies under, 51–52; scope of, 52; enforcement of, 54; archaeology under, 256, 268; segmentation under, 268
National Folk Festival, 429
National Forests Management Act (1976), 225
National Heritage Area (NHA), 37, 243–45, 465–67, 479–80, 531 (n. 20); and sense of place, 438–41; federal funding for, 439; National Park Service and, 439–40; social benefits of, 440; holistic approach to, 461; evaluation of, 466; cross-jurisdictional boundaries in, 479; planning controversies in, 479; design arts in, 480; future of, 535 (n. 37)
National Heritage Areas Policy Act, 243–44
National Heritage Corridor (NHC), 16–17, 243, 439
National Heritage Fellowships, 445–46, 531 (n. 22)
National Historic Landmarks (NHLS), 245; during Great Depression, 8; under National Park Service, 36, 498 (n. 4); under Section 110f, 50–51; under Section 106, 51; grants to, 59; nomination to World Heritage List, 380; African American, 387–88
National Historic Landmarks Survey (NCPTT), 498 (n. 4)
National Historic Preservation Act (NHPA): creation of, vii, 19, 35; incentive value of, 11; early years of, 11–12; organizational framework of, 35; property owners under, 44; states' implementation of, 58; surveys by, 81; grants programs of, 97,

and trails programs of, 479; American Indian Liaison Office, 498 (n. 4); communication with tribes, 498 (n. 4); National Center for Recreation and Conservation, 498 (n. 4); National Historic Landmarks under, 498 (n. 4); landscape evaluations of, 514 (n. 3); Cultural Landscape Initiative, 516 (n. 28)

National Park system: landscape issues in, 69; threats to, 69; rural settings of, 197

National Preservation Conference (Charleston, S.C., 1990), 148, 490

National Preservation Conference (Miami, Fla., 1992), 390–91

National Preservation Conference (San Francisco, Calif., 1991), 18, 128, 183, 490; cultural diversity in, 389, 390

National Preservation Conference (Savannah, Ga., 1998), 395

National Preservation Conference (Washington, D.C., 1999), 395

National Preservation Conferences: diversity at, 390–92

National Preservation Coordinating Council, 10

National Preservation Loan Fund, 323

National Public Television, 479; historic properties on, 535 (n. 33)

National Register, History, and Education Program (NCPTT), 498 (n. 4)

National Register Bulletin Guidelines for Evaluating and Documenting Rural Historic Landscapes, 202

National Register Information System (NRIS), 271, 499 (n. 12)

National Register of Historic Landmarks, 245; concept of, 452; review procedures for, 462; criteria for, 499 (n. 11); tax credits for, 500 (n. 23). *See also* National Historic Landmarks (NHLS)

National Register of Historic Places, 41–44; nominations to, 11, 42, 43, 57, 423; postwar sites in, 11–12, 88, 90; Criterion A of, 23; owners of, 29; standards for, 29, 30; National Park Service and, 36, 42; criteria for, 42, 44, 203, 482; impact on preservation, 42, 43–44; inclusivity of, 44; protective procedures of, 44; Section 106 protection for, 48, 77; federal property on, 67; as benchmark, 77; local sites in, 82, 88, 119, 121; state sites in, 82, 83, 87–88; local review for, 86; Determina-

tions of Eligibility for, 88; fifty-year threshold for, 88, 112, 461; as planning tool, 90; negotiation of criteria, 103; as model for landmark ordinances, 132; planning context of, 136; educational programs of, 145; landscapes in, 188, 192, 196, 202–6; landscape publications of, 193, 197, 202; rural landscape criteria of, 203; cultural landscapes in, 239; historic landscapes in, 244–45; archaeological sites in, 256, 267, 271, 275; ethnic diversity in, 388; strategy of, 443; effect on diversity, 463; gay/lesbian sites in, 471; integrity of, 481–82; political pressures on, 481–82; funding for, 482, 485; criteria for historic districts, 485; demolition of listed properties, 511 (n. 2)

National Road: surveys of, 98

National Science Foundation, 67

National Society of Colonial Dames of America, 2, 317–18, 521 (n. 1)

National Trust for Historic Preservation (NTHP), 4, 322–27; chartering of, 9, 318, 322; impact on preservation movement, 10; Main Street programs of, 13, 15, 20, 113, 130, 145, 146–48, 155, 157, 211, 287, 324, 453; maritime preservation programs, 13; publications of, 13, 208; Charleston Principles of, 18; in ACHP, 38; federal grants to, 55; matching grants for, 58; "Most Endangered Properties Lists," 97; and Disney theme park, 106; workshops of, 108; minority representation in, 111; work with nonprofits, 112; advocacy by, 114; partnership with states, 114, 145, 325–26, 348, 453; comprehensive planning by, 137; Community Partners Program, 145, 325; Office of Statewide and Local Partnerships, 145, 462; initiatives of, 155, 332, 452–53; partnership initiatives, 155; congressional funding debate on, 157–58, 159, 166–67, 183, 511 (n. 1); federal funding for, 157–58, 323, 455; audits by, 165; on sprawl, 168; Rural Project of, 189, 191; Western Regional Office of, 190; and Smart Growth movement, 233; model easements of, 241; documentation of economic benefits, 295; Organizational Development booklets of, 316; economic impact studies of, 320; membership of, 322; Law Department of, 323; Legal De-

fense Fund, 323; in *Penn Central* decision, 323; challenge grant program of, 324; museum properties of, 324; financial services programs, 325; Heritage Property Investors program, 325; Independence Fund, 325; loss of federal funding, 325; regional offices of, 332, 486; Statewide Initiatives Program, 332; revolving fund forums of, 338; capital fund for, 348, 349; fund-raising by, 348; Statewide Partners program, 348, 462, 474, 486; international activities of, 367, 381; International Relations Committee, 367; Louise du Pont Crowinshield Award, 387; diversity under, 391, 469; minority scholarships of, 393; heritage corridors programs of, 440; leadership of, 462, 468; training programs of, 475; educational material of, 478; Board of Advisers, 486; *Forum Journal*, 490; Williamsburg seminars, 490; organizational studies by, 522 (n. 10); work with local organizations, 522 (n. 10); historic tax credit fund for, 523 (n. 15); Board of Trustees, 532 (n. 10); inclusiveness in, 532 (n. 10)
National Trust for Places of Historic Interest and Natural Beauty (Great Britain), 232
National Wilderness Preservation System, 224–25
A Nation of Nations (exhibit, Smithsonian Institution), 388
Native American Graves Protection and Repatriation Act (NAGPRA), 37, 76, 265, 419–20; coordination of activities under, 419; revisions to, 420; human remains under, 472; cultural affiliation under, 527 (n. 9)
Native Americans: role in preservation, ix, 24, 405–21; in federal preservation programs, 19; in ACHP, 39; and federal land management, 54, 76; HPF funds for, 58; human remains protection for, 76, 420, 472; preservation professionals, 111; cultural recognition of, 164; pre-Colombian, 235; of Colonial era, 235–36; cultural sites of, 388, 410–11, 418, 421; assimilation of, 405; federal policy toward, 405, 407, 409–11; historic places of, 406–9; European displacement of, 407–8; paleological ancestry of, 408–9, 527 (nn. 7–8); cultural secrets of, 410–11, 413; anthro-

pological study of, 411; traditionalist, 411; religious practices of, 414–15, 423; under NHPA, 415–17; relations with federal agencies, 420; folklore of, 426, 427; folk arts of, 446; whaling tradition of, 489. *See also* Archaeological sites, Native American; Historic preservation programs, tribal; Sacred sites, Native American; Tribes, Indian
Native Hawaiians: preservation activities of, 396; historic places of, 421
Natural heritage programs, 229
Natural Lands Trust (Philadelphia, Pa.), 233
Natural resources: conservation programs for, 224; destruction of, 226; of local communities, 232; and cultural resources, 234–42, 247. *See also* Landscapes, natural
The Nature Conservancy (TNC), 227, 246–47; nature sanctuaries of, 228; scientific emphasis of, 228–30; public image of, 229; objectives of, 246
Nature sanctuaries, 228, 230
Navajo Nation: Historic Preservation Department, 418; sacred places of, 527 (n. 11)
Naval Historical Center, 98
Neal, Richard, 157
Neighborhood conservation districts, 141–42
Neighborhood Conservation Initiative, 165
Neighborhoods, historic: disinvestment in, 168, 319; highway projects through, 170; revitalization of, 280, 523 (n. 15); destabilization of, 289; tax credits for, 292–93; public-private partnerships in, 302; in Smart Growth movement, 305; property values in, 320; revolving funds for, 334; partnerships for, 377; ethnic, 385, 386; African American, 387; traditional, 467; teardowns in, 511 (n. 6)
New Deal: National Park Service during, 8; cultural preservation in, 428
Newell, William Wells, 426
New England: natural resources of, 228; land trusts of, 232
New Jersey: building codes of, 166; historic rehabilitation investment in, 310; Pine Barrens, 437
New Jersey Conservation Foundation, 242
New Mexico Heritage Preservation Alliance, 239, 511 (n. 7)

New Orleans, La.: historic district of, 7, 16, 120

Newport Folk Festival, 429

New River Gorge National River, 437

Newton, Norman, 515 (n. 17)

New urbanism, 469

New York, N.Y.: Central Park, 3; theater preservation in, 15–16; St. Bartholomew's Church, 16, 175; Landmarks Commission, 172, 394; Lower East Side Tenement Museum, 324; African Burial Ground, 393–94; preservation-related businesses in, 523 (n. 14)

New York Historical Association (Cooperstown), 433

New York Landmarks Conservancy, Professional Circle, 523 (n. 14)

Nixon, Richard M., 12, 71, 359

Nongovernmental organizations: environmental, 225–31; international, 372; international congresses of, 374

Nonprofit organizations: boards of, 314; definition of, 314; incorporation of, 314; staff of, 314, 315; tax status of, 314, 315; legislative advocacy by, 315; board-staff relationships in, 315–16; role in inner cities, 476

—preservation, ix, 313–51; heritage educational programs of, 97; work with National Trust, 112, 351; partnerships with public sector, 117, 349, 351, 453; educational programs of, 131; of early twentieth century, 316–17; historical role of, 316–20; of later twentieth century, 318; incorporation of, 319; professionalization of, 319, 343, 344; local prerogatives of, 320, 322; relationships among, 320, 322; in Smart Growth movement, 320; work with affordable housing, 320; statewide, 325–32, 337, 461, 522 (nn. 6–10); advocacy by, 327; public education programs of, 327; technical assistance by, 327; of Vermont, 328; of Indiana, 329–30, 337; staff of, 332, 343–44; local, 332–35; revolving funds of, 333, 336–39, 459; leadership of, 334, 343; affinity groups of, 335–36; lobbying by, 336; risk averseness of, 338; easements held by, 340, 342; organizational issues for, 342–47; boards of, 344; endowments of, 344, 347; goals of, 344–45; long-term projects of, 345; volunteers in, 345–46; effect of technol-

ogy on, 346; maintenance function of, 346; minorities in, 346–37; planned giving to, 347, 523 (n. 13); funding for, 347–49; policy issues for, 347–51; charitable deductions for, 348; entrepreneurship of, 349; and land conservation organizations, 460; and heritage areas, 480

North Carolina: preservation responsibilities in, 25; preservation legislation of, 240–41; heritage legislation of, 244; natural area registry of, 246; tax credits in, 290; nonprofit preservation organizations of, 330–31; Main Street program of, 331; revolving fund operation of, 339, 522 (n. 8); preservation diversity in, 465; mill villages of, 476

North Carolina Coastal Land Trust, 238

North Carolina Society for the Preservation of Antiquities, 330

Office buildings, federal: preservation of, 70

Office of International Affairs, 362

Old and Historic Charleston District, 7–8

Old Homes and Gardens of North Carolina, 330

The Old-House Journal, 12–13

"Old Indian House" (Deerfield, Mass.), 406

Old Sturbridge Village (Massachusetts), 6, 188, 316

Old World Wisconsin, 195, 196

Oley, Pa., 202; landscape projects at, 191

Olmsted, Frederick Law, 3, 4, 191

Olmsted and Vaux (firm), 191, 193

Olmsted Center for Landscape Preservation, 193

One Space, Many Places: Folklife and Land Use in New Jersey's Pinelands National Reserve (1986), 437

1000 Friends of Oregon, 207

Organization of Lesbian Architects and Designers, 335

Organization of World Heritage Cities, 360

Outdoor museum villages, 5–7; in National Trust, 9; in 1990s, 17; educational function of, 144; interpretive programs of, 400–401

Out-migration: effect on landscape preservation, 207

Pacific Asian Tourism Association (PATA), 370, 381

Paleo-Americans, 408–9, 527 (nn. 7–8)
Paradise Valley Folklife Project (Nevada), 436
Parker, Patricia: *Keepers of the Treasures*, 418
Park History Program (NCPTT), 498 (n. 4)
Parks: urban, 3, 211; state, 197; as historic landscapes, 211; design of, 515 (n. 16)
Parr, Alfred Eide, 465
Partners for Sacred Places (Philadelphia, Pa.), 336, 513 (n. 37)
Past Meets Future, 128, 536 (n. 38)
Pei, I. M., 308
Penn Central Transportation Co. et al. v. New York City Co. et al., 14, 15, 468; effect on local government, 119; landmark regulation under, 132; takings clause under, 172–73; Justice Brennan on, 183, 495 (n. 1, Introduction); National Trust in, 323
Pennsylvania: Latino historic sites in, 395–96; German culture of, 433; heritage corridors in, 439
Pennsylvania Folklife, 433
Pennsylvania Folklife Society, 434
Pennsylvania Station (New York, N.Y.), 318
Peters, Christine Capella, 516 (n. 28)
Peterson, Charles, 514 (n. 4)
Philadelphia: Independence Hall, 2; Centennial Exposition (1876), 3; Historical Commission, 120; Natural Lands Trust, 233
Photography: aerial, 200–201, 204; large-format, 515 (n. 21)
Piedmont Environmental Council (Virginia), 207, 233, 234; British exchange program of, 367
Piedmont Land Conservancy (North Carolina), 239
Pigeon Island National Landmark, 372
Pine Barrens (New Jersey), 437
Pioneers of American Landscape Design (National Park Service), 197
Pipelines, historic, 499 (n. 16)
Pittsburgh, Pa.: volunteer programs in, 474
Pittsburgh History and Landmarks Foundation, 319, 320, 337; revolving fund of, 336
Place theory, 465, 479–80, 488; associative values of, 466

Planning: comprehensive, 136–40, 167, 474–75, 509 (n. 20); small area, 139; archaeological resources in, 267; long-term, 357; environmental, 421, 438, 488, 531 (n. 18)
Planning, preservation: federal, 17, 259; local, 17, 113–14; state-mandated, 17, 91; under Section 4(f), 52; for projects, 136; through CLGs, 140; cultural landscapes in, 219–20; predevelopment, 285–86; in foreign venues, 354; British, 355; tribal programs in, 417
Plant material: extinction of, 225, 226; endangered, 228–30
Plant material, historic, 188; genetic duplication of, 201; documentation of, 201–2; and rural landscape preservation, 206; in historic landscapes, 217–18
The Politics of Culture (Bradford, Gary, and Wallach), 534 (n. 26)
Poplar Forest (Bedford County, Va.), 217, 275, 516 (n. 29)
Postepowa Synagogue (Cracow, Poland), 372
Post offices: preservation of, 70
Power of Place (Los Angeles, Calif.), 16
Prairies: of Colonial era, 236
Presenting Nature: The Historic Landscape Design of the National Park Service, 1916–1942, 197
Preservation Action (PA), 114, 335–36, 453; lobbying by, 126; collaboration with National Trust, 462
Preservation Alliance of Virginia, 212
"Preservation and Conservation Principles and Practices" (conference, 1973), 367
Preservation Brief 36: Protecting National Landscapes (NPS), 215–16, 516 (n. 28)
Preservation commissions, local, 132–34; number of, 122; property owners and, 134; membership of, 134–36, 145; conflicts of interest in, 135; training for, 135–36, 145, 155, 486; antipreservation members of, 143; minority representation on, 152; judicial review of, 160; as "taste police," 174; economic hardship decisions of, 178; and heritage areas, 480. *See also* Historic preservation programs, local
Preservation Law Report (National Trust), 323
Preservation North Carolina (PNC), 330,

331; revolving fund of, 337, 339; Endangered Properties Program, 522 (n. 9)
Preservation Services Fund (PSF), 323
Preservation Society of Charleston, 333
Preservation Trust of Vermont, 328
Preservation Week, 478, 535 (n. 32)
"Preserving the Architecture of Historic Cities and Sacred Places" (conference, 1999), 366
Private Property Rights Implementation Act (proposed), 150–51
Private sector: in historic preservation, ix, 159, 167, 279–311, 453, 477; public partnerships of, 114, 117, 281, 301–2; in American society, 313; in international historic preservation, 366–72; in information sharing, 376–77; multicultural efforts by, 398; role in inner cities, 476; and heritage areas, 480. *See also* Rehabilitation, commercial
Procter and Gamble: historic plant of, 499 (n. 16)
Professionals, preservation: in preservation community, 84, 460; in local preservation programs, 122; in nonprofit organizations, 319, 343, 344; diversity among, 398–99; qualifications for, 461–62
Project Weeksville (Bedford-Stuyvestant, Brooklyn, N.Y.), 387
Properties: noncontributing, 30, 140, 205, 466; tax-foreclosed, 121
—historic: threshold tests for, 31; protective processes for, 31–32; stabilization of, 32; federal ownership of, 36, 40, 41, 70, 103; federal threats to, 40; federal criteria for, 44; federal protection of, 45, 499 (n. 9); Section 106 protection for, 48–49; adverse impacts on, 48–49, 63; federal grants for, 56, 97; in Tax Reform Act of 1976, 59–60; tax credits for, 60–61, 127; rehabilitation of, 61, 62, 312; of NPS, 67–70; federal management of, 67–77; urban encroachment on, 68; federal lease of, 73; loss of, 78; federal tax incentives for, 94; tax relief for, 98; in Review and Compliance program, 107–8; twentieth-century, 112; effect of market on, 118; local, 119, 482; of postwar era, 131; urban context of, 141; role in economic development, 144; deterioration of, 151, 178–79; maintenance of, 151; religious, 175–77; easements for, 180–81; rural,

203, 205; lands adjacent to, 213–14; adaptive use of, 237, 459; in conservation easements, 241–42; commercial development of, 281; development process for, 282–86; private investment in, 283; depreciation of, 290, 500 (n. 38); investment analysis for, 299; cash flow from, 300; internal rate of return on, 300; capitalization rates for, 300–301; social history in, 397; interpretation of, 399–401; multiracial, 399–401; effect of federal development on, 415; under NHPA, 415; tribal registers of, 418; on military installations, 499 (n. 15); impact of highways on, 500 (n. 28); media coverage of, 535 (n. 33). *See also* Buildings, historic; Historic sites
Property owners: of National Register sites, 29; expectations of, 33, 497 (n. 3, Chapter 1); financial assistance for, 33–34; under NHPA, 44; tax incentives for, 61, 292–93, 298; states' aid to, 95; grants to, 97, 354; and local preservation commissions, 134; hardship provisions for, 151; consent and objection by, 179–80; easements for, 180–81, 234; land-management agreements with, 239; easement donations by, 297; benefits from nonprofits, 314–15; architectural advice for, 376; British, 378
Property rights: and societal good, 150–51, 171, 173–74; in preservation legislation, 157; in historic preservation, 157–58, 163; advocacy of, 170, 173, 457, 485; litigation over, 171, 175–76; legislation concerning, 173–74, 513 (n. 29); and religious liberty, 181–82; in rural landscapes, 203–4; in real estate, 296; easements in, 297–98; during Reagan administration, 360; regulation of, 474
Providence, R.I.: College Hill area, 120; Preservation Society, 334, 337
Public policy: and preservation legislation, 157–85; historic preservation as, 158, 182–83; states' role in, 163; religious groups in, 175; and commercial rehabilitation, 281, 286, 305–11
Public works projects, 40, 428, 446, 531 (n. 23)

Quincy Market (Boston, Mass.), 13

through easements, 180; effect on rural resources, 207–8; in Vermont, 325. *See also* Growth management

State historic preservation officers (SHPOS), 42–43, 82, 100–104; in Section 106 process, 47, 48, 83, 499 (n. 22); grant allocation by, 55, 56; in certification process, 61; standards used by, 62; mitigation strategies of, 66; and amendments to federal law, 83; and CLGs, 84; tribal programs of, 86–87, 103, 416, 417, 418; review of state activities, 93; aid to property owners, 95; relationship with DOT, 98; political influences on, 100–101, 109, 115; in preservation community, 101, 114; implementation of federal law, 101–2; and NPS, 102–4; autonomy for, 103; authority of, 105; under Review and Compliance program, 105–10, 116; workload of, 109; minority representation among, 111, 507 (n. 73); economic impact studies by, 113, 115; in growth management programs, 113–14; accomplishments of, 116; operational resources of, 116; use of landscape guidelines, 197, 220; archaeological guidelines of, 267–68; conflicts facing, 457–58, 528 (n. 20); compromises by, 458, 531 (n. 4); cross-training with THPOs, 503 (n. 13); qualifications for, 532 (n. 9)

States: sovereignty of, 26, 28, 131, 485; police power of, 26, 29, 239, 485; registries of, 31, 88; inventories by, 42–43, 110; matching fund appropriations, 57; funding for historic preservation, 57, 97–98, 349, 454, 485, 504 (n. 37); implementation of NHPA, 58; preservation surveys by, 81; enabling legislation of, 81, 131–32, 135, 151; environmental review processes of, 92; mitigation procedures of, 93; federal tax incentives for, 94; public education assistance to, 94–97; technical assistance to, 94–97; housing codes of, 109; partnerships with National Trust, 114, 145, 325–26, 348, 453; role in public policy, 163, 165; property rights laws of, 173, 513 (n. 29); religious freedom acts of, 176; natural heritage programs of, 229; land trust of, 232; natural area registries of, 246; archaeological standards of, 269; excavations permits of, 277; transfer of development rights, 297;

preservation advocacy by, 319; nonprofit preservation organizations of, 331–32; revolving funds of, 339, 459; cultural agencies of, 444; devolution of authority to, 458; governmental reorganizations in, 483–84; due process procedures of, 485; preservation incentives for, 485; archaeological surveys of, 502 (n. 6). *See also* Historic preservation programs, state

Stipe, Robert, 137

"Stop H-3" (Hawaii), 318

Stratford Hall (Virginia), 3, 187, 317

Streetscapes, 211

Suburbs: preservation of, 169, 470

Surface Mining Control and Reclamation Act, 499 (n. 19)

Surface Transportation Policy Project (STPP), 18

Surveys, 29; evaluation of, 30–31; NHPA, 81; information retrieval from, 87; by state programs, 87, 502 (n. 6); ISTEA, 98; in Main Street programs, 147; minority resources in, 152; rural, 203

Takings, constitutional, 171, 172–73, 178, 296; bills for, 455; historic designation as, 513 (n. 340)

Tallgrass National Preserve (Chase County, Kans.), 218

Task Force on New Jersey History, 113

Tax credits: federal, 15, 107, 289–90; for historic properties, 60–61; impact of, 62; for housing, 127; for affordable housing, 127, 290, 521 (n. 4); rehabilitation, 166, 279, 287, 289, 325, 349, 356, 521 (n. 4); under NPS, 279; for low-income housing, 290; state, 290, 292; for homeowners, 292–93; for neighborhood revitalization, 351, 523 (n. 15); standards for, 459; for National Register listings, 500 (n. 23)

Taxes: property, 289; inheritance, 347; flat, 348

Tax incentives: federal, 37, 56, 77, 94, 127, 166, 204; for historic preservation, 37, 59–63, 166, 454–55; depreciations, 60, 500 (n. 38); for property owners, 61, 292–93, 298; for private investment, 107–8; for urban renewal, 127, 207; state, 166; for easements, 180, 242; for National Register properties, 204; for development, 286; for commercial rehabilitation, 287–88; socio-cultural value of, 310; in

Union of Archaeological Field Technicians (UFAT), 264

United Kingdom: Town and Country Planning (Amendment) Act, 354; historic preservation in, 354–55, 401, 403; Town and Country Planning Act of 1949, 355; Countryside Acts, 378; folklore in, 424; Conservation Area legislation, 480

United Nations (UN), 359

United Nations Educational, Scientific, and Cultural Organization (UNESCO), 358, 366; Cultural Heritage Division, 359, 362, 379; U.S. National Commission for, 359; U.S. withdrawal from, 359, 375, 379; during Reagan administration, 359–60; during Clinton administration, 360; during second Bush administration, 361; standards issued by, 374–75; publications of, 376; International Safeguarding Campaigns, 379; preservation contracts of, 379. *See also* World Heritage List

United States: in international historic preservation programs, 358–65; demographic change in, 403–4; folklore studies in, 424, 425; arts policies in, 534 (n. 26). *See also* Federal government; Government, United States

United States Agency for International Development (USAID): historic preservation programs of, 364, 368, 380

United States Bureau of American Ethnology, 425–26, 427, 429

United States Bureau of Land Management: historic properties of, 43

United States Coast Guard: lighthouses of, 73–74

United States Conference of Mayors, 10

United States Congress: debate on Main Street programs, 157; debate on National Trust funding, 157–58, 159, 166–67, 183, 511 (n. 1); conservatism in, 375; Appropriations Committees, 439; recognition of sacred sites, 471

United States Constitution, 24, 26; federal government in, 28; individual rights in, 170; taking clause of, 171; Fifth Amendment, 171, 172, 456; due process under, 174; First Amendment, 176; equal protection under, 179

United States Department of Commerce: Economic Development Administration of, 309

United States Department of Defense: historic properties of, 43; Legacy Program of, 98–99; Bureau of Educational and Cultural Affairs, 362

United States Department of Housing and Urban Development (HUD), 10; block grants of, 63–64, 125; Demonstration Cities of, 120; Model Cities program, 120; establishment of, 309; in international historic preservation, 380

United States Department of State: historic preservation activities of, 362; Office of Overseas Buildings Operations, 363–64; Cultural Resources Committee, 364; Secretary's Register of Culturally Significant Property, 364; international preservation activities of, 381

United States Department of the Interior, 5; preservation programs of, 100, 390, 459, 483, 535 (n. 37); international activities of, 381. *See also* Secretary of the Interior

United States Department of the Treasury: in international preservation projects, 366

United States Department of Transportation (DOT): scenic highway program of, 16–17; relationship with SHPOs, 98; property development programs of, 309

United States Department of Transportation (DOT) Act (1966), Section 4(f), 50, 163; historic preservation under, 52–54; federal agencies under, 53; enforcement of, 54; as model for states, 93; local governments under, 119; project planning under, 136; excavation under, 267

United States Forest Service: historic properties of, 43

United States General Services Administration (GSA), 393; historic properties of, 41, 43

United States Information Agency (USIA), 362; role in historic preservation, 361; international preservation activities of, 381

United States National Committee of the International Council on Monuments and Sites (US/ICOMOS), 355, 363, 374, 381; exchange program of, 368; Specialized Committee on Cultural Tourism, 368

United States Postal Service: preservation policies of, 165

United States Supreme Court: property rights decisions of, 172–73; on tribal sovereignty, 410; on takings, 456; land-use decisions of, 485

University of Florida, Department of Architecture, 372, 373

University of Hawaii, Department of American Studies, 372–73

University of Pennsylvania, Department of Folklore and Folklife, 433

Urban Homesteading Program, 120–21

Urbanism, new, 169

Urban Land Institute, 301, 467

Urban Redevelopment Program, 119

Urban renewal, 119–21, 154; in postwar era, 9, 10; and commercial development, 13, 119–21, 154; of downtowns, 13; grants for, 63–64; preservation activities in, 120; tax incentives for, 127; in Smart Growth movement, 305; demographics of, 307; federal funding for, 318; ethnic groups in, 386; in inner cities, 470, 476

USS *Huron*: protection of, 98

Utah: nonprofit preservation organizations of, 337

Uwharrie Lakes coalition, 244

Valley (Shenandoah) Conservation Council, 233

Vaux, Calvert, 3

Venice, Italy: flood of 1965, 369

Venice Charter, 463

Vermont: Growth Management Act (1988), 17; impact of sprawl on, 325; Housing and Conservation Board, 328; nonprofit organizations of, 328; Preservation Trust, 328

Vernacular Architecture Forum, 335

Viewsheds, 211; of historic sites, 214

Vila, Bob, 13

Virginia: Cultural Coordinating Council, 106; Garden Club of, 187; Piedmont Environmental Council, 207, 233, 234; Preservation Alliance of, 212; Board of Historic Resources, 239; Department of Historic Resources, 275

Virginia History Initiative, 106

Virginia Landmarks Register, 105

Virtual reality, 154

Visitors' centers, 65

Voice of America: World Net broadcast system, 363

Volunteers: in local preservation programs, 129–30, 474; in land trusts, 231; in nonprofit organizations, 345–46; in information sharing, 376

Walden Wood (Massachusetts), 16

Washington, George: birthplace of, 6

Washington Charter for the Preservation of Historic Towns, 355

Water pollution, 226

Watson, John Fannin: *Annals of Philadelphia and Pennsylvania in Olden Times*, 425

Watt, James, 439

Wave Hill, New York: landscape archives at, 193

Wealth: intergenerational transfer of, 523 (n. 12)

Wells, Albert, 6, 316

Wells, Meryl, 104

West: landscape preservation in, 3; national monuments in, 74, 501 (n. 57)

West Baden Lakes hotel (Indiana), 329

Westmoreland, Carl, 387

White, Kevin, 146

White House: historic plant material of, 201; Millennium grants of, 445

White House Conference on Natural Beauty, 10

Wild and Scenic Rivers Act (1968), 225

Wild and Scenic Rivers Program (NCPTT), 37, 498 (n. 4)

Wilderness areas: human management of, 237

Winterthur Museum (Wilmington, Del.), 316

Wise-use movement, 150–51

With Heritage So Rich, vii, 10, 11, 117; on federal leadership, 35; central elements in, 41; federal agencies in, 45, 78; on incentives, 54; easements in, 62; core recommendations of, 77; societal values in, 162; European influence in, 358

Women's history: sites of, 110

Woodlawn Plantation (Virginia), 9

Workshops, preservation, 95–96

Works Progress Administration (WPA), 428, 446, 531 (n. 23)

World Bank, 365–66, 381

World Conference on Cultural Parks (1984), 374

World Heritage Convention (1972), 358, 456; U.S. ratification of, 359, 361; NPS